PERSIAN STUDIES SERIES

Edited by Ehsan Yarshater
Number Eight

THE TRIUMPHAL SUN

Photograph by Dr James Dickie

Mowlānā Rumi's tomb in Konya, called *al-qubbat al-ḥaḍrā*, the Green Dome.

THE TRIUMPHAL SUN

A Study of the Works of Jalāloddin Rumi

ANNEMARIE SCHIMMEL

FINE BOOKS LONDON
EAST-WEST PUBLICATIONS THE HAGUE

ISBN: 90.70104.27X

Typesetting by Malvern Typesetting Services
Printed and Bound in Great Britain by the Pitman Press, Bath

PERSIAN STUDIES SERIES

The Persian Studies Series consists of scholarly works which explore various aspects of Iranian history and culture.

This volume has been published with the assistance of the Iranian Ministry of Culture and Arts and the Royal Institute of Translation and Publication, and the Center for Iranian Studies, Columbia University.

A complete list of the books published in the Persian Studies and Heritage Series appears on page 514 onwards.

Contents

LIST OF ILLUSTRATIONS

NOTES ON TRANSLITERATION

The transliteration system used in this work is that adopted by the Corpus Inscriptionum Iranicarum, Persian Heritage Series, Bibliothèque Persane, Meisterwerke der persischen Literatur and Encyclopaedia Persica for the transcription of Persian, and Arabic elements in Persian.

PUBLISHERS' NOTE

The publishers wish to thank Professor Schimmel for her tolerance and immense effort in the production of this book, which has been extended over a considerable period. Also they thank the contributors for the use of the illustrations, especially the Mehmet Order for allowing us to reproduce a page of the oldest extant Mathnowi for the first time.

Most especially they wish to thank Professor Yarshater for his advice and encouragement without which publication would have been impossible.

Preface

Faridun Sepahsālār (d. ca. 1319), the author of Rumi's most famous biography, claims that he had been in the master's service for forty years.

If that were true, he would have been about a hundred years old when committing his notes to paper. We have to surmise that here, as in many other cases, 'forty' denotes the number of trial and patience: just as the mystic, in the course of his training, has to undergo a forty-day seclusion (*chilla*) in order to mature spiritually, many a Sufi has said that he served a master for forty years until he was blessed with true enlightenment. We may understand Sepahsālār's remark as a statement of this kind.

Yet, the present writer has to confess that she has been interested in Rumi's work for exactly forty years: beginning in my early schooldays when, for the first time, I read some of Rückert's marvellous verse-translations from the *Divān* of Mowlānā Jalāloddin, German verses which never ceased to fascinate me. Later, when I was a very young student of Islamic languages in war-time Berlin, the moment that my venerable professor H. H. Schaeder recited to us the first lines from Rumi's *Mathnavi* proved decisive for the development of this old love, and it took only a few weeks until my first verse-translations from the *Divān-e Shams-e Tabrizi* were ready; R.A. Nicholson's edition of the *Divan*, carefully copied by hand, became a faithful companion for many years, and the first money earned in compulsory work in a factory during the semester vacations was immediately transformed into the eight volumes of Nicholson's edition of the *Mathnavi*.

The text of the *Mathnavi* was one of the few items I took out of Berlin in April 1945, when our exodus began—an exodus which ended, eventually, in an American internment camp in Marburg. Here, the *Mathnavi* served as a soothing balm during the long days of waiting and preparation for a new chapter in our life. It is small wonder that the *ghazals* and *robāʿiyāt* which I composed during those years bear the distinct flavour of Rumi's poetry; their title, when published in 1948, *Lied der Rohrflöte,* alludes to the introductory verses of the *Mathnavi,* 'The Song of the Reed'. Other smaller studies, mainly connected with Mowlānā's symbolical language, and with the problem of prayer, followed in the next years.

Then came my first visit to Konya in May 1952—this fragrant spring day suddenly made literature alive. Two years later, my mother and I belonged to the lucky few (and we were the only Westerners!) who participated in the first festival arranged in honour of the anniversary of Rumi's death in December 1954: there, the *samāʿ*, the whirling dance of the dervishes which had been banned since 1925, like all manifestations of the religious orders, was celebrated for the first time after the great break—an experience never to be forgotten.

Thus, Konya became a second home-town for me; during the five years of my stay in Ankara I often visited the place, taking friends from all over the world with me. Historians of religion like Friedrich Heiler and C. J. Bleeker were among them; and poets, like Hanns Meinke, intoxicated, in spite of his great age, by the presence of the mystical poet whose verses he had transformed into German lyrics. The then director of the Mevlâna Müzesi, Mehmet Önder, enjoyed showing us every corner of the town, and thanks to his efforts the area around Rumi's mausoleum and the few monuments left from the 13th century were restored and beautified so that the inhabitants of the town learned, once more, to admire their haunting beauty. The Mevlevi musicians were among our close friends: the ney-player Halil Can as much as Sabri Özdil and Kani Karaca who used to recite the *naʿt-e sharif* and the Koran, and many others as well. Mehmet Dede, the last dervish, aged and weak, still lived in his little cell in the compound of the former *tekke* and present-day museum; he died in 1958 at the age of nearly 90; a little fountain close to the memorial of Shams-e Tabrizi reminds the visitor to Konya of this remarkable man. And there was 'my brother' Ismail, a carpenter by profession, who, in his simple purity, was an embodiment of the best dervish tradition; he always reminded me of the numerous medieval artisans who once followed Rumi in veneration and devotion, and his mystical wisdom was deeper than that of many learned masters. A few days before his departure for Germany, where he suddenly passed away, he saw in a dream that he was sitting at the feet of Hazrat-e Mowlānā, who smiled at him. I am sure that his dream was fulfilled—he certainly deserved such a gentle gesture . . .

Turkey brought me in contact with innumerable lovers of Hazrat-e Mowlānā, who were recruited from the most divergent social classes, ranging from illiterate village women to ministers of state and diplomats. New aspects of Rumi were unveiled during the ensuing years when my work concentrated on Pakistan, and on Muhammad Iqbal (d. 1938) who has been called —though with undue exaggeration—the 'Rumi of our age'. Iqbal's dynamic interpretation of the work of his spiritual master, who appears as his guide and master in all his poetical works, is of vital importance for the modern approach to classical Islamic Sufism; it seems, to me, closer to Rumi's original thought than many of the commentaries which were composed in the course of seven centuries under the influence of Ibn ʿArabi's philosophy. Wherever I went in Pakistan, Rumi's spirit was alive: be it in the musical sessions in Peshawar, or in the powerful Punjabi translations of his verses; it permeated the poetry of the Sindhi mystics, headed by Shāh ʿAbdul Laṭif, and was palpable in Bengali religious folk-songs.

Mowlānā Jalāloddin proved indeed a faithful companion throughout the years. His poems—the lyrics as well as the *Mathnavi*—yielded new results at every new reading, whether during lonely evening-hours, or during seminar-sessions with my students.

What, then, can be said about Rumi from the view-point of a modern interpreter? The response of our students to his verses is absolutely positive, although his poetry seems to offer difficulties to those who have not lived long enough with him. His language many times breaks the borders of normal Persian imagery. In Rumi's ghazals there is nothing of the nicely trimmed gardens of Shiraz which we like to take for the very essence of the Persian ghazal. His verses resemble rather the miniature paintings in Turcoman style with their almost incredible movement of flowers, bushes, demons, and animals than the well organized perfection of Bihzadian painting. Rumi's wide reliance upon a vocabulary taken from everyday life, and his switching from one topic to another without apparent logical sequence tends to confuse the readers at first; but the strong rhythm (which is part of the cosmic dance) always carries them away and helps them finally to overcome the obstacles. The fact that the poet, probably almost unconsciously, uses rhetorical devices, puns and wordplays of a high order in the midst of outwardly plain verses adds as much to the difficulty as the application of dialectical expressions or Turkish and Greek words in some of his verses. Rumi's language can be compared, in its rich and varied vocabulary, only to that of the greatest panegyrist of Persian literature, Khāqāni (d. 1179) whose use of the language was, however, much more logical.

Can we extract a mystical philosophy out of Mowlānā's work? The number of commentaries which have attempted to do so is extremely great, and each commentator, beginning with Solṭān Valad, has seen in Rumi what was closest to his understanding. Was Mowlānā a pantheist or monist, a defender of the theory of *waḥdat al-wojud* as systematized by his older contemporary Ibn ʿArabi (d. 1240) whose foremost interpreter Ṣadroddin was a friend of Mowlānā's in Konya? The oft-used imagery of the ocean out of which the waves and the foam emerge seems indeed to point to a pantheistic tendency. Are Mowlānā's words about the ever-rising movement of created beings to be interpreted as evolutionist, or as emanationist, as many scholars particularly in our century want to explain them? Or do they not rather express the simple truth visible every moment: that only through death new life can arise, and that sacrifice in the way of love is the only way that leads to survival? Was Rumi a philosopher who saw the activity of the First Intellect permeate the whole world, or considered non-existence a box in which all possibilities, including matter, were hidden from pre-eternity, waiting for God's call to become realized in time and space? Or was he simply a lover who had been burnt, putting aside intellect and external forms in the higher unity of lover and beloved?

He was, most probably, something of each of these possibilities. It would be worthwhile investigating his use of several central concepts in detail, the two most important being *ʿadam*, non-existence in both negative and positive meaning, often bordering on the definition of Nirvana as 'bliss, unspeakable', and *kibriyā*, the glorious Divine grandeur, manifest in the sun and in everything radiant and powerful. But if we understand him correctly, the moving force even beyond *kibriyā* and *ʿadam* is love—love as the Essence of a God who reveals Himself in Beauty and Majesty to His creatures.

Rumi was a human being, and very much so: his use of images proves that, and his very personal remarks, his short poems born out of rapture or sudden anger prove that as well. But he knew that the spiritual ladder which he described so often in his verses does not consist in killing the base qualities, and doing away with the world of matter but rather in integrating them into the human progress. The little devil of a soul becomes a faithful Muslim, Satan himself turns into a Gabriel once love has performed its wonderful alchemy. Then, man sees *faqr*, spiritual poverty and denudation from every created quality, as a red ruby, comparable to Dante's *balascio* at the end of the Divine Comedy. Annihilated in the light and fire of this ruby he is led into the very heart of love. And returning once more, he sees the world changed, filled with meaning, and no longer as the dunghill which it appears to be in the eyes of the ascetic.

Simple as Rumi's thought may be, it is impossible to exhaust his work. The variety of expressions, the rich embroidery of the simple material, the opaline quality of the images makes him intriguing anew every time one approaches to his work.

When an author has to deal with such a complex personality the question arises: how to organize the material found in the nearly 60,000 verses of his work?

It seems to me that a purely descriptive approach might yield the most unbiased results. Since Mowlānā is primarily a mystical poet, it seemed logical to interpret his work from different angles, the first being that of poetical language, the second one that of mystical thought. Both facets taken together can reveal at least part of his personality and of his inexhaustible poetical work.

Like his predecessors and followers on the mystical path, Rumi lived deeply out of the eternal truth revealed in the Koran. We therefore tried to develop each chapter in the context of a Koranic saying, which is reflected in his utterances in various colours. The whole problem of his imagery can be understood from a Koranic verse of which the Sufis were particularly fond: 'We shall show them Our signs in the horizons and in themselves' (Sura 41/53), a word that gave the mystics endless possibilities to experience God's creative power in each and every aspect of life, revealing itself in mineral and rainbow, in flowers and birds, in man and angel.

Rumi's favourite symbol among all images is the *Sun*, all the more because it is connected with the name of his mystical beloved, Shamsoddin, the 'Sun of religion'. And the Koranic phrase 'By the morning-light . . .' (Sura 93/1), so often applied by earlier Sufi poets to the radiant face of the Prophet of Islam, gives a Koranic clue for this symbol.

Water has been the sign of Divine grace in all countries of the Middle East, and the Koran proclaims: 'We made everything alive from water' (Sura 21/30); Mowlānā, too, elaborates this image in its various, even contradictory, aspects. That leads logically to the imagery of the *Garden*. Did not the Koran promise the faithful in many of its verses that they would dwell in 'gardens of delight', in 'gardens underneath which flow rivers'? The garden and what is in it became a symbol of God's creative power, of His grace, and a prefiguration of the paradisical bliss which the faithful will experience at the end of times.

The Koran had called the faithful to see God's signs everywhere: 'Do they not look at the camel, how it was created?' (Sura 88/17). Here is the starting point for Mowlānā's imagery of *Animals*. He was particularly fond of these images, and his verses prove his keen observation, encompassing even the most insignificant creatures which reveal to him God's power, or constitute lively examples of human behaviour, as it was known from the fables of *Kalila va Dimna* upon which Rumi, like many other mystics, heavily relied in his tales. In his work, no animal is left aside—from lion to ant, from camel to gnat, from sea cow to porcupine, and the various birds that were used as symbols by his predecessors in mystical poetry, Sanāʾi and ʿAṭṭār, form an important aspect of his imagery.

But more than the world of inorganic beings, of plants and of animals the world of man attracts Rumi, and there is barely an aspect of human life that he has not touched. The Koran mentions the miraculous creation of man more than once. It is 'He who created you from dust, then from a drop of sperm, then from a blood clot, then brought you forth as children' (Sura 22/5). Mowlānā dwells upon this idea and shows man's spiritual growth in terms taken from the life of *children* in medieval Konya, painting a lively picture of their games and their aversions and predilections; he knows that 'He makes clear His signs to the people: haply they will remember' (Sura 2/221)—signs which the eye of the saint can detect in every moment of *daily life*, even in the Turkish bath or in the shop of the butcher or the cobbler. They can also be found in contemplating one's daily bread: the Koran had ordered man 'Eat and drink of God's providing' (Sura 2/60), and Mowlānā, though according to his biographers very strict in fasting, did not hesitate to use every kind of *food* for his imagery so as to enable us to find an almost complete 'mystical menu' as prepared in the kitchen of 13th century Konya.

It would be surprising if we did not find the imagery of *diseases* in Rumi's verses: outward diseases are signs of inward defects, but the faithful Muslim knows 'And when I was ill, He healed me' (Sura 26/80). The professions and activities of the inhabitants of Konya inspired Mowlānā to some of his most beautiful verses; the age-old imagery of *weaving and sewing*, along with the Koranic promise 'And their garment there, will be silk' (Sura 22/23) provided many opportunities to show God, or Love, under the symbol of the great weaver of fate, or tailor of life, as much as the imagery of *calligraphy*, so cherished by all poets of the Muslim lands, shows the Lord as the master calligrapher. Did He Himself not say in the Koran: '*Nūn*, and by the Pen, and what they write' (Sura 68/1)?

But even the pastimes of the grandees at the Seljukid court of Konya could serve Rumi as examples for religious ideas. The Koran had declared that 'The present life is naught but a sport and a diversion' (Sura 6/32 and others); thus, sports and games as practised all over the medieval Muslim world could well serve to symbolize higher mental stages and spiritual experiences.

That the Koran itself contributed hundreds of images to Arabic, and consequently to all Muslim languages, is well known; 'We have indeed displayed for men in this Koran every manner of similitude' (Sura 18/54). The heroes of the Koranic tales became as much part and parcel of the daily speech of the Muslims as became its most impressive verses which were incorporated without difficulty into the various Islamic idioms. The Koran teaches man also to look at the *history* of the bygone nations; 'That is a nation that hath passed away'

(Sura 2/128) and a poet like Rumi did not restrict himself to the use of the standard names of some cities, rivers, and mountains but was well enough versed in contemporary and near contemporary history to include allusions to it in his poetry.

That a mystic should largely draw upon the sources of the *mystical tradition* goes without saying. The saints, described in the Koranic revelation with the consoling words; 'Verily, God's friends—no fear shall be upon them, neither shall they sorrow' (Sura 10/69), form the 'golden chain' that leads from the poet-mystic back to the Prophet. Their stories were widely known in the medieval Islamic world, and it was easy for any poet to allude to them; Rumi remains faithful to this tradition and highlights their personalities in sometimes surprising verses.

But perhaps the most typical expression of Rumi's personality is the imagery connected with *music and dance:* the initiator of the Whirling Dervishes knew the enrapturing character of music, and the Song of the Reed at the beginning of his *Mathnavi* is related to the Koranic story of creation when God says about Adam; 'And I have have breathed into him from My breath . . .' (Sura 15/29): man is the flute which speaks when touched by the breath of the Divine Beloved.

These groups of images occur most frequently in Rumi's verses, and a careful study of their application to various aspects of mystical thought may lead us to a deeper understanding of his way of thinking. As to his mystical theology, it is almost impossible to draw a clearly outlined picture; too widely divergent are his utterances about the same topic at various times.

There is no doubt that his whole life was directed by the overwhelming Majesty of God that revealed itself to the pious Muslim best in the Throne verse (Sura 2/256): 'God—there is no god but He, the Living, the Everlasting . . .' Rumi's theology is a constant dialogue with this living God who has created the world and is able to create every instant something new from the abysses of non-existence; but what ever He may create, it is meant to worship and praise Him: 'Nothing is there that does not proclaim His praise' (Sura 17/44). The highest and noblest place in creation is given to *man,* as the Koran states: 'And We have honoured the children of Adam'

(Sura 17/70); for man is the only creature endowed with the possibility of choosing between good and evil, and is hence superior to both beast and angel. Mowlānā has not developed a mystical psychology but sometimes gives deep insights into the human heart and soul.

If man in general is the highest manifestation of God's creative power the *Prophet* of Islam occupies a special rank among men: God proclaimed about him; 'We have not sent thee, save as a mercy to all beings' (Sura 21/107). His sacred personality is the centre of every Muslim's piety, and the mystics soon surrounded him with innumerable qualities of miraculous character.

Man's whole way into the Divine presence is seen, by the mystics of Islam as of other religions, as a constant spiritual progress, a *ladder* that leads to heaven, as the Koran says; 'You shall surely ride stage after stage' (Sura 84/19). But such a progress is impossible without sacrifice: death is the prerequisite for eternal life, destruction the condition for new building. God's activity reveals this constant change; 'He brings forth the living from the dead and the dead from the living' (Sura 30/19 and often). This constant sacrifice in order to gain access to higher stages of beings, the unending experience of *Stirb und werde* would be impossible were not *love* the force behind every movement in the world. The Sufis had early discovered the Divine word 'He loves them, and they love him' (Sura 5/59) and understood from it the truth that God's love precedes human love. This feeling of mutual love, and the knowledge that love is indeed the only thing that matters in the whole life of creation, forms the cornerstone of Rumi's thought, and is echoed time and again in his verses in every possible tune. But the last and highest experience of this mutual love between man and God is found in *prayer,* when man obeys the Divine invitation 'Call, and I shall answer' (Sura 40/62) and reaches a perfect union of will through loving surrender.

This book is the result of a dialogue of forty years with Mowlānā. A very personal dialogue, to be sure—that is why he will emerge not so much as the mystical master whose verses bear the stamp of neo-Platonic speculations, but rather as a human being of great sensitivity, a 'man' in the highest sense of the word, grounded firmly in the Koran and in classical Islamic mysticism. The light of the Divine Sun, in its Beauty and Majesty, manifested itself for him through the person of Shamsoddin of Tabriz. Transformed by this light, consumed by this fire, Mowlānā Rumi saw the world in new light: everywhere he detected the traces of God's Grandeur and His Grace, listening to the praise of everything created; and he reminded his followers in unforgettable verses that true life is possible only by surrendering to love.

I

The Outward Setting

THE HISTORICAL BACKGROUND

The 13th century is perhaps the most fascinating and, at the same time embarrassing period in the history of the Muslim world.

After the death of the Prophet Moḥammad in 632, the Muslims had extended their rule from Arabia over large parts of the then known world: Syria, Egypt, and Iran were soon incorporated into the new empire; in 711 the Muslims reached Spain, the Indus Valley, and Transoxania. The kingdoms they founded in the Eastern and Western outposts of the empire waxed stronger and more independent in the course of time. The Iberian peninsula is an exception—the slow *reconquista* of Spain by the Christians was completed in 1492, and the Spanish inherited a brilliant civilisation that was to influence deeply the development of Christian Europe.

Many different rulers had come and gone; the 'Golden Age' of the four righteous caliphs ended in 661 when ʿAli ibn Abi Ṭāleb, Moḥammad's cousin and son-in-law, was murdered. The following dynasty, the Omayyads, who shifted their residence from the homeland of Islam to Syria, waged successful wars and extended the borders of the empire further and further, although the pious disliked their worldly, luxurious life and accused them of not following the injunctions of the Koran as strictly as they were expected in their capacity as leaders of the faithful. In 680, ʿAli's cadet son Ḥoseyn was killed, together with most members of his family, in the battle of Karbala; the tragic event resulted in a deep popular veneration for him. The *shīʿatu ʿAlī* (Shiites), ʿAli's party, who mainly fostered this love, soon developed into different branches and at times (thus in the 10th century) ruled large parts of the Muslim world, attracting the masses by a more emotional interpretation of some facets of Islam and also segments of the intelligentsia by their combination of philosophical and theological hermeneutics.

In 750, the Abbasids, related to the Prophet through his uncle ʿAbbās, took over the rule and shifted the capital to Baghdad; hence, Iranian influences upon Islamic culture became palpable in every area of life. The Abbasid period is considered the heyday of Muslim civilisation, literature and art. Translations from Greek, Indian, and Persian medical, philosophical and mathematical works were produced and elaborated by Muslim scholars; the theoretical foundations of Muslim law were laid, the four schools of law, *madhhab*, developed; theological thinking, armed with the new weapon of hellenistic philosophical terminology, grew in different directions. The Muʿtazilites, who first used the tools of philosophy to defend the pure monotheism of Islam against the threat of Persian dualism and Christian trinitarian thought, were eventually banned; orthodox currents, with their unshakeable faith in the Koran as the uncreated, eternal word of God, became firmly established in Muslim lands.

At the same time, the more pious Muslims turned to stricter asceticism—in opposition to the growing luxury of everyday life; the name for Islamic mysticism, *tasavvof*, Sufism, is derived from their woollen (*ṣuf*) frocks. In Khorassan and Iraq, in Egypt and Syria people of ascetic inclinations gathered in small groups, and out of this movement, which centred around constant meditation on the Koran, poverty and complete trust in God, true mysticism emerged. The ideal of perfect love of God, without any selfish wish—be it hope for Paradise or fear of Hell—was accepted and elaborated to its utmost consequences. Rābeʿa al-ʿAdawiyya, the woman saint of Basra, is credited with the introduction of these thoughts. As early as the 10th century one finds representatives of different trends in Sufism: there is the Nubian Ẕuʾn-Nun in Egypt (d. 859) whose enthusiastic poetical prayers belong to the finest products of classical Arabic Sufi literature, and there is the lonely, weird Bāyazid Besṭami (d. 874) in Western Iran, noted for his 'negative way of union' and his stress upon *fanāʾ* 'annihilation from human qualities' in God; we find Yahyā ibn Maʿādh (d. 871), the preacher from Reyy who 'had a tongue in hope', and the sober scholars of the Bagdhadian school, headed by Moḥāsebi (d. 857) whose surname is derived from the stern psychological self-control (*moḥāsaba*) he advocated: this system of Sufi psychology which shaped the spiritual training of the later moderate Sufis finds its first expression in his writings. Among the leaders of the Baghdadian school the name of Joneyd (d. 910) is most prominent; he was the 'sheykh of this group', 'the peacock of the poor', and most of the spiritual genealogies of the later orders can be traced back to him. It was he who—according to legends—predicted that his former disciple Ḥoseyn ibn Manṣur al-Ḥallāj would meet a terrible end: indeed, Ḥallāj, the greatest representative of early Sufism was cruelly put to death in 922. The reasons were mainly political—not so much, as one usually tends to believe and as legend asserts, orthodox aversion to his utterance *anā'l-ḥaqq* 'I am the Truth' or, 'I am God'.

Although the mystical movement spread over almost every Muslim country, Ḥallāj's ideas were kept alive, under the surface, mainly in Iran. They became once more conspicuous in the work of ʿAṭṭār (d. 1220), the mystical poet of Nishapur, who became spiritually initiated into mystical life by the Baghdādian 'martyr of Divine Love'.

Persian poetry, from its very beginning—e.g. from the 10th century onwards—had been influenced by Sufi thought; the first author to use Persian for his beautiful poetical orisons was ʿAbdollāh-e Anṣāri (d. 1089), the patron saint of Herat and author of an important Persian biography of saints. Other mystics of Eastern Iran used the quatrain (*robāʿi*) as means of expression for their mystical thought. Again in the same area—present-day Afghanistan—the first comprehensive didactic work was composed: Sanā'i of Ghazna (d. 1131), a former court poet converted to Sufism, wrote his *Ḥadiqat al-ḥaqiqa*, 'The Orchard of Truth' around 1120; he thus set the model for all later mystical *mathnavis*, e.g. didactical works written in rhyming couplets, which contain numerous stories, anecdotes and parables without fixed order to illustrate different aspects of mystical and practical life. Sanā'i's example was followed by Faridoddin ʿAṭṭār, whose numerous epics are much more artistic than those of his predecessor. They soon became standard works of mystical instruction, widely read wherever Persian was spoken.

In the meantime, moderate Sufism had produced a number of handbooks in which mysticism was explained in accordance with orthodox teachings (as in the case of as-Sarrāj, d. 988, al-Makki, d. 996, al-Kalābādhi, d. 995, al Qusheyri, d. 1074, and, in India, Hojwiri, d. c. 1070). Abu Ḥāmed al-Ghazzāli (d. 1111) of Tus, Sanā'i's contemporary, created the *summa* of moderately mystically tinged Muslim thought in his *Iḥyāʾ ʿolum ad-dīn. The Revivification of the Sciences of Religion*—a book which has not lost its paramount importance for Muslim piety up to our day.

It was, however, Abu Ḥāmed's younger brother, Aḥmad Ghazzāli (d. 1126) who should be remembered as one of the greatest masters of mystical love theories. Mystical love, first directed exclusively towards God without any object in between, was now sometimes blended with the admiration of a beautiful face in which God's Beauty reveals itself to the loving mystic: the oscillation between heavenly and earthly love became then, a standard aspect of Persian and related poetry. Aḥmad Ghazzāli's *savāneḥ*, as well as the works of his disciple ʿEynolqozāt Hamadhāni (d. 1137) show this love-mysticism in highly artistic form; the union of lover and beloved in Love, the mirror-like relation with each other is described in words the subtlety of which defies translation. In the words of Ruzbehān Baqli of Shiraz (d. 1209) nearly one century later than Aḥmad Ghazzāli, these ideas reached their apogee.

Already in very early times the Sufis were attacked because of their fondness for music: a beautiful voice might induce them into ecstacy, whether the content of the text was the Koran, the Divine word, or a profane love poem. They often indulged in whirling movement to attain ecstasy, and as early as the late 9th century *samāʿ*-sessions were held everywhere. Here, the Sufis, intoxicated by music and recitation, whirled around their axis, often rending their garments so that not only orthodox circles, but also more sober groups among the mystics were scandalized. All these movements reached maturity in the 12th century—and this is the time when Sufism, consolidated in theory as well, began to be converted into a mass movement.

The first mystical fraternities came into existence—it may be that they were a counterweight against the Ismaili movement, which, as an extremist Shia sect, had attracted large masses in earlier days; in the 11th century, the orthodox, like al-Ghazzāli, afraid of the political and spiritual consequences of Ismaili theories, relentlessly fought against them with pen and sword. Yet the common people craved for a closer communion with God which they could not find in the outward forms of religion: the lawyer-divines and theologians had put every movement of body and soul into such a narrow framework that the free soaring of the soul was often hampered; that is why people from all strata of society sought some outlet for their feelings in more emotional forms of religion. Such forms were offered by the orders, which, from around 1120 onwards, slowly developed in the Muslim East and soon spread everywhere. The spiritual leader, the sheykh—always highly respected and absolutely obeyed by his disciples—was now considered the sole and infallible guide on the path towards salvation: he was 'the ladder to Heaven', as Rumi says. His influence over his disciples grew tremendously. Many members of Sufi orders wandered through the Muslim world; they reached distant provinces like India, founding little centres (*dargāh*) which soon grew into veritable nuclei of Islamic missionary work, and they won over to the simple basic teaching of Islam thousands who would have never been attracted by the official legalistic forms of this religion, but who enjoyed the warm, loving surrender as taught and practised by the mystical leaders.

Thus was the 'spiritual' situation around 1200.

On the political plane, many things had changed. The Abbasid caliphat once so powerful, had lost many of the border lands. Spain had become independent in 926, when ʿAbdorraḥmān III from the Omayyad family declared himself caliph; the Eastern provinces were more or less nominally under Bagdhad suzerainty. In 945 the Persian Shiite family of the Buweyhids took over de facto rule in the central provinces so that the Abbasid caliph became a mere puppet in their hands. The powerful Turkish ruler Mahmud of Ghazna, who conquered large parts of Northwestern India after the year 1004 and whose court was a centre of learning and Persian poetry, remained a loyal vassal of the Abbasid caliph and defender of Sunnite orthodoxy. Ghaznavid predominance was followed in the East by the Ghurids, in the central countries by the Seljuks, another Turkish clan who entered the realms of Islam in the mid-11th century and whose members soon became stern defenders of orthodoxy in the Eastern and central provinces. The names of Alp Arslān and Malekshāh as well as that of the capable vizier Neẓāmolmolk, Ghazzāli's protector, mark the zenith of this dynasty in the second half of the 11th century. Their army succeeded also in 1071 in entering Eastern Anatolia at the expense of the Byzantines; in spite of the Crusaders, who often crossed Anatolia, these Rum Seljuks were able to build up a flourishing rule in Turkey, their capital being Konya, the old Iconium.

Egypt was separated from the Abbasid empire in 969—after the short interlude of the Tulunids and the Ikhshidids—when the Fatimids (again a Shia dynasty) conquered it to rule there for two centuries. The country was brought back into the fold of the Abbasids, or at least to Sunni Islam, by the Ayyubid dynasty in 1171: the Ayyubids are known, to Western readers, as the main supporters of the Muslim cause during the Crusades, their sultan Ṣalāḥoddin (Saladin) being regarded as a model of Muslim virtue and chivalry.

The highly confused history of the Islamic Empire, in which religious and political movements interacted and worked against each other in ways not easily disentangled cannot be told in detail. Suffice it to mention that once more a revival of the Abbasid caliphate was attempted around 1200. The inaugurator of the movement was the last truly active member of the dynasty, an-Nāser li-Din Allāh. He tried to build up an organization of Muslim princes who should co-operate in the spirit of *futuvva*, 'virtue'. This is a basically mystical ideal, which he used as basis for a chivalric organization, insignia of which he sent to the neighbouring rulers at the hand of one of the leading mystics of his time, Abu Ḥafṣ ᶜOmar Sohrawardi (d. 1232). Caliph Nāṣer's main aim was to call the Muslims to reunite against a power rising on the Eastern horizon during his lifetime, i.e. the Mongols under the leader Genghiz Khan. But the unwise behaviour of the Khwarezmshah, the ruler of Eastern Khorassan and parts of Central Asia, provided the Mongols with the pretext—if they needed any at all—for moving towards the Muslim lands. It need not be told how their hordes over ran Asia and parts of Eastern Europe in the 13th century, occupying an area between the Eastern borders of Germany to the shore of the Japanese Sea, leaving death and ruin wherever they went. They soon conquered Iran and adjacent countries, and reached Central Anatolia as they had already descended to the Indus Valley. The final blow came when Hulagu conquered Baghdad in 1258. The last member of the Abbasid house was killed, all traces of Baghdad's former glory wiped out. Two years later, in 1260, the Mamluks, a dynasty of Turkish slaves recently established in Egypt, succeeded in stopping the Mongols in ʿAyn Jālut in Syria. Yet, Mongol supremacy was established over large parts of the Muslim world. The whole political situation changed in the second half of the 13th century—not to mention the economical changes that took place after the ruin of so many flourishing cities and the destruction of irrigation works in agricultural areas. Yet, out of the Mongol rule new, and in part very attractive, facets of Islamic culture were to develop in the following centuries.

Strangely enough this period of the most terrible political disaster was, at the same time, a period of highest religious and mystical activity. It seems as though the complete darkness on the worldly plane was counteracted by a hitherto unknown brightness on the spiritual plane. The names of poets, scholars, calligraphers could be enumerated, but it is mainly the mystics who dominate this century. The supreme figure is the Spanish-born Ibn ʿArabi, *ash-sheykh al-akbar* (d. 1240 in Damascus); he developed a most consistent theosophical system, which was to be adopted by most of the later mystics of Islam. His contemporary in Egypt, Ibn al-Fāreḍ (d. 1235) sang highly refined poems to praise eternal spiritual love. Somewhat later the founder of the Shadhiliyya order settled in Egypt; his second successor, Ibn ʿAṭāʾ Allāh (d. 1309) is the author of words of wisdom (*ḥikam*) which have provided spiritual food for thousands of mystics in the Western Islamic world. In Iran, Faridoddin ʿAṭṭār, who died in 1220, left a rich spiritual heritage of poetry and prose (among them his biography of saints, *Tadhkerat al-owliyā*); in the same year the Mongols killed Najmoddin Kobrā, the founder of an extremely interesting mystical order in Khwarezm. His disciple Najmoddin Dāyā Rāzi, like so many other scholars and saints, including Jalāloddin Rumi's family, fled to Anatolia where he composed his mystical work *Mirsād ol-ʿebād* under the Seljuks. In India, Moʿinoddin Chishti (d. 1236) introduced the Chishtiyya order; from the long list of Chishti saints in 13th century India we may mention Faridoddin Ganj-e Shakar (d. 1265), Neẓāmoddin Owliyā of Delhi (d. 1325) and his faithful disciple and biographer Amir Ḥasan as well as his poet-friend Amir Khosrow. Bahāʾoddin Zakariya founded a branch of the Sohrawardiyya in Multan, and in his presence

Fakhroddin ʿErāqi, the mystical minstrel of overbounding love, spent twenty-five years of his life before his return to Anatolia. There, he found Ṣadroddin Qunavi, Ibn ʿArabi's foremost interpeter in Konya; a little while earlier Owḥadoddin Kermāni had died, a poet who had sung about the love of beautiful human beings and had written a mystical mathnavi *jām-e jam*. Antolia was filled with groups of mystics striving for social and political changes. Many of them had migrated from the Eastern lands, fleeing from the Mongol threat. Among them we may mention Hājji Bektash to whom the Bektashi order of dervishes trace back its origin; slightly later the first great poet of mystical songs in the Turkish tongue, Yunus Emre, wandered about the country.

In short, in almost every corner of the Islamic world were found great saints, poets, and mystical leaders, who, in the darkness of political and economical catastrophes, guides the people towards a world which was unhurt by change, telling them the secret of suffering love, and taught that God's inscrutable will and His Love may reveal itself in affliction even better than in happiness.

That was the spiritual environment into which Jalāloddin Rumi was born.

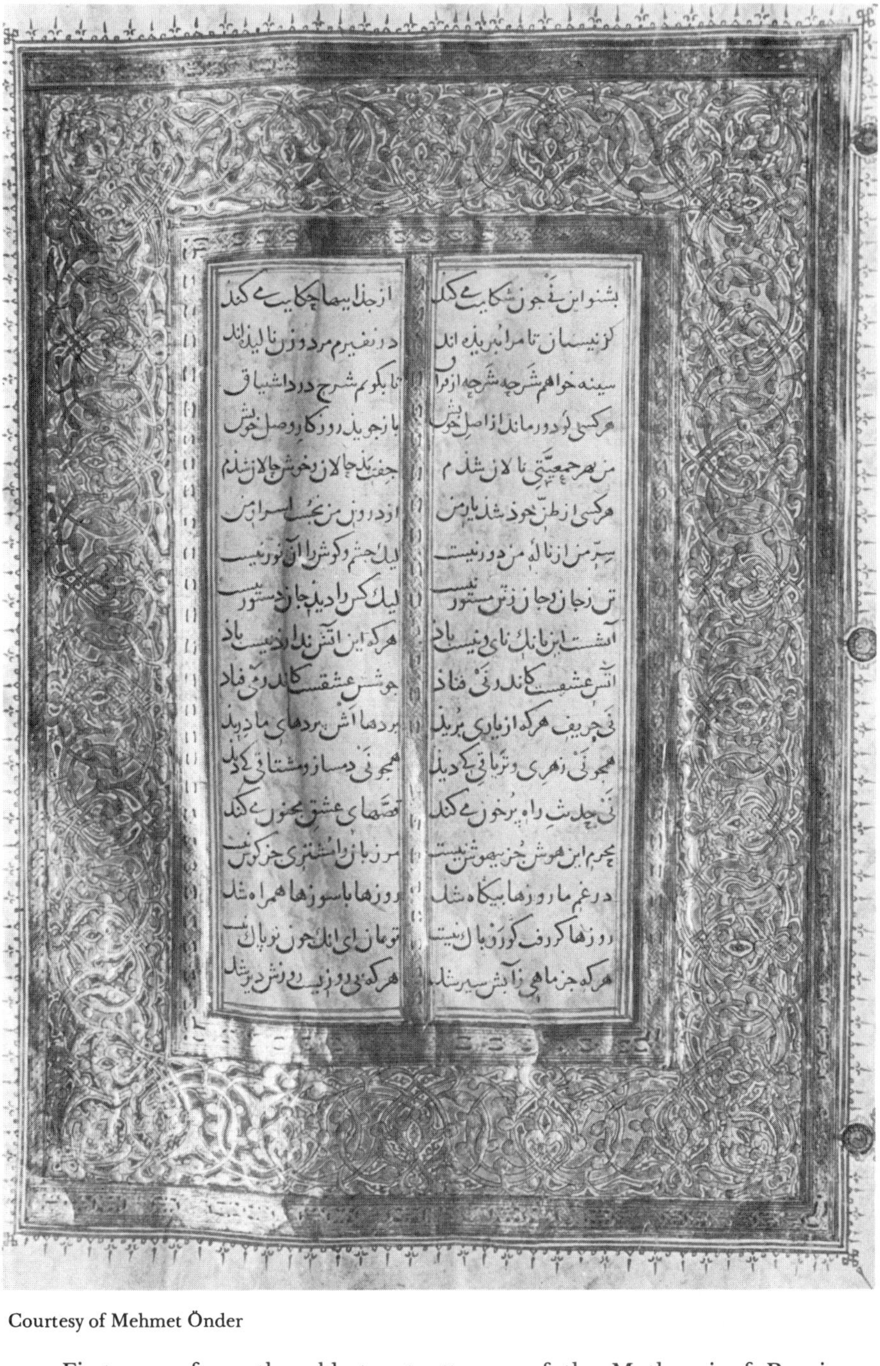

Courtesy of Mehmet Önder

First page from the oldest extant copy of the Mathnavi of Rumi, preserved in the Mevlâna Müzesi, Konya.

BIOGRAPHICAL NOTES

The inhabitants of Konya were seized with fear during the first half of December 1273. For days and days, the earth continued to shake and tremble, and Mowlānā Jalāloddin Rumi was feeling weak and exhausted. Eventually he declared: 'The earth is hungry. Soon, it will get a fat morsel and then give rest.' His illness increased, but he consoled his friends who surrounded him with some poems:

> The lovers who die well-informed,
> die before the Beloved like sugar . . .[1]

melting away in the eternal sweetness of God. And:

> O birds which are at present separated from your cage,
> show again your face, and say: 'Where are you?'
> O you who were born when you arrived at death—
> This is a second birth—be born, be born![2]

On December 17, at sunset, Jalāloddin passed away, to become united with the Eternal Sun; but his radiance remained behind him, never fading away throughout seven centuries.

How did this life unfold itself in the realm of time?

Jalāloddin was born in Balkh, present-day Afghanistan. The generally accepted date is September 30, 1207, although a remark in his prose-work *Fihi mā fihi* may indicate an earlier date, since he mentions the Khwarezmshah's siege of Samarqand (1207) as if speaking as an eye-witness.[3] An earlier date would also agree better with his father's age. His father (born ca. 1148 or somewhat later) was a noted theologian, Moḥammad ibn al-Ḥoseyn Bahāʾoddin Valad, surnamed *Solṭān al-ʿolamā*. This title was conferred upon him, according to his grandson, by the Prophet himself through a dream which all the scholars of Balkh saw on the same night. Bahāʾoddin was a mystic; according to some sources, he belonged spiritually to the school of Aḥmad Ghazzāli (d. 1126). In how far the subtle love-mysticism as described by Aḥmad in his *Savāneḥ* may have influenced him and, through him, his son's spiritual formation cannot yet be judged. If Aflāki's remark about Bahāʾoddin Valad's verdict on 'looking at beautiful young men' as 'spiritual fornication' is correct,[4] it would be difficult to believe in his affiliation to the Ghazzālian school of love-mysticism. Close relations with Najmoddin Kobrā, the founder of the Kobrāviyya, are more likely.

Some claims have been made that Bahā'oddin's paternal family descended from Abu Bakr, the first caliph of Islam. This may or may not be true; nothing certain is known about the racial background of the family. It has also been told that Bahā'oddin's wife belonged to the house of the Khwarezmshahs who had established their rule in the Eastern provinces about 1080; but this tale can be dismissed as a later invention.

Jalāloddin's hometown was captured in 1206 by the Khwarezmshah from the Ghurids; Rumi himself later alluded in his poetry to the bloodshed in the wars between the Khwarezmians and the Ghurids when he attempted to describe how separation had drowned him in blood . . .[5]

Balkh was, at that time, still one of the centres of Islamic learning. The ancient city had played an important part during the formative period of Eastern Sufism and is the hometown of many Muslim scholars during the first centuries of the hegira. Since it had formerly been a centre of Buddhism, its inhabitants—or its atmosphere—may have served as mediators of some Buddhist ideas which are reflected in early Sufi thought: was not Ibrāhim ibn Adham, the 'prince of spiritual Poverty', a highborn inhabitant of Balkh whose conversion was told in terms of the Buddha-legend?

During Jalāloddin's childhood, one of the leading scholars in the town was Fakhroddin Rāzi, the philosopher and commentator on the Koran who enjoyed great popularity with Moḥammad Khwarezmshah. It is said that he instigated the ruler against the Sufis and was the cause of the mystic Majdoddin Baghdādi's being drowned in the Oxus (1209). Bahā'oddin Valad, too, was apparently not on friendly terms with him, as his writings prove: the pious, mystically minded theologian 'whose blessed character had become stern, and filled with awe due to the large amount of manifestations of Divine Majesty'[6] had a heartfelt aversion against philosophy and the cerebral approach to religion; this attitude, already palpable in Sanā'i's poetry one century earlier, was inherited by Jalāloddin as well, strengthened even more by his friend Shamsoddin who called Rāzi 'a red infidel'.[7] Half a century after Rāzi's death, Jalāloddin Rumi could not help writing in the *Mathnavi:*

> If intellect could discern (the right way) in this discussion, Fakhr-e Rāzi would have been the mystery-keeper of religion.[8]

We have, however, to dismiss those legends which attribute Bahā᾿oddin Valad's migration from Balkh to the growing influence of Fakhroddin; for the philosopher died in 1210, whereas Bahā᾿oddin and his family left Balkh only c. 1218 or 1219.

At that time, the threat of the Mongols from Central Asia must have made itself felt. The Khwarezmshah himself, by killing some Mongol merchants, had played a most fatal role in the drama which was to develop during the ensuing years in the whole Near and Middle East. Whatever the reason for Bahā᾿oddin's travel to foreign lands was, he, his family and his disciples (Sepahsālār speaks of 300!)[9] were far away from his hometown when it was sacked by the Mongols. Balkh was reduced to mere ruins in 1220; thousands of people were killed.

> When you are in Balkh, make a move towards Baghdad, oh father,
> So that every moment you get farther away from Merv and Herat . . .[10]

The way led the family through Khorassan; legend tells that they paid a visit to Faridoddin ᶜAṭṭār in Nishapur; and the aged mystical poet, impressed by young Jalāloddin's ability, presented him with a copy of his *Asrārnāme.*

Then the family performed the pilgrimage to Mecca and probably lived for a while in Syria, again one of the centres of Islamic civilization. Information about the length of this journey, and of the stay in different places is contradictory; it seems most likely, however, that Jalāloddin stayed for a while in Damascus, the seat of learning, perhaps also in Aleppo; for it is mentioned that he studied under the famous historiographer Kamāloddin Ibn al-ᶜAdim, the chronist of Aleppo.[11] In one story of the *Mathnavi,* he alludes to that way in which ᶜAshurā was celebrated at the Antioch gate in Aleppo[12]—since the rule of the Hamdanids in the 10th century, the Shia creed had been established at least in part in the north Syrian town.

In the mid 1220's, Bahāʾoddin Valad and his family reached Central Anatolia, Rum—hence Jalāloddin's surname *Rumi*. They stayed for a while in Laranda, present-day Karaman. Here, Jalāloddin's mother passed away: the little mosque built in her honour is still visited by the people. The young scholar himself was married to Gowhar Khātun, a girl from Samarqand; his son Solṭān Valad was born in Laranda in 1226. As to the birth of his other son, ʿAlāʾoddin, some sources place it before that of Solṭān Valad; exact information is still lacking. Solṭān Valad was Rumi's favourite son, and was to become his father's most faithful interpreter, biographer, and at an advanced age his second successor; it was he who finally institutionalized the Mevlevi order.[13]

Karaman is situated about 100 km south-east of Konya, the capital of the Rum Seljuks. To this place, Bahāʾoddin Valad was called by Solṭān ʿAlāʾoddin Kaykobād, who gathered around himself scholars and mystics from all over the world. Anatolia, after recovering from the invasion of the Crusaders, had developed into a flourishing country, peaceful, and at that moment still far from the reach of the Mongols.[14] In 1220-21, Solṭān ʿAlāʾoddin (1219-1236) had built the Great Mosque on the hill in the heart of Konya, adjacent to the castle and overlooking the plains. The large, simple building bears the stamp of true greatness; it has room for 4000 men to pray under numerous pillars in front of the beautifully elaborated prayer-niche and most exquisitely carved wooden pulpit. There was no dearth of flourishing mosques and madrasas in Konya; some more were erected during Rumi's lifetime.

This was the place where Bahāʾoddin Valad and his family settled about 1228 and where the learned theologian began his preaching and teaching activities with great success. After only two years, however, he died at an advanced age (January 12, 1231), and his son Jalāloddin was appointed his successor.

Up to that time, the young scholar seems to have been interested mainly in the outward sciences; he was fond of Arabic poetry, especially of the highly difficult verses of Motanabbi (d. 965); probably he had taken part in mystical activities only so far as this was 'in the air' in his family. Shortly after Bahāʾoddin Valad's death, however, a former disciple of his entered Konya: Borhānoddin Moḥaqqeq at-Termezi, who had fled from Balkh first to his hometown Termez and then farther west, began to introduce Jalāloddin into ᶜ*ilm ladoni,* inspired wisdom, and the deeper mysteries of mystical life. He got his disciple interested in his father's collection of prose-works, the *Maᶜāref,*[15] in which the teachings and thoughts of Bahāʾoddin were laid down. It is told that Borhānoddin made Jalāloddin keep many *chilla*'s, e.g. forty days' periods of seclusion and meditation, until he reached the higher stages of illumination. But it is also told that Rumi spent, on Borhānoddin's advice, a long time in Syria to meet the mystical leaders: Sepahsālār relates that he had seen there Ibn ᶜArabi (di. 1240), Saᶜdoddin-e Ḥamavi, Owḥadoddin-e Kermāni and many other Sufis of Ibn ᶜArabi's circle.[16]

It is difficult to combine the two accounts. We may guess that Rumi indeed spent some time, though not too much, in Syria to refresh his mystical learning; at that time he may have met Shamsoddin of Tabriz for the first time without, however, being aware of his importance. A passage in Shams' *Maqālāt* seems to indicate such a first encounter.[17] Borhānoddin Moḥaqqeq left Konya around 1240. According to legend, he foresaw the coming a of 'great spiritual lion' with whom he could not live in one place.[18] He went to Kaiseri where he asked God to take away the soul which He had entrusted to him:

> O friend, accept me and take my soul!
> Intoxicate me and take me from both worlds!
> Into everything in which my heart has rested with Thee
> Cast fire, and take that (impediment) away![19]

Rumi came to Kaiseri to look after the remnants of his master's library; to his relation with Borhānoddin a line in a later ghazal may allude:

> When our Caesar is in Caesarea —
> do not place us in Albestan![20]

Borhānoddin Moḥaqqeq's modest tomb, surrounded by flowers, lies in the centre of the old cemetery, above which the majestic snow-covered Erciyes mountain rises. Pious Turkish Muslims still visit the place. Borhānoddin was a stern, extremely ascetic teacher; in his *Maqālāt*, which in many respects resemble those of his master Bahāʾoddin, one detects a strong influence of Sanāʾi—an influence which was to become again felt in Jalāloddin's poetry.

The topic of the soul's journey, sung so eloquently by Sanāʾi and then even more beautifully by ʿAṭṭār, recurs in Borhānoddin's verses as well:

> The way has an end, but not the stations—one thing is the journey towards God, and something else the journey *in* God.[21]

During the years when the master stayed with Rumi, and at the time of his death, Anatolia had become shaken by internal troubles. The Seljuk ruler Ghiyāsoddin Keykhosrow, who ascended the throne in 1237, was weak. A main problem was caused by the group of Khwarezmians who had fled their country to seek shelter from the wrath of Mongols in Eastern Anatolia. Solṭān ʿAlāʾoddin had settled them in Akhlat, not far from Erzerum—an act which drew the Mongols to Eastern Anatolia in 1232; subsequently, the Khwarezmians were resettled in Kaiseri. Neglected by ʿAlāʾoddin's successors, this group became again troublesome; some of their leaders were imprisoned by the government, an action which added to the difficulties. The Khwarezmians in part joined hands with some of the mystically inclined groups whose members wandered through Anatolia and some of whom tried to introduce social changes by attacking the ruling classes. Strange saints, like the Qalandaris, the Heydaris, the Abdāl of Rum with partly strong Shia tendencies swarmed through the country and attracted the lower strata of the population. Among them, the followers of Bābā Esḥāq even succeeded in conquering Tokat and Amasya; their leader was hanged in 1240.[22] All these groups worked together, more or less unintentionally, to weaken the Seljuk power to such an extent that the Mongols eventually found the country an easy prey: they finally conquered Erzerum in 1242; Sivas, one of the cultural centres of Anatolia, was handed over to the Mongol army by its Qāzi; thus, human lives were spared. In Kaiseri, which was pillaged soon afterwards, all male inhabitants were killed.

> People flee from the Tartars—
> We serve the Creator of the Tartars . . .[23]

The rulers in Konya understood that they were incapable of resisting the Mongol forces under these circumstances; they agreed in paying heavy tributes to them, and had, for all practical purposes, lost their political independence. The weak Ghiyāsoddin Keykhosrow died in 1245, leaving three sons who were recognized, after many struggles, in 1251 as a triumvirate by Möngke Khan, the Mongol ruler. Only a short while afterwards one of the three was murdered, and long feuds between the remaining two brothers ended in a chaos in which the last surviving brother, Roknoddin, became a mere toy in the hands of his minister Moʿinoddin Parvāne.

It was during those days, when the Rum Seljuks had to accept Mongol suzerainty, that the life of Rumi was likewise completely changed—as if the catastrophe on the political level was counterbalanced by an illumination on the spiritual level.

> Do not talk any more of the catastrophe of the Tartars—
> Speak of the (scent of the) navel of the Tartar muskdeer![24]

Although 'fire fell into the world, the smoke of the Tartar army',[25] Jalāloddin saw the eternal sun rising before him: in late October 1244 he met Shamsoddin of Tabriz, the 'Sun of Tabriz' in Konya.

> Your lovely dream-image was in our breast—
> The dawn gave a sign from the Sun![26]

Many legends have been woven around this first meeting, and it is difficult to decide which one is closest to the truth—perhaps we may accept the report that the two mystics started discussing the difference between Moḥammad the Prophet and Bāyazid Besṭâmi: Moḥammad, though a prophet called himself 'His slave' whereas Bāyazid the mystic exclaimed *Sobḥāni* 'How great is my glory' (both expressions, 'His slave' and *Sobḥān*, belong to the same Koranic passage, the allusion to Moḥammad's heavenly journey in Sura 17/1).

This topic would be much in keeping with the interest of both and echoes of meditations about these words can be found in Rumi's later verses. For six months, the two mystics were inseparable, so much so that the family and the disciples complained—Rumi neglected his classes, his friends, everybody, completely lost in the company of Shamsoddin.

> For six months they sat in the cell of Ṣalāḥoddin Zarkub, discoursing, without eating, drinking, or any human needs . . .[27]

Who was this man who transformed Rumi so completely?

We do not know much about him. The legends woven around him show him as an overpowering personality who, with immense spiritual pride, wandered through the Near Eastern countries in search for a master—none of the living mystics could evade his biting criticism. He himself tells in his *Maqālāt* that he was for a while the disciple of a certain basket-weaver in Tabriz whom he left later:

> In me there was something which my sheykh did not see. Indeed nobody had ever seen it. But my lord Mowlāna saw it.[28]

Shams met the important masters in Iraq and Syria. Famous is the story of his encounter with Owḥadoddin Kermāni, one of those who 'worship Divine Beauty in created forms', e.g. who saw Divine Beauty manifested in youthful human beauty.

> He told Shams: 'I see the moon reflected in a vessel with water!' Whereupon Shams rebuked him: 'If you have not got a boil on your neck, why don't you look at the sky?'[29]

It seems that Shams has also met Ibn ᶜArabi, of whose work and attitude he was rather critical—the Doctor Maximus of theosophical speculations, whose works were to exert such a tremendous influence upon later Sufism, seemed to him immature and arrogant; he saw his behaviour not fitting to the Divine Law, and compared the Great Sheykh to a pebble, Rumi being a pearl . . .[30]

This witness as noted in his *Maqālāt* is of importance insofar as it helps us to limit the extent of Ibn ᶜArabi's influence upon Rumi: although Ibn ᶜArabi's main interpreter Ṣadroddin Qunavi lived in Konya and was Rumi's colleague, the possible influence of his teaching or of his whole attitude upon Jalāloddin was probably counterbalanced by Shams' aversion to these theories as well as against all theoretical burden—even the most important classics of Sufi literature were, for Shams, less valuable than a single authentic Prophetic tradition.[31]

We have no information about Shamsoddin's affiliation to one of the accepted chains of Sufi spiritual genealogy; indeed, he claimed to have received the *kherqa*, the dervish-frock, from the Prophet himself—but not an ordinary frock which would tear away and get dirty, but the frock of *ṣoḥbat*, e.g. of companionship beyond the limits of time.[32] We may assume, following Gölpınarlı, that he was in fact a *qalandar*,[33] a wandering dervish without proper affiliation, closely related to the group of Malāmatiyya, 'those who try to draw people's contempt upon themselves by outwardly blameworthy actions'. There are utterances by Shams which fit well into this picture, and Rumi's later praise of the *qalandar* seems to point to the same fact.

But even more: Shamsoddin claimed to have reached the stage of 'the Beloved'. He was no longer an *ᶜāsheq*, an enthusiastic lover (as they are found in three degrees), but had passed all lower stages and reached this highest possible station to become 'the Pole of all Beloved', *qoṭb-e hama maᶜshuqān*.[34]

Sepahsālār relates that Shams, in his early prayers, had asked God:

> Is there not a single created being among Thy elect who could endure my company?

And he was directed to take the way to Rum . . .[35]

There he arrived, at a ripe age—perhaps in his late forties, overwhelming, like a burning sun, or a wild lion. Rumi found him in a caravanserai, for he always used to stay in such places, as it was convenient for homeless travellers, and avoided mixing with the society of the learned or the theologians.

We can well imagine how shocked the inhabitants of Konya were when they saw their venerated master neglecting his religious and social duties and giving himself completely over to the company of this wandering dervish who did not fit at all into the Konya society. Thus, after long months of mystical love, Shams felt that he had better leave Konya, fearing the wrath of Rumi's entourage. He disappeared from the town.

Rumi was heartbroken. He who had formerly rarely cared for Persian poetry and music began to sing his passionate longing and his pain in verses:

> What place for patience? For if patience were the world-encircling Mount Qāf,
> It would become annihilated like snow by the sun of separation![36]

He took to music and mystical dance, searched for Shams everywhere—Tabriz is the magical word:

> If our clay and water had wings like our soul and heart,
> It would come to Tabriz this very moment, it would cross the desert![37]

He wrote letters to the Beloved which, perhaps, never reached him; a few verse-letters have been preserved:

> I wrote a hundred letters, I showed a hundred ways—
> Perhaps you do not know the way, or do not read a letter![38]

But eventually, news came from Syria—Shamsoddin had gone there. Solṭān Valad was sent to bring him back, his hand filled with gold and silver. Rumi began to sing of his joy; Damascus, the place where the Beloved was found becomes the centre of his world:

> We are enamoured and bewildered and enraptured of Damascus,
> We have given our soul and bound our heart to the passion of Damascus . . .[39]

And indeed, Shamsoddin yielded to his friend's wishes, and returned with Solṭān Valad to Konya. The sources describe the meeting of Shams and Rumi after the separation—embracing each other; nobody knew who was the lover, who the beloved . . .[40] For the attraction was mutual; not only saw Jalāloddin his Beloved in Shams, but Shams had found in Jalāloddin the master and friend for whom he had been searching throughout his life. And the line in the *Mathnavi*:

> Not only the thirsty seek the water,
> but the water seeks the thirsty as well,[41]

which condenses Mowlānā's whole philosophy of love and longing may well be interpreted as a reflection of this measureless spiritual love between the two mystics.

In the hope to keep the friend close to himself, Jalāloddin married Shamsoddin to one of the girls who had been brought up in his house. Shams loved this Kimiyā deeply. A small room in Mowlānā's house was given to the couple. When Jalāloddin's son, the learned ʿAlāʾoddin, passed thereby, Shams rebuked him, telling him not to intrude upon his father's friends. Whatever the character of this accident may have been, it certainly added to the aversion which ʿAlāʾoddin felt for the foreigner who had become his father's most intimate friend. For again, weeks and months passed in ecstatic conversation between the masters, and again the jealousy of the family and the disciples waxed stronger. Kimiyā died in the late fall of 1248, and not much later Shams disappeared, never to return.

The circumstances of this event have been related in different form in our sources—Solṭān Valad barely touches it; other sources say that Shams left for an unknown place, as he had predicted it;[42] but Aflāki boldly states that he was murdered—in connivance with Rumi's son ʿAlāʾoddin, 'the pride of professors'. This version has been doubted until recent years; too strange seemed it that a member of the family should have committed such a crime. One can, however, reconstruct the drama which took place on the night of 5 December 1248, approximately as follows: Rumi and Shams talked till a late hour, when someone knocked at the door and asked Shams to come out for some purpose. He went, was stabbed, and then thrown into the well opposite to the back entrance of the house—a well which still exists. Solṭān Valad, informed about the action, hastened to take the body out of the well and bury it in a hurriedly dug tomb nearby, which was covered with plaster and then with earth; later the *maqām* of Shams, his memorial, was erected there. Recent excavations in the *maqām* in the course of some repair have indeed proved the existence of a rather large tomb covered with plaster from the Seljuk era. Thanks to this discovery by Mehmet Önder, the then director of the Mevlâna Müzesi in Konya, the truth of Aflāki's statement has been proved.[43]

Rumi's entourage tried to conceal the friend's death from him for a long while; yet, one may feel in some of Rumi's darkest verses an echo of this shock, and perhaps a subconscious knowledge of the event:

> This earth is not dust, it is a vessel full of blood,
> from the blood of the lovers, from the wound of checkmate . . .[44]

People told him, that Shams had gone, perhaps to Syria—and Jalāloddin went to seek him there.

> Someone said: 'I have seen Shamsoddin!'
> Ask him: 'Where is the way to Heaven?'[45]

Poem after poem about separation and longing was written; but Shams was not to be found in Syria.

> My housemate fled from my cries of despair,
> my neighbour wept from my lamentations . . .[46]

It is told that Rumi went a second time to Syria, again without result; but he returned in a more peaceful state of mind. Eventually, he had found Shams in himself, 'radiant like the moon'.[47] The process of complete identification between lover and beloved had come to its end: Jalāloddin and Shamsoddin were no longer two separate entities, but one forever.

> When I went to Tabriz, I spoke with Shamsoddin
> Without the letters of a hundred *maqālāt*, in the Divine Unity . . .[48]

Rumi's poems which resulted from this experience show all the stages of mystical passion—longing, yearning, searching, and again and again hope for union, love without limits. Many ghazals are born out of the dancing rhythm in which the master used to indulge more and more often.

> Not alone I keep on singing Shamsoddin and Shamsoddin—
> But the nightingale in gardens sings, the partridge in the hills,
> . . . Day full of splendour: Shamsoddin, and turning Heaven: Shamsoddin,
> Mine of jewels: Shamsoddin, and Shamsoddin is day and night.
> Shamsoddin is Jamshid's goblet, Shamsoddin the endless sea,
> Shamsoddin is Jesus-breathéd Shamsoddin is Joseph-cheeked . . .[49]

More than once he addresses Shams:

> In my hand was always the Koran—
> Now I seized the *cheghana* out of love—
> In my mouth were always the words of laud—
> Now it is poetry and quatrains and songs . . .[50]

His whole being was transformed into poetry and music. Music became the only expression of his feelings; music, echoed in the enthusiastic words, vibrating in the rhythms of his lyrics. Even though he may later have realized that Shams was indeed dead on the earthly plane, he never admitted it, for

> Who said: 'The eternally Living is dead . . .'
> Who said: 'Oh, the Sun of Hope is dead . . .'
> That is the enemy of the sun, who climbed upon the roof,
> Put a bandage on his two eyes and said: 'The sun is dead!'[51]

He sensed that ʿAlāʾoddin had had his share in the tragedy; many stories tell, and his letters prove, that he never afterwards cared for this son. When ʿAlāʾoddin died in 1260, the father even refused to attend his funeral. Only later, it is said, did he forgive him. One of his letters speaks of ʿAlāʾoddin's heritage and his family members who should not be kept in strained circumstances;[52] but it seems that even after decades Rumi's other children never accepted ʿAlāʾoddin's descendants as legitimate part of Mowlānā's family.

There are many questions about Shamsoddin of Tabriz—some critics have even doubted his very existence. But the huge dervish cap preserved in the Konya Museum would be a sign of his corporeal existence, even if we did not know cases of a similar infatuation among Muslim mystics. Rumi's meeting with Shams, however, was unique, since it was not the usual adoration of Divine Beauty in the shape of a youthful person, so common as inspiring factor in Sufism, but the meeting of two mature mystics of great personal strength. Shams has been compared to Socrates who, without leaving anything written, was the cause of Plato's greatest writing: he, too, drank the cup of martyrdom at the hand of those who did not understand his spiritual fire. Shams was like a spark which kindled the fire in the lamp which was Rumi. A. Gölpınarlı has described the relation of the two mystics with this image:

> Mowlānā was ready for the enthusiastic experience. He was, so to speak, a purified, cleaned lamp in which oil had been poured, the wick had been placed. To make this lamp burn, a fire, a spark was needed. And there was Shams to do this. But when the light of this candle the oil of which does not end became so strong that it could not even show Shams, he turned into a moth and went into the light, giving up his life . . .[53]

Taking into consideration the fiery nature of their relation, the intense spiritual light, and the world-embracing glow of the poetry which emerged from their meeting—short as it was in terms of human time—the comparison is quite poignant.

> The result is not more than these three words:
> I got burnt—and burnt—and burnt . . .[54]

In the light of Jalāloddin's overwhelming love experience everything in the outward world seems to fade away, and one is easily tempted to forget that Mowlānā was also a human being whose deep and strong humanity and his understanding of the sensual world is reflected in his verses in perfect lucidity. One also tends to forget the historical background against which this candle unfolded itself, and to neglect the numerous social activities in which the mystic was involved on the 'worldly' plane.

During the same years when Shams appeared and disappeared, one of the most fascinating buildings of Konya was erected, the Qarātay Madrasa, completed in 1251. It bears the name of Jalāloddin Qarātay (d. 1254), the viceroy, stemming from Byzantine family background. This great politician was a close friend of Rumi, noted for his unusual piety and sincerity, so that Jalāloddin addressed him as 'of angelic qualities, Qualified with the qualities of the angels who are closest to God', 'the mine of goodness and justice'—qualities which were certainly rare among the statesmen of the decaying Rum Seljuk empire . . .[55]

Not long after Mowlānā had discovered his identity with Shamsoddin, he found a new source of mystical inspiration. It is told that one day he walked through the goldsmiths' bazaar in Konya. Listening to the melodic hammering in the shop of master Ṣalāḥoddin Zarkub, he began to turn in mystical rapture, asking Ṣalāḥoddin to join him, and both danced for a while in the bazaar. Ṣalāḥoddin then returned to his work, but Rumi continued whirling around for hours . . .

This story may well be true, but it should not be forgotten that Jalāloddin had been acquainted with Ṣalāḥoddin the Goldsmith for many years. The young man from a village in the Konya plains had come to the capital in the 1230s. He became a favourite disciple of Borhānoddin Moḥaqqeq, Jalāloddin's own mystical instructor; he seems to have resembled this *sheykh* in his austere and ascetic outlook. Therefore he was elected by Borhānoddin to become his only *khalifa*, his spiritual successor, in spite of his being illiterate. Ṣalāḥoddin later went back to his village where he married and had several children. Then he returned once more to Konya and remained close to Mowlānā Jalāloddin whom he deeply admired and loved; the meetings of Jalāloddin and Shams sometimes took place in his cell. Thus, a twofold relation between the two mystics existed long before Rumi felt that, after experiencing the miracle of perfect love, he needed a mirror—and he found this mirror in the simple minded Ṣalāḥoddin, who, completely purified from worldy concerns, gave him the company he needed, helping him, thus, to find himself again. Rumi describes the change of the outward forms in which the beloved manifests himself:

He who came in a red frock in years past,
He came this year in a brown garb.
The Turk about whom you heard that time,
Appeared as Arab this year.
The friend is one, only the dress changes—
He exchanged the garb and returned!
The wine is one, only the bottles are different—
How beautifully does this wine intoxicate us![56]

It goes without saying that the inhabitants of Konya who had just rejoiced at Shamsoddin's disappearance, were deeply dismayed when the learned Mowlānā Jalāloddin directed his love to this goldsmith who could not even recite the *fāteḥa* correctly, as jealous people claimed: Shams, after all, had been an educated person whose influence one could accept, though grudgingly. But Mowlānā and the goldsmith did not pay heed to the gossip and the slander; their spiritual union was deep and pure, and at times Rumi would praise the new friend—who must have been approximately his same age—in tender and loving verses. In a chapter of *Fihi mā fihi*, Rumi scolds a certain Ibn Chāvush who had apparently talked against Ṣalāḥoddin:

> Men have left their own country, their fathers and mothers, their households and kinmen and families and have journeyed from Hind to Sind, making boots of iron until they were cut to shreds, haply to encounter a man having the fragrance of the other world . . . As for you, you have encountered such a man here in your own house, and you turn your back on him. This is surely a great calamity and recklessness . . .[57]

In order to cement the new relationship, Jalāloddin married Ṣalāḥoddin's daughter, Fāṭema, to his son Solṭān Valad, who was then in his mid-twenties. It is revealing that Rumi admonished his son by letter to treat his wife well[58] (and Rumi's ghazal sung at the occasion of the wedding is still known).[59] At a time when a tension had taken place between the couple, he consoled his daughter-in-law with heartfelt words:

> If my dear son Bahā'oddin strives to hurt you, I shall verily verily take away my love from him; I will give up loving him, I shall not respond to his greetings, I do not want him to come to my funeral . . .[60]

Rumi looked also after the second daughter of his friend,

Hadiyya Khātun who was married to a certain Neẓāmoddin, known as The Calligrapher: he helped procure the dowry through the minister Moʿinoddin Parvāne's wife, a remarkable woman who was one of his admirers.[61] Rumi's letters reveal that the couple did not live in prosperity, and thus he several times asked his well-to-do acquaintances for financial assistance for Ṣalāḥoddin's son-in-law.

During the years of Rumi's company with Ṣalāḥoddin, many political events took place in Anatolia, and in the whole Muslim world. In 1256, the Mongols under Bayju approached Konya once more. Legend tells that they did not enter the 'city of saints' thanks to Rumi's spiritual presence.[62] Power was then assumed by Roknoddin Qılıcharslān IV, a mere puppet in the hands of the powerful minister Moʿinoddin Parvāne.

In 1258, the Mongols conquered Baghdad and extinguished the ruling house of the Abbasid caliphs. In the same year, Ṣalāḥoddin Zarkub fell ill, and after a prolonged suffering Jalāloddin eventually 'allowed' him to leave this world and join the realm of pure spiritual life. The friend's illness kept him away from his own work, and he rarely left Ṣalāḥoddin's room. But when the dead friend was buried, Rumi, and with him his family members and friends, joined in a glorious *samāʿ*, a mystical dance accompanied by drums and flute—for death is not a separation but, as the dervishes say, an *ʿors*, a spiritual wedding. A wonderful threnody celebrates the deceased friend:

> O you because of whose emigration earth and sky have wept!
> Hearts sat in the midst of blood, reason and soul have wept!
> Since there is none in the world to take your place,
> Place and No-Place, in mourning you, have wept.
> Gabriel's wing and feather and that of the holy ones have turned blue,
> The eyes of prophets and saints have wept . . .
> O Ṣalāḥoddin! You have gone, you fast-flying homā-bird—
> You have leapt from the bow like an arrow—and that bow has wept.[63]

Events like a *samāʿ* after a funeral must have shocked the orthodox circles of the population:

> He said: "From *samāʿ* veneration and high rank diminishes!"
> High rank be yours—love is my fortune and rank![64]

Yet, Mowlānā Rumi's influence over Konya was fairly well established. Although he was so fond of mystical dance that he even gave correct legal decisions (*fatvā*) during his whirling dance,[65] he led an extremely ascetic life; and Sepahsālār, who served him for many years, describes his fondness for ritual prayer as well as for prolonged periods of fasting. This strict adherence to the law, and his personal charm and sincerity attracted many people to his threshold. Among them was also the minister Moᶜinoddin Parvāne who waited upon him not rarely, and was even kept waiting for a while until he was admitted into Rumi's presence; he is also the addressee of most of Rumi's letters that have been preserved, for, in his position, he could always help the needy.[66]

Moᶜinoddin was of Deylamite origin, and for 17 years (1259–76) he was *de facto* ruler of Konya. His attitude towards his Seljuk masters was as shifting and unreliable as that towards the Mongols and their enemies, the Mamluks of Egypt. He had secured the throne for Roknoddin Qılıcharslān IV, first asking to divide the country between Roknoddin and his brother ᶜEzzoddin Keykawus. ᶜEzzoddin ruled in Konya between 1257 and 1261, but spent most of his time in Antalya, the lovely town on the Mediterranean coast; he even invited Mowlānā to join him there (Jalāloddin declined the invitation, however).[67] ᶜEzzoddin tried to co-operate with the Byzantines against the Mongols, but was imprisoned by his 'helpers' and eventually died, after many adventures, in the Crimea in 1278. As to the Parvāne who more or less openly took the side of the Mongols, he had Solṭān Roknoddin killed at the hands of his overlords in order to put his infant son Ghiyāsoddin Keykhosrow III on the throne in 1264. Despite his friendship with and admiration for Rumi, Moᶜinoddin Parvāne was several times blamed by word and letter for irreverent behaviour (he talked with some visitor while Rumi was engaged in *samā*ᶜ, whereupon a long blaming ghazal was issued)[68] and mainly for his double-faced policy, and his unreliability.

> It is told that he visited Mowlānā to ask for a good advice. Rumi said: 'I hear that you memorize the Koran and take *ḥadith* classes from Sheykh Ṣadroddin.'—'Yes', replied the minister.—'Then, said Rumi, if God's word and the sentences of the Prophet do not impress you—what shall I say?'[69]

Ṣadroddin Qunavi, from whom the minister took these lessons, was the favourite disciple of Ibnʿ Arabi, an intellectual, highly sophisticated master of mystical, or rather theosophical theories, admired by some members of high society. Contrary to Rumi's modest way of life, Ṣadroddin lived in a rather luxurious setting, and not always approved of Jalāloddin's enthusiastic behaviour, or his unconditioned love and his overflowing poetical effusions. Neither did Rumi think much of Ibnʿ Arabi's theories; we may well believe the story that one day Mowlānā's friends talked about Ibnʿ Arabi's *Fotuḥāt el-Makkiyya, The Meccan Revelations*, describing this huge work (it contains 560 chapters) as 'a strange book; it is not clear what its goal is'. At that very moment a well-known singer, Zaki-ye Qawwāl, entered and began to sing a beautiful tune, whereupon Rumi said: 'Zaki's *fotuḥāt* (revelations) are better than the *Fotuḥāt al-Makkiyya*' and started dancing . . .[70]

Yet, the two great mystics got along without outward friction, and Ṣadroddin later showed much admiration for Rumi, who must have been slightly junior to him. 'They were connected by special friendship' writes Jāmi,[71] and it seems that Jalāloddin, too, became more interested in theoretical thought towards the end of his life. When Ṣadroddin was asked to lead the funeral prayer of Jalāloddin, he fainted; only a few months later he too died. His modest tomb with an open ceiling lies in the centre of Konya.

Ṣadroddin was the mystic to whom Moʿinoddin Parvāne was particularly attached. The influential minister was also fond of another, though more poetical, interpreter of Ibn ʿArabi's ideas, e.g. Fakhroddin ʿErāqi.[72] This poet, whose Persian lyrics belong to the most lovely expressions of mystical love, returned from his prolonged stay in India after the death of Bahāʾoddin Zakariyya of Multan (d. 1262); he passed through Konya. We have no account of his visit there, but may surmise that he paid visits to all the mystical leaders in the late 1260s. Moʿinoddin Parvāne erected for him a small tekke in Tokat, a flourishing town in the northern part of the Seljuk empire. After the Parvāne's death in 1277 ʿEraqi went to Syria, at that time politically more stable than Anatolia; there he died in 1289 and is buried close to Ibn ʿArabi in Damascus.

Another mystic who visited Konya during Rumi's lifetime—rather during his earlier years—was Najmoddin

Dāyā Rāzi, the leading disciple of Najmoddin Kobrā who, fleeing like Rumi's family from the Mongols, had settled in Sivas.[73] There he wrote his *mirṣād al-ᶜebād*, a mystical work which was soon translated into Turkish, and was accepted as the best handbook of Sufism in the Kobrāvi interpretation in every part of the Eastern Muslim world, mainly in India. Najmoddin Dāyā was given a tekke in Kaiseri by Moᶜinoddin Parvāne.

> An anecdote relates that during his vitit to Konya he was asked to lead the prayer, and he recited twice the Sura 'O ye infidels . . .' Jalāloddin turned to Ṣadroddin Qunavi with the words: 'With the first one he intended me, with the second 'Infidels', you . . .!'[74]

Rumi had many contacts with the higher strata of society; we mentioned his predilection for the minister Qarātay, and a younger politician in the crumbling Seljuk Empire who sometimes acted against Moᶜinoddin Parvāne belonged to his friends as well: it is 'our brother', 'the lofty and pious' Fakhroddin Ṣāḥeb ᶜAtā (d. 1288), who built many madrasas, monasteries, and fountains. The lavishly decorated madrasa in Konya which bears his name, was completed one year before Rumi's death. It is a fine building although it cannot match in beauty with the Ince Minareli, a madrasa famous for the huge band of Koranic sentences which surrounds its portal in exquisite stone carving (built 1258).

Rich merchants participated in Rumi's meetings; it is told that one of them used to give away trunks full of precious material to the singers and musicians at the *samāᶜ* gatherings. But basically, Rumi's sympathy belonged to the middle and lower classes. Some 'high-brow' people blamed him for his friendship with the artisans:

> Wherever a tailor or a weaver or a greengrocer is, he will accept him!

Whereupon Mowlānā reminded him—with full right—of the Sufi leaders of the classical period, whose surnames indicate that they came from the artisan class: Abu Bakr an-Nassāj 'the weaver', the 'glass-maker' (Joneyd al-Qawāriri), the blacksmith, Ḥaddād, or the cotton-carder, Ḥallāj.[75]—Others would remark that he gathered bad people around him; but his reply was:

> If these around me were good, I would become their disciple; but since they are bad, I take them as disciples.[76]

Quite a number of poor and indigent people sought shelter at Mowlānā's door, and many of his letters ask help for them: could they not be exempt from taxes, or given a little job in the vizier's entourage, or granted some money to pay their debts?

> He has no place where to go at night, his mother is poor. His mother's husband is a bad-tempered, stingy person. He has thrown the child out, telling him "Do not come to my house, do not eat my bread . . ."[77]

Or he may request the vizier or a high-standing jurist to allot a post in a certain mosque or madrasa to this or that person, or ask the minister to buy some copper vessels from an honourable, poor merchant and to pay him immediately . . .[78] And he would always remind his audience of the Koranic word contained in Sura 5/32: 'And who quickens one person, it is as if he had quickened all people'.

It should however be remembered that Rumi, with all his compassion for poor artisans, disliked the crude and misbehaving villagers and spoke against the life in the countryside, which makes people stupid.[79] And he certainly had no sympathy with anarchistic trends of any form, as they showed themselves in some of the groups led by wandering dervishes; he always underlined the importance of the orderly built cosmos in which every created being had a particular function. As he saw that outward forms were only the 'pith', through which the seeing eye of the perfected faithful can penetrate and recognize the eternal 'kernel', so did he know that 'forms' and 'piths' have their function in life as well:

> If you plant in the earth only the kernel of an apricot stone, nothing will grow; if you plant it along with the pith, then it will grow . . .[80]

And outward forms of behaviour show the inward attitude of a person, comparable to the frontispiece of a letter that shows the addressee:

> From outward respect, bowing the head and standing on the feet, it may be realized what respect they have inwardly, and in what manner they respect God . . .[81]

His was a refined way of life, and thus he became the leader of the urban population whereas the villagers and nomads were attracted by his contemporary Ḥājji Bektāsh and by the smaller bands of dervishes who wandered through Anatolia. Out of this urban attitude developed the more aristocratic form of culture which characterizes the Mevlevi order in later periods.

It should also not be forgotten that Rumi had quite a number of female disciples and admirers; some of his letters bestow high praise on pious and charitable ladies.[82] One lady founded a *zāviyye* where she acted as *sheykh* (or rather *sheykha*), and a pretty dancing girl from the Ziyā Caravanserai—a place noted for some 'unfitting' events—was induced by Rumi's visit to a saintly life.[83] Aflāki tells that the wife of Aminoddin Mikāʾil, once viceroy, invited Rumi to meetings in her house and used to shower roses on his head during the *samāʿ*;[84] Solṭān Ghiyāsoddin's wife, who went to Kaiseri, even had a picture of her venerated master made by a Byzantine painter because she could not bear the separation from him.[85]—In later times, ladies—like Solṭān Valad's own daughter—acted quite successfully for the spread of the order.[86]

Rumi's own wife, Kerā Khātun (d. 1292), whom he had married after his first wife's death, is praised as

> the beauty of her time in loveliness and perfection, and a second Sarah and the Mary of her age in virtue and purity.[87]

She bore him two children, one son and one daughter. When the son, ʿĀlem, was born, Rumi celebrated the event, according to Aflāki, with seven days of *samāʿ*, and a lovely ghazal welcomed the new flower in the garden.[88] ʿĀlem later joined first government service, but then, to his father's joy, 'put on the dervish garb'.[89] Rumi's daughter Malike Khatun was later married to a certain Shehāboddin. The master's days passed in worship and meditation, in discussion and at times in *samāʿ* meetings; in summer days, he went out to Meram to picnic with his friends and disciples, enjoying the sweet sound of the watermill on the hill, and once a year he liked to visit the hot springs in Ilgın.

The inspirational process in Rumi repeated itself three times—after the glowing and burning experience of his love of Shamsoddin he found spiritual peace in Ṣalāḥoddin's company. The last expression of his fully-matured mind was produced through the influence of Ḥosāmoddin Chalabi. After the ascent in the love of Shams, and the calmness of his friendship with the goldsmith he now showed himself as the inspired teacher, entering into what the mystics call 'the arch of descent', returning to the world as guide and master.

Ḥosāmoddin ibn Ḥasan Akhi Turk belonged to the middle-class of Konya. His father's name indicates that he was probably a member of the *akhi* organization. This sodality of artisans, merchants and other people, renowned for immaculate life, constituted a kind of offspring of the Arabo-persian *fotuvva*-groups which were again permeated with Sufi ideals. The *akhis* cared for the welfare of their brethren, offered hospitality to foreigners, and formed a closely-knit group who looked after the needs of the community.

Ḥosāmoddin did not enter Mowlānā's life unexpectedly. He had been associated with him for many years; it is said that Shams-e Tabrizi had been very fond of the ascetic and striving young man, who was later appointed *sheykh* of Vizier Ziyāʾoddin's *tekke*, despite the objections of some rivals.[90] Sepahsālār praises the mildness of Chalabi, who would feel the pains of his friends in his own body, and who was a model of good and descent behaviour: even in winter nights he would never use his master's privy but went back to his own house to 'renew the ablutions'.[91] In his letters Rumi generally calls him 'Joneyd of his time', and some of the letters reveal the love he felt for the friend with whom he was spiritually completely united, who was

> both father and son to me, both light and eye . . .[92]

It was Ḥosāmoddin who inspired Rumi to commit to paper his thoughts, ideas, teachings, in short, his whole wisdom, for the benefit of his disciples, to whom he belonged. These were engaged in reading Sanāʾi and ʿAṭṭār's mystical epics (mainly the *Manṭeq oṭ-ṭeyr* and the *Moṣibatnāme*) but wanted to know the master's authentic teaching for their instruction. Rumi acceeded to this wish of his beloved disciple, and began to write what has become known as the *Mathnavi-ye maʿnavi, The Spiritual couplets*. Ḥosāmoddin took the charge of the writing:

> O Ḥosāmoddin, write you the praise of this prince of love,
> although the renegade goes on begging in the air of his love![93]

as he says at the end of one of the most glowing praise-poems written in memory of Shams.

For years, Ḥosāmoddin accompanied the master, noting down every verse that flowed from his lips, be it on the street, in the bath, during the *samāᶜ*, or in the house. He would recite the verses once more; then, they were corrected and distributed to the disciples.

The poem which thus came into existence is written in the easy, flowing and simple meter *ramal mosaddas* (*fāᶜelāton fāᶜelāton fāᶜelon*), used, after Sanāʾi and ᶜAṭṭār, for mystical didactic poetry.

It is difficult to say when the *Mathnavi* was begun: it is usually assumed that Ḥosāmoddin appeared as an inspiring force only after Ṣalāḥoddin's death, but we would rather accept the chronology of A. Gölpınarlı who proves rightly that one story in the first book of the *Mathnavi* alludes to the Ābbasid caliphs in Baghdad as still being in power.[94] Since the last Abbasid caliph was killed in 1258 by the Mongols, the first book, with its 4000-odd verses, may have been dictated some time between 1256 and 1258. This can be supported by one of the dated poems in the *Divān*, which in a strange visionary recital alludes to the Mongol attack near Konya. It is dated 5. Dhu'l-qaᶜdā 654/25 November 1256 and bears, as *nom-de-plume* Ḥosāmoddin's name:[95] he was already then close to Mowlānā's heart. A remark at the beginning of the second book of the *Mathnavi* would also become clear: Rumi complains that quite a long time has elapsed since the first volume was finished: during the years between 1258 and 1263 (this latter date is given in *Mathnavi* II 5-6) Ṣalāḥoddin's death had caused in Jalāloddin a deep feeling of bereavement which disabled him from continuing his poetical teaching, and Ḥosāmoddin was afflicted by his wife's death, which, again, caused a break in the inspiration. It was in 1262 that Ḥosāmoddin was officially appointed as Rumi's *khalifa*: the young friend who appears, in the discourse about the mystery of Shams at the beginning of the *Mathnavi* as still comparatively immature,[96] could now be accepted as his true spiritual successor.

The dictation of the *Mathnavi* continued almost until

Rumi's last illness. The book is not built according to a system; it lacks architectural structure; the verses lead one into the other, and the most heterogenous thoughts are woven together by word associations and loose threads of stories. The imagery is protean: the same image can be used in contradictory sense. Rumi has used all kinds of associations from everyday life in this book, as he had done in his lyrics; he expounded the layers of tradition from Khorassan and from Anatolia where Hittites, Greeks, Romans, and Christians had lived and left traces of their spiritual legacy. He takes his topics from historical events, legends, hagiography, folktales; he inserts theoretical discussions about free will and predestination, about love and prayer, or muses about proverbs and Prophetic traditions. Sometimes he seems to follow the lead of one of the chapters of Ghazzāli's *Iḥyā*ʾ ʿ*olum ad-din*; at other times he inserts bluntly obscene stories which are then interpreted in a spiritual sense. Centuries-or millenia-old stories, as were alive between India and Byzantium are mixed with remarks pointing to contemporary Iranian or Turkish customs.

Rumi knew when he began the sixth book of the *Mathnavi* that this would be the last part of the great work; the final story even lacks a logical conclusion. He was exhausted after a life in which he reached the loftiest summits of spiritual love. After tasting the most ardent longing, the deepest homelessness, and final spiritual union, and after pouring out more than 30,000 verses of lyrical poetry, more than 26,000 verses of didactic poetry, talking to his friends as is noted down in *Fihi mā fihi*, composing numerous letters for the benefit of his countrymen—after all this, he felt tired.

Besides, the political situation in Anatolia grew worse every year. Even the most marvellous buildings, like those which were erected in Sivas just during the years before Mowlānā's death (combining every conceivable artistic means to decorate the façades in the most superb way by ornament and writing)—even those buildings could not conceal the fact that the Seljuks not only had lost their independence and were constantly paying tribute to the Mongols, but that they were also weakened by internal political struggle and internecine feuds. Rumi complains about the misbehaviour of soldiers who broke into the houses and about unpleasant events which preoccupied the learned inhabitants of Konya.[97] Many of those who had a deeper insight into the political scene left Anatolia after Rumi's death and went to Syria or Egypt. Syria had become part of the Mamluk kingdom, founded in 1250, and proved to be a solid wall against the Mongols after Baybars had been the first to stop them in the decisive battle of ʿAyn Jalut in 1260.

Rumi was fading away in the autumnal days of 1273, and the physicians despaired of diagnosing his illness; they found water in his side, but otherwise an overall weakness. Mowlānā's friend, the physician Akmaloddin Ṭabib—known as a commentator of Ibn Sinā's *Qānun*—stayed with him, as did his closest friend, Serājoddin al-Tatari whom he had visited and with whom he had talked about Shamsoddin. Other friends, disciples, and colleagues came to call upon him. He consoled them, reciting poems about death as the door towards a new life—a subject which he had touched time and again during his lifetime. The earthquakes in Konya made people restless, and all those who learned about Mowlānā's illness came to the town to show him their love and veneration. He passed away on 17 December 1273, at sunset.

His burial was attended by all communities of the province; Christians and Jews joined in the funeral prayers, each according to his own rite, for he has always been on good terms with the large non-Muslim population of the town . . . They praised him: 'He was our Jesus, he was our Moses . . .'[98] After the funeral prayers were over, *samāʿ* and music went on for hours and hours:

> When you come visiting my grave,
> my roofed tomb will appear to you dancing . . .
> Do not come without tambourine to my tomb, brother!
> For a grieved person does not fit in God's banquet![99]

Then, Konya became silent.

It is told that Jalāloddin's cat refused food and died one week after him; his daughter buried her close to him. How often had he mentioned in his poetry the animals whom he saw engaged in constant praise of God, and which could so easily serve as models or symbols of human behaviour!

Jāmi relates that shortly after Rumi's death, Ṣadroddin Qunavi, Shamsoddin e-Iki, Fakhroddin ʿErāqi and other Sufi leaders were sitting together, remembering the late master, and Ṣadroddin, the great theosophist, said:

> If Bāyazid and Joneyd had been alive at this time, they would have seized the hem of this virtuous man and would have considered this a boon; he is the *majordomo* of Muhammadan Poverty, and we taste it through his mediation . . .[100]

The stream of visitors to his tomb never ceased to this day. Although Rumi did not want a complex construction over his tomb but would have preferred, like many dervishes, the sun and rain to touch the dust of his grave, his wealthy admirers soon built a magnificent dome over his tomb, known as *al-qubbat al-khaḍrā*ʾ or *yeşil kubbe*, the Green Dome, the centre of a complex which contains a whole monastery with cells, a large kitchen, and a library. Under this dome, Mowlānā Jalāloddin is buried, together with his family members and his most faithful friends. On his coffin, some of his most 'intoxicated' verses are inscribed, and Arabic words praise his greatness. Black velvet shrouds with gold-embroidery cover the coffins.

Mowlānā Jalāloddin's teaching was continued by Ḥosāmoddin Chalabi, the last 'reflection' of the spiritual Sun which first appeared in Shamsoddin of Tabriz.[101]

POETIC TRADITION, INSPIRATION, AND FORM

Jalāloddin was deeply influenced by his two predecessors in the field of mystical poetry, and primarily *mathnavis*, i.e. by Sanāʾi and ʿAṭṭār. The verse:

> Sanāʾi was the spirit, and ʿAṭṭār his two eyes;
> We have come after Sanāʾi and ʿAṭṭār.

has been often quoted as proof of his high estimation of the two masters. However, A. Gölpınarlı has recently shown that these words should be read differently, the second line beginning:

> We have become the *qebla* of Sanāʾi and ʿAṭṭār.

a version which places Rumi himself on a higher level than the previous poets.[1]

Whatever be the correct version, it cannot be denied that Mowlānā has underlined the importance of both his predecessors in various connections. Playing on the meaning of their names, he speaks of Sanāʾi's *sanāʾ*, 'splendor, eminence', and Faridoddin's *fardiyyat*, 'uniqueness';[2] or he combines them with Bāyazid Besṭāmi.[3] ʿAṭṭār appears to Rumi as the *ʿāsheq*. 'lover'; Sanāʾi as the 'king and superior' (*fāʾeq*), whereas he himself is 'neither this nor that' but has lost himself completely.[4] It is revealing that he calls Sanāʾi 'superior' or 'paramount'—he was indeed more influenced by the Sage of Ghazna than by ʿAṭṭār. This is perhaps—at least in part—due to Borhānoddin Moḥaqqeq's influence, as people even blamed him for 'quoting Sanāʾi frequently in his discourses.'[5] On the whole, Sanāʾi's powerful and direct diction seems to have appealed particularly to Mowlānā, who in his approach to mystical problems, in unquestioning faith and love, is perhaps closer to the Ghaznavid poet than to the restless seeker ʿAṭṭār, over whose mystical epics there always hangs a cloud of melancholy. Sanāʾi is more matter of fact, often cruder in his expression than ʿAṭṭār—echoes of his style, though refined, can be easily detected in Rumi's poetry.

Jalāloddin's elegy on Sanāʾi is one of his best-known lyrical poems, impressive in its simplicity:

> Someone quoth: Master Sanāʾi has died!
> The death of such a master is not a small thing . . . .[6]

However, this ghazal is nothing but an elaboration of a *qeṭʿa* by Sanāʾi himself (who had in turn imitated an elegy by Rudaki) which he composed shortly before his death:

> Sanāʾi died who has not yet died—
> The death of this master is not a small thing.[7]

Allusions to the Sage of Ghazna occur frequently in Rumi's *Mathnavi*;[8] verses from both his lyrics and his various *mathnavis* serve as starting points for Rumi's own stories;[9] they were often inserted in the conversations recorded in *Fihi mā fihi*. Strangely enough, Rumi several times associates the *Ilāhināme* with Sanāʾi, not with its real author, ʿAṭṭar.[10] In many cases, similarities with or variations of verses of Sanāʾi can be found;[11] they range from very tender love-verses to the famous lines in the *Mathnavi*:

> One does not sleep with such an idol with a shirt,[12]

and to utterly crude remarks inspired by the satirical *Kārnāme-ye Balkh*[13] 7. Sanāʾi, like Rumi, praised the *ney*, the reedflute; likewise the story behind the proem of the *Mathnavi*, that of the reed which tells the secrets of the king that were entrusted to the lake is found in detail in Sanāʾi's *Ḥadiqa*.[14] The story itself goes back to the Greek tale of King Midas[15] (who lived not too far from Konya, in Gordion); in Islamic lands, it has been transferred, through another stream of tradition, to ʿAli ibn Abi Ṭāleb who disclosed the secrets entrusted to him by the Prophet to the reedbed in the lake; the reed, then, made them public after being cut from the reed-bed. The originally Indian story of 'The Blind and the Elephant' is likewise inherited from Sanāʾi, who may have learnt it from Abu Ḥāmed al-Ghazzāli, his elder contemporary.[16]

Some of Rumi's favourite expressions have been coined by Sanāʾi, thus *barg-e bi-bargi*, spiritual poverty and contentment, a combination which both poets like to combine with the generally known word *barg*, 'leaf':

> You have not got the foot (suitable) for this arena: don't don the garment of the Men (of God)!
> You have not got the *barg-e bi-bargi*—don't talk about the state of the dervish![17]

Another allusion common to both Sanāʾi and Rumi (which seems to occur rarely, if at all, in ʿAṭṭār's poetry) is that to Abu Horeyra and his miraculous bag, into which he put 'the hand of faithfulness' (*ṣedq*) to take out wonderful things.[18]

Sanāʾi, though probably in poetical technique and rhetorics superior to Rumi—his early career as court panegyrist proves his skill in most difficult poetical expressions—sometimes uses in his verses catch-words for the Arabic meters, or those of musical modes, like *tan tanna tanin tan tannana tan tanin*[19]—a practice of which Rumi, too, is fond; with him, however, it is the genuine expression of musical intoxication. Both mystical poets use a common stock of proverbs and anecdotes. Of course, one can also easily detect quite a number of allusions to or adaptations from ʿAṭṭār's poetry. The very meter of Rumi's *Mathnavi*, i.e. *ramal mosaddas*, suggests that of ʿAṭṭar's *Manṭeq oṭ-ṭeyr*. The sources tell that Jalāloddin was particularly fond of this epic and of the

Moṣibatnāme, which relates the spiritual journey through the forty stages in which everything created expresses its yearning for return to the Lord until the hero finds God in the ocean of his own soul. Both these epics with their central theme of the mystical journey, or Pilgrim's Progress appealed to Rumi's dynamic *Weltanschauung*. Whole stories from ᶜAṭṭār's epics have found their way into Rumi's *Mathnavi*; that of the Hindu boy and Maḥmud of Ghazna is described by the poet as adopted from ᶜAṭṭār.[20] One of Rumi's deepest words on prayer is taken almost verbally from the *Manṭeq oṭ-ṭeyr*:

> Both prayer is from Thee, and answering is also from Thee . . .[21]

ᶜAṭṭār sings of the fire of love which consumes everything:

> Finally, nobody should be without love in this valley,
> He who is not fire, his life may be not agreeable —[22]

just as Rumi addresses his audience in the very beginning of the *Mathnavi*:

> He who does not possess this fire, may be naughted!

The image of the cross-eyed person who sees everything double and cannot imagine that there is only one, is also taken from the *Manṭeq oṭ-ṭeyr;*[23] it is a good symbol of the unbelievers who are unable to recognize God's unity.

But Rumi had not only studied the poetical works of the Sage of Ghazna and the master of Nishapur. He was well-versed in both Arabic and Persian literatures — as every educated person in those ages would have been — and now and then reminiscences of his readings can be found in his verses. Among them, the collection *Kalila va Demna* occupies the most prominent place: these fables, ascribed to Bidpai, were translated into Arabic in the late 8th century, and formed one of the most important sources of inspiration not only for Muslim scholars, poets, and mystics who used the fables of animals' behavior to elucidate their theories, but also for generations of philosophers and literates in Europe, up to Lafontaine. *Kalila va Demna* certainly inspired Rumi whose predilection for animal-imagery is remarkable, and many a story in the *Mathnavi* is taken from this book. As he himself says:

> You may have read it in *Kalila,* but that was the husk of the story and this is the kernel of the soul.[24]

Nevertheless, in a fit of anger, he calles the *Kalila*-stories, in another place, 'all falsehood',[25]

Rumi was of course well acquainted with the Persian national tradition of the *Shāhnāme,*[26] although the heroes of Ferdowsi's epic figure comparatively rarely in his work, except Rostam, the central hero as symbol of the 'true man' who rescues people from the hermaphrodite[27] and shows his power in destroying everything mean. As in the verses of other Persian poets, Rostam is often linked or equated with ᶜAli, since both are paragons of humanity, of manly virtue and heroism, in short, models of the 'man of God'. Compared to the general tenor of Persian literature, however, allusions to the *Shāhnāme* are not too common in Rumi's verses although they cover almost all the traditional scenes.

Jalāloddin had read the famous love stories of medieval Persian literature—Gorgāni's *Vis u Rāmin,*[28] as well as *Vāmeq uᶜAzra;*[29] the heroes of both tales became standard types of lovers in his poetry. Rumi further quotes from Neẓāmi,[30] alludes to his *Makhzan al-asrār;*[31] the figures from Neẓāmi's romantic epics, Leylā and Majnun as well as Farhād, Khosrow and Shirin, also Iskandar (Alexander) play a prominent role in his poetical symbolism—a role which is completely consistent with the general imagery of 13th century Persian poets:

> You may be a hardworking lover, taking bitterness and drinking bitter,
> So that Shirin (sweet) may give you medicine from the imperial *(khosravi)* honey . . .[32]

It seems from Rumi's imagery that he was well acquainted with Khāqāni's poetry; some unusual expressions in his work can be traced back to the great panegyrist's lines which excell by their incredible strength and imaginative power.

From the Arabic tradition, Rumi sometimes quotes the *Kitāb al-aghāni*, the famous collection of poetry and literary history as compiled in the 10th century—but these poems are only 'the branch of longing for union'[33] since they talk about earthly love. Whether the allusions to BuᶜAlāʾ intend the Arabic philosophical poet Abuʾl-ᶜAlaʾ al-Maᶜarri can not be decided; it would be possible since this person always figures as a negative symbol,[34] sometimes along with Buʿ Ali, e.g. Ibn Sinā, the philosopher-physician: both of them are in the 'sleep of heedlessness'.[35]

There are allusions to Abu Nuwās, the wine-poet of the Abbasid court,[36] and the traditions agree that Rumi greatly admired the Arabic poet al-Motanabbi (d. 965) whose panegyrics constitute the apex of traditional Arabic poetry. He was fond of him to the extent of quoting his verses verbally.[37] And which Muslim scholar of the 13th century would not have enjoyed reading the masterpiece of Arabic rhetoric, the *Maqāmāt* of Ḥariri, this firework of puns, word-garlands, and witty remarks which was studied in every madrasa between Egypt and Muslim India? Rumi addresses his Beloved:

> As long as I saw your kindness *(fażl)* and your high stations *(maqāmāt)* and miracles,
> I am helpless, fed up with the *fażl* and the *Maqāmāt* of Hariri.[38]

We may safely admit that Mowlānā, according to the traditions of his time, studied the whole bulk of Arabic literature as well as theology, and of course mysticism; he had read Makki's *Qut al-qolub* and Qosheyri's *Resāla*, and certainly Ghazzāli's *Iḥyā ʿolum ad-din* which seems to have provided some inspiration for his *Mathnavi*. Many other works have enriched his vocabulary and his imagery.

But, as he says:

> I read the story of the lovers day and night—
> Now I have become a story in my love for you . . .[39]

The meeting with Shamsoddin changed him completely and although formerly he had enjoyed poetry, he had probably never written any verses, perhaps with the exception of a few lines—for every student of Arabic and Persian writes for technical purposes to acquire some skill and taste. The change brought about by his spiritual experience is best reflected in a chapter in *Fihi mā fihi* in which he, years later, put down his reflections. It begins with a verse from the *Divān* where the last question is put in Turkish:

> Where am I and where is poetry? But into me breathes
> that one Turk who comes and says to me: 'Hey, who are you?'

> Otherwise, what have I to do with poetry? By Allah, I care nothing for poetry, and there is nothing worse in my eyes than that. It has become incumbent upon me, as when a man plunges his hands into tripe and washes it out for the sake of a guest's appetite, because the guest's appetite is for tripe.[40]

These words sound very harsh, and one wonders in how far one should take them at face value. The mystic probably thought of the Koranic verdict against the poets who 'say what they do not do' (Sura 26/226) and of some alleged Prophetic traditions condemning poetry. Poetry, understood in the sense of panegyrics, love- and wine-songs which belong to the category of the religiously prohibited things, was indeed, for a scholar, considered a most despicable profession in the Eastern lands of the caliphate, as Rumi attests at the end of this passage:

> I have studied many sciences and taken much pain, so that I may be able to offer fine and rare and precious things to the scholars and researchers, the clever ones and the deep thinkers who come to me. God most High Himself willed this. He gathered here all those sciences, and assembled here all those pains, so that I might be occupied with this work. What can I do? In my own country and amongst my own people there is no occupation more shameful than poetry. If I had remained in my own country, I would have lived in harmony with their temperament and would have practised what they desired, such as lecturing and composing books, preaching and admonishing, observing abstinence and doing all the outward acts.

Yet, after meeting Shams, Rumi could not help expressing himself in verses: 'It was a great urge that compelled me to compose'[41] – an urge which grew weaker in the course of time, as he attests. We may understand the term 'poetry' here as merely designating 'lyrics', for his urge to compose the *Mathnavi* certainly did not become less in the later years of his life . . . And he knew, notwithstanding his verdict on poetry, that:

> After a hundred more years this ghazal
> will be an evening-talk, like Joseph's beauty.[42]

In many a verse he describes his state:

> Can't they speak in their dreams words without tongue?
> Thus I speak in my state of wakefulness.[43]

> Every hair of mine has become due to Thy love verse and ghazal,
> Every limb of mine has become due to Thy relish a barrel of honey.[44]

We encounter here the central problem of every mystical writer: to what extent is mystical poetry written consciously, and to what extent does the poet feel that he is merely an inspired instrument, deprived of his own will, and giving himself over completely to the inspiration which leaves him no choice and which he cannot resist:

> When I do not recite a ghazal, He splits my mouth . . .[45]

When pondering this problem one usually thinks of the verse from the *Mathnavi* where Jalāloddin addresses Ḥosāmoddin:

> I think of rhymes, but my beloved says:
> Don't think of anything but of my face![46]

The beloved is the inspirer who induces the lover into poetry; without his radiance, the mystic is silent.[47] The same is even more true about Shamsoddin, the first and decisive force of inspiration:

> You sit down and shake your head and say:
> Shams-e Tabriz shows you the secrets of the ghazal . . .[48]

The mystic is like Mount Sinai, which echoes the voice of the Divine Beloved;[49] or like David, burning in the heart's fire and producing lovely psalms, whereas the imitator only regurgitates foreign words, like a wall or a parrot.[50] The inspiration that overwhelmed Rumi after Shams had disappeared is beautifully expressed in the line:

> The pre-eternal moon is his face, verse and ghazal are his scent—
> the scent is the portion of him who is not intimate with the view.[51]

Just as the relation between the Prophet Moḥammad and Oweys al-Qarani was established by the 'breath of the Merciful', the scented breeze which came from Yemen and informed Moḥammad about his friend's saintliness (although he had never seen him), thus the very scent of Shamsoddin's love inspired Rumi to write so that he might feel his presence in his poetry—to draw him, so to speak, closer by the magic of words. If he could but enjoy the concrete view of the beloved, ghazal and verse would be superfluous, word and sound would become silent.[52]

When the ghazal is washed from the heart's tablet,
Another ghazal without form and letters is heard from the soul.[53]

Rumi's poems reflect every mood of his soul in the long months of yearning. At times, he may joke with the beloved:

You tell me every moment: 'Say some nice, witty words!'
Give me a kiss for every verse, and sit beside me![54]

But this light mood is rare; the mystic rather speaks of his 'blood-stained' ghazals from which the odor of the heart's blood rises.[55] He was sure that the word which has been entrusted to him, was something weighty, even heavenly.[56]

Since the flute can only talk when touched by the musicians' lip, Rumi often—in almost all his verses connected with music—calls for the friend's breath, or hand, to enable him to sing again:

If I could only be joined to my Reason, then I would say whatever is to be said.[57]

Sometimes he tires of scanning verses. He probably never gave much time to correct scansion, and metrical or grammatical flaws can be easily detected in his poetry, for the rhythms flowed without intellectual effort. But sometimes—mainly in the last one of two verses of a ghazal—he inserts the catchwords for the meters when he lacks proper words, or else uses them as symbols of outward intellectual fetters:

This *moftaʿelon fāʿelaton* has killed my soul . . .[58]

Would it not be better to become active (*faʿʿāl*) instead of repeating *fāʿelāton fāʿelāt*?[59] For poems (*sheʿr*) should be torn like old pieces of hair-cloth (*shaʿr*)[60] so long as they are devoid of real meaning. True meaning, however, can be granted only by the inspiration of the beloved.

Although Shamsoddin, Ṣalāḥoddin, or Ḥosamoddin inspired poetry, yet,

letters and breath and rhyme are all foreigners;[61]

when the *ʿaṣida* (a sweet cake for festive occasions) arrived, why still write a *qaṣida*?[62] And when the veritable Sun arrives, the 'snow of words' will melt.[63]

Poetry grows only in separation, words die in union. Rumi has expressed this mystery of mystical poetry very often, and has lived through it for many years:

> To speak words means to close that window, the manifesting of word is exactly its veiling.
> Sing like nightingales in front of the rose in order to divert them from the scent of the rose;
> So long as their ears are occupied with *qul* 'Say!', their understanding does not fly towards the face of the rose(*gol*).[64]

The mystic who was once blessed with union, and has seen the deepest light, knows that he cannot express his vision in human words: 'Who knows God, becomes dumb', as the *ḥadith* says, and the true gnostics 'put a seal on their tongues'.[65] On the other hand, overwhelmed by the beauty and greatness of Divine Majesty, the mystic cannot help conveying at least fragments of his experience to the world, because he wants everyone to get at least a pale image, a weak scent of this final Reality, and therefore, as another *ḥadith* attests: 'Who knows God, his tongue becomes long (in talking).'

Every mystic in the Muslim world—and not only there!—experiences this dilemma, and exactly those who claimed time and again that silence is the only way of speaking of God—constantly reminding themselves, like Rumi, at the end of their ghazals to become silent—have written most voluminous works on mystical topics in verses or prose . . .

Rumi was well aware that silence is the language of the angels which is without words,[66] and that

> silence is the ocean out of which the stream 'speech' is derived.[67]

He calls himself no longer to knit the net of speech,[68] to close his lips although his words make the mouth fresh and lovely like a toothbrush (*mesvāk*) made of odoriferous wood. [69] But the wave of love and longing was so strong that it overpowered him and carried him away into ever new poetical expression. It is the wave of a primordial experience, of a love which was sealed at the day of the Pre-eternal Covenant:

> Leave the ghazal, and look into pre-eternity (*azal*),
> for our grief and passion came from pre-eternity![70]

In more sober moments, then, he tried to ponder upon the role of language in the expression of mystical experience. One of the finest passages in this respect—which is, in fact, a key passage for his whole understanding—is noted down in the first book of the *Mathnavi* when Ḥosāmoddin, still unexperienced, asks him to speak about Shams. But Rumi refuses: this Sun is so radiant that its secrets can be only told in metaphors, stories, parables:

> It is better that the secret of the Friend should be disguised: do thou hearken in the contents of the tale.
> It is better that the lovers' secret should be told in the talk of others.[71]

For nobody can look at the sun without veils; if this sun, unveiled and naked, as young Ḥosāmoddin wanted it, should draw nearer, it would burn the whole world. All the stories invented in the *Mathnavi*, all the lovely images in the *Divān* are nothing but a veil to hide this overpowering sun of Shamsoddin, in whom Divine Love and Majesty revealed itself. The eye is incapable of seeing this sun in its brightness—its very brightness constitutes its greatest veil; but he who has seen it for a moment, and has been transformed by its rays, must invent colourful images, like stained glass-pieces, to show the world how marvelous the Sun is. Rumi very clearly recognized this twofold function of the poetic word, its role in veiling the extremely bright beauty and in revealing parts of it:

> The jealousy of love uses the words to hide the beauty of the beloved from the strangers, speaks His laud without five and seven,[72]

without outward images. But the common people cannot enter the Divine Fire without mediation: images and examples serve, for them, as a hot bath which shows them how hot the fire beneath may be . . .[73]

Rumi's store of symbols is almost inexhaustible: he relies upon the stories of yore, the *asāṭir-e awwalin*,[74] or takes examples from Arabic grammar to show in how far a symbol can be useful. The Arabic proverb *mā lā yudraku kulluhu lā yutraku kulluhu* 'When the whole of a thing is unattainable the whole of it is not (therefore to be) relinquished' is applied to a defense of symbols: although one can never reach the full reality, one should not refrain from at least attempting a certain approximation—although one cannot drink the flood from the cloud, yet, one cannot refrain from drinking water either.[75]

Common man is comparable to a child whose parents explain the secrets of life in simple images,[76] or give a wooden sword or a doll in his hand:[77] he is a child who still reads books for instruction[78] and talks much, while a mature person leaves books, and is silent.[79]

Rumi comes always back to the relation of word and meaning: you may call a man 'a lion' in braveness—how great the difference between the outward form of man and lion may be: the interior meaning of both, e.g. the essence 'bravery', is the same.[80] The corporeal senses have to serve as a vessel for understanding,[81] and too much water may break the vessel. The tongue is like the earth in relation to the heaven 'heart':[82] yet the tongue, fertilized by the heaven, will show finally what is hidden in it. Or, in another image, the tongue, like the kettle's lid, reveals what is cooked in the kettle 'heart'.[83] A story may be likened to a measure-vessel in which the meaning is contained like grain.[84]

The poet can only express the husk, but the kernel, the marrow, is meant for those who can understand.[85] Or: words are like the tresses which veil the face of the lovely idol and should be opened so that the sun-like face can be seen[86]—but tresses and curls are also part of that very beauty.

Certainly, there are correspondences between experience and expression—experience is like the hand, expression like the instrument through which the hand acts,[87] like the pen or brush by means of which are painted on a wall pictures, which are mere reflections of true beauty, shades which man thinks to be real. Expressions are beacon-lights which are needed only so long as one has not arrived at the port;[88] they are the scent of heavenly apple-trees,[89] or stars which work by God's permission.[90]

Rumi has often tried to solve this riddle of the relation between words and meaning, of experience and expression, but always returns to the feeling that words are merely dust on the mirror of 'experience',[91] dust brought forth from the movement of the broom 'tongue' . . .[92] and the true meaning, the 'soul of the story' can be found only when man loses himself in the presence of the Beloved where neither dust nor forms remain.[93]

It does not matter, therefore, whether the words are spoken in Arabic, Persian, or Turkish—the 'Arabic meaning' is important, not the Arabic word.[94] Rumi himself often turns to Arabic expressions and has composed a considerable number of skilful Arabic poems. He also liked writing verses in both languages alternatively, and the languages of his environment, Turkish and Greek, are used in his lyrics as well. What difference does it make?

> Love has a hundred different tongues![95]

He tells the story of four quarreling persons: the Arab wanted *ʿinab*, the Persian *angur*, the Turk *üzüm*, the Greek *estafil*—but eventually they discovered that they all desired 'grapes' in their different languages.[96] And the blind who fail to describe the elephant properly are in the same position as the mystic who tries in vain to describe his experiences in an created language . . .[97]

The whole *Mathnavi* is an attempt to show the way that leads towards the inner meaning which is 'hidden like the lion in the forest',[98] dangerous and overwhelming. Or, to put it differently:

> The word is a nest in which the bird 'meaning' rests.[99]

Notwithstanding all his remarks about words as veils, Rumi apparently felt a certain pride when composing his *Mathnavi-ye maʿnavi*: even if the trees were pens and the ocean ink, the *Mathnavi* could not be completed—it is infinite, since it tries to expound the infiniteness of God.[100] But not always the poet found an ear to listen;[101] people even objected to the style of the book,[102] so that the poet, in a fit of anger, sighs:

> This discourse is now left like a donkey on ice, since it is not fitting to recite the Gospel to Jews.
> How can one speak of 'Omar to Shiites? How can one play the lute before the deaf?[103]

The *Mathnavi* is, according to its author, 'the shop of Poverty', and the 'shop of Unity';[104] here, lovers can find spiritual nourishment and precious rubies and a source of life.[105] The highest mystical stages are noted down in this poem, although the 'true wakefulness of the heart' cannot be described even in a hundred *Mathnavis;*[106] yet, it is an island into which the stream of God flows.[107]

Rumi, under the waves of inspiration, must often call himself back to continue a story; he feels that forty camels would not be able to carry this book if he were to tell everything that is in his mind,[108] and if he were to explain the secret of love, inspired by God, it would become eightyfold . . .[109]

To be sure, the person intended by the *Mathnavi*, its source and its goal is Chalabi Ḥosāmoddin.[110] As inspirer of the poem, he is addressed at the beginning of each of the six books—only the first one is built up differently—and at times also in the course of a story. Ḥosāmoddin took the place of Shamsoddin; but he is only 'sunlight' (*ziyā*), not the Sun itself.

It would perhaps be easier to understand and appreciate Rumi's full greatness as a mystical poet if his poetry had always remained on the highest level, speaking of nothing but heavenly things, of union and love, of God, angels and prophets, without descending into the lower strata of life. Indeed, quite a few Western critics have felt in Rumi's verses the perpetual repetition of high soaring ideas which can be enjoyed only for a certain span of time due to their enthusiastic flights. This judgment is mainly based upon the translations of those selected poems from the *Divān* which are available to Western readers. But once we take a close look at Rumi's poetry we will be surprised to discover the range of human—and very human indeed!—stories, allusions and images the poet has compiled.

First of all, Rumi is a good story-teller. He cannot compete, though, with ʿAṭṭār, whose main epics show a comparatively logical architectural structure, and whose stories are generally well-knit. Rumi's stories are without beginning and end; he often starts with one tale, then is carried away by a loose association of words or thought, and may insert a second, and even third story until he reminds himself to return, once more, to the basic anecdote. This looseness of the *Mathnavi*, which most Western readers find difficult to appreciate, is reminiscent of the form of mystical sessions: the master gives some advice, or expresses an opinion; some visitor or disciple may utter a word; he takes it up, spins a new tale out of it, is caught by some verbal association—very common in the Islamic languages with their almost infinite possibilities of developing different meanings from one Arabic root—then, he may become enraptured and recite some verses, and thus the evening passes in an enchanted atmosphere; but it would be difficult to remember the wonderful stories and points the next morning in any logical sequence.

In 1251—i.e. before the *Mathnavi* was begun—Mowlānā's friend, the minister Jalāloddin Qarātay, founded the Qarātay madrasa, a small edifice which, in my opinion, better reflects the character of the *Mathnavi* than any rational explanation could do: its inside is covered completely with the turquoise blue tiles that are so typical of Konya and of Seljuk art; its walls join the tambour-zone by means of five so-called 'Turkish triangles' in each corner; on these triangles, the names of the Prophet, the first four caliphs, and some prophets are inscribed in black quadrangular Kufic. The tambour zone itself is covered with an exquisite Koranic inscription in plaited Kufic of the most complicated style so that only the initiate may decipher it. The knots and stars in the letters lead the spectators' eye higher to the dome whose white, bluish, black and turquoise tiles form a pattern of most complicated stars which are connected with each other and yet remain separate entities so that the eye wanders, without finding a beginning or end, until it reaches the apex of the dome which is open so that at night the real stars can be seen; these are, in turn, reflected in a tiny pond in the middle of the madrasa.

This decoration corresponds directly with the character of the *Mathnavi*: the same greater and smaller units of artistically connected stars and starlike motifs, rising from the foundation of Koranic words—as Rumi has always relied upon the Word of God—and leading, finally, to the heavenly stars which every literary work, or work of art, can only imitate in the hope of leading man to the original.

If we regard the *Mathnavi*, and part of the lyrics, from this viewpoint we may understand it better.

Mowlānā Jalāloddin himself had a very fascinating way of getting his audience interested in a topic. His art of story-telling shows itself, of necessity, mainly in the *Mathnavi*, where his subjects range from highest meditations on prayer and resurrection to the lowest aspects of life, like pederasty, fornication, and similar topics. He can describe in glowing words the day of resurrection,[111] and, matured in the pangs of love, knows how to depict the lover who has eventually returned to his beloved Bukhara.[112] The tenderness of his style reaches an acme in the description of the annunciation of Mary, a story which could be easily taken out of a medieval Christian book of devotions;[113] it contrasts with the sarcastic description of Kharaqāni's hideous wife which is so colourful that even the least mystically minded person can enjoy it.[114]

The liveliness of all tales in the *Mathnavi* is remarkable, even though they sometimes lack logical sequence, and even though the symbols show an almost protean variance so that the same image can be used sometimes in a positive, at other times in a negative setting. The imagery is fresh, and the discussions of the persons are lively as if taken from the spoken word. Amazingly enough, the uniform meter does not hinder the poet from giving a different flavour to his stories; the wording and even the structure of the sentences is so variable that one does not easily tire of reading, despite the monotony of the meter.

Rumi's art as a story teller and his way of attracting people's attention can be witnessed in his lyrics, too.[115] He belongs to the poets who prefer a strong *maṭlaᶜ*, first verse, for their poems—it is as if a lightning strikes him and sets him on fire. Take for example the line:

bāz āmad ān mahi ke nadidash falak be-khāb
āvord ātashi . . .[116]

with its sequence of strongly stressed long *ā* at the beginning. Sometimes the fire continues through the whole ghazal—there are poems which seem to be spoken almost in one breath, each line beginning with *agar* 'if' . . . The initial fire may develop so that one can almost feel the movement of the whirling dance becoming faster and faster until, all of a sudden, the inspiration is broken—but the poet, fettered by rhythm and rhyme, still continues speaking in verses which, however, are much weaker and less attractive than those before the climax.[117]

One of Rumi's most frequently-used poetical techniques is the repetition of words, or groups of words. Anaphora, so abundant in ᶜAṭṭār's later epics in order to describe the ineffable, are common in Rumi's lyrics as well; hammering questions in the rhyme—like the constant *ku? ku?* 'Where?' Where?'—serve the same purpose. He repeats the call to the lovers or the Muslims twice, even thrice, in each hemistich so that sometimes only the rhyme-word changes, or he uses long chains of *radifs* in which his longing, his rhythmical shouting is echoed. How many poems follow the pattern of this one:

bahār āmad, bahār āmad, bahār-e muskhbār āmad
negār āmad negār āmad negār-e burdbār āmad . . .

The spríng has come, the spríng has come, the spríng with loáds of musk has come,
the fríend has come, the fríend has come, the búrden-beáring fríend has come . . .

Or he may call the Beloved through the whole poem *biyā biyā biyā biyā* 'come, come, come, come', or ask him *kojāʾi kojāʾi*? 'Where are you, where are you?'[118]

This technique is made possible by his use of meters which are easy to scan; often, meters are applied which allow of a caesura in the middle of the hemistich: that enables the poet to insert interior rhymes as well (*mosammaṭ*). The single verse is thus split up into four smaller units and becomes quite similar to Turkish popular folksongs with four line verses in the rhyme-scheme *aaaa bbba ccca* etc.[119]

Frequent also are meters with a large amount of short syllables, reflecting the breathless excitement and the quick heart-beats of the poet; in many such cases, the closing last two long syllables then bear a very heavy stress as if they were to be extended for a long while. Full statistics of the verse forms used by Rumi as well as his rhyming technique, his use of alliterations is still a *desideratum*; but everyone who reads his lyrics will be carried away by the strong rhythmical movement which, in many cases, even suggests that the verses can be read according to stress, not according to *ʿaruż* (although they adhere firmly to the rules of classical quantitative meters).

Rumi has sometimes coined unusual forms, like comparatives of nouns: *āhutar* 'more gazelle than a gazelle' or *sowsantari* 'you are more lily than a lily', etc.;[120] he has also rhymed whole ghazals—of satirical character—in diminutives.

His imagery is inspired by the events in his environment. He may start with the question:

Did you hear? Our neighbour was ill last night?

and then goes on to describe the symptoms of his illness, not sparing the reader some rather unspiritual details, until he discovers the true reason for the illness, i.e. love. The rather common occurrence of the government confiscating wealthy people's goods—often accompanied by all kinds of tortures—leads Rumi to compare Love to a police-officer who enacts fines and confiscation from the whole world.[121] The ragman who walks around the town, shouting in Turkish *eski babuj kimde var?* 'Who has old shoes?' becomes likewise a symbol of Love, which carries away everything old and rotten.[122] The 'bald man of Baalbek' who carries trays with pinches of drugs and herbs on his head appears as the model of man who is loaded with pinches and pieces out of the treasures of the Divine Attributes—a pinch of speech, a pinch of generosity, etc.[123]

Rumi takes us to the bazaar to test earthen pots: if they give a good sound, one should buy them, but those with hidden cracks sound different—why not discern the faithful and the hypocrites by the words and sounds they produce?[124]

Mowlānā Jalāloddin knows the charming but thievish *luḷis*, the gypsies who come to Konya, enchanting and confusing people with music and rope-dance; they remind him of the rope-dance which his soul performs on the black tresses of the beloved.[125] His aversion to villagers finds expression in the fact that they are used as symbols for the uneducated base faculties which create all kinds of trouble in the bazaar and are eventually arrested by the market-superintendent 'Reason'.[126] His mystical beloved Shams appears even in the image of a bleacher who scolds the sun which hides behind clouds—but at his word, the sun will appear and do his work for ever . . .[127] Rumi may close a poem by comparing himself to a water-carrier's horse—once the water-carrier has found a customer, he takes off the little bell from his horse: silence is the end . . .[128]

After the happy days of Ramadan and the ʿ*Id*, daily life begins anew and makes the poet sigh:

> The festival has passed, and everybody has returned to work,
> the intelligent have gone to the bazaar for the sake of the capital.
> You are the bazaar and profession of the lovers—
> The lovers have despaired from any bazaar but you!
> The silly have gone to their meetings for sex and stomach,
> the jurists have gone to the madrasa for the sake of arguing . . .[129]

Rumi knows the kitchen and the weaving places, the art of

calligraphy and music. The stone-figures—man or beast—which are found in the caravanserais and on the highways pouring water out of their mouths prove to him that the so-called 'secondary causes' are deceiving: water does not issue out of the mouth of a stone-bird, but comes from a higher source.[130]

Just as everything in his daily life could become a symbol for a higher reality, he also animates everything, be it pain, sleep, love, or grief. Grief is a market-superintendent whom the lover sends away;[131] it may also appear as a thief who runs away when he sees that the lover is a friend of the police-officer 'Love',[132] if he is not hanged by the police-master 'Union'.[133] His grief is growing fatter and fatter, whereas he himself becomes emaciated in longing; 'Union' too has become so lean that it needs nourishment from the friend's goblet;[134] or else, when the lover becomes mad, grief will decrease in weight.[135] Who would not think of John Donne's complaint in 'Love's Diet':

> To what a cumbersome unwieldiness
> And burdenous corpulence my love had grown . . .

Rumi looks for his lost heart, and

> when I searched house by house, I found a wretched thing . . .
> . . . in one corner, prostrating itself and crying 'O God!'[136]

The most tender verses are addressed to sleep—Rumi who according to Sepahsālār slept little and spent most of his nights in prayer, has used the sweetest words to describe this state of sleeplessness: he warns sleep lest he be drowned in the ocean of tears:[137] sleep only looks at him and flees to sit with someone else;[138] glancing at his heart, he found this roast meat too tasteless (*bi namak*) and therefore did not stay;[139] or the fists of love mistreated him so much that he became wounded and ran away.[140] Perhaps:

> My sleep drank the poison of separation and died . . .[141]

There are lines of unforgettable beauty in which Jalāloddin addresses his beloved:

> Open the veil, and close the door,
> I am and you, and empty the house . . .[142]

or, in a verse inspired by a line of Sanā᾿i:

Without your word the soul has no ear,
without your ear the soul has no tongue . . .[143]

And he is afraid that nothing is soft enough for his beloved:

When the shade of a rose petal falls on you,
A mark will remain on your delicate cheek . . .[144]

Descriptions of spring and flowers, of the sweet sleep of the lovers belong to this category:

Under the shade of your tresses—how softly slept my heart,
Intoxicated and lovely, so peaceful and so free . . .[145]

But there are those verses of tremendous darkness—the subconscious remembrance of Shamsoddin's blood in the dust may loom behind lines in which he exclaims:

Make a mountain of skulls, make an ocean from our blood . . .[146]
kuh kon az kallahā . . .

with a remarkably hard alliteration in the first hemistich.

The image of the world as a cauldron filled with blood out of which he brings forth a ladle filled with spiritual experience, or the statement

We make the cup for our wine only from a skull . . .

belong to this category.[147] Terrible loneliness, and haunting fear of separation are voiced:

O dog of the butcher 'Separation', lick my blood nicely![148]

This aspect of his poetry should never be forgotten—the dance in blood, the dark night of the soul after the Sun has disappeared, the separation of the reed from the reedbed are the painful experiences out of which his poetry grew.

Yet, Rumi had also a good sense of humour, and when he claims that even his dirty jokes are instructional, he is certainly right.[149] Here, he is again close to Sanā'i, whose language was anything but chaste. He ridicules the market-inspector, the laughing-stock of most love-intoxicated poets,[150] and sees people in ridiculous situations, like the man who seeks cheese from an empty tray,[151] or the Sufi who becomes enamoured of the empty food-vallet.[152] Most amusing is his description of the poor dervish who was most heartily welcomed by the inhabitants of a Sufi convent, who then sold his donkey in order to procure sweetmeat for the *samāʿ*-party: one almost hears the hand-clapping which accompanies their cheerful song:

> *khar beraft u khar beraft u khar beraft . . .*
> Gone the donkey, gone the donkey, gone is he . . .[153]

Or take the story of the drunken Turk who asked a musician to sing before him and then mocked at the negative way of description 'not like this and not like that . . . neither . . . nor . . .'[154]

Surprising remarks or comparisons put forth to shock or at least awaken the auditors are sometimes reminiscent of the paradoxes (*koan*) in Zen Buddhism.

> Why should the bald man comb himself? He has no hair![155]

Rumi is most critical of the common people—'men like animals', as the Koran asserts (Sura 7/179). The tale of the cow which entered Baghdad exemplifies this view.[156] Stupid human behaviour is often described in not very decent language,[157] and one of the targets of Rumi's attacks is the self-complacent and proud Khāja, the teacher or merchant, and often, in this poetry, an image of the 'bourgeoisie':

> You call him red gold, though he is yellow-handed and painful;
> You call him the khāja of the town, and he has not even pants![158]

In Rumi's descriptions of the 'world'—the world of base instincts—his language becomes even more expressive:

> Who is this shabby little old woman? A tasteless little hypocrite,
> Layer upon layer like an onion, stinking like a little garlic . . .[159]

And his words against the philosophers do not lack spice either.

Rumi loves to insert proverbs and popular expressions into his poetry; Arabic proverbs are sometimes translated,[160] but were probably well enough known to everybody to be used in the original. Expressions like 'to come out like a hair from the dough'[161] or 'the vessel fell from the roof', i.e., a secret was revealed (or will be revealed after nine months, for 'nights are pregnant')[162] are used without difficulties in his verses. Popular beliefs, superstitions and customs become evident from his allusions.

Everything became a symbol for him, from rotten onion to the radiant beauty of the full moon, from a donkey's excrement to the life-giving breeze of spring; and, strangely enough, even the uncouth expressions do not form an impediment for our enjoyment of his poetry. One may indeed say that Jalāloddin had the gift of transforming everything that came into his hands. He often speaks of the sun which transforms, by means of its Divine rays, the hard stone into a ruby, making it partake of the eternal sun-light. Thus, Rumi, united with the spirit of Shamsoddin and seeing through his light, discovered the spark of the Divine in everything—for everything has been created by God in order to proclaim His glory. By his poetry Rumi set this spark free. That is why his poetry is both human and full of spiritual life, an instrument leading from metaphorical existence towards Real Existence.

Mowlānā Jalāloddin knew well that all the symbols are but weak 'astrolabes' to point the way towards the Divine Sun. But how should the movement of the hidden breeze which keeps the world alive become visible if there were no dust stirred up, or if the leaves in the garden would not dance? Nothing is outside this dance—and thus Jalāloddin sang in ever new verses that:

> the whole world is charged with the Grandeur of God.

II

Rumi's Imagery

We shall show them Our signs in the Horizons and in themselves . . .

'By the morning light!'

THE SUN

One of the most revealing verses in Rumi's *Divān* is the last line of a ghazal in which he describes his mystical meeting with Shamsoddin:

> As the sun moving clouds behind him run,
> All hearts attend Thee, O Tabriz's Sun![1]

Man has always been overwhelmed by the power and glory of the created sun—a sun, which, however, could easily find its peer,[2] if God had willed. For the visible sun, beautiful and useful as it may be, is only God's cook, not anything to be worshipped. What would happen if man would seek the sun at midnight?[3] Then, only 'the Sun of the Sun of the Sun' remains . . .[4]

Yet, this created sun offers itself as a fitting symbol for anyone who tries to describe the Divine Majesty and Glory, and is, indeed, one of the most common images in religious literatures throughout the world—not to mention the numerous religions in which the sun itself was worshipped as 'the God', or at least one of the leading deities. But for Rumi, the combination of this ages-old symbol with the very real experience of his love for Shamsoddin gives his sun-imagery a fresh, and very personal, note. Whenever we find in his poetry allusions to the sun we may be sure that he, consciously or unconsciously, thought of Shamsoddin whose light changed his life so completely. He was right to call himself 'a messenger from the sun' and a slave of the sun, who talks constantly about the sun, not about sleep and night.[5] Thus, he addresses the Sun of his life in words overboarding with enthusiasm:

> Bravo, o limitless sun about which your atoms say:
> "Are you the Divine Essence? Are you God?" . . . I do not know![6]

It is not only the brilliant and gracious sun which Rumi praises, that friendly luminary which ripens the fruits and fills creation with happiness: he knows all too well the tremendous power, the destroying strength of this sun. The key passage in the beginning of the *Mathnavi* when Ḥosāmoddin asks him to speak of the secrets of Shams, reveals much of his feelings: he refuses to talk openly about the lost friend, for:

> If this sun should become naked and visible,
> neither you would remain nor your breast or hem.
> The sun through which the whole world is illuminated—
> if it would draw slightly closer, the whole world would be burnt.[7]

That is a statement which he repeated almost verbatim in *Fihi mā fihi*.[8]

The sun is both *tremendum* and *fascinans*, and thus the perfect symbol of that God who is kind and loving and, at the same time, a consuming fire.

The Koran endowed Rumi with new possibilities of combining the sun-motif with God: did not God call Himself 'the Light of the heavens and the earth' in the famous light-verse of the Holy Book (Sura 24/35)?[9] This verse, which is amply quoted by the mystics in different interpretations, serves Rumi i.a. to describe the spiritual sun, Shamsoddin, who 'radiates from the zodiacal sign "Neither Eastern" . . .',[10] e.g. the sun which is not bound to any spatial relations but reveals the Divine Light in its fullness. Another Koranic verse—the beginning of Sura 93 'By the Morning-light!'—points to the same end. It was generally used, in Sufi circles, to describe the glory of the Prophet; Rumi, however, combines it with Shamsoddin as well, for in him the eternal light of Moḥammad—which is light from the Divine Light[11]—is reflected in perfect purity. And it is this *sura* which speaks of the miraculous morning-sun of Eternity which is used, in Islamic folklore, to cure headache and repel grief.[12] Thus, the connection with the Beloved who heals every pain is given in the background.

There is no doubt that the meeting with Shamsoddin was the one decisive experience in Rumi's life. He has never ceased to see Shams in the various manifestations of the sun—he is the Sun of *maʿāref* (gnostic knowledge) in the foreplace of inner meaning,[13] and he is, like real sunlight, separate from everything and yet miraculously connected with everything.[14]

Rumi's friendship with Ṣalāḥoddin and later with Ḥosāmoddin are mere reflections of this first encounter with the spiritual sun; Jalāloddin clearly expresses in the *Mathnavi* what he sees in his younger friend Ḥosāmoddin Chalabi:

> I have called you *żiyā* (light) *ḥosām od-din* (sword of religion) for this reason,
> because you are a sun, and these two (words) are epithets (appropriate for the sun).[15]

Żiyā᾿ is the Koranic expression for sunlight, and *ḥosām*, 'sword' reminds the reader of the rays of the sun which destroy everything mean, be it the snow which covers the frozen and loveless earth, be it the uncertain greyish dawn.[16] Żiyā᾿ ol-ḥaqq, the Sun of Reality, is a new manifestation of Shamsoddin, the Perfect Beloved; hence he performs the same miracles as Shams, and as the sun does: the rubies in the mountains prove his power of transforming raw minerals into precious gems, the garden smiles when he looks at it.[17] For the stone, touched by the sun, assimilates into himself the sun-like qualities; likewise man, under the spiritual influence of the Divine Sun as revealed in Shamsoddin and Żiyā᾿ al-ḥaqq, becomes purified and gains some approximation to the Divine qualities, following the Prophetic tradition:

> Qualify yourselves with the qualities of God (*takhallaqu bi-akhlāq Allāh*),

until he becomes a transparent vessel for the Divine Light.[18]

There is no end of descriptions of the miraculous power of the sun in Rumi's poetry, and often he invents tender and sweet images:

> The sun addresses the sour grape: "I came into your kitchen for that purpose
> that you should not sell vinegar anymore, but take up the profession of a sweetmeat-confectioner".[19]

It should be remembered that in Turkey a very sweet thick and nourishing jam is prepared from ripe grapes (called *pekmez*)—hence the sweetmeat. Just as these grapes participate in the power of the sun, selfish and sour human beings become sweetened through the meeting with Shams. Man will melt, like heaven and stones and mountains, once he is touched by this spritual sun;[20] but at the same time he will gain a new life thanks to its kindness: annihilation is followed by eternal life. But this holds true only for those who lovingly surrender to the sun: the fresh tree gains power from its warm light so that its fruits ripen; but the dried-up branch will become even drier under its burning heat, and will be eventually destroyed[21]—the Sun of Divine Grandeur leads spiritually barren people not towards life but towards death. The Beloved is indeed the true sun, other people being flighty and short-lived like the lightning—and:

> What letter could one read in the lightning's light?[22]

Night falls over the human heart when He disappears, just as the moon is eclipsed when the sun hides itself . . .[23]

The created sun offers still more analogies to the poet, although it is subject to changes whereas the Sun of Inner Knowledge has its East in the soul and spirit and enlightens the spiritual world day and night.[24] But the setting of the sun is a symbol for man's death and resurrection: the heavenly light appears, in renewed beauty, the next morning—will not man be resurrected and reborn in a similar way?[25]

Much as medieval astronomers computed the sun's way by means of an astrolabe which serves to indicate the station of the Divine Sun—how could a word or a speech give true news about the worldly, not to mention the Divine Sun?[26] They are useful to a certain degree, but ineffective like the signs of the astrolabe. For the true sun which dwells in the heart of the lovers is beyond time and space. It is the *mehr-e jān*, 'sun of the soul' with no *mehrejān* 'autumnal feast'.[27] How could one expect scholars like Avicenna to explain this light and its mysterious ways?[28]

Nobody can describe this sun properly. The shade may point to its existence, since things are known through their opposites[29]—but the shadows which seek light become annihilated when the sun appears in full radiance, just as reason disappears when God manifests Himself, for 'Everything is perishable save His Face' (Sura 28/88). And the Koranic expression 'how the shade extended' (Sura 25/45) points to the saints who tell people of the existence of the Divine Sun by their own shadowy existence: Rumi describes himself as circumambulating the sun like a shade, sometimes prostrating himself, sometimes standing on his head.[30]

The created sun, again, shows how easily man can be deceived: when he puts only one finger upon his eyes the sun disappears.[31] That is what the infidels do in respect to their spiritual eyes and the spiritual sun. Closing their eyes with very meaningless devices, they resemble also bats which deny the very existence of the sun, even hate it. Their hatred against daylight is comparable to the hatred the infidels nourish against the Prophet, or against God: it does not detract from the luminosity of those spiritual lights but rather proves that the hated object is in fact a veritable sun.[32] However, these poor creatures who blindfold their eyes believe that they can hinder the sun from reaching others, that they can jeopardize the prophets' activity which consists in illuminating people.[33] And how stupid is the person who asks proofs from the sun when it rises—is not daylight itself proof enough? He who does not see that, is blind.[34]

If they would but look . . . every atom, every particle of dust gives news from the sun, moves thanks to it, is its servant.[35] Thus those who praise the sun praise themselves, for from their laud one understands that they are endowed with insight and willing to see, being capable of receiving illumination,[36] whereas the enemy of the sun is, finally, his own enemy.[37]

The atom which is annihilated in the sun, becomes part of it. After realizing the truth of the Koranic assertion 'Verily we belong to God and to Him we return' (Sura 2/156), the atom now fully co-operates with the Divine Sun,[38] and

> every atom touched by the Sun of the Soul, robs cloak and hat from the created sun,

i.e. it is infinitely higher than anything created.[39] For to love the Sun means to love the eternal values; but he who loves this world is comparable to the man who is enchanted by a wall upon which he enjoys the reflections of the sunrays—an application of Plato!—until he discovers that the light spots do not originate from the wall but from a source higher and purer.[40] When these sun rays hear the call 'Come back (*irji'ī*, Sura 89/28) they return to their origin, and neither the colours of the rose garden nor the ugliness of the ash-house remains; for only by the light of the sun the world is alive and visible.[41]

This sunlight is not defiled by any outward dirt or darkness;[42] it remains pure wherever it reaches—the spiritual cannot be polluted by the material.

Is not the sun a model of the illuminating intellect?

> When the sun of the sky goes the wrong way,
> God makes it blackfaced (disgraced) by an eclipse . . .

Likewise human intellect will experience an eclipse if man deviates from the God-given spiritual rules.[43]

Rumi's sun-imagery is not only the result of spiritual experiences—the sunrises and sunsets in Central Anatolia are so splendid that he was inspired by their beauty time and again:

> The sun drew its sword, and spilled the blood of the dawn—
> the blood of thousands of dawns is ritually permitted to its countenance (*ṭalʿat*, also: appearances).[44]

> The heart which was like dawn drowned in blood
> became now filled with sun, like the sky . . .[45]

> When the sun came out of the pit of black water,
> hear from every atom (the profession): 'There is no deity but God!'[46]

Whosoever has once experienced the true sunrise which annihilates the bats, e.g. the senses, is completely filled with sunlight and will bring this light wherever he goes; the East will envy his West, so full of light has he become:[47] that is what Rumi felt after his meeting with Shamsoddin who permeated his whole being and shone through him. His point of sunrise is beyond the Orient and not bound to the particles which reflect the light: he and all those who have experienced a similar sunrise in love, have become suns without rising-place in both worlds.[48]

Rumi had experienced what other mystics called 'the sun at Midnight', the sunrise beyond time and space which is preceded by the pangs and loneliness of the 'dark night of the soul': only out of its depths can this eternal and everlasting sun of love rise.[49]

Then, no one has the right to speak;[50] the stars are extinguished, and the shades dissipated, or at least called to disappear in the sunshine.[51] The dark material existence of man is annihilated in its splendor.

> Be silent so that the preacher Sun may talk,
> For he came to the pulpit, and we all are his disciples.[52]

It is natural that Rumi should have tried to explain the experience of *fanāʾ*, annihilation, with the symbol of the sun and the stars, or the sun and the candle: *fanāʾ* is not a substantial union, but resembles the state of a candle in front of the sun—its light, though still materially existent, is no longer visible and has no power of its own; it is existent and non-existent at the same time.[53] Thus, human qualities no longer count when the Divine Sun fills every corner of the spirit.

Rumi has, of course, also alluded to the Prophetic tradition that Moḥammad himself is like a sun, and his companions like stars, radiant, and helpful for the traveller, throwing stones —like meteors—against the devils. But the real light comes from the sun;[54] the stars are but helpers and reflections of its majesty. And since 'the scholars are the heirs of the prophets', the perfect scholar is also comparable to the sun,

> whose whole function is giving and dispensing universally, converting stones into rubies and cornelians, changing mountains of earth into mines of copper and gold and silver and iron, making the earth fresh and verdant, bestowing upon the trees fruits of diverse kinds. His trade is giving: he dispenses and does not receive.[55]

Whatever the sun means—the Divine Light, the Prophet who guides his people, the Perfect Man, the Spiritual Beloved—it is, no doubt, the central symbol in Rumi's poetry through which the name of Shamsoddin is echoed and re-echoed thousands of times.

Connected with the image of the sun is that of the colours. Rumi never tires of expressing the truth that the sunlight in itself is much too strong to be seen, and that its very strength and brilliance is a veil in itself.[56] Things can be recognized only by their opposites, and pure light can be seen either by the contrasting darkness, or broken in different colours.[57] Red and green and russet are only veils for the unmixed light[58] which is, so to speak, filled in glass vessels of different hue[59]—an image long since known among the mystics. As soon as the vessels break, as soon as the material world disappears, the sunlight remains in its purity, and no colour or shade is left.[60]

But besides this general explanation of the colours as veils for the pure invisible light, which occurs repeatedly in the *Mathnavi*, Rumi plays with the traditional colour concepts very frequently. He has, however, not developed a colour mysticism like that of his elder contemporary Najmoddin Kobrā or his colleague in Sivas, Kobrā's disciple Najmoddin Dāyā,[61] in whose works the mystical meaning of colours, and a whole polychromatic system of mystical experiences is systematically described. Rumi merely sees the various colours, like everything else in the world, as symbols for his mental state, or for generally accepted truths. In his descriptions he often invents images which can be understood best when one thinks of the glowing colours of Central Anatolia.

There are his descriptions of the night, when the sun has disappeared:

> When the face of the sun became absent from the eye of the earth,
> In consequence the night put on, out of grief, a black dress.
> When the sun in the morning lifts its head (the sky) puts on a white garb—
> O you whose face is the sun of the soul, do not be absent from your court![62]

> The night put on this black dress, like a wife donning a black dress for the sake of her husband who has gone under the dust—[63]

verses which show that black was, at that time, the colour of mourning, white being for Rumi the colour of joy.—The poet may compare the blackness of the night sky to the smoke of the fire of his yearning for the Sun which has gone.[64] Only when the moon—again the beloved—wanders about, the night puts on a joyful white dress.[65]

Spring is, of course, the time when everything dresses in green, the colour of Paradise—it is as if heavenly beings in green gowns had descended upon earth to greet the faithful,[66] reminding them of the happiness of the eternal gardens.

Red is, for Rumi, the best colour, and he even alludes to an alleged Prophetic tradition that God could be seen—if at all—in a red garment.[67] For red is the colour of the radiant and happy beloved, connected with sun and with love, whereas yellow is the sign of the pale and lean lover who resembles a piece of straw . . .[68]

In a lovely passage of the *Mathnavi* Mowlānā describes the activity of the sun and the various colours, particularly in spring time:

> The King's sun, in the zodiacal sign of reproach, makes faces black as a piece of roasted meat.
> Our souls are leaves for that Mercury (to write on): that white and black (writing) is our standard (criterion).
> Again, he writes a patent in red and green, that our spirits may be delivered from melancholy and despair.

> Red and green are Spring's cancellation (of winter); in regard to their significance (they are) like the lines of the rainbow.[69]

Rumi uses the traditional wordplays connected with the different colours as cleverly as any other Persian poet: he speaks of the red wine to be poured in the head of —black—melancholia;[70] and he marvels at the wrong behaviour of his hair which puts on a black dress in the time of youthful gaiety but a white one in the time of grief and separation.[71] But he has no special predilection for a certain colour like some other poets (such as Mirza Ghalib) in whose lines one peculiar colour taints the whole poetry. All the different colours are caused by the blandishments of the beloved; the sky binds its blue cummerband for His sake (due to its blue frock, the sky is often equated with a Sufi), and the dusk is red-faced from the blood of the liver (which the sky sheds out of love).[72] Only thanks to the activity of the Divine Beloved the various colours appear and disappear, as reflections of the one great light:

> Through Him the greenery of the leaves becomes yellow,
> Through Him the twigs of the trees become green,
> Through Him the cheeks of the beloved become red,
> Through Him the cheek of the free becomes yellow,[73]

as he sings in a little Arabic poem, which best summarizes his attitude to the manifold colours which reveal the Sun's unceasing activity and, at the same time, hide the pure light from the eyes of the common people. The end of all colours is the dyer's vat of what the Koran calls *ṣibghat Allāh*, 'the baptism of God' (Sura 2/138). In this vat a dress with a hundred colours becomes clean and lucid, like the sunlight itself.[74] Here is the beginning and end of all colours.

Another aspect of the imagery connected with the sun is the poet's use of the names of stars and terms from astronomy and astrology. Rumi displays, in his verses, the normal knowledge of the medieval Muslim intellectual about the stars, their astrological qualifications and their importance for human life. He likes to play with their names and qualities describing them as living personalities:

> Jupiter takes out of his pocket the finest kind of gold,
> Mars says to Saturn: 'Bring out your dagger against me . . .' etc.[75]

However, his imagery is not remarkably original: the inherited ideas about the stars are faithfully reproduced: Jupiter the Greatest Fortune, Saturn the Great Misfortune, Mars the Warrior, etc. Neither is Rumi's connection of the blood-shedding Mars with the Turks[76] and of black Saturn with the Hindus by any means novel. One may mention, as somewhat more original, Rumi's numerous puns on the name of Jupiter, *moshtari*, which means also 'the buyer', 'the customer'; this word is, then, combined with the Koranic promise that God will 'buy your souls'[77] (Sura 9/111)—which constitutes, of course, the true 'great fortune' for man.

Soheyl, the small but radiant star connected with Yemen is generally mentioned as a symbol of spiritual beauty: the possible combination with the 'breath of the Merciful' which comes from Yemen as well as with the cornelian, the Yemenite gem which symbolizes the friend's lip made this star a happy augury for the lover;[78] perhaps a remembrance of the 'Yemenite wisdom' as taught by Sohravardi Maqtul can be detected in allusions of this kind. Soheyl, appearing at the *rokn-e yamani*, the south-east corner of the Kaʿaba, can even work upon the process of tanning raw hide and making it into delicate *ṭāʾefi*-leather;[79] that means it symbolizes the Beloved and his miraculous power.

Mercury, the intelligent secretary of heaven,[80] and Venus, the playful dancing and singing star, could likewise be used in connection with the experience of love which makes even Mercury break his pen.

Among the signs of the zodiac *ḥamal*, Aries is most prominent, since it is the spring-sign in which the sun becomes most radiant,[81] hence the equivalent for the lover's heart in which Shamsoddin finds his true home, to dwell in full glory.

> When the sun of union with you comes one day into Aries,
> it will find in my heart another sign Aries![82]

The other signs of the zodiac are likewise used in appropriate connections, and their application by the poet would perhaps yield some interesting observations for the specialist in medieval astrology.

That Rumi uses the old image of the radiant moon for the 'moon-faced' beloved, goes without saying, and innumerable verses sing of the eternal beauty of this moon who kisses those who spend their nights wakeful, counting the stars . . .

Mowlānā is fully conversant with the medieval idea that the world rests upon a cow, the cow upon a fish, and claims that in love even those mythological creatures beneath the seventh layer of the earth have become happy, just as the signs of the zodiac up to the fishes stamp their feet in enthusiastic dance:[83] again, the whole world is created to worship and love the eternal Beloved, and express their constant adoration in an intoxicated dance which embraces fish and moon (*az māh tā māhi*), atom and sun.

The lover, then, can claim to be the astrolabe of the world, which accepts the forms of the whole firmament,[84] and Rumi closes a great poem filled with astronomical images with the words:

> This sky is an astrolabe, and Love is reality—
> Whatever I may say about it; turn your ear toward the inner meaning![85]

The power of the spiritual Sun, and the attraction of love, is not restricted to the skies but works in stones and minerals as well.

> The Prophet of God said: 'Humans are like mines'—
> there are mines of silver and gold and surely full of jewels.[86]

This prophetic tradition gave Rumi a means to explain the differences in human beings,[87] since their *jowhar*, their 'jewel' or 'essence' is different. Basically, God Himself is the true mine which contains everything; so we may find gold, copper, and cornelian in it.[88] Or else the lover's heart is comparable to minerals:

> For a while I tremble on the hand of his love like mercury,
> For a while I become gold in the mine of all hearts.[89]

This imagery gains more weight when Rumi compares the soul to iron pieces and the beloved, or love itself, to the magnet which attracts them:

> You are the magnet, and the soul, like iron,
> comes intoxicated and without hand and feet.[90]

All the images and dreams of the world run in front of the dream-image of the Beloved like iron pieces attracted by the magnet,[91] for:

> Where would there be iron which is not in love with the magnet?[92]
> The soul of the poor turns around annihilation like iron and magnet.[93]

Indeed, there is no better symbol for the mysterious power which draws man close to God—even though one must be apprehensive of the danger that love, a very personal Divine force in Rumi's view, might be interpreted here as a purely mechanical attraction. But the numerous equations of the magnet with a person, namely Shamsoddin, make such an interpretation quite unlikely, although it would conform to some philosophical doctrines of Rumi's contemporaries.

Rumi also speaks of the attraction exerted by the *kahrobā* 'straw-robber', e.g. amber, upon the piece of straw; indeed, the tiny straw pieces are comparable in their weak yellow appearance to the frail, pale, and submissive lover who is carried by every draft in a new direction.[94]

> The threshold of His tent became the amber of the lovers—
> O lean lovers, make yourselves like a piece of straw![95]

Rumi often mentions the sparks hidden in the stone—as long as iron and stone will co-operate, they can produce something higher than themselves, namely fire and light, and thus the world will never be without light.[96] These hidden sparks serve to illustrate man's power to perceive the yet unborn possibilities in the gross matter; to see the sparks in the stone, to recognize the wine already in the grapes are the signs of the perfect spiritual leader who sees through the light of God.

In the tradition of worldy love poetry, Rumi speaks of the golden, e.g. pale, face of the lover as contrasted to the silver-limbs of the beloved:

> The six directions became like gold due to my face—
> so that I might see the silver of your seven limbs . . .[97]

Rumi knew well how to discern the false and the true, and often uses the image of false gold, *qalb*, which is put on the touchstone to test it.[98] The identity of the word *qalb* 'counterfeit' and *qalb* 'heart' offers an excellent way of introducing the idea that the heart has to be tested by the touchstone of love and grief, or in the fire of afflictions and pains,[99] so that its true value can be discovered by the beloved. The idea itself is not novel, but fits very well into Rumi's world-view.

Mystics of all countries have tended to see man's experiences on the mystical path in the image of alchemy. And Sepahsālār tells that Rumi, to the amazement of one of his disciples, was able to transform base matter into precious gems . . .[100] No wonder that *kimiyā*, spiritual alchemy, plays an important role in Rumi's imagery as well. Man feels himself to be a piece of copper which has no right to attest its own base qualities.[101] The beloved, or the hand of Love, can change this lowly metal into pure gold:

> Why do you seek gold? Make your own copper into gold,
> and if it is not gold, then come with a silver-breast![102]

The Divine call *irjiʿi* 'Return!' (Sura 89/28) is the great alchemy which transforms the low material beings into spiritual gold;[103] only after such a transformation has taken place, the copper will become aware of its previous miserable state.[104] In one of his ironical poems, Rumi ridicules the worldly people who think only of sleep and sensual joy, things forbidden for whose who long for spiritual growth (and he may well have thought of the erotic symbolism of alchemy):

> We have melted like copper thanks to our search for alchemy (e.g. Love)—
> You, for whom the bed and bedfellow are alchemy, keep sleeping![105]

For only when the black stone is transformed by chemical processes and loses its identity, when it so to speak experiences *fanāʾ*, it turns into precious metal and can be used as money.[106] Only after the annihilation of his base qualities it becomes useful in the world.

This alchemy is a painful process—even more painful than the testing of gold by touchstone and fire; it requires long and patient work and suffering. The gold ore has to be put into the furnace to become purified; the lover has

> to live together with the fire in the midst of the furnace like gold.[107]

Hearts which are like iron are melting in this fire, and with full right is the experience of annihilation, in which man feels himself completely united with God, compared to the state of the red-hot iron which calls, with its whole being 'I am the fire'.[108]

Rumi knows that it is alchemy for the heart to look at God's saints,[109] or at the Beloved, the most perfect manifestation of Divine Grace:

> From myself I am copper, through you: gold;
> From myself I am a stone, through you, a pearl . . .[110]

The transformation of ordinary stones into precious gems is one of Mowlānā's favourite images—it is an old Oriental belief that stones can be changed by the light of the sun into rubies.

> Every stone which you seized, you have made into jewels,
> every fly which you brought up, you made like a hundred *homā*-birds![111]

The *laʿl-e badakhshān*, the most esteemed species of ruby, is the product of the look of the beloved:[112]

> When the sun entered Aries, its rays became active:
> look at the ruby of Badakhshan and the alms-tax on garnet![113]

Rumi never tires of describing this miraculous power of his Sun, Shamsoddin, who is the treasure of rubies and cornelian and can transform even the stone-hearted into gems.[114]—The ruby is, on the other hand, produced from the heartblood of minerals being poured, when stones lie for ages in darkness, patiently waiting for the ray of the sun which, eventually, will recompense their endurance by making them transparent for its own light. The connection of blood and ruby—much more frequent in later Persian poetry than in Rumi's lines—is openly expressed in a dark and hopeless verse in the *Divān*:

> 'Blood' became the name of the mountain whose name had been 'ruby',
> when shame, because of you, fell into mountain and hill range.[115]

Whoever has seen the mountains of Anatolia or Iran at sunrise and sunset, glowing in deep crimson and purple hues, feels that these images were not only cerebral plays but inspired by the nature which surrounded the poet.

The most beautiful poem in which Rumi speaks of the ruby connects this stone not, as usual, with the power of love and the mine of beauty, but with *faqr*, 'spiritual poverty':

> I saw Poverty like to a mine of ruby,
> so that I became, thanks to its colour (some grandee who) dons (crimson) satin.[116]

Perfect spiritual poverty is the most valuable royal gem which grants those who gather around it the royal garment, the red majestic satin.

It adds to the special charm of stone-imagery that ruby, rarely garnet, and often cornelian, the Yemeni stone, are metaphors for the lips of the beloved (who is often asked to pay the alms-tax due on these stones, e.g. a kiss).[117] Especially the precious cornelian has served Rumi for many comparisons.

> Without his cornelian, the market of existence be destroyed, stone by stone![118]

The emerald is mentioned always in the Oriental tradition as the gem averting evil by blinding the eyes of serpents and dragons; thus it becomes a symbol for everything spiritual, be it the *sheykh*, the beloved, or love itself.[119]

Whatever images Rumi has taken from the mineral world, he knew that, as the Koran has attested, every stone is praising its Lord, and that even in this inanimate part of the world there are likenesses for those who see. The stone itself, representative of the lowest natural kingdom will become, in the course of time, either a valuable gem, like the ruby, or it will be polished to be used as a mirror, or else it becomes dust, modest and soft, out of which plants can grow: minerals are the starting-point of the constantly rising movement of the created beings which leads, through long periods of time, to plants, animals, and man to end, finally, in God. (cf. ch. III, 4).

We made everything alive from water . . .

THE IMAGERY OF WATER

The poets and mystics of the Islamic world have delighted in using the imagery of water in all its aspects, and the Koran gave them ample justification for this use—did God not attest, time and again, that

> We made everything alive from water (Sura 21/30, and many similar instances).

The idea that Divine Grace, or even the Divine Essence itself, reveals itself in the image of water is therefore one of Rumi's main topics; but in his usual protean style he applies the water symbolism to different levels, although the breadth of variations is not as large here as in other symbols.

Created water reminds the poet of the water of life, the water of grace and many other beautiful and life-bestowing things which are sent down, like rain, from heaven to refresh the world.

> What is the call of water? It is like the call of Israfil, quickening the dead, or like a dervish in the days of religious almsgiving, or like the sound of freedom for a prisoner, like the breath of the Merciful which reached the Prophet from Yemen, or like the scent of Joseph's shirt which cured Jacob's blindness . . .[1]

The whole world and existence can be compared to a stream of water—the Ashᶜarite theory of the atomic structure of the universe which is annihilated and recreated every wink, could be easily represented under the image of water in a river which looks always the same and yet, is different every moment.[2]

The main object of this water is to clean the dirty (cf. Sura 8/11)—rain is sent down in order to purify man.[3] Should the dirty hesitate to enter the water to clean himself, because of his fear lest the water be polluted, the water will call him back and promise help: only shame hinders faith, as the *ḥadith* says.[4] Thus is God's treatment of his sinful servants: he is the limitless ocean of grace in which everyone who dares enter will be purified and sanctified. What would the water do without the dirty? It needs them to show its kindness . . . a theological thought not alien to Christian ideas.

But water has many other functions besides, like supporting the plants or carrying boats without hands and feet, etc.[5]

Water is always the symbol of the Divine—but not everyone understands its secret: the water of the Nile became blood for the infidel Egyptians, but was helpful for the Israelites[6]—God revealed Himself to the faithful in His grace as water of life, to the infidels and hypocrites in His wrath as poison, danger, and death.

Even more: there are people who are not even aware of the existence of sweet water, for they dwell in places with brackish water, like certain birds—how could they understand that there is a water of greater purity and limpidity than the one they know? Thus, the people bound by this world will never understand the sweetness of mystical experience, they rather prefer to remain in their dwelling-places in the salty, stagnant pools of this world.[7] In fact, they do not understand water at all, for:

> The ocean is a home for the duck, but death for the crow.[8]

Rumi has often confronted the 'ocean of inner meaning' and the external world: outward manifestations and all forms visible to the eyes are nothing but straw and chaff which cover the surface of this divine sea.[9] He has repeatedly elaborated this image, though calling the sea by different names, be it the 'water of Life',[10] or the 'ocean of Unity',[11]—but whatever be its name, the outward material forms are always conceived as something accidental which hides the fathomless depths of this ocean.

In other places, and quite often, Rumi uses the image of the foam on the sea to express this very idea—in his great ghazal on visionary experience[12] he sees the world and its creatures emerging from the divine ocean like pieces of foam, clapping their hands (an often-used *tajnis* between *kaf* 'palm of the hand' and *kaf* 'foam'), and disappearing again at the call of the abyss. He visualizes

> people clapping their hands like the sea, and prostrating themselves like waves.[13]

The ocean which is hidden behind this veil of foam is the Divine attributes,[14] and it behoves the mystic to enter into the water without caring for the foam.[15] Yet:

> This world is but foam full of floating jetsam; but through the turning about of those waves and the congruous surging of the sea and the constant motion of the billows that foam takes on a certain beauty—,[16]

this world is 'decked out fair' (Sura 3/13) for a moment, but the eye which perceives reality, cannot be deceived by its temporal charm. And the poet juxtaposes those who look at the foam and those who behold the sea, those who are still 'in the world' and those who fix their eyes on God, breathless with adoration:

> He that regards the foam tells of the mystery, while he that regards the Sea is bewildered.
> He that regards the foam forms intentions, while he that regards

> the Sea makes his heart (one with) the Sea.
> He that regards the foam-flakes is (engaged) in reckoning, while he that regards the Sea is without conscious volition.
> He that regards the foam is in (continual) movement, while he that regards the Sea is devoid of hypocrisy.[17]

Divine Mercy is an ocean which produces its effects without reason and without explanation,[18] and man is called to dwell upon the sea-shore so that maybe the wave of grace will fill his little vessel.

Rumi has described also the world of sleep using the image of a big sea which covers everything and in which a dark leviathan swallows thoughts and individualities until man is rescued, again, when the morning-sun rises in the East.[19]

More than any other image that of the ocean of God lends itself to a pantheistic interpretation:[20] the world appears here only as an outward aspect of the hidden Divine reality, whereas in most of his verses Rumi underlines the mystery of Divine power which works upon not-being, and creates out of nothing.

This personalistic interpretation of the relation between God and man becomes more explicit in the idea that the human body is like a fish in the ocean World; hidden in this fish, the soul lives like Jonah, waiting until God leads it out of its dark prison; the poet then turns to say that the souls are likewise like fishes in this ocean—those who have ears to hear can listen to the permanent laud and praise which the soul-fishes utter in the depths of the sea.[21] (This example shows clearly how easily Rumi changes his application of images to particular facts or states.)

Man's movement towards God is, as in other mystical works, often compared to the journey of the torrent, or the river,[22] towards the ocean:

> Prostrating myself I run towards the sea like a torrent,
> On the face of the sea we go afterwards, clapping our hands (or; producing foam).[23]

The reader acquainted with German literature will immediately recognize the motif of Goethe's poem *Mahomets Gesang* in which the life of the Prophet of Islam has been symbolized by this very image—it is a poem which has in turn inspired the Indo-Muslim poet-philosopher Muhammad Iqbal to imitate it in Persian verses,[24] thus uniting the two major influences under which he composed his lyrics, that of Goethe and of Mowlānā Rumi.

The imagery of river and sea is mainly used in Rumi's lyrics; the ocean is the river's true homeland, and like the drop which emerges from the sea of ᶜOman (a well-known catch-word for the ocean) man goes back to this place.[25] His wish is to break the vessels of material externals, to be reunited with this source of being.[26]

Those who have finally arrived in the ocean are submersed in the Essence—how could they still regard the Attributes? Lost in the abyss, how could they know anything about the colour of this Divine water?[27] This infinite and fathomless sea is Love—that is why the lover makes his own breast (*kanār*, also 'shore') an ocean of tears.[28] The love which man experiences, is a branch of this ocean which reaches his heart; he is called to leave the shore of the lower soul, of his ego, and to enter into this sea in which he has no longer to fear the crocodiles.[29] Numerous verses use this imagery; love can even be called 'an ocean of fire'.

The motif of the spiritual journey which underlies the image of the torrent returning into the sea, is even more outspoken in the image that out of the sea humidity rises to take a place, for a while, in the clouds; thence, it returns to the ocean and becomes, if Divine Grace wills, a precious pearl[30]—for pearls are produced, according to Oriental belief, by the drops of April rain which fall into choice oysters. The oyster thus represents the saint whose perfect contentment is recompensed by his silent mouth being filled with such a jewel.[31] Or else the oyster becomes a sign of God's mercy: He feeds it with most wonderful food although it possesses neither ear nor eye . . .[32] The twofold imagery of the drop and the sea as used by the mystics in all religions appears very lucidly in Rumi's verses: the drop either returns to the ocean to become united with its own source once more and to disappear completely in the all-embracing water, or it lives as a pearl, embraced by the sea and yet distinct from it. Both images have been utilized in later times by the Sufis: the confessors of *waḥdat al-wojud*, 'Unity of Being' preferred that of the drop which loses itself in the ocean, whereas the followers of a more personalistic interpretation of the Divine liked to speak of the pearl: the drop returns into its proper element after being purified and elevated by its journey, and lives in God though distinct from Him in its substance.

Rumi sees the distribution of the 'water of intellect', the 'water of Universal Reason' through different channels into man as Divine water flowing into a garden.[33] In a similar strain of thought he may also imagine the body to be the canal through which the spirit flows like running water: only by water the canal gains its proper importance, and man should beware of covering the surface of this water with sticks and straws of useless thought, but rather keep this spiritual water clean, sweet, and unpolluted.[34]

Again, the senses resemble an ewer which can contain a certain quantity of water; or material man is like a vessel with five spouts, e.g. the five senses. The ewer and the water preserved in it have to be kept pure so that it can be brought as a gift to the king who will appreciate its fine taste and limpidity.[35] Rumi applies this simile to man's restricted sense-perception which is like the ewer; the caliph to whom the simple-minded bedouin offers his water, is the huge river Tigris of Divine knowledge—if man were only aware of the existence of such a river, he would break his ewer without hesitation!

That the 'rain of mercy' occurs frequently in Rumi's imagery, goes without saying: the traditional relation of the Prophet who was sent as a 'mercy for the worlds' (Sura 21/107) and the rain which is likewise called *raḥmat,* 'mercy', in the Middle Eastern countries, could easily serve to interpret the activity of the Prophet or of the perfect saint, the Beloved who quickens the thirsty land of the souls by his advent. And the tears of the lovers are likewise comparable to the blissful rain which causes the garden to open its blossoms in spring. . .

One can certainly not draw a clear picture of Rumi's religious ideas by relying only upon his imagery connected with water—in this field, his expressions are very much like those of the mystics of all times and religions, who lovingly used the image of the Divine Ocean which indeed offers itself to everybody who has eyes to see. In Rumi's poetry verses praising the unlimited ocean of God, or of Love, stand side by side with clearly personalistic images like that of the Divine Sun.

A particular aspect of this imagery are verses speaking of

ice: here, Rumi seems to be close to Ibn ʿArabi who had described the relation of God and the world like that of water and ice. Rumi, however, takes the image in a very realistic sense and usually connects it with the image of the sun—as long as ice remains in the shadow, it is immovable, only the sun can melt it.[36] Thus, the human body and whatever man possesses, is like ice; God will buy it and give, instead, a sweet melting in annihilation.[37]

The ice and snow in the solidified world of winter[38]—be it the winter of corporeal life, or that of the congealed minerals and inanimate beings—would immediately melt if it only knew the strength and beauty of the sun, and would turn once more into water, running in brooklets towards the trees to do useful work in quickening them—for being frozen is the state of the selfish and egotistic person.[39]

Rumi's *Divān* is replete with verses in which he sings the deplorable state of those who, far from the sun, become like snow[40] and long to be melted:

> That snow says every moment: 'I will melt and become a torrent, I will roll towards the sea, I am a being which belongs to the sea and the ocean.
> I am alone, I have become stagnant, I have become frozen and hard so that I am chewed by the teeth of affliction like snow and ice.[41]

The sigh of the frozen, isolated human heart which yearns to be dissolved in spiritual union is here expressed in an image which was at once understood by those who know the hard winter in the Central Anatolian provinces and the sudden outbreak of spring, when the sweet murmuring of the brooks fills the hillside. And how beautifully does the poet indicate the secret of true annihilation:

> In the essence of annihilation I said: 'O King of all kings!
> All images have melted in this fire!'
> He spoke: 'Your address is still a remnant of this snow—
> As long as the snow remains, the red rose is hidden![42]

As long as the smallest trace of self-expression and self-will is left (be it even a word of praise for the Beloved), the rosegarden of perfect union is still closed to the lover.

The whole world is like ice—it will melt on Doomsday, and if people would know that, the partial intellect would behave like a donkey on ice.[43] For who could believe that ice and snow will become water? And yet, they will set free the water hidden in them, just as the body's dissolution will set free the soul which is concealed behind its frozen surface.

And the annihilated snow will turn to earth and will be richly decorated by flowers which praise the power of the Sun . . .[44]

And Gardens beneath which flow rivers . . .

THE SYMBOLISM OF GARDENS

Joseph von Hammer-Purgstall, the Austrian orientalist, was the first to translate some of Rumi's poems into German in 1818. One of these translations begins with the line:

> Mondnächte sind wieder gekommen, aus Gräbern die Gurken,
> Und aus dunkelem Sand ist Geile des Bibers gekommen . . .[1]

I am quite sure that his readers must have accused him of having mistranslated Rumi's verse: for who could imagine that a mystic like him would use the words 'reed and 'cucumber' in his poetry? However, Hammer's translation is not too far off the mark, and we have here an example of the garden imagery which abounds in Jalāloddin's poems—though indeed, a rather weird one. Gourds, cucumbers, and other products of the gardens of Konya can, however, be found several times in his lines in various combinations: for instance he ridicules the would-be Sufi who shaves his head like a gourd or a cucumber,[2] an image which fits well with the descriptions of certain groups of the *qalandar* dervishes who roamed about the country.

Of course, vegetables like gourds are 'slowfooted' and have still a long way before them in their pilgrimage towards the beloved;[3] but even they partake in the constant upward movement of life. Rumi may compare the self-complacent person to a high growing gourd[4] whereas the stupid one is like a gourd unaware for which purpose the gardener binds its throat:[5] but on this rope, the silly fruit may even learn rope-dancing.[6] The bitter gourd, often compared to man's head,[7] becomes useful when used as a drinking-vessel in which unexpected wine may be contained.[8]

For Jalāloddin the garden is full of life. He dreams of the garden of which heaven is but one leaf,[9] and yet, the earthly garden is at least a tiny reflection of this uncreated garden. Only those who have spent some days in May in the Konya plain can fully understand the truthfulness of Rumi's imagery; they know how all of a sudden a thunderstorm arises and heavy rains flow; then, the sun breaks through the dark clouds, and the trees open their buds; the whole air is filled with the fragrance of roses, *iğde,* and fresh grass, and the town is covered with a lovely green veil. The fields surrounding the city are filled with hazelnut-bushes: poppies, mint and fenugreek grow soon beside the brooklets which rush down from the two hills[10] that limit the plain towards the Southwest.

> The rosegarden and the sweet basil, different kinds of anemones,
> a violet-bed on the dust, and wind, and water, and fire, O heart![11]

The four elements participate in the Festival of Spring (as a translator has called his verses inspired by Rumi), and the countryside becomes like paradise where the cypress drags from the earth the sweet water of *kowthar*[12] (for in poetical imagery the cypress is always connected with a brook or pond).

Indeed, one of Rumi's favourite comparisons in his enrapturing spring poems is that of springtime with the day of resurrection: the wind blows like the sound of Israfil's trumpet, and whatever was hidden and apparently rotten[13] under the dust, is quickened again and becomes visible. The poet is a faithful interpreter of the Koranic invitation to witness the proof for resurrection in the revival of the dead earth in spring.[14]

> The grace is from God, but the bodily people do not find grace
> without the veil 'garden'.[15]

The new green leaves show God's eternal grace and life-bestowing power which will manifest itself once more and for ever on the Day of Resurrection: thus, the true lover sees behind this new life of the garden 'the beauty of the gardener'.[16]

Trees and flowers are perfect symbols of human beings; for the changes in the garden 'human heart' which bears spring and fall in itself—if man would only look!—are reflected in the external world;[17] and once the beloved approves of the heart, hundreds of thousands of roses will open, nightingales will sing.[18] For just like man, the world, too, is some times patient, sometimes grateful, and that is why the garden now wears a lovely dress, and then, again, becomes naked.[19]

In winter, the trees are like Jacob who patiently waited to see his beloved son Joseph, practising 'fine patience'[20] (Sura 12/18), as the Koran attests. This winter, mainly the month of December, is a mad[21] thief from whom the plants and trees hide their goods:[22] but as soon as the police-master (*sheḥna*) Spring comes, this thief disappears and hides himself.[23] Then, the army of rosegardens and odoriferous herbs becomes victorious, thank God: for the lilies have sharpened their swords and daggers[24] which act as veritable *ẕu'l-feqār,* the mysterious sword of Ali.'[25] It was indeed high time for such a victory, for winter had closed the ways which lead towards the beloved, and all the lovely buds were imprisoned in the dark dungeon Earth[26]—winter in Central Anatolia is hard, and snow prevents communication.

But winter is also the season of gathering for the sake of spending: all the riches which the trees have collected in their dark treasure-houses will be spent when spring comes.[27] The lover himself becomes like fall, yellow-faced[28] and shedding his foliage,[29] when separated from the beloved, or else he turns into winter, frozen and unhappy, so that everyone suffers from him. But as soon as the Friend appears, he is transformed into a rosegarden in spring.[30] In fact the Beloved *is* spring-time for the whole field of creation, and it is only thanks to him that anemones can blossom.

To be sure, everything longs for warm April days, but one should not ask the secret of spring from stones and clods of earth, but rather from hyacinth and boxtree for they know better what this season means.[31] They know that now the patient seed which had been waiting under the dust will be recompensed by hundredfold fruit,[32] that it eventually will ripe into corn; and then, finally, the beloved may separate the grain Joy from the straw Grief.[33]

Spring in the Middle East, is the messenger from the invisible Paradise,[34] when the 'green-dressed' i.e. the paradisical people, arrive from the blue hall of heaven.[35] And it means the arrival of warm rains. The clouds which come slowly over the hills are 'pregnant from the ocean of love',[36] just like the mystic himself: they will shed their tears on the dust and praise God:[37]

> As long as the cloud weeps not, how could the garden smile?

That is one of Rumi's central ideas. The manifestations of nature correspond exactly to human behaviour: Smiling happens in proportion to weeping—the smile of the garden is the compensation of the cloud's weeping.[38] For as the rain drops are instrumental in producing the beauty of the garden, the lover's tears will eventually result in a manifestation of Divine Lovingkindness.[39] And does not the complaining water wheel attract the water from the darkness and makes greenery sprout in the field of the soul?[40] The cloud's weeping, together with the heat of the sun, grants the garden new splendour, just as the 'weeping eye and sunlike intelligence' give the heart real life.[41] The thunder's wrath, again, helps to unfold the hidden possibilities of the heart.[42]

> Until there is the lightning of the heart and the rain-clouds of the two eyes,
> How shall the fire of Divine menace and wrath be allayed?
> How shall the herbage grow, (the herbage) of the delight of union,
> How shall the fountains of clear water gush forth?
> How shall the rose-beds tell their secret to the garden,
> How shall the violet make an engagement with the jasmine?
> How shall a plane-tree open its hands in prayer?
> How shall any tree toss its head in the air (of love-desire)?
> How shall the blossoms begin to shake out their sleeves full of largesse in the days of Spring?
> How shall the cheeks of the anemone flame like blood?
> How shall the rose bring gold out of its purse? . . .[43]

These poetical images were known in Sufi circles since at least the early tenth century: but in Rumi's verses they gain a new actuality. Was he himself not weeping like a cloud after the Sun of Tabriz had disappeared?[44]

In a sweet and melodious ghazal Jalāloddin describes his loneliness and helplessness after the sun has gone:

> O you, from whose cries and callings 'O Lord!'
> the heaven wept the whole night . . .!
> I and the sky were weeping yesterday,
> I and he have the same religion.

What grows from the sky's weeping?
Roses and violets nicely arranged.
What grows from the lovers' weeping?
A hundred kindnesses in that sugar-lipped beloved . . .[45]

There is no end of these spring songs in Rumi's *Divān*. The lightning laughs only for a short moment and remains imprisoned in the cloud,[46] but the thunder comes like a drum to announce the great wedding party of the earth.[47] The *hieros gamos,* the ancient myth of the marriage of heaven and earth, is spiritualized in Rumi's garden poetry:

You are my sky, I am the bewildered earth,
For what things make you grow every moment from my heart! . . .
How knows the earth, what you have sown into its heart?
It is pregnant from you, and you know its burden . . .[48]

When man wanders thirsty through the burning sand of the desert, the water-carrier Love consoles him with the voice of the thunder which promises rain.[49] However, only when the seeker becomes like dust, breaking his stone-like nature, can roses grow out of him.[50]

Using an old comparison Rumi describes the lover who is

> like a cloud weeping for an hour, like a mountain at the time of endurance, like the water prostrate, and lowly like the dust of the road.[51]

In ever-changing images he sings of the beauty of flowers, water and trees which come into existence by the tears of the cloud—

> Where are the compassionate tears of spring, that they may fill the hem of the thorns with roses? —[52]

and which are quickened by the breath of the spring-breeze.

The breeze, again, is a fitting symbol of the life-giving breath of the Beloved: the twigs and branches become intoxicated and dance, touched by the wind,[53] stamping their feet on the tomb of January,[54] and clapping their hands.[55] Even more: the spring breeze becomes visible in the rosebeds and sweet herbs: invisible waves of roses hidden in the breeze need the medium of the earth to become visible to the human eye, just like man's qualities must be revealed by outward means, be it speech, fighting, or peace-making.[56]

Thus, every leaf and tree is a messenger from non-existence[57] which proclaims the creative power of God, talking with long hands and green fresh tongues.[58] Later, in Fall when the plane-tree sheds its leaves (*barg*) God grants it the grace of *barg-e bi bargi, barg* denoting also 'sorrow' or 'possession': this is the state of perfect spiritual poverty and selflessness which the mature Sufi should attain.[59]

In a fine pun the poet speaks of the wind which moves the twigs, whereas the tree-Heart is moved by an interior breeze (*bād*), namely the recollection (*yād*) of the Beloved.[60] This breeze keeps it steadily a-dancing. Only those trees which are sapless and dry can no longer be moved by the wind of love and recollection; either their roots must be watered by the water of life, which is repentance,[61] or else they must be cut off to be used as fire-wood for the ash-house:[62] who would not think of Sura 111 where Abu Lahab's wife is called, for her faithlessness, 'the carrier of fire-wood'? As in her case, every heart that is not moved by love (and, as Rumi says, only Abu Lahab, the Father of the Flame, has no share in the fire of love)[63]—every heart that is filled with envy[64] and other base qualities will be thrown into the depths of the ash-house. The *golkhan* 'ash-house' where dead dogs are also thrown,[65] is the lowest conceivable place, always contrasted with the rose-garden (*golshan*): thus, the hypocrite's praise of God is comparable to greenery growing out of the ash-house.[66]

The dried-up branch, though it be close to the sun, will dry up even more when touched by the warm rays:[67] thus the loveless heart will receive not life but death from the Eternal Sun. This image of the dried-up, lifeless, and hence loveless, tree was taken over by most of the poets in the Muslim East. But not only such sapless trees, but also the steadily growing thorn-hedge of evil qualities should be rooted up, the earlier the better.[68]

The trees are like dervishes, slowly advancing, slowly growing and smiling until they bear full fruit;[69] and their leaves bear witness of the root's character and tell what kind of nourishment they have imbibed.[70] As long as the branches are dry, they resemble ascetics who become refreshed (*sarsabz* 'green-headed') and intoxicated when the friend's lip touches them—asceticism is transformed into love.[71]

Even though the tree moves and trembles in its branches, it is firmly grounded:

Even though I am restless, I am at peace in my soul.[72]

The classical philosophical discussion as to whether the tree precedes the fruit or vice versa is elaborated or alluded to in several passages of the *Mathnavi*, and is solved in the sense that although the tree was earlier in its outward form, the fruit is its meaning and end;[73] without fruit it will be ashamed—'the last will be the first' *al-ākhirun as-sābiqun,* as Rumi adds with a well known *ḥadith.*[74] The whole world is like a tree on which the fruit 'man' is ripening;[75] and the yellow leaves are signs that the fruit is ripe—so man's white hair shows that he has reached maturity, whereas the *barg-e bi bargi* is the state of the perfect gnostic.[76]

This equation of trees with the world, or with human beings, leads Rumi frequently to describe the trees as 'pregnant';[77] they therefore can be compared to Mary who became pregnant by the Holy Spirit[78]—do not the trees in their youthful beauty and virgin innocence surrender to the Divine breath as manifested in the spring breeze which fertilizes them so that they bring forth delicious fruits?

In a different strain of comparisons, Rumi sees the beloved as the tree on which the lover is the fruit:

We went away from your town and did not see our fill of you,[79]
From the branch of your tree did we fall, quite unripe . . .

For such a fruit can be ripened only by the sun of His mercy.[80] The beloved is a marvellous palm-tree—that tree under which Mary experienced the miracle of Divine grace, when fresh dates were showered upon her during her birth pangs (Sura 19/25)—and the lover attests:

Since I sleep in the shade of his palmtree,
I became sweeter than dates, O yes![81]

Man in general is called not to remain in the dust, but to lift his head and become fresh and lovely like a branch of the peach,[82] full of tender blossoms and sweet fruit. The apple and apple-tree are likewise used in Rumi's imagery: Rumi has also utilized the famous image of the apple with its yellow and red cheek[83] that was known as a symbol of lover and beloved, or of the lovers' farewell, to the Arab poets in the Abbasid period, and which has found its classical expression in the *Golestan* of Rumi's contemporary—and, if we can believe the sources, his admirer—Sa'di of Shiraz.[84]

Yet there are less common images as well: the beloved is a strange tree which produces now apples, now gourds,[85] or the ascetic who performs many acts of piety without experiencing spiritual relish, is like a nut without marrow.[86] The custom of putting odoriferous herbs into an earthen flower pot—often mentioned by earlier poets, especially by Khāqāni—is mentioned in Rumi's *Divān* as well.[87]

Whatever plants he chooses, all of them have only one function: to praise without tongue the grace of the water which quickens them[88]—comparable to the faithful who are free and happy like cypress and lily, praising God in different tongues. Yet, compared to His garden, the gardens of this world are as lifeless as a picture in the bath house, without the fruit of Eternal Life or fresh branches.[89] The Beloved is the great gardener; he gives every day a new colour and a new form to the garden-Heart so that, finally, the heart has no longer its original form (which is called *ṣanowbari*, shaped like a pine-tree's fruit).[90]

In Rumi's garden, every flower has its function in representing various states and aspects of human life, functions invented partly by his predecessors, the Arab and early Persian poets. The tulip with glowing cheek has sometimes burnt its heart from wrath,[91] or reflects the splendour of his friend's fiery cheeks;[92] or perhaps it has performed its ablutions with blood like a true martyr (the tulip has often been connected with the martyrs in Islamic lore).[93] The carnation tells the story of the rose,[94] the waterlily is like the lover, restless on the foam of the Divine Sea;[95] the lotus flower rests fresh and peaceful in the garden of Beauty.[96] The jasmine reminds the poet of the separation from his beloved, for this flower says—if we analyse its name—*ya's-e man* 'My hopelessness'; already in medieval Baghdad it was considered bad taste to give jasmine-flowers to friends for the possible combination of its name with *ya's* 'despair'.[97]

The lily has a brilliant sword;[98] but even more, it possesses a hundred tongues which it uses to explain the beauty of the Rose[99]—comparable to the lover, adoring and praising the beloved without words. Sometimes it praises also the cypress which represents the slender stature of the beloved.[100]

Rumi does not add any new dimensions to the usual imagery

of the lily or of the narcissus, symbol of the languid intoxicated eyes; he adds only little to the inherited image of the 'bent' violet: this flower may represent the lowly person sitting in the dust;[101] it is bent under the burden of the beloved,[102] full of grief.[103] In general, the violet is the symbol of the ascetic in his dark blue frock, who sits meditating, or in the position of genuflexion in ritual prayer.[104] It is the mature believer:

> When the base soul has become old, and heart and soul are fresh and green,
> (you are) like a violet with fresh face and hum-backed . . .[105]

Rumi not only listens to the constant laud and praise uttered by the flowers and by all the inhabitants of the garden, but visualizes them in the various positions of prayer:

> See the upright position (*qeyām*)from the Syrian rose, and from the violet the genuflexion,
> the leaf has attained prostration—refresh the call to prayer![106]

It would be surprising if Rumi had not reserved the central place in his garden lyrics for the rose. As much as he has described the various flowers—the rose is different; it is the most perfect manifestation of Divine Beauty in the garden. The vision of Ruzbehān Baqli, the mystic of Shiraz who saw God's glory radiating like a majestic red rose, may have been known to him.[107] Thus he admonishes himself to become silent:

> When the Lord of the *Qul* ('Say'!) speaks—how could the nightingale sing?
> This (Divine) Rose is eloquent and creative in His talk.[108]

Yet, the rose, in its absolute perfection, was known as the flower representing the beloved long since; it was the finest symbol for his/her cheeks. Of course, even the centifolia tears its dress when thinking of the face of the Friend (a beautiful phantastic aetiology for the opening of the rose, which reminds the Muslim reader also of the torn dress of Joseph, the paragon of beauty, and of the healing scent of his shirt).[109] And if even the rose is ashamed how should the lover, who has seen the friend's Beauty, look at the created garden, unless it be out of heedlessness?[110]

The rose was loved by the Prophet, was perhaps even created from his perspiration, as legend tells, and therefore every Muslim would certainly be fond of this flower . . .[111]

Rumi's poetry abounds in rose-poems, beginning with the famous ghazal:

> Today is the day of joy, and this year is the year of the rose . . .[112]

Only rarely the 'faithlessness' of the short-lived flower is mentioned in accordance with the usage of earlier Persian poetry,[113] or the adept is warned not to sit 'with open mouth like the rose, with closed eyes like the bud'.[114] The smiling flower[115] rather becomes a symbol of the happy soul:

> Like a rose, I smile with my whole body, not only by way of the mouth,
> For I am — without myself — alone with the king of the world.[116]

When Rumi sees the rose, he remembers the description of Arab writers who saw it like a royal prince, riding into the garden, surrounded by the grass and the herbs as if they were an army of foot-soldiers.[117] But he knows that the true rose-garden, the rose-garden of love, is eternal and needs no support from Spring to unfold in its beauty.[118] Nevertheless, he may complain:

> That rose which is in the centre of the soul's garden did not come into our embrace tonight . . .[119]

And he connects the external roses with his own state of mind:

> Every red rose that exists has become thus by the help of our blood,
> every yellow rose which grows is from our yellow gall-bladder,[120]

so that from his bleak cheek a yellow rose will grow after his death . . .[121] But hundreds of thousands of centifolia will blossom when he dies in the shade of the cypress in the Friend's rosegarden,[122] for the feelings of the lovers are manifested, after their death, in the flowers that grow from their tomb, as many Persian poets have claimed.

And why should it not be like that? Rumi admonished himself — and repeats the expression in the *Mathnavi* — :

> Die with a smile, like the rose, although you are more excellent . . .[123]

Slowly dropping its petals, the lovely flower fades away, without complaint, in perfect serenity, and leaving sweet fragrance behind it . . . And when the rosegarden has vanished — how to find the rose? From the rose-oil: its scent reminds the lover's heart of the friend.[124]

Out of the feeling that the rose is the highest possible manifestation of God, Rumi may invent expressions like 'the rose of Poverty',[125] or 'the rosegarden of gratitude'.[126] The rose as a sign of Divine grace is also the basis of the post-Koranic legend according to which the pyre into which Abraham was cast, turned for him into a rosebed, 'cool and pleasant' (Sura 21/69); and Rumi, like every Persian poet, has not hesitated to apply this beautiful story to the state of the perfect lovers who are saved, in the midst of the fire of worldly afflictions, by the Beloved who can transform a flame into a rose, a rose into a flame.

At the end of the oft-recited story of the lover who after a year's separation was transformed into his beloved, the lover is addressed by the beloved

> Come, enter the house, O you completely I,
> no longer opposing each other like rose and thorn in the garden![127]

Rose and thorn are generally considered to be enemies, but both belong to the same plant—why should they fight?[128] Rumi has often pondered upon the strange relation of rose and thorn in which God's Beauty and Wrath manifest themselves. He asks the rose to send away the thorn, but the flower answers that it has become sanctified by performing many circumambulations around its face.[129] Both are inseparable—the thornlike lover in all his destitution belongs to the rose-like beloved.[130] Even more: the thorn boasts of its sharp weapon by which it protects the lovely rose against the host of its enemies.[131] The rose, touched by the faithful behaviour of this thorn,[132] bestows grace upon it, and thus even the thorn is transformed into a rosebed, thanks both to its faithful adherence to the rose and the endless kindness of the Divine flower.[133] (In the hand of the sinner, however, every rose turns into a thorn.)[134] He who has realized the secret of Unity, can no longer distinguish between rose and thorn;[135] for in the cypress-garden of *Hu* 'He' the thorn loses its base qualities and opens like a rose:[136] God grants the naked thorns a gala dress of roses.[137] Thus, the saints and initiated who see everything with the eye of unity apprehend the All (*koll*) from the atom, and the rose (*gol*) from the thorn . . .[138]

Rumi has used this pun on *gol* and *koll* several times; it is particularly appropriate, since every rose gives, by its very scent, news of the mysteries of the Whole, carrying at least a slight fragrant message from the rosegarden of Union.[139] Thus the rose (like all the flowers in the garden) reminds man of the Garden of Paradise, of creation and resurrection; it allows a first glance on Divine Beauty, and hides this beauty again with a colourful veil:

> The remembrance of rose and nightingale and the lovely (inhabitants) of the garden
> Is all pretext—why does He make it?
> It is the jealousy of love—otherwise the tongue
> comments upon the graces of God . . .[140]

Do they not look at the camel, how it was created . . .?

IMAGERY INSPIRED BY ANIMALS

No one who has travelled in Anatolia will forget the long rows of camels lined up along the road, carrying their heavy load from the Salt Lake to the city, or bending under the burden of grass, straw, or wood. Mentioned in the Koran as a sign of God's creative power, this animal—so familiar to the medieval Muslim—became a favourite symbol for Mowlānā Jalāloddin.

> The Prophet said: Know the faithful as a camel, always intoxicated by God who leads it as the camel driver. Sometimes he puts a mark on it, sometimes he puts fodder before it, sometimes he bends its knees, bends them prudently. Sometimes he opens its knee for the camel's dance, until it tears its *mehār* (the piece of wood put in the camel's nose through which the leading rope goes), and it is bewildered.[1]

These lines summarize Rumi's approach to the patient animal which is so similar to man:

> Although I am of crooked nature, yet I lead towards the Kaʿba like the camel . . .[2]

The human body, too, may be compared to a camel whereas the heart itself is the Kaʿba.[3]

The poet is the *nāqat Allah,* God's she-camel which, like Ṣāleḥ's she-camel in the Koranic story (Sura 7/70 ff.) performs miracles and dances upon wild roses and carnations.[4] When the faithful hear the sound of the spiritual leader's voice, they start their journey towards the Kaʿba of truth, intoxicated by his sweet song—classical Arabic tradition has often told stories about camels which died from excitement when listening to the lovely voice of the *hādi,* the driver.[5] Rumi can, hence, interweave the camel-motif with that of the spiritual journey, and that of *samāʿ*, mystical music and dance. The intoxicated camel which tears the rope of intellect[6] and its dance belong to his favourite images, denoting the mystic who, out of himself, hurries towards the beloved. For:

> Whereas intellect still seeks a camel for the pilgrimage,
> Love has already gone to the hill *Ṣafā* (purity).[7]

Our poet realistically describes the animal, chewing its rope[8] and, like himself, eating only the thorns which God gives it, even though it were grazing in the garden of Iram.[9] He sings in a light rhythm *(ramal mosaddas* with a strong stress on the third syllable) as if he were dancing:

> O you in whose hand the *mehār* of the lovers is,
> I am in the midst of the caravan, day and night,
> Intoxicated I carry your burden, unwittingly,
> I am like the camel under the burden, day and night . . .[10]

And thus he walks to the resting-place where he is free from both just and tyrannical people,[11] or runs towards Tabriz, the spirit being the camel, the body the chain.[12] Grief and joy, too, resemble two camels which are led by the beloved's reins.[13]

Rumi gets his audience interested by telling them:

> A camel went up on a minaret and cried; 'Alas!
> I am hidden here—please don't reveal me!'[14]

and then explains this incredible event:

> The camel is the lover, the top of this minaret is love,
> For all the minarets are perishable, but my minaret is eternal.

The camel on top of the minaret designates something very conspicuous,[15] something strange to which people point with their fingers[16]—and that is what happens to the poor lover. In a variation of a well known saying Rumi again tells:

When you make a house for the chicken,
the camel does not fit into it, since it is too tall.
The chicken is reason, and the house is this body—
the camel is the beauty of your love with uplifted head and stature.[17]

And he elaborates this very idea by telling the story of the poor hen which invited a camel into her humble den and was destroyed . . .[18] Rumi alludes also several times to the evangelical-Koranic parable of the camel and the needle's eye (Sura 7/40):[19] here, again, love is the camel which does not fit into the narrow hole of human intellect. He tells the little story of the Kurd who had lost his camel, and finding it again in clear moonlight, thanked the revealing moon;[20] and he compares those who try to describe the Divine Essence to well-meaning people who give a Bedouin an approximate description of his lost camel—'and you know that the signs are wrong'.[21]

The soul-camel is described best in the touching verses which speak of the herdsman who takes the animals every night into the pastures of Non-Existence, where they graze on the greenery of Divine gifts, with their eyes bound so that they cannot recognize the Divine Path on which they walk when the body sleeps.[22]

There are a few other images which do not match the general tenor; for Rumi's imagery is always ambivalent, and the same image can be applied to completely different realities. Thus, the poet may see himself as a camel ready to be sacrificed;[23] the camel—once compared to the body—can represent the base faculties as in the story of Majnun who tried to drive his camel towards his beloved whereas the animal always returned to its kid: thus, reason seeks the way toward the beloved, and the instincts are bound to their earthly relations.[24]

And in one of his poems which starts with the description of the Beloved, guiding the soul-camel by its nose-ring, he closes his musing with the charming little joke:

The first line of the ghazal was a camel—that is why it became long—;
Do not expect shortness from a camel, O my sober King![25]

Rumi's camel-imagery is typical of his whole poetical approach to mystical truth. Not only the animal fables as found in *Kalila va Demna* but everyday life in Konya inspired him to give animal-symbolism an amazingly large room in his poetry.

He saw the signs which God had put into the world, and interpreted them. He saw the animals in the stable telling each other proud stories about their ancestry—the ram remembers that he had shared the pasturage with Ishmael's sacrificial ram; the ox was yoked together with Adam's ox when he began to plough the earth; but the Bactrian camel needs not even a historical date since it is so high and impressive . . .[26] And he heard the poor little gazelle's sigh when the hunter had put her into the donkey's stable . . .[27]

Rumi is aware that

> Wolf and rooster and lion know what love is—
> He who has no love, is less than an ass . . .[28]

The comparison of human beings not touched by love with animals is commonplace in Sufi writings; the mystics could rely upon the Koranic verdict that many people are 'like animals, nay, even more astray' (Sura 7/179). In Rumi's poetry, the cow or ox symbolizes the body or the carnal soul which has to be slaughtered,[29] and those who 'worship fodder' are comparable to the cow and will die like asses.[30] The story of the golden calf which induced the Israelites into idol-worship may have added to the negative aspect of these comparatively rarely mentioned 'stupid' bovines. Yet, even such animals are sometimes more intelligent than humans:

> Would the cow eat from the hand of her future murderers, or give them milk, if she knew what her end will be?[31]

Man, however, though aware of death, refuses to draw the consequences. Divine grace can elevate the bovines as well:

> When Thou transformest animal and cow into humans, it is no wonder,
> Since Thou changest the excrements of the cow in water into amber.[32]

The strange animal commonly known as the sea-cow becomes, thus ,a symbol of the lower soul, the *nafs ammāra,* which is transformed, by Divine grace, into the 'soul at peace', the *nafs moṭmaʾenna.*[33]

That the pig—ritually unclean in Islam—should become a symbol of the lowest qualities in man, is but natural, and is not typical only of Islamic imagery. Sensual dirty pleasures are attributed to this animal, and man is rather a pig, dog, ass and cow when following his lusts.[34] Sanāʾi and ʿAṭṭār had visualized the grave sinners transformed into pigs at the day of Judgment,[35] an idea to which Rumi alludes.[36] He mainly connects the pig with the Europeans, the *ferangi* who have desecrated and defiled the holy city of Jerusalem with their pigs (a reminiscence of the Crusades).[37]

Rumi is, at times, convinced that everything is bound to return to its origin, and that outward changes can not modify the innate character of man:

> Even if a pig would fall in musk, and a man into dung,
> Everyone goes back to his own origin from (these outward) provisions and dresses.[38]

Yet, at other times he believes that the leather bottle filled with spiritual wine is so potent that even the pig can reach a place superior to the Lion of the Sky (the zodiacal sign Leo) from trying one sip of this wine.[39]

The goat is used in a proverbial setting still common in Turkey:

> If one would become a man by virtue of beard and testicles,
> every buck has enough hair and beard![40]

The setting of rural Konya is reflected also in the negative allusions to the wolves as they are still found in Anatolia; the Koranic story of Joseph and the wolf has, of course, contributed to the images in which the *nafs,*[41] or sensual lust,[42] and even separation[43] are compared to a ferocious wolf. Only those who trust the shepherd, the Eternal Beloved, will find safety from the ruses and claws of these animals. Did not the Prophet say that every prophet was, for a while, a shepherd tending his flocks before he became a shepherd of men?[44] Hence, the image of the good shepherd is extended to the Beloved.[45] From this idea, Rumi develops the eschatological hope—so often expressed since the times of Israel's prophets—that 'wolf and lamb will lie together': when the kindness of the King will manifest itself, eternal peace will reign; peace will be between fire and water, and the wolf will nurse the lamb;[46] for the Beloved enchants flock, wolf, and shepherd together.[47]

In an impressive and unique image Rumi compares thought *(andisha)* to a forest in which hundred wolves run to catch one lamb—a hopeless and useless affair, not fitting for him who is intoxicated by the One who gave him thought.[48]

Other animals as found in the steppes are not so frequently met with in Rumi's poetry—the hare plays a prominent role in a story taken from *Kalila va Demna* where it represents the base soul.[49] Lovely is the story of the jackal who went into a dyer's shop and then revealed himself to his astonished colleagues as a peacock, and the jackals, in amazement, gathered around him 'like moths around a candle'.[50]—The fox is, as always in literature, the prototype of cunning, well aware of the danger of life:

> A fox saw a tail in the meadow and said:
> 'Never has one seen a tail without a noose in the grass . . .'[51]

Generally,—though not as often as in later Persian poetry—the fox is contrasted with the brave lion. But even this animal could induce higher inspiration: it is told that a salesman came to Rumi to sell a fox, and the Turkish name of the animal, *tilku,* made the mystic exclaim *del ku*? 'Where is the heart?', words, by which he immediately started a new ghazal.[52] We have no reason to doubt the truth of this story which is fully in tune with the reactions of medieval, and even modern, Muslim mystical poets.

The mice run through the granaries, and are comparable to those who stay in the dust of this world for the sake of food, intoxicated by cheese, pistachio and syrup,[53] instead of leaving this material world like birds.[54] Those who silently try to steal some 'spiritual morsels' are blamed because they 'make their way towards the kitchen in the dust, like mice'.[55]

Mice are generally similes for unintelligent people in the fables of the *Mathnavi*: whether the mouse *(nafs)* falls in desperate love with a frog,[56] or leads a camel and then shuns the water which was shallow for the camel, but as deep as an ocean for the tiny creature . . .[57]

Where there are mice, the cat is not far. Rumi has included many cats into his poetry, though not always favourably. There is the famous story known from Naṣreddin Khoja, that a wife told her husband that the cat had eaten the meat for dinner; the man weighed the cat and, finding it exactly the same weight as the meat, became perplexed:

> If this is the cat—where is the meat?
> And if this is the meat—where is the cat?[58]

This deliberation leads to a discussion of the relation between body and spirit . . .

'The cat dreams only of (sheep's) tail' says the poet ironically when telling the story of a Jew who claimed to have been blessed by a vision of Moses in his dream.[59]

The cat is generally mentioned as the enemy of the mice; that is why God has created this animal;[60] the mice may be as numerous as the stars, the cat, like the sun, will never be frightened by them.[61] When the house of religion is pierced by the mice 'envy', these will flee as soon as they see the cat's tail:[62] the cat is the police-master[63] and, as such, the representative of the Universal Reason that keeps the world in order.[64] But if the cat sleeps and the mice eat holes into the box, the cook will put both in a bag and cast them in the fire to punish them, since the mice have transgressed their limits and the cat has neglected her duties.[65]

The cat can also be an image of the hypocrite who feigns fasting in order to catch more reward[66]—that is the story of the 'pious' cat who, dressed as an ascetic, tried to seduce the mice. Their *qebla* is either the mouse-hole or the top of the roof—according to the way in which they catch their prey.[67] And death can be compared to a cat which suddenly jumps upon her prey, illness being its claw;[68] likewise heaven and earth produce in their marriage children whom they devour again, like cats which eat their kittens.[69]

These images are not novel; they offer themselves to everybody and are partly elaborated from proverbial sayings. But now and then Rumi invents strange similes. He sees the branches in spring:

> like a cat each of which has taken her kitten into her mouth—
> why do you not come to look at the mothers in the garden?[70]

The soul 'licks its lips like a cat' remembering the taste of the Beloved;[71] and when Love comes, grief chirps like a mouse in the claws of the cat.[72]

The soul is a cat, produced—as legend says—from the lion's sneezing; but once this cat miaows, even the lion trembles.[73] Born from such a noble animal, the poor soul-cat is imprisoned in the bag *(anbān)* 'world': this connection is frequent in Rumi's poetry.[74] Now and then, interrelations between this bag and the mysterious bag of Abu Horeyrah are made—the name of the companion of the Prophet 'Kitten-father' could invite poets to such plays of words which were sanctioned even by prophetic tradition.[75] Rumi uses the image very realistically: when the cat 'lower soul' says 'miaow' it will be put in the bag;[76] and his heart is, in the hand of love, like a cat in the bag, now low, now high.[77] But eventually cats and mice go together into the bag Eternity.[78] Yet, there is still hope for the poor creature:

> Yesterday His kindness asked me: 'Who are you?'
> I said: 'O Soul, I am the cat in Thy bag!'
> He said: 'O cat, good tidings for you,
> For your King will make you a lion!'[79]

Strangely enough, more than the cat, the Prophet's favourite animal, it is the 'unclean' and lowly dog that is used as a symbol in Persian poetry. There are many different shades in the dog's relation to humans. Inserting a well known proverb, Rumi alludes more than once to the dogs which bark while the moon,[80] or the caravan, continues its way without being disturbed by their noise;[81] the dogs of the world can neither sully the radiant purity of Eternal Beauty, nor threaten the caravan of hearts on its ways towards God.

The dog is, first of all, an animal connected with the world:

> The world is a carrion, and those who seek it, are dogs,[82]

says a *ḥadith* often repeated by the early ascetics of Islam. It is the typical animal representing the greedy lower soul[83] which was even seen by some early Sufis in the shape of a black dog accompanying its owner.[84] Man's inclinations are like sleeping dogs which awake when some carrion is brought: incited by the trumpet of Resurrection which is, in their case, greed.[85] We really see the half-starved Anatolian dogs when looking at Rumi's descriptions: as the dogs feed on tripes and dung[86]and enjoy it, waving their tails, common people are bound to disgraceful wordly pleasures; smelling fried meat they run for the pot,[87] and when you throw some bread before them, they first sniff and then eat it[88] (later, Rumi adds 'the dog sniffs with his nose, we with our intellect')[89]

They come, running after the broth[90] or bread—why should man exhaust himself for a crust of bread? On the other hand, Rumi has told man not to sit in indolence waiting for a Divine gift, be it material or spiritual nourishment—

> after all—you are not less than a dog which is not content to sleep in the ashes and say 'If he wills, he will give me bread of himself', but entreats and wags its tail. So you do wag your tail and desire and beg of God . . .[91]

And Sepahsālār tells that his master Mowlānā Jalāloddin did not drive away a sleeping dog from his way but rather waited until the poor creature got up . . .[92]

We hear the terrible barking and howling of dogs in the Anatolian villages at night—but that is meant to scare away only the hermaphrodite: the true spiritual rider, the perfect lover, could not care less for this noise;[93] still, we will certainly agree with Rumi who blames these ugly and repellent sounds.[94] From here, a connection with the lovers who enjoy beautiful voices which inspire them to mystical dance, is easily possible:

> If you deny the *samāʿ* of the lovers,
> then you will be resurrected at Doomsday with the dogs![95]

Jalāloddin knew, however, that the *kalb-e moʿallam*, the well-trained dog—even though he can never deny his wolfish nature[96]—is indispensable for the shepherd and the hunter;[97] for he awakens the shepherd in times of danger.[98] The Turcomans have extremely vicious dogs, but their children can pull their tails,[99] since the animal is acquainted with them. In a lengthy tale, Rumi has compared the Turcoman watch-dog, which has to be driven away with a formula for protection, to Satan who sits at God's door, threatening the wayfarers unless they send him off with the word 'I seek refuge by God . . .'[100]

However, even this despised animal remains at the 'door of fidelity',[101] if you only give him some bread.[102] Rumi does not yet indulge in the fashion of praising the dog of his beloved's street, envying that wretched cur and kissing its paws (as Majnun did with Leyla's dog,[103] and as Jāmi has done hundreds of times in his poetry). But he respects the faithful animal, best represented in the dog of the Seven Sleepers: by staying with his masters in the cave, this dog became endowed with almost human qualities;[104] he is, thus, the model for the man who, through keeping company with saintly persons and mainly with the mystical guide becomes purified and reaches a state formerly unknown to him. Then, as Rumi points out by ingeniously changing the proverb 'A wakeful dog is better than a sleeping lion':

> A loving dog is better than sober lions![105]

This imagery serves Rumi perfectly to illustrate one of his central theories, e.g. that man can become a new creature through love:

> And the heads of all the lions in the world are lowered, since a hand was given to the dog of the Seven Sleepers, (e.g. since God showed His grace to this animal).[106]

The *nafs* and its education can be symbolized as horse or donkey as well. The 'restive horse'[107] offered itself as favourite image to the early Sufis: the *nafs* has to be trained properly in order to carry its owner towards the goal (although even the best trained horse is of no avail for reaching the Shah: only by giving up one's horse may one attain to his Presence).[108] The *nafs*-horse has to be beaten[109] and taken under the rein of faith and reason,[110] and the burden of patience and gratitude must be put on its back.[111] The princely rider *(shāhsowār)* who marvellously directs the steed of his instincts is a fine image of the Perfect Man, or the Beloved *par excellence*.[112] And in this lofty state the perfect lover may even pass beyond the two horses 'day' and 'night'.[113]

The animal which occurs most in this connection is the ass, which chews *zhāzh* i.e. talks nonsense.[114]

> The renegade *(monkar)* is for your eye a blow
> like an ass's head(=scare-crow) in the midst of a rose-garden.[115]

For a moment, the poor ass may serve as the model of the faithful who patiently carries everything God puts on his back.[116] In general, however, Rumi delights in telling stories of people who lost their donkeys:

> Where is my ass? Where is my ass? For yesterday, woe, died my ass . . .[117]

This lost or dead ass turns, then, again into a symbol of the base soul at whose death or loss man should rejoice rather than complain. For

> He who let the donkey go due to his drunkenness,
> has no grief of pack-saddle and crupper![118]

Perhaps one should read under this aspect the amusing story of the Sufi whose donkey was sold by his Sufi brethren in order to procure the sweetmeat required for a musical party . . .[119]

The donkey which gets stuck in the mire, resembles intellect in its attempt to explain love;[120] and is not man, unaware of himself, like a person sitting on a donkey and asking: 'Where is the donkey?'[121]

Time and again Rumi advises the vulgar to join the company of asses, describing in amusing and often outrageous details how these animals gather on the pasture ground.[122] But the donkey, stupid as it may be, still gets used to its driver, knows his voice and recognizes the way he binds and feeds it:

> It has eaten from his hand nice fodder and good water—
> strange, strange, that you have not got such a relish from God![123]

If even the unintelligent beast can recognize the servant who feeds it how much more should man be grateful to the Eternal Nourisher!

The donkey is very often connected with Jesus—ox and ass stood at his cradle, and out of modesty he rode to Jerusalem on a donkey. Thus, 'Jesus—donkey' is a firmly rooted topos in Persian poetry, particularly used by Sanāʾi from whom Rumi takes some verses almost verbatim.[124] The images point to the contrast of the animal soul and the spiritual master: Jesus is intoxicated by God, his donkey by barley,[125] and:

> When you have reached Jesus' village, don't say anymore 'I am a donkey.'[126]

Jesus' spiritual wine can even produce two wings for his donkey[127] so that he (we extend the comparison) resembles Borāq, Moḥammad's winged steed. This is the mysterious power of love, for the donkey is generally 'human nature' which remains earthbound:

> Jesus, son of Mary, went to heaven, and his donkey remained below;

> We remained on earth, and our heart went up to the higher side . . .[128]

for its final station is Heaven, not a stable.[129]

> He comes running towards Mary, if he is Jesus,
> and if he is a donkey, let him smell donkey's urine.[130]

This foul image—the smelling of the donkey's excrements—is common in Rumi's poetry;[131] and to this category belong also the verses which speak of the *kun-e khar,* lit. 'the ass's arse' and then also 'unworthy person'.

> Far be the dog's eye from the lions' banquet!
> Far be from Jesus' cradle the *kun-e khar*![132]

> He who kissed the *kun-e khar*—
> how could his lip be worthy of the sugar-kiss of the Messiah?[133]

It is slightly embarrassing to see how often this image occurs in Rumi's verses. He has not invented it; already Sanāʾi was fond of the expression. It is from him that Rumi has almost verbatim taken over the beginning of his description of how he did everything wrong:

> I called the *kun-e khar* 'Neẓāmoddin',
> I called the dung precious amber ;
> In this stable 'world' out of foolishness
> I called every excrement (*chamin*) a meadow (*chaman*)[134]

a poem which leads us back to the old Sufi imagery of the world as a dunghill which only the mean visit and appreciate. For how would the call to prayer come from the plectrum of the *kun-e khar*?[135]

Another story, inspired by Apuleius' *Golden Ass,* about the love-making of a maid with an ass of her mistress, serves Rumi to allude to the deepest mysteries of initiation . . . for the donkey, here, is 'the animal soul which becomes manifest in the resurrection in this shape'—[136] again an idea borrowed from Sanāʾi.

Another animal from the same family had better luck than the poor donkey: it is the mule Doldol, 'Ali's riding-animal. In a fine pun (*tajnis-e zāʾid*) Rumi has connected this noble white mule with the human heart: *del* 'heart', becomes a *doldol* when written twice.[137] The heart which can be called 'the lion of God', comparable to 'Ali, is of necessity connected with Doldol.[138]

Jesus' donkey could become winged through the power of love—but the veritable animal of love is Borāq, the winged steed which carried the Prophet into the Divine Presence.[139] It is always contrasted to the ass 'base faculties' and the horse 'intellect' which is, in its presence, only a wooden horse, a children's toy. Why should man remain a donkey-driver, (*kharbanda*) instead of becoming God's slave (*khodābanda*) and mount the Borāq 'Love'?[140] (the *khodābanda* in this connection is certainly meant as an allusion to the expression *ᶜabduhu* 'His servant', which occurs at the beginning of the Sura that speaks of Moḥammad's heavenly journey, Sura 17/1). Why not leave the donkey 'outward body' when the king—Shams-e Tabriz—rides the swift Borāq 'Love'?[141] Only this Borāq and the help of Gabriel, can bring man to the stations which the Prophet passed in his way towards God.[142] And Rumi heaves a sigh in one of his little ghazals:

> From my satin-like bloody tears
> one can make a covering for the Borāq 'Love' . . .[143]

The horse knows the roar and the smell of the lion,[144] and contrary to the equines which in general represent the lower faculties of man, the lion is the almost unchangeable model of the holy man: was not 'Ali called "God's Lion"'?

> The lion of this world seeks prey and provision,
> the lion of the Lord seeks freedom and death.[145]

The Sufi, striving for perfection will follow his example; he is 'in immediate communication with the jungle of Godhead',[146] and the souls of these spiritual lions are united in God whereas the souls of wolves are separated, remaining in this external world.[147]

It is typical of the strength of Rumi's love-experience that he often compares Shamsoddin to a lion or a panther who dwells in the forest of the lover's soul.[148] He is the master of all lions:

> I see a caravan of lions like camels,
> in whose noses is His nose-ring . . .[149]

Identified with the beloved, the lover no longer hunts hares, partridges and gazelles;—now, male lions lay with lowered heads before his lasso.[150]

Rumi alludes so often to the 'lion in the box' that we may surmise that sometimes lions were brought in cages to

Konya:[151] the lion 'soul' wants to break the box 'body',[152] but even though he be in fetters, he is still the master of all those who enchain him.[153]

Not only the Perfect Man, the Beloved, is a lion, but love itself is voracious: in grand and haunting verses Rumi describes the black lion 'Love',[154] bloodthirsty and wild, who lives exclusively on the blood of the lovers.[155] When this lion roars, the whole flock 'grief' runs into the desert, trembling like a fearful prey.[156]

The weak hare is often contrasted with the powerful lion, just as the cunning fox is opposed to the majestic lion.[157] But one of the strangest comparisons—taken over from Sanā'ī[158]—is that of the blood-drinking wild lion and the meek, tame cheetah (*yuz*), who is said to live on cheese, even on rotten cheese. This idea evades explanation so that we can only guess that the poets allude to a story unknown to us.[159]

The lion and the gazelle, or muskdeer, are often mentioned together—the latter shy animal from Turkestan or Tibet,[160] famous for its navel filled with musk can represent, like the lion, the soul or the 'inner meaning'. Thus strange combinations are sometimes invented by the poet:

> What a gazelle am I that I am the guardian of the lion?[161]

Though the lion on the worldly plane usually hunts gazelles, the spiritual lion with his live-giving Jesus-like breath is different:

> He takes the image of a gazelle and breathes into it and makes it a real gazelle![162]

The eschatological significance of the advent of the Beloved is seen again in the peaceful communion of panther and gazelle: they shout together *Yā Hu* 'O He!'[163]—the words of the intoxicated dervish; and the rhyme *āhu* 'gazelle' and *yāhu* enabled the poet to insert this combination several times in his poetry.[164]

The noble gazelle which feeds on jasmine, carnations and roses can produce musk and thus become a symbol of the gnostic who feeds on Divine Light in God's garden to bring forth beauty,[165] and the Beloved, grazing on wild roses and lotos, is addressed:

The whole desert became roses and *arghowān*
from that one moment that Thou hast breathed in the desert![166]

Turning back once more to the lion, we should remember that Rumi alluded also to the 'secondary lions', as we may call them: the lion embroidered on the flag, dancing in the air[167] is a sight well known to the poets since at least the mid-eleventh century: the Lion of the Sky, the zodiacal sign Leo, is usually thought to be under the rule of the spiritual lion,[168] weak like a mouse before him.[169]

Rumi varies in this connection also a verse by Motanabbi:

> When the lion shows his teeth do not think that the lion smiles! Even when he smiles, don't be secure: he will be more bloodthirsty . . .[170]

The last of the big animals occurring in Rumi's as in other poets' verses is the elephant. He was known to the Muslims from Sura 105 in which Abraha's siege of Mecca is described: the elephants of the enemy were miraculously killed by the *abābil*-birds (symbols of the true faithful).[171] Thus, the elephant becomes, first, a symbol of the body or the lower qualities which are subdued by the lion 'heart' or the miraculous soul-birds. Even the powerful will be destroyed by surprise, or killed for the sake of their wealth: in the elephant's case, for his ivory.[172]

Rumi knows the old tale according to which the *karkadann,*[173] the rhinoceros or unicorn, kills the elephant by lifting him upon its huge horn. He could see this scene every day represented on a stone freeze in the wall of the castle of Konya.

> If you became an elephant, love is a unicorn![174]

But when eschatological peace reigns thanks to the power of the Friend elephants become the companions of unicorns.[175]

Rumi knows almost innumerable ways to describe the soul's longing and the moment of illumination when the heart, lost in the sleep of heedlessness, is suddenly reminded of its original home. One of them is that of the elephant who sees India in his dream—not invented by him, but already in use in Khāqāni's and Neẓāmi's poetry. Yet, in Rumi's work, the beautiful image takes a central place:

The elephant who yesternight saw India in his dream
leapt from his fetters—and who has the strength to keep him?[176]

as he asks in one of his quatrains. He never tires of repeating this marvellous experience of the 'vision of home' which is, however, granted only to the spiritually strong:

One has to be an elephant to see the land of India in one's dream
A donkey does not see any India in his sleep;[177]

for he does not even know that such a country exists. Therefore his dream is connected in the *Mathnavi* with the great Sufi-leaders: Ibrahim ibn Adham broke the fetters of his worldly kingdom and returned to the spiritual Hindustan,[178] and Bāyazid Besṭāmi encountered Khidr, just as the elephant sees, all of a sudden, Hindustan.[179]—In his lyrics Rumi sometimes speaks of sleeplessness—that is the state which befits the intoxicated elephant who has seen the vision of his native country, and enters the 'passage to more than India . . .'

* * *

Legend tells that Rumi one day wanted to meditate at the side of a pond but the frogs disturbed him by their noise. So he addressed them: 'When you can say something better, then talk—otherwise listen!' And for a long time no croaking of frogs was heard in that area . . .[181]

This little story shows that his interest was not restricted to the big animals but embraced everything created. For using even the smallest insects in his imagery, he had Koranic sanction: had not the Holy Book mentioned the bee and the ants as models of God's creative power and inspiration?

The bee, feeding on pure things—like the believer who is nourished by Divine light—possesses a house full of honey;[182] since 'Thy Lord has inspired the bee . . .' (Sura 16/68) the house of its revelation is filled with sweetness; and thanks to this Divine gift the bee, in turn, fills the world with honey and candles.[183] If this small animal can do such wonderful things, how much greater is the influence of Divine inspiration upon man! Therefore, the world can become filled with sweetness and light by the inspired saint.

The body may be a beehive in which the wax and honey of

God's love are stored. The bees are our fathers and mothers; although they are only a means for our life, they are tended by the gardener who also builds the beehive.[184] The comparison of the world to the bee's hexagonal cell was all the more apt, since the created world was usually described as a cube in which man is kept.[185] But man in spite of the treasure of honey he possesses, often complains, like humming bees,[186] and his breast can become restless and full of turmoil like a beehive for:

> The heart has sipped from the friend's nectar every night . . .[187]

The movement of the bees is reminescent of the *samāʿ*.[188] Indeed the 'dance of the bees' is used as a modern scientific term to denote this movement.

As to the mosquito, it is mainly known in Muslim legend as that insect which caused Nimrod's death, and as such, a sign of God's way of destroying the mighty tyrant by seemingly small causes. Rumi compares the intellect which is useless in the cold storm of love to a helpless mosquito;[189] he also knows the colloquial expression 'to bloodlet a mosquito in the air' for useless intellectual work or excessive greed.[190]

Ants are connected—faithful to the Koranic revelation—with Solomon. They depend upon his grace—the grace of the Beloved[191]—or are frightened when the army 'mystical dance' announces the arrival of the Solomon 'Love':[192] tiny earthbound souls, afraid of the power of enrapturing love. They are also the first messengers of spring when their caravans are called to come out of the dust which does not know of spring yet.[193] Rumi does not fail either to apply the traditional pun *mur,* 'ant', and *mār* 'snake', in his teachings; the ant 'lust' becomes like a serpent once one gets accustomed to it, and should be killed before it develops into a dragon. But who would not claim that the serpent in his head is in fact only a tiny innocent ant?[194]

Whoever has travelled in Middle Eastern countries will certainly appreciate—though not like!—Rumi's comparison:

> They fell at the door thronging each other
> like insects in fetid sourmilk . . .[195]

and the lovers fall like flies from honey into the bag with butter milk.[196]

Since the beloved, or his lip, is always described as extremely sweet, the lovers, or the longing hearts, will gather around him like flies around the sugar[197]—what does it harm him, when one or two flies fall from the confectioner?[198] Yet, the Beloved can give even the fly the glory of the Anqā, the mythological Phoenix[199] (the combination fly—Phoenix is rather common in Rumi's poetry). For the fly is an image of the human soul which can grow into a wonderful angelic being and reaches annihilation and peace: when it falls in honey, no movement of its single parts remains; it is perfectly collected—a 'soul at peace' in the sweetness of union.[200] And when flies fall into sourmilk, no difference remains between them either:

> The fly 'spirit' fell into the sourmilk 'Eternity'—
> neither Muslim nor Christian, neither Zoroastrian nor Jew (remained).
> Now say! The word is the fluttering of that fly,
> and they can no longer flutter when going down into the sourmilk![201]

In the unity of the eternal God, men are no longer distinct; they no longer have any power to express their divergent views, since they are drowned in the element for which they have yearned.

The spider resembles the selfish person who does not know anything besides enjoying and boasting of his own art, without attributing the true art to God.[202] Lust which spins veils before the soul, is again a spider,[203] and in one of his finest verses Rumi compares the soul which weaves a net from its own thoughts and plans to the spider whose house, woven from its saliva ('the weakest of all houses', Sura 29/41) is soon destroyed, whereas the fabric God weaves by His plans, remains in eternity.[204]

Even different species of worms serve Rumi to describe man, who sits in the midst of his prison of filth and is very happy there without knowing the outside world;[205] for if the worm in the wood would know that there are blossoming twigs in spring, it would be 'reason in the shape of a worm'.[206] The silkworm, on the other hand, is sometimes cited as an example of Divine Grace: from the storehouse of God's kindness he gains the power to produce lovely silk:[207]

When the worm eats leaves the leaf becomes silk—
we are the worms of love, for we are without the leaves (provision or sorrows, *barg*) of this world.[208]

Yet, the same animal can also serve as a symbol of partial human reason because it is fond of exhibiting its art, e.g. the production of fine material, which should be attributed to the true artist, God.[209] It will die in the garment which it has produced itself, unable to escape from its silken prison, just as worldly people are fettered by their love of silk and precious things.[210]

Completely different—and perhaps inspired by a sight in the gardens of Konya—is Rumi's idea that Love is a worm which appears in a tree to eat it completely—a worm which does not leave Joneyd or Baghdad but devours everything.[211]

And grief is a scorpion which can be dispatched only by a certain spell written in the street of love.[212] Similarly the sensual appetites may be compared to locusts which live in the dust 'body' and eat the seed . . .[213]

The bat occurs frequently in Mowlānā's verses—mainly in the *Mathnavi*: for it well represents the ordinary benighted human thought which does not understand, nay even dislikes Shamsoddin: as the bat denies the existence of the sun, or hates it, common people deny and hate the Sun of Truth.[214] However, they cannot be called enemies of the Sun, but are rather their own enemies.[215] Yet, even the bat is invited to join the great spiritual dance. It may dance in darkness whereas the morning-birds stamp their feet till sunrise—but it will at least feel that the dancing movement comprises the whole nature from its lowest to its highest manifestations.[216]

It would be surprising if Rumi had not used the image of the moth and the candle in his poetry:

O lover, do not be less than a moth—
when would a moth avoid the fire?[217]

Compared to the number of his poems, however, this image is by far not as often used as in later Persian poetry. The allegory of moth and candle was known, in Islamic mysticism, at least since the days of Ḥallāj who had given it its classical form in the *Kitāb aṭ-ṭawāsin*; it was then, inherited by the later mystics to denote the grades of approximation to and annihilation in the light and fire of God.[218]

The snake, again, is a *nafs*-animal, for

> the ugly snake to which you give milk now
> becomes a dragon which is by nature, man-eating.[219]

It is often mentioned in connection with treasures; for snakes are thought to live in ruins, and ruins are supposed to contain treasures. Thus, if man kills the snake 'base soul' he will find the treasures of love; and the soul, finally deified, leaves serpenthood and becomes a fish, no longer creeping in the dust, but swimming in the paradisical fountain *Kowthar*.[220] The snake's annual skin-shedding induces Rumi to compare a superficial person to a snake which seems to consist only of skins without marrow, of outward show without reality.[221]

In most cases, the serpent appears along with the emerald; for according to Oriental belief, serpents and dragons can be blinded when they are made to look at an emerald.[222] Thus, the serpent 'grief' is blinded by the emerald 'love'.[223] The eye of the perfect saint can destroy everything worldly which is symbolized as 'serpent',[224] be it wealth,[225] the base soul,[226] and low qualities.

The emerald 'Love' kills every dragon in the road[227]—but love itself can be compared to a dragon, man-eating and stone-eating;[228] if it is not compared to a crocodile which either destroys the boat 'intellect'[229] or scars away man's sleep.[230]

The crocodile, again, may represent this world, waiting with open mouth for its prey,[231] or those insatiable lovers who want to drink, like Bāyazid, the whole Divine Ocean,[232] or else the greedy person whose mouth is never filled:

> Close your mouth in the ocean like the oyster—
> how long will you sit with open mouth like a crocodile?[233]

For the oyster is always praised for its perfect contentment which results in its mouth being filled with lustrous pearls.[234]

The ocean 'world' or the ocean 'God' is a common image; yet the fish imagery—which is found already in the very first chapter of the *Mathnavi*[235]—is not used by Rumi too often; he adds little to the traditional comparison of the soul, or the dervishes as fishes in the ocean of God, or the ocean of love; separated from Him, they feel like fishes on the burning sand[236] — and how long can they stand this?[237]

Fascinated by fiery rather than by watery images, Rumi has preferred to compare the perfect lover to the salamander which sits in the midst of the fire — the possibility to combine the *samandar* with the *qalandar,* the carefree perfect dervish (since both words have the same meter) must have made this comparison particularly attractive for him.[238]

But the largest group of animals which appears in Rumi's work are the birds of different kinds and colours.

The expression 'soul-bird'[239] is still used in Turkey in common speech, as it was current in Persian in old times; the idea that the soul is a bird which flies away at night and at the moment of death, was known in the religions of mankind from time immemorial. The Koran has attested that the birds have their special language which is understood by Solomon (Sura 27/16) — for the mystics, Solomon thus became the model of the sheykh, of the perfect saint who can interpret the secret language of the soul, the language of inspiration which the common folk does not understand.[240]

Rumi heard and understood the laud and praise of the birds in every place[241] — here he often follows Sanā'i who had written the lovely 'Litany of the Birds' where he interprets the different cries of the birds as words for seeking and praising God.[242] A few decades later, ʿAṭṭār composed his *Manṭeq oṭ-ṭeyr* which has remained the standard source for bird-imagery in Persian literature since 1200. This story of the pilgrimage of the thirty birds who discover, eventually, that they, being *si morgh,* are themselves the *Simorgh,* is the most subtle and beautiful allegory of the unity of the individual souls with the Divine Essence.

Thus, the bird-imagery was prefigured long before, and Rumi could use it to represent different human qualities. Here again he is indebted to *Kalila va Demna* and other tales. He muses extensively upon the Koranic word 'Take four birds and slaughter them' (Sura 2/262) — these birds are explained as the duck 'greed', the peacock 'eminence', the crow 'worldly desire', and the rooster 'lust'.[243]

The story of Adam's fall is seen as the faux-pas of a Divine bird,[244] and the main weakness of birds is their greed for the grain which is always hidden as a bait in a snare — was not Adam seduced by a grain of wheat?[245] He is thus the prototype of the heedless bird who could be caught by a grain of wheat. Mowlānā therefore warns man time and again not to follow any worldly attraction, any lust and appetite:[246] they all hide a snare to capture him for ever in this world of matter, in this cage whence there is no escape. And even if the immature bird would try to fly away, he would become the cat's prey.[247]

Why do these captured birds not break their cage? The other, free, birds may fly around them telling about the beauty of the garden,[248] just as the prophets and saints inform people about the happiness of Divine life; but they are too weak—only in the state of intoxication might they be able to break their cages.[249] And who knows whose voice reaches the birds? The hunter may also learn to imitate their voices, to seduce them so that they fall into his snare[250]—and such an unhappy bird must be excused for he longs for the company of those who sing the same tunes as he: 'Birds of one feather flock together'.[251] Those with high ambitions follow the heavenly birds whose melodies sound familiar to them, reminding them of the lost rose garden, whereas the lowly ones are easily seduced by the sound of imitated voices, or follow the ugly sounds of crows and ravens.

> Where should the bird 'sick heart' fly?
> Only the paradise of the beloved's face is his place . . .[252]

Rumi speaks of the bird's egg: the lover's heart hurries out of the egg[253] after patiently waiting.[254] He may also hold that the bird 'good works' produces the egg which is Paradise which, itself, is the final cause of the bird.[255] This is a suitable image to explain the mystery of resurrection when out of the outwardly similar eggs birds of different colour and size will appear. In a similar strain, Rumi sees the created world—earth and time— as an egg, in which infidelity and faith are the yolk and the white between which is situated 'a *barrier* which both cannot transgress' (Sura 55/20). But when God takes this egg under the wings of His Grace, yolk and white disappear, and the bird 'Unity' is hatched.[256] Could there be any better place for the lover than under the wings of God where he becomes annihilated?[257]

In addition to descriptions of birds in general there are then descriptions of the particular kinds of birds—from the nightingale to the raven scarcely a species is lacking.

The nightingale, *bolbol,* had been the favourite bird of the lyrical poets since old times; the fact that it most comfortably rhymes with *gol*, 'rose' made the classical combination of rose and nightingale even more popular. Both are connected with spring, both with love. The nightingale is the soul-bird *par excellence,* since the rose is a reflection of God's glory, or of the face of the beloved. And the longing bird suffers from the thorns which surround the rose . . . Rumi invites the nightingale to come to the pulpit (branch) and to deliver a sermon about the beauty of the rose.[258] The nightingale is also 'the head of the musicians',[259] or can be connected with the *bolbola,* the long-necked bottle which makes a nice sound when wine is poured out of it during cheerful drinking parties in spring.[260] It is the bird of intoxicated love:

> The cow does not know how to produce the cry of the nightingale,
> the sober intellect does not know the taste of intoxication.[261]

The nightingale can also be matched with *Doldol,* ʿAli's wonderful mule:

> O you Doldol of that arena, how do you feel in this prison?
> and O you nightingale of that garden, how do you feel in the company of those who do not hear?[262]

Both are here symbols of the lover who is imprisoned in the company of uncongenial souls.

How beautifully the poet describes his own status:

> My heart became a hundred pieces, each one complaining,
> so that from each piece you can make a nightingale.[263]

The adventure of rose and nightingale, so often recalled by Rumi (and even more by later mystical and non-mystical poets) is, together with that of moth and candle, a particularly fitting symbol of the eternal story of love.[264] But the rose in its everlasting beauty cannot be described properly—the real topic of poetry, and of the whole *Mathnavi*, is

> the explanation of the nightingale who was separated from the rose.[265]

It is the story of Rumi himself, separated from the eternal fiery rose Shamsoddin. And it is again his own story when he says:

> The nightingale of those whom He grants a mystical rapture has its own rosegarden in itself.[266]

For the soul-bird eventually experiences his identification with the beloved who lives in his heart, and through whom he lives and loves. Can the stork and the crane, the crow and the raven understand at all the complaint of the intoxicated nightingale, its *golbang*[267] (this lovely word for 'loud shout' could be easily associated with the rose, *gol*)? Can common people become aware of the wonderful songs of saints and lovers? They rather enjoy the unpleasant sounds to which they are used and cannot understand that the nightingale, finally, will return to the rose garden for which it has been longing throughout its life.[268] Did this bird's arrival not always announce spring-time—the time of resurrection—whereas the crow talks only in the heart of winter?[269]

> The nightingale 'heart' be intoxicated in eternity,
> the parrot 'soul' be always sugar chewing![270]

Thus Rumi connects two favourite soul-birds of Persian poetry. The parrot—topic of one of the first stories in the *Mathnavi*[271]—is endowed with a breath like Jesus, because he is so eloquent and life-giving;[272] he is intelligent, and his green colour reminds man of Paradise. He is taught to speak by means of a mirror which is put in front of him, and behind which a person speaks: assuming that another parrot is talking he imitates him. Likewise the disciple learns from the mirror of his spiritual guide's heart the art of the 'language of the birds', i.e. the secret Divine conversation.[273]

Parrots are always associated with sugar, and thus with the sugar-lips of the beloved:[274] the bird preaches about the eternal cane-sugar which his beloved represents,[275] and tears himself into pieces if one takes away from him even one piece of sugar—like the lover, when deprived of his friend's lip.[276] And:

> The helpless heart which remained without you is a parrot, but has got no sugar.[277]

Rumi never tires of repeating this topic and sometimes reaches grotesque results in his description of mystical rapture:

> When the parrot 'soul' chews sugar, suddenly I become intoxicated and chew the parrot . . .[278]

Rumi's favourite bird, however, is neither the plaintive

nightingale nor the playful baby-parrot, but rather the *bāz,* the falcon or hawk. This noble bird, popular in the Middle East for hunting purposes since ages past, became an appropriate symbol for the high-born soul. When the soul-falcon falls into the hand of the old crone 'world' and is captured, its eyes are covered by means of a hood;[279] therefore the beloved is asked to take off the hood so that the falcon may be able to fly in the desert and bring the prey.[280] However, in *Fihi mā fihi,* Rumi explains the trapping of a hawk with the intention of training him as the 'acme of generosity'—here, the mystical leader is compared to the true master of the hunt who educates the bird by different, and outwardly cruel, measures.[281]

The falcon of the empyrean is often described in lyrical verses which sing of the trapped bird's longing for home.[282] One of the most touching descriptions in the *Mathnavi* is devoted to the homesick falcon who had fallen into the company of owls and ravens—symbols of the lower instincts—and tells them about the beauty of the eternal castle where his King resides—, but they do not believe him . . .[283]

> How should the falcon not fly from the hunt towards its King,
> when he hears the news 'Return!' when the drum is beaten?[284]

says Rumi with an allusion to Sura 89/28 'Return ,o soul at peace.' The return of the falcon with the wing 'We have honoured'[285] (Sura 17/70) at the sound of the heavenly drum forms the main subject of all his stories, verses and images connected with the *bāz* (for the raven does not return at the sound of the drum,[286] he goes rather to the graveyard);[287] so much so that the poet invents a rather daring *tajnis*: the very name of the falcon, *bāz*, shows that he comes back, *bāz*, to his master.[288]

> I am Thy falcon, I am Thy falcon, when I hear Thy drum,
> O my king and Shahenshah, my feather and wing come back.[289]

And once he has returned,

> the falcon rubs his wings at the Shah's hand—
> without tongue he says 'I have sinned'—[290]

a beautiful image for the soul which, eventually finds rest in God's hands.

In the company of crows and raven, the falcon may have

been induced to do things which contradict his royal nature; imitating the other birds when he hunts mice, he becomes despicable[291]—the true men of God seek a higher prey, they hunt angels, not mice. But the white falcon was indeed in bad company in his exile: how would the owl, inhabitant of ruins, listen to the description of Baghdad and Tabas?[292]

The vulture, living on carrion, and still a common sight in Anatolia, is only rarely mentioned in images similar to those of the crow.[293]

As for the crows, they belong to the hibernal-material world. After summer is over,[294] when everything is congealed, the crow puts on its black dress and feels happy while the loving soul longs for eternal spring.[295]

> If the crow would but know its own ugliness,
> it would melt like snow from grief and pain,[296]

and would, thus purified, be able to participate in the flight towards the rose garden—that is 'the time when the crow "grief" is killed'.[297]

In a cruel image Rumi advises man not to look at this world:

> Since the Living, Self-sustained is the customer of your eyes,
> Do not give your eyes into the crow's claw, as if they were carrion.[298]

And he complains that the beloved has taken away his heart to give it to the crows.[299] This bird feeds on unclean food, like the base instincts, and should be educated by being kept hungry:

> Prescribe the crows "Nature" a fast from their carrion
> so that they may become parrots and hunt sugar.[300]

These two birds are contrasted by our poet in a ghazal which is rather outspoken in its criticism:

> You have prepared the food of the crow from dung and carrion;
> How should the crow know, what that parrot has gotten in his chewing of sugar?—
> What says this foolish crow when Thou makest it eat dung?
> O God, preserve us from that world and from evil opinion!
> What says the green parrot, when Thou givest him sugar?
> By Thy grace, open our mouth for such a word!
> Who is this crow that tastes dung? Someone who has become afflicted with knowledge outside religious knowledge for the sake of worldly reputation!

> Who is that parrot and sugar? Conscience, the fountain of wisdom!
> For God (or: truth) is his tongue, like Aḥmad, at the time of speaking. . . .[301]

The lowly crow, *zāgh*, which normally resides in the lowland of winter, can, however, be changed by Grace and Love into the falcon 'high ambition', which will then attain the place of *mā zāgha* 'the eye did not rove . . .' (Sura 53/17), i.e. the station of the Prophet during his vision as described in the Sura 'The Star'.[302]

This is the effect of the miraculous power of the beloved, as Rumi says with an image inherited from Sanā'i:[303]

> It would be a mistake if crows would come into my ruined heart—
> Putting Thy reflection upon it, He makes this crow a *homā*-bird . . .[304]

As for the falcon, his high rank is also understood from one of Rumi's deepest ghazals in which the enrapturing power of Love is seen in the image of the mysterious moon which

> like a falcon who seizes the bird at hunting time . . . took me out of myself and began to run over the sky . . .[305]

Like lion and dragon, the falcon overwhelms all the hearts and seizes them heavenward;[306] he may, logically, also symbolize death.[307]

The majestic bird is juxtaposed, in Rumi's and other poets' verses not only with the mean crow but, as in modern language, with the pigeon or dove as well.[308]

> The whole world is a pigeon through the love of Him whose prey are falcons.[309]

The *fākhta*, ring-dove, repeats *ku ku?* 'where where'? until it finds the way towards the beloved,[310] and:

> every bird has put on, in your love, a necklace like the ring-dove.[311]

The dove's necklace, *ṭauq al-ḥamāma,* as Ibn Ḥazm had called his book on chaste love,[312] binds the soul-bird for ever to the beloved.

The pigeon, kept in houses or little towers, either as messengers or for pleasure (as still today in the Indo-Pak Subcontinent) can easily be likened to the soul which, born in the tower of the Beloved, is nourished by His grace and love:

> Since we are baby-pigeons, born in your pigeon-house,
> we always circumambulate in our journey your portico.[313]

How should the pigeons fly to any other place? With fluttering hearts, the lovers approach the beloved, called by his voice or whistling[314] like pigeons thronging with flapping wings around the balcony.[315] A pigeon which has dwelt on the roof of the beloved is more precious than anything in the world.[316] Likewise the *kabutar-e ḥaram,* the pigeon which lives in the immediate presence of the central sanctuary in Mecca and is not allowed to be killed, is comparable to the heart that lives in the Friend's presence, endowed with eternal life,[317] as Rumi has described in a beautiful letter 'the soul-pigeons that rest on the roof of the Kaʿba 'hope' . . .'.[318] And in a rare image he speaks of the pardons which fly every night from the hearts to God, like pigeons, until He sends them back to imprison them again in the bodies.[319]

Although pigeon-post was common in medieval Anatolia, as it had been for centuries in the world of Islam, Rumi does not describe the pigeon as letter-carrier, as almost all the later Persian poets do; nor does he use the image of the *morgh-e besmel,* the ritually slaughtered, shivering and shaking bird (preferably a pigeon or chicken, but also a peacock) which recurs in hundreds of verses during the following centuries; only once he speaks of the trembling of the bird with cut-off head.[320]

The peacock—lovely as an idol[321]—has always fascinated the poets. Originating from India, he is related in legend to Paradise. Even more than other birds, the peacock is ambivalent in Rumi's imagery. He can serve as a symbol of pride,[322] ignorance and showing off; boasting of his beauty, he forgets his ugly feet. He is carnal nature, removing man from his spiritual aims.[323] And again, a long story tells how the peacock wants to practice asceticism by tearing out his radiant feathers; thereupon a sage admonishes him that this, again, would be lack of gratitude since his feathers make not only pretty fans but are even honoured by being put into the Koran.[324] Owing to his shimmering plumage which makes him a valuable prey,[325] the peacock is endangered, as much as the muskdeer owing to its navel filled with perfume, or the elephant due to his ivory.

But Rumi, apparently, liked peacocks.[326] His imagery sometimes reminds me of the bewilderment of some villagers from Konya who saw for the first time, in the modest zoo of Ankara, the dazzling beauty of this bird, and broke out in hymns of praise for the Creator . . .

He is a symbol of miracles—how could he fit in a narrow pit? Thus, miracles do not agree with the pit 'body'.[327] Spring becomes, for Rumi, a lovely peacock opening his feathers[328] out of love for the friend's face;[329] for 'both garden and peacock partake of His loveliness'.[330] The bird opens his marvellous feathers 'like the hearts of the lovers';[331] dancing, he brings the soul into dance.[332]

When the peacock appears in the company of serpents, the poet has in mind the legend of Paradise:

> When love flies away like a peacock, the heart becomes a house filled with serpents, just as you have seen.[333]

And in the ruins of metaphorical existence, the soul, once a glorious peacock in the rose garden of coquetry, has become like an owl . . .[334]

The rooster is highly praised for calling man to prayer.[335] One of Rumi's ghazals, in which he uses Greek rhyme words, well reveals his way of reasoning:

> That rooster is (busy with) exclamation, and you are still nicely sleeping;
> You call him a bird, your own name is *atharbos.* (probably azerbor 'bitter')
> That rooster which invites you towards God
> may be in the shape of a bird, but is in reality an *angelos.*[336]

The poet boasts that, in the quick and punctual fulfillment of his ritual duties he resembles a rooster who knows the exact time, not a crow whose screaming 'cuts off union'.[337] This is an allusion to the Arabic expression *ghurāb al-bayn,* the 'raven of separation' which is so often scolded in classical Arabic poetry since he separates the lovers; but the rooster brings the lover closer to his Beloved by calling him to prayer. Hence the poet can speak of the rooster 'soul',[338] that soul which knows the 'real morning' and crows for God's sake, not deceived by the false morning and thus deceiving the Muslims.[339] For a bird which crows before dawn and thus cheats the faithful *(morgh-*

e bi hangām) is worthy of being slaughtered.[340]

Amusing images are not lacking either in this context:

> The moon spread out his wings like a rooster
> behind and before him the stars like hens . . .[341]

The comparison of human beings with the duck, or any other waterfowl, offered itself easily and is therefore often used by Rumi: half born out of the ocean of the Divine Spirit, half bound to the earth, he is indeed like a duck which is at home in both places.[342] How long should man remain like a chicken, picking corn,[343] since he belongs to the ocean? He does not even need a boat but is himself the vessel![344] On doomsday, these ducks will swim once more on the Divine Sea whereas the ordinary cattle will be slaughtered.[345]

The most prominent bird among those which frequent Anatolia is the stork, *laklak,* regarded, in Oriental folklore, as particularly pious, because he is reported to perform the pilgrimage to Mecca every year, and preferably builds his nest on mosques. Rumi sees him as a preacher on top of the minaret,[346] praising his Lord after he has returned from foreign countries.[347] A typical soul-bird returning in spring,[348] he announces happiness; his *lak lak* means, as Rumi repeats with Sanā'i's words, *al-mulk lak, al-amr lak*' Kingdom belongs to Thee, Order belongs to Thee!';[349] With these words the stork casts the fire of *towḥid* into doubtful hearts.[350] And if such a noble bird should fly, or walk, together with a crow the wise will soon detect that both are lame.. . .[351]

The Koran mentions several other birds: the *abābil* birds which killed Abraha's elephants are comparable to the true faithful;[352] the *hodhod*, hoopoe, acted as messenger between Solomon and the Queen of Sheba (cf. Sura 27/20); to our surprise, Rumi uses this bird but comparatively rarely in his verses.[353]

But he likes fanciful allusions to the ostrich (which are found almost exclusively in his lyrics). This creature, called in Persian *oshtormorgh* 'camel-bird', is a strange thing, comparable to the poet's strange heart;[354] it is fire-eating, and thus related to the fire of love.[355] And Rumi shapes an old Arabic saying into a ghazal in which he attacks the useless Khāja, the laughing stock of many of his verses:

O Khāja, what kind of bird are you? What is your name? For what do you fit?
You do not fly, nor do you graze—o you confectioner's birdie!
Like the ostrich: when they say 'Fly!' you say:
I am a camel, and how could a camel fly, oh Arab of Tayy?'
When the time of burden comes, you say: 'No, I am a bird,
How could a bird carry the burden? Why do you cause inconvenience?[356]

Outside the realm of 'natural' birds two mythical birds are dear to Rumi as to Persian writers in general—the Homā and the Simorgh or ᶜAnqā. The Homā is a mythological animal whose shade is said to convey kingship to those whom it touches; it lives exclusively on dry bones (a feature never mentioned by Rumi). The Simorgh dwells on the Mountain Qāf at the end of the world, and represents, since ᶜAṭṭār, the Divine ruler. Sometimes this bird is called with its Arabic name ᶜAnqā, the long-necked; living far away from human company, he had gained fame like a true ascetic.[357]

The true lover does not seek the shade of the Homā; for his kingdom is with his Beloved.[358] (ᶜAṭṭār had told the story of Ayāz who sought only the shade of his king, Maḥmud of Ghazna, when everybody rushed to catch the Homā's shade).[359] Rumi therefore compares Ṣalāḥoddin to the Homā,[360] and the utterance of the Beloved 'I am the Homā . . .' is repeated in several ghazals.[361] The carefree, *qalandar*like dervish no longer thinks of the crow, the bird of grief and sorrow, since in daring love he himself has been transformed into the soul of the Royal bird—the juxtaposition of crow and Homā is frequently found in Rumi's verses and has been taken over by later poets up to Ghālib in the 19th century.[362]

Allusions to the Simorgh, probably due to ᶜAṭṭār's influence, are more frequent. The beloved is the Simorgh of the Qāf of the Lord of Majesty,[363] nay, in front of Him the Simorgh which crosses the skies becomes lowly like a fly[364]—just as the created ᶜAnqā is only a fly before the ᶜAnqā Love. How could the spider 'intellect' spin its web in such a place?[365] Or else the lover's heart is a Simorgh which cannot be captured but flies beyond everything created.[366]

There is no end to these comparisons; sometimes Rumi blends the different birds into each other—the Homā sits on the Mountain Qāf of Divine proximity,[367] and the shade of the ʿAnqā is called 'blessed'.[368]

Love and the beloved can both be represented by each of the mythological birds—but when other poets complain that Simorgh and alchemy have disappeared from this world, Rumi adds a third element: the station of the *qalandar* has likewise disappeared, for a true *qalandar* is higher and rarer than alchemy and Simorgh together . . .[369]

He who created you from dust, then from a drop of sperm, then from a blood clot, then brought you forth as children . . .

CHILDREN IN RUMI'S IMAGERY

It is told that our Master Jalāloddin one day walked in the streets of Konya when some children came and prostrated themselves before him, and he kissed them. One little boy, however, shouted from a distance: 'Lord, let me first finish my work, then I'll also come'. So Mowlānā waited for him to finish his 'work', and then accepted his greetings and embraced him.[1]

It is indeed likely that such an event took place—and Rumi, the father of three sons and one daughter, knew the ways of children well enough to use them in his poetry as images of the behavior of man.

> God is able to do all things. After all, the child when it is first born is worse than an ass; it puts its hand into filth and carries it to its mouth to lick; the mother beats it and prevents it . . . Yet . . . God most High is able to make it into a man . . .[2]

Rumi follows, as always, in many respects the Koranic way of arguing: the growth of the embryo in the mother's womb serves as a model to prove God's grace and His wonderful way of nourishing His creatures first with blood, and then with milk.

> He bestowed on thee a form within her body, He gave ease to her during pregnancy and accustomed her (to the burden).
> She deemed thee as a part joined (to herself); His providence separated (from her) that which was joined.[3]

All creatures are, in a certain way, God's children and family whom He feeds in His all-embracing kindness.[4] Basically, every act in the world can be conceived as a birth: every cause is the mother of a result, and everything, from mineral to human, is a mother—they only are not aware of each other's pangs and pains.[5]

The slow development of the embryo—which transforms the drops of sperm into a handsome king[6]—becomes, first of all, the symbol for spiritual development:

> If anyone were to say the embryo in the womb 'Outside is a world exceedingly well-ordered,
> A pleasant earth, broad and long, wherein are a hundred delights, and so many things to eat,
> Mountains and seas and plains, fragrant orchards, gardens and sown fields . . .
> Its marvels come not into description: why art thou in tribulation in this darkness . . .'
> It, in virtue of its present state, would be incredulous, and would turn away from this message and would disbelieve it . . .[7]

Man is like this unborn child; he disbelieves the saints when they tell him in the dark and bloodstained prison of this world of the glory of the spiritual world. As for the lover, he is like the embryo in the womb of Annihiliation, turning his back to outward existence.[8]

Rumi describes the state of pregnant women in extreme terms: they tremble at each smell[9] and want to eat clay[10]—but all the pain is forgotten once the child is born:

> For the woman is in pain, but for the child, birth is a release from the prison.[11]

Spiritual birth is likewise a difficult process for the wordly mind, and requires corporeal pain. Yet, not to forget:

> Even if a woman has twenty children, each of them will remind her of the lovely moments of union . . .[12]

The child can grow only after the union of husband and wife has taken place—likewise the soul ripens after the touch of grace has sanctified the seeker, and is, eventually, born to the new world of light. That is why Rumi can compare the state of the lover to that of the unborn child:

> Like a child in the womb am I, being nourished with blood—
> A human being is born once, I have been born several times.[13]

Blood is 'the food of the hearts'[14]—thus the symbol is perfect. The newborn—being helpless and confounded[15]—is then given a name which often designates his lineage, like Ḥajji or Ghāzi, but has no reality;[16] yet, as the Prophet said 'The son is his father's secret'.[17] Once the child is born, it is nourished with his mother's milk instead of blood[18]—the development of—ritually unclean—blood into pure milk is one of the marvels caused by God who changes everything to the better. Thus, even the inspiration of the *Mathnavi* can be compared to the transformation of blood into sweet milk when fortune gives birth to a new spiritual child.[19]

The baby's crying causes the mother to move the cradle[20]—the cradles in Konya hang from the ceiling, and the baby is tightly swaddled, and

> he feels perfectly at ease with his hands bound. But if a grown man were cribbled in a cradle, that would be torment and a prison.[21]

Thus, the loosening of the outward fetters at the day of resurrection, when earth will shake off what is in it (Sura 99), will be a release for human beings, at least for those who are spiritually grown up.[22] Rumi compares the child's weeping to the call of the lover who hopes thereby to attract his friend's attention so that he gently moves the cradle 'heart' in which the soul lies, or gives him spiritual food.[23] For when the child cries, the mother's milk begins to flow, and thus the lover has to cry and weep:

> As long as the child in the cradle does not weep,
> how would the grieved mother give him milk?[24]

The child knows nothing but milk—like the lover who knows only his beloved.[25] How would it care for the beauty of the nurse?[26] Thus, most people look exclusively at their worldly welfare without considering the grace of Him who bestows nourishment upon them (a typical example of the contradictory use of one and the same image in different contexts). The milk from the 'teat of Grace' is one of Rumi's favourite expressions:[27] he thinks that the true word of religion is 'like milk in the soul's teat' and needs people who are thirsty to taste it.[28] Sometimes the mother has to rub the baby's nose to awake and feed it—for it is unaware that the milk is ready:

thus God awakens the non-existent beings to show His primordial lovingkindness.[29] Yet, every food is dependent upon the child's age—if you give an infant bread instead of milk, the poor thing will die; but once his teeth have developed—the teeth of intelligence[30] which defy the blackened teat of the nurse 'world'[31]—he will ask for bread himself. Likewise the spirit has to be nourished according to its capacity.[32] Divine Grace which is the true mother or nurse of the soul,[33] knows how to handle this child and how to feed it. Rumi uses similar imagery once more in one of his letters, when he describes *taqlid,* blind imitation:

> The blind child knows his mother, sucks her milk, but it could not answer when asked what she looked like, whether she was dark or fair, whether her eyebrows were like bows, whether her neck was long or short, whether her nose had this or that shape, whether she was tall or short . . .[34]

he can only describe her from hearsay, if at all. Such is the case with worldly people whose spiritual eyes have not yet been opened.

In one of his most touching verses Rumi alludes to a scene which he must have seen often, i.e. the death of infants:

> Like a child which dies in the mother's lap,
> I die in the lap of the mercy and forgiveness of the Merciful.[35]

The topic of the dying children and the bereaved mother is elaborated several times in the *Mathnavi* where the grieved mother attests that her children, though far away from the change of times, are 'with me and play around me',[36] and every dust particle of the grave seems to listen to her lament.[37]

Love is the mother who protects her child,[38] the friendly nurse who hinders him from eating clay,[39] and the true Muslim trembles to preserve his faith as much as a mother trembles for her child.[40] Only rarely is the traditional image of the world as a cruel and miserable mother who devours her children used in his poetry.[41]

Jalāloddin loves the image of the mother: he may even call 'fasting' a mother, and admonishes the children not to give easily out of their hands the veil of this lovable mother[42]—a somewhat strange image which, however, indicates the importance he attributed to fasting for the education of the soul. Even though the mother may look angry at times, her wrath is kindness: thus the prophets who guide their people like children can be compared to loving mothers:

> That wrath of the prophets is like the anger of mothers, it is an anger full of mildness for the pretty child.[43]

Does any mother lead her child to bloodletting for the sake of hatred? No, this action is a sign of absolute Mercy which manifests itself, now and then, in painful operations.[44] Therefore the child comes always back to his mother, even though she thrashes him at times, for he knows no refuge but her—a beautiful symbol for the behaviour of the believer who always comes back to God.[45] Gratefulness towards the mother who is inspired by Divine Charity, is both a sacred duty and a worthy task.[46] Yet:

> Although the mother is complete mildness,
> See the Mercy of God from the father's wrath.[47]

This idea is explained in the end of the *Mathnavi*[48] in the statement that the mild, yet foolish mother is the *nafs,* the lower soul, whereas father Reason's stick is required for proper education; the child would remain stupid if it were to obey the comforting mother (Rumi gives, in this chapter, a lively description of a family argument!).

As long as the infant cannot move about properly, 'his riding-animal is only daddy's neck';[49] he is first 'completely ear' to listen to the address of his parents—if he would try to say *titi*, he would never learn to speak properly, just as the spirit needs to be first addressed by God and only later can answer correctly.[50] In the beginning, however, the child imitates the grown-ups without thinking, so that the *moqallid*, the imitator in religious matters, can be compared to a sick child.[51] Out of ignorance, babies chew their sleeves,[52] but once they grow, the time of play and games begins; but it is also the time that they become more independent and may go astray in the bazaar. The lover feels like such a lost child:

> I am like a child, lost between street and bazaar: for I do not know that street and this bazaar—I do not know them.[53]

Lost in the bazaar of worldliness the mystic longs for home and cries, and may be compared to the child which has broken a plate and now cries from grief.[54] For a while, he may forget everything in worldly play, like the little boy who stripped off his clothes when playing; someone carried away his mantle and shirt but he was so annihilated (*fānī*) in that game that he did not remember anything of his outward apparel and only later found himself naked and bewildered.[55]

The children in thirteenth century Konya indulged apparently in the same games as everywhere in the world, filling their laps and skirts with rubbish, 'and if you take a piece away, they would cry'[56] (just like the earthbound person who complains when losing anything from his goods). They played merchant,[57] played at dice,[58] and were possessed by 'greed of enjoyment' so that they rode a cockhorse, until they reached the age of discretion and this greed vanished.[59] The game *qalʿa bizim*—thus with it Turkish name 'The castle is ours'—reminds the poet of the constant influx of new favours from the soul into the body.[60] The children were particularly fond of walnuts because they spin along so nicely—but they refused to take out the kernel which they did not recognize as belonging to the nut (comparable to many Koran-readers who toy only with the lovely outward recitation of the Holy Book and refuse to understand the deeper meaning),[61] and they would weep for their nuts[62] (although these are only comparable to the exterior body). Girls had their dolls, boys their wooden swords,[63] and all of them were impatient to eat the lions and camels baked from sweet dough.[64]

But they also shouted names at their playmate, and when he called bad names back, they were encouraged to continue, for they saw the effect of their words—thus, answering an enemy's evil deeds by hatred rather encourages him to continue in his bad actions.[65] Rumi is indeed right: the wise understand the deeper wisdom even behind the children's tales and their foul language.[66]

But life is not only a game—as the Koran attests—; proper education is required, and just as the morning breeze in spring stirs up the strong perfume (*lakhlakha*) in order to teach the 'children of the garden', e.g. the flowers, good manners,[67] thus the child has to be brought to school. 'It does not go, it is brought', says Rumi,[68] for it does not yet understand the meaning of this action.[69] So one has to tell him:

> When you go to school I'll buy you a birdie, or I'll bring you raisins and walnuts and pistachio nuts;[70]

for his mind is set, like that of the donkey, on the stable, on food and comfort; that is why he laughs frequently, not considering the end of affairs.[71] Man, however, does not care for such deceptive sweets.[72] There are different schools: the school of love, made of fire,[73] is a school in which the lover hopes not to remain stupid;[74] there, the child 'soul' becomes the teacher of all teachers.[75] But this child may become naughty when Patience is the teacher, just as school children take pleasure in disobedience.[76] And when in the school of love even old people are rejuvenated, in the school of intellect the child is growing old, trying to learn the alphabet.[77] The school as symbol of outward learning as contrasted to inspired wisdom is a topic frequently used in later Sufi poetry, however, not too much by Rumi; the comparison of Love with a teacher, so common with later mystical poets, is again not too often found in Jalāloddin's verses.[78] He generally sees in education and schooling systems appropriate symbols for the spiritual development. With expressions taken from the Koran-school where one begins with the last part of the Koran, he congratulates the growing spirit:

> Your child 'reason' has reached *tabāraka* 'Blessed be . . .' (Sura 67/1)
> Why are you, in the school of 'Joy' still (busy with) ʿ*abasa* 'He frowned . . .'? (Sura 80/1).[79]

Rumi describes the advancing stages in schools in *Fihi mā fihi*:

> So, a teacher is teaching a child how to write. When he comes to writing a whole line, the child writes a line and shows it to the teacher. In the teacher's eyes that is all wrong and bad. The teacher speaks to the child kindly and cajolingly: 'That is all very good and you have written well. Bravo bravo! Only this letter you have written badly, this is how it ought to be. That letter too you have written badly' . . . The child's weakness gathers strength from that approval, and so gradually he is taught and assisted in his way.[80]

That is how God acts with weak human beings, slowly correcting their faults and perfecting them. Of course, the teacher sometimes beats the child.[81] The school can therefore also be regarded as an image of the spiritual difference between humans—even though all the pupils are in one school, they are in different classes according to their spiritual progress.[82] That even girls were sent to the *maktab* can be understood from a line in the *Mathnavi*.[83] And school life is, for Rumi, not only a high symbol: he delights in telling the story of the naughty boys who suggested to their teacher that he was ill so that they might have a day off . . . It is highly amusing to read this realistic description of a school which was, probably, not too different from what modern pupils sometimes invent . . .[84]

And we can follow the child—presumably a young girl—going out alone into the streets, accompanied by the mother's warning:

> Maternally said the mother: 'When you see a corn and trap,
> Walk along your way, repeating: "We do not submit, we don't!"'
> (*lā nusallim lā nusallim*)[85]

Likewise the soul should not submit to any flatterings and insinuations, but keep aloof from all worldly deceptions and attractions. But eventually, neither the child's affection for milk, nor its antipathy against school will remain: they disappear like shades which the sun has cast on the wall, and being grown up, man learns to turn towards the Sun.[86]

And he makes clear His signs to the people; haply they will remember . . .

IMAGERY FROM DAILY LIFE

Rumi does not hesitate to use images from even the most intimate spheres of life and from sensual love to express the secret of love, longing, and separation, and the requirements of spiritual growth. The love-play is well known to him,[1] as is the 'hand-play of husband and wife'.[2] In his most secret love-chamber, nobody may enter 'but the eunuch "His Grief" or the messenger of his remedy'[3]—as if his innermost heart were a harem into which only eunuchs were admitted. To designate 'grief' as a eunuch shows both the poet's contempt for external grief and sorrow and the close association of grief with love. The eunuch, *tavashi*, occurs but rarely; but Rumi often recurs to stories of or allusions to the *mokhannath*, the hermaphrodite, a word which merely designates the eunuch who serves as male prostitute. This *mokhannath* constitutes a model of unreliability: sometimes he poses as man, then again as female. Thus, he is generally contrasted with the true man,[4] the man of God: does not the proverb equate those who seek this world, with a woman, and those who yearn for the otherworld, with a *mokhannath*? Although this formulation was coined a few decades after Rumi's death, it expresses the general attitude of the Sufis very correctly.[5] The *mokhannath* is even the laughing stock of the animals: Rumi tells a joke about such a person who complains to a shepherd that one of his bucks has strangely gazed at him and laughed at him whereupon the shepherd tells him that his buck will of course be amused to see such a ridiculous creature, but would never dare to laugh at a true man . . .[6]

Rumi knows of dreams which are 'sometimes lovely and coquettish like nightly pollution, sometimes evil like an unfitting dream',[7] and he warns man lest he indulge too much in sexual intercourse: the love-games the Divine Spirit plays with him, strengthen his soul, but to play the love-game with women, will weaken him, as one can witness every day in the exhausted people of this world.[8]

According to the *sharīʿa*, sexual intercourse requires a ritual bath (and the sweet scent of the bed-fellow is so strong that it fills the *ḥamām* when the lover enters it next morning)—:[9]

> By the touching of body and body, man will need a bath—but in the touching of the spirits—where would a bath be needed?[10]

Rumi describes his longing in a strange though appropriate image taken from this sphere:

> Even stranger is this that my eye did not sleep out of longing for thee,
> and yet goes to the bath every morning owing to its union with thee![11]

The longing for the beloved in which the lover spends his sleepless nights makes him weep in the morning, as if his eye had seen the friend and enjoyed the fruits of union with the beloved which would require a bath . . . To the same stream of ideas belongs a verse which is typical of Mowlānā's imaginative power:

> The dream-image of my beloved came into the hot bath of my tears
> and the little man of my eye (e.g. the pupil) sat there as a watchman . . .[12]

Rumi was very fond of the bathhouse imagery, and compares the world to the bathhouse where man feels the heat of the fire which he sees only after leaving the bath—thus, man will see the real causes of his life only after departing from this world.[13] And the story of an apprentice in the bathhouse who produced a fine heat in the stove by 'the nimbleness with which he obeyed the master's orders' leads him to the explanation of a true *sheykh*-disciple-relation.[14]

He even speaks of the soap by which the soul is being cleaned;[15] and mentions a *solṭāni* soap which remained apparently very long on the body, for an unwelcome guest is compared to this kind of soap . . .[16]

Very frequently occurs the image of the 'picture of the bathhouse', *naqsh-e ḥamām, naqsh-e garmābe*, which was common in early Persian poetry, as with Sanāʾi, and which remained popular even in a time when it was no longer fashionable to decorate *ḥamāms* with pictures, as it had been in early Islamic days (the bath-rooms of Syrian Omayyad castles like Quṣayr Amra are fine examples of this art).[17] The pictures in the bathhouse are lifeless; they are nice to look at, but that is all—[18] even if there were a picture of the hero Rostam,[19] one could not fight with it.[20] Man, too, resembles the picture in the bathhouse, and he gets a soul only when the Beloved appears.[21] Then, all the figures painted on the wall will become intoxicated and start dancing, as Rumi describes it in a lovely and cheerful ghazal.[22]

> How can the figure in the bath enjoy the hot bath?
> What makes a form without soul in the place, where the soul is visualized?[23]

The whole world is comparable to a bathhouse—compared to the Divine Spacelessness, Orient and Occident are like the dark ashhouse, the most despicable place in the world, and he, whose nature is cold, is called to fill the cup of his heart (e.g. the cup which is used to pour water over the body). He should look first at the lovely figures painted at the walls with beautiful forms and colours—but then, he should turn his eyes towards the window, for only through the light that falls through this upper window the painted figures become animated and gain their special charm.[24]

> The six directions (e.g. the created world) is the bath, and the window the Placelessness (*lā makān*),
> and on top of the window is the beauty of the hero—

a beauty which illuminates the whole world.[25]

There are other pictures and images as well. One knows that according to Prophetic tradition angels do not enter a place in which figurative paintings are found:—what shall the poor lover do when the picture of his beloved is found with him?[26]

Rumi, like other poets, alludes not rarely to the old imagery of statues and idols produced by Azar, Abraham's father, and by Mani, the founder of Manicheism, who is credited with beautifully illuminated and illustrated manuscripts and with the cave paintings in Western China. Mani's very name became a catch-word for artistic painting,[27] and thus, the connection with the idol-temple, located in Central Asia (the home of the lovely Turks) or in China, is easily established in poetry.[28] The poet asks, therefore:

> Since we are purer than the pure heart,
> why are we filled with images like China?[29]

And he reminds the readers of the famous story of the contest between the painters of China and Byzantium (*Rūm*)—a story known from Ghazzāli and Neẓāmi—in which the highly artistic achievement of the Chinese painters is surpassed by that of the Greek artists who did nothing but polishing their own wall so perfectly that the images drawn by the Chinese were fully reflected on that wall, and their beauty even enhanced.[30] That he changed the roles of the two parties is indicative of his poetical and mystical ingenuity, for China was the country of colourful painting in Persian poetry. This story illustrates the situation of the true mystic who has purified and polished his heart so perfectly that no personal dust or colour remains, thus making visible the reflections of light in all its different shades and hues . . .

God, too, is as much a painter as He is a calligrapher, and man's way towards God is comparable to that of the picture towards its painter;[31] it was He who painted it first, and has shown His perfection in its beauty or in its ugliness, a quality which is required as a contrast to make beauty more radiant.

Other everyday images are inserted to point to the state of the soul which Rumi tries to describe in ever new forms. One of his favourite images is that of the compasses, known to the Western reader also from John Donne's poem *A Valediction: forbidding mourning* which almost looks like a transcription of a Persian ghazal. For this image well describes the lover who turns around his beloved,[32] performing the sacred circumambulation.[33] This circumambulation 'makes me end where I began'—'In my beginning is my end'[34] was the traditional rule of the Sufis: coming from God, they hoped to return to God, and the good end of things would be visible already in the very first step of the Path.

Only rarely are the compasses used in a different context; the application of this image to the mystery of speach which turns around the still heart and tries to circumscribe and hence to describe its states, is particularly beautiful:

> The point of the heart is without number or turning,
> The speaking of the tongue is not by a circle . . .[35]

The restlessness of the lover which underlies a number of the circle-verses is represented quite often by the movement of the millstone.[36] Or else the poet thinks that this world is like the millstone, the other world like the harvest: human existence is, here, like an old bag. When man regards himself as wheat, he should bring himself to the mill to become crushed by the millstone—the result will be seen in the otherworld, where he has to go in any case, whether he be wheat or only pulse-grain.[37] For the grain's suffering and being killed under the millstone is required for it to be transformed into something more valuable.[38]

The seven or nine skies are often compared to seven constantly revolving millstones: the mystic, however, does not want his bread from them but from God directly, without secondary causes, much as he does not want water from that green waterwheel, the sky . . .[39]

The *dulāb,* the waterwheel which turns with a characteristic shrieking sound in all the countries of the Middle East, can likewise symbolize the lover:

> Like a *dulāb* did we turn full of complaint and lamentation, like thought without complaint and words did we turn.[40]

Man is like a mill; he gives what has been given to him—so why blame him if he speaks although he ought to be silent? He has to grind his corn . . .[41] Or else the body is like the mill-stone, the thought the driving water—but even the water does not know how and why the miller has directed it towards the wheel; and Rumi, looking at the water-mill in the garden of Meram near Konya listened to the melodious sound of the wheels and the refreshing murmuring of the water and sang:

> The heart like grain, and we alike to mills,
> How knows the mill, why it is turning round?
> The body like the stone, the thoughts like water,
> The stone says: 'O, the water knows well, why!'
> The water says: 'You better ask the miller
> Who makes the water flow towards the low . . .'[42]

Daily life provides Mowlānā with innumerable similes: God put the soul into the mortar Body and beats it there—but the collyrium (*sorma*) of Love can not be produced in this mortar; it is too fine, and requires other measures.[43]

And God is the great locksmith: it is He who builds the door and closes it, and then produces mysterious keys with letters[44] which open the doors again— 'the key whose teeth bear the letters Joy':[45] does not the proverb attest that 'Patience is the key to joy'?

The whole world is nothing but dust, moved by a hidden sweeper and a secret broom.[46] Thought and selfishness too are like dust; therefore the poet asks the beloved carpet-sweeper to clean from the assembly the dust of thought,[47] or else he describes the impossible situation of the lover in similar household expressions:

> That beloved gave me a broom into my hand;
> He said 'Stir up the dust from the sea!'
> Then the broom burnt from fire,
> and he said: 'Bring forth a broom from fire!'[48]

He speaks of the beating of felt mats which, as he asserts, does not imply any enmity against the felt, but is only meant to take out the dust[49] (does not the beloved make the lover suffer in order to purify his heart?): or, as he says in a different connection: such a beating is not meant as a reproof for the inanimate carpet; but when a father beats his beloved child, then it is a proof of his love.[50]

One stuffed cotton into one's ears to protect one's self from noise—thus, heedlessness which makes people insensible to the Divine Call, can be compared to cotton; or the intoxicated poet calls out:

> I put some cotton of Carefree Behaviour into the heart's ear,
> I do not accept good counsels, from patience, and tear the fetters[51]

We learn from Rumi's verses that all kinds of old folk beliefs were alive in thirteenth century Konya: linen was thought to be destroyed by moonlight—an idea often used in early Persian poetry;[52] Geomancy was applied: the Divine soothsayer is shown drawing the lines on the human dust.[53] The moon was called back from its eclipse by the noise of drums and vessels.[54] In order to protect the house from the evil eye, wild rue-seed (*sepand*) is still being burned in Middle Eastern houses, and Rumi who not infrequently protects his beloved in his verses with the words 'May the evil eye be far!' often speaks of the burning of *sepand*:

> We constantly burn *sepand* because of His coming.
> What *sepand*? We burn ourselves like aloes wood![55]

The wild rue wards off the evil eye from the approaching friend, and the scent of aloes wood in the censer welcomes him. The burning hearts of the lovers happily dance like rue-seed in the flames of love[56] lest the beloved be affected by any evil; or the lovers burn rue and odoriferous woods on the censer of their hearts.[57]

But the heart is not only a censer but also a fragile bottle, made of precious glass, ready to weep,[58] and often endangered by stones which may break it. Rumi connects this wellknown image often with the fairy in the bottle, a legend telling that Solomon, the king of fairies, put all the ghosts and jinns into bottles which he sealed and cast into the sea. Oriental folklore is very fond of stories connected with these little spirits (which have even been revived recently on American television . . .) Rumi tells a longish story of the man who had lost himself in *parikhvāni*,[59] calling the ghosts, and he himself very often tried to call a fairy with the incantation of his verses—a fairy who represents the hidden and mysterious beloved:

What can I recite magic, o king of the fairies—
for you do not fit into bottles and magic![60]

The glass heart is, quite naturally, an abode of the fairy which he tries to make visible:[61] the *dulcis hospes animae* of mystical thought is transformed, here, into a fairy from the Arabian Nights—once more an example of Rumi's talent to spiritualize every conceivable image in an ingenious way.

Eat and drink of God's providing . . .

THE IMAGERY OF FOOD IN RUMI'S POETRY

The reader of Persian and Turkish verses soon gets used to the poets' constant complaint that their hearts have become roast (*kabāb*) in the flames of love, and that their blood turns into wine—wine always being red in Oriental tradition. There is scarcely a writer who has not used these stereotyped expressions which provide him with an easy rhyme (*sharāb—kabāb*) but sound, to the Western ear, at first slightly embarrassing, and often form a serious impediment to the attempt to translate Persian love poetry into our languages in truly poetical style.

Jalāloddin Rumi is no exception, as far as the use of *kabāb* and *sharāb* for the descriptions of the lover's state is concerned. A nice example of the use of contrasting pairs is the line:

The smell of *kabāb* comes up from my heart, full of lamentations, the scent of *sharāb* comes up from your breath and your complaint.[1]

He becomes even more substantial when speaking of the roasting-spit (*sikh*) for the *kabāb* 'heart'—a spit which consists of repentance that pierces men's breast; if he is not roasted this way, he will be cooked on hell-fire.[2]

We can safely assert that Rumi's imagery is filled, to an amazing extent, with images taken from the kitchen, although he always calls his disciples to fasting to the extent of starving, and spent many weeks every year in strict fasting discipline. To be sure, he considers wine, roast, and sugar to be 'coloured dust' which drag man again to the dust[3] yet, the act of eating becomes for him a symbol of spiritual nourishment. When he asks his companions and friends: 'What did you eat—or drink yesterday?'[4] he holds that the kind of nourishment reveals man's character, and that the smell of food can be detected very easily from the mouth of the person concerned. But the word 'yesterday', *dush*, immediately connects this seemingly worldly enquiry with the pre-eternal banquet at the Day of *Alast*: the spiritual food which man's soul has tasted that day shows itself in his actions in this life. For a poet who relies strongly upon the sense of smell, and uses the word *bu*, 'scent, smell' so frequently in connection with spiritual experiences, this combination—smelling the food—was natural.[5] Just as the very smell of food informs of man's predilection, the spiritual intoxication caused by the beloved can be detected from the lover's 'scent', even if he does not speak. The poet may also ask the beloved about his special diet so that he may eat the same food throughout his whole life.[6] Images taken from eating and cooking are found in the strangest combinations—thus in the interpretation of the old saying 'Hurrying is from Satan': one should not act too hurriedly, for cooking requires slow and careful action, otherwise the stew will boil over and get burnt . . .[7]

Although poems in exuberant praise of fasting are numerous in Rumi's poetry, his *Divān*—together with the *Mathnavi*—enables us to draw up a whole list of dishes which were in use in thirteenth century Konya—a place which, by the way, is still renowned for tasty food. To give some examples from the 'mystical menu':

The heart becomes not only *kabāb*, but also *beryāni*,[8] a dish of broiled meat, usually eaten with rice. And love offers at night a delicious dish of *totmāj* (a kind of vermicelli) to the lover which it has cooked.

> 'Now say bismillah!' (i.e. start eating!)
> When I drank from his *totmāj*, he put me down like vinegar,
> I made my face bitter like pickles (*tuzluq*) since I became separated from the sweet one![9]

Such is the *totmāj* of love but those who dance the whole day for the sake of worldly *totmāj* and *ḥarira* (a kind of pap) do not know how the lover's heart enjoys poetry and passion (*ḥarāra*)![10]

The true lovers are comparable to *ḥarisa-ye rasida,* a nourishing thick pottage made of boiled bruised wheat which, perfect in taste and consistency, needs no addition of water or oil.[11]

The cooking of chickpeas is used as an appropriate symbol for spiritual development (cf. Ch.III, 5)

Boiled ox-feet occur in Rumi's verses,[12] and the mystic warns people not to eat too much of them, nor of *sanbusa*,[13] those delicious triangular small pies with meat stuffing (to which he even compares the heart hidden in the breast)[14] which are known all over the Muslim world. This dish, together with 'marvellous *beryāni*' was apparently used in festive gatherings, for it is mentioned along with 'candle, wine, and the lovely beloved' (three words beginning with sh—*shamᶜ, sharāb, shāhid*—which are used in poetry almost as an unit).[15]

Lablabu, explained by Steingass as 'beet boiled and eaten with whey and garlic' are perhaps already for Mowlānā those small roasted chickpeas (*leblebi*) which are still a favourite with Turkish children.[16] Meals made of bruised wheat, *bolghur,* were apparently in Rumi's time as popular in Anatolia as they are today; but

> the spiritual wine is better than *bolghur* dishes.[17]

Qadid, dried meat cut in stripes, and *tharid,* bread soaked in gravy, as well as lentils belonged to the ordinary everyday dishes.[18] Rumi warns his compatriots not to eat too much eggplant, for that would induce them into 'the sleep of heedlessness or smaller impurity', for:

> Who is the friend of the eggplant? Either head (of lamb) or garlic![19]

Perhaps he himself did not like this vegetable too much? Otherwise he would scarcely have compared the 'sour' renegade (*monker*) to the eggplant (probably in pickles) which is always connected with sour things.[20]

Rumi may also ask his Beloved to regard him as his spinach which can mix with sweet or sour according to the wish of the cook,[21] and he does not hesitate to blame the boiled turnip that it looks, in the service of bread, like a forelock of

Iblis[22] — verses which seem to foreshadow the strange poems of Busḥāq-e Aṭʿema in fourteenth century Iran, or the almost surrealistic verses of Qaygusuz Abdāl in fifteenth century Turkey. Even though our poet may be saltish like cheese he is in reality full of kindness like milk which can easily be swallowed,[23] or he melts like sugar in the milk.[24]

The relation of body and soul can be seen as that of sour milk and butter: the butter is invisible, and becomes conspicuous and tasty only after separating it from the milk by different tribulations[25] and finally by death. And the difference of pulse and rice is only due to the squint-eyed: if their eyes were normal they would no longer see duality and recognize that everything is one.[26]

Various kinds of fruits were brought to the capital — the peaches that come from Laranda (Karaman) make the whole town smile,[27] and the poet feels like a pomegranate whose 'teeth', i.e. the small round kernels of the fruits, constantly smile. Since he is made of finest sugar, he cannot stand the sight of *somakh*, the herb of bitter aroma which is used with roast, for these two tastes can not be combined.[28]

Rumi warns people not to expect the scent of musk when they put garlic and onion before their noses.[29] Rotten onion in general becomes a symbol of worldly pleasures: the child who has not yet seen an apple, will not give away his rotten onion,[30] just as a man who knows nothing about the spiritual world, clings to the miserable and rotten enjoyments of this world; in the eyes of the wise, however, even the most attractive girls and boys are not better than a stinking onion.[31] — In a different strain of thought, Mowlānā may contrast the 'onion Separation' which causes tears with the 'saffron Union' which gladdens the heart.[32]

Sometimes Jalāloddin's imagery becomes even more grotesque: which other poet would compare the house of his Beloved to a butcher's shop who trades in hearts and heads?[33] These little shops selling intestines could be seen in Anatolia still a few years ago, and Rumi, overstressing the image of the lover's heart and head being sacrificed to the Beloved, found them an appropriate symbol for his terrific power.

But the Beloved is also sweet and gentle. He pleases the patient lover with confections full of walnuts, sugar and almonds (*luzina*) to sweeten his mouth and throat and to give him light.[34]

In fact, verses connected with sugar, honey, and sweets abound in Rumis's *Divān* as in the verses of almost every other poet looking for a perfect image of the sweetness of his beloved. Honey is always 'licked[35]—a quite naturalistic image! —and if man

> licks the honey of Spiritual Poverty (*faqr*), even the generalissimo of the Empire has in his eyes no more importance than a fly.[36]

Rumi intends to show with this verse, that spiritual poverty is better and sweeter than all worldly ranks—a somewhat surprising image for an idea expressed hundreds of times by Sufi poets.

The Beloved, of necessity, has been compared innumerable times to sweet milk, sugar, sugar-cane, and candy (*qand*), although he may be, at the same time, bitter like colocynth.[37]

> If the sugar but knew anything of the taste of love,
> it would turn water from shame, and no more show its sugar-quality.[38]

And the bitterness of separation makes the lover's teeth blunt (*kond*) until the sugar (*qand*) of union can be tasted again.[39]

Egypt was the province with the largest sugar exports; thus Egyptian caravans carrying sugar wander through Rumi's verses—here, the internal relation of Egypt with Joseph, the prototype of youthful beauty and thus symbol of the beloved, should always be taken from granted, all the more when the Beloved is addressed as carrying a whole Egypt in himself. Once the poet mentions sugar from Khuzistan,[40] rivalling Egypt as a producer of sugar but rarely used as a poetical topos since it lacked a symbolic figure like Joseph who could be connected with it. The pun between *qand* and the city of *Qandahar*—frequent in early Persian poetry—seems to be lacking in Rumi's poems; he prefers the similar combination of *qand* with *Samarqand.*[41]

Among the hundreds of lines speaking of sugar and candy, one image is worth mentioning: this is the connection of the sugar cane with the reed flute. The reed is empty, it has given up its own will,[42] and made its heart narrow; therefore the Beloved can breathe into it and fill it with sugar—the two functions of the reed are put together in an ingenious combination[43] (to which the image of the reed-pen, both sweet and complaining, can be added).

Sugar was sold in small quantities, wrapped in paper, like candy;[44] for the poet says:

> When I write the name of Shams-e Tabriz, I put my heart's desire
> like sugar into the belly of paper—,[45]

as if the name of the Beloved would make the paper sweet! Or he calls the Beloved:

> O you the grief for whom is like sugar, and my heart like paper![46]

These little paper bags filled with sugar as sold by the druggist serve him, later, as symbols for God's grace: the customer should not think that the merchant has only this small amount of the coveted sweet—nay, his stores are filled with sugar which he, however, distributes according to the customer's need and capacity, just as God grants only small pieces from His endless Mercy.[47]

We learn from Rumi's verses that the practice of keeping sweet dishes cool in snow and ice (as it was common in Abbasid times, and still in Mamluk Egypt) was known in Konya as well:

> In this snow do I kiss his lips—
> for snow and sugar keep the heart fresh.[48]

Paluda, a dish of milk, fine flour, and some spices, was popular enough in the thirteenth century to be mentioned several times as a symbol of spiritual sweetness:[49] compared with the Beloved, everything is as tasteless as *paluda* bought in the bazaar.[50] *Paluda* is also mentioned along with *qaṭāʾef,* a delicious kind of sweet cake, as a meal for a festive occasion.[51]

How lovely is Rumi's idea that even the sweetmeat is engaged in prayer!

> Be silent, for sugared almonds *(jowzina)* and sweetmeat with almonds *(luzina)* are engaged in prayer:
> the *luzina* offers the prayer, the *halva* says 'Amen'.[52]

May we think of the saying I often heard in Ramadan in Turkey that the food which is brought from the kitchen before the breaking of the fast at sunset, praises God as long as it is on the table?

Mowlānā makes the Beloved tell the lover the secret of being broken and thus, as we may surmise, reaching a higher level of existence:

> You will become broken like old nuts, when you taste my almond-sweet . . .[53]

For 'the friend is like *luzina*'.[54]

Among the sweets, *ḥalva* is Rumi's favourite object—an object comparable to the taste of spiritual experience: just as the villager who tasted *ḥalva* for the first time, would no longer like the carrots he used to chew formerly for the sake of their sweetness, man will despise wordly pleasure once he has tasted spiritual bliss.[55] That is why Rumi does not even hesitate to see the love of Shamsoddin in his heart inseparably blended 'as *qand* and sugar in the *ḥalva*'.[56]

One should not forget that the Sufis were indeed always notorious for their fondness of sweetmeats, and many an earlier poet has ridiculed this tendency in his verses. Rumi himself has several times alluded to Sufi parties with *ḥalva.*[57] His most unusual poem in this respect is that with the rhyme-word *ḥalva,*[58] in which he tells that God Himself has cooked some *ḥalva* for the Sufis, and that the angels produce it in the heavenly kitchen . . . Of course, the true mystic thinks of the *ḥalva* of his friend's lip, and takes the scent of *ḥalva* from his mouth: 'Do not talk too much of *ḥalva*!' he admonishes himself, because the word itself reveals the secret of loving union which must be kept secret.[59] And the *ḥalva* should be chewed with closed mouth like a fresh fig, chewed 'in the heart' without contaminating hand and lip.[60]

Jalāloddin goes even further in his fondness for this image: as soon as the Beloved lits the fire of His love, the whole world becomes like a big pan in which *ḥalva* is cooked;[61] the night is turned into a *ḥalva* pan[62] (probably an allusion to the sweetness of nightly prayer, the conversation between lover and Beloved), and the trees carry trays with *ḥalva* on each branch and twig:[63] a miraculous sweet has been prepared in the pan of the wood, without outward fire, without oil and syrup. Man, once tasting of the friend's *ḥalva* will boil like a *ḥalva* kettle on the fire.[64]

Rumi speaks of the '*ḥalva* of contentment'.[65] Turkish readers will here remember the 'morsel of contentment' *rıza lokması*, which is praised in subsequent centuries in Bektashi religious poetry: after the trial of boiling, man understands that contentment is sweet and palatable. But the base soul may even remain *ammāra,* inciting to evil, instead of becoming peaceful, if it has tasted too much earthly *ḥalva.*[66]

In this connection one should not forget that Konya has always been famous for its *ḥalva* and one of the stories of Naṣroddin Khoja attests that 'in Konya they thrash you to make you eat *ḥalva*'. One is reminded of this saying on finding a remark in the *Mathnavi*[67] where beating a child and feeding it with *ḥalva* are contrasted to show the eternal wisdom which manifests itself better in pain than in grace:

> If I am slapping an orphan, while a mild-natured person may put *ḥalva* in his hand,
> Those slaps are better (for him) than the other's *ḥalva,* and if he be beguiled by the *ḥalva,* woe to him!

Rumi's cuisine does not only comprise sweet items—salt becomes an emblem of spiritual regeneration:[68] the beloved is the Mine of Salt,[69] or the salt cellar,[70] and by partaking of this salt—which means at the same time 'loveliness, charm'—the lover himself becomes more lovable and spiritual.[71] The image that everything that falls into a salt-mine is transformed and thus purified—found first in ʿAṭṭār's epics—has been used by Rumi in several connections,[72] i.e. in his description of the Prophet who is 'more salty and elegant' than material salt.[73] In many cases, the beloved is asked to sprinkle some of his salt upon the roasting heart or liver of the lover to make it more tasty.[74]

Rumi who sang the praise of hunger and spiritual food so often, holds that

> bread is the architect of the prison 'body',
> wine is the rain for the garden 'soul'.[75]

Notwithstanding his warnings against too much eating which induces man into sleep and sexual desires,[76] the imagery of baking and bread occupies much room in his vocabulary. The world is like a furnace in which different kinds of bread are baked—but he who has seen the Baker Himself, what should he care for the world?[77] For him, bread is only a pretext; it is the Baker who enraptures him.[78] God reveals Himself here under the attribute of *ar-Razzāq,* He who bestows the daily bread. Those who love Him, take His gifts only as a means to increase their gratitude.

The lover's heart is comparable to a furnace.[79] But he should rather resemble the furnace of the old woman of Basra (which, according to Muslim legend, caused the Flood) and cover the whole earth with the hot water of his love instead of baking bread.[80]

To mature, that is the duty of the lover; as long as he is raw there is no use for him. But once he is baked—be it in the fire of tribulation or of separation—he becomes 'the head of the most precious part of the table'.[81] But the same person who was once honoured like baked bread, may experience that he becomes, on his way, like breadcrumbs, scattered and worthless.[82]

In the otherwise rather uniform imagery of baking and bread in Rumi's work, one instance attracts our special attention, since it is an interesting example of the mystic's imaginative power:[83] he compares lovemaking to the baker's dealing with the dough and describes it in such amusing style that it is difficult to detect here anything but sheer sensual joy—although, of course, some may interpret the passage also as the Divine action of kneading and apparently mistreating his friends for the sake of spiritual union . . .

This whole complex of images leads, quite naturally, to the feeling that man is constantly in a kitchen,[84] being treated like one of the ingredients of food: Rumi speaks of the kitchen of Love,[85] but also of the kitchen of God out of which comes only precious food, like manna and quails, as attested in the Koran (Sura 2/57; 7/160; 20/80). For the whole sky is God's kitchen, the stars the servants, and since water and fire are always at His disposal He can feed everything created. In his visions, Rumi enters a kitchen full of light,[86] a kitchen full of honey in which the kings lick the vessels.[87] Mortals, however, are not allowed to taste from it even a ladleful; rather, their hearts and souls become roasted.[88]

Mowlānā compares almost everything to a kitchen: the soul,[89] the heart,[90] the head, the stomach[91] and even intellect in whose kitchen the poor Sufis remain hungry.[92]

In a charming play of contrasts Rumi once more highlights the importance of fasting for the true Sufis:

> Since the lovers' life became dark as an effect of the kitchen 'body',
> He prepared for their kitchen the fasting.[93]

Fasting makes the kitchen empty, cleans it thoroughly, and

Mowlānā Rumi, turning in front of Ṣalāḥoddin Zarkub's shop. From a manuscript of Sultan Ḥoseyn Bayqarā's *majāles-e ʿushshāq*, 17th or early 18th century.

allows man to taste spiritual food, so that he becomes similar to the angels who live exclusively on adoration and worship.[94]

Jalāloddin likes to compare the most divergent objects to a kettle or cauldron (*dik*; rarely the Turkish *qazghān* is used). This is a convenient image for the human heart which is constantly boiling from the fire of Divine love or wrath—and how could a kettle be silent when the water starts boiling? The tongue is therefore well comparable to the lid of the pot—when it moves, one smells what kind of food is contained in it, whether sweetmeat or vinegar-spiced stew. Does not the proverb attest that 'Man is hidden under his tongue'?[95] The motif of the kettle 'heart' became even more prominent in later Sufi poetry—when Rumi complains that the Beloved should not ask the lover to be silent, for that would be impossible, later Sufis have compared Ḥallāj's utterance 'I am the Truth' to the sound of the kettle in which the water was still in the process of boiling and not yet evaporated as silent steam: to voice one's experiences is only the median stage on the mystical path.[96]

We may place here also the verse:

> I put a lid on the cauldron 'faithfulness'
> so that not every raw person may smell it.[97]

Rumi describes the handling of the kettle in all details, beginning from lighting the fire with the match (or rather the piece of sulphur) in the friend's hand.[98] The kettle itself is always black; this fact allows many cômparisons to the black heart, or to black-faced, i.e. disgraced, people. But if its material were gold, this external blackness would not diminish its value.[99]

Again, we find unusual, even sinister, images in this connection: man, in his constant movement in the cauldron 'world' can be compared to a skimmer,[100] and the soul goes round like a ladle in the kettle 'heart' to become filled with *ḥalva*.[101] But the true lover sings:

> I want to draw up a spoon *(kafak)* with blood from the kettle 'soul' . . .[102]

The kettle filled with blood was already known earlier, thus to ʿAṭṭār, and occurs in several places in Rumi's lyrics.[103]

There are still many other images taken from kitchen and household:

The world is a sieve, and we like flour;
when you can pass, you are pure, otherwise you are chaff.[104]

To be sure, as many people dance out of love of bread and soup, as dance in pure love.[105] But for Rumi himself all the delicious kinds of food he has so often mentioned in his poetry are hardly attractive:

I do not eat head, for that is heavy,
I do not eat feet, for that is bones,
I do not eat *beryāni*, for that is a loss,
I eat light, for that is the nourishment of the soul.[106]

He knew, however, that once a person becomes drunk, he cannot remain silent, and when bread reaches the hungry, one should not say 'Do not eat!'[107]—the intoxication by love or, on the lower level, by the sight of food is too great to be counted in terms of normal behavior.

It is revealing that one ghazal in which imagery of bread and wine has been used in a style reminiscent of Omar Khayyam and other not exactly mystical poets has been inscribed, among other verses, on Rumi's sarcophagus: here, he follows the example of all those poets who claimed that their intoxication—real or metaphorical—would last beyond the grave:

When wheat grows out of my dust,
and when you bake bread from it, then intoxication increases,
the dough and the baker become intoxicated,
and the furnace sings, drunken, poetry . . .[108]

It would indeed be astonishing if Rumi had not used the age-old symbolism of the sacred intoxication which better than any other symbol expresses the overwhelming power of the mystical state[109]—a state in which man is strangely transported to higher levels of consciousness. Already in the first lines of the *Mathnavi* he confronts the reed flute which speaks through the fire of love with the wine, agitated by the fermentation of love.[110] The heart, comparable to grapes, is beaten for years and squeezed until the sap flows out and wine is made,[111] for only if the husk of the grapes is removed can union be experienced: out of thousands of grapes emerges one wine.[112]

One finds verses in Jalāloddin's poetry in which ordinary drunkenness is described in very matter-of-fact images—the drunkard walks around falling, creeping, and vomiting,[113] a laughing-stock for the children who do not know the real nature of his intoxication.[114] But:

> He whom Thou makest drunk and lion hunting—
> accept his excuse, if he walks crooked from intoxication![115]

An amusing description of the meeting of a drunk person with the police-inspector serves the poet as starting-point to come from earthly to spiritual intoxication:

> The Inspector said to him 'Come now, say Ah!' But the drunken man at the moment of utterance, said 'Hu, Hu!'
> 'I told you to say 'Ah'', said he; 'you are saying 'Hu'!—'Because I am glad', he replied, 'while you are bent with grief.
> Ah is uttered on account of pain and grief and injustice, the Hu 'He' of the wine drinkers is from joy.'
> The Inspector said: 'I know nothing about this. Get up, get up! Don't retail mystic lore, and leave off this wrangling . . .'[116]

Rumi often applies the Koranic promise that God will offer pure wine, *sharāban ṭahuran*, to the faithful in Paradise (Sura 76/21) to descriptions of the mystical wine which, by virtue of its intoxicating power, takes out of man's heart grief and sorrow.[117] It is the wine of *ladon,* of immediate Divine experience which endows every hair with vision. Therefore the mystic wants that even the *moḥtaseb,* the model of sober orthodoxy,[118] should taste this Divine wine which is licit[119] and whose fragrance makes all the saints *(abdāl)* both visible and invisible among people.[120]

The *kowthar,* the abundant paradisiacal fountain, is equated with the wine of the soul whereas the 'wine of the body' is given from the goblet of *abtar* ('he who has no offspring')—this is a most elegant application of the *Surat al-kowthar.* For the Prophet was inspired by this spiritual wine, not by the material wine which his enemy (who was doomed to be *abtar*) used to drink. This verse can be considered a clue to Rumi's wine symbolism which is so prominent in his poetry.[121]

The outward forms are like the vessel,[122] the inward beauty is the wine which, never changing in substance,[123] intoxicates the lover. Without the grace of the Friend's wine, the whole world is nothing but an empty vessel.[124] A single sip of this wine mingled with dust made Majnun loose his intellect—how much higher, then, must be the pure and unalloyed intoxication which the true lover enjoys when he is not fascinated by an earthly beloved![125] Rumi knows that the radiant glory of the cupbearer transforms the must into sparkling and potent wine,[126] and his verses are understood as responses to this intoxicating experience.[127] He has described this marvellous event in one of his finest and most musical ghazals, a poem which reflects the magical quality of the wine of love and the Divine cupbearer in perfect lucidity:

I saw my Beloved wandering about the house:
He had taken up a rebeck and was playing a tune.
With a touch like fire he was playing a sweet melody,
Drunken and distraught and bewitching from the night's carouse.
He was invoking the cup-bearer in the mode of Iraq:
Wine was his object, the cup-bearer was only an excuse.
The beauteous cup-bearer, pitcher in hand,
Stepped forth from a recess and placed it in the middle.
He filled the first cup with that sparkling wine—
Didst thou ever see water set on fire?
For the sake of those in love he passed it from hand to hand,
Then bowed and kissed the lintel.
My Beloved received it from him, and quaffed the wine:
Instantly o'er his face and head ran flashes of flame.
Meanwhile he was regarding his own beauty and saying to the evil eye:
'There has not been nor will be in this age another like me.
I am the Divine Sun of the world, I am the Beloved of the lovers,
Soul and spirit are continually moving before me.'[128]

It is a poem which reveals the identity of Beloved, cup-bearer, wine, and music in unforgettable images and tells better than any explanation of the magic of Shamsoddin's intoxicating love and beauty and shows how the wine of love leads him proudly to reveal his status as the Beloved.

Rumi was probably acquainted with Ibn al-Fāreḍ's *khamrīyya,*[129] the great Arabic ode in which the Egyptian mystic had praised the wine of love which he quaffed before the grapes were created:

If in the Maghreb the scent of this wine would appear out of Non-Existence,
the ascetics in Herat and Taliqan would become intoxicated . . .[130]

This motif is a poetical interpretation of the events at the Day of the Covenant, when the soul accepted the Divine address *Alastu* 'Am I not your Lord?' and responded by answering *balā* 'Yes' (Sura 7/171)—intoxicated, as the Sufis would say, by the goblet of *alast.* This image has been used by mystical poets time and again, but the similarities between some of Rumi's verses and the words of his elder Egyptian contemporary are so close that a direct influence cannot be ruled out. The poet describes the saints who have drunk wine and experienced excitement before the creation of grapes, and who perceive, with inner vision, the wine already in the grape, the existent already in non-existence[131] (verses which have been imitated, six hundred years later, by the Indo-Muslim poet Ghālib in one of his most impressive *qaṣidas*).[132] The *sāqi* of the day of *alast* is a standing figure in Rumi's poetry. Even more: whoever saw a dream of this primordial covenant is intoxicated, but—and that is important!—intoxicated in the way of works of obedience, so that he carries the burden of religious obligations which God loads upon his back happily like an intoxicated camel.[133]

Mowlānā alludes not rarely to the tradition that God kneaded Adam's clay for forty days, and connects this kneading of the dough and its fermentation with the intoxication which still permeates man—verses, echoed most perfectly by Ḥāfeẓ.[134]

The drink of love is a wine which makes the dead jump out of their graves,[135] and the lovers realize that there must be only one goblet—no duality is left for those who drink this wine.[136]

The intoxication caused by the pre-eternal wine makes Rumi exclaim:

> I am so drunk, I am so drunk in this moment
> that I cannot tell Eve from Adam . . .[137]

It is this primordial wine that flows through all the lovers in the world—be they the Seven Sleepers who were taken out of time for three hundred and nine years, or the Egyptian women who cut their hands when gazing at Joseph's beauty, or Jaʿfar aṭ-Ṭayyār, the hero of early Islamic battles.[138] This wine enraptures the lovers, purifies spirits and angels so much that they have broken the wine-jar of this world—with the exception of a few infidels in their hopelessness—;[139] for the true lovers do not need any more external wine:

> The wine became intoxicated with us, not we with the wine . . .[140]

And when I was ill, He healed me . . .

IMAGERY CONNECTED WITH DISEASES

> Yesterday our khāja fell ill . . .
> He has no bile (*ṣafrā*) he has no melancholia (black gall), he has neither colic nor dropsy—
> from this event a hundred uproars have fallen into every corner of our town . . .[1]

What is the poor khāja's illness? It is, of course, the illness of love which can only be cured by the skillful physician, the beloved. Rumi, faithful to the tradition of Islamic poetry and mysticism, uses medical terminology rather frequently; for a proper knowledge of this terminology belonged to the general education. It is always love which is discovered as the real illness, as the poet describes it so well in the first story of the *Mathnavi*, love,

> the illness which is more agreeable than health . . .[2]

The lovers have fallen ill from the physician's 'ill', e.g. 'languishing' eyes,[3] and since every lover wants to behold the Eternal Physician, there is only one way out: one has to become ill so that He may come to visit the suffering lover.[4]

That Mowlānā himself apparently did not care too much for external school medicine becomes clear from a rather amusing story told by Sepahsālār: the master whose disciples were sick took the medicine and acted in every respect contrary to what the physicians would have advised—dancing in ecstatic *samāʿ*, going to the hot bath after swallowing some purgative pills, and yet, he felt perfectly well.[5] He knew, however, enough about concrete ailments and their symptoms and cures to use them as symbols for higher spiritual experiences.

Illness is one of the so-called 'secondary causes' of death, created by God to divert man's eye from Azrāʾil, the angel of death who had first refused to slay human beings. But God consoled him: He has invented fever, colic, delirium and spear to preoccupy man so that the angel himself remains invisible.[6]

Sowdā and *ṣafrā*, the illness of black gall and yellow bile, i.e. melancholic and choleric temperament and their results are the external signs of the lovers. When a man eats too many dates, it becomes phlegm and produces bile:[7] one of Rumi's favourite comparisons is that sugar is dangerous for those infested with bile, or those with fever:

> If is difficult to play tanbour for the deaf,
> or to perform the custom of sugar-strewing on a bile-infested person![8]

Those suffering from *ṣafrā* are the loveless people who cannot enjoy the sugar, or *ḥalva,* of union, whereas the Sufis can indulge in eating sweetmeats since they seek purity *(ṣafā),* not gall *(ṣafrā).*[9]

The person deceived by wordly interests is comparable to one dying of consumption who melts like ice and yet thinks that he gets better every day.[10]

The most frequently mentioned illness in Rumi's vocabulary is dropsy, since its symptoms could be connected with the insatiable thirst of the lover for more 'water of life'.[11] The idea that the lover is never satiated was common with the Sufis, beginning, at least, with Bāyazid Besṭāmi, and even the first lines of the *Mathnavi* speak of this metaphysical thirst which can never be quenched.[12]

> Heart and soul, more feverish than dust,
> seize the jar like dropsied people, 'Water! Water!'[13]

The swollen body of the dropsied person is even compared to a drum which constantly repeats the call for more water, an image perhaps taken over from Khāqāni.[14]

Comparable to dropsy, but less often mentioned, are *juʿ al-kalb,* 'canine appetite',[15] or *juʿ al-baqar* 'voracity',[16] which make people hungry for the bread which comes from the bakery of the soul or leads them to the pasture ground of eternal life *(baqāʾ)* to graze there like a never satiated cow:[17] both images express the spiritual longing of the lover in rather crude form.

The unrest produced by colics which makes man restless so that he 'falls from the dwelling place of the patient'[18] serves as much as a symbol as toothache,[19] which is treated with heat and steadfast trust in case it is caused by wind;[20] but if a worm has fallen into the tooth it should be torn out, just as evil qualities have to be uprooted lest they cause more pain to the spirit.[21]

There are different ways of diagnosing illness: by smelling the sick person's breath one may find out what he has eaten, and Rumi does not hesitate to insert a story known from folklore into his lyrics:

> A man went to the physician complaining of stomach ache; he had to confess that he had eaten burnt bread whereupon the physician prescribed him an eye-salve so that he could recognize, the next time, whether his food was edible or not . . .[22]

The physician in this story acts like the spiritual master who opens the eyes of the worldly minded who cannot discern what is good for their soul.

For the cure of eyes, *sorma,* collyrium, was used; the best quality came, according to Rumi's allusions, from Isfahan.[23] It was produced by grinding pearls in a mortar. Thus, the days of life could be compared to such a mortar in which precious jewels are pulverized in order to make the spirit see,[24] and this, again, leads Rumi to the conclusion that to be broken is the pre-condition for becoming a useful medicine.[25] The most common method of diagnosis was by examining the *qarura*, the vial,[26] and Rumi, alluding to the Light-Verse of the Koran (Sura 24/35) says in rather direct language:

> That glass which has not got the light of the soul
> is urine and bottle, do not call it a lamp![27]

By feeling the pulse, the classical method of detecting secret diseases, and ailments of the heart, most of the 'beloved' physicians in Persian poetry find out the secret illness of the heart, as the first story in the *Mathnavi* describes in detail.[28] And the poet can admonish his disciples to apply these practices to their spiritual life as well:

> Take the pulse of your heart and religion, and see how you are,
> and look once into the vial of actions![29]

By examining one's thoughts and the result of one's religious attitudes one may be able to find out what is wrong with one's faith.

Ailments were often cured by bloodletting, and Rumi sees those who long to be slain in the way of love in a somewhat strange image:

> The slain one comes to the slayer as quickly
> as blood runs from the body into the bottle of the cupper . . .[30]

In many cases, a mixture of honey and vinegar would be given to the sick; this is a medicine appropriate for liver diseases;[31]

for Mowlānā, it becomes a symbol of the saints and prophets in whom the spiritual honey and the wordly vinegar are mixed so that they can cure, by their very nature, the diseases of the soul.[32] But:

> When you are cured from your illness,
> leave the vinegar and eat only the honey![33]

The slow introduction into the world of spirit is described in another similar image: some people cannot digest pure honey; only when it is mixed with rice, dressed with turmeric and *ḥalva* are they able to swallow it, until they have fully recovered: not every heart is able to enjoy immediately the spiritual sweetness offered by the saints.[34] Opium, mainly mentioned as intoxicating matter along with wine, was given to the sick to quiet down their pain.[35]

Worldly qualities should be spit out, or vomited:

> When man does not spit out the blood of boasting,
> the blood will become agitated, and diphtheria will result.[36]

And just as this blood should be cleaned away, Rumi, or the beloved, offers his services to those who have eaten rotten food[37] or have drunk devil's milk[38] and want to vomit: he gives them the medicine but warns them lest they eat such stuff any more. Thus, the soul has to give up, even if by force, the rotten worldly pleasures. Even grief can be called an 'evacuation' which leads the soul, eventually, to joy.[39] The beloved is very often described as the eternal physician,[40] a second Galen, nay, even more than Galen, or Galen and Avicenna in one person;[41] he is a wise physician coming from Baghdad[42] and heals ailments even Galen did not know.[43] He quickens the sick with his Jesus-like breath, and is himself the medicine for the soul, he is:

> A hundred wormwoods and medicines for the heart full of pain . . .[44]

For once he opens even his mouth to show his lovingkindness, he sends a *mofarraḥ*—a kind of tranquillizer—to the hearts of all those who are sick for his sake.[45] But his quality as physician implies also that he sometimes prescribes bitter medicine which the lover will take without hesitation, for he firmly believes in his wisdom: whatever the physician does, is good in itself.[46]

That is why Rumi applies the image of the physician to God in order to solve the enigma that He wills both good and evil, but approves only the good:

> He desires that people should be ill, since he desires to practice his medicine, and he cannot display his medical skill unless people are ill. But he does not approve of people being ill, otherwise he would not attend them and treat them . . .[47]

And their garment there will be silk

WEAVING AND SEWING

One of my favourite verses in Rumi's lyrical work are the lines in which he describes the lover who

> weaves satin and brocade from his liver's blood
> in order to put satin and brocade under the beloved's feet—[1]

a verse which has numerous, though less artistic, parallels elsewhere in his poetry. Thus the tears of blood are often compared to red shimmering satin[2] (*aṭlas* 'satin' is generally synonymous with 'brilliant red'). The lover's heart-beats may remind the poet of the constant movement of the loom, weaving a garment of thought and hopes[3]—provided the beloved helps him. For if the Friend is not present in the weaving factory,

> by God, neither woof remained—by God, nor warp remained![4]

Otherwise, when He mixes with it,

> *one* thread becomes a dress, *one* brick a castle![5]

It is but natural that Rumi uses allusions to weaving and sewing comparatively often. In a place like Central Anatolia, long famous for its colourful woollen carpets, with brocades and silk imported from all over the Islamic world, such imagery offered itself very easily to a poet. Besides, the symbolism of weaving and of dresses goes back to the oldest times of religious expression and is common to almost all religions in the Ancient Near East, including Judaism and Christianity.[6] It was often used by the ancient Greeks, who would see the starry sky as a richly decorated garment of the gods, just as the Hebrew psalmist regards light as the dress Divine (Psalm 104), and as Christianity imagines Mary in a star-embroidered gown of heavenly blue . . . Earlier poets in Iran had elaborated the imagery of weaving and woven material by comparing flowers and desert, clouds and water to precious silken material[7]—not to forget Farrokhi's *qaṣida-ye ḥolla* in which he skillfully describes the process of 'weaving' a poem.[8] Rumi, adopting a famous ancient motif, uses images pertaining to weaving and clothing to symbolize many aspects of mystical life. He jokingly warns people not to be deceived by the dark blue frock of the sky which pretends to be, in this dress, a stern ascetic, but 'has not trousers under it . . .'[9]

What does the outward appearance of man mean? Nothing; it behoves one to look into the possibilities hidden behind the husk, for:

> satins are hidden under the leaves of the mulberry tree.[10]

Jalāloddin knows the silk form Shoshtar[11] (or Sus),[12] and speaks of the most precious satin which is put before the tailor to test his skill.[13] The 'silk of felicity'[14] is decorated by the *ṭerāz*, whose inscriptions bear the royal names and titles and thus honour the woven material. The lover is the best *ṭerāz* on Adam's dress;[15] therefore Rumi compares the saint leading the congregational prayer to a wonderfully embroidered *ṭerāz* which makes the silk more valuable,[16] and the very view of the *ṭerāz* of the Friend's robe of honour tears a thousand dresses of pain, anguish and grief in pieces.[17]

Man's outward qualities—noble and mean—are like woven material. The poet speaks of the 'garment body which is the lowliest dress',[18] although he may think at other times that the four elements are only like a dress, the true work of the creator being visible in the human body itself.[19] He tells about the 'cloak of holy attributes' which Adam put on and gave up again[20]—images known to other Muslim and non-Muslim poets as well. Whatever man does, becomes a garment for him—we may remember the old Indian tale of the King and the Corpse in which each work of the King contributed to the perfection of the beggar's frock.[21] Good thoughts become the fabric of the outward form,[22] so that man is dressed, finally in a garment (*ḥolla*) made from the warp and woof of works of obedience,[23] e.g. in a material which he himself has woven by his actions. He may sometimes put on the frock of patience—but this will be torn to pieces the very moment love enters his heart.[24] The dress is something 'other'; it is a veil which covers the perfect nudity required for the last union between lover and beloved.

> I am better naked, and put away the garment 'body', so that the lap of Thy grace becomes a cloak for my soul.[25]

For:

> Whatever the dress be, hairy wool or *shoshtari* silk: to embrace Him is better without this veil.[26]

Rumi uses these images in an interesting combination: God taught Adam the names, e.g. the attributes of things out of jealousy, weaving, thus, the 'veils of the particulars' whereas He comprises the fullness of things;[27] every name covers a reality, partakes in it as the garment partakes in the character of its owner, and yet veils this reality from the views of the strangers. Love tears this dress (as it was, in fact, often the case in mystical dance when the Sufis rent their frocks), whereas reason tries to mend it—a useless task when the Beloved sews hearts . . .[28]

Thought and word are therefore a garment which man should take off—he should 'tear the dress of speech'.[29] The humans weave or spin words: later Indo-Muslim poets have compared the *ẕekr,* the recollection of the Divine Names, to the movement and sound of spinning by which the heart becomes soft like the most valuable yarn.[30] But the 'dress of thought',[31] the cloaks (*kherqa*) spun by intellect[32] will all be naught before the Sun which burns everything so that neither warp nor woof is any longer required.[33] Then, the lover will put on the *qabā*, the long robe of honour which the Sun itself grants him; that is, he will partake of the Sun's own nature (for the original meaning of bestowing a garment upon somebody was to grant him part of one's own spiritual power, *baraka*). The Sun weaves golden brocade for those who give up their external existence and stand before it in perfect poverty and nudity, to dress them in its own golden light.[34]

On the level of ritual religion, the yellow cheeks of the fasting Muslim which were formerly red like satin will be covered by the robe of honour given by fasting.[35] The lover will be dressed in the 'cloak of felicity'[36] which is taken from the 'treasure-house of Mercy'.[37] Rumi calls the 'pacified soul' (Sura 89/28) to put on this gown of Divine Reality instead of its old sackcloth;[38] for the *aṭlas* and *eksun* (red and black satin of superior quality) which love grants man already in this life are more precious than that green velvet and silk promised to the pious in Paradise.[39]

The light of the Sun which bestows golden dresses upon the naked is able to transform everything—rocks and thorns become, thanks to its power, soft like Chinese silk (*parniyān*, as Rumi says in his imitation of Rudaki's *qaṣida* about the *āb-e Muliyān*);[40] the contrast between *khār,* 'thorn' and *ḥarir* 'silk' is not rarely used in his poems.[41] In fact, he sees how all nature in spring puts on a robe of honour which needs neither warp nor woof,[42] granted by the Almighty King[43] who bestows on every thorn the gala-dress 'rose'.[44] Or else: Spring is a tailor who stitches lovely dresses of green brocade,[45] or brings them forth from the 'shop of the Invisible';[46] one of his masterpieces is the tulip's dress with its sun-coloured collar and its evening-coloured hem.[47]

But the poet may also joke, addressing his beloved in autumn:

> O idol, look at the fall, see those naked (creatures)!
> Give the naked a cloak of wine (red) like satin![48]

The admiration for the strange weaver and tailor who bestows the gala robe of existence on the non-being[49] and who embroiders the moon on the blouse of the evening[50] overwhelms Jalāloddin from time to time. He may hear the Creator's address who informs him about His marvellous grace:

> I put a hundred *aṭlas* and *eksun* before the silk-worm![51]

And He can change cotton into fine silk, as Rumi says in a 'spinning' ghazal,[52] as much as He can put on the dress of wrath and again change it into that of the Guide.[53]

Certainly, the tailor Fate never cut a shirt for a man which he did not turn eventually into a full dress,[54] and Rumi elaborates this idea in the well-known story, taken from Arabic literature, of the tailor who cleverly stole large parts of his customers' material. His hero, a foolish Turkish soldier who brings a lovely Istanbuli satin to him, is deceived by the vulgar tricks of this tailor 'Fate' who cuts the satin of life with the scissors 'months' . . . and although he had relied upon his intellect, he is as helpless as every other human being against these ruses which are enhanced by his own heedlessness.[55]

At times man wonders what all this cutting and sewing means by which the invisible tailor can change in a wink a pious man into an infidel, a heretic into an ascetic.[56] But reasoning cannot help much here:

> For instance, you have an uncut cloth which you want to have cut into a tunic or a cloak. Reason has brought you to a tailor. Until that moment reason was fine, for it brought the cloth to the tailor. Now in this very moment reason must be divorced and you must abandon yourself wholly to the control of the tailor . . .[57]

The poet describes his way towards this mysterious tailor in a ghazal:

> Tomorrow I will go to the cell of the tailor of lovers,
> I, in a long gown with a hundred yards of black (or: melancholia, passion)—:
> He cuts you from Yazid and he sews you upon Zayd,
> He makes you a companion of this and takes you from that other one—
> With this one he stitches you that you may put your heart (on him) through your whole life—
> Praised be the silk and the quilting, praised be the White Hand![58]

This means: man is like a piece of silk in the hand of this Eternal Tailor who stitches him with the unique and endless thread Love so that the needle—as much as its movement causes pain for the separated pieces—eventually grants the single pieces lovely union.[59] Man may also be compared to a doll on which the master has put artistic golden embroidery.[60]

Eventually, the lover recognizes the hand of the Great Weaver everywhere:

> That dark blue veil has a wind which makes it move—
> that is not the wind of air, but a wind which God knows.
> The cloak of grief and happiness—do you know who weaves it?
> And this cloak—how could it think itself separate from the Weaver?[61]

Who would not be reminded here of William Blake's lines:

Joy and grief are woven fine,
a clothing for the soul divine . . .

Man has to give himself completely into the hands of this great master, he has to tear the garment of thought, intention, speech, and self-will. His own willing and striving are comparable to the fragile and useless spider web:

> Like the spider, do no longer weave a circle from the saliva of thought,
> for the woof and warp are rotten.
> When you do not speak, He becomes your speech,
> When you do not weave, the Creator becomes the Weaver—[62]

a wonderful consolation: the spider web of human pursuits and plans will be replaced by the eternal masterpiece of the Weaver who knows how the final fabric will look at the end of time.

Nun, *and by the pen, and what they write . . .*

DIVINE CALLIGRAPHY

In his review of Mowlānā's *Mathnavi,* J. von Hammer-Purgstall remarked in 1851, when discussing verse 311 of Book V:

> dass Dschelalleddin Rumi inmitten seiner mystischen Begeisterung dem schlechten Geschmacke von Wort—und Buchstabenspiel huldigt. Ohr, Aug', Augenbraunen (sic!) und Maal werden mit den Buchstaben des Alphabetes verglichen, deren Figur den Leser an jene Schönheiten erinnert . . .[1]

It is astonishing that just this small passage, in which Rumi uses the traditional comparisons of the different letters with parts of the head, aroused Hammer's wrath against the poet's 'bad taste';—he could have easily found dozens of examples of this imagery in the *Mathnavi* and even more in the *Divān*.[2]

Rumi is only faithful to the Islamic tradition in which the letters of the alphabet were used, throughout the ages, for comparisons with things human and Divine. He also plays with the names of the master calligraphers, like Ibn al-Bawwāb,[3] or sees the lover's bent body as the *toghrā* at the beginning of the document (*manshur*) of love;[4] the long nights become ink for the lover who slowly matures in his longing.[5]

In general, Jalāloddin follows the inherited interpretation of single letters: *alef* a straight line which designates the long *ā* or, at the beginning of the word, any vowel, has always symbolized the slender figure of the beloved. At the same time, it was considered the ideal cypher for Divine Unity and Uniqueness, both owing to its form which does not accept any changes, and to its numerical value, 1.[6] The old Sufi idea that *alef* in its 'Divine' likeness is the only 'sincere' letter is alluded to by Rumi:

> Sometimes He makes you straight like an *alef,* sometimes crooked like the other letters . . .[7]

letters which were, according to Sufi lore, disobedient and therefore lost their beautiful original shape. *Alef* is the upright letter, resembling those who go to say *labbayka* 'At Thy Service' in the Divine presence.[8] It is thanks to its unity and sincerity that *alef* is the head of the alphabet; and the lover who emulates this model-letter by becoming endowed with the Divine attributes will be the first in line as well;[9] for *alef* is bare of all qualifications, stripped of attributes like the Divine Essence, and similar to the Sufi who has reached annihilation.[10]

Thanks to its grammatical peculiarities, *alef* becomes the symbol of the lover who annihilates himself in God—when one writes *besm* 'in the name of . . .' the *alef* of *esm* disappears between the *b* and the *s* and is both existent and non-existent, comparable to the person who experiences *fanā*' in the Divine Names and to whom the Divine word 'You did not cast when you cast' (Sura 8/17) is applicable,[11] e.g. who does no longer act by himself but exclusively through God.

Other interpretations of the *alef* are possible though less frequent. Its connection with the narrow-hearted *mim* produces for Rumi, the word *omm* 'mother' or 'basic substance', which induces him to a long deliberation about the meaning of these substances.[12] He sees the *alef* disappearing when it is united, in pronounciation and after certain particles, with the *lām* of the article,[13] as tyranny and darkness disappear when the sun rises.[14]

The ambiguity of Rumi's use of metaphors is demonstrated by comparing his verses about the letter *alef*: once he admonishes his reader to become an *alef* and to sit alone, upright and sincere,[15] whereas in another line he tells him not to be an *alef* which is stubborn, nor a two-headed *b,* but rather a *jim*[16] — this letter has, usually, no specific significance in mystical symbolism, if not as a symbol for the ear, or is thought to be related with *jamāl*, 'beauty' and *jām,* 'goblet', as once in Rumi's *Divān*.[17] One may also remember the line in which the poet speaks of the splitting of the moon at the hand of the Prophet and tells that an *alef*-like stature became like a *jim*.[18] That means: the power of Love, represented in the previous verse by the Prophet, produces changes even in the letters: through love, the crooked *d* can become a straight *alef,* just as the demons can become angels when they are lovestruck: without love, however, even the noble *alef* becomes bent like a *d*.[19]

On the whole, Rumi does not indulge as much in the symbolism of *alef,* as do most of the later Sufi poets — although he speaks of the necessity of giving up the alphabet as soon as one has finished school, he has rarely praised the *docta ignorantia* which consists of knowing the one letter *alef* to the exclusion of the whole alphabet — which means that to know God, the One, the Beloved, is enough.

The letter *d,* crooked and modest,[20] is once connected in a clever *tajnis,* with *del* 'heart'.[21] But in most cases Rumi uses it in a device of which Sanāʾi and other early poets had been very fond, i.e. the invention of a connection of the first letter of the word with the meaning of that very word. The poet can say, with a meaningful word-play, that man who turns to God in prayer, *doʿā*, should become bent like the letter *d* by which the word *doʿā* begins.[22]

The Western reader will certainly not appreciate the combination of the letter *sin, s* — usually connected due to its shape and name with the teeth — and the Sura Y*āsin* (Sura 36) of which the poor lover is reminded when thinking of the teeth of his Beloved,[23] for the Sura *Yāsin* is recited for the dying or the dead. Thus this combination, not unknown to other poets either, points to the overwhelming power of the Beloved who almost kills the lover when he opens the mouth to address him or to smile at him . . .

The letter *kāf,* rarely used in poetical language, becomes, with Rumi, a symbol for 'narrowness of the heart',[24] or lack of intelligence:[25] it is important to notice that the poet speaks in this context of the *kāf-e Kufi,* the *k* as written in the Kufic style where indeed this letter is generally represented by three horizontal lines between which almost no space is left. This *kāf-e kufi* was used mainly in the poetic imagery of earlier poets[26] who still knew examples of Kufic handwriting, which disappeared in the twelfth century.

In other cases, the narrow and helpless heart is connected with the bent and split figure of the *lām-alef.* But normally it is compared with the *mim, m,* the ringlet with a very narrow opening (usually used to symbolize the small mouth of the beloved):

> A heart like the heart of the little *mim,*
> a stature like the stature of a little *dāl*—[27]

that is the state of the lover, crushed under the burden of afflictions.

As for many other mystical poets, the letter *nun, n,* leads Rumi to Sura 68, *Nun, wa'l-qalam,* 'N, and By the Pen!' for, as he says in a beautiful verse:

> When you are in genuflexion like a *nun,* and in prostration like a pen,
> then you will be joined, like *Nun wa'l-qalam* with (the Divine word) 'And what they write' . . .[28]

E.g. when man is lost in constant prayer and adoration, he will become an instrument—a pen—which gives itself completely into God's hand, so that He may write with it His own words. And most fascinating is Rumi's image—which would fit in well with later practices of contemplating the letters of the word *Allāh*—about the letter *h*:

> In both worlds have I emptied my sides—
> Like a *h* I am sitting besides the *l* of *Allāh* . . .[29]

The different secret letters at the beginning of twenty-nine Suras of the Koran were a subject of meditation for many a mystic; Rumi, too, devotes to them several passages in the *Mathnavi.*[30] He sees in them the signs of Divine acticity, comparable to the rod of Moses which contained unknown powers. Even skillful plays on the name of the

Prophet—besides the generally accepted *ḥadith qodsi* 'I am Aḥmad without m, e.g. *Aḥad*, *"One"*'—can be found in his lyrics.[31]

As mentioned in connection with the *d*, Rumi likes to play with the meaningful first letter of a word: the *qāf-e qorbat*, well-known since Sanā'i, occurs in his poetry: *qāf*, representing both the first letter of the word *qorb* 'proximity', and the name of the world-embracing mountain-range, could serve the poets to express the closest possible proximity to God:

> And when the flight of your love does not find room in this world,
> fly towards the Qāf of proximity, for you are the Simorgh and 'Anqā.[32]

In similar combinations are mentioned the *kāf-e kofr* 'infidelity' (without any deeper meaning, however),[33] and the *ʿayn-e ʿaṭā*, the first letter or the 'essence' of 'generosity' into which all needs and wants will eventually turn.[34]

Rumi also follows another favourite play of Sanā'i, namely to enumerate the disjoined letters of a word and then to explain that the reader can not reach the true meaning from these bare, husklike letters. Has anyone ever plucked a *gol*, 'rose', from *g* and *l*?[35] And he addresses the Beloved in a charming verse:

> Wherever I go without you, I am a letter without meaning,
> I opened my two eyes like a *h*, and sat like a *sh* in Love (e.g. like the central letter of the word *'eshq*, "Love")
> Since I am a *h*, since I am a *sh*—why have I lost my reason (*hush*)?
> Because reason demands a combination (e.g. the word *hush* is generated by combining letters),—and I have cut myself from combination.[36]

The lover who has reached the perfect collectedness has left the world of combinations and compounds.

The most famous example of this kind of reasoning is in the letters *k* and *n*, which form the word *kun* 'be!' by means of which God created the world. The lover, separated from his original home, sighs:

> You ask me: 'How are you?'—Look, how I am:
> I am destroyed, out of myself, drunk and mad.
> He brought me into the noose by (the letters) *k* and *n*,
> and from that awe I am now twofold like *k* and *n*—[37]

that means, he has lost his primordial unity and lives in the twofold world of body and spirit, longing for the original unity. And the poet addresses his beloved in a charming line:

> You are the *q* of *qand* (sugarcandy) and I the *l* of the bitter lip
> From our *q* and *l* one can make (the word) *qul* 'Say!'[38]

Qul is the Divine address often repeated in the Koran: the lips of the beloved are so sweet and powerful that they almost convey a Divine message when united with the bitter lips of the lover . . .

In similar ways, Rumi puts together the word *shakkar*, 'sugar',[39] the name of Rostam,[40] *ᶜeshq*, 'love',[41] *moʾmen*, 'faithful',[42] the prayer-call *Rabbanā*, 'Our O Lord!',[43] and plays with the word *bot*, 'idol'.[44] He may even allude in an elegant *tajnis* to his own age: he would like to leave this body,

> for my life became sixty (*shast*), and I am like the *s* and the *sh* in this net (*shast*)—[45]

Life is a net knitted from letters to keep the fish which cannot escape.

The favourite pun of Persian poets, i.e. the connection of *khaṭṭ*, 'line, script, letter' with *khaṭṭ*, 'down' (on the cheeks of the young beloved) almost never occurs in Rumi's verses;[46] it is worth noticing that this kind of comparison was for him only a remnant of the inherited poetical tradition, but not a living image or meaningful symbol.

The alphabet, *abjad wa huṭi*, which is part of the education of every school child, should be discarded by the mature who are intoxicated in *samāᶜ* and love;[47] for in the school of the dervishes, this alphabet is not taught.[48] Even Mercury, the scribe-star, has broken his pen in intoxication and does no longer write the alphabet on his heavenly tablet, as the poet emphatically asserts.[49]

Letters are but outward signs and do not reach reality;—the blind men who tried to give their impression of the elephant, partly described the animal as an *alef*, partly as a *dāl*, according to the part their hands had touched.[50]

Rumi wrote a number of letters to Shamsoddin after he had disappeared for the first time, and the complaints of the lover who never gets a reply fill his poetry.[51] It is certainly not his invention to compare his tears to letters written on the yellow face with red ink; this image—indicative of the lover's state—is much older.[52] When the beloved writes a document (*manshur*) about separation, the *toghrā* weeps blood[53] (for the head piece of a document was sometimes calligraphed in coloured ink). Finally the poet understands:

When I write a letter towards the friend,
He is paper and reedpen and inkpot . . .[54]

The pangs of separation exist not longer: everything has been transformed into the Beloved.

The script on paper becomes the symbol of human or Divine activity: the little ants admire the flowerlike beauty of the letters until they discover, step by step, that the letters exist neither by themselves, nor through the hand or the arm, but are caused by man's mental activity.[55]

The purified heart of the Sufi is compared to white paper on which the eternal designs of destiny are written[56]—for God can write only on pure white paper.[57] Man's face is likewise marked by the dots of love, which only lovers can read.[58] But the comparison of the lines on the face with the letters of destiny, *sarnevisht,* 'what is written on the forehead' does not occur in Rumi's verses.

Man's heart is like paper; but it is also like the pen which is turned in God's hand. The famous *ḥadith* that man is between two fingers of the Merciful Who turns him as He pleases[59] provided a good starting point for numerous verses about man's following the movements of God's finger.

My heart is like the pen in the fingers of the Beloved
who writes tonight a *z,* tomorrow a *r.*
He cuts the pen for *req*ʿ*a* and *naskh* and other scripts:
The pen says 'Greetings!'—you know where I am![60]

The comparison with the pen enables the poets to insert hints at the lover's suffering: the beloved splits the pen's head as is required for correct writing,[61] and the lover runs with cut-off tongue and head, making his head a foot, like the pen.[62] He then puts his head on the script of His order, or dances headless on the paper[63] (no doubt an allusion to Ḥallāj's fate!).

God is the great calligrapher—and the rank and ability of a pen depends upon the rank of the writer!—;[64] human beings are as different as the letters between *alef* and *yā*:[65] He can produce whatever form He wants; can unite the letters and separate them again[66] (just as His pen can draw now a leopard, now a mouse)[67]—but eventually they will return into the undivided unity, the 'eternal inkpot', as a Persian-writing mystic called this state one century after Rumi.[68]

A peculiar combination, which was probably invented by Rumi but imitated by many later poets, is that of the reed pen with the reed flute in the hand of the Beloved: the pen writes strange images and words, and animated by His breath, the flute sings and irritates the poor intellect.[69] Both of them are hollow, empty-stomached (for otherwise they would be unable to tell the secrets of love);[70] both are filled with sweetness thanks to the breath of the Friend (hence the cross-relation with the sugarcane). And, as later poets would continue with an allusion to Rumi's first verses in the *Mathnavi*, both are able to cast the fire of love into the world.

The lover knows that 'the image of Shamsoddin was drawn in the books of love in pre-eternity',[71] and although he possesses a whole library of wants which the Beloved is supposed to read,[72] he cleans the tablet of his heart of all the letters of the alphabet—even the letters of creation, *k* and *n*, should be washed off by him who concentrates upon the mole of the Beloved.[73] For letters are like thorns in front of those who have reached union.[74] The 'splendour of the cupbearer's forehead' intoxicates the mystics so that he breaks the pen,[75] and every pen is bound to break once it reaches the word 'Love' . . .[76]

The present life is naught but a sport and a diversion . . .

PASTIMES OF THE GREAT

Persian poets were always fond of images taken from the pastimes of the ruling classes. Since Persian poetry is basically connected with court life, its authors had to provide themselves with a sufficient knowledge of the terminology of chess, *nard* (backgammon) and other games in which the grandees indulged. The mystics willingly took over this imagery—was not the whole arena of life a big game in which the Divine Beloved played with His creatures?

Many mystics have used the shadow-play as an excellent

model of life. Rumi, however, does not follow ʿAṭṭār or Ibn al-Fāreḍ's example but only once or twice mentions the puppets and the screen without, however, entering into detailed descriptions as did his predecessors and, even more, later mystics.[1] On the other hand, allusions taken from chess and polo abound in his lyrics; less frequently similes taken from *nard* occur. This latter game provided the mystics with a fine image of the world and man's closed situation, e.g. the *shashdara* 'six doors', the player's most hopeless situation in *nard*—the world, made of the six directions, resembles a closed cube, and keeps the hearts and souls of human beings imprisoned, as if man were indeed in a *shashdara.*[2] But there is still hope:

> If the door becomes closed in the six-doored monastery,
> that moon-faced one shows his head from No-Place in my window—[3]

the Divine beloved can pierce the closed wall of created things and bring the lover to a luckier position in his life's game. The sunlike beloved is also the player himself: when he casts the dice on the plate of heaven, all the stars will be checkmated[4]—when Shams appears, every thing else in heaven and earth vanishes before the eyes of the lover. His is the *mohra-ye mehr,* the 'die of lovingkindness' or 'of the sun'.[5] Besides many scattered allusions to the *shashdara* and the rescue from this station, Rumi devotes a whole lovely ghazal to his state of mind after having played *nard* the whole night with his beloved: it was the *nard* of the heart which has been going on and has made the lover pale . . .[6]

Chess is more prominent in Rumi's poetry. The imagery was well elaborated long since—to think only of Khāqāni's artistic combination of six technical terms from chess in one single verse of his *Madāʾin-qaṣida.* This predilection for the chess imagery can be easily explained not only from the fondness of the Persians for this game, but even more from the ambiguity which could be produced by using chess-terminology in different connotations. Thus the Persian word for 'tower/rook', *rokh,* means literally 'cheek', and the checkmate, *shāh māt* 'the king is dead' is exactly the state for which the lover longs: the radiant cheek of the beloved can easily cause the heart to become checkmate.

When you have seen the *cheek* of the *Shāh*, go out of your house like the *pawn* (footman),
When you have seen the sun, then disappear like stars![7]

On the *leather*, I am *afoot*, I do not need a *horse*,
I am *killed* by Thee, O *Shāh*, put Thy *cheek* on my *cheek*![8]

The changes in the evaluation of figures brought forth by the King's approach are signs of spiritual transformation:

When the *Shāh* showed his *cheek*, the *horse* became the companion of the *elephant*,
The poor intellect became *checkmate*, and the soul ?? and *died*.[9]

Rumi compares himself to the Shah:

Though we are kings, for your sake we put our *cheeks* straight, so that we, on this *leather*, become more intelligent *(farzāna)* than your *queen (farzin)*.[10]

The movable *farzin*, 'queen' is several times connected with intelligent *(farzāna)* movement owing to the similarity of the two words,[11] or else blamed as the figure with crooked ways.[12]

Whatever different images Rumi has taken from the chess game, his goal is always the same: to become *māt* thanks to the cheeks of the king, to become annihilated thanks to the radiance of the Divine Beloved. Rumi has devoted a long ghazal to chess, completely filled with mystical allusions and worthy of a detailed analysis.[13] It may be mentioned at random that in later times chess, and similar games, were played by some mystics who saw in them models of life and of the progress on the mystical path—Nāṣir ʿAndalib of Delhi has composed, in the eighteenth century, a whole book on spiritual chess to teach his disciples the stations, pitfalls, and means to progress on the Path,[14] just as the Neʿmatallāhi dervishes in Iran still use a similar game.[15] Rumi certainly did not dream of inventing such games; yet, he knew how well the chess imagery suited his purposes.

We have not seen any chess, and yet are *māt*,
we have not drunk a single sip, and yet are drunk . . .[16]

The imagery taken from chess involves the movement of the figures and their constant progress and thus corresponds to a comparatively regular and regulated journey in mystical experience until the moment of checkmate overwhelms the figure. Another favourite pastime of the grandees offered the poet the opportunity of showing himself as completely helpless, left to the mercy of his beloved: this is polo. Rumi describes the game in *Fihi mā fihi* to explain the secrets of the mystical concert and dance which, like the polo play, are the mere astrolabe of an interior movement and a certain intention:

> Kings play with the polo-stick in the *maydān,* to show the inhabitants of the city who cannot be present at the battle and the fighting a representation of the sallying forth of the champions and the cutting off of the enemies' heads, and their rolling about just as the balls roll in the *maydān,* and their frontal charge and attack and retreat. This play in the *maydān* is as the astrolabe for the serious business in the fighting. In like manner, with the people of God, prayer and spiritual concerts are a manner of showing the spectators how in secret they accord with God's commandments and forbiddings special to them . . .[17]

Images taken from polo were first used by Persian panegyrists to show their patrons their complete submission and dependence (Goethe has therefore pronounced a negative judgment about this image in his *Noten und Abhandlungen zum West-Oestlichen Divan*!).[18] As for the mystics, they regarded the polo-ball as a perfect example of the lover who, without hands and feet rolls in the hook of the friend's polostick.[19] This polostick was usually, in the tradition of court- and erotic poetry, equivalent with the curved black tresses of the beloved. Rumi uses this combination comparatively rarely; for him the aspect of absolute submission to the beloved is paramount:

> We are your ball with turning head in the convexity of your polostick,
> sometimes you call us towards joy, sometimes you drive us towards affliction.[20]

The ball 'heart' is never lost sight of in the desert;[21] it dances in the polostick under the rider's blows although it suffers. But by doing so it becomes the first *(sābeq)* in the arena, and is the goal of every player.[22] The ball suffers all these afflictions gladly since the rider looks at it—as long as this is the case, it will follow the movements of his stick,[23] running in the playground of bewilderment:[24] the lover happily dances, without head and feet, under the strokes of affliction in which he feels the hand of his Beloved, and is sure that the friend's eye rests upon him and knows where to drive him.

The imagery of the cut-off head rolling on the sand, which usually shocks those who begin their study of Rumi with the first poem in R.A. Nicholson's selections from the *Divān-e Shams,*[25] is only part of this large field of polo imagery which so superbly expresses the mystic's loving submission to all the blows coming from the Beloved, the Royal Rider who has trained the horse 'soul' and acts as representative of God.

> *We have indeed turned about for men in this Koran every manner of similitude . . .*

KORANIC IMAGERY

> The Koran is a double-sided brocade, some enjoy the one side, and some the other. Both are true, inasmuch God most High desires that both people should derive benefit from it . . .[1]

Indeed, Rumi's work can largely be explained from the Koran.

> Ask the meaning of the Koran from the Koran alone, and from that one has set fire to his idle fancy,
> and has become a sacrifice to the Koran and is (laid) low (in self abasement) so that the Koran has become the essence of his spirit.
> The oil that has wholly devoted itself to the rose—smell either the oil or the rose as you please![2]

As a good thirteenth century Muslim our mystical poet stands completely and wholeheartedly in the Islamic tradition, and it is small wonder that he has inserted innumerable words and sentences from or allusions to the Holy Book into both his lyrics and his *Mathnavi,* quoting them partly in their Arabic original, partly in Persian version. Did not his son Ṣolṭān Valad attest:

> The poetry of God's friends is all explanation and secrets of the Koran, for they are annihilated from themselves and exist through God—[3]

as if he were paraphrasing Rumi's just quoted verses?

Mowlānā uses the Koran in theological discussions as well as in verses which sound like sheer love-poetry. A close examination of his work would certainly yield even more Koranic allusions than can be detected in the registers and during a cursory reading of the *Mathnavi*. Even a simple Arabic expression which can easily be overlooked by the general reader may remind the initiated of a whole sentence in the Holy Book. Rumi has not the slightest difficulty writing a whole ghazal in which the second hemistich of each verse consists of Koranic quotations most ingeniously wrought together, and combined with Prophetic traditions.[4]

There was no doubt for Jalāloddin that the Koran was the perfect and final Divine revelation:

> Although the Koran is from the Prophet's lips—yet who says 'God did not say it!' is an infidel![5]

But only rarely does he utter opinion about theological problems, like that of the abolished verses *(mansukh);*

> Every law He abolished—
> He took away grass and brought a rose as substitute.[6]

Rumi, like every mystic and poet, had his favourite verses in the Koran which he loved to insert into his poetry to the exclusion of others. But even Koranic sentences rarely quoted by other poets can be found in his verses. That the Light-verse (Sura 24/35), the allusions to the pre-eternal Covenant (Sura 7/171) and verses which point to the marvellous qualities of the Prophets, as well as those which indicate God's creative power are particularly frequently cited, goes without saying; one of the favourite verses of later mystics, however—

> Whithersoever ye turn your face, there is God's face—(Sura 2/109)

occurs surprisingly rarely in his work. The Throne-verse (Sura 2/256) to which Muslim piety attributes so many wonderful qualities makes him exclaim:

> We have flown with the Throne-verse towards the Divine Throne,
> so that we saw the Living, and reached the Self-Subsistent—[7]

These two attributes of God, *al-ḥayy al-qayyum,* described in the Throne-verse are mentioned time and again in his work.

Rumi, like other Persian mystics, knows how to play with the Koranic sentences, and changes them to attain, now and then, surprising results—thus he describes (in words taken from Sura 69/25) the state of man who is given two books of actions—not only at Doomsday but already here on earth, for he carries

> the book of sensual feeling in the left hand, the book of reason in the right hand,[8]

and has now to choose between the two lest the wrong book be given into his hands on the Day of Judgment.

Jalāloddin, like other Persian and Turkish writers, compares the perfectly beautiful face of the beloved to a masterfully calligraphed copy of the Koran; it is a manuscript from which he reads 'the *surat al-qeṣaṣ* and rare verses'.[9] For the friend's beauty is as flawless as a Koran copy has to be, and, exactly as the Holy Book reveals Divine wisdom and power, the beautiful face reveals God's beauty and creative power; it is, indeed, a Koran for those who know how to contemplate God's wisdom in its lines.

In a less usual image, love is described as an exquisite Koran which the poet reads in his dreams so that he, eventually, becomes demented from enthusiasm. He also speaks of the Koran-copy of madness out of which he had read a verse so that his knowledge and his art as Koran-reader became abolished.[10] And in a lovely verse he calls the beloved to look at him, for:

> I am a faulty *(bāṭel)* copy, but
> I'll be corrected when you recite me.[11]

For the Beloved overlooks the faults which spoil man, once honoured more than the angels; he corrects him by accepting him as he is.

Every Muslim poet and writer had utilized as symbols the personalities mentioned in the Koran—here, again, Rumi follows the traditional pattern. These figures are, in Islamic lore, a sort of counterpart to the heroes of Greece and Rome in Western literatures, transformed into half-mythological beings whose stories are retold throughout the centuries and appear in different guises. To assume such a role was all the easier for these personalities since the Koran had indeed stressed the exemplary role of the various prophets who prefigure the Prophet of Islam whose behavior sets the ideal pattern for every Muslim's way of life. Rumi could, therefore, easily interpret them in the inherited way; but they become, for him, more or less identical with the Beloved ,or else teach the faithful in ever changing images complete surrender into the hand of his Lord and Beloved. That is why the imagery inspired by the Koranic figures is comparatively uniform and even slightly monotonous in Rumi's verses, although allusions to the prophets and the events connected with them abound in his poetry. Suffice it to mention the stories of Noah and Moses, of Solomon and Jesus as told in the *Mathnavi*.

These spiritual heroes have performed hundreds of thousands of miracles, beyond human understanding, without intermediate secondary causes, as pure instruments of God; for if the capacity were the condition for God's acting, nothing non-existent would come into being.[12] They reveal the creative power of God in every moment of their lives. We may restrict ourselves here to enumerating only.a few less common comparisons with Koranic figures in Rumi's works.

Noah's ark, the saving vessel in the flood, is still a veil when the wave of ecstasy carries away man's body and drowns him completely in the abysses of the Divine Ocean.[13]

Ibrāhim Khalil, the 'friend of God' is the true Muslim who 'does not love those who set' (Sura 6/76). He is usually mentioned in connection with the story of Nimrod's casting him into the blazing pyre—but the fire became 'cool and pleasant' for him (Sura 21/69): the lover experiences the fire which is meant to destroy him as a rose-garden[14] which he does not want to leave.[15] This traditional motif of Persian poetry fits very well into the 'fiery' imagery of Rumi, who sees love as a consuming fire which frightens those who do not completely rely upon their Lord. —Rumi also mentioned Abraham's sacrifice of the 'fat calf' in honour of his angelic guests (Sura 11/69) in a few places.[16]

A poet fond of music and poetry must find the figures of David and Solomon particularly attractive: Rumi compares himself to David who addresses the birds (a motif essentially connected with Solomon), singing his ghazals as though they were a psalter.[17] The legend that David gained his livelihood by producing iron coats of mail is applied to a pleasant spring-description:

The face of water which was in winter like iron has become, through the wind, coats of mail—
The new spring is perhaps the David of our time, weaving coats of mail from iron.[18]

I.e. the frozen water is again dissolved into little ringlets which constantly move like a coat of mail (a comparison used by earlier poets as well but, as far as I can see, not in connection with the Prophet David).

The relation of King Solomon with fairies, genies and demons, his dealing with the ants, his miraculous seal, offered many images to all poets. Love can be equated with Solomon, the ruler of everything animated, or else love of God is Solomon's seal which holds everything under its spell;[19] the mystical dance is his army which scars away the little dark ants, models of earthbound humans.[20] For the vulgar cannot stand the victorious army of the *samāʿ*; they run away, hiding themselves from the spell of the Solomon Love. Solomon is often the spiritual king to whom the hoopoe soul returns, full of happiness;[21] the story of Belqis, the Queen of Sheba, though told in the *Mathnavi* at some length,[22] is rarely alluded to in the lyrics. One of the famous stories of Oriental lore is again applied to Solomon to prove the inevitability of human planning and scheming:

At morn, to Solomon in his hall of justice
A noble suitor came, running in haste,
His countenance pale with anguish, his lips blue.
'What ails thee, Khwaja?' asked the King.
Then he: ''twas Azrael—ah, such a look he cast
On me of rage and vengeance.'—'Come now, ask
What boon thoü wilt.'—'Protector of our lives,
I pray thee, bid the wind convey me straight
To Hindustan: thy servant, there arrived,
Shall peradventure save his soul from Death.'

Solomon bade the Wind transport him swiftly
Over the sea to farthest Hindustan.
On the morrow, when the King in audience sat,
He said to Azrael: 'Wherefore didst thou look
Upon that Musulman so wrathfully
His home know him no more?'—'Nay, not in wrath',
Replied the Angel, 'did I look on him;
But seeing him pass by, I stared in wonder,
For God had bidden me take his soul that day
In Hindustan. I stood there marvelling.

Methought, even if he had a hundred wings,
'Twere far for him to fly to Hindustan . . .[23]

The suffering of the Prophets, repeatedly mentioned in the Koran with the purpose of strengthening Moḥammad in the afflictions he had to undergo is, of course, meant as a pattern for the mystic's life as well. Does not the *ḥadith* attest:

Those who are afflicted most are the prophets, then the saints, then the others and the others.[24]

Job is patient in suffering; longing for Joseph, the paragon of beauty, Jacob became blind from grief and was miraculously healed by the scent of his son's shirt—thus, the lover's soul will be healed when the fragrance of the beloved, the breeze of the Merciful, comes and opens his eyes to behold the everlasting spiritual beauty. Jonah, imprisoned in the whale, was rescued after praising his Lord even in the darkness of his living dungeon: that is a theme often varied by Rumi, for the lover feels at times like Jonah, at other times like Joseph in the depth of the well.[25]

Contrary to ʿAṭṭār, and even more to later mystics, stories about these suffering prophets only rarely serve Rumi to express some feeling of revolt against God.[26] He does not ask why God afflicts his friends but sees the triumphant end: He made a comfortable cell for Jonah in the fish, and He eventually took Joseph out of the well.[27] What is important for him is the Divine act of rescuing grace which works only on those who live in the deepest despair, in 'non-existence'. Suffering, being broken, is nothing but a prerequisite for greater joy, and in the heart of darkness the 'Sun at Midnight' will radiantly reveal itself. The fate of Joseph, representative of the soul, will certainly end positively:

Which ewer went down and did not come back filled?
Why should one lament about the Joseph 'Soul'?[28]

Death, going down into the 'well of the tomb', is indicative of the soul's future return in a more glorious state, since Joseph, after patiently enduring his tribulations, was blessed with happiness and reached the highest office in Egypt.[29] When the faithful persevere in their way towards Divine Glory, they will experience the same.

Joseph is not only the prototype of the soul but more often

the model of Divine Beauty. Just as the women at Zolaykha's banquet cut their hands unwittingly when gazing at his bewildering beauty, the soul is unaware of any pain when looking at the Divine Beloved. Zolaykha had become rejuvenated thanks to Joseph—thus the old world will also find new youth from this radiant star.[30] In his quality as Beloved, Joseph is the 'true food' for those suffering from dearth; they will not run after bread and water, for he gives them spiritual nourishment[31] (as he gave nourishment to the famine struck people). And as interpreter of dreams, he personifies another aspect of the Perfect Man, e.g. the beloved who understands the mysterious working of Divine power in this dreamlike world and tries to explain it to his followers.[32]

There are few allusions to Benjamin in Rumi's lyrics.[33] further to Harut and Marut, the disobedient angels, and to many other Koranic figures. The rebellious tribes of ᶜAd and Thamud represent wordly interests:

> We do not decorate with stalactites the castle and the four porticoes on this field of annihilation like ᶜAd and Thamud.[34]

Most of Rumi's images in this area, however, are inspired by the Koranic stories about Moses and Jesus. Moses' experience with the Burning Bush—when Mount Sinai was agitated into an ecstatic dance—is a central topic for him, since:

> Everything is rose, even though its exterior is like thorns,
> The light appeared from the bush of Moses like fire.[35]

The Divine Light hides itself in the form of fire—Divine Mercy conceals itself under the guise of wrath.[36] But Moses—the soul—should know that once he enters the Most Holy, everything is sheer beauty and loveliness:

> O Moses 'soul', put off your two shoes (Sura 20/12)
> For in the rose garden of the soul there are no thorns![37]

Rumi's favourite story from the Moses-tradition is that of his miraculous rod which was turned into a serpent. Shams, called the Moses of his time, is the prototype of the Beloved in whose hand the lover is like the rod—sometimes a support for people, sometimes a wild dragon;[38] he applies the tradition that 'the faithful is between two of God's fingers' to the Moses-image: the faithful and lover is one moment a rod, the next moment a serpent.[39] But he may also say in a slightly lighter variation that the stick 'separation from the friend' resembles the rod of Moses which brings water out of stones, namely ,out of the lover's eyes . . .[40]

The figure of Khiżr occurs—at least expressis verbis—not as frequently as one would expect although—or perhaps because?—Legend tells that Rumi used to talk to Khiżr and was instructed by this hidden guide of the faithful, this model of saintliness.[41]

Both the Jewish and the Christian community of Konya were very fond of Rumi and regarded him as 'their Moses and their Jesus'. Konya, the ancient Iconium, had been the scene of Christian life since the first abortive attempts of St. Paul at converting its inhabitants (Acts 14); it later became a Christian town, probably influenced by its proximity to Cappadocia, the stronghold of medieval monastic Christianity and native place of some of the greatest of the mystically inclined early Christian theologians (Gregory of Nyssa, Gregory of Nazians, St. Basil the Great etc.) The cave monasteries of Göreme were inhabited till the late Middle Ages. Small Greek settlements with their churches were flourishing in the neighbourhood of Konya till the end of World War I. Rumi certainly availed himself of the opportunity of talking to the numerous priests and monks living in the area. In fact, in reading his poetry one gets the impression that he was not only acquainted with the image of Jesus and Mary as depicted in the Koran (an image which has inspired thousands of Muslim writers to compose tender and graceful verses), but had also at least some knowledge of the biblical tradition. One may even surmise that he might have taken some of his unusual images from popular religious songs—but this problem needs further elucidation. Whether the mentioning of the ox and donkey in Jesus' company alludes to the nativity, seems doubtful;[42] but Rumi translates Matthew 5/49 in the last line of a poem in which he had earlier confronted the Christian grape-wine and the Islamic Mansuri-wine:

> When you get one blow on your cheek, go and seek another blow—
> What does Rostam do in the battle-row with a handful of roses and wild roses?[43]

'Doubtful thought', *gomān,* is called *tarsā,* e.g. 'Christian' and 'afraid' because the true believer does not think that he has put his messiah on the cross (cf. Sura 4/151).[44]

The imagery inspired by Jesus generally centres around three subjects: the first one being Jesus who left his donkey behind him and went to heaven (cf. Ch. II 4). This was an appropriate symbol to express the relation of body and soul:

> When Jesus was freed from his donkey, his prayer was heard:
> Wash your hands, for table and food arrived from heaven! (Sura 5/112, 114).[45]

Jesus was granted heavenly food which nourishes the soul, as the Koran attests. Jesus' life-bestowing breath is compared to the kiss of the beloved by Rumi as often as by other Persian, Turkish, and Urdu poets.

> When he asks you about the messiah, how he quickened the dead,
> give in his presence a kiss on our lips: 'Thus!'[46]

Such light and sweet sounds are rare in Rumi's poetry, and the reader enjoys them all the more. Jesus makes the blind see and the deaf hear, and by his breath induces them into mystical dance.[47]

The lover is like a bird of clay which is made alive by Jesus' breath (Sura 5/110):

> As much as you blow into me, that much do I fly upwards.[48]

He is the kind physician of the soul, and Moses the shepherd:[49] Jesus does not leave anyone blind from birth but cures him, and the sea does not leave any way closed for Moses.[50]

Jesus constantly smiles firmly trusting in God's mercy, whereas his friend John the Baptist is sinister, fearing the wrath of God:

> John said to Jesus: 'You have become exceedingly secure against the subtle deceits, that you laugh so much!' Jesus replied: 'You have become exceedingly unmindful of the subtle and mysterious and wonderful graces and lovingkindnesses of God, that you weep so much.'—One of God's saints was present at this incident. He asked God: 'Which of these two has the higher station?' God answered: 'He who thinks better of Me . . .'[51]

Since the beloved is Jesus, idle thought is comparable to the Jews who molested him [52] (for the Jews left manna and quails and chose instead onions and leeks and thus resemble the uninitiated).[53]

But when Rumi's beloved is represented praising himself as Jesus, he underlines at the same time that he, whose sweet smile had enlivened the whole world, is not related to any Mary, but only to God:[54] his is the immediate experience of unity with God, without any human medium in between. And the lover addresses him in terms which, if understood by the Muslim orthodox scholars of Konya in their real theological implications, might have proved dangerous for Rumi:

> Show the pre-eternal Divine nature (*lahut*) through your human nature (*nāsut*)![55]

Sometimes Jalāloddin alludes to the old Sufi legend underscoring the absolute necessity of freedom from anything worldly, i.e. the story according to which Jesus took with him one needle. This apparently innocent act proved that he had not yet attained absolute poverty and perfect trust in God so that he was placed only in the fourth heaven, not in the immediate Divine presence . . .[56] For the saint, one needle from 'the world' is as dangerous as the whole treasure of Qārun.

Jesus is, in most of Rumi's verses, the symbol of man's soul which lives in the bodily form like a Divine child in the cradle;[57] the body is also comparable to Mary.

> Every one of us has a Jesus within him, but until the pangs manifest in us our Jesus is never born. If the pangs never come, then Jesus rejoins his origin by the same secret path by which he came leaving us bereft and without portion of him.[58]

How close are these lines to the words of Rumi's younger German contemporary, Meister Eckhart, about the birth of Christ in the soul!

From ideas like this, the paramount importance of Mary in Rumi's work becomes clear. The veneration of the Virgin pregnant from the Holy Spirit belongs to the essentials of Islam. It was, and still is, particularly popular in Turkey. Mary is the soul who, in silence[59] accepts her fate, the inspiration from God. The lovers' soul is 'light upon light' (Sura 24/35) like Mary the beautiful who carried Jesus in her womb,[60] for the Divine light makes the mystic spiritually pregnant like her.[61] Her patience and trust were recompensed again by Divine grace, when the dried-up palm-tree showered dates upon her: thus, the grieved soul, smarting under the pangs of spiritual birth, finds the fresh fruits of grace.[62] (Sura 19/25).

Rumi loves to compare the garden in spring to Mary: the warm gentle breeze acts like the Holy Ghost so that the virgin branches become pregnant, producing blossoms, leaves and eventually fruits out of the unseen.[63] The chapter about the annuncation as told in the *Mathnavi*[64] belongs to the tenderest and most poetical versions of this story, and could easily form part of a medieval Christian book of devotions. Here Muslim and Christian legend and mystical interpretation are woven, by the art of a great poet, into a wonderful unit.

One should not overlook, however, that slightly negative judgments and remarks about Christianity and especially about the church are not lacking in Rumi's work—what should Jesus do with the church, since he went to the fourth heaven?[65] Rumi who had told the story of the confusion of the Christian sects in the very first book of the *Mathnavi*[66] contrasts Islam, the religion of war and glory, with the religion of Jesus, in which cave and mountain, e.g. monastic life, are desirable.[67] The long winded superficial talk of the Arabs when they speak of pastures and forsaken remnants of former resting places reminds him of that of a Christian who confesses before the priest all the sins of one year in one long deceitful talk . . .[68] And Rumi connects the cross with a refusal of the world of matter which is distinct from God:

> Far be the portico of joy from fire and water and dust and wind!
> The composition of the true confessors of unity be as far away from these four simple (elements) as from the cross![69]

The true believer who has realized the Divine unity is no longer bound to the four elements which constitute the material, composed and hence perishable world; he has become part of the spiritual world which cannot be represented under the symbol of the cross.

That is a nation that hath passed away . . .

IMAGERY TAKEN FROM HISTORY AND GEOGRAPHY

Rumi's poetry, like that of other writers of his time, contains quite a number of allusions to figures from Islamic History, and it is revealing to notice which personalities he selects out of the long historical tradition of the Muslims, and for which poetical purposes they serve him.

There are, in the first line, the *kholafā-ye rāshidun,* the first four righteous caliphs,[1] beginning with Abu Bakr aṣ-Ṣiddiq, Rumi's alleged ancestor, the 'seal of loyalty'[2] or 'the friend in the cave', *yār-e ghār,* who spent the night with the Prophet in the cave on their way from Mecca to Medina where they were miraculously protected by God. Abu Bakr's relation to the Prophet can therefore prefigure that of Rumi and his Beloved with whom he lives 'in one cave', far away from the people, in intimate spiritual communion.[3]

> If you are not a Fāruq (e.g. 'Omar al-Fārūq)—how could you be saved from separation (*ferāq*)?
> If you are not a *ṣiddiq*—how could you become a friend in the cave?[4]

'Omar ibn al-Khattāb is the hero of war, the model of justice,[5] the faithful servant of the Prophet.[6] Alluding to a *ḥadith,* Rumi compares the overwhelming beloved to this powerful caliph:

> Intellect and soul flee due to the majesty of this ruler, like the demon who fled from ʿOmar al-Khattāb'.[7]

The days come and go, just as the caliphs succeeded each other:

> As yesterday went, today is still here,
> when ʿOmar went away, ʿOthmān came in.[8]

Rumi knew that the Shia, though at his time not yet the official religion of Iran, hated the first three caliphs, to the extent of even avoiding the company of any person bearing the names Abu Bakr, ʿOmar, or ʿOthmān. The impossibility of finding a man named Abu Bakr in a Shia environment is told in a most lively story in the *Mathnavi*:[9] 'more longely and lost than an Abu Bakr in Sabzvār' is indeed the state of utter destitution, the state of the spiritual man in this world of matter, whence he is rescued by the spiritual ruler and beloved, represented in our story by the Khwarezmshah, the king under whose rule Jalāloddin himself was born. But when love comes,

> even the extreme Shiite (*rāfezi*) becomes confused, biting his finger in amazement: ʿAli and ʿOmar are mixed up![10]

ʿAli Ḥeydar is the hero of innumerable Islamic tales in both Sunni and Shia environment. It is he who opens the doors of the fortress Kheybar by his mysterious power,[11] that means, he is the veritable 'lion of God' who breaks through the outward forms and reaches spiritual freedom.[12] His sword is *ẕu'l-feqār,* the two-edged weapon which, by its very name, is connected with *faqr,* 'spiritual poverty'[13] (at least in Rumi's imaginative etymology). Is not the human soul comparable to this divinely blessed sword to which the body serves as a mere scabbard? Why, then, should man grieve, when the scabbard is broken?[14]

Or else, the lovers are the *ẕu'l-feqār* that lies in the hand of love,[15] and the poet kills grief by it when he comes out of the forest of the soul like (the spiritual lion) Ḥeydar-e karrār.[16] By its very shape *ẕu'l-feqār* resembles the word *lā*, 'No', the first word of the profession of faith; that means that it cuts everything besides God. In dramatic verses Rumi describes the holy war when the drum is beaten and the soul takes *Ẕu'l-feq*ār from its scabbard to conquer the eternal kingdom of Love.[17]

ʿAli is often—and this, again, is not a novel invention—combined with the greatest hero of Persian tradition, with Rostam: both of them symbolize the superman who leads the spiritual warfare and conquers this world.

The tragedy of Karbala in 680 during which ʿAli's cadet son Ḥoseyn and his family were killed, is mentioned in Rumi's verses as well as the image of utmost grief (just as the expression *shām-e gharibān* which was later used for the mourning-session on the eve of the tenth of Moḥarram, became, since Ḥāfeẓ, an expressive symbol for the forsaken lover's mood):

> The night died, and became alive—there is life beyond the death!
> O grief, kill me, I am Ḥoseyn, and you are my Yazid![18]

To be sure, the heart is like the martyred Ḥoseyn, slain by the cruel Yazid 'Separation' and martyred two hundred times in the desert of pressing *karab,* and affliction, *balā,* as Rumi says with an ingenious wrong etymology of Karbala.[19] Since Ḥoseyn is the model of the martyred lover[20] he is at times, mainly in later poetry, mentioned along with his namesake, Ḥoseyn ibn Manṣur al-Ḥallāj, the martyr-mystic.

The different factions of early Islam occur now and then in Rumi's imagery. To express the uselessness of speaking to the uninitiated, he says:

> How could I speak to the Rafeżis about the Bani Qoḥāfa?
> How could I tell the Kharijites my grief of Abu Torāb?[21]

For it was a Kharijite who assassinated ᶜAli, surnamed Abu Torāb. ᶜAbbās, the ancestor of the Abbasid dynasty is mentioned in some stories,[22] but out of the figures of early Islam—among them the Prophet's black moezzin, Belāl—,[23] Jalāloddin shows a predilection for two, e.g. Abu Horeyra and Jaᶜfar aṭ-Ṭayyār.

> Abu Bakr pawned his head, ᶜOmar pawned his son,
> ᶜOthmān pawned his liver, and that Abu Horeyra his bag.[24]

Every early companion was willing to give away what was dearest to him—and Abu Horeyra had this mysterious bag in which one finds whatever one wishes. Jalāloddin apparently loved this bag which was mentioned by Sanāʾi as well, and the name of the 'kitten-father' Abu Horeyra never occurs in his verses without this bag.[25]

A whole ghazel confronts Abu Horeyra, the faithful companion of the Prophet, and Abu Lahab, the 'father of the flame',[26] Moḥammad's arch-enemy who has become the paragon of evil, deprived of the fire of love. In an ingenious verse Rumi tells how happy he was once, but then

> the Abu Lahab 'Grief' bound my neck with a rope of straw.[7]

The connection with Sura 111 which describes the future fate of Abu Lahab and his wife in Hell, fettered with a rope of straw, well describes the poet's miserable state of mind at this very moment. As to Jaᶜfar aṭ-Ṭayyār, he was a cousin of the Prophet who excelled in bravery and was killed in 630: his hands and feet were cut off, and he flew to Paradise, as legend tells. His surname 'The Flying' may have contributed to characterizing him as a model for those who fly through the strength of love and surrender, even though outwardly broken and crippled.[28]

Ḥamza, the Prophet's uncle and one of the heroes of the early Islamic wars, represents, now and then, the beloved in his manifestation as hero.[29] He was to become, in later times, the subject of an extended romance cycle which was often decorated with large size paintings in India.[30] — On the other hand Rumi mentions Ḥātem aṭ-Ṭā'i, the pre-Islamic model of hospitality and generosity,[31] as comparable to the beloved in his manifestation as generous host; or else the lover can even surpass Ḥatem by generously giving his soul to the guest of his heart, to the beloved.[32]

Some personalities of early Islamic centuries have become subjects of longish tales which Rumi knew from historical or literary works, and which he applied to his world-view — even the *Divān* contains some narrative passages, thus a story of Abu Ḥanifa,[33] the lawyer of early Abbasid times. The representatives of the different sects (Jabrites, Qadarites, Muᶜtazilites etc.) occur and are refuted in short allusions. Even the Ismāᶜilis are mentioned.[34]

One of the religious groups, however, has been transformed in Rumi's poetry into a symbol of spiritual purity and loyalty: these are the *Ikhvān aṣ-Ṣafā*, the 'Pure Brethren', a Shiite learned sodality of the early tenth century whose encyclopedic works were widely read. For Rumi, their very name usually designates the initiates with whom he can freely speak about the mysteries of love.[35]

Among the later rulers, the Seljuk king Sanjar (d. 1157) had apparently been transformed into a model of the successful worldly ruler in the early thirteenth century; the story of Sanjar and the old woman became commonplace in Persian literature, and was a favourite subject for painters. The frequency of his name in Rumi's poetry seems to indicate that he could be treated exactly like any of the ancient kings, comparable to the heroes of pre-Islamic Persian mythology, like Sohrab, Kaykobad and Kaykaus along with whom he is often mentioned.[36] (The latter two names may perhaps also pertain to the Seljuk rulers of Rumi's own time, or at least conceal allusions to them).

> Come, o soul of the soul of the soul, you shelter of the soul of the guests!
> O solṭān of solṭāns, why do you grieve about Sanjar?[37]

The true *faqir* has a hundred kingdoms like that of Sanjar,[38] for:

> Since I came into your shade, I am like the sun in the sky,
> Since I have become a slave of love, I am the Khaqan and the Solṭān Sanjar,[39]

or:

> The ruler of the Kingdom has unfolded the banner of the lovers so that nobody has the ambition (to gain) Sanjar's kingdom.[40]

The worldly ruler Sanjar is humiliated before the conquering power of love and of the lovers. But the most marvellous story about the king changed by love is that of Maḥmud of Ghazna and his slave Ayāz. Maḥmud, stern warrior and defender of Sunni Islam, conqueror of Northwest India and ruler of a court filled with poets and scholars, is mentioned by Persian writers rarely for these achievements. Rather he has become the model of the lover, infatuated with his slave Ayāz, a Turkish officer of the Oymak tribe in whose honour Farrokhi wrote a fine *qaṣida.*[41] This love between king and slave, the subject of many later romantic poems, has inspired the mystics as well. Aḥmad Ghazzāli alludes to his story, Sanāʾi knew of it, ʿAṭṭār was likewise fond of retelling it.[42] It is therefore small wonder that Rumi, too, has inserted a long tale about Maḥmud and Ayāz into his *Mathnavi,* not to forget the numerous allusions to their love in his lyrics.

Ayāz, the faithful Turkish slave, had become, in the work of the mystics, the symbol of the loving soul who, by surrendering completely to his master, wins his love: lover and beloved, king and slave become mutually interdependent. In Rumi's story,[43] Ayāz every morning visits a secret cabinet so that the courtiers eventually suspect him of hiding treasures; but his treasure is nothing but his old frock and a pair of worn-out sandals which he contemplates every day to remind himself of his destitute state before Maḥmud chose him for his service. To know himself, i.e. one's former miserable state, means to know one's Lord, i.e. the endless bounty of the Lord without which man would be nothing. This unusual elaboration of the famous tradition 'Who knows himself knows his Lord' (*man ᶜarafa nafsahu faqad ᶜarafa rabbahu*) shows, that Rumi did not interpret this *ḥadith* in a pantheistic sense, as was usually the case.

The name of Maḥmud, i.e. 'praiseworthy', gives Rumi unending opportunities to repeat a pun: he who acts in perfect obedience and love, like Ayāz, will reach the station that 'his end is praiseworthy', *maḥmud,* which can also mean that his end is Maḥmud: being identified with the royal beloved and source of love, Ayāz' end is, indeed, praiseworthy to the highest degree.[44]

(For allusions to contemporary events, like the Mongol invasion, vide the Introduction, I 3,4.)

Besides images of or allusions to historical or legendary persons Rumi also utilizes the names of the countries of Islam as poetical similes. Some of them are used in quite concrete setting and are not yet fossilized into clichés, as they often were in later Persian poetry.

Thus it is natural that Rumi remembers Khwarezm, his homeland, and the wars of the Khwarezmians of which he was, at least in part, an eye witness.[45] His way of dealing with 'realities' can be understood from his transformation of the actual Khwarezm into a spiritual realm. The remark of a friend who spoke of the beautiful women of this country, who are so numerous that no one can become a real lover, because every wink prettier and more attractive women appear before his eyes, caused him to answer:

> If there are no lovers for the beauties of Khwarezm, yet Khwarezm must have its lovers, seeing that there are countless beauties in that land. That Khwarezm is poverty, wherein are countless mystical beauties and spiritual forms. Each one you alight upon and are fixed on, another shows its face so that you forget the former one, and so ad infinitum. So let us be lovers of true poverty, wherein such beauties are to be found.[46]

Baghdad is often mentioned, usually as seat of the caliphate—for Rumi's lyrical poetry is mostly composed before the destruction of the capital of the Abbasid Empire in 1258. Thus, the heart is Baghdad, the capital of the caliph Love;[47] or the city becomes a symbol for power and wealth, and thus for the endless treasures of the Beloved:

> If one basket has got lost from the whole of Baghdad—what does it matter?[48]

Yet, in the ruined village, i.e., the heart of the lover, a treasure is hidden which renders the ruins more valuable than the whole of Baghdad:[49] for the treasure is the Divine Beloved who promised 'I am with those whose hearts are broken for my sake'.

Baghdad is sometimes for some reason connected with or juxtaposed to Hamadan which seems to constitute its spiritual counterpart.[50]

The name of Amol at the Caspian Sea offers the poet a nice occasion to insert a pun with *amal,* 'hope':

> From your Ah Ah! the sea of Divine Kindness became agitated:
> The traveller of your hope (*amal*) has reached *Amol*![51]

as if the fragile boat Hope has eventually reached the haven where it is safe from the dangers of the journey.

Rumi's allusions to Qeyruwan[52] have been explained by R. A. Nicholson as pertaining to the arabicized form of *karvān*;[53] perhaps one may also think in this connection of the combination used by earlier Persian poets who like to juxtapose Qandahar and Qeyruwan, the two most distant places of the then-known Islamic world.[54] For Sohrawardi Maqtul Qeyruwan represents the place where the human soul suffers in its 'Western Exile', an idea which would fit into the connection of this name with the 'veil', i.e. separation, in one of Rumi's ghazals.[55] Other parts far distant are China and Constantiniyya—that is why the morning breeze is asked to bring the scent of Shamsoddin's beauty to these two places.[56] The name *Istanbul,* however, occurs as well in Rumi's poetry: an infant who does not know his homeland and place of birth wants only a wet-nurse; what do Istanbul or Yemen mean to him?[57] Andalusia and Hormuz are contrasted as the utmost East and West:[58] but generally it is only the distance of Iraq and Khorassan, or Marv and Reyy which denotes utter distance of the lovers:

> Stranger is this that I and you are here in one corner
> and at the same time in Iraq and Khorassan, I and you.[59]

Or: soul and body are as much strangers to each other as people from the Maghreb and Tus, or from Marv and Reyy,[60] and everyone will return to his birthplace after death, the Byzantine to Rum, the Ghurids to the wilderness of Ghur.[61]

The city of Reyy, destroyed in 1220 by the Mongols, is remarkable for houses underground—the lovers build their domiciles out of fear of the evil eye like these houses.[62]

Isfahan only occurs as the centre of production of the best eye salve, which enhances the sight,[63] whereas Shostar produces fine silk and brocades.

Syria, mainly Damascus—*demashq-e ᶜeshq,* the city of love, as he calls it once[64]—is always connected with Rumi's search for Shamsoddin—the relation between the proper name *Shām*, Syria, Damascus, and the evening, *shām,* of the friend's dark hair is easily established.[65] Aleppo, on the other hand, is once described as destroyed, like the heart of him who is deserted by his friend.[66] This allusion dates the poem after 658/1256 when Hulagu devastated the town completely. The Aleppine glass, famous in the Middle Ages, and a topos in later Persian poetry, occurs as well.[67]

Lebanon is remembered as the seat of pious monks and ascetics—it has been, indeed, a centre of early Sufism and meeting place of Christians and Muslim ascetics:

> At the entrance of the village of your grief has my soul a monastery (*ṣowmaᶜa*)—
> When it has no foot, how should it go to the Mount Lebanon?[68]

Kashmir is the place of lovely beauties of idol-like charm, as usual in Persian poetry.[69]

Yemen offered many elegant cross-relations due to its conection with Oweys-e Qarani, with the red cornelian which represents the friend's lips, with the star Soheyl, canopus, and with the delicate *ṭā'ifi* leatherware: all these allusions, to which one may perhaps add the Yemenite Wisdom as preached by Sohrawardi Maqtul, contributed in giving this province a quite prominent place in Rumi's poetical geography.

The traditional allusions to the different parts of Central Asia, the homeland of the beautiful Turks, are not lacking either—Saksin and Khita, Bolghār and Qutu, Chāplus etc.,[70] occur in Rumi's verses exactly as in those of any worldly Persian poet: Tartarian musk and Bolgarian curls,[71] the narrow eyes of the Qipchaq[72] and the splendour of the

Romean cheeks[73] all point to the beauty of the Beloved:

> If you see in your journey Rum and Khotan,
> the love of your homeland leaves your heart.[74]

China brings the Chinese mirror and the lovely *loᶜbat-e Chin*, Chinese dolls as used in shadow plays,[75] and all the thoughts of the lover which formerly were as ugly and dangerous as Gog and Magog turn into houri-like beauties and Chinese dolls when the Beloved appears.[76] China is also the home of the painter Mani—hence the story of the contest of the Chinese and Byzantine painters—and of elegant mirrors.[77]

Sometimes Rumi uses proverbs connected with a place:

> How should I carry dates to Basra, how should I carry cumin seeds to Kerman?[78]

equivalent to 'carry coals to Newcastle'.

To compare the river of tears to the Jeyhun is a commonplace with Persian poets; sometimes the Euphrates is used in the same simile. That the holy city of Mecca is not lacking in Rumi's geographical vocabulary goes without saying. In one interesting verse Mecca, the obedient, is contrasted with Acca, the rebellious[79]—a remembrance of the days of the Crusaders who, for a long time, were in possession of the Syrian port Acca.

And like Mecca, all the other famous places of the Muslim world, like Samarqand, Bokhara, Ghazna etc., occur frequently in various stories. thinking of Rumi's experience, we may take allusions to Qeyseriyya for expressions of his own feelings rather than of inherited topoi: Kaiseri, connected with the *qeyṣar*, *caesar*, was the place where Rumi's master Borhānoddin was buried, and hence dear to his heart.

As for Tabriz, it is of course always connected with Shams. Rumi combines it with the Arabic root *barraza*, 'to manifest one's self', and thus could produce clever puns about the home of Eternal beauty, the place where he wants to run, like an intoxicated camel, nay, rather to fly. Tabriz is his central sanctuary; nevertheless he knows that

> the faithful regard God—they do not see Khwarezm and Dehestan.[80]

And after his perfect spiritual union with Shamsoddin, even Tabriz is no longer important, He has reached a stage,

> that from Konya the light of Love may shine for an hour till Samarqand and Bokhara . . .[81]

One of the geographico-historical topics is the contrast of Turk and Hindu. It was used from the earliest days of Persian poetry; but it is interesting to see Rumi's application of this traditional pair of correlatives in his works, since the Turks are absolutely convinced that Mowlānā himself was a Turk, quoting one of his lines in favour of this claim. However, we shall probably never be in a position to reach any definite conclusion in this respect. Rumi's mother tongue was Persian, but he had learned, during his stay in Konya, enough Turkish and Greek to use it, now and then, in his verses. We may ask, therefore, how he represents the Turks, or the usual pair Turk-Hindu. To be sure, these words and combinations occur so frequently in his verses that one has to restrict oneself to some of the most characteristic passages from both the *Divān* and the *Mathnavi*:

There is one revealing poem, beginning with the lines:

> A Hindu came into the *khānqāh*.
> 'Are you not a Turk?—Then throw him from the roof!'
> Do you consider him and the whole of Hindustan as little,
> pour his special (part) on his whole (i.e. let him feel that he is part of infidel Hindu India).
> The ascendent of India is Saturn himself,
> and though he is high, his name is Misfortune.
> He went high, but did not rescue (man) from misfortunes—
> What use has the bad wine from the cup?
> I showed the bad Hindu the mirror:
> Envy and wrath is not his sign . . .
> . . .
> The *nafs* is the Hindu, and the *khānqāh* my heart . . .[82]

The last hemistich gives the clue: the Hindu, always regarded as ugly, black, of evil omen (like the 'black' Saturn, the Hindu of the Sky, in astrology), and as a mean servant of the Turkish emperors, is the *nafs,* the base soul which on other occasions is compared to an unclean black dog.[83] Yet, even the *nafs*—if successfully educated—can become useful, comparable to the little Hindu-slave whose perfect loyalty will be recognized by the Shah.[84]

Rumi plays with the inherited imagery very skilfully, and uses it surprisingly often: he speaks in the strain of love-poetry of the Hindu-black 'broken' curls which set out towards

Turkestan,[85] i.e. the radiant face of the Beloved. 'Turk' is from Ghaznavid times onwards equivalent with the beloved; the word conveys the idea of strength, radiance, victory, sometimes cruelty, but always beauty; Rumi's mystical friend is 'the Turk'.[86] Addresses to 'the Turk' are therefore frequent in the *Divān,* no matter to which of Rumi's inspiring friends the verses are written. Ideal beauty is described in a little Arabic verse as:

> of Hashimite face, Turkish head,
> Deylamite hair, and Roman (Byzantine) chin.[87]

To be sure, Rumi indulges in telling stories about the Turk in Balasaghun who lost one of his two bows,[88] of the stupid Turkish amir who was easily cheated by the tricky tailor,[89] or of the drunken Turk (always a favourite topic of Persian writing poets!) who disliked the music played by the mystical singer.[90] But these stories in which the Turkish warrior—not endowed with too much intelligence—is slightly ridiculed, are by far outweighted by those allusions (not stories) in which the Turk is contrasted to the Hindu as the representative of the luminous world of spirit and love, against the dark world of the body and matter.[91] Sometimes, though rarely, the Turk is contrasted with the Tajik, the city dweller in the Central Asian countries, who is generally described in such poems as soft-hearted:

> Show activity and act like a Turk, not softness and the way of the Tajiks![92]

The allusions to the *torktāz*, the attack by night of Turkish warriors against Hindustan,[93] is a common topic, and Rumi may even use the Borāq 'Love' for such a heroic 'Turkish' flight towards the beloved, with the intention to destroy the dark Hindu curls[94] which cover the eternal beauty, i.e., to leave behind and overcome everything besides the Beloved.

The Hindu 'Night' flees from the attack of the Turk 'Day' which had been hidden among the Hindus,[95] or the Hindu 'Night' complains when the Turks enter his tent to pillage it;[96]—hence the relation with Shams, the Sun of Tabriz, can be explained without difficulty: his face can burn the Hindu 'Night'.[97] Variations on this theme are largely used in the *Divān*.

Charming applications of the motif of the Turk to other phenomena of nature are not rare either:

> The Turks with fairy-cheeks have now decided to travel away: one after the other has gone to the winter-quarters (*qishlaq*), unknown of plundering —[98]

That is the time of fall, when the yellow foliage disappears. But in spring, when 'all the Turks turn towards the *yaylā*',[99] the 'Turks of the garden' return as well — the lovely leaves come back. This constant migration of the Turcoman tribes between *kishlā* and *yaylā* becomes, with Rumi, a symbol of the relations of soul and body: once the spirit goes to the eternal *yaylā*, the green summer-grazing-places, then it can leave the winter quarters of the body. The birds — again in connection with the soul bird — resemble the Turcomans and their coming.[100]

For the other world is like Turkestan, whereas the world of clay and water is a mere dark Hindustan.[101] This symbolism culminates in the intoxicated line:

> When you are intoxicated from pre-eternity, take the sword of endless eternity,
> In Turkish style sack the Hindu-beg 'Existence'![102]

How far is this explanation of Hindustan as the world of matter from the other image in which the elephant dreams of the Hindustan of the soul!

Rumi's imagery is quite in tune with that of other Persian writing poets who have elaborated this subject throughout the centuries, with the difference that he, taking his images in part from the daily life of the Turcoman tribes whom he saw around Konya with their tents, their fierce dogs and their colourful dresses, added greater realism to this stereotyped topic. His application of the Turk-Hindu contrast to high mystical experience is also remarkable.

But what does he say about himself?

> Leave the word (which is) a Hindu, see the Turks of inner meaning:
> I am that Turk who does not know a Hindu, who does not know.[103]

Then, describing his moon-faced Turkish beloved who addresses him in Turkish, he continues in another ghazal:

> You are a Turkish moon, and I, although I am not a Turk, know that much, that in Turkish the word for water is *su*.[104]

Rumi is Turk insofar as he belongs to the world of spirit, beyond the world of Hindu-like dark matter; but on the outward plan he knows no what he is: maybe the water in which the Turkish moon can reflect its own beauty . . . The differentiation of races belongs to the world of matter; their origin is pure white sperm, and only after birth do they appear as Byzantine and Abyssinian.[105] More than once he has attested that:

> I am sometimes Turk and sometimes Hindu, sometimes Rumi and sometimes Negro,
> O soul, from your image is my approval and my denial.[106]

For in love, differences completely vanish:

> Everyone in whose heart is the love for Tabriz,
> becomes—even though he be a Hindu—a rose-cheeked inhabitant of Ṭarāz (i.e. a Turk).[107]

The difference between Turk and Hindu, or Turk and Negro, or Byzantine and Negro is part of the material world: when they look into the mirror, they see their own beauty or ugliness, though sometimes without recognizing it. But as they were alike before being born, all the Hindus, Qipchaq, Romans and Abyssinians will look alike again behind the wall of the grave.[108] On the spiritual plane, the Prophet is the mirror, in which Turk and Hindu, i.e., faithful and infidel, can see their true nature.[109] Mowlānā connects this very idea of the mirror with the thought of death which will appear like a mirror before man to show everyone his true face: it looks lovely for the Turk, ugly for the Negro.[110] The idea of the black and white faces which will become visible in the Otherworld at Doomsday is transformed here into a fine poetical image, and transplanted from the end of times to the very personal experience of death.

Strangely enough, one of the numerous later Indo-Persian poets who played on the contrast Turk-Hindu, has put a famous line by Rumi into the mouth of a Hindu sage whom he claims to have met at the door of Somnath, the temple destroyed by Maḥmud of Ghazna, and from whom, as he says, he learnt this verse:

> The result of my life is not more than three words:
> I was raw, I became ripe, I burnt—[111]

lines often quoted as Rumi's summary of his life, and here cleverly connected with the 'death through fire' for which the Indians were noted in the Islamic world.

The Hindu is usually described as lowly and ugly. The *zanji*, Negro, blackfaced like him, is generally a model of spiritual happiness (the cheerfulness of the Negroes was mentioned in many a book and verse as early as Abbasid times).[112] In spite of his black face, he is smiling and apparently happy[113]—an idea which Sanāʾi has used to interpret the inner meaning of the Prophetic tradition according to which 'Poverty is blackness of the face'.[114] Rumi is slightly more critical and thinks that such happiness as experienced by the Negro lasts only as long as the superficial person does not see his own face in the mirror.[115] The Byzantines, specifically their emperor, and the Zanji are several times contrasted, probably in part due to Rumi's personal acquaintance with the Byzantines, in part also in the tradition of Neẓāmi's *Iskandarnāme*. The Abkhazian, i.e. Georgian infidel occurs once.[116]

While the Turks, Hindus, and Zanjis belong to the general stock of classical Persian imagery, the Europeans are of course not too often mentioned as a poetical topos in early times (only in post-sixteenth century poetry they play a more conspicuous role). Rumi remembers them in connection with the crusaders who passed through Konya[117] several times in a rather unfriendly way: Not less than four times he combines them with the pigs which they allegedly brought to the holiest town, Jerusalem.[118] He probably took over this image from Khāqāni, in whose first *qaṣida* the pigs which entered Jerusalem are set parallel with the elephants that attacked Mecca under Abraha. For Mowlānā, the sanctuary of the heart filled with dirty qualities is comparable to Qods, the Holy City filled with Europeans tending their pigs. Rumi does not hesitate to address those who deny Shamsoddin's glory:

> The love (*havā*, also 'air') of Shams-e Tabrizi is like Jerusalem You are the pig which not (even) the European accepts . . .[119]

There is however, one Jerusalem, one sacred place which has not fallen into the hands of the *ferangis*: that is the sacred banquet of the true saints (*abdāl*). Even reason, which is the foundation of religion, is like an ignorant king at the door of this place: how could the impure Europeans enter this sanctuary?[120]

Thus Rumi's imagery contains several glances at political and social values and far transcends the purely academic use of inherited images.

Surely God's friends—no fear shall be on them, neither shall they sorrow

IMAGERY TAKEN FROM SUFI HISTORY.

The tradition of Sufism was firmly established when Jalāloddin set out on his spiritual journey. The names of the mystical leaders and saints of yore had become part and parcel of the language. Allusions to their legend, quotations from their sayings permeated the speech of every adept on the Path. Yet, every mystic had a peculiar way of appropriating into his *Weltanschauung* these early representatives of religious life. From the frequency of their occurrence as well as from their situation in the whole work of the individual author it is possible to draw some conclusion which may help to define the predilections and inclination of the writer. That holds true not only for Rumi, but for all the later mystics and poets of Iran, Turkey, and Muslim India.

Rumi is particularly fond of the figure of Oweys al-Qarani who, according to legend, lived in Yemen and never met the Prophet—yet the scent of his holiness reached Moḥammad who recognized 'the breath of the Merciful coming to him from Yemen'. Oweys became the prototype of those mystics who enter the spiritual path without proper initiation through a human master.

Rumi, though not exactly an *oweysi* mystic himself, loves allusions to Oweys' legend.[1] The inspiration coming from the 'luster of the Ahmadian cornelian', i.e. the lip of the Prophet, brings the 'scent of the Merciful' to him:[2] he feels this very scent of the Merciful in the spring breeze which turns the buds into cornelians.[3] The old poetical expression of the 'carnelion-like lips of the beloved' is strengthened, in such connections, by the introduction of the well-known *ḥadith.* For a poet like Rumi who sensed Divine Beauty and Majesty everywhere, but particularly in the gardens, images related to this heavenly fragrant breeze must have been very attractive indeed; — they are among Rumi's numerous verses connected with the sense of smell.[4]

Another early Sufi whose legendary life always fascinated the mystics is Ibrāhim ibn Adham, the master of the Khorassanian ascetics. Born in Jalāloddin's birthplace, Balkh, about 500 years before our poet, Ibrāhim was, naturally enough, very dear to Rumi's heart. Of princely origin, Ibrāhim was miraculously converted to the life of poverty.[5] One legend, similar to that of St Hubertus, tells that a gazelle addressed him during the hunt; according to others, his conversion took place in the following way:

On a throne, that man of good name heard at night a
  noise of tramping and shrill cries from the roof.
Loud footsteps on the roof of the palace, and said
  to himself; 'Who dares to do that?'
He shouted at the palace-window: 'Who is it?
  This is not a man, belike it is a genie.'
A wondrous folk put their heads down (saying) 'We
  are going round by night for the purpose of search.'
'Eh, what are ye seeking?' — 'Camels', they replied. He said:
  'Take heed! Who ever sought camel on a roof?'
Then they said to him: 'How are thou seeking to meet with God on
  the throne of state? . . .[6]

Ibrāhim thus became the model of the Sufi who, once struck by the Sun of Reality,[7] or intoxicated by the Eternal wine,[8] was transformed completely and wandered into homelessness, forsaking crown and throne for the sake of true gnosis. He returned to the realm of Absolute Poverty which he recognized as his true home, comparable to the elephant who saw India in his dream . . .[9]

Ibrahim's younger contemporary, the Basrian woman Rābeʿa al-ʿAdawiyya, is credited with introducing the concept of pure love into Islamic Mysticism. Although the ideas which she uttered in public were perhaps known earlier among some Sufis, she has become, in Islamic hagiography the paragon of pure, disinterested love. Strangely enough, Rumi never mentions her by name; even the story which ᶜAṭṭār tells as pertaining to her, is converted into a general Sufi story in the *Mathnavi*: a Sufi sitting in the midst of the garden had put his head on his knee and contemplated God, for—as Rābeᶜa had told her servant who called her to admire God's work in the glory of a spring day—:

> The gardens and fruits are in the heart,
> (Only) the reflections of this kindness of His are on this water and clay.[10]

This saying does not perfectly agree with Rumi's personal attitude, since he was endowed with the gift of discovering Divine traces everywhere in the world, especially in the beauty of nature in spring. Yet, he knows that this inner vision can be so overwhelming that a blind saint might refuse medicine because his interior world is much superior to everything he would see in the outward creation . . .[11]

Rumi sees himself in the company of the great masters: he has reached such a state that normal people will be amazed, a state in which even Joneyd, Sheykh Besṭāmi, Shaqiq, Karkhi and Ẕu'n-Nun would be bewildered.[12] Shaqiq al-Balkhi is the main representative of the Khorassanian school of *tavakkol,* perfect trust in God: Maᶜruf al-Karkhi was one of the early Baghdad mystics, whose strong spirituality worked upon the formation of Sari as-Saqaṭi, Joneyd's uncle and teacher; this Sari is also mentioned along with a similar group of Sufis elsewhere.[13] And there is Beshr al-Ḥāfi,[14] the Barefooted, and Shibli, Ḥallāj's friend who, at times, feigned madness in order to escape punishment. Their names are once philologically explained in elegant puns.[15]

With all those saints Rumi drinks 'the wine of the pious' (Sura 56/6).[16] When a man seeks companions like Besṭāmi and Karkhi, he should not drink wine in this ash-house, but rather on the highest roof,[17] that is, he must leave this world and what is in it and climb to the summit of spiritual life where the eternal cupbearer will quench his thirst with pure wine of love.

Rumi shows special sympathy for Ẕu'-n-Nun, the master of Egypt (d. 859), who was, indeed, one of the most powerful and intriguing personalities in early Sufi history.[18] This mystic, whose very surname 'He with the Fish' enables the poet to create associations with the prophet Jonah, occurs several times in Rumi's lyrics, and is often seen in connection with enthusiasm and dance. His love, like that of Majnun, is a sign from the Divine Grandeur, as Jalāloddin sings in an enthralling, highly rhythmical poem.[19] Ẕu'n-Nun, the man without head or tail,[20] is also the topic of several stories in the *Mathnavi,* although the historical context is not always correctly given.[21]

Joneyd, the master of the Baghdad school, is rarely mentioned independently; he generally figures along with Bāyazid Besṭāmi.[22] In fact, the sober Baghdad sheykh was highly critical of the theopathic locutions of the master of Besṭām. But for Rumi, both constitute models of perfect spiritual life in its different aspects.[23] That is why he could call his friend Ḥosāmoddin 'the Joneyd of his time and the Bāyazid of his age'—although associations with Bāyazid occur more often in his descriptions of Ṣalāḥoddin Zarkub.

Among the later mystics, Rumi often mentions Abu'l-Ḥasan-e Kharraqāni, the illiterate saint of Kharraqan in Khorassan who was initiated by *oweysi* succession by the spirit of Bāyazid Besṭāmi. As Rumi tells in accordance with traditional hagiography, Bāyazid, sensing the birth of this saint more than one hundred years ago, had given his disciples the glad tidings of the future arrival of his spiritual heir.[24] Kharraqāni, in turn, showed every possible reverence to Bāyazid's tomb. He is noted for his asceticism, his patience in endurance of hardships, and his strong love. This is illustrated by a tale which contains, indeed, one of the most amusing descriptions in the *Mathnavi*—a tale according to which this perfect saint, smarting under the misbehavior of his perfectly ghastly and horrid wife, was seen riding on a lion, using a snake as his whip: his steadfastness in tribulations was recompensed by miraculous powers.[25] He belonged to those perfect saints about whom Jalāloddin says:

> Neither greed for knowledge and honour remained for them, nor greed for Paradise—
> Such a one seeks not a donkey or a camel, for he rides on lions.[26]

A more important role than any given to these figures, however, is that assigned in Rumi's work to Bāyazid Besṭāmi and Ḥoseyn ibn Manṣur al-Ḥallāj, the martyr of Divine love.

These two were generally yoked together by later mystics, although their theoretical approaches to the central problems of Sufism are quite different.

Rumi tells several stories about Bāyazid.[27] The most beautiful account of his miraculous power, and a poignant description of the true saint, is this:

> The flood of bewilderment swept away his reason: he spoke more strongly than he had spoken at first,
> 'Within my mantle there is naught but God: how long wilt thou seek on the earth and in heaven?'
> All the disciples became frenzied and dashed their knives at his holy body . . .
> Every one who plunged a dagger into the sheykh was reversely making a gash in his own body.
> There was no mark on the body of that possessor of the (mystic) sciences, while those disciples were wounded and drowned in blood . . .[28]

In spite of his claims 'Glory be to Me' and 'There is nothing under my cloak but God'—claims which deeply shocked the orthodox—Bāyazid is, for Mowlānā, the ideal Muslim, a paragon of faith. More than once he admonishes pretenders to Sufism not to call themselves Bāyazids.[29] A philological pun allows him to contrast Bāyazid (Abu Yazid), this prototype of asceticism, self abnegation, and religious strength, with the detested Omayyad ruler Yazid, who had caused the martyrdom of the Prophet's grandson Ḥoseyn in 680: the carnal soul is like Yazid, but can be changed, through hard labour and love, into a Bāyazid:

> By the light of the Beloved the night of infidelity became a Day of Religion (or: Day of Judgment),
> And Yazid became from his breath a Bāyazid.[30]

Another 'philological' combination is that of Bāyazid's name with the word *mazid,* 'more, increase', derived from the same root as Yazid. Here, we may discover a subtle allusion to the famous correspondence between Bāyazid and his contemporary Yaḥyā ibn Moʿāẕ, the 'preacher of hope', who sent him a letter saying:

> Someone has drunk one sip from the water of His love and is satisfied . . . Bāyazid answered: And someone has drunk the seven seas of heaven and his thirst is not yet quenched, and he says 'Is there not more?' *(hal min mazid).*[31]

The 'increase' which he experienced is unique in the world,[32] for he was the true *faqir,* the spiritually poor.[33] Man's fall can also be described in images taken from this circle:

> Yesterday you were a Bāyazid, you were in increase,
> today you are in ruins, and a dreg-seller, and drunk![34]

Even in Rumi's lyrics — which do not lack narrative trends — we find a story of Bāyazid: the saint met on the way a donkey driver, *kharbanda* (lit. 'servant of the donkey') and exclaimed:

> O God, make his donkey die so that he becomes a servant of God *(khodābanda)*[35]

The most impressive poem in honour of the sheykh of Bestām is found in Book V of the *Mathnavi.*[36] It contains a poetical enumeration of his lofty qualities as well as the story of how a Zoroastrian was asked to embrace Islam: he, though expressing his basic willingness, yet remarked that if true faith were that which Bāyazid showed, he would not be able to bear it, and would rather not try it; for such faith is too strong for a normal human being. These very verses have been quoted by Muhammad Iqbal in his *Javidnāma* (1932) when he tried to show the strength of true Islamic life and the perfection of the veritable Muslim.[37]

The central place which Bāyazid occupies in the history of Sufism is described, in lovely words, in one of Rumi's dancing-poems:

> The body is like the monastery of the soul, the thoughts are like the Sufis,
> they form a circle, and in the centre is my heart like Bāyazid.[38]

Bāyazid's exclamation *sobḥāni* 'Glory be to me' and Ḥallāj's expression *anā'l-Ḥaqq,* 'I am the Truth' or 'I am God' are generally regarded as pointing to the same experience. Thus, Rumi could compare his mystical friend Ṣalāḥoddin to Bāyazid, and sometimes also to Manṣur (as Ḥallāj was generally called with his father's name, meaning 'The Victorious').[39]

Mowlānā has described his own situation with symbols taken from these two mystics:

> The heart, before his face, is like Bāyazid in constant increase,
> The soul had, hanging upon his tresses, the character of Manṣur:[40] (for he was hanged in 922).

When the beloved becomes to him like Bāyazid, the increase of Manṣur's happiness can be applied to himself.[41]

Allusions to the martyr-mystic of Baghdad constitute the greatest part of Rumi's symbols taken from Sufi history. He is reported to have said on his deathbed:

> As the spirit of Manṣur appeared, a hundred and fifty years after his death, to the sheykh Faridoddin ʿAṭṭār, and became the sheykh's spiritual guide and teacher, so, too, do you always be with me, whatever may happen and remember me, so that I may show myself to you, in whatever form that may be.[42]

Rumi follows the general Sufi tradition in describing as 'intoxication' the state out of which both utterances, that of Bāyazid and Ḥallāj, were born.[43] This intoxication has supplied the poets with images like 'Manṣur's wine', 'Manṣur's goblet' etc—images which were used by Sufi and profane poets alike for centuries. The 'drum of Victory' belongs to this festive imagery in connection with the name Manṣur 'the Victorious'.[44] How often Rumi has spoken of the Mansuri wine, of the cup 'I am the Truth'![45] He goes so far as to claim that everyone else has drunk only a cupfull of wine of *anā Allah* and *anāʾl-Ḥaqq* respectively, while he has quaffed this wine with vat and bottle—so great is his love-intoxication![46]

A story related by Aflaki on the authority of Solṭān Valad points to this feeling: when Rumi's son wondered why Ḥallāj and Bāyazid had been persecuted whereas his father, who uttered so much more daring words in his poetry, enjoyed a good reputation, Jalāloddin told him that these two Sufis had remained in the state of 'lovers', and therefore had to suffer affliction, whereas he had reached the station of the beloved . . .[47]

> How many a lordly Simorgh whose litany was *anāʾl-Ḥaqq*
> burnt his wings and feathers when he flew to that side![48]

Even the king of birds—an expression possibly taken from ʿAbdul Qāder Gilāni's remark about Ḥallāj—will get burnt when reaching the station of Absolute Unity in love, just as Gabriel would burn his wings were he to come closer to the place where the Prophet enjoyed intimate conversation with his Lord.

Like almost every mystic, Rumi has pondered upon the secret of *anāʾl-Ḥaqq*, and its relation to Pharaoh's claim

Anā rabbukom al-aʿlā, 'I am your highest Lord' (Sura 79/24). Ḥallāj himself had compared himself to Pharaoh and Satan, for each of them had made a daring claim in which he said 'I am . . .'[49] Rumi defends Ḥallāj: his word was light, that of Pharaoh tyranny, and,

The I of Manṣur became surely grace,
that of Pharaoh became a curse, look![50]

He must have been deeply concerned with this problem, for he took it up years later, in Book V of the *Mathnavi*, to stress once more the same truth.[51] For the first 'I' was spoken out of idle boast, whereas the other one was the utterance of union with the Divine light, not—and this is important—a union achieved by *ḥolul*, incarnation. Rumi thus rebukes those who saw in Ḥallāj a representative of the heretic teaching of God's incarnation in man. During those years—between 1262 and 1270—Mowlānā has also explained the *anāʾl-Ḥaqq* several times in his conversations:

> Take the famous utterance 'I am God'. Some men reckon it as a great pretension. But 'I am God' is in fact a great humility . . . He has naughted himself and cast himself to the winds. He says 'I am God' that is 'I am not, He is all, nothing has existence but God, I am pure non-entity, I am nothing' . . .[52]

> So when Manṣur's friendship with God reached its utmost goal, he became the enemy of himself and naughted himself . . .[53]

The same idea is expressed in the last book of the *Mathnavi*.[54]

But Jalāloddin has explained this famous utterance in a different way as well, one similar to the method of the Christian fathers: He speaks of the pieces of cloth which exclaim full of intoxication 'I am the vat' after falling in the dyeing-vat 'He' and experiencing the *ṣibghat Allāh* (Sura 2/138), the dyeing of God in which all colours disappear, and then proceeds to compare the mystic to the piece of iron which, heated by the fire, becomes red and fiery until it finally exclaims 'I am the fire': its form and outward appearance are, indeed, fiery. Yet substantial union is not achieved: fire remains fire, iron iron, as much as the fire may lend its attributes to the raw material, as much as the iron, following the Prophet's word 'Qualify yourselves with the qualities of God' assumes the qualities of fire.[55]

In some of Rumi's verses, again, later interpretations of the *anāʾl-Ḥaqq* are prefigured, thus in his description of the feast of union: the sun dances and claps its hands on the sky, the atoms play like lovers, the fountains are intoxicated and the roses open in smiling—then, the spirit becomes Manṣur and exclaims '*anāʾl-Ḥaqq*'.[56] These glowing images conform with descriptions of the mystical intoxication and cosmic consciousness as expressed in later Sufi poetry.

Since Shamsoddin is the most perfect manifestation of God in this world, his radiance completely transforms the soul of the lover who gains union with him, so that everyone who prostrates himself before this Beloved and is accepted by him, will say *anāʾl-Ḥaqq*.[57] The same motif is transferred upon Ḥosāmoddin: he is the cupbearer who quickens the soul with the morning drink from Manṣur's wine.[58] For the *bāda-ye Manṣuri* is the privilege of the true believers:

> That grape wine belongs to the nation of Jesus,
> but this Mansuri-wine belongs to the nation of *Yāsin*
> (i.e. Moḥammad),[59]

for it is the wine of spiritual love and self-negation, of absolute surrender and the strength resulting from surrender.

Again in accord with later Sufi poetry Rumi applies many allusions to the gallows—just as David will greet in reverence the Beloved from the height of his throne, Manṣur will speak the words of greeting from the gallows.[60] The atoms, touched by the sun of the beloved's face, exclaim *anāʾl-Ḥaqq* (an idea which became later a standard topos in Persian, Turkish and Urdu poetry), and Manṣur is hanging on the gallows at every corner:[61]

> As long as you show your cheek and rob intellect and faith,
> so long has the Manṣur 'Soul' another gallows at every side.[62]

This gallows means good tidings, i.e., the promise of union which can be achieved only through death. It is therefore the goal of the lovers[63] who are 'killed but are, in reality, alive' (Sura 3/169 about those martyred in the way of God). That Rumi uses the common puns, like the combination *deldār* 'beloved' and *del dār* 'heart—gallows' is natural.[64]

The dilemma of the mystics and the orthodox—namely, whether God and creation are separate or identical—can be solved, according to Mowlānā, only by accepting a higher unity in love. None of the two parties is right on the worldly plane:

> We put on the gallows everyone who says 'We are one' —
> We cast fire into every one who says 'We are two',[65]

for the persecution of some representatives of Persian dualist ideas during the early Abbasid period was well known to him.

It is the custom of the Divine Beloved to afflict those who love him:

> He dragged the foot of Ẕuʾn-Nun into fetters,
> the head of Manṣur went to the gallows,[66]

says Rumi with words first spoken by ʿAṭṭār, and then echoed in numerous verses of Persian, Turkish, and Indo-Muslim mystics.

Other mystics might ask God why Ḥallāj was put to death, since it was not he who uttered the word 'I am God'—it was God himself who spoke through him as He once had spoken through the Burning Bush. Rumi, though he alludes to this idea,[67] yet accepts that this cruel death is a necessary prerequisite for true life. He therefore compares Ḥallāj to the ripe apple hanging on the tree[68]—the double-sense of *dār*, 'gallows' and 'branch' facilitated, or perhaps even caused, such imagery. The apple, even though one throws stones at it, refuses to come down, replying with mute eloquence:

> I am Manṣur, hanging from the branch of the Merciful,
> far away from the lips of the evil, such a kiss and embrace comes to me![69]

A combination which is found at least since Sanāʾi in religious poetry[70] is that of gallows and pulpit, *dār u menbar,* well-known in present-day Indo-Pakistan, thanks to Ghalib's oft imitated verse:

> The secret which is in the heart, is not a sermon:
> You can utter it on the gallows, but not on the *menbar.*[71]

The underlying idea that the pulpit in the mosque is not the proper place to speak out the secret of love and union permeates Rumi's poems even when Ḥallāj's name is not mentioned: for the problem of enraptured love versus institutionalized religious forms was well known to him after he had experienced illumination through Shamsoddin. There are many hidden Manṣurs, who, relying upon the soul of Love, have dismissed the *menbars* and have proceeded to the gallows;[72] since all those who preferred the immediate life of the spirit have been persecuted by the established orthodoxy. The true lover is a gypsy-like rope-dancer:[73]

> Hark, give me leave, O chosen house, that I may perform a rope-dance, like Manṣur![74]

For Ḥallāj on his way to the gallows and rope danced in his fetters. Death was a festive occasion for him, and Rumi has well understood the secret of Ḥallāj's joyful suffering. That is why the main source of his inspiration is one Ḥallājian poem which he repeats in different variations so often that it becomes a veritable key-word for his own mystical teaching:

> *uqtulūnī yā thiqātī, inna fī qatlī ḥayātī . . .*[75]

> Kill me, O my trustworthy friends, for in my being killed there is my life . . .

By their very rhythmical structure, these verses are most convenient to be used in spiritual dance. In the *Mathnavi*, Rumi had to fit the line into the rhythm by adding a three-syllabic word at the end which was not difficult.[76] He also invented new Arabic verses fitting into the whole context, and adds another line from one of Ḥallāj's lyrical poems:

> *li ḥabibon* . . . I have a friend whose love roasts my interior:
> if he wanted it I would walk on my eyes.[77]

But in such cases the poet, suddenly aware of the fact that he has been talking in Arabic all the time, eventually reminds himself to return to Persian:

> though Arabic is nicer—but love has still a hundred tongues.[78]

Everyone has to learn the secret that 'in being killed is my life'—then, as the poet continues with an allusion to a saying attributed to ᶜAli ibn Abi Ṭāleb:

> Sword and scimitar become, like for ᶜAli, his sweet basil,
> whereas narcissus and wild rose are the enemy of his soul.[79]

The gallows is in fact the Borāq, the heavenly steed which carries man towards union, for life is hidden behind the image of death.[80]

Rumi has exemplified one of his favourite ideas, that of the upward movement of the created beings, by these very verses,[81] for the 'drum of love' constantly repeats the rhythmical words of Ḥallāj.[82] Rumi knows the wonderful Divine promise by which Shibli was consoled when he asked God the reason for Ḥallāj's execution—God spoke to him:

> Whom I kill, I become his blood money,

and the lover will remind Him who is going to slay him of His promise[83] which transforms every pain into a beatitude.

Allusions to Ḥallāj are scattered throughout Rumi's work.[84] He thus points to the original meaning of Ḥallāj's name, i.e., 'cotton carder'.[85] The lover is asked to cast fire into the sorrow of tomorrow which is like cotton in the soul's ear, and thus become like Ḥallāj.[86]

But for all his admiration of the Baghdad martyr-mystic, the overwhelming personality of the Sun of Tabriz extinguishes even the traces of Ḥallāj: who has failed to recognize Shams, and has remained far from him, is lower than an ant *(mur),* even though he be Manṣur.[87] For, as Solṭān Valad and following him Sepahsālār tell, Mowlānā saw in Ḥallāj only a lover:

> The lovers of God are in three degrees, and the beloved have three degrees as well. Manṣur Ḥallāj was in the station of 'being a lover' on the first degree. The middle one is magnificent, and the last one even more magnificent. The states and words of these three degrees become visible in the world. But those three degrees of 'being beloved' are hidden . . . Shamsoddin was the leader of the beings in the last degree . . .[88]

At times, Rumi saw himself as superior to Manṣur, having attained the station of a beloved. What he accepted from the Baghdad mystic and incorporated into his work, was his sacrifice which led him to higher union—like the unitive state of the moth in the flame. By his call to become annihilated for the sake of eternal life, Ḥallāj appears as a forerunner of Rumi himself, a true lover, dancing on the rope of the beloved's tresses . . .[89]

We have breathed into him from Our breath . . .

THE IMAGERY OF MUSIC AND DANCE

One day—thus legend tells—a man objected to Rumi's interest in music; an interest which was, indeed, not justified by orthodox standards. But our master Jalāloddin replied:

> 'Music is the scratching of the doors of Paradise.'—Said the man: 'I don't like the sound of scratching doors!'—Whereupon our master answered: 'I hear the doors as they open—you hear them when they close . . .'[1]

This story, poetically reworked about 150 years ago by Friedrich Rückert in German verse, is the best introduction to Rumi's approach to music. Music was something heavenly for him;[2] not in vain did he describe the house of Love as having doors and roof made of music, melodies, and poetry.[3] Musical imagery permeates his whole work from the very moment that Shamsoddin's love carried him away from bookish learnedness and his heart, instead, 'learned poetry, song, and music.'[4]

The most famous expression of this love of music is the eighteen introductory verses of the *Mathnavi,* commonly known as *sheʿr-e ney*, 'The Song of the Reed'—a title which has inspired several European versions of Rumi's poetry, and of verse inspired by his teachings.

> Listen to the reed how it tells a tale, complaining of separation
> Saying: 'Ever since I was parted from the reed-bed, my lament has caused man and woman to moan.
> I want a bosom torn by severance, that I may unfold the pain of love-desire.
> Every one who is left far from his source wishes back the time when he was united with it . . .
>
> This noise of the reed is fire, it is not wind: whoso hath not this fire, may he be naught!
> 'Tis the fire of Love that is in the reed, 'tis the fervour of Love that is in the wine.
> The reed is the comrade of every one who has been parted from a friend: its strains pierced our heart.
> Who ever saw a poison and antidote like the reed? Who ever saw a sympathiser and a longing lover like the reed?
> The reed tells of the Way full of blood and recounts stories of the passion of Majnun.
> Only to the senseless is this sense confided; the tongue hath no customer save the ear . . .[5]

The reed flute was known to Islamic musicians from the beginnings of their history; it belongs to the oldest instruments used by man. The ancient Greeks spoke of the melancholy sound of the Phrygian flute, and the role of this instrument, as well as of musical therapy for mental diseases, was known to them and was inherited by the Islamic peoples: the Shefāʾiyya-asylum in Divrigi, completed in the very year of Rumi's settling in Konya, in 1228, contains a wonderful basin in which the melodious sound of falling water-drops was utilized for mental treatment.

Jalāloddin certainly knew of the psychic effect of music, and of the role the flute played in such rituals. On the other hand, the story of the reed which divulges the king's secrets can be traced back to the tale of King Midas of Gordion, although it was known to the Sufis previous to Rumi who probably adopted it from Sanāʾi's version.[6] The Anatolian tradition, however, may have strengthened his love for the complaining sound of the reed which could be cut in different sizes, from the simple small ney (similar to a recorder) to the larger Manṣur-*ney* (by its very name alluding to Manṣūr Ḥallāj), and the huge *shāh-ney,* to mention only the most prominent types used in the Mevlevi orchestra.

The reed flute provided Rumi with an ideal symbol of the soul which can utter words only when touched by the lips of the beloved, and moved by the breath of the spiritual master,[7] an idea expressed before him by Sanāʾi.[8] Man, cut off from the eternal ground of his existence, like the flute from the reedbed, becomes resonant in separation and tells the secrets of love and longing. Jalāloddin often saw himself, in the pangs of separation, passionately complaining like the reed,[9] and felt the inspiration through Shams enter into his empty heart like the breath of a flute player.[10] Does not the flute open nine or ten eyes in order to behold the Friend?[11] In repetitious verses Rumi has alluded to the enrapturing power of the *ney* which, hands and feet cut off, deprives people of hands and feet,[12] i.e., carries away their reason.

The reed flute has suffered; its head has been cut, exactly like that of the reed pen—hence both instruments are media to convey information about the Beloved, one by singing, the other by writing.[13]

Likewise the *ney* is connected with the sugar cane—both are filled with the friend's sweetness; both are dancing already in the reedbed or in the field in the hope of the lip of the Beloved.[14]

Everyone is infatuated by the complaint of the *ney* which tells the story of eternal longing:

> The sound of the *ney* calls from non-existence one hundred Leyla and Majnun, two hundred Vāmeq and ᶜAzrā . . .[15]

as Rumi says with an allusion to the two most famous loving couples in Islamic poetry. Later commentators have regarded this instrument as the symbol of the Perfect Man who informs people about their primordial state reminding them of the greatness and beauty of their eternal home so that they, remembering their past happiness, join in his complaining songs, and are carried away from this land of separation. For the sound of the flute casts fire into the world;[16] we may assume that the traditional image of the burnt reedbed has played a role in shaping these similes.

> We are the reedbed, and your love is fire,
> waiting that this fire may reach the reed flute.[17]

The fire produced by the lovesick reed flute or the intoxicated reed pen will cover the whole world, leaving nothing intact—this idea has become a standard topos in later, mainly Indo-Muslim, poetry.

Rumi sometimes specifies the wind instruments and mentions the *sornā,* a sort of trumpet or clarion, which, like the *ney*, speaks and sings only when touched by the friend's lips,[18] waiting with nine eyes for these lips which endow it with life. Otherwise, there is no meaning or complaining in this 'veil' or 'musical mood' (the usual pun on *parda* which has both meanings).[19] This instrument—which was apparently often played by the wandering musicians, the *lulis,* —reminds Rumi of the Divine word: 'I have breathed into him from my breath' (Sura 15/29); it is like man who tries to repeat the pre-eternal melody of love.[20]

As the wind instruments are alive only when touched by the breath of the beloved, the *rabāb,* rebeck, a small four-stringed instrument, can produce sounds only when the musician puts it onto his breast and touches it with his bow[21]—it thus becomes, in the language of Persian poets, an appropriate symbol for the human heart and mind. As such, it is often mentioned along with the *ney*. Rumi complains, alluding to the process of inspiration:

> Being sober, no story comes from me —
> (I am) like a *rabāb* without a bow . . .[22]

for:

> All my questioning and answering is from him, I am like the *rabāb*,
> He beats me 'Hurry up!', he tells me 'Complain!'[23]

The lover's veins can easily be compared to the strings of the *rabāb* (ʿAṭṭār had used this simile, comparing the instrument to dried up bones and his veins to strings):[24] he vibrates as soon as the beloved touches him.[25] The heart, too, can be represented by the *rabāb* the 'ear' of which is twisted by the musician's hand to tune it properly:

> When you twist the ear of the rebeck 'Heart',
> then I start saying *tantantan tan* . . .[26]

The sound of the *rabāb*, at first difficult to appreciate for the Western listener, is prominent in the Mevlevi orchestra, for this instrument is, in Rumi's word, 'the nourishment of the consciences and the cupbearer of the hearts'.[27] We know that he was particularly fond of the *rabāb*, the use of which was prohibited by the orthodox lawyer-divines (a legend tells how a sober-minded theologian was punished for his denial of rebeck-music!).[28] The name of the *rabāb*-player Abu Bakr-e Rabābi occurs not only in the sources but also in Rumi's poetry.[29] And one should not forget that the word *rabāb* constitutes a very practical rhyme with *kabāb* 'roast' (the general simile for the lover's heart) and *sharāb* 'wine' and was, therefore, used wherever a festive gathering was described.

The *chang,* the little harp, often connected with the *ney*, functions, exactly like the *rabāb,* as a sign of close union: the harp leans in the lap of the beloved, with its back bent,[30] and is touched by his fingers (or the plectrum 'love-pain'),[31] thus producing sweet songs, day and night.

> In the lap of your grace I am like the melodious harp,
> place the plectrum softer and more tenderly, so that you do not tear my strings![32]

Thus sings Rumi in melodious verses.

The lamentation of each and every string—be it that of the harp, or that of the large *qanun*—is subject to the order of the Beloved;[33] it is he who produces the complaint of the harp which the lover has learned to play in his love.[34] The *chang* is also the instrument of Zohra, the star Venus who, in poetical imagery, still bears the character of an attractive love-deity and had, as such, caused the fall of the angels Harut and Marut; the sound of her harp resounds in heaven.

Wind and string instruments are more or less caressed by the hand of the player, but the percussion instruments have to suffer from his strength:

> I have surrendered my face like the tamburine (*daf*),
> strike hard strokes and give my face a neck-stroke![35]

The poet has become like a tamburine from the blows of separation, his body being crooked like the frame surrounding this instrument—why, then, does the friend not keep his tamburine-like heart in his hands to play with it?[36]

Yet the hard blows of the musician add to its perfection so that Jalāloddin implores God to grant the musicians honey and a hard blow for beating it.[37]—In a different strain of imagery he speaks also of the tamburine of Divine Wisdom which makes everybody dance.[38]

The large drum, *ṭabl,* is the instrument of information:—the love of the lovers has two hundred drums[39] and pipes (since their state is so conspicuous), and the proverb that it is useless to play a drum under the cover is often alluded to in Rumi's lyrics.[40] The drum is the instrument of the ruler, i.e., Love,[41] or of the army, hence in poetic imagery sometimes connected with Manṣur, the Victorious, or with the banner:

> When the drum tears the existences,
> you bring the banner from the hidden non-existence.[42]

As a war-drum, it announces separation;[43] yet, during the royal hunting party it is used to call the hawk or falcon back by the Divine message 'Return!' (Sura 89/28)—this message for which the exiled soul-bird has been long waiting.

The *ṭabl* can be used also as the symbol of loud, noisy, but empty people: to be silent and not to play 'the drum of talk' is required from the lover; for speech is an empty drum.[44]

This imagery is even more used in connection with the smaller drum, *dohol,*[45] whose sound can be heard during festivities.[46] Thus, several verses speak of the drunk drummer[47] — apparently not an unusual sight on festive occasions. In a strange ghazal, Mowlānā imitates the sound of the 'drum of gratitude':

> My tear has become a *dohol* from the cup moment for moment (*dam ba-dam*)
> Beat the drum with a grateful heart, *lam u lam u lam!*
> Beat the big drum of gratitude, for you have found the wine of the drum,
> Sometimes beat the high pitch (*zīr*), o heart, and sometimes the low one (*bam u bam u bam*).[48]

This image is brought to its utmost limit when the poet speaks of the person afflicted by dropsy who plays 'the drum of love for the water' on his swollen body . . .[49]

Alluding to the proverb 'The drum sounds good only from afar', and connecting it with the emptiness of created talk, Rumi finds that:

> Every sound we heard in the world
> was the voice of the drum — except love.[50]

Or else, the whole world is a big drum, played by the master — and could one find one's way if one deserts the drum which leads the army of souls?[51]

The drone-instrument, *tanbura,* was used, as still in modern oriental music, to give the background-sound for the orchestra — again the connection with the heart that makes sounds at the striking of the beloved can be easily established.[52] The *barbaṭ,* a large lute-like instrument should be twisted at its ears, for it is very lazy,[53] complaining and yet without knowledge of its own lamentations.[54] Rarely, the *musiqār,* the 'pandean pipes', is mentioned.[55]

The number of verses with musical allusions is almost unlimited in Rumi's poetry. The poet cleverly connects the different instruments all of which serve, more or less, as symbols for his own spiritual experience: only the Eternal Musician can inspire him to sing and to speak poetry.

It would be amazing if Mowlānā had not used allusions to the musical modes which, with their meaningful names, have offered welcome material for puns throughout the history of

Persian and Turkish poetry. Whole poems are made up by witty combinations of moods and instruments.[56] Often the heavy and solemn Iraqi-mood is mentioned: other moods, again with names of towns or landscapes like Isfahan or Hejaz, can serve to indicate the long way of the lovers:

> You beat the drum of separation, you play the flute of *Iraq,* you combine the mood *busālek* with the *Hejāz*![57]

Of course, the *parda-ye oshshāq*, the mood (or veil) of the lovers, is Rumi's favourite mood, often connected with his love of Shamsoddin,[58] and he,

> whose heart is not a *zangula* (a bell on the tamburine), and a mood from the 'mood of the lovers'
> what shall he do with *zir* (highest pitch), and *Irāqi* and *Sepāhān*?[59]

The charm of all these comparisons is enhanced by the double meaning of the word *parda:* it is both 'musical mood' and 'veil', a fact to which Rumi points in the very beginning of the *Mathnavi*: the flute's *parda* has torn the *parda* 'veil' of human thoughts.[60]

This 'tearing of the veils', this opening of new horizons by means of music is one of the central ideas in Mowlānā's musical imagery, an idea found already in neo-Platonic thought, notably in the works of Iamblich. Music reminds the soul of the primordial address at the *ruz-e alast* which endowed it with love and life:

> A call reached Not-Being; Not-Being said: 'Yes, (*balā*),
> I shall put my foot on that side, fresh and green and joyful!'
> It heard the *alast,* it came forth running and intoxicated,
> it was Not-Being and became Being (manifested in) tulips and willows and sweet basil.[61]

Music leads the soul back to this moment, and Rumi is certainly right to repeat several times the idea that:

> It is from the water of life that we turn in circles, not from the handclapping or from the flute, not from the tamburine, O God![62]

That is why the musical side of the Mevlevi ritual—the expression of this eternal experience in time and space—has so deeply influenced Turkish musical tradition. It was for the *samāʿ*, the whirling dance, that the greatest composers have written their music. The sixteenth century composer ʿItri set to music the *naʿt-e sharif,* Mowlānā's hymn in honour of the Prophet, which forms the introductory part of the ritual; it is of breathtaking beauty. Different musical moods have been used for the music accompanying the dance; at the very end, generally a simple Turkish melody is added which culminates in the assertion:

> *samāʿ* is the nourishment of the soul, *ruha gıdādır* . . .[63]

Indeed, the *samāʿ* has become the distinguishing feature of the Mevlevi order. For Rumi himself, the whirling movement was an expression of his enraptured interior state which he, in most cases, could not control. Yet, regular *samāʿ* meetings were also held in his own house or in the houses of his friends.

That was not unusual or novel; as early as the mid-ninth century rooms for *samāʿ*-meetings were established in Baghdad. However, the problem of the extent to which participation in musical performance and dance was licit formed a major theme of controversy even among the Sufi leaders.[64] Some of the orders strictly rejected any emotional musical gatherings, for they clearly saw the danger of such performances which were liable to attract many people whose sole interest lay in enjoying the music and dance, not in the religious edification. We certainly cannot blame the orthodoxy who sternly disapproved of acts like that of Owḥadoddin Kermāni, a friend of Ṣadroddin Qunavi, who used to tear the dresses of young boys in mystical dance, pressing his breast upon their breast.[65]

Rumi—if we belive the sources—danced in his decisive meeting with Ṣalāḥoddin Zarkub breast to breast and closely embracing him in the bazaar of the goldsmiths in Konya: at other times he whirled alone, or surrounded by his faithful disciples. Only later, the dance in the Mevlevi order was institutionalized.[66] Here, the behaviour and movements of the dervishes were rigorously prescribed: after the participants, in black gown and high felt caps (*sikke*) have completed three circumambulations and the exchange of devotional greetings with the sheykh, they cast off the black coats, and the whirling movement begins in which one hand is opened toward heaven, the other one toward earth, and the white dancing gowns (*tannura*) open widely as if white moths were circling around a flame. The turning, on the right foot, is performed both around the dervishes' own axis, and in a larger circle; should one of the participants become too enraptured in his spinning, a dervish in charge of maintenance of order ever so softly touches his widely opened skirt to curb slightly the movement which continues accelerating until, at the last sound of the music, it stops abruptly and is finished by long and melodious prayer.

To understand the central place of the whirling dance in Rumi's life, it suffices to go through the *Divān* and look at the poems with the *radif pā kufta* 'foot stamping', or *samāᶜ*, and related rhyme-words which point to the dancing movement.[67] Rumi sees his beloved, walking around his house, carrying a *rabāb* with him to act as dancer, musician and cup-bearer;[68] he sees him again in his dream, dancing on the screen of his heart,[69] for he is the master who teaches the created beings to dance.[70]

> The beloved radiates like the luminous moon,
> The lovers around him like atoms—
> When the spring breeze of Love begins blowing,
> Every twig which is not dry starts dancing.[71]

Of *samāᶜ* this much is certain (and Rumi agrees with the classical authorities): it is licit only insofar as the beloved is present. Divine Presence was required by the Sufis of the earlier centuries, but later mystics would need the beloved in visible form to complete the inspiration. Rumi's poetical letters to Shams speak of his presence which he misses for performing the mystical dance;[72] and later, he sometimes would not begin the *samāᶜ* as long as Ḥosāmoddin Chalabi was not present.

Samāᶜ becomes the antidote for every illness—it gives rest to the restless soul by inducing it to experience a new freedom which carries it out of its prison here in water and clay:

> . . . the spirits bound in clay, when they escape glad at heart from their (prisons of) clay,
> Begin to dance in the air of Divine Love and become flawless like the full moon's orb,
> Their bodies dancing, and their soul—nay, do not ask (how their souls fare); and those things from which comes the soul's delight—nay, do not ask (of those things!).[73]

This is the same experience which made the mystics in most religious traditions choose dance as a form of religious expression (not to mention the 'primitive' religions in which dance is in fact the central cult). Dance frees the soul from the fetters of earthly gravitation by directing it toward a different centre of gravitation, namely the beloved around whom the eternal dance revolves.[74] Thus, a strange union between the attracting power—imagined as that of the Sun—and the attracted particles is formed. The fact that the highest representative in the mystical hierarchy was called the *qoṭb*, 'axis' or 'pivot', can be interpreted also such that around him the souls revolve in mystical dance, kept in equilibrium by his presence.

Rumi knows that this dance is born out of separation, just like the song of the reed:

> Clap with the hand and understand that from here comes every sound:
> for this sound of two hands comes not without separation and union.[75]

That means, the rhythmic clapping of the hands which accompanies music and dance, is a symbol of the constant tension between separation and union, attraction and repulsion, without which no movement and no sound would be possible.

All nature partakes in this dance:

> The sky is like a dancing dervish frock, and the Sufi is invisible—O Muslims, who has seen a dancing frock without a body?
> The frock dances due to the body, and the body dances due to the soul,
> The love of the beloved (*jānān*) has bound the neck of the soul (*jān*) into a rope.[76]

Not only the revolving sky and the stars dance[77]—an idea which is reminiscent of the classical theories of the harmony and dance of the spheres as put forth by a number of Greek and Hellenistic philosophers—the inhabitants of heaven dance as well:[78]

> Gabriel dances in love for the beauty of God,
> The horrible demon (*ʿefrit*) dances, too, in love of a she-demon.[79]

Every movement can be explained as dance—even the Koranic dictum that during God's revelation on Mount Sinai the mountain trembled (Sura 7/143) is interpreted as its entering into ecstatic dance, comparable to the perfect Sufi in the Divine Presence.[80] Did not Abraham dance in the fire, and Jesus, and whoever partook in the spiritual pilgrimage?[81]

Rumi's main topic is—as it is the case in other Persian-writing poets as well—the dance of the *zarrāt,* the tiny dust particles which are seen moving in the sunlight; the word *zarra* can also be translated as 'atom' which gives this imagery a very modern, but appropriate flavour. These particles are thought to dance around the sun; the Sun of Tabriz is the centre around which everything turns so that the Sufis can almost be called sun-worshippers.[82] It is out of love for this sun that the atoms of this world came dancing forth from Non-Existence.[83]

Creation is seen as a great cosmic dance in which nature, dreaming in non-existence, heard the Divine call and ran into existence in an ecstatic dance, and this dance represents, at the same time, the well-established cosmic order in which every being has its special place and function—comparable to the dervishes who follow the rigid rules of *samāʿ* in perfect ease. For nothing could be more opposed to Mowlānā's strong feeling of cosmic harmony than even a single sign of anarchy and orderlessness.

The trees, flowers, gardens which have come dancing into being, continue their dance in this world, touched by the spring breeze, and listening to the melodies of the nightingale:

> The twigs started dancing like repentants (who have just entered the mystical path), the leaves clap their hands like minstrels,[84]

led by the plane-tree.[85] The nightingale comes back from its journey and calls all inhabitants of the garden to join her in *samāʿ* to celebrate spring.[86] The common people perhaps do not see this dance which begins as soon as the spring breeze of love touches the trees and flowers,[87] but these latter experience the truth of the Koranic promise that 'After difficulty comes ease' (Sura 94/5-6), after winter, spring.[88] The leaves, dressed in green like paradisical houris, happily dance on the tomb of January . . .[89] Only dried-up twigs are not moved by this breeze and this lovely sound, comparable to the dry hearts of scholars and philosophers. Even the fruit ripens dancing before the sun.[90]

Wherever Shamsoddin appears, the garden is called to participate in the spring of his beauty by dancing:[91] the poet, who has become like the wild rue-seed (burned to ward off the evil eye) dances in the fire of love,[92] and when Shamsoddin should glance once at the Koran-copy 'Heart', all the declension signs start stamping their feet in joy . . .[93]

The call for *samāʿ* comes from heaven,[94] and thus, dance constitutes a ladder which leads the lover to the seventh heaven.[95] That is why it possesses miraculous powers: wherever the lover puts his foot in dance the fountain of life will gush forth;[96] or else his dancing and treading the ground is compared to the pressing of grapes which will produce spiritual wine.[97]

The *samāʿ* is a window which allows a view towards the rose garden of the Beloved—that is why the lovers put eye and ear to this window. It is news from those who are hidden, and the lonely heart finds consolation in their letters.[98] But one should not forget that this *samāʿ* is only a branch of the eternal spiritual dance in which the soul will join one day.[99] Its connection with the world of spirit allows that it should be performed any time and everywhere—it is not restricted to time, place, or age. Rather everything created should wittingly partake in this great cosmic dance in which it is already involved unwittingly:

> No one dances until he has seen your favour,
> in the womb the children dance through your grace,
> be it in the womb, be it in non-existence,
> in the tomb the bones have a dance thanks to your light![100]

It is only Shamsoddin who reminds the soul of the source of love:

> Say Shams-e din and Shams-e din and Shams-e din, and that's enough,
> So that you may see the dead beginning to dance in their shrouds.[101]

Through *samāʿ* the greatest mystery of life, that of annihiliation and eternal life, can be, though inadequately, expressed in this world. For: 'The true men of God dance in their own blood'.[102]

Rumi alludes to the legend that Ḥallāj went dancing in his

fetters towards the gallows—such a dance in the arena where the martyrs are killed, is Rumi's wish.[103] The constant movement of the whirling dance indicates the movement of life, losing itself in union and returning to separation. As long as he is lost to himself, the whirling dervish participates in the Divine Life, the source of every movement.

In one of his English versions of Rückert's German translations from Rumi, W. Hastie has expressed this secret of *samāʿ*:

> Sound drum and mellow flute, resounding *Allah Hu*
> Dance, ruddy dawn, in gladness bounding, *Allah Hu*
> Sun exalted in the centre, o thou streaming light;
> Soul of all wheeling planets rounding *Allah Hu* . . .
>
> Who knows love's mazy circling, ever lives in God,
> For death, he knows, is love abounding: *Allah Hu*![104]

Later, Hugo von Hofmannsthal, the Austrian poet, has alluded to the 'wonderful word of Rumi:' 'Who knows the power of *samāʿ*, knows how love kills' and has seen life as the great mystical dance in which everything partakes.[105] This dance goes through all spheres of existence—some people see it; others do not understand the secret of life, love, death and resurrection symbolized in its movement. In the dervish ritual, this mystery of life and death is symbolized by the black gown that is cast off as is earth and the darkness of the grave to reveal the white dancing frock, the heavenly body' which moves in freedom round the Sun of Life.

III

Rumi's Theology

God—there is no god but He, the Living the Everlasting. Slumber seizes Him not, neither sleep; to Him belongs all that is in the Heavens and the earth . . .

Nothing is there that does not proclaim His praise . . .

GOD AND HIS CREATION

If the seven seas became all ink,
there would be no hope of an end (to God's words),
and if gardens and forests became all pens,
this word would never become less;
all this ink and pen would disappear,
but this word without number would remain.[1]

Thus sings Rumi, variating a Koranic saying (Sura 18/109) about the greatness of God and His creative words which can never be adequately described.

His whole work is permeated with verses praising God, whose praise nobody can tell; in fact, one may say without exaggeration that Rumi's poetry is nothing but an attempt to speak of God's grandeur as it reveals itself in the different aspects of life. God, as He revealed Himself to Mowlānā Jalāloddin, is the Living God, *al-ḥayy al-qayyum,* not a *Prima Causa* or a first principle which once brought the world into existence and now moves it according to prefixed schedules; it is the God who wanted to be known and manifested Himself out of His eternal richness. He is the immeasurable treasure; through His creative word everything originates, and He can be approached by faithful observation of His traces in the cosmos, each of which bears witness to His creatorship, Power, and Lovingkindness.

I was a hidden treasure and wanted to be known
for the sake of the soul of the longing, in spite of the jocose carnal soul.[2]

The famous *ḥadith qodsi* in which God was heard to attest that he wanted to be known means that the treasure of Eternal Wisdom wanted to be seen and recognized:[3] the fullness of Divine Love and Grace should be revealed although God is not depending upon human appreciation.[4] But everything longs for manifestation; the scholar tries to show his scholarship, the lover his love, etc,[5] and thus God, the treasure of hidden mercy also longed to show this mercy of His to those who accept right guidance.[6] The created world is a mirror the face of which can be poetically compared to heaven, its backside to the earth, and His eternal Beauty is reflected, though imperfectly, in this mirror, which should lead the contemplating eye towards the uncreated and everlasting Beauty and Majesty.

God is closer to man than his jugular vein (Sura 50/16),[7] and He has put signs on the horizons and into men (Sura 41/53)[8]—these were always favourite Koranic descriptions of God in which the mystics of Islam could find the foundations of their worldview. Rumi, indeed, saw God's signs everywhere. He, however, uses comparatively rarely another Koranic saying which later became a focal point of mystical theology, e.g. 'Whithersoever ye turn, there is the Face of God' (Sura 2/109)—a verse which lent itself easily to the so-called 'pantheistic' interpretation of Islam. For Mowlānā, God appears mainly in His personalist aspects as the Powerful, Almighty, Merciful, as He was described most beautifully in the Throne-verse (Sura 2/256). He does what He wants (Sura 14/27),[9] and can change man's states every moment, if He pleases. Rumi never tires of repeating the marvels of God's creation, the results of His never resting Will and Power, and his verses sometimes remind the reader of the most beautiful psalms or of those passages in the Koran in which the Creator, Sustainer, and Judge is described in glowing images. It is He who lowers and uplifts everything, and without secondary causes turns fire into Satan and dust into Adam.[10]

God's immediate creatorship is Rumi's favourite subject:

> The whole Koran means the cutting of the secondary causes,[11]

i.e. attests God's immediate act of creation out of nothing. This *creatio ex nihilo* is the basis of Islamic theology, and Rumi is absolutely faithful to this view. Secondary causes are nothing but veils; yet, they are necessary—and thus again a sign of Divine Wisdom—because not everybody is allowed into God's workshop. God has created the heavens and the earth—but this statement means, according to Rumi, only a particularization,

> since He created all things in general. Undoubtedly all bowls travel on the surface of the water of Omnipotence and the Divine Will. But it is unmannerly to relate to It a despicable thing, such as 'O Creator of dung and farting and wind-breaking!' One only says 'O Creator of the heavens!' and 'O Creator of the minds!' So this particularisation has its significance; though the statement is

general, yet the particularisation of a thing is an indication of the choiceness of that thing . . .[12]

Heaven and earth are singled out as the noblest part of His creation, and to acknowledge God as Him 'who taught the Koran' (Sura 55/2) is equal to attesting that He has in fact taught man every possible science, the choicest of which is that of the Holy Word.

The whole world is created for God's sake; it is wide and spacious (Sura 4/97), and every leaf on the trees, every bird in the bushes praises God's greatness and utters thanks for His feeding him.[13] Everywhere in the six directions are the signs of His Kindness;[14] all atoms are His army which act for Him—whether they be called fire, water, wind or earth, or birds and insects[15]—so that nothing happens but by His Will: fire burns only when He permits it; therefore man need not fear entering it for God's sake[16] (an idea derived from the Koranic story of Abraham, for whom fire turned 'cool and pleasant' (Sura 21/69), and often mentioned in Sufi hagiography since the tenth century, when Ashʿarite theology had supplied it with its theoretical basis).[17]

Thus, if man loves God's creation in patience and gratitude, he acts as a true monotheist, because he sees in the 'world' nothing but an expression and manifestation of God's creative power (that was Ghazzāli's argumentation as well);[18] but if he loves creation for its own sake, he becomes an infidel, an idolatrist—and that is why the 'world' is so often depicted as something distracting from God.

Look at the cupbearer, not at the intoxicated!
Look at Yusof, not at the (wounded) hand![19]

Nobody will ever understand the miraculous way in which God has created, and does not cease creating, things: although man is created from dust, he does not remain bound to dust, nor does the fairy resemble the fire which is her origin, nor the bird the air which is his appropriate element—the relation of the 'branch' man, or bird, with their original matter can not be explained by logical reasoning; it is 'without how' and shows God's eternal wisdom.[20] The Lord knows what is required in each and every moment: were not the earth in need of dust and mountains, He would not have created them; were not the world in need of sun and moon and stars, He would not have brought them forth from nothing.[21] And if He willeth, and regards it to be necessary, He can transform water into fire, fire into a rosegarden; He can make the hills fly like carded wool (Sura 70/9; 101/5) and can turn the clot of blood in the navel of the gazelle into fragrant musk.[22]

> From the very thorn you see wonderful blossom,
> from the very stone you see that it is the treasure of Korah (i.e. full of jewels),
> for Grace is eternal, and out of it a thousand keys
> are hidden between the *kāf* and the boat *nun*.[23]

The Divine Grace which is concealed behind the two letters of the creative address *kun* 'Be!' is without end, and can still produce more marvellous things and events.

God is involved in permanent creation out of the 'treasure-house of Not-Being': He produces the different kinds of creatures according to the necessity of time and place. Everything has its fixed place in the cosmic order, and is bound to its limits which to transgress is impossible: the fish belongs to the water, the beast to the dust—that is a limit given to them against which every ruse and attempt at change is useless.[24] Only man, strangely created as a mixture of angel and animal, is torn between the two extreme limits of his being, unless he completely leaves the world of matter and reaches the world of spirit.[25] Whatever happens, has been decreed according to the Divine Wisdom: be it the turning of the sky's wheel, or the raining of the inanimate cloud—for how could they know how to behave if God were not to inspire them to fulfil their duties in the maintenance of the great Divine plan, as He had inspired the bees to build their houses (Sura 16/68).

God has created things in special ranks and orders, slowly raising from mineral towards man. The meeting of two elements of a lower order can produce something higher—thus stone and iron belong to the mineral kingdom, but their co-operation produces fire, which is higher than both.[26] For everything under the sky is a mother (*umm,* also primary matter),[27] be they mineral, animal, or plant, unaware of each other's birth pangs and sorrows: but the goal of all of them is to produce something higher and more permanent.

To be sure, God has brought forth the world from non-existence by the single word 'Be!', and has created and shaped it in six days; but 'every day of His has a thousand years', and the development of creatures to their perfection takes a long, long time—just as the development of the sperm into a living child takes nine months before it can be born.[28] God could have finished creation in a wink, but He preferred a slow and steady growth—does not man need forty years until he reaches spiritual maturity?[29]

God is 'everyday in a new work' (Sura 55/18) and carries forth every moment new armies from the loins of non-existence toward the prime elements, from the female womb towards the earth, and, again, from dust to heaven.[30] He never rests in this creative movement—sleep and slumber do not touch Him (Sura 2/256), and the faithful should follow His example by acting patiently and without rest.[31] Perfection of nature and man can be attained only after long periods of time, when matter and spirit patiently undergo the process of painful 'alchemy' or 'fermentation' before reaching the utmost limits of their innate capacities. Sanāʾi and ʿAṭṭār had often expressed the idea that it takes centuries and requires the sacrifice of millions of lower existences, until a single perfect rose can blossom in the garden, or until a single perfect man, a prophet, can grow out of the amorphous masses who are still bound to the material world.[32] And just as the miracle of God's creative power becomes visible in the beauty of the unique rose which was the meaning and end of the garden,[33] thus humanity gains its full value only by the perfected saint who manifests God's creative light through his whole being.

> The treasures of the heavens belong to God, and the treasures of the earth, but the hypocrites do not know (Sura 63/7).

It is He who changes stones into rubies, who gives the revolving skies clarity, and endows water and earth with the power to produce plants out of the darkness.[34] He created the mother, the breast and the milk. His is what man knows and what he does not know.[35] Stones and wood are obedient to Him, and can become alive if He orders them to do so as can be witnessed in the miracles of the prophets.[36] The leaves receive their wealth (*barg*) from Him, the nurses are provided with milk by His all-embracing mildness, and 'He gives nourishment to the nourisher'.[37] Therefore, man should always be aware that only God gives him what he needs:

> The amir gives a cap, and You a head full of intelligence,
> he gives the dress, and You the tall stature![38]

that is why man is called to leave his affairs to the ruse (*makr*) of God, for his own little contrivances are meaningless when God appears as the Best of plotters (Sura 3/54; 8/30).[39]

Rumi does not hesitate to recur to the famous grammarian Sibawayhi (d. ca 770) in his definition of the word *Allāh,* for his explanation seems to show the deepest truth about God:[40]

> That Sibawayhi said (that) the meaning of (the name) Allah (is that) they take refuge (*yawlahuna*) with Him in their needs.
> He said: 'We have repaired for succour (*alehna*) unto Thee in our needs and have sought them (and) found them with Thee.'

And he explains the statement of this scholar in an almost hymnical passage:

> In the hour of affliction hundreds of thousands of intelligent persons are all crying before that unique Judge.
> Nay, all the fish in the waves, all the birds in the lofty region
> The elephant and the wolf and also the hunting lion, the huge dragon and also the ant and the snake,
> Nay, earth and wind and water and every spark gain subsistence from Him both in December and spring.
> This heaven is making entreaty unto Him incessantly—'Do not forsake me, O God, for a single moment!'
> . . . . .
> And this earth says 'Preserve me, O Thou who has caused me to ride upon the water!'
> . . . . .
> Every prophet has received from Him the guarantee: seek help with Him with patience or prayer (Sura 2/153).
> Come, ask of Him, not of any one except Him: seek water in the sea, do not seek it in the dry river-bed.
> And if you ask of another, 'tis He that gives; 'tis He that lays generosity on the open hand of his inclination . . .

God is the great artist without instrument and bodily members, the great painter who sometimes produces the image of a demonic being, sometimes that of man; sometimes He paints happiness, sometimes grief.[41] But only this constant interplay of what looks to human eyes as positive and negative aspects and colours can produce real life: although pain and happiness look outwardly contradictory, they inwardly work toward one goal which God alone knows.[42]

Rumi's favourite idea is that things can be known only

through their opposites[43]—if a bird has tasted sweet water he will understand the brackish taste of the water in his native brooklet.[44]

God's twofold aspects are revealed in everything on earth: He is the Merciful and the Wrathful; His is *jamāl*, Beauty beyond all beauties, and *jalāl*, Majesty transcending all majesties (twentieth century Western history of religion invented the juxtaposition of the *mysterium tremendum* and the *mysterium fascinans* to come closer to God's attributes). His is *lotf*, Grace, and *qahr*, Wrath, and by these attributes He manifests Himself in His world—the perfect *coincidentia oppositorum, kamāl*, is found only in the inaccessible abysses of the Divine Essence.[45]

Is not God called the *khāfiḍ* 'He who lowers' and *rāfiʿ*, 'He who raises (men and things)'? Without these two contradictory qualities nothing can come into existence—the earth must be lowered, the sky raised so that life can exist. The same Divine Names work also together in the change of night and day, of grief and joy, of illness and health—although for eyes that see only the outward husk these states seem to be in constant struggle with each other.[46] Divine Grace and Wrath are like morning breeze and pestilence: the one carries away straw, the other iron, i.e., they are like amber and magnet.[47] Everything visible and tangible hides another quality behind it—behind every nothingness the possibility of Existence is concealed; iron and steel though looking dark and dull, are able to produce fire from their insides to illuminate the world.[48] And does not legend tell that the water of life is found only in the darkest valley at the end of the journey?[49]

In the world of Reality everything is still undifferentiated, but in the world of forms separation and union are possible[50] whence the seemingly contradictory behaviour of all created things. It behoves the eye—the inner eye which has been illuminated by the Divine Light—to recognize the interior aspect of things: for man usually sees only the movement of the waterwheel but not the water which causes it to turn.[51] The fluttering of the lion embroidered on the flag tells whence the wind comes,[52] and the dust tower is a sign of the whirlwind which remains invisible.[53] Rumi loves to compare outward events to the dust moved by the hand of wind, an image which was conveniently taken from everyday scenes in the dusty

Central Anatolian landscape. But he also speaks of the foam, visible in the surface of the water, whereas the bottom of the sea remains hidden.

> The souls are before His face all dreams,
> The world is dust at the feet of His horse, and out of the dust of the hoof of His horse grows steppe after steppe with lovely cheeks.[54]

The exterior appearances—forms, scents, sounds—easily tempt man to misunderstand the Divine acts: but God, in His absolute perfection, can not be recognized without the dust, i.e., the veil of created things; these, again, have to be revealed in contrasts—only by the contrast of light one recognizes light.[55]

Rumi's trust in God's wisdom and mercy and power is infinite; it is the trust that

> no leaf falls from the tree without His will, and no morsel enters the mouth without God's permission.[56]

He always acts in a way which will prove, finally, useful for His creatures even though it might look, at first sight, like loss:[57]

> He takes away half a soul and gives a hundred souls,
> and bestows what man cannot imagine.[58]

How often is man misled by the illusion and delusion of outward forms and appearances and will only later recognize the wisdom of God's dealing with him in an outwardly cruel way:

> How many enmities that were friendship! How many destructions that were renovation![59]

Thus, the true believer can repeat ʿAli's saying:

> I recognized my Lord by the annulation of my intentions.[60]

Man sees with utter amazement that the cold wind that destroyed the people of ʿAd served as a servant and bearer for Solomon,[61] just as poison is proper to the snake and is part of its strength, whereas the same poison means death for others;[62] and the Nile that turned into blood for the Egyptians protected the Children of Israel.[63] One man may call Zayd an infidel liable to execution, the other one sees him as a faithful Sunnite or even an exalted saint—not two aspects of life bear the same meaning for different people.[64]

Man, being 'between two fingers of the Merciful' experiences these contrasting expressions of the Divine power in every breath—taking breath into the lungs and breathing it out belong as much to the essentials of life as depression (*qabż*) alternates with spiritual dilation (*basṭ*) or grief with joy. The masculine and the feminine aspects of things, or the positive and negative energy, are working together to weave the visible garment of the invisible Divine Will under which He is concealed and through which He manifests His attributes; but the divergent aspects of being will rest, eventually, in God's Perfection.

This trust enabled Rumi to believe that there is no absolute evil:

> Wherever there is a pain, the medicine goes there;
> wherever there is poverty, help goes there.[65]

Good and evil come both from God, although they are created for different purposes. For He never does anything without purpose—has any potter ever made a jar for its own sake, not for carrying water? Or

> does a calligrapher write exclusively for the sake of letters, not for the sake of the reading?[66]

God is like the painter who portrays both beautiful and ugly things, showing His masterly hand in the perfection of both, so that the image gets its proper and intended character.[67] For even the ugly picture proves His creative power,[68] and a true artist never paints a picture without a purpose: be it to amuse children, be it to remind people of departed friends (a not very fitting idea in an Islamic environment, but probably influenced by Rumi's Byzantine neighbours).[69] Thus the poet can attest:

> I love both His kindness and His wrath—
> Strange that I love these two opposites![70]

Even if God seems to destroy a thing, He does it with the purpose of replacing it with something better: this side of His activity is revealed, in the Koran, by the strange and apparently destructive acts of Khiżr, the prototype of sainthood, (cf. Sura 18/65-83). Did he not abolish some

Koranic verses in order to replace them by better ones, taking away the grass and bring a rose instead?[71] This idea—destruction for the sake of renovation, annihilation for the sake of duration, loss for the sake of gain—forms the cornerstone of Rumi's thoughts about the development of the whole world.

God's acting with man is therefore also described, in Koranic imagery, under the simile of a merchant:[72] He buys man's body, his outward existence, and if man willingly sells to Him whatever he possesses, he is rewarded by the most wonderful spiritual gain:

> God says 'I have bought you, your moments, your breaths, your possessions, your lives. If they are expended on Me, if you give them to Me, the price of them is everlasting Paradise. This is your worth in My sight.' If you sell yourself to Hell, it is yourself you will have wronged just like the man who hammered the dagger worth a hundred pounds into the wall and hung a gourd upon it.[73]

God's wrath and His mercy both help the development of the world—and in the midst of wrath, mercy is hidden like a precious cornelian in the midst of dirt.[74] God's wrath may, in many cases, be more useful than the mildness or friendliness of the creatures, for He knows what is good for the spiritual growth of man.[75] Eventually He will turn the left, unlucky side, into the right, lucky side.[76]

Both wrath and mercy, majesty and beauty are necessary to reveal God's true greatness. This idea has been elaborated by Mowlānā several times in his prose-work as well:

> A king has in his realm prison and gallows, robes of honour and wealth, estates and retinue, feasting and merry-making, drum and flags. In relation to the king all these things are good. Just as robes of honour are the perfect ornament of his kingdom, so too gallows and slaying and prison are the perfect ornament of his kingdom.[77]
>
> The king puts a man on the gallows, and he is hung up in a high place in the presence of the assembled people. He could also suspend him indoors, hidden from the people, by a low nail, but it is necessary that the people should see and take warning, and that the execution of the king's decree and the carrying out of his order should be visible. After all, not every gallows consists of wood. High rank and worldly fortune are also a gallows and a mighty high one. When God most High desires to chastise a man He bestows on him high rank in the world and a great kingdom, as in the cases of Pharaoh and Nimrod and the like . . .[78]

Certainly, God orders good and evil, but wills only good—comparable to the physician who needs man's illness in order to prove his skill, or the baker who needs the hungry to feed them: and still He wills that everybody should be good, healthy, and satiated. Rumi spins out this idea to a conclusion which is not too far from certain Christian concepts: 'God needs the sinner to show His mercy'[79]—this, too, is part of the mystery of the Divine Treasure which wanted to be known. And even those who suffer in Hell, praise Him, for everything has been created to praise God, and

> inasmuch as the unbelievers in the time of their ease do not do this, and since their purpose in being created was to recollect God, therefore they go to Hell in order that they may remember Him.[80]

Everything has to attest God's Greatness; evil and good, suffering and joy are nothing but instruments to lead man towards his duty and to the goal of his life which is permanent adoration of God as it is said in the Koran: 'Verily We created spirits and men that they might worship' (Sura 51/56)

That is why Rumi praises God's power in ever new verses, in glorious hymns and short lines, in heartfelt sighs and strange similes. Take the lovely words in the story of the poor Sufi:

> He who turns the fire into roses and trees is also able to make this (world fire) harmless.
> He who brings forth roses from the very midst of thorns is also able to turn this winter into spring.
> He by whom every cypress is made 'free' (evergreen) has the power if He would turn sorrow into joy.
> He by whom every non-existence is made existent—what damage would He suffer if He were to preserve it for ever?[81]

When He wants, the essence of grief becomes joy, the very fetters of the foot become freedom.[82]

Rumi knows that the angels are the treasurers, or the mines, of Divine mercy and kindness, whereas the demons act as the mines of His wrath, and he firmly believes in the *ḥadith qodsi* 'My Mercy precedes My wrath'—finally, the angelic side will win.[83] Yet there must be some people as well to satisfy Hell; otherwise it would not have any meaning and that is inconceivable.[84] Man may be unable to understand these contradictory movements of the Divine Wisdom and Power, and is left bewildered and hopeless in between. He knows, there is no place to flee from this amazing confusion—only in God's solitude is eternal peace and calmness, and in the vision of the Divine Beloved all the opposites rest and fall together.[85] The Prophet's saying: 'Show me the things as they are' is the call of the human soul which is dumbfounded and helpless before the contrasting outward aspects of life, and longs for a vision, higher and purer, by which he may, perhaps, draw closer to an understanding of the working of the Divine workshop.[86]

Part of the Divine creation are the angels who are mentioned in many a story of the *Mathnavi*, in verses and prose-passages; Isrāfil, the angel of resurrection is, now and then, connected with the perfect saint or with the beloved, who calls man back from the prison of the tomb, i.e. rescues him from the material world and revives him in the realm of spiritual glory.[87] The story of ʿAzrāʾil, the angel of death, is told with many touching details in harmony with popular beliefs, and Gabriel, often mentioned as the messenger-angel who brought inspiration to the Prophet, can become a symbol of reason, which is denied the last and highest union with God, which was the Prophet's prerogative.[88] And there is Mikāʾil who dispenses nourishment to created beings and looks after man's needs.[89] Numberless choirs of angels are engaged in constant worship and prayer; jinns and demonic powers belong to the fullness of creation as much as the higher ranks of angelic beings—each and every one has his function in the cosmos to prove God's creative power and to glorify Him through his works.

There are passages in the *Mathnavi* and in *Fihi mā fihi* which point to the Universal Intellect as the power acting behind the multiplicity of phenomena, and in such passages Rumi uses a language developed by the mystics of his century. However, his use of these terms is not fully consistent, and an elaborated system is lacking in his poetry. It seems that he was interested in these speculations in the 1260s and introduced a terminology into his poetry which was basically not very congenial with his own feeling, but rather appealed to those who had imbibed the rigid systematization brought about by Ibn ʿArabi and developed by Rumi's fellow-citizen Ṣadroddin Qunavi. But these problems have still to be studied in detail.

In general, Mowlānā has spoken comparatively little about

theological problems, or about God's essence. He was mainly preoccupied with God as the Creator who never ceases continuing His wonderful work. Did not the Prophet warn the faithful: 'Think little about the essence of God but think about His attributes?'[90] And His attributes could be detected best as working in the various aspects of creation so that everyone tries to find his way through them:[91]

> After all, surely the Creator of thought is subtler than thought. For instance, the builder who has constructed a house is subtler than the house, for that builder, a man, is able to make and plan a hundred such buildings other than this, each different from the other. Therefore he is subtler and more majestic than any fabric; but that subtlety cannot be seen save through the medium of a house, some work entering the sensible world, that that subtlety of his may display beauty.[92]

Rumi refuses the anthropomorphism uttered by some of the orthodox on behalf of God, and blames those who attribute to God hand and feet in the human meaning; this is as blameworthy as calling a man Fāṭema. What is an honour for woman is a shame for man; and although hands and feet are an honour for human beings, it does not apply to the Divine Being.[93]

> Just as a person is in relation to you a father and in relation to another either son or brother—
> So the names of God in their number have relations:
> He is from the viewpoint of the infidel the Tyrant (*qāher*); from our viewpoint, the Merciful.[94]

What can be said about God?

> He is the First, He is the Last, He is the Inward, He is the Outward—.[95]

The Divine Names which have formed a source of inspiration or of meditation for so many mystics in Rumi's time are understood by him in an ethical sense: God has called Himself 'the Seeing' to prevent man from sinning, or 'the Hearing' so that man should not open his mouth for foul and disgusting talk, etc.; but all these names are only derived, whereas the qualities designated by them are primordial and eternal in God.[96] Mowlānā's treatment of the Divine Names is, in some way, similar to that of Ghazzāli's discussion of these Names in the *maqṣad al-aqṣā*.[97] They work upon man as models and warning; thus when man wants to avoid God's wrath, the heaviest of all things imaginable, he has to give up first his own wrath,[98] for man is called to 'qualify himself with the qualities of God'. The qualities of God can be recognized through His Names, and through the contrasting qualities as revealed in the created world, but His essence is hidden, since He has no contrast through which He can be recognized.[99]

What can be said about Him is that He is one—not begotten nor begetting, as Rumi repeats with the words of Sura 112.[100] For He is the creator of everything begetting and begotten—they are *moḥdath*, 'created in time', and therefore subject to decay, whereas He is never touched by any change.[101] Past and future are not applicable to Him.[102]

It was ᶜAṭṭār who invented the story of the squint-eyed person who saw two moons and could not imagine that there is actually only one—an example utilized by Rumi to show the spiritual illness of those who cannot see that God is One, and not two or three.

> If you tell the squint-eyed person that the moon is one, he tells you: 'It is two, and there is doubt in its being one . . .'[103]

The two letters *k* and *n, kun* 'Be!', the word of creation, are like a two coloured yarn; they are like a twisted rope to bring things out of the abyss of Non-Existence into existence, but they hide the reality of the Divine Unity.[104] Once man has realized this Divine Unity, and has undergone what Rumi calls with the Koranic expression *ṣibghat Allāh,* 'the colouring' or 'baptism of God' (Sura 2/138)[105] in which the differently coloured pieces of cloth become one colour, he knows that 'seeker' and 'sought' are no longer separate.

> Faith and infidelity are only His doorkeepers,[106]

they are the chaff which hides the clear, fathomless water—an idea which Sanāʾi had elaborated in one of his great hymns to God at the beginning of the *Ḥadiqat al-ḥaqiqa.*[107] Man has to go a long and difficult way to recognize this Divine Unity behind the colourful interplay of opposites which may lead him slowly to the truth. True existential realization of the confession of Divine Unity implies man's annihilation:

> What is *towḥid*? To burn one's self before the One![108]

No matter how much a lover or theologian may try to describe, or rather circumscribe God, they could not describe a single mole of His Beauty.[108] Men know that everything goes back to Him, that 'God's hand is above their hands' (Sura 48/10), that from Him the clouds take their water and into Him the torrents return.[110] This is certainly not a philosophical statement but the unshakable faith in God's absoluteness as Creator who granted not-being the robe of honour of existence and will order the world to end and return into not-being whenever He deems it necessary. To give any definition of Him, however, is impossible:

> Whatever you think is liable to pass away—
> That which cannot be thought, that is God.[111]

His name flees from utterance; whatever man thinks about Him, He is different, now clear like the moon on the sky, now shimmering like the moon's reflection in a pool of water; at one moment He gives the hem of His grace into man's hand, and then becomes invisible like an arrow that flies from the bow, as Rumi sings in one of his most beautiful ghazals.[112] There is no place where He can be found—not even in the *lāmakān,* the 'place beyond places', outside time and space. But still, Rumi, like every faithful Muslim, knows that there is one place where man can hope to find God. Did not God Himself inform the Prophet in a *ḥadith qodsi:*

> Heaven and earth do not contain Me, but the heart of my faithful servant contains Me?[113]

The heart, broken in constant service of God, smashed under the blows of affliction, is comparable to a ruin which contains the most precious treasure—that treasure 'God' who wanted to be known. By recognizing his own worthlessness and absolute poverty, man finds the Treasure closer to him than his jugular vein, according to the tradition: 'Who knows himself, knows his Lord.'

The central point in Rumi's view about creation is that of a *creatio ex nihilo*—God has produced everything from *ʿadam,* 'nothingness' or 'non-existence'. Only in rare cases does he claim that *ʿadam* does not accept *hasti*, 'existence'—but such a connection occurs, as far as I can see, only in an ethical sense, i.e., when you plant colocynth you cannot expect sugarcane to grow out of it.[114] Mowlānā has never tired of repeating that the Divine Creator and Beloved has brought forth man and everything for ʿ*adam:*

> 'I' and 'We' were ʿ*adam*, to which God, out of kindness, granted the robe of honour 'I' and 'We'.[115]

ʿ*Adam* is like a box from which creatures are called[116] (we may think of ʿAṭṭār's parable of the puppet-player and his box from which he takes his puppets and then throws them back into it, as told in the *Oshtornāma*):

> Hundreds of thousands of birds fly nicely out of it,
> hundreds of thousands of arrows spring from that one bow![117]

Without the Divine Beloved, man is ʿ*adam,* or even less than this, for ʿ*adam* is capable of existentialization—but without the beloved, man is not capable of existence at all.[118]

> The beloved gives birth to man from ʿ*adam,* puts him on a throne, gives him a mirror.[119]

Out of this ʿ*adam* thousands of worlds come forth,[120] and not a single drop can disappear and hide itself in ʿ*adam* when God addresses it and calls it into existence.[121] Every leaf and every green tree in spring becomes, for Jalāloddin, a messenger from ʿ*adam,* for they point to God's power to create lovely things from nothingness.[122]

ʿ*adam* is the treasure-house and mine from which God, as *mubdi*ʿ, 'Originator' brings forth everything, producing the branch without the root,[123] which is why everyone seeks not-being as prerequisite for being.[124]

> You have bound our existence to absolute non-existence,
> you have bound our will to the condition of having no will.[125]

The ʿ*adam,* is the hidden ground which God has concealed under the veil of existence; it is the sea of which only the foam is visible, or the wind which can be perceived only through the movement of the stirred up dust.[126] ʿ*adam* is Solomon, and the creatures are like ants before it.[127] The Koran has attested that God 'brings forth life from death', (Sura 6/95 etc.), and that means, in more scholarly language, that He produces being from not-being.[128] He utters magical words upon ʿ*adam* and transforms it, the poor 'nothing without eyes and ears', into beings, to call them back, by another magical word, into the second non-existence.[129] Hundreds of thousands of hidden things are waiting in that *ʿadam* to spring forth by Divine grace,[130] to come out in an intoxicated dance at the sound of the Divine word, and to grow into flowers and beauties, for

> He has shown the joy of existence to non-existence.[131]

In *ʿadam,* love, kindness, power and sight are hidden, and its agitated movements make existences appear like waves,[132] or make a hundred mills turn.[133] Caravan after caravan comes out of *ʿadam* day after day so that the two contrasting manifestations—being and not-being— are always visible.[134] One never knows whether the manifestations that are called out of the undifferentiated not-being will be good or evil with respect to what is created—they may prove sugar for the one, but poison for another.[135] But even if a thousand worlds were to appear out of *ʿadam,* they would not be more than a mole of His cheek.[136]

The deserts of not-being are filled with longing—the image of the caravan occurs once more at the very end of Rumi's life.[137] All those armies of the thought of the heart

> are one banner from the soldiers of *ʿadam.*[138]

God knows all these forms which are still hidden in non-existence so that He can call them at the moment they are required:[139]

> There are still suns in *ʿadam,* and what appears here as sun, is there a tiny star like Canopus.[140]

The lover, however, experiences *ʿadam* differently; he feels completely non-existent without the force of love[141] which causes him really to exist:

> O Prince of Beauty, make the eye smiling,
> grant existence to the handful of non-existence![142]

The image of non-existence, *ʿadam,* as a box, mine, or ocean could lead easily to the conclusion that creation consists in giving form to entities already existent at least in the Divine Knowledge. Rumi is not clear upon this point, but his whole approach shows rather the *ʿadam* as an unfathomable depth of nothingness which is endowed with existence only so far as God speaks to it and looks at it; he has certainly not pondered upon the philosophical implications of this imagery.

But there is another point: ʿ*adam* is not only the first and initial station which is the prerequisite for being—it is likewise the final position and end of everything. In many cases one would like to substitute for ʿ*adam* the term *fanā*ʾ, 'annihilation', but in other cases ʿ*adam* seems to lead even deeper. Just as the puppet-player in ʿAṭṭār's *Oshtornāma* puts the puppets back into the box of Unity, Rumi has at times expressed the feeling that ʿ*adam* is the abyss of Divine Life, which is beyond everything conceivable, even beyond the 'revealed God'. We may call it the *deus absconditus,* or the Positive Non-Being, or the sphere which is beyond everything and in which contrasts fall once more together.

> If you could only know what is before you,
> all existence would become ʿ*adam*![143]

The 'desert of ʿ*adam*' is equated, therefore with the *bāgh-e Eram,*[144] the fascinating gardens described in the Koran. There is no end of poems which tell, often in dancing rhythms, the beauty of ʿ*adam*—like these lines:

> The moment I became annihilated through you, and became what you know,
> I seized the cup of ʿ*adam* and quaffed its wine cup by cup . . .
> This moment, every wink, give me the wine of ʿ*adam,*
> Since I entered into ʿ*adam* I do not know the house from the roof.
> When your non-existence increases, the soul performs a hundred prostrations before you,
> O you, before whose ʿ*adam* thousands of existences are slaves!
> Bring a wave up from ʿ*adam,* so that it may carry me away—
> how long shall I go step by step on the shore of the sea?[145]

Rumi has once said that ʿ*adam* is like the East, whereas the end *(ajal)* is like the West, man wandering between the two towards another, higher heaven.[146] We may call this 'other heaven' the 'positive ʿ*adam*', the last station of man on his way through the world:

> Put your two eyes on ʿ*adam* and see a wonderful thing—
> What marvellous hopes in hopelessness![147]

It is this positive non-existence which is almost equated with the Divine Essence in the famous lines about the rising gamut of existence:

Then I became ʿ*adam;* ʿ*adam,* like an organ
speaks to me 'Verily unto God we are returning!' (Sura 2/156)[148]

This ʿ*adam*

is a sea, we are the fishes, existence the net—
the taste of the sea knows he who has left the net.[149]

In ʿ*adam,* the caravan of souls wanders to graze every night on the hidden path which connects them with God;[150] it is the place where the saints and lovers go—they see a dream without dreaming, and enter ʿ*adam* without a door.[151] In this ʿ*adam* the lovers 'pitch their tents', united completely without distinction,[152] for it is the mine of the purified soul.[153]

Here, in the way of complete silence, man can become non-existent *(maʿdum),* lost to himself, and in his silence, completely transformed into praise and laud.[154] In ʿ*adam* all 'knots' and complications are resolved.[155] Rumi sings of the beauty of this state:

Thanks to that ʿ*adam* which carried away our existence,
Out of love for this ʿ*adam* the world of the souls came into existence.
Wherever ʿ*adam* comes, existence diminishes,
Well done, ʿ*adam;* for, when it comes, existence increases!
For years I took away existence from non-existence,
ʿ*adam* took away with one single glance all this from me.
It saved (me) from myself, and from before, and from the soul that thinks about death,
It saved me from fear and hope, and saved me from wind (*bād*) and being (*bud*).
The mountain 'existence' is like straw before the wind of ʿ*adam;*
Which is the mountain that ʿ*adam* did not carry away like straw?[156]

We may perhaps see in Rumi's extended imagery of ʿ*adam*—which, in fact, is one of the central expressions in his whole poetical work—an echo of Joneyd's theory, well known to all mystics, that man should eventually become as he was before being. One of Rumi's verses is a variant on a famous dictum of Joneyd:

Become nothing, nothing from selfishness, for there is no sin worse than your existence.[157]

For since ᶜ*adam* was the state of things when God addressed them with the words 'Am I not your Lord?' (Sura 7/171) then the goal of the mystic is to return once more to this very ᶜ*adam,* into the undifferentiated nothingness out of which everything existent jumped forth in joyful obedience to the Divine order.

But there is something higher and more comprehensive even than ᶜ*adam,* and that is Love:

> Love has the ear of ᶜ*adam* in its hand, and Being and Non-existence are dependent upon it.[158]

Rumi has described the world in different images. There is no doubt that it is a manifestation of God's creative power, and a bridge which leads man again to God, yet, even he, though looking with the eye of faith at its manifestations, could not help seeing its outward disharmony. The world is a place of struggle and strife, in which

> atom struggles with atom, just as religion with infidelity,[159]

and the centrifugal forces of the various atoms threaten its harmony in case they forget their absolute dependence upon God and try to rely solely upon their own deceptive power. Sometimes, Rumi sees the whole world as frozen, waiting for the spiritual sun to set it again in motion;[160] the numerous images connected with the hibernal aspect—crows, raven, snow, darkness—belong to this picture of the created world. Mowlānā even voices at times the old Sufi hatred of the world, which was described as carrion,[161] or as a dunghill, visited only in cases of need; those who frequent it or are attached to it are lower than dogs. Such a description of the created world is applicable, however, only in so far as materially minded people consider it as valuable in its own right, and forget that it has been brought into existence by God in order to manifest His power. In the hope of leading such people toward the spiritual background of creation, Rumi dwells intensely upon the old ascetic imagery which shows itself mainly in his animal-similes. (Ch. II 4)

There is also a famous passage in the *Mathnavi* in which he claims that the world is the external form of the First Intellect, ᶜ*aql-e koll,* who is the father of everyone addressed by the Divine word *Qul* 'Say!'. But this description is as little consistent as Rumi's other images of the world.[162]

The poet may also explain the world as a dream. Here, he has Prophetic sanction—a favourite *ḥadith* of the mystics was that 'People are asleep and when they die they awake', and another one claiming that the world is 'like the dream of a sleeper'.[163] Does not this world disappear when man blindfolds his eyes[164] or goes to sleep,[165] when he is led into other worlds beyond that of sensual perception?

> The world is nothing, and we are nothing; imagination and sleep, and we are perplexed—
> If the sleeping person would know 'I am asleep'—what grief would it be?[166]

Life is indeed like wandering in a dream;[167] and, when one considers the woes and afflictions to be really painful, one is wrong—they are as little real as the pain one suffers in a bad dream. These 'dreams' are only a derivation from the original source of life, but nothing independent;[168] yet, they are signs which point to a deeper reality.[169] Rumi therefore speaks of the 'second sleep' in which man acts;[170] but he is realistic enough to warn man not to think that these so-called dreams, i.e. his actions and passions on earth, are of no value: they are rather signs of a hidden spiritual reality; and whatever man has 'dreamt' here will become prominent on the morning of eternity, when God will interpret human dreams and lay open their purport.[171]

> The night's departed: yet my friend,
> Our story's not yet at an end,[172]

as Mowlānā says with the old and oft-repeated combination of 'story' and 'sleep' which was to become so prominent in later Sufi poetry. Later Sufi poets enjoyed this theory of 'the world a dream' as a consolation for the sufferings of life. On the one hand, such ideas might induce them to heedlessness and indifference; on the other hand, during times of disaster, they might give them a little hope, hope that they were going only through a nightmare without reality. Rumi, however, transforms even the idea that the world can be likened to a dream into something positive: for man's awakening on the glorious morning when eternity dawns upon him will be in accordance with his dreams: he who has seen a rose garden in his wordly dream will wake up in that very garden.[173] Only the prophets and the saints are able to discern the true character of these dreams on earth, as the Prophet of Islam said: 'My eyes sleep, but my heart is awake'.[174] They know that even dreams are directed by God, and see through their veil to the Reality, recognizing the Creator of dreams and sleep who will call them on the morning of Doomsday. The story of the elephant's dream of India belongs to this imagery: in the midst of the sleep of heedlessness which covers the majority of people, the elect suddenly see the decisive dream which reminds them of their lost and long-forgotten homeland, and, tearing the ropes of material existence, they set out wandering to seek this country, the country of God which is beyond dream and wakefulness.

But, whatever Rumi's verses attest about the world, he returns from every possible digression to his main idea that the world is valuable as a place of Divine manifestation:

> The world is like Mount Sinai; we are seeking like Moses;
> Every moment comes a manifestation and splits the mountain.
> One piece become green, another jasmine-white,
> One piece becomes a jewel, others ruby and amber . . .[175]

Man, in this world, is completely dependent upon God's will:

> If He makes me a goblet, I become a goblet,
> and if He makes me a scimitar, I become a scimitar;
> if He makes me a fountain, I give water,
> if He makes me fire, I give heat;
> if He makes me rain, I produce harvest;
> and if He makes me an arrow, I dash into the body,
> if He makes me a serpent, I spew poison;
> and if He makes me a friend, I serve.[176]

Man should acknowledge that God is the source of everything, that without His word he would not be able to speak, that without His attraction, he could not love Him. Whatever man possesses—and that holds true not only for man but for the whole of creation—is God's gift and a sign of His creative power, strange as His manifestations and revelations may appear to the eye of the uninitiated. But, looking behind the husk of material forms, those with enlightened hearts see the wise arrangements of events; having lost themselves in Him, they understand His will. All the various images and similes, the long chains of anaphora and the prayers and supplications, the praises and philosophical treatments of the problem 'how to describe God' can be summed up, for Jalāloddin, in the trusting verse:

> And if He closes before you all the ways and passes,
> He will show a hidden way which nobody knows . . .[177]

And We have honoured the children of Adam . . .

MAN AND HIS POSITION IN RUMI'S WORK

> The situation of man is like this: They took the feathers of an angel and tied them to the tail of an ass, that haply the ass in the ray and society of the angel might become an angel.[1]

Thus Rumi describes the strange situation of man—man, the central figure in God's creation, the vicegerent of God on this earth and yet, the most endangered creature. Jalāloddin has never ceased reminding man of his original high position, as is attested by several Koranic revelations.

> We have been in heaven, we have been the companions of the angels
> Let us go again there, master, for that is our city.[2]

Man was created, as Rumi says in a mythological image, from the first sip of Divine wine that fell into the dust, whereas Gabriel the Archangel was created from that sip which fell into heaven.[3]

Did not God address man with the words *karramnā* 'We have honoured the children of Adam' (Sura 17/70)? This *karramnā* is like a crown for man, just as the Divine word *Aᶜṭanāka*, 'We have given you the *kowthar*', (Sura 109/1) is his necklace.[4] Or else, Love can be seen as the robe of honour combined with the chain of *karramnā*[5]—i.e. man alone of all creation is capable of loving truly. He has become, by this twofold honour, the true essence of creation for whom the sky is nothing but an external accident,[6] for the heavens never heard such a Divine address.[7] To be sure, God offered the special trust *(amāna)* to heaven and earth, but only man accepted it (Sura 33/72):

> I took the trust which heaven did not accept with the firm belief (*eᶜtemād*) that Thy kindness would support me.[8]

For:

> although heaven and earth carry out many wonderful tasks, God did not say 'We honoured heaven and earth'. God has set a great price on man: would any one use a precious Indian sword as a butcher's knife, or a fine dagger to make it a nail for a broken gourd?[9]

Man has become, by this trust—be it explained as love, or as free will—the most valuable part of creation, which should not be misused, so that God will buy his soul, finally, to bring it to the loftiest spiritual heights.

The greatest gift God bestowed upon man was that 'He taught him the names' (Sura 2/31)—Rumi has often alluded to this wonderful act of grace which gave man the highest rank in the universe,[10] and made him the *ʿallamaʾl-asmāʾ-beg,* (as he says with a strange Arabo-Turkish compound) so that he has thousands of sciences in each vein.[11] The names which God taught him first were not the outward names 'in the dress of *ʿayn* and *lām*', i.e. of written and pronounced letters,[12] but those which are not veiled by outward letters; it was the wisdom that was on the *lowḥ-e maḥfuẓ*, the Well-preserved Tablet, so that man indeed became higher than the angels, even those who carry the Divine Throne.[13]

For to know the name of a thing means to possess power over it, and to work on it: thus, by enabling man to call everything by its name, God has made him the true ruler of the earth and what is in it. Yet, after his fall man knows only part of the names—the secret hidden behind them is known only to God:[14] Moses called his miraculous rod by the name of 'stick', but God knew its name to be 'dragon'; 'Omar, though first called by his compatriots an idol worshipper, had been named 'faithful' already in pre-eternity. In spite of Adam's being acquainted with the secret of the names, man, in his present state, can only name the visible parts of everything, and as much as names can reveal the true character of a person, they can serve as well to veil and hide a secret: the story of Zoleykha who intended with thousands of names only one essence, i.e. her beloved Joseph, is a fine example of the veiling quality of man-made names.[15]

Man was elected for his special relation with God when the future humanity was still concealed in the loins of the yet uncreated Adam, by the Divine address *Alasto bi-rabbikom*

'Am I not your Lord?' as the Koran states (Sura 7/171). The future generations answered *balā, shahednā* 'Yes, we witness it'; and since that day—the Day of the Primordial Covenant—they have grown and lived under the spell of this first Divine address. This Koranic verse, romantically interpreted and elaborated by the poets and mystics as the 'banquet of *alast*' has formed the cornerstone of mystical theology from at least the days of Joneyd (d. 910).[16] It is small wonder that Rumi always has recourse to the story of this covenant, which shows so clearly that the very first word was spoken by God, addressing man and thus establishing once and for all His rule over human life; man can only speak, or rather answer, if God has enabled him to do so. The Divine *alast* and the human answer is the seal of the heart,[17] so that this organ is forever bound to acknowledge God's infinite power and love. Human hearts are imagined as intoxicated from the goblet of *alast,* from the pre-eternal wine;[18] they are, as Rumi says once, 'intoxicated in the path of works of obedience'.[19] Man's whole being is suspended between this beginning of history—or rather meta-history[20]—and the end of time, the Day of Judgment: poets and mystics would therefore speak of the one day of human life between the Yesterday of the *ruz-e alast* and the Tomorrow of Resurrection, following the Koranic idea that Doomsday is for every human being the true Tomorrow.

> He who has seen the happiness of pre-eternity,
> has no fear of the eternal.[21]

The drink man tasted that day will help him to discern between good and evil—comparable to Moses, who recognized the milk of his own mother from among all wet-nurses, man will recognize what is good for him.[22] This primordial Divine address leads man into conscious and responsible life, but it leads him also, if understood correctly, into *fanā*ʾ. For the goal of the mystic is, as Joneyd had expressed it, to become as non-existent as he was at the day of the covenant—his end (in ʿ*adam)* is the return to his beginning (in ʿ*adam*). That is why Rumi is reminded of the covenant of *alast* by the Friend's light;[23] for it is He who leads the seeker towards the final state of union. *Alast* means the moment when Unity still prevails—out of it the souls spring forth like rivers;[24] but once the address is heard again, the way of the rivers into the ocean is finished:

> The wave *alast* came, the boat of the outward forms broke, when the boat is broken, that it is the time of union and meeting.[25]

The Sufis have invented a beautiful pun on the human answer to this Divine address: the word *balā* 'Yes' was interpreted as meaning *balā* 'affliction'.

> One moment we are affliction-drinkers of the primordial love,
> one moment we are those who say *balā* to the address of *alast*.[26]

> He said *alast,* and you said *balā* –
> What is the thank for the *bālā*? To undergo affliction *(bala)* ![27]

This affliction is meant as a touchstone for man: only if his primordial answer was sincere, will he be able to take gratefully the burden of affliction,[28] and the higher his rank at the Divine banquet, the greater the amount of suffering he will have to endure: that is why the prophets are those who suffer most. Rumi sees his Beloved Shams as among the first to pronounce this answer,[29] who were, so to speak, closest to the Divine fountain.

This *alast* is, however, not a unique act–God repeats it every moment for the world is created anew every wink according to Ashʿarite theology; even though the essences and accidents do not explicitly answer *balā*, which is the prerogative of man alone, their very appearance out of nothing (*ʿadam*) is the attestation of their positive answer to the Divine address 'Be!'[30]

But man forgot his primordial oath very soon, notwithstanding all the favours God bestowed upon Adam who had been kneaded for forty days by the hands of the Almighty, and had been the eye of the primordial light, and that is why his first transgression–his step into sensual pleasures–was considered so heavy, so painful–comparable to a hair in the eye.[31] His fall from Paradise was caused by his mixing too freely with the serpent[32]–a warning for everyone who mixes with uncongenial and bad companions who keep him matter-bound and jeopardize his spiritual pursuits.

The way home could be found only by constant weeping –'For the sake of weeping Adam came to earth';[33] he should be a model of the pious who, in constant repentance, will try to find the way back to Paradise Lost, to the place whence they were exiled. Adam wept for 300 years to re-attain God's satisfaction,[34] trusting in the Divine promise *la taqnaṭu* 'Do not despair' (Sura 39/53)—and the rose garden, lonely in the heart of winter, follows his example and does not despair.[35]

Man, fallen into the enclosure of the four elements, considers this world his prison:

> I have remained for the sake of betterment in the prison World—
> What have I to do with the prison? Whose money have I stolen?[36]

In his present life, man can be compared to the spark hidden in the iron; he is bound to sleep and food; his soul invisible, without leaving its dark prison. The spark is nourished first by cotton, and once it is freed by the master's hand, the soul's fire extends up to the skies and he is, once more, higher than the angels.[37]

Rumi, like most of the Sufis, has often meditated upon the twofold state of man: thanks to the Divine trust he has become 'half honey-bee and half snake': whatever the faithful eats—be it material or spiritual—will be turned into life-giving substance, whereas others produce by each and every act deadly poison for themselves and for others.[38]

> The angel was saved by knowledge, and the beast by ignorance—
> The son of man remained in between in the struggle.[39]

Man is at times like a sun, then like an ocean full of pearls which carries inside the glory of heaven, but outwardly he is lowly like the earth.[40] And in an image used in later times by many Persian poets, and known to English readers from John Donne's *Devotions,*[41] Rumi says:

> Man is a mighty volume; within him all things are written, but veils and darknesses do not allow him to read that knowledge without himself. The veils and darknesses are these various preoccupations and diverse worldly plans and desires of every kind . . .[42]

But man usually forgets the high rank which God bestowed upon him; he does not know himself, and sells himself cheap: he was a piece of valuable satin and stitched himself on a tattered cloak.[43] Rumi illustrates this sad truth with the amusing story of a man who ran into a house to seek shelter since outside hunters were hunting asses. The landlord had to persuade him that he was not at all an ass and need not fear the hunters, but was rather a 'Jesus', whose place is in the fourth heaven, not in the stable.[44] This shows how man seeks his place in the stable of this material world instead of going to his heavenly resort.

To be sure, 'not every human-faced creature is a human being', as Rumi attests, following Sanāʾi's verdict.[45] People are quite different—did not the Prophet compare them to mines with different contents? They differ like the letters of the alphabet, all of which are required to produce a sensible script and text;[46] or else the poet may see the bodies as vessels into which the sweet and bitter draughts of ethical qualities are poured,[47] hence the differences among human beings of which the seeker should be aware.

Why is man so negligent of his high rank? Everything was created for him, as the Koran attests:

> the angels prostrated themselves before him, because the sky was made his water-bearer and servant;[48]

for him the sea and the mountains were created, tigers and lions are as afraid of him as if they were mice, and the crocodile trembles in fear; the demons hide themselves from him. Many are his hidden enemies but, if he acts reasonably, he will certainly be saved.[49] Rumi thinks that the animals are inferior in degree in so far as they disobey him.[50]

It is only in relation with God, however, that this high rank of man becomes again visible; so long as he takes his light from God, he remains the being before whom the angels prostrated.[51] Only in the hands of God is he comparable to the rod of Moses or to the life-giving messianic spell, being able to perform miracles such as devouring the whole created world, just as Moses' serpent devoured the snakes of the magicians.[52]

If man would only remember that God has created him in the most beautiful form (Sura 95/4) and even, according to a famous tradition, in His Own form, that He has breathed from His Own breath into him (Sura 38/72 and others)! Endowed with these qualities, man becomes the astrolabe of the lofty, Divine Attributes, reflecting the Divine qualities just as water reflects the moon; upon him the operations of Omnipotence are carried out and become visible; the dial of this astrolabe perpetually gives news of Divine greatness, provided one knows how to read and to interpret its position. In his outward form, Adam may be called a microcosm; but, as to his internal meaning, he is a macrocosm.[53]

> . . . the human being 'We have honoured the Children of Adam'—is the astrolabe of God. When God causes a man to have knowledge of Him and to know Him and to be familiar with Him, through the astrolabe of his own being he beholds moment by moment and flash by flash the manifestation of God and His infinite beauty, and that beauty is never absent from his mirror.[54]

Or else, Rumi may compare man's substance to a flag—

> He first sets the flag fluttering in the air, and then sends troops to the foot of that flag from every direction, as God alone knows—reason, understanding, fury and anger, forbearance and liberality, fear and hope, states without end and qualities unbounded. Whoever looks from afar sees only the flag, but he who beholds from close at hand knows what essences and realities reside in it.[55]

The central problem is that only a few human beings try to re-establish their previous high rank, or are even aware of it. Most of Rumi's interpreters have derived these ideas about the high rank of man from currents as systematized in Ibnʿ Arabi's philosophy and theosophy: the return of man to his origin, the growth and development of the Perfect Man as goal of creation. But it would suffice to trace these ideas back to the Koran, where sentences about man's twofold role—God's viceregent on earth, and the ignorant, lost creature and sinner—are found side by side, encompassing almost all the possibilities of human behaviour. Man was conceived by God as the highest manifestation of His qualities in His creation; and since he, in his perfection, is the goal of this creation, everything moves towards him, yearning for 'The Man'. Everything, from mineral to human, wittingly or unwittingly aspires to the rank of the Perfect Man; but only few are called to attain it. The true man (*mard,* or, as the Turkish Sufis would say, *er*) is often contrasted with the *mokhannath*, the hermaphrodite, in the language of the mystics, and especially in Rumi's verses: the eunuch is still bound to worldly pleasures, and does not concentrate exclusively upon the spiritual path, does not surrender completely to Divine love.

The profession of being a man I have learned from God;
I am the hero of Love and the friend of Aḥmad (Moḥammad).[56]

Such 'man' who has developed all his noble qualities to the utmost possibilities in the constant service of God, is rarely found in the world; that is why Rumi repeats his word in quest of Man in all stages of his work: Both in his lyrics and twice in the *Mathnavi* he tells the story (which goes back to Diogenes) of the man who went around the town with a lamp in search of a true man[57] — for among those vulgar who are 'like animals, nay even more astray' (Sura 7/179) it is almost impossible to find the Man. Whether one interprets such verses as the search for the true believer, or as search for the *insān-e kāmel*, the Perfect Man in the technical sense, it amounts almost to the same: what is needed is the man of God who has completely surrendered his will into God's will and acts through Him, leading His community on the spiritual highway like a beacon filled with Divine Light. It should be remembered, by the way, that the technical term *insān-e kāmel*, so dear to the mystics of the Ibn ʿArabi school, never occurs as such in Rumi's work.

To a truly perfected man the tradition 'Who knows himself knows his Lord' can be applied. This *ḥadith* is usually explained as alluding to internal gnosis: to know one's own, innermost self means to find that it is identical with God. For Rumi, however, it shows another aspect of mystical experience, as he relates in the story of Ayāz,[58] who every morning contemplated his old outworn clothes in order to remember how destitute he had originally been and to recognize that everything had been given to him by the Lord in His endless bounty and lovingkindness. Thus, for Rumi, the *ḥadith* rather expresses the feeling of the perfect poor before the Eternally Rich, but not a substantial union.

One of the problems in the creation of man is his relation with Satan, Iblis, who refused to prostrate himself before Adam (Sura 2/34 and others) and consequently was cursed by God. Adam and Iblis, as Rumi says in a poetical image, are like two flags in the cosmos, one white, the other black:[59] man, as most perfectly manifested in the Prophet Moḥammad, is the 'treasurer' of God's mercy; Satan, of God's wrath. Early Sufism developed strange and touching theories: he is represented as the great lover who did not want to worship anything other than God and therefore refused to prostrate, obedient to the Divine Will, yet disobedient to the Divine Command.[60] One of the most beautiful ghazals by Sanā'i, 'Satan's Lament'[61] may have inspired the passage in Rumi's *Mathnavi* where Satan complains of his sad lot.[62]

On the whole, Rumi's viewpoint is much more in tune with orthodox Muslims about Satan, the principle of disobedience, than with the high-flown speculations of Ḥallāj and Aḥmad Ghazzāli about Iblis' unique role as the only true monotheist in the world—who was almost 'more monotheist than God Himself'.[63] Rumi views Satan as the manifestation of the great sins of pride and haughtiness: he was cursed by God because he said 'I am better than Him'. Likewise, man's fall is brought about by his own pride, by carnal desires, sexual lust and the stomach.[64] Satan's destructive actions in human history are dramatically described,[65] and Mowlānā accuses him of being the first to use *qeyās* 'analogy' in considering the fire from which he was created to be superior to the clay from which Adam was formed.[66] Consequently, Iblis could be regarded as the principle of 'one-eyed' intellect, of 'lovelessness': he saw only the outward, earthly form of Adam, but ignored the Divine spark hidden in him, using an illicit method of comparison.[67] Eventually, Rumi's satanology culminates in the lines:

> (Cunning) intelligence (*ziragi*) is from Iblis, and love from Adam—[68]

a line which constitutes, in our own time, the pivot for Iqbal's philosophy of humanity. Following Rumi, Iqbal thinks that intelligence without love is *the* satanic illness of the world, an illness which brings about not only man's fall but also the destruction of everything beautiful. The eye of intelligence can not recognize true beauty hidden behind outward form, as the Divine Breath was hidden behind the form of Adam; it behoves Majnun, the man demented by love, to see the unique beauty of Leyla behind a form which looks completely uninspiring to loveless, intelligent, hence inhuman, people.

One creature in which Satan can hide his ruses and which he often uses to lead man astray, is woman. Classical Sufi tradition was by no means very positive with regard to woman—not much more than medieval Christianity, although the Prophet's fondness for 'the fair sex' and the important role of the women of his family, mainly his daughter Fāṭema never allowed the pious to completely disavow women's religious role. Women were accepted as saints and their spiritual capacities were, though sometimes grudgingly, admitted. Rābeʿa al-ʿAdawiyya is the first famous example of a Muslim woman saint. But Rumi, faithful to the medieval tradition, makes one of his heroes sigh:

> First and last my fall was through woman![69]

The ruse of women is great, and they cause the spirit to descend into the realm of corporal existence by seducing man into sexual intercourse. Since the animal quality prevails in woman, she brings things into the material, i.e. animal, world. Was not the first blood on earth, that of Abel, shed for the sake of women?[70]

Rumi agrees with the Prophetic tradition that one should seek counsel with women and then act contrary to their advice,[71] for women have less intelligence than men; even a woman's dream is less true than a man's.[72] And she cannot fully understand the secrets man has to learn:

> What should the servant of outward forms do with the belt of Divine Love?
> What should a poor female do with shield and mace and spear?[73]

Woman is a trial for man, as Rumi has underscored in a longish passage of *Fihi mā fihi* where he describes a good way leading to God:

> What is that way? To wed women, so that he might endure the tyranny of women and hear their absurdities, for them to ride roughshod over him, and so for him to refine his own character. 'Surely thou art upon a mighty morality'. By enduring and putting up with the tyranny of women it is as though you rub off your own impurity on them. Your character becomes good through forbearance; their character becomes bad through domineering and aggression. When you have realized this, make yourself clean. Know that they are like a garment; in them you cleanse your own impurities and become clean yourself . . .[74]

An illustration of this maxim is the story of Kharraqāni's bad wife in the *Mathnavi*,[75] a story the likes of which can be found quite often in Sufi hagiography. To what extent we should take such words for Jalāloddin's own opinon is not certain; his two marriages seem to have been not unhappy, and the tender letters which he wrote to his daughter-in-law show his feelings as much as other letters addressed to high born ladies of Konya who worked for the mystics and led a model religious life . . .

Again, Rumi does not hesitate to see the *nafs,* the carnal soul, in the old image of a disobedient woman and uses extremely vulgar language in describing the 'World' as an ugly old crone who paints her ghastly face in order to seduce as many men as possible, not even refraining from tearing to pieces a beautifully illuminated Koran to rub its golden and coloured ornaments over her wrinkles . . .[76]

And yet, all of a sudden Mowlānā speaks in a different mood: Did not the Prophet say that women often prevail over the intelligent? Out of this critical and somewhat ironical *ḥadith* the poet develops a description of women who produce mildness and love, which are distinctively human qualities, whereas man, possessed of wrath and lust, has more animal qualities than such a mild motherly woman. He concludes:

> She is a ray of God, she is not that (earthly) beloved:
> she is creative, you might say she is not created.[77]

This is an astonishing interpretation of the role of women who reflect the mercy of the Creator best and are, in some way, creators themselves when giving birth to a child for which they care just as God cares for His creatures. We need not combine this praise bestowed upon women by Rumi with the high-flown mystical theories about the role of the feminine in spiritual life as described by Ibnʿ Arabi—Jalāloddin may have well taken his example from the everyday life of his family and his compatriots in Konya.

The Divine order of *karramnā*, and the Koranic sentence of the Divine trust, which only man can bear, forms Rumi's starting point for his teachings on free will and predestination.[78] This problem never ceased to puzzle Muslim theologians from the very beginning of theological discussion.[79] For Mowlānā, this problem was not theoretical, for he was not interested in mere speculations; it had a bearing on practical life and was thus important for the Muslim community.

There are verses in which he jokingly alludes to the differences of the schools of thought in Islam, the *jabri,* the defender of absolute predestination, and the *qadari,* who believes in free will:

> The perfect description of the lord Shams-e Tabriz is beyond the imagination of *jabri* and *qadari* . . .[80]

He also contrasts the Sunni Muslim with the predestinarian—both of them have their own ways of praising God:

> This one (the *jabri*) says 'He (the (*sunni*) is astray and lost, unaware of his (real) state and of the (Divine Command) 'Arise (and preach)'.
> And that one (the *Sunni*) says 'What awareness has this one?' God by fore-ordainement, hath cast them into strife.[81]

Or else he says, tongue in cheek:

> In my ghazals is *jabr* and *qadar*—leave these two,
> for out of this discussion only agitation and evil emerges![82]

A much deeper definition of these two currents is given in another passage where Rumi contrasts the prophets (here, as quite often, standing for the perfected believer) and the infidels:

> The Prophets are *jabris* (necessitarians) in the affairs of this world,
> the infidels are predestinarians for the sake of the other world,
> to the prophets the works of the other world are a matter of free will,
> to the ignorant the works of this world![83]

True believers act in what later writers called *jabr maḥmud,* 'praiseworthy predestination', i.e. in full accordance with the God-given laws and with God's will, whereas the infidels imagine they can act against these laws and follow their own lusts and imaginations, denying the machinery of evil which carries them deeper and deeper into sin and rebellion as a corollary of their alleged 'freedom of will'.

Mowlānā firmly relies upon the Koranic promises that good and evil are bound to bring forth fruits, even though they be like a mustard seed (Sura 21/47), and he repeatedly recurs to the Divine promise that good works are like sheaves which bear seven-fold fruit (Sura 2/263).

> See the face of faith in the mirror of actions![84]

or, as he expresses it elsewhere 'in the vial of actions':[85] what is in the heart, should find expression in pious acts and useful works; these, however, can be performed only if man possesses a certain quantity of free will. The camel can refuse to follow his driver's stick, and the dog at which you throw a stone is agitated and acts against you, not because it dislikes the stick or the stone, but because it acknowledges man's capacity to act this way or the other.[86] As a good psychologist, Rumi explains man's reaction to the concept of free will: when he likes something he says it is his free choice so to act but, when he dislikes something which he is bound to do, he sees God's unpleasant constraint in it.[87] But man is, in fact, like a camel on which the pack-saddle of 'free will' is put, and in his prayer the poet asks God to use this pack-saddle the right way.[88] If there were no free choice, man could not be angry with his enemies and gnash his teeth against them.[89]

Few mystical poets have underlined the incompatibility of true faith with the acceptance of a blind fate by which everything has been pre-destined since pre-eternity more insistingly than Mowlānā. One of his nicest stories in this respect is that of a man who climbed upon a tree and ate the fruits, assuring the angry gardener that 'This is God's garden, and I am eating from God's fruits given by Him'. The gardener reacted cleverly: he thrashed him soundly 'with the stick of God' until the man had to acknowledge that the transgression was caused by his own will, not by God's order, and repented from his predestinarian views. In the same way, man cannot claim that his infidelity is chosen and preordained by God: it is his own choice, for infidelity without man's active partaking is a contradiction.[90]

Rumi refuses to believe in the oft-quoted *ḥadith* 'the pen has already dried up' in the sense that there is no change possible in human fate and that whatever was noted down on the Well-preserved Tablet is no longer subject to change. According to him, revealing his practical mind, this *ḥadith* means rather that the laws given by God are invariable: God has ordered once and for all time that the good deeds of the faithful should not be lost, but not that good and evil actions are of equal value;[91] for that would lead to dangerous results: the absolutely passive trust in God as developed in the very first centuries of Islamic piety and the acceptance of everything as an unchangeable Divine order was to prove quite destructive in at least parts of the post-thirteenth century Sufism.

Mowlānā believed in action, and the Prophetic tradition that 'This world is a seedbed for the next world' is one of his favourite quotations.[92] He taught his disciples:

> If you have done evil, you have done it to yourself—how could your wickedness reach out to affect God?[93]

Every human act bears fruit for man himself, be it in this world, be it in the world to come:

> Onion and leek and poppies will reveal the secrets of winter—some will be fresh (*sarsabz*), others with lowered head like violets.[94]

Garden imagery lends itself perfectly to an interpretation of the Prophetic tradition in ever new variations:

> If you plant bitter gourds, no sugar cane will grow from it,[95]

or:

> Dress in the material which you yourself have woven, and drink the produce you have planted.[96]

Man's actions, which spring from himself, are like his children who grasp his hem to follow him; and he is responsible for them as he is for his own offspring.[97]

> Whether there be sugarcane or reed in the soil of the earth, the interpreter of each kind of soil is its fruit. Now in the soil of the heart, whose plants are thoughts, the thoughts reveal the secrets of the heart.[98]

Thoughts and works shape man's future. Did not the Prophet himself admonish people, saying: 'Happy is he whose good works remain when he leaves the world'?[99] Rumi elaborates this idea in his letters:

> The good luck of this world is like a whirlwind; it blows very hard, very fast, comes and takes a handful of dust into the air, casts it again to the ground and rushes off. How happy is he who prepares the wheat of good works for the mill Death during this storm. . .[100]

What has been sown in the wintertime of this life will be reaped in the harvest of eternity; death brings man the fruits of what he has planted.[101] Rumi follows Sanāʾi, who thinks that every act, nay every thought embedded in the heart will become a visible form on Doomsday, just as an architect's idea becomes visible in the plan of the house, or like a plant growing out of the seed hidden in soil.[102] Death will meet man like a mirror which shows either a beautiful or an ugly face, depending upon man's good or evil deeds—beautiful before the Turk, ugly before the Negro.[103] Mowlānā, however, goes scarcely as far as Sanāʾi and ʿAṭṭār, who see people who have followed their bestial nature transformed eventually into pigs and other unclean animals.[104] He explains the same thought with a more poetical image which reminds the reader of the Zoroastrian idea of the virgin who meets the dead at the Chinvat bridge and reflects again his good or evil actions:

> Your good ethical qualities run before you after your death;
> like ladies, moonfaced, do these qualities proudly walk . . .
> When you have divorced the body, you will see houris in rows,
> Muslim ladies, faithful women, devout and repenting ladies
> (Sura 66/5)
> without number run your characteristics before your bier,
> Your patience 'and by those that pluck out vehemently' and
> your gratitude 'by those that draw out violently' (Sura 79/1 2)
> In the coffin these pure qualities will become your companions,
> they will cling to you like sons and daughters,
> and you will put on garments from the warp and woof of your
> works of obedience . . .[105]

For from the very day of the Covenant man's whole life is directed towards the Divine Tomorrow, the Day of Judgment. One would expect that Rumi, being a mystic, would not be so interested in death, resurrection, and other worldly recompenses, yet his poetry clearly shows that he believes in Hell and Paradise as real, as the Muslim creed prescribed. He certainly sees both as states produced by man's actions and thoughts rather than places;[106] and he believes that the light of the faithful can extinguish the fire of Hell,[107] for the fire of Hell is created whereas the true faithful exists from the uncreated Divine Light.

Descriptions of death, however, and dramatic visions of Doomsday in the *Divān* certainly belong to Mowlānā's most impressive verses; the whole eschatological apparatus as described in the Koran is alive with him, and the trembling of the earth which will bring forth whatever is hidden in it (Sura 99) serves him as a wonderful image for the moment when not only graves but also hearts are opened, and everything hidden in them is laid bare.[108] That is why he never tires of exhorting his friends and disciples to work for Paradise, to act according to God-given laws, and to prepare during the winter of this life for the eternal Spring, or to believe during the nocturnal anguishes of this world in the dawn of Eternity which will dissipate the shade and blind the bats.

Notwithstanding this firm belief in the reward of each action, Rumi knows that God will not judge man according to his actions, but rather according to his good intentions, and that He gives from His endless bounty not according to man's capacity and receptivity, but rather grants man the capacity to receive His bounty, and then transforms this stream into useful action.[109] The interaction of man and God is beautifully defined: Free will is the endeavour to thank God for His Beneficence.[110] The *ḥadith* of the dried-up Pen is therefore, in Rumi's view, not an invitation to laziness and passivity but on the contrary an impetus to work harder and to act in perfect sincerity so that one's service at the Divine threshold becomes purer and more efficacious. By saying *inshāʾ Allah* 'If God willeth', man is incited to work more and better.[111]

It is natural for free will and free choice to be limited to the innate capabilities and capacities of the creature: nobody would address a stone to ask it to draw near, nor would one ask man to fly, or a blind person to look at someone.[112] Would a teacher beat a child if it were not capable of learning to choose between two possibilities? He would certainly never treat an unfeeling stone like that![113] And:

> One beats an ox when it refuses to carry the yoke, but not because it does not put on wings![114]

God has given man his faculties so that he may use them for good purposes and develop them properly; and every species is endowed with a certain free-will which he can use to act upon those below him (as the carpenter works on wood, the locksmith on iron, etc.), but all of them gradually rise to the supreme Divine Will.[115] Thus man will reach ever higher levels of approximation to the Divine Attributes, and particularly to the Divine Will. If man proves grateful on every step, his gratitude induces God to bestow upon him new gifts,[116] and his endeavour to reach Heaven is strengthened by Divine Grace; both co-operate, and the more man strives to reach his lofty goal the more will he be supported:[117] thus Rumi applies the famous *ḥadith an-nawāfil*, in which God promises:

> When my servant draws nearer to Me by means of supererogatory works I draw nearer to him; when he advances one span, I advance one cubit; when he comes walking, I come running; and I become the hand by which he grasps, the eye by which he sees, and the ear by which he hears . . .

By constant struggling with the lower faculties, and by eliminating base qualities, man can reach annihilation (*fanā*ʾ) in the Divine Will, *fanā*ʾ being basically an ethical concept. Purified through love, he then acts in conformity with the Divine Will, similar to the Prophet in the Battle of Badr when the Koranic verse was revealed 'Thou cast not when thou cast, but God' (Sura 8/17). This is the *jabr maḥmud,* 'praiseworthy necessitarianism, the free will and predestination of the saints who, like pearls in oysters, live in the ocean of Divine Life and are moved by its motions.'[118] Eventually, after giving himself up man will drink of the goblet of God which makes him selfless and volitionless. Whatever he does, intoxicated by this wine, it is in accordance with the Divine Decree so that he experiences higher predestination.

It should not be forgotten that in this way the communion with other faithful is of great help: tradition attests that 'The faithful is the mirror of the faithful'. True believers understand from the behaviour and actions of their companions the reflection of their own feelings and actions. When the mystic sees a fault in his neighbour, he should correct this very fault in his own character. Thus the mirror of his heart will become clearer and purer, and the constant purification leads him closer to God.[119] For he should know that every word and every action is like an echo reverberated by the mountain of this world, and nothing is lost.[120]

As far as one can understand from scattered remarks in Rumi's poetry and prose he firmly believed in the Ashʿarite doctrine of constant re-creation:

> God most High creates a man anew every moment, sending something perfectly fresh into his inner heart.[121]

In general, however, Mowlānā does not dwell upon the theoretical foundations of man's being; he rather tries to describe the relation of man's different parts to each other in poetical imagery. In the first verse of the *Mathnavi,* which may be considered a kind of general introduction to his thoughts, he writes about the relation of body and soul:

> The body is not hidden from the soul, nor the soul from the body, but nobody has the right to see the soul.[122]

Both are interdependent, like husk and kernel, and as little value as a husk has without kernel, it is impossible for a kernel not protected by a husk to survive and give fruit:[123] spirit without matter cannot be imagined in our material world.

Rumi describes the body, according to the classical tradition, as constituted of the four elements, and thus liable to decay and corruption like every compound of these elements. Only the perfect saint is beyond air, earth, fire and water, for he lives already here in the world of spirit. In a charming pun alluding to the seventy-two sects (*mellat*) which form, according to tradition, the body of Islam, Rumi expresses the view that in the human body there are seventy-two 'illnesses' (*ʿellat* instead of *mellat*), produced by the working of the four elements which manifest themselves in the different regions of the body.[124] A pale, yellowish face comes from too much movement of the bile, a red face means too much blood, a white face too much phlegm, and a dark face too much black gall (melancholia), signs taken by the ordinary people at face value, but which, in fact, point to the inner substance of man and his characteristics.[125]

The outward body and these elements are like a tent for the spirit,[126] a tent in which the 'inner meaning' lives in full beauty like a Turkish prince.[127] The body is a husk, and he who cares for it resembles a child who plays with nuts and almonds without caring for their sweet kernel.[128] This husk is perishable—that is why the lover's outward appearance is burnt by the Beloved.[129] And if the exterior had any deeper meaning, then the Prophet and Abu Jahl, his grim enemy, would have been the same, for both were Arabs from the same clan.[130] This body gains its value only through the interior forces. Often the corporeal and spiritual forces are conflicting: the eye of the head, *sar,* struggles with the eyes of the innermost heart, *serr,* as Rumi says with a pun.[131] The body may be compared to a lamp with six spouts, i.e. the senses: in this case the soul is the light which illuminates it.[132] Or else it may be likened to a vessel into which the water of the soul is poured but the contents vary: some bear the water of life, others deadly poison.[133] The poet may also see the body as a rope which fetters the soul's foot, constantly dragging it towards the earth while the soul wants to fly heavenwards: this is the solution of the long-winded story about the she-mouse who, falling in love with a frog, tried to tie up her beloved to her own feet with the result that both perished.[134] The body is also like a boat which will be broken once man cuts himself loose from his ego which holds him like an anchor until the wave of Divine love carries him forcefully away.[135]

Rumi at times becomes even more negative in describing the body and its weaknesses—it is as ugly as a donkey's head in a garden;[136] it is the fuel for Hell, and the disciple should strive to diminish it lest he become 'a carrier of fire-wood' like Abu Lahab's wife in the Koranic revelation (Sura 111/4).[137] If the body is fondled too much, it will certainly drag man to Hell, not to the *sedra*-tree in Paradise. To water this tree, or thornbush, 'Body', is sheer tyranny and injustice; the believer should rather water his soul which will lead him to the paradisical lotus-tree.[138] For whatever one tries, the body will always remain like a dog, and can never resemble a lion, i.e. the soul, or spirit.[139]

However, this absolutely negative judgement is not the rule in Rumi's verses. He sees the body as a Sufi frock full of patches, and the soul as a true Sufi. As soon as the Sun (of spiritual enlightenment) appears, the Sufi washes his frock, i.e. purifies himself.[140] The tree 'Body', so called in some verses, can be accepted as something similar to the rod of Moses, which should be thrown away according to the Divine order; then, after regarding its very essence, it should be taken up again for noble purposes. Once man learns to treat this body properly and in congruence with the Divine Law, it will become a useful instrument—a description otherwise used for the carnal soul (*nafs*).[141]

There is no end to Rumi's images for the relation of body and soul, or, more rarely, body and spirit. He may see the body as a dark piece of dust which carries in itself the qualities of light, so that interior and exterior are engaged in constant fight.[142] The body is the dust on the pure mirror 'Spirit',[143] and the relation of the two components is described under very realistic images: the soul is hidden in the body like butter in sour milk,[144] or 'the body is pregnant with the soul—a Negro pregnant with the Byzantine "Heart"!'[145] This image recurs in the *Mathnavi,* where Rumi compares corporeal death to the birth pangs which will eventually set the child 'Soul' free.[146] The body may be likened to a bag from which the soul should poke its head[147] (the image of the lion breaking his cage belongs to the same strain of thought, and of course, that of the soul-bird which flies away from the cage).

> If He breaks this cup of mine, I do not drink grief,
> I have another cup from this cupbearer under my arm.
> The cup is the dust-made body, the soul is the pure wine;
> He grants me another cup, when this cup is infirm.[148]

As the earthen cup is of no value, and can be easily broken and replaced by a more valuable vessel, so also is the body alike to a house which should be destroyed in order to discover the treasure hidden beneath the ruins[149]—treasures which are much more precious than the whole building. But as long as man is attached to the house which is decorated with colourful paintings and figures, he will never find the treasure 'Soul'.[150]

In applying his usual winter-terminology to everything connected with the world of matter, Rumi sees the behaviour of men comparable to that of a caravan sitting in the caravanserai in fear of snow; eventually the sun will come to melt the snow and open the way to the caravan of souls which will then be able to move about freely.[151]

Rumi has also utilized the Koranic dictum that the 'creation' (*khalq*) and the Command (*amr*) belong to God (Sura 7/54) to indicate the difference between body and soul, form and content: for creation is connected with the form, whereas Command is meant for the soul.[152] Not only the soul but also the spirit (*ruḥ*) is contrasted with the body, though less frequently—the spirit, usually represented by the image of the sun, can be detected by means of the body which acts like an astrolabe and shows its stations and movements.[153] In a completely different imagery, Mowlānā has described spirits as an ocean out of which bodies emerge like foam.[154] This image leads to the idea of the Universal Spirit, *ʿaql-e koll*, out of which creation manifests itself to become its outward garment[155]—an idea which probably belongs to a later period of his life, since all the relevant verses are found in the third book of the *Mathnavi* and the following parts of this work.

More in the traditional, Koranic, vein is Rumi's comparison of the body to a camel and the spirit to the prophet Sāleḥ, who miraculously produced a camel from a rock (Sura 91/13 and others); only the camel can be hurt by the infidels, but not the saint, who represents the spirit.[156] The image of the spirit as a white falcon imprisoned in the dwellingplace of crows and ravens is exactly the same as that often used for the soul: the snow of the corporeal world has to be dissolved by the Sun of Reality so that the bird can fly homeward. The summer and winter are 'states' of the body, that is to say of the material world, which spiritual man transgresses.[157]

In a beautiful application of the image of husk and kernel, Mowlānā has spoken of the pressing of the grapes by which the individual husks and thus the differences between the individual grapes, disappear, and only the pure wine of spirit remains.[158]

Jalāloddin likes to contrast the corporeal and the spiritual limbs of man, for man has five outward and five inward senses—there is, for instance, the stomach which drags man towards the straw-barn; as for the 'stomach of the heart', it leads him towards sweet basil with the result that whoever eats straw will become an animal which will be sacrified (*qorbān*) whereas he who feeds on Divine Light becomes himself a *Koran,* united with God.[159] When the body eats material food it forms an impediment to the soul's 'eating' of light. The soul sits like a merchant, and the body is a highway-robber who attempts to take away this merchant's goods.[160] Similar images are used for the inward and outward ear etc.

What is the body but a guest-house into which various visitors come, e.g., thoughts of joy and sorrow? Every morning a new guest appears who will fly back into non-existence if man does not receive him with cheerful countenance, like Abraham. Man should care well for those guests who come from the Unseen into his heart and make their home there.[161] The outward senses have their duties in this world, but they are useful only to a certain extent—once the spiritual world dawns like the sun, they vanish like stars;[162] or they become ridiculous like a hobby-horse ridden by a child.[163] Man can experience the needlessness of the senses in sleep:[164] once the senses fall asleep, the outward world no longer exists for him.

Likewise the senses are deceiving—a crooked sense cannot perceive anything but in a crooked way: the squint-eye cannot see a single thing correctly.[165] Certainly, the five senses are intrinsically bound to each other and work together in a mysterious way.[166] It is however, necessary for man to recognize their weakness; he can shed them off like leaves for a while and then discover that they are dependent upon intellect; intellect, in turn, is a prisoner of the spirit, and the last instance is the soul, which sets free the hand of intellect so that it can operate through the medium of the senses.[167] In a longish passage Rumi describes the senses as horses which are under the command of the rider: the problem is to find the rider of Divine light who can direct the horses in the right direction, otherwise they would go only to the meadows to graze there and enjoy food and rest. But if the secondary, derived light of the senses is enhanced by the light of the spirit, then the Koranic promise of 'Light upon light' (Sura 24/35) will be fulfilled. The spiritual rider may remain invisible, but the actions of the 'horse-senses' will show his presence and his skill.[168]

On the pure water of mystical experience, the senses, like human thought and deliberations, are like tiny straw particles which should be skimmed away by the hand of reason so that the limpid water becomes visible: otherwise it will become brackish due to the augmentation of chaff.[169]

In a strange comparison those who follow the senses are compared to the Muʿtazilites, a sect that denied the possibility of beholding God in the Otherworld—Rumi accuses them here as relying completely upon sense-perception, denying a spiritual vision even in Paradise:

> They are Muʿtazilites, though from misguidedness they represent themselves as Sunnites.
> Anyone who remains in (bondage to) sense-perception, is a Muʿtazilite; though he may say he is a Sunnite, 'tis from ignorance.
> Anyone who has escaped from (the bondage of) sense-perception, is a Sunnite: the man endowed with (spiritual) vision is the eye of a sweet-paced Reason.
> If the animal sense could see the King (God), then the ox and the ass would behold Allah . . .[170]

In many cases, verses directed against the body can be applied as well to the *nafs,* the base faculties, or carnal soul. *An-nafs al-ammāra bi'ˀs-su,* the self inciting to evil (Sura 12/53) is the principle against which man was called to struggle relentlessly. Rumi is not less energetic in his struggle against the *nafs* than his predecessors on the Sufi path who saw here the root of every evil.

> The *nafs* is of this kind, and therefore it must be killed—
> 'Kill yourselves' or 'your *nafs*' said that High One . . .[171]

That can be done by casting the fire of 'renunciation of passions' into the thornbush of the *nafs.*[172] Did not the Prophet himself call the *nafs* the most dangerous enemy of man, which is located between man's sides, an enemy which has to be conquered in the 'greatest holy war'?[173]

The whole Koran consists, according to Rumi, of an explanation of the evils of the carnal soul in its various manifestations.[174] Mowlānā applies the Prophetic tradition 'Die before ye die' to this struggle against the carnal soul, which should be slain so that the higher faculties may live.[175] This 'greater holy war' has to be waged day by day, moment by moment, for the 'old enemy will never become man's maternal or paternal uncle', even though it behaves friendly and feigns peace.[176]

The *nafs* has to be trained by constant fasting and ascetic exercises until it becomes an obedient animal—hence the comparison with the trained dog, with the cow or fat calf that has to be slaughtered, with the donkey, with the ferocious wolf, or the cunning hare;[177] a very common image is that of the restive horse which eventually can become obedient and carry its owner along the spiritual path towards the ultimate goal.[178] There is no end to poetical, although at times rather crude, comparisons: the *nafs* is like Pharaoh, unwilling to listen to the call of Moses the prophet, but claiming that he himself is divine,[179] it is a dragon that can be blinded only by the wonderful power of the spiritual master's gaze.[180] Or else it is like a woman, so disobedient and troublesome that man had better act against her advice—this comparison was all the easier since the word *nafs* is feminine in Arabic. Only through the help of the intellect, the father of spiritual man, can it be educated properly.[181] And an amusing image:

> When the *nafs* says *miouw* like the cat, then I put it, like a cat, into a bag . . .[182]

The greedy little beast must be put in a bag and kept starving for a while, or even be drowned. For the *nafs* is as insatiable as Hell.[183] Was it not together with Satan in the beginning of human history?[184] Their joint efforts caused Adam's fall; therefore equations of *nafs* and Satan occur now and then in Rumi's and in other mystics' works.

If the *nafs* has been properly trained, one must be careful and wary of its ruses, for more dangerous than its overt actions manifest in sensuality, hatred, greed etc., are its fine tricks by which it tries to overcome the pious in their devotions. Even to take pride in devotional acts, or to feel happy and secure in constant fasting and prayer may be a feeling caused by the *nafs,* for

> The *nafs* has a rosary and a copy of the Koran in the right hand and a dagger and sword in the sleeve.

When the *nafs* behaves like a pious Muslim and pretends to bring man to the pool for his ritual ablution it will certainly throw him into the dark well the very moment he becomes heedless, seduced by his pious work.[185]

It requires long and hard struggle to tame the *nafs*, but eventually, by the grace of God, it will pass over the stage of *nafs ammāra* and *nafs lavvāma* (comparable to 'conscience', cf. Sura 75/2), and reach the state of *nafs moṭmaʾenna,* the 'soul at peace' (Sura 89/28). When it has become a true lover, it is no longer 'inciting to evil' and holy war is no longer needed to keep it under control.[186] It then hears the call of its Lord and Beloved *irjiʿi* 'Come back', and returns, like an obedient falcon, to its master's hand.[187] After experiencing the wonderful power of the Sun of love, the *nafs* is transformed by Divine alchemy into a peaceful and loving being and is nourished upon silence, returning into the eternal silence, contrary to the *nafs nāṭeqa*, which turns towards speech.[188] (This is, indeed, a strange juxtaposition, but the combination of two basically unconnected items in an ingenious way is typical of Rumi's mode of thought.) Then, the *nafs* is so quiet that the poet may admonish his disciples not to scratch its lovely face with the poisonous nail 'thought'[189] . . . for it is completely absorbed in God.

But this is the final state of man. Much more frequent are the passages in which Rumi blames the *nafs* in its primary stages, and amazingly often the image of the *nafs* as mother and reason as father of man occurs in his poetry.

The constant struggle between the base faculties and reason is a main topic of the *Mathnavi*. This struggle is comparable to that of the Prophet with Abu Jahl and his companions (the contrast of *jahl,* 'ignorance' with reason is well intended); sensual experience is likewise inimical to the spirit, and should be blinded by casting dust into its eyes.[190]

Rumi may call reason the camel-driver and man the camel; then the saints are the 'reason of reason', leading man's caravan along the unquestionable right path.[191] Reason is made from light and qualified by luminous characteristics, contrary to the *nafs,* which is part of darkness and shade. They stand in the same relation as a lion and a blind dog.[192] Reason is also the gift with which the angels are endowed[193] and which keeps them in permanent obedience, whereas the *nafs,* as we have seen, is part of the Satanic realm.[194] Rumi never tires of telling by means of various images how terrible it would be if a person's reason were to act like a female and fall under the sway of the *nafs,*[195] or if the carnal soul were to keep reason imprisoned.[196] If reason joins with reason, it increases in light; whereas the *nafs,* joining with another *nafs,* will increase in darkness and veil the right path.[197] One can therefore only hope that the dog-like *nafs* will be chased by reason and be killed.[198]

Reason, in passages like this, is by no means the intellectual approach to the world or the faculty rational. Rumi has connected sheer intellectual endeavour with Satan. *ʿaql,* as understood here, is 'the opposite of lust and passion';[199] it is comparable to the sun: when it disappears, there remains stupidity which covers the world like a dark night.[200] In this respect, reason is the touchstone of the Prophets and the faithful, who are called to act according to the Koran. It is the prerequisite for every religiously valid act, teaching man how to follow correctly and consciously the principles laid down in the Koranic law. Here Rumi is perfectly in harmony with the traditional Islamic theological attitude. The person who turns away from sensual pleasures, leaving body and *nafs* behind, is like the one who forsakes his donkey and joins Jesus, this model of wisdom and understanding. Let him no longer listen to his deserted donkey's complaints![201] Mowlānā has often attempted to describe the relation of this positive faculty with the body and the other faculties of man. Often, reason and *nafs* are, as in Sanā'i's work,[202] considered father and mother of this world. Rumi views reason as the power which sets in notion the lifeless figures of the body.[203] Together with the soul, reason means spring-time; whereas passion, lust and *nafs* are the signs of an autumn which will deprive the spiritual garden of all its beauty and announce the hibernal material aspect of life.[204] *ᶜaql*, in this respect, is like an anchor which helps the wise during their life by keeping them steadfast;[205] in its solar quality, it burns darkness and even brings the water of life into the night of this world.[206] Reason may also be likened to a bird which carries man to higher levels of existence—quite different from the bird of 'imitation' which keeps man on this earth.[207]

A person endowed with this reason, which enables him to discern between good and bad, can take examples from the life of others: he understands that death is before him, and consequently acts prudently obeying the Divine word.[208] Reason is like a key which opens the door, or like wings to carry man higher;[209] it bears a certain rose-scent in order to lead man to the eternal Rosegarden.[210] Eventually, the reason of the *abdāl*, the high ranking saints, is so subtle that it can bring them to the Most-Distant Lotus-tree in Paradise, far away from this carrion 'world'.[211] Rumi even compares the angel Gabriel to the highest embodiment of reason, which ends, however, at this very Lotus-tree; for here, before the arcane chamber of God, lies its very limit.

Reason connected with faith is indeed the watchman of the town 'Heart'. It sits like a cat waiting to kill the mice which try to enter this town to steal faith and love from it, and the very sound of this cat scares the trespassers away.[212]

Rumi alludes to the idea that there are different degrees of reason: one is like the sun, others like Venus or like meteors.[213] Behind all the individual manifestations of the partial intellect is hidden the Universal Reason. This is the secret power from which the 'partial Reason' can create immortal works and produce gardens which never fade.[214] Rumi has invented an interesting disputation between Adam and Iblis in one of his ghazals where Adam is made to say:

> . . . but someone in whose hand the lamp of reason is,
> How could he leave the light, and how could he go towards the smoke?
> He (Satan) said: 'If it were me, I would kill that lamp!'
> He (Adam) said 'The wind can not carry off the lamp of sincerity . . . Thousand thanks to God that the Universal Reason again after the distance of separation came with a happy ascendent!'[215]

The Universal Reason is the fountain-head of spiritual life; it is like a town, surrounded by the Universal Soul, *nafs-e koll,* and the particulars come and go like caravans.[216] This image sounds almost too technical in the context of Rumi's imagery; but he speaks also, in other verses, about the *ʿaql-e koll* as the royal court whence the flags of the heart proceed,[217] and as an *ʿidgāh* (the spacious place where Muslim festivals are celebrated) whence the drums sound.[218] Rumi praises the *ʿaql-e koll* as manifested in the perfect beloved, Shams; and the concept occurs in several ghazals, sometimes even as a kind of *makhlaṣ* (nom-de-plume) in the last line as in the following example:

> Be quiet and do not talk any more, so that perhaps Universal Reason
> may show a way and pass from partial reason.[219]

Partial reason can err, whereas Universal Reason is safe and secure from every defect and fault.[220] A number of passages in the *Mathnavi* are devoted to an explanation of this Universal Reason, a concept alien to primitive Islam, but later influenced by neo-Platonic speculations. Yet Rumi has not built up a consistent system, like his elder contemporary Ibn ʿArabi, to bring the emanations from Universal Reason into a logical order and relation. It is almost impossible to draw a clear picture of his ideas on the *ʿaql-e koll* from the scattered, though rather numerous, remarks in his poetry. One thing is certain, however: that for him even Universal Reason is subordinate to love; it needs 'the healing sugar from Love'[221] and dances, clapping its hands, when the beloved appears.[222]

Although Universal Reason overwhelms everything created so that even 'Plato would be only an animal before it',[223] and though the skies are nothing but an umbrella for the Soltan

Universal Reason,[224] Rumi addressed this highest power, asking it to 'become intoxicated and to open its face instead of hiding its secrets'.[225]

Universal Reason is steadfast and invariable, it is both 'judge and generous Ḥātem',[226] and is never sullied by outward events, thus comparable to the radiant moon.[227] It is this power to which the word 'The eye did not rove' (Sura 53/17) is applicable; that leads to an identification of the Universal Reason with the Prophet in the moment of highest vision:[228] one of the rare theoretical statements in Mowlānā's poetry.

Mowlānā often contrasts this Universal Reason with the partial reason—the latter is busy with all kinds of scholarly pursuits and studies but is not able to receive inspiration;[229] it is the planning intellect, and what does planning help in the midst of fire?[230]

> Intelligence consists of two intelligences: the former is the acquired one which you learn, like a boy at school.
> From book, teacher, reflection and memory, and from concepts and from excellent and virgin sciences
> your intelligence becomes superior to others; but through preserving that (knowledge) you are heavily burdened . . .
> The other intelligence is the gift of God; its fountain is in the midst of the soul . . .[231]

Acquired intelligence is, compared to that divinely inspired one, like water gushing from the streets into a house, and one should not rely too much on this partial reason which can lead man into an impasse—that happened even to the angels Harut and Marut, who relied too much upon their angelic reason. Therefore man should take Universal Reason as his vizier, for that is infallible;[232] its light illuminates the horizons, whereas human partial reason 'blackens the books', i.e. it induces man into useless, even dangerous intellectual activities.[233]

In some verses Mowlānā speaks of the *nafs-e koll,* the Universal Soul, which is, however, seen before the royal rider of the Divine Order 'Say', i.e. before the Prophet, as helpless as a baby chewing its sleeve . . .[234]

Rumi poetically describes man's way in this world:

> From the inclination of man and woman the blood became agitated and turned into sperm,
> and then from those two drops a tent came up in the air.

And then came the army 'man' from the world of the soul,
Reason became his vizier, the heart went and became king.
Until after a while the heart remembered the town of the Soul,
Back turned the whole army and went into the world of permanence.[235]

Reason is certainly as necessary as a vizier for the functioning of the kingdom, and it is typical that Rumi has often used images from the legal sphere to point to reason's natural duties: it is the *mofti*[236] or the police-master who keeps the heart clean,[237] or the watchman of the town—but when the Soltan himself appears, what has the policeman to do? When the night of senses is illuminated by the radiant Sun what has a watchman to do?[238]

Reason is only a shade and will disappear when God Himself appears like the sun, or it will fade away like a candle before the sun.[239] To bring reason as gift before God, is as if you bring something lower than dust.[240] And:

> Once you have reached His door, divorce reason; for in that hour reason is a sheer loss to you, a highway-robber. When you have reached the king, surrender yourself to Him . . .[241]

Reason will be utterly disturbed and amazed ('it bites its finger from amazement' as the Persian poet says) when it sees this wonderful spiritual intoxication to which entrance is denied to any but the true lover.[242]

Rumi depicts *ᶜaql* as the useful, though somewhat pedestrian, educational force in life which is absolutely necessary to overcome the temptations of the lower soul and which is of great value insofar as it is connected with the source, with Universal Reason, the principle of movement and growth. But higher than reason is the soul, animated by love and longing:

Neither like the gleaning reason, nor like the carnal soul full of hatred,
nor like the animal spirit of earth—you go to the place of the soul![243]

The soul goes homewards, like water in the canal;[244] the image of the soul-bird has also been used hundreds of times in Rumi's verses. But as the partial reason lives through its connection with Universal Reason, the soul, too, needs constant relation with the *jān-e jān*, the Soul of the Soul, the innermost principle of spiritual life: Rumi wonders how this piece of flesh, man, is capable of splitting mountains with the help of body and soul? But in fact, the light of Farhād the mountain-digger's soul could split only rocks; the light of the Soul of the Soul splits the moon,[245] as the Koran tells about the Prophet (Sura 54/1), who, the highest manifestation of humanity, is the embodiment of the soul-principle which moves the world; for the soul of the Soul is the theatre of God Himself.[246]

In poetical images Rumi has described the 'lady Soul' who is the true housewife of the body:

> When the soul goes, make room for me under the dust —
> Dust is in the house, when the lady goes away.[247]

Just as Mowlānā feels that a certain amount of reason is hidden even in the lowest creatures, as in minerals,[248] he knows that the soul manifests itself differently in the various layers of existence: the human soul is higher than that of the animals, the angelic soul, again is higher than that of man; but higher than the angelic soul is the soul of those whose hearts are purified: that is why Adam was the object of prostration for the angels.[249] Yet, this soul is alive only as long as it is connected with the Divine Light:

> If the soul were alive without this light,
> God would not have said about the infidels 'They are dead'.[250]

It is like a candle burning with a Divine flame,[251] or else like a window which can be opened towards God so that His letter, i.e. the inspiration, can come through the window.[252] A house without such a window is like Hell, and the real meaning of religion, the sole content of the prophetic and mystical teaching, is that man should open this window of the soul. Only then can he participate in the great universal movement. The individual human soul cannot understand this universal movement of the Soul-principle as long as it remains closed; only after opening the window and partaking of the Divine Soul will it feel that the faithful, though separated by the barriers of bodily existence, are one in soul, vibrating in a single harmony.[253] There is no difference left between the souls of the saints, as Rumi beautifully describes the lovers who are one soul and die in each other.[254]

In a long passage of the last book of the *Mathnavi*, at a time when he was apparently more interested in theoretical discussions, Rumi has tried to depict the different parts of man and to give their limitations; but the lines are not always clearly drawn.[255] Sometimes he calls the animating principle *jān* 'soul', sometimes *ruḥ*, 'spirit': thus, he writes in the last part of the *Mathnavi* extensively about the spirit, which is, during man's sleep, hidden and uplifted, for it is 'by the order of my Lord' (Sura 17/85),[256] and:

> Sleep comes with the intention of carrying away your reason—
> How would the demented sleep? What does the demented know of the night?[257]

But in *Fihi mā fihi* he says exactly the contrary:

> The soul is one thing, and the spirit is another. Do you not see how in sleep the soul fares abroad? The spirit remains in the body, but the soul wanders and is transformed . . .[258]

That is why it is difficult to develop a true psychological system from Rumi's often conflicting statements. Sometimes he calls the soul the moving principle, at other times the spirit to which the limbs are obedient as the earth is obedient to heaven.[259] The *ruḥ* is, no doubt, higher than male and female, nor is it bound to outward limitation;[260] it is capable of receiving the Divine revelation and is, therefore, much more hidden than reason.[261] Layer by layer of man's body, carnal soul, intellect must be put aside until all the veils which cover the organ which is capable of receiving Divine inspiration are removed.

But higher than all these parts is the heart, the seat of love. There are numerous verses about the heart, *del*, which is described most poetically, and the qualities of which are praised, the griefs of which are told in touching verses. For the *ahl-e del*, those endowed with heart, are the true lovers and initiated, far from the body which drags man into mere water and clay.[262]

The heart is often imagined as a child which calls for the milk of love; it is born from the body, but is the king of the body, just as 'man is born to woman'.[263]

From the basin 'Heart' the whole body is watered and cleaned, although between the ocean 'heart' and the ocean 'body' a 'barrier which they shall not transgress' (Sura 55/20) is erected.[264] But provided man gives alms from his body, God will cause a lovely garden to grow in his heart.[265]

The heart should be restless for many years, for it is like water which will become putrid when it rests;[266] but it is also fiery like Hell; nay, even more so: its glow can burn Hell and does not shun the water of the ocean.[267] In his lyrics, Rumi never ceases addressing this heart which is restless and homeless, longing and loving, and which deserts the body and follows the beloved wherever he may go:

> I shouted: 'Where does my intoxicated heart go?'
> The King said: 'Quiet! It goes towards me!'[268]

Lost in the ocean of love,[269] it illuminates the eyes so that 'the light of the eye is produced by the light of the hearts,'[270]

This heart is, at the same time, the Throne of God for which the Koranic word 'And the Merciful stood on His throne' was revealed (Sura 20/5).[271] It is the place to which God looks;[272] he who possesses a true heart has a mirror which reflects the six sides of the world so that God can see this world in the human heart.[273] The image of the mirror is common: it has to be polished by piety, good works and love until man can see in it 'the science of the prophets without books and without preceptor and master'.[274] Such a steady polishing makes the heart resemble a 'Chinese mirror'[275] so that it is able to receive inspiration, the light of God.[276] Owing to its relation with the Divine Light which radiates in the purified mirror, the heart can also be compared to a lamp of God,[277] alive only by the Divine Light, and transparent for its rays, as Rumi says with an application of the Light-verse (Sura 24/35).[278]

The most common comparison is that of the heart and a house, known to the Sufis from at least the late tenth century, when Abuʾl Ḥoseyn an-Nuri wrote his allegories.[279] The house awaits 'the sweet guest of the soul', the Divine Beloved to dwell in it, as God promised:

> Heaven and earth contain me not, but the heart of my faithful servant contains me.[280]

Whether the heart is cleansed so that no idol remains when the Divine visitor wishes to enter, or whether it is completely ruined under the strokes of affliction so that suddenly the treasure appears—it makes no difference as to the result. For God has promised:

> I am with those whose hearts are broken for my sake.[281]

And His image—the image of the Beloved—rests in the 'oyster-like heart like a pearl'[282] so that the lover himself has no room in it; only the name remains from him, nothing else.[283] For 'two "I" cannot be contained in his narrow house.'[284]

The heart is also a lovely garden, again a classical image from at least Nuri's days: it may be outwardly a desert but it contains flowers and gardens, watered by the rain of Grace, quickened by the breeze of Divine messages.[285]

The image of the house is extended to that of the sacred building: the heart is the mosque in which the body worships, and no enemy should enter this sanctuary to pollute it;[286] it is the *masjed-e aqṣā*, the mosque in Jerusalem,[287] or even the Kaʿba itself.[288] And, like the soul it opens a window towards the Unseen so that the lover may listen to the words which are spoken by the invisible Beloved.[289]

There are ever fresh images, full of poetry and sometimes strange: the heart is a glass bottle, in which the Divine Beloved dwells like a fairy, and man thus becomes a magician, calling this fairy with magical incantations.[290] Or else:

> His love put my painful heart on its hand and smelled it:
> If this heart is not nice, how could it become a bouquet of flowers for him?[291]

When the heart is nicely burnt in the flames of love,[292] when it is roasted like *kabāb*, as the poet says, different smells will rise from it by which the beloved recognizes its true character. In a ghazal devoted to the marvels of the heart, Rumi praises this tiny heart, which is so strong that it squeezes the skies like a napkin, and hangs the eternal lamp unto itself as if it were a minute candle. Is not the heart like Solomon, possessing his mysterious seal, under whose sway was everything created?[294] It leads man towards *baqāʾ*, eternal life in God, whereas the body goes towards annihilation;[295] and everything beautiful is, in fact, nothing but the reflection of the heart, for 'from its cheek God's Beauty appears'.[296]

Thus Rumi's anthropology—if it can be called by this scholarly name—is the description of man's high rank, a rank which he tends to forget and which to rediscover he is called to leave the veils of the body, the carnal soul, and the partial intellect until he reaches the wonderful world of the heart, which reveals to him God in His beauty and love.

We have not sent thee, save as a mercy for the worlds.

MOWLĀNĀ'S PROPHETOLOGY

Man is the apex of created beings; but among men, the prophets in general, and the Prophet of Islam in particular, constitute the highest possible point of spiritual development, which means that they enjoy ultimate proximity to the Creator.

Love of the Prophet Moḥammad, called by honorific names Aḥmad and Moṣṭafā, is one of the outstanding features of Muslim life in general and of Sufi thought in particular. One often overlooks the strong relationship of the Sufis, and thus of Jalāloddin, to the Prophet of Islam, to whom he 'clings like Abu Bakr to Moṣṭafā' when they spent a night in the cave on their way from Mecca to Madina.[1] The closest possible relationship of a trusting and trustworthy friend with the leader of the faithful is a model for the Sufi's relation with the Prophet.

> If I deny the morning-time, I am a bat,
> If I deny Aḥmad, I am a Jew.[2]

Rumi admonishes man to look around him: is not the Prophet's work still alive after 650 years?[3] He should become 'a servant of *laulāka*, take a morsel from *laulāka*',[4] i.e. he should accept the tradition according to which God addressed Moḥammad, saying:

> *Laulāka mā khalaqtu'l-aflāka*—If not for thee, I would not have created the spheres.

This Divine dictum is, indeed, the true source of creation, of movement, and of love,[5] for Moḥammad Moṣṭafā is the goal and meaning of existence. He claimed, as tradition holds:

> I was a prophet when Adam was still between water and clay[6] —

and yet he sighed:

> Would that the Lord of Moḥammad had not created Moḥammad!

for:

> in comparison with that absolute union which he enjoyed with God all this prophetic work is but burden, torment, and suffering.[7]

To be sure, every prophet and saint has a special method to teach mankind, but in God they are one;[8] and they are only brokers, who mediate between man and God, who is the Buyer. Their reward is, then, the vision of the Beloved.[9] Moḥammad is the seal of prophets (Sura 33/40) and fulfills what his predecessors have taught.

Rumi sees the Prophet as helper and leader; and when he tells the story of Moḥammad's nurse Ḥalima, who was grieved when the infant had been lost to her, he quotes the saying of the old man who tried to console her:

> Do not grieve: he will not be lost to thee, nay, but the whole world will become lost in him.[10]

That was, no doubt, the feeling of every pious Muslim in the thirteenth century.

Rumi has firmly relied upon the Prophetic traditions in his work, which he either inserts overtly or to which he alludes hundreds of times. Reminiscences from Moḥammad's biography permeate his poetical language and his *Mathnavi* abounds in stories about his life: how the infidels came to visit him, how he talked to his beloved young wife ʿAʾesha, and how a glutton came and utterly misbehaved after having eaten 'with seven stomachs' so that the Prophet himself had to clean the room in which the uninvited guest had spent the night,[11] and many other tales. Moḥammad is the paragon of mildness and wisdom, and anecdotes concerning his personality are frequently quoted in *Fihi mā fihi,* where they are explained, as in the *Mathnavi,* in a mystical sense.

Moḥammad's hegira from Mecca to Madina becomes the symbol of the spiritual journey:

> Did not Moṣṭafā go to travel towards Yathrib,
> found a kingdom and became the ruler of a hundred countries . . .?[12]

Similarly, man can find his spiritual kingdom only by leaving the country in which he was born, i.e. the material world, and wander along the difficult roads as taught by the masters of the Path to obtain the kingdom of Spirit and finally to conquer the world. Returning to Mecca, the Prophet smashed the idols;[13] following his example, the seeker who has established his spiritual kingdom will proclaim the rule of the Lord everywhere, will transform the material world into the kingdom of God. The motif of the journey, so dear to the mystics of all religions, has often been used by Rumi in different contexts; but this combination with the Prophet's migration seems particularly revealing.

The tribulations which Moḥammad encountered are usually symbolized in the figure of Abu Lahab, the 'Father of the Flame' who, according to Rumi, is the only human being who lacked the flame of Divine Love.[14]

The whole complex of legends told about the Prophet for centuries is echoed in Rumi's poetry. He is particularly fond of the story of the weeping palm-trunk: Moḥammad had used this trunk for a while to support himself during his preaching; when a pulpit proper was built, he left the palm-trunk—and the deserted thing began to sigh. Is man lower than a palm-trunk that he should not sigh when separated from his beloved?[15] The sighing trunk, the speaking stones are all endowed with life. Only the common people regard them as lifeless and without feeling; but before God (and we may add: before those who live in God) they are intelligent and submissive.[16]

There are other miracles which serve to illustrate the Prophet's high rank: the napkin which he used to wipe his face and hands was not burnt in the oven, for the Mohammadan light with which it was impregnated proved stronger than the flames,[17] as in the tradition that attests that Hell addresses the true faithful with the words 'Your light extinguishes my flames'. The Divine light manifest through the Prophet and the faithful is uncreated, whereas Hellfire is created and thus inferior, and bound to perish.

Jalāloddin agrees with the Persian poets of Shiraz who knew, through another *ḥadith*, that the rose was created from Moṣṭafā's perspiration.[18] Since the Prophet's whole body was free from any outward impurity, and his heart had been taken out and cleansed by the angels, he was fragrant, beautiful and, transparent for the Divine Light, he cast no shade.[19] Having perfectly tamed his lower instincts, he could proclaim that his '*sheyṭān*', his base soul, had become a Muslim and followed him in every respect:[20] here, again, he is the model for the mystic who has to train his lower faculties to bring them into the service of God where they will prove useful (much as a former thief will become an excellent police-master because he knows all the tricks of the trade . . .)[21]

The Koranic allusions to the Prophet's visionary experiences were always a central theme for mystical writers, who recognized in Sura 53 'The Star' the perfect description of the Prophetic status: a two-bow length was the distance[22] between the Prophet and the Ineffable on the clear horizon; but Moḥammad's eye did not rove in the presence of God, the radiant Divine Sun:[23] this is exactly the state of one who has reached a full life through God and sees only Him, undistracted by outward forms and things other than Him. Rumi includes also allusions to Sura 80 'He frowned' in which the Prophet's unfriendly attitude towards a blind guest was blamed.[24] That allusions to the role of Moḥammad as the seal of prophets are frequent goes without saying:

> The seals which the (former) prophets left were removed by the religions of Aḥmad.
> The unopened locks had remained: they were opened by the hand of 'Lo, We have opened (unto Thee)' (Sura 48/1)
> He is the intercessor in this world and in yonder world: in this world for guidance to the true religion, and yonder (for entrance) to Paradise . . .[25]

Moḥammad has come

> as mercy for the worlds (Sura 21/107), and from the Ocean of Absolute Certainty he grants pearls to the inhabitants of this world, peace to the fishes.[26]

Here, the combination of 'mercy' with the rain cloud, so common in Islamic poetry, is at least intended: the Prophet, gaining his strength from the Divine Ocean, just as the cloud is nourished by the sea, transforms the rain-drops of wisdom, mercy, and certainty into pearls. In him, God's working through the human instrument without secondary causes is most conspicuous: thus the Koran mentions the miracle of the battle of Badr in 624: 'Thou cast not, when thou cast, but God casts' (Sura 8/17). Since Moḥammad lived in and through God, every action was not his own but produced by God[27]—thus the motif of the arrow which comes from the world of the Unseen without bow frequently denotes the activity of the Prophet or those who have reached the final stage of sainthood.[28]

One of the supernatural events connected with the Prophet

is the splitting of the moon. This miracle, interpreted from a short remark at the beginning of Sura 54, was always regarded as one of his highest achievements:

> Moṣṭafā split the moon at midnight,
> Abu Lahab talks nonsense out of wrath.
> That Messiah quickens the dead,
> That Jew plucks out his moustache out of anger.[29]

Moḥammad's miracle is set parallel to that of Christ, since both of them negatively impressed the unbelievers, arousing their anger. To become split by the Prophet's finger is the highest beatitude the moon can attain.[30] Why, then, should men remain like clouds, hiding his beauty?[31] But not only the moon, nay, heaven and earth burst from happiness when Moḥammad appeared on earth:

> The sky is bursting from his happiness,
> the earth becomes like a lily from his purity.[32]

He is 'more than moon',[33] and that is why he calls his companions 'stars',[34] stars which surround him who leads the way[35] and who is not affected by the dog-like enemies who bark at him without hampering his glorious journey.[36]

The mystic who has reached union with the Light of Moḥammad can therefore claim:

> I split the moon with the light of Moṣṭafā![38]

The concept of the 'Moḥammadan Light' developed in the first half of the tenth century and forms the subject of many learned treatises of Sufis and theologians:[38] it is light from the Divine Light, previous to all created lights; it permeates the whole creation, and leaves no room for any darkness:

> Infidelity put on a black dress: the Light of Moḥammad arrived, the drum of Eternal remaining (*baqā*ʾ) was beaten, the eternal kingdom arrived.[39]

It is to this light that Sura 93 'By the Morning-Light' alludes, as the earlier Sufis always maintained: Sanaʾi's poetical interpretation of this *sura* in a long *qaṣida* in Moḥammad's honour is the most eloquent expression of this feeling.[40] Rumi has adopted this idea as well. In wonderful images he praises this light, which illuminates travellers and whose luminous shade embraces everything.[41] This light is found in thousands of derivations all over the world, and

> When Moḥammad tears the veil from one derivation,
> then a thousand monks and priests tear the infidels' thread.[42]

His beauty embraces the world,[43] and his light is opposed to black melancholia as much as to passion for wife and wealth; it makes the soul radiant[44] and, so to speak, polishes the different species of darkness, unifies all the shades of different length, all the colours of different hues, so that eventually all shadows are 'given in pawn', to, i.e. absorbed by, that sun.[45]

Moḥammad's light is the source of every love: 'the mystic's love and longing for God emanates from the pre-existent light of Moḥammad which is the essence of all prophecy and saintship . . .'.[46] The Prophet is therefore often described as the veritable embodiment of love,[47] and the lover is called to seize Aḥmad's cloak and to listen to the call to prayer of love from the heart of Belāl,[48] the Prophet's faithful Abyssinian muezzin. Love is, as Rumi says, comparable to 'Moṣṭafā's coming in the infidels' midst'.[49]

This Divine Love manifested itself best in the experience of the *isrā*, the Night-Journey, the ascension to heaven to which the Koran (Sura 17/1) alludes: 'Praised be He who travelled with His servant at night'. This night-journey has been interpreted from at least the days of Bāyazid Besṭāmi as the prototype of the mystic's flight into the immediate Divine presence and thus as symbol for the highest spiritual experience. The Prophet who 'dedicated his day to work and gain, and his night to (Divine) love',[50] because his 'heart was awake even though his eyes slept', as the *ḥadith* says, was uplifted on the miraculous steed, *Borāq*, whose very name became among the mystics and particularly with Rumi equivalent to 'love'.[51] Aḥmad's Borāq is the lot of those true lovers who do not care for thousands of Arabic steeds which may belong to others.[52]

In connection with the Prophet's ascension, Rumi has coined one of his finest images: according to tradition, Gabriel, the guide of the heavenly journey, remained outside the Divine Presence into which the Prophet was admitted; for even the angel of inspiration did not dare to fly further lest his wings be singed: thus he becomes the symbol of reason which cannot transgress a certain point.[53] Where the intimate discourse of love and the gnosis of the lover begins, reason is no longer admitted, even though it appear in angelic shape. The Prophet, however, enjoyed 'a time with God'.[54] In this interpretation of the *meʿrāj*, the ascension, Rumi has summed up his whole attitude towards discursive reason which, though useful, and necessary like Gabriel as guide on the ascending steps of the Path, becomes useless once the seeker has reached the chamber of union where the ineffable mystery of love takes place.

According to Islamic tradition, the Prophet is announced in the gospels as Aḥmad,[55] the paraclete (Sura 61/6), and his name, Aḥmad, is the name of all prophets.[56] Rumi knows the *ḥadith qodsi* according to which God said 'I am *Aḥmad* without *m*' i.e. *Aḥad*, 'One', a tradition probably invented in the late twelfth century, since it is found several times in ʿAṭṭār's work,[57] but not in Sanāʾi's poetry. Jalāloddin not rarely alludes to the wordplay *aḥad-Aḥmad*:

> The *Aḥad* wove feathers around his face out of jealousy,
> the soul of Aḥmad exclaimed out of longing for Him: 'Woe longing'.[58]

In *Fihi mā fihi*, Mowlānā mentions Moʿinoddin Parvāna's name, which has become, due to the letter *m moʿinoddin* 'Helper of Religion' instead of *ʿeynoddin* 'Essence of the Faith': that proves, for him, that addition to perfection is diminution. That is the case in the relation of *Aḥmad* and *Aḥad*:

> *Aḥad* is perfection, and *Aḥmad* is not yet in the station of perfection; when that *m* is removed it becomes complete perfection. That is to say, God comprehends all; whatever you add to Him is a diminution.[59]

Rumi, however, does not allude in this context to the numerical value of *m*, being forty, as pertaining to the forty grades of emanation which separate man and God, this being left to later Sufi theoreticians.[60] In an interesting line Mowlānā speaks of Shams-e Tabriz, 'the companion of Aḥmad' who is 'surely one of the greatest things' (Sura 74/35).[61] Should this line contain a subtle hint to the first discussion of the two mystics which revolved, as legend tells, around whether Moḥammad was greater than Bāyazid Besṭāmi? Moḥammad had called himself 'a servant of God' whereas Bāyazid had exclaimed: 'Praise to me, how great is my Majesty'. The discussion was resolved, of course, in favour of the Prophet. But the master from Tabriz, famous for his burning love of the Prophet, becomes, for Jalāloddin, the true interpreter of the 'Mohammadan spiritual wine.'

> When out of the Aḥmadian barrel scent emerges and becomes apparent,
> the soul and eye of the infidels becomes ebulliating like wine.
> When you want complete scent and colour from the Aḥmadian wine,
> then, Oh caravan leader, rest for a moment in Tabriz![62]

But again, the poet changes his mind: Moḥammad was in reality neither wine nor cupbearer:

> He was the goblet replete with wine, and God was the cupbearer for the pious —[63]

a fine distinction of the role of the Prophet, who does not convey any intoxicating doctrine himself, but brings only what God has put into him, being a mere instrument for Divine action, the immaculate vessel for the Divine wine. He was called *ummi* 'illiterate' to show that his wisdom was not nourished by intellectual effort and bookish learning, but exclusively by God's inspiration.

> He was illiterate, but hundreds of thousands books filled with poetry were nothing before him.[64]

In a later, more scholarly explanation in prose, Rumi has dwelt once more on the Prophet's 'illiteracy' which leads almost to an equation of the Prophet and the Universal Reason, an idea alluded to in the *Mathnavi* as well:

> Moḥammad . . . is called 'unlettered' not because he was incapable of writing and learning; he was called 'unlettered' because with him writing and learning and wisdom were innate, not acquired. He who inscribes characters on the face of the moon, is such a man unable to write? And what is there in all the world he does not know seeing that all men learn from him; what then, pray, should appertain to the partial intellect that the Universal Intellect does not possess? . . . Those who invent something new on their account, they are the Universal Intellect. The partial intellect is capable of learning and is in need of teaching! The Universal Intellect is the teacher, and is not in need . . . It is the prophets and saints who have effected union

> between partial intellect and Universal Intellect so that they have become one . . .[65]

But by and large, Rumi's verses rather reflect the deep trust in the Prophet who is 'the helper of both worlds'[66] and who makes the faithful 'one soul' like a gentle mother.[67] He is God's scales on earth on which the light and the heavy are weighted and judged,[68] and he is like Noah's ark, rescuing everyone who clings to him (the same saying is also applied to his community).[69] The Koran in his hand is like the rod of Moses, endowed with life-giving qualities for the faithful, but turning into a dragon against the infidels whom he devours.[70] Thus, the Prophet, that Unique Pearl, can well be called an 'alchemy for man'; they are like base copper, but his light changes them into gold.[71] Once they have tasted from the *Kowthar*, the paradisiacal fountain which was given to Moḥammad (Sura 108) they are transformed and acquire his qualities: such people should be chosen as companions, for they have an apple from the Aḥmadian tree.[72] And whosoever seizes one corner of Moṣṭafā's cloak will be saved from the depths of Hell and brought to Paradise.[73]

Rumi has never ceased to express his love and trust in the Prophet, whom he surrounds with many beautiful names and epithets. In a small Arabic ghazal in an almost dancing rhythm, he praises him:

> *hādha ḥabibi, hādha tabibi, hādhā adibi, hadhā dawāʾi* . . .
> This is my beloved, this my physician, this my tutor, this my remedy . . .[74]

words, usually applied by mystical poets to their beloved; and indeed, in the following centuries the Prophet more and more assumed the character of the mystical beloved.

We may sum up Jalāloddin's attitude towards the Prophet in a line from one of his most enraptured ghazals where he describes the soul's journey to its original homeland:

> Young fortune is our friend, to give up our soul is our profession,
> our caravan-leader is the pride of the world, Moṣṭafā![75]

And no one who has ever listened to the *Mevlevi*-ritual will forget the haunting beauty of the introductory passage, the *naʿt-e sharif*, the song in honour of the Prophet, in which

Jalāloddin expressed his love and veneration for Moḥammad: the whole mystical dance develops out of this hymn which sings of the greatness and beauty of the leader and friend of the faithful.

You shall surely ride stage after stage . . .

THE SPIRITUAL LADDER

Rumi saw life as a constant upward movement. Both the development of the whole creation from the lowest to the highest manifestation and the progress of individual life can be regarded in this light. Such movement could be expressed by the image of the journey which, indeed occurs frequently in his poetry, as in that of other mystics; but his favourite symbol, again in tune with Sanā'i's imagery, is that of the ladder or staircase (*nardabān*), which will eventually lead the lover to the roof, where the beloved is waiting.

God has put different ladders into the world, destined for different people to climb,[1] and the worldly senses may also serve as a ladder, which ends, however, in this world, whereas religious feeling leads towards heaven.[2] That even the spiritual leader should be called a ladder is not too surprising, for he leads the adept, slowly, in well prepared stages, towards higher realities until the doors of grace are opened and in love a ladder is no longer required.[3] But even death—be it the corporeal or the spiritual death in annihilation—leads, as a ladder, to the roof of the Beloved;[4] *samāʿ*, again, is a ladder towards Heaven.[5]

Rumi sees steps and ladders everywhere: the branches and twigs which in spring appear from the depths are like a ladder which those who travel to heaven have put into the garden,[6] as if the buds and leaves were spirits who have reached paradise, having left the dark dust, i.e. the body. The friend's roses address the lover in the garden that the ladder which leads to the Beloved is to sacrifice one's soul in affliction,[7] and the branches which attract the water from the roots are images of the beloved who attracts the soul without outward ladder.[8]

Man should transform himself into a ladder when he sees that all the doors of peace and rest have been closed before him — then he will find his beloved on the roof, radiant like the moon . . .[9] Even though the image of the journey downwards, into one's own heart is used at times in his work, this imagery of ladders and stairs is almost without limits in Rumi's poetry.

The first step in this ladder which leads man towards God is essential: the beginning of a minaret is made with one brick, and if man neglects one single brick in the foundation, the whole building will be ruined soon.[10] This first step is the strict adherence to ritual duties as taught in the Koran and explained in the tradition. Fasting, prayer, religious alms and pilgrimage are indispensable, for they are the expression of true faith:

> This prayer and fasting, pilgrimage and holy war
> give witness to the faith,
> This alms and gifts and abandonment of envy
> give witness to your own secret (thought).

Besides prayer, which will be discussed separately, it is the fasting during Ramadan on which Rumi's main interest is concentrated.

> Although faith is built upon five pillars,
> yet, by God, the greatest pillar of those is fasting.
> But He has hidden in all the five the value of fasting,
> just as the blessed Night of Might is hidden in fasting.[12]

On the mountain Qāf of fasting even the sparrow becomes a Phoenix;[13] the stone turns into a wonderful ruby, during fasting, and this religious practice is a fast horse running swiftly towards the source of life, as Mowlānā says in a long ghazal rhyming in *ṣiyām* 'fasting'.[14] Those who fast drink the wine of the Spirit,[15] or, to put it differently those who have broken the (mundane) bottle with stones of 'fasting' and 'holy war' will be granted pure wine from the goblet of the Feast of Fastbreaking (cf. Sura 76/21).[16] Fasting means, indeed, to sacrifice one's self so that the two feasts are basically one great Feast of Sacrifice, for the month of Ramadan is like an honoured guest for whom something valuable has to be slaughtered.[17] In an artistic pair of contrasts says the poet:

> Kill the fat cow of your greed by fasting,
> so that you reach the blessing of the lean crescent of the ᶜId![18]

Fasting is, as Rumi says with a military expression, the war machine (*manjanik*), which destroys the fortress of darkness, tyranny and infidelity.[19]

Numerous single verses and whole poems highlight the importance of fasting, which Rumi himself kept very strictly, even beyond the prescribed measure. Other lines interpret fasting and feasting differently: so long as the poet is with his beloved, the Moon, he enjoys a festival every day, day and night.[20] When the beloved scolds him, he feels that

> after the pain of fasting the day of the feast will come![21]

In fact, one should break the fast only with the sugar of the friends lip[22]'-what is one to do when this sweetmeat is not available? The two ʿ*id,* at the end of Ramadan and at the end of the pilgrimage to Mecca, are enough for the normal believer; but whoever knows the beloved has two hundred ʿ*id* every moment.[23] Rumi complains, addressing the Friend, in charming imagery:

> You are like the day of ʿArafāt and ʿ*id*, I am the beginning of Ẕu'l-ḥijja (the month of pilgrimage; the two festive days fall between the 8th and 10th)—
> I can never reach you, nor can I cut myself off from you.[24]

Rumi has sometimes described the pilgrimage, the long tiresome way when the pilgrim

> in sand and deserts gets used to camel-milk and sees the plundering of the bedouins . . .[25]

He sees even the sky performing the circumambulation around the Kaʿba in its dark blue Sufi-gown,[26] and knows of the journey of those who come back, having left their hearts in Mecca, with exhausted bodies;[27] but all fatigue is meaningless as long as the heart is not present during the pilgrimage. Thus Mowlānā calls the pilgrims to tell of their experiences and what they saw in Mecca:

> O people gone to pilgrimage—where are you? Where are you?
> The Friend is in this very place—come hither, come O come!
> Your Friend, he is your neighbour, his wall and yours are one—
> Bewildered in the desert, what do you seek and roam?
> When you behold, without forms, the form of this your Friend
> Then master, house, and Kaʿba will you become yourself . . .[28]

Although the *ḥajj* is obligatory, its spiritual value is higher than its external value; to kiss the black stone at the Kaʿba is a mere symbol:

> The pilgrim kisses the black stone from his innermost heart because he feels the taste of the lip of his beloved from it.[29]

It is a sign, nothing more. Therefore Rumi—like most of the Sufis—spiritualizes the pilgrimage; he sees the camel 'body' wander towards the Kaʿba 'heart', and describes the long way towards the Kaʿba of union on which thousands have perished from longing. Man does not need a candle to see this spiritual Kaʿba at night—its foundation is all light which radiates over the whole world.[30]

The 'Kaʿba of the soul', and the '*qebla* of the friend's face' are common expressions with him. And in a famous passage towards the end of the *Mathnavi* he enumerates the *qebla* (direction of prayer) of all kinds of people who see the direction of their wishes and hopes by no means in Mecca, but:

> The Kaʿba of Gabriel and the spirits is a Lotus-tree,
> the *qebla* of the belly-slave is a table-cloth.
> The *qebla* of the gnostic is the light of union;
> the *qebla* of the philosopher's intellect is phantasy.
> The *qebla* of the ascetic is the Gracious God;
> the *qebla* of the flatterer is a purse of gold.
> The *qebla* of the spiritual is patience and long-suffering
> the *qebla* of form-worshippers is the image of stone.
> The *qebla* of those who dwell on the inward is the Bounteous One.
> The *qebla* of those who worship the outward is a woman's face.[31]

The great festival, the Feast of Offering, provides the lover with a wonderful opportunity to offer himself to the Beloved. Thus Rumi repeatedly regards Shamsoddin as the Great Feast itself, and himself as the offered lamb.[32]

> He said with a smile: 'Go and render grace
> for my feast, O you who have become my sacrifice!'
> I said: 'Whose sacrifice am I?'—The Friend said:
> 'Mine, mine, mine!'[33]

Turned into a sacrificial animal at *ʿid*, burnt like aloes-wood in the flames of love to produce fine fragrance—that is the lover's state.[34] He is slaughtered by the sword of God,[35] or by the sword *Allāhu Akbar* which will find everybody, wherever he may flee.[36] The lover, lean and skinny,[37] may once, in a moment of weakness, request from his friend a sign of mildness, for according to the *shariʿa* a bony animal should not be slaughtered; but then he rather prefers to show himself as nice and plump, since the 'butcher of the lovers' likes to slay good-looking animals.[38]

Rumi applies the motif of the sacrificial animal also to natural events:

> The black cow 'Night' became a sacrifice of the dawn, that is why the muezzin afterwards said: *Allāhu Akbar*—[39]

the call to morning prayer is compared to the formula *Allāhu Akbar* as spoken when slaughtering an animal. Or else the poet may offer all the animals of the zodiac to the Moon, his Beloved, for his great feast.[40]

When Rumi saw in the black stone of the Kaʿba a symbol of the lip of his beloved, he has interpreted the *zakāt,* the legal alms, in a similar way and several times asks his beloved to pay the *zakāt-e laʿl,* the tax due on rubies,[41] i.e. to grant him a kiss from his ruby-like lips. This image is not rare in Persians lyrics in general. It is worth mentioning that Mowlānā alludes several times to the *shab-e barāt,* the night in mid-Shaʿban during which sins are forgiven and destinies fixed—this night is regarded even today in Turkey as very auspicious.[42]

* * *

> Every iron is valuable, not that it has no use; but reason understands how much a piece of iron must be polished until it becomes a mirror.[43]

The way towards God which begins with the fulfilment of ritual duties requires this constant struggle,[44] the polishing of one's heart, as Mowlānā says with an image common to all Sufis. He knows that all kinds of dangers lie in ambush for the faithful one who tries to climb up the ladder leading towards perfect faith and towards God.

On this path, one needs true companions:

> The longer the way, the more companions are necessary—the way to the Kaʿba is hard, one needs a long caravan and a caravan-leader . . . and how much more difficult is it to come closer to God through so many veils, steep mountains, and highway-robbers![45]

Man should therefore be careful not to mix during his journey with those who do not understand the higher realities of life. How many people are there, travelling to Syria and Iraq, who do not see anything but infidelity and hypocrisy; how many others have gone to India and Herat without looking to anything but trade, or did not find in Turkestan and China any goods but ruse and hatred![46] They detect only colour and odour, wherever they be, but are not aware of the realities hidden behind the forms. Such superficial persons can easily become laughing-stocks of Satan, who induces them more and more into worldly affairs, or leads them to stonier and more slippery impasses.[47]

It is dangerous to follow such people, for they are like children who do not see the moon in the sky but reflected on water and thus mislead the caravan by their lack of insight: when the stupid become leaders, the intelligent, out of fear, cover their heads with their carpets.[48] These stupid people are blind or at best one-eyed; and, though an ox is excused when he looks only to his stable, man is different; he is expected to look through the eyes of the Divine Beloved. Fate makes such a person blind and causes him finally to fall into a well so that he perishes.[50] For a blind man is prone to fall again and again; if he falls in filth, he cannot even discern whether the bad smell comes from himself or from the polluting matter (just as he considers the scent of the musk which someone may shower upon him to be his own, not understanding it to be the gift of a friend).[51] Such are the people animated by self-will who refuse to see through the Divine light. The bad smell of their outward filthiness reaches only a few yards, but the odour of their spiritual filth permeates the world from Reyy to Damascus, and makes even the houris and Rizvān, the doorkeeper of Paradise, feel sick.[52] Their blindness veils to them the fact that everything in this created world is alive and points to a higher goal—they regard the parts of the world as dead, where as the Prophet, and the saint, experiences them as alive.[53]

A lowly and mean person of this kind turns black like false coins when the touchstone is put to him; although he bears the garb of a lion, he is soon discovered to be a wolf with all his greed.[54] He cannot discern the real greatness of things: when he sees a mountain, he becomes impressed, so that his thought becomes like a tiny mouse in front of a huge wolf; instead of fearing God he trembles at the very sight of clouds and thunders, as stupid as an ass.[55]

Since the unbelievers are destined to go to the deepest hell, *Sejjin*, they really enjoy the prison (*sejn*) of this world, whereas the prophets and faithful, determined to reach the paradisical height, *ᶜilliyun*, always turn to higher levels (*ali*).[56]

Rumi does not spare his imaginative vocabulary in describing such a person who 'has eaten donkey's brain':[57] though outwardly aged and decrepit, he is like an unripe fruit among yellow leaves, or like a kettle which has become black and ugly in the fire whereas the meat that was to be cooked is still raw—such is the state of a person who has not matured in the sufferings of life, and in the fire of love, but has remained earthbound.[58]

Mowlānā therefore admonishes his readers to flee from the stupid just as Jesus fled from them, for these people steal man's religion exactly as a cloud slowly steals the light of the sun.[59] Man must definitely not be deceived by the friendly behaviour of the ignorant, who are as unreliable as a hermaphrodite, sometimes posing as a man, sometimes as a woman.[60] Such people, and of course even more those who are open enemies to man's religion, are dangerous to the extent of drinking man's blood, even if they be his relatives. Did not Abraham break his father's idols and part with him because of his infidelity? He is the true believer's model for his actions against those who do not partake of his faith and love.[61]

Indeed, such people are, to use the Koranic expression 'like animals, nay, even more astray than those' (Sura 7/179), and as Rumi concludes:

> It is lawful to slaughter animals for man's benefit, or in order that he may not suffer injury from them. The same rule applies to infidels and those who violate the Divine commandments. Such persons are virtually animals, since by indulging their selfish, sensual, and bestial natures they place themselves in antagonism to the spiritual reason which is the crown of humanity.[62]

Among the evil qualities which man, and especially the future mystic must avoid most, Rumi regards greed and avidity as the worst—greed is a dragon, exactly the counterpart of spiritual poverty.[63] And the scent of greed and avidity appear like the smell of onion in speaking:

> when you eat them and say: 'I swear, I have avoided onion and garlic,'
> the breath of your oath will witness against you.[64]

These base and mean qualities have often been allegorized in the *Mathnavi*: one needs only think of the long story of the four birds which have to be slaughtered,[65] or the strange tale of the three persons of which the farsighted and yet blind man represents greed, which sees other people's faults, but not his own; the sharp-hearing and deaf hope which does not think of its own death, although it hears the mourning for others every moment; and the naked one with long skirt is the worldly person who thinks of his own affairs.[66]

It goes without saying that sensual lust and concupiscence belong to the most dangerous qualities in man; they are so dirty that they can be called 'the menstruation of men'.[67]

But not only the stupid, ignorant, sensual, greedy and faithless people who, out of greed, 'let a gnat's blood in mid air' are man's enemies on the way towards perfection; even more dangerous are the superintelligent individuals, mainly the philosophers, with their useless hair-splitting logic.

Jalāloddin himself had studied all the sciences of his time, and he was not completely anti-intellectualistic, as one may conclude from some of his verses. He is, to say the least, not as anti-intellectualistic as his spiritual master Sanāʾi, whose verse, written at a time when the consolidating Muslim orthodoxy became more and more suspicious of intellectual and mainly philosophical delvings, reflects the strictly legalistic mentality which distinguished the Eastern fringe of the Muslim world during the later Middle Ages. Rumi knows, and does not deny, that there is agreement that

> a wise man (*dānā*) is a mercy for the two worlds.[68]

We saw, that *ʿaql*, reason, is appreciated as the faculty which enables man to fulfill his religious duties and to understand the Divine Law. Logically, Rumi praises reason as long as it serves religion. But he is afraid, and that is again in congruence not only with the early Sufis but with the main body of orthodoxy that intensive intellectual activity without religious background is dangerous for man's spiritual progress. The intellectuals who split hairs are ridiculed,[69] and *ziraki*, 'intelligence, cleverness' is once described as Satan's quality as contrasted with man's love;[70] it should be sacrificed before the Prophet.[71] To devote one's self to outward sciences is nothing but to build a stable in which animals can remain for a couple of days; to weave gold-embroidered garments, to dive for pearls at the bottom of the sea, to occupy oneself with the intricacies of geometry and astronomy, of medicine or philosophy means to be still bound to this perishable world; the only true science, the wisdom which is an ocean without limits,[72] is that which leads to God, and that is known only to him who possesses a pure heart.[73] At the moment of death, all the outward sciences and crafts will be of no avail, required is only 'the knowledge of *faqr*', of spiritual poverty.[74]

The wisdom of this world is good only for augmenting thought and false imaginations, whereas religious wisdom flies beyond the spheres.[75] So long as religious science remains at the surface and is concerned exclusively with legal problems and theological disputations, it is not only superfluous but dangerous (we may think of Ghazzāli's verdict against his theological colleagues!): a person who indulges in false scholarly interpretation of the Divine word, relying upon his intellect but without religion, is comparable to a fly; his imagination is like donkey's urine, his conceptions like straw . . .[76]

In order to curb the claims of these scholars, Rumi quotes the *ḥadith*:

> Most of the inhabitants of Paradise are the unintelligent.[77]

Unintelligent, *ablah,* means here 'not bothering with outward religious sciences', but not 'ignorant of religious duties'. Or, if we follow Solṭān Valad's interpretation of the same sentence, it means that the perfection of human reason is reached when God reveals Himself to man, so that the recipient of this grace looses his rational faculties, being overwhelmed by this wonderful light. Just as a five years' old child will not faint at the sight of a beautiful beloved, but the grown up man will forget everything in the contemplation of his friend's beauty, thus the state of being without reason (*ablah*) is that of the most mature minds.[78]

Rumi, and following him his son, believes in immediate knowledge, in *ᶜelm-e ladoni* (Sura 18/65), not in traditional, *naqli,* sciences: traditional science which only relates from hearsay is, if brought into the presence of the Divinely inspired master, like performing the ablution with sand instead of running water, i.e. it is not only unnecessary but prohibited by law. Why use dry sand when the water of life, manifested in the spiritual guide, is available?[79]

Even more: when man says 'We do not know', like the angels (Sura 2/30), God's word 'We have taught him' (Sura 18/65) will rescue him; and when he does not know the alphabet in this school, he will be filled with Divine Light like Moḥammad, the 'unlettered' Prophet.[80]

Rumi's main targets in his attacks are the philosophers; the *feylasufak*, the 'little philosopher' or 'philosophiser', as he sometimes calls him, sees only the outward figures on the wall, and does not understand, and even less believes, that the palm tree spoke to Muhammad; for he relies upon his senses and thus does not hear the interior, spiritual voice of everything created.[81] He denies demons, yet falls prey to demons at that very moment.[82] Did not God say: 'I am closer to you than your jugular vein' (Sura 50/16)? Why should man then cast the net of his thoughts and ideas so far? And that is exactly what the philosopher tries, since he does not recognize the treasure which is so close at hand.[83]

> The poor little philosopher became blind, the light be far away from him!
> From him the hyacinth of religion does not bloom, for you don't plant it, O Idol![84]

This verdict against too much intellectual activity is particularly weighty when man enters, on his way towards God, the narrow path (*ṭariqa*) 'Sufism' which branches out of the great trunk road *shariʿa*, 'Divine Law'. But here, other dangers lie in ambush for the innocent disciple: the would-be Sufis seduce harmless travellers and discredit the whole mystical movement.

Such people, as Rumi describes them in his satirical verses (following again Sanāʾi's unfriendly remarks about self-styled Sufis), claim high spiritual rank; they shave their heads and necks as if they were gourds, and confuse the poor visitor with highfalutin talk about gnosis and poverty so that he thinks his companion must be a veritable Joneyd or another of the great masters of the Path.[85] In fact, however, such people show three qualities which are not found in a true Sufi: they talk too much, like a bell; they eat more than twenty people, and they sleep like the Seven Sleepers.[86] The word 'Sufi' is often used in a pejorative sense, as it was almost a rule in Persian literature. Clad in his dark blue cloak, this 'Sufi' resembles the sky: both are, as we may surmise, unreliable.[87] The stories in the *Mathnavi* depict some of these would-be saints in a rather negative light. As for the true Sufi, it is he who seeks purity (*ṣafvat*), not he who dons a woollen (*ṣuf*) garb or a patched frock and indulges in pederasty[88]—a sheykh who 'sews dervishes' frocks' is not becoming for the lovers.[89]

But how would Jalāloddin define Sufism at its best?

> What is Sufism?—He said: 'To find joy in the heart when afflictions come'.[90]

It is not to be learnt from books but from experience: Noah, although he spent nine hundred years thinking of God, lived exclusively on the recollection of his Lord, without reading Qosheyri's *Resāla* or Abu Ṭāleb-e Makki's *Qut al-Qolub*, the two standard-works of moderate Sufism![91] For only the Sabians and *ahl al-ketāb* ('People of the Book') are instructed by books—the Sufi enjoys immediate knowledge.[92]

> The Sufis came from left and right,
> Door by door, street by street: Where is wine? . . .
>
> The Sufi's door is his heart, his street the soul,
> The Sufi's wine is from God's barrel.[93]

Jalāloddin himself had grown up in an atmosphere completely saturated with mysticism; he had undergone formal training under the guidance of Borhānoddin Moḥaqqeq who made him study intensely his father's writings on mystical subjects. One would therefore expect that his poetry should bear the distinct flavour of this Sufi training, overflowing with technical terms and concrete instruction which, however, it does not. And in fact, some of his adversaries in Konya criticized the *Mathnavi* from this viewpoint:

> There is no mention of (theosophical) investigation and the sublime mysteries towards which the saints make their steeds gallop,
> (That) from the stations of asceticism to the passing away (from self-existence) step by step to the union with God, (It contains not) the explanation and definition of every station and stage, so that

by means of the wings thereof a man of heart should soar . . .[94]

To be sure, Mowlānā alludes to these states and says, i.e.:

If you perform a complete ablution with the water of asceticism.
You can transform all the pollution of the heart into purity,[95]

and he often speaks—overtly or in allusions—of the hard work that is required to polish man's heart:[96] does not the Koran attest 'Man possesses only that for which he strives' (Sura 53/39)? Yet, the experience of love through his meeting with Shamsoddin was so overwhelming that the early stages of the Path occur comparatively seldom in his poetry:

When you see running water, leave the ablution with sand;
When the festival of union comes, leave ascetic practices.[97]

There are a few allusions to Sufi practices in Mowlānā's imagery: e.g. to the Sufi's meditative position in his seclusion:

Since the school of the Sufi is his knee
the two knees are crafty in solving problems.[98]

And he has often underscored the power of the mystical guide (viz. below) whose presence is absolutely necessary to guide the novice. To the numerous definitions of early Sufism concerning the changing states (*ḥāl*, p. *aḥwāl*) and the lasting stations (*maqām*) through which the mystic passes on his path, Rumi adds a lovely sentence:

The *ḥāl* is like the unveiling of the beauteous bride,
while the *maqām* is the (king's) being alone with the bride,[99]

a verse which is then elaborated to explain the various degrees found among the high-ranking mystics.

The beginning of the mystical path is *towba*, repentance:

a strange mount which jumps up to heaven in one moment.[100]

Rumi has described the *towba-ye Naṣuḥ* in a rather drastic story. The expression taken from the Koran (Sura 66/8), where it means 'firm repentance' is here applied to the bath-keeper Naṣuḥ, who, in the guise of a woman, served in the woman's bath and eventually repented from his immoral deeds at the moment of mortal peril.[101] But this is not a truly Sufi act of repentance comparable to the 'repentance' which made a future saint like Ibrāhim ibn Adham renounce his kingdom;[102] Naṣuḥ's repentance is the simple duty of every

Courtesy of the Museum of Fine Arts, Boston

Mowlānā Rumi distributing sweetmeats. 17th or 18th century Turkish.

sinner.

For Mowlānā, as for every faithful Muslim, repentance is not a unique act: he knows that the door of repentance, situated in the Maghreb, is open till Doomsday, when the sun will rise in the West. Man should never despair of finding this door, which is, according to our poet, one of the eight doors of Paradise.[103] Does not Rumi's mausoleum bear the inscription:

> Come back, come back, even though you have broken your repentance a thousand times . . .

In his attitude towards the world, Rumi is close to the Sufis of the first generations, so long as the 'world' is thought to distract man from his sublime goal; for those endowed with insight, it is a mirror of God's activities. At times he has used very strong language to describe the lower world, words which remind the reader of the disharmonious sounds in the sermons of Ḥasan al-Baṣri (d. 728) and other ascetics of the eighth and ninth centuries, sounds which were echoed by most of the great Sufi writers in the later Middle Ages as well. The world is thus a stinking crooked crone who adorns herself to attract ever new lovers, who, overcome by sensual lust,[104] forget her repelling ugliness for a moment—

> Don't look at her foot-rings, see her black leg:
> The nightly game is nice—but behind the curtain.[105]

After a short while, this old toothless woman will kill her lovers as she has killed millions before them. This image, which occurs frequently in early Sufi texts, is also common in medieval European literature.

However, who would expect Rumi to compare the world to a pig which is the prey of the immature, whereas the true faithful would hunt the gazelle 'Soul'?[106] In such cases, he relies upon the *ḥadith* 'The world is carrion, and those who seek it are dogs';[107] it is a dunghill[108]—hence the numerous combinations of crows and ravens,[109] representatives of the dark matter and base instincts which populate the world. What should the ascetic do here? Weeping is required: weeping being one of the steps towards enlightenment. The ascetics of the eighth century were even known as *bakkā*ʾ*un* 'those who weep much', and tears are if we believe Rumi, as valuable as the blood of the martyrs.[110] The whole effort on the first steps of the spiritual ladder should be concentrated upon man's fight with his *nafs,* the lower soul, or 'base instincts, upon this 'real greater Holy War'.

One of the best ways to train the *nafs* properly is to fast, or even to starve, and to sleep little,[111] according to the old Sufi maxim, *qellat at-ṭaʿām, qellat al-manām, qellat al-kalām*— the latter device, 'little talk', is rarely mentioned by Rumi, unless we look at the numerous verses in which he advises himself to be silent. Sepahsālār's stories about his master's unusually long periods of fasting explain his poetical evaluation of hunger. Mowlānā knew well the 'alchemy of hunger' which the early ascetics had practised and preached. One must not eat one's fill, otherwise one will become Satan's donkey,[112] a vehicle for the seducer who can easily carry man to worse sins. Only when empty the reed can sing . . .[113]

There is no reason why man should eat so much. The body is nothing but a morsel for the tomb, and should therefore be lean.[114] In early times the Sufis invented traditions according to which

> Hunger is the food of God with which He quickens the bodies of the very faithful,[115]

and:

> Hunger is a treasure which is preserved with God who gives it to His special friends.

The animal grazes on straw and barley, and as a consequence will be slaughtered one day, but the pious lives on the light of God, following the example of the Prophet who said:

> I stay with my Lord who feeds me and gives me to drink;[116]

for, as Mowlānā asserts:

> Gabriel's strength was not from the kitchen,
> it was from looking at the Creator of Existence.
> Thus know that this strength of the saints (*abdāl*) of God
> is also from God, and not from viands and trays.[117]

The true mystic's food is constant praise of God, and then he experiences,

> that we eat lovely and sleep sweetly
> in the shade of never-ending grace—

a food, not by means of throat and stomach,
a sleep, not the result of nights . . .[118]

For the lover who has lost reason does not sleep—in his spiritual frenzy he 'sleeps with God', that means, he is without sleep like God Himself[119] (cf. Sura 2/256).

If man has to eat at all, he should be careful to take only that food which is ritually pure;[120] he should not even touch the morsels of sinners, as Rumi, faithful to the Sufi tradition, explains in a story in *Fihi mā fihi*.[121]

One of the basic stations on the mystical ladder is *tavakkol,* trust in God. Rumi relies, in this respect, upon the Prophet's word:

First tie your camel's knees, and then trust in God![122]

He does not believe in sitting idly under the pretext of *tavakkol*; his trust in God is active and means man's heartfelt acceptance of God's will and acting in harmony with His will. The higher he climbs on the spiritual ladder, the more he will understand the mystery of the Divine work and will annihilate himself so that God can work with him and through him. *Tavakkol*, understood thus, is a state of the highest order, not a state of the beginners who may interpret it in the wrong way.

One of the basic and fundamental qualities of the mystic is *ṣabr,* patience: it is 'a ladder towards higher stages',[123] or the *ṣirāṭ*-bridge which leads to Paradise,[124] the unfailing alchemy.[125] God Himself has indicated the importance of patience several times in the Koran; the mystics were particularly fond of hinting at this station by the expression 'the end of *al-ʿaṣr*' i.e. the last word of the *Surat al-ʿaṣr* which is '*ṣabr*', (patience).[126]

In describing patience, the poet has found ever new images, for 'Patience is the key to joy' as he repeats the old Arabic saying dozens of times. Man is like Joseph in the well of this world, who waits for the rope to take him out;[127] patience is an iron shield on which God has inscribed the words 'Victory has come',[128] for 'patience goes to the male, complaint towards the female'.[129]

When you do not ask, it will be revealed to you all the sooner:
The bird of patience is faster-flying than all the others![130]

And the uselessness of impatient screaming and crying is

illustrated in amusing imagery by the story of the man who wanted to have a lion tattoed on his back and could not stand the pain, so he decided first to have a lion without head, then without tail, then without belly . . .[131]

The importance of patience is particularly revealed in Rumi's spring-poems when he describes how birds and trees, after patiently waiting during the harsh times of winter, are rewarded with beautiful colours and aromas. The heart in the winter-landscape of the material world should wait for the spring of the soul, or the eternal joyful spring of Paradise, as it will become visible on the day of resurrection.

The correlative of patience—connected with the body—is gratitude, *shokr*—growing in the heart—;[132] and Rumi has evaluated these two states in a fascinating image:

> Patience says always: 'I give news of union with Him'.
> Gratitude says always: 'I have a whole store from Him'.[133]

Patience lives still between man and God, whereas gratitude speaks out of the state of union when man has experienced the immeasurable amount of Divine kindness and fills his store with it.

> Patience shows itself from the yellow face,
> Gratitude from the radiant red face.[134]

Gratitude should be the collar of each neck,[135] for:

> Gratitude for kindness is better than the favour received.[136]

And Mowlānā, whose first letter to Solṭān ᶜEzzoddin contains an impressive passage about the necessity of gratitude,[137] explains the different modes of this central virtue:

> Gratitude is a hunting and a shackling of benefits. When you hear the voice of gratitude, you get ready to give more. When God loves a servant He afflicts him; if he endures with fortitude, He chooses him; if he is grateful, He elects him . . . Gratitude is a sovereign antidote, changing wrath into grace . . .[138]

Two other correlatives on the mystical path are fear and hope, considered to be the two wings by which the human soul can fly toward God. Rumi knows the Divine ruse which may overcome man when he feels safe:

> Know that the station of fear is the one in which you are safe,
> Know that the station of security is that one in which you tremble.[139]

But as important as fear and hope are, they constitute for Rumi only preliminary states to be drowned in spiritual wine;[140] they may bring man closer to God during a certain portion of his journey, but:

> The seaman is always on the planks of fear and hope—
> when the plank and the man get annihilated, there is nothing but immersion,[141]

for in the Ocean of the Godhead neither fear nor hope, neither patience nor gratitude are any longer existent. Rumi highlights in one of his discourses the necessary interrelation of fears and hope with the image of the peasant who sows corn and hopes that it may grow but fears a crop failure; but in his poetry he once praises hope as the true mover of life:

> Is there anyone who has sown the corn of hope in this soil, to whom the spring of His grace did not grant a hundredfold (fruit)?[142]

This seems to be his last word about hope.

Rumi, who has experienced the different stages of love and has expressed in his poems both happiness and despair, sometimes uses the technical terms for the two states between which man is usually torn: *qabż*, 'depression', 'spiritual contraction' and *basṭ,* 'expansion, overwhelming joy'. These are, as he says, God's two fingers between which man is held, and which manifest themselves in sadness and joy.[143] In his acceptance of the overall tension of the two poles of life, or the constant manifestation of the Divine Unity under two seemingly contrasting aspects, he sees that both states are as necessary as breathing: there can be no joy without prior sadness, and *vice versa.*[144] The concept upon which Rumi's mystical theories focus insofar as we can detect any substantial theories at all is *faqr,* 'poverty'. The Prophetic saying 'Poverty is my pride' occupies a central place in his thought.[145] Did not Ṣadroddin Qunavi call him 'the *majordomo* of Mohammadan poverty'?[146] This poverty is not to be construed in the outward appearance of the dervish:

> Seek poverty in the light of God, don't seek it in the coarse cloth:
> If every naked person were a true man, then garlic would be a man too.[147]

True poverty is often combined with the Light of Divine Majesty;[148] it is a miraculous goblet,[149] or else is a wine to fill the dervish who has emptied himself from his self.[150] The whole world is nothing but a tell under which the treasure of 'poverty' is buried.[151] This is the treasure which Rumi saw in his dreams as 'a mine of rubies',[152] or as 'a beauty from the light of whose cheek the whole world becomes light'.[153]

In lovely verses Rumi underlines the importance of this mystical poverty, which is 'a powerful physician' to heal the illness of the self[154] and which means to possess nothing and to be possessed by nothing.

> The hearts of the lovers have formed a circle around poverty,
> Poverty is like the *sheykh ash-shoyukh*, and all the hearts are his disciples.[155]

And he combines the different mystical stations which are nothing but reflections of the Friend's transforming power which manifests itself on all levels of creation:

> Aloe (*ṣabr*) remained patient (*ṣabr*) through you, sugar (*shakkar*) saw your gratitude (*shokr*),
> Poverty became pride, for it became right through you.[156]

Faqr is a man's nurse and teaches him how to behave.[157] He, the absolutely poor being, is contrasted with the eternally rich Lord, and after reaching perfect poverty, becomes annihilated in Him. *Faqr* with Rumi is almost a coterminus of *fanāʾ* 'annihilation',[158] as it was prefigured in the poetry of Sanāʾi and ʿAṭṭār. He who flies form '*faqr* and not-being' leaves, in fact, true happiness.[159] In the last stage of poverty the alleged *ḥadith* 'When *faqr* becomes perfect, it becomes God' can be applied to the mystic.[160] This saying, known among the Persian-speaking mystics from probably the late eleventh century, became later very popular in the Eastern fringe of the Muslim world. It is interesting to see that Rumi has utilized it as well.

At the beginning of the *Mathnavi*, when Rumi refuses to talk about Shamsoddin, Ḥosāmoddin reminds him that *aṣ-Ṣufi ibnu'l-vaqt,* 'the Sufi is the son of Time', i.e. the moment of inspiration, and is not supposed to leave anything or any thought for tomorrow.[161] This traditional Sufi saying, often combined, as in Ḥosāmoddin's urging sentence, with the other dictum 'Time is a cutting sword',[162] alludes to the fact that the mystic has to leave himself to the coming inspiration and illumination. But even this according to Rumi is only a preliminary stage: although the Sufi may be *'ibnu'l-vaqt'*, the *ṣāfi*, the one who is completely purified, no longer has states or times. Immersed in the light of Majesty, he is no longer the 'son' of anybody; his relations with time and space are severed once he has entered the Eternal Now.[163] It is this last stage that matters for Rumi:

> A fire of piety (*taqvā*) burnt the world which is besides God:
> A lightning from God struck and burnt piety.[164]

When union comes, the small gifts of the lover, like fasting and ritual prayer, are merely outward signs.[165] They are like golden and silver ladders put before the lover[166]—but no ladder reaches to the roof of Poverty and Absolute Certitude.[167]

The goal of the mystic is generally called *fanā*ʾ 'annihilation', a central concept in Sufism and interpreted in different ways. Rumi once alludes to the famous saying of Kharraqāni, the eleventh century Khorassanian master who plays a rather prominent role in his work:

> There is no dervish in the world, and if there were a dervish, this would not be a dervish.[168]

A true dervish, as understood by Kharraqāni and his followers, is non-existent; he has experienced *fanā*ʾ and lives only through and in God. For he knows:

> Whence do we seek Existence? From renouncing existence.[169]

Everything limited is so to speak non-existent before Him who has no limits; 'everything but His face is perishing', as the Koran has said (Sura 28/88). Whatever man sees in the external world is nothing compared with God; faith and infidelity are only husks of different colours.[170] And even more: not-being becomes annihilated before Him, a state which the pen is incapable of describing.[171]

Therefore, to become annihilated in the Face of God, the only thing permanent, is true life, a life which rises from the *lā*

'No' of negation (i.e. negating one's self) to the *illā*, the affirmation that only God's existence is permanent.[172] To say *anā* 'I' is licit only when God speaks through man, for, as classical Sufism had stated, only He has the right to say 'I'.[173] That was the case of Ḥallāj; but in general such a claim is a sin. The human 'I' has to be eliminated in God's presence. Rumi has illustrated this point in a tender story of a lover who, after maturing on a long journey, was admitted by the beloved; for after having lost his identity he answered the friend's question 'Who is there?' saying 'It is you!'

> A certain man knocked at his friend's door: his friend asked: 'Who is there?'
> He answered 'I!' — 'Begone', said his friend, 'tis too soon: at my table there is no place for the raw.'
> How shall the raw one be cooked but in the fire of absence? What else will deliver him from hypocrisy?
> He turned sadly away, and for a whole year the flames of separation consumed him;
> Then he came back and again paced to and fro beside the house of his friend.
> He knocked at the door with a hundred fears and reverences, lest any disrespectful word might escape from his lips.
> 'Who is there?' cried his friend. He answered, 'Thou, O charmer of all hearts!'
> 'Now,' said the friend, 'since thou art I, come in: there is no room for two 'I's in this house . . .[174]

The lover in this oft-quoted story is the model of all those seekers who search for the palace of God; but when God arrives in his awful Majesty, the seeker becomes *lā* 'no', for

> although this union is 'remaining in remaining', (*baqāʾdar baqāʾ*)
> but first it is remaining in annihilation (*baqāʾdar fanāʾ*).[175]

Fanāʾ is the basis for *baqāʾ* 'permanent life in God',[176] as Rumi often repeats in accordance with the classical masters.

The true dervish has to cut the neck of egotism, of selfishness, of I-ness so that he may experience one day the mystery of God's action through him, similar to the Prophet, who was addressed in the battle of Badr 'Thou didst not cast when thou cast' (Sura 8/17).[177] So long as the self is still conscious, it is comparable to a cloud which covers the moon, but selflessness is cloudlessness.[178] Wonderful is Rumi's simple line which tells of a state which transgresses even love, longing and union:

> I am so submerged in not-being (*nisti*), that my beloved keeps saying:
> 'Come, sit a moment with me!' Even that I cannot do.[179]

The mystics have invented all kinds of images to allude to the ineffable mystery of this annihilation: man resembles the water in a narrow vessel which is cast into a mighty river; the quality of 'water in the vessel' becomes annihilated, but the essence 'water' remains for ever.[180]

In this state the mystic is like iron cast into fire, so filled with heat that it feels itself to be the fire;[181] or *fanāʾ* can also be compared to the disappearing of the stars at sunrise,[182] or to the situation of the candle before the sun: the light of the candle is still existent, but becomes invisible, since it is overwhelmed by the light of the sun which is, indeed, its origin.[183]

Besides these common images which were more or less known to all mystical writers, Rumi has also applied a grammatical symbol to *fanāʾ*: in the sentence *māta Zeydun* 'Zeyd has died' Zeyd is the subject, but not the acting subject—that is exactly what happens to the mystic in the experience of *fanāʾ*.[184]

Words cannot explain this mystery; the only thing possible is that man after experiencing this wonderful annihilation of human qualities—which is, however, not a substantial union!—can become a translator of the Divine truth, since his whole being becomes transparent for those mysteries which are beyond limit and word.[185]

Only rarely has Rumi attempted to describe the ecstatic state which the mystic may experience at times. We have his strange account of a vision in *Fihi mā fihi,* without being able to solve completely the enigma hidden behind it.[186] The most illuminating poetical expression of a mystical vision is no doubt the wonderful story of Daquqi:[187] the seven candles which appear before him are transformed into human beings, and again into trees: here, the psychologist of mystical experience would certainly find highly interesting material worthy of a detailed study. The rare occurrence of true visionary recitals in Jalāloddin's work is all the more surprising since his father has described in his *Maʿāref* some visions and raptures of extraordinary power.

To be sure, the true state of rapture defies description. The mystics of the whole world have spoken about intoxication, love-union, or being drowned to symbolize at least partly the experience they have undergone. And if we believe the chronicles, Rumi himself had experienced ecstatical raptures, was able to transgress time and space, or to be present in several places at once.[188] His lyrics overflow with verses in praise of the ineffable union, of this wine of love, with descriptions of his union with the beloved, although they may be separated as far as Iraq from Khorassan. Numerous lines describe the cosmic consciousness of the lover who feels that he is neither from the North nor from the South, neither from earth nor from heaven, neither Christian nor Jew—or that he is everything and above everything. One of the truly poignant descriptions of ecstatical rapture is found no doubt in a ghazal which R. A. Nicholson included in his selection:

At morning-tide a moon appeared in the sky,
And descended from the sky and gazed on me.
Like a falcon which snatches a bird at the time of hunting,
That moon snatched me up and coursed over the sky.
When I looked at myself, I saw myself no more,
Because in that moon my body became by grace even as soul.
When I travelled in soul, I saw nought save the moon,
Till the secret of the eternal Theophany was all revealed . . .[189]

Here, the sudden flight of the soul in the claws of the moon-bird leads the mystic to the vision of the world as an ocean out of which the foam rises only to disappear again at the call of the abyss . . . all this thanks to the miraculous power of Shamsoddin.

A second poem in which the reader can almost feel the rising intoxication uses the same imagery of the sea, describing the slow arrival of the call of love which, then, in accelerating rhythm carries the lover towards the ocean until the boat of his body is shattered in the wave '*alast*', the Divine address of the primordial covenant to which he finally returns'.

Every moment the voice of Love is coming from left and right.
We are bound for heaven: who has a mind to sight-seeing?
We have been in heaven, we have been friends of the angels;
Thither, sire, let us return, for that is our country . . .

Came the billow of 'Am I not?' and wrecked the body's ship;
When the ship wrecks it is the time of union's attainment;

'Tis the time of union's attainment, 'tis the time of eternity's beauty,
'Tis the time of favour and largesse, 'tis the ocean of perfect purity.
The billow of largesse hath appeared, the thunder of the sea hath arrived,
The morn of blessedness hath dawned. Morn? No, 'tis the light of God . . .[190]

This poem speaks of *kibriyā*, 'Divine Grandeur' or, as Nicholson puts it 'majesty supreme'. This is one of Rumi's favourite expressions when describing the place to which he wants to return. There is no end of verses which allude to this *kibriyā*—the true lover who has left his self and no longer boasts of his personal existence, of his 'I' and 'We', is intoxicated by the wine of *kibriyā*;[191] and the house of his heart, purified from every outward thing, will be illuminated by the light of *kibriyā*.[192] Those who go two steps forward from the dwelling-place of lust, can enter the sacred realm of *kibriyā*;[193] for this Divine Castle *kibriyā* is destined only for those who have experienced annihilation.[194]

Kibriyā comes like waves;[195] now it is comparable to the Phoenix whose shade conveys kingdom to man;[196] then it can be described as a banquet in which all the drums are broken from awe,[197] or again as a police-master who cuts the neck of all quarrels which show that men are not yet of one heart.[198] The two worlds are like a grain before the rooster whose eyes have witnessed *kibriyā* . . .[199]

It is difficult to say to what extent Rumi relies upon the *ḥadith qodsi* according to which God declares:

Kibriyā is my cloak, and Majesty (*ʿaẓmat*) is my undergarment.[200]

In his poems *kibriyā* is the place of Divine Grandeur, a world beyond the 18,000 worlds,[201] or the rising place of the spiritual sun: Shams-e Tabriz rises from the East of *kibriyā* to illuminate the whole world.[202] And 'we are alive from the light of *kibriyā*'.[203]

The cannon *kibriyā* destroys everything in man and is thus almost equal with Divine love;[204] and enamoured by this Divine grandeur the lover knows nothing more about being and not-being, about religion and infidelity.[205] But someone who is still possessed by *kibr*, 'worldly pride' will certainly never reach this state.[206]

In many cases where other mystical poets would have spoken of the eternal life in God, or of the Divine Essence, Mowlānā prefers the word *kibriyā*:[207] the lover's soul must be coloured by *kibriyā* in order to bear the affliction which will come down upon him;[208] and the poet, who has reached the last stage of union, may boast that his words are 'mixed with *kibriyā*'.[209] *Kibriyā* is for him the best symbol for God in His overwhelming radiant greatness and His dynamic and forceful actions; it is indeed a key word for the understanding of Rumi's mystical thought, reminiscent, in its many glorious aspects and by its very sound, of a triumphant chord in C-major.

Closely connected with Rumi's ideas of the mystical path are those about the saints and about the mystical leaders which occupy a large portion of his poetry. One of the most famous ghazals attributed to him—though probably not his own—is the poem *Mard-e khoḍā mast buvad bi sharāb*, 'The man of God is intoxicated without wine'.[210] This poem, which describes so eloquently the state of the true saint, has been translated several times into Western languages, since it conveys a most impressive view of saintliness. This 'man of God' who is no longer bound to the four elements, and who is an unlimited ocean which produces pearls out of itself without the help of secondary causes, is indeed a central topic of Rumi's poetry. To be sure, we will certainly not find a full-length discussion of the qualities of the saint in his poetry; Rumi's description of the saint, the sheykh, the beloved, the pir, the true Muslim or whatever he calls the ideal man, are scattered throughout his work, mainly in the *Mathnavi*.

Now and then Rumi speaks of miracles wrought by the saints. He does not doubt that everyone who has completely surrendered his will into the Will of God is capable of performing miracles, for 'everything in the world obeys him who obeys God'.[211] Mowlānā illustrates this old Sufi saying with numerous stories: Kharraqāni, who can ride on a lion and use a snake as a whip, is the model of a saint who has perfectly mastered his base soul and is therefore master over all the lower animals in the world, who are bound to serve him just as his *nafs* has learned to serve him.[212] The story of Ibrahim Adham, who miraculously produced golden needles out of the sea after one needle had been lost by a fellow traveller,[213] belongs to the large treasure of stories and legends inherited from earlier Sufi authors which serve to explain Rumi's view-point with regard to God's unlimited creativity and the saint's acting as a kind of relay between God and the creatures; these stories sometimes lead to unexpected conclusions.

Mowlānā knows: the saints are 'the children of God';[214] the Lord keeps them away from Himself for a while to test them, as if they were orphans; but they are as close to Him as His own children. Rumi enumerates also the different types of saints: those who pray constantly and 'tear and sew human conditions' by their prayer, and those who have closed their mouths from prayer, sitting in perfect peace and contentment, accepting the vicissitudes of fate as signs of special grace.[215]

From the early tenth century, the grades of saintship had been systematized by Sufi authors, and a whole hierarchy had been constructed, culminating in the *qoṭb,* the 'Pole' or 'Pivot', around whom everything revolves: Rumi describes this Pole in more detailed form, comparing him to reason; in relation to him, the ordinary people are like the limbs of the body which are moved and set in action by reason;[216] it is he around whom the skies revolve, the centre of the created universe, the Perfect Man. The only other category of saints which are mentioned by their technical name are the *abdāl*, the category of forty, or sometimes seven, high ranking saints who were particularly popular in Islam, as many allusions to their names and their activities may be found in the lands of Islam. The *abdāl* are those whose breath gives spring;[217] and Rumi explains their name 'substitute' by their being *mobdal* 'changed', so that their wine has turned, thanks to God's grace into ritually pure vinegar.[218]

But the highest term he uses for the perfected mystic is *qalandar:* no created being can become a true *qalandar*, as he claims,[219] and from his use of the word one may understand that he means by *qalandar* the veritable *maʿshuq*, the Beloved: that would be in harmony with Shamsoddin's *qalandar*-character and his role as *maʿshuq*.

The transformation of the *abdāl*, and that means of all saints, is brought forth by interior change: the house of the heart which God has chosen as His dwelling-place, must be purified before He can descend there:

I have cleaned the house from good and evil,
my house is filled with the Love of the One.
Whatever I see in it other than God,
that does not belong to me; it is a reflection.[220]

Only when man cleans his house completely from himself and from all things other than God, using the 'broom of *lā*, "No"',[221] can the Lord descend there; only when he purifies himself, renouncing all outward apparels, and comes poor and naked into the presence of the King will the bounteous Lord bestow upon him a robe prepared from the qualities of holiness, a robe which is woven from the attributes of the King Himself,[222] and will his homeland become the Divine Grace.[223] Then, everything is changed: infidelity turns into faith, and the demons embrace Islam (according to the Prophet's saying *aslama sheyṭāni*, 'my Satan has become Muslim'), since the measureless light leaves no room for otherness. Man, once more becomes the place of manifestation of Glory and is loved by God; once more the story of creation will become realized: the angels will prostrate themselves before him.[224]

In this state, the sanctified person can be compared to the tree of Moses, the Burning Bush through which God revealed Himself in the form of fire, although it was in reality the Divine Light which was manifested.[225] Man becomes like the niche and the candle, pure glass as described in the Light-verse of the Koran (Sura 24/35): his body is the niche and his heart, the glass filled with the primordial light, illuminates the world and the heavens so that all other small lights are annihilated and bewildered, like stars when the Morning-light, *aḍ-ḍoḥā* (Sura 93) appears.[226] It is this light of the true faithful which extinguishes the fire of Hell.[227]

This transformation of man into light is one of Rumi's favourite themes. Reaching this state, the saint sees through God's light, or even through God Himself, who is the source of all light.

This light enables the saintly person to see through things and beings, to perceive the innermost thoughts of men:[228] the *ferāsat*, cardiognosy, is one of the distinguishing features of the mystical leader.[229] He is a lion, and the thoughts of others are like a forest which he can easily enter.[230] He will be able to discern the Sun of Duration already in the atom, the all-embracing ocean in the drop,[231] existence in seeming non-existence,[232] and he discovers in the unpolished stone the wonderful figures which people see in the polished mirror.[233] That is why he can show the novice the path which leads him best towards self-realization and approximation to God, calling the figures out of the stone 'heart'.

Such sanctified people no longer need a special call and seclusion, or times of training and meditation: their cell is the sun itself, and they are never covered by night. Neither secondary causes nor infidelity are left in this radiant Divine sun.[234] The saints have lost their earthly qualities.[235] Annihilated in the eternal richness of God, they can give without hope of gain;[236] for the saint is like the sky, scattering his light everywhere, but also like the cloud which brings the rain of mercy to the thirsty people.[237]

The saints work without secondary causes, for having qualified themselves with the qualities of God, as the old Sufi saying required, they act through God:

> Thus was day and night the exertion of the Pirs
> that they rescued people from pain and corruption.
> They complete somebody's work and pass by,
> so that no one knows it but God—praised be the Lovingkind, the Generous!
> Like Khiżr towards the sea, like Ilyas in dryness,
> Thus they prepare (help) for those who are gone astray.[238]

Their actions are performed without movement, even without their own knowledge;[239] they are comparable to the Seven Sleepers, who were drawn by God's grace into their wonderful state of perfect peace. Their perfection is such that they can even 'take the arrow back to the bow'.[240] Insofar as the saints are unconscious instruments of God's unintelligible will,[241] one understands why they sometimes commit acts which look like sheer destruction but are meant for the betterment of human conditions: in such cases, they are like Khiżr, the prototype of saintliness,[242] whose three outwardly destructive acts were described in the Koran (cf. Sura 18). Their behaviour can not be measured by human standards; the obedience of the common people is the sin of the elite; the union of the masses is, for them, a veil, as Rumi says in a variation of a famous saying by Z̲u'n-Nun.[243]

The saints are beyond human conditions. They are always young, smiling, sweet; a hundred years and one hour are equal to them, since they have broken the ring of created time and participate in the Divine Eternal Now.[244]

How should he be grieved, whose eyes are kissed by the Soul?[245] Their whole life is praise of God, like that of the garden which permanently proclaims laud and praise with the 'tongue without tongues'[246] Like flowers they wait in the dark forest of this nightly world;[247] like lions in the thicket they long to show the Divine glory; like roosters, they watch the sun at night time to inform people of the true sunrise so that they can direct their morning-prayer to God.[248] But they are veiled from the ordinary people's eyes. God is jealous and does not allow anyone to see his beloved friends, as the *ḥadith qodsi* says:

> My friends are under my domes, nobody knows them but I.[249]

Only those who have eyes to see know that in the morning angels and holy spirits circumambulate their bed and talk with them without human words.[250]

The saint *par excellence* is, for the Sufi, the master, whom he is bound to follow. *Ṣoḥbat*, the company of a spiritual master or of pious and elevated friends, was always considered a must for man's spiritual welfare.[251]

> Whoever desires to sit with God most High, let him sit with the people of Sufism.[252]

Just as the dog of the Seven Sleepers was purified by his keeping faithful company with these saintly persons until he became almost a human himself, thus people can derive spiritual nourishment from the company of the saints, and become purified by their purity. They kindle the spiritual spark in him until it becomes a veritable light, but this spark would die in the company of the ashes and become extinguished, to return to the dust out of which it was created. Man is called to use the dust of the feet of the true men, the men of God, as collyrium for his eyes; thus they will be cured from worldly blindness and become capable of accepting spiritual light.[253] Man is protected from error if he follows a saintly person, and the novice is called to 'become a servant of the camel of the saint's body so that he may fit the company of Ṣāleḥ's spirit'.[254] (Ṣāleḥ was the prophet who produced a she-camel out of a rock, Sura 7/70).

It is worth noticing that the verses about the determining role of the mystical leader, the *sheykh* or *pir*, are almost exclusively contained in the *Mathnavi*; the earlier lyrics, abounding with love and intoxication, are much more a witness of the prime importance of the free movement of love. Mowlānā himself had been prepared by his guide Borhānoddin through all kinds of mortifications for the last experience, the meeting with Shamsoddin—nothing more. Yet, he stresses the importance for man's progress of the guidance of a mystical guide in his later years. His own growing duties, when many people flocked around him and when the group of his adherents developed into a closely-knit unit, certainly contributed to this change in emphasis. The fact that Ḥosāmoddin Chalabi, the inspiring force in the *Mathnavi*, was his disciple (though he figures as perfected saint) shifted the centre of gravity in his late poetry of necessity from passionate love to edifying charity. Hence the repeated praise of the master and the stress upon his role in the orderly cosmos of the advancing Sufi.

> Whosoever goes on the path without a guide,
> for him a way of two days becomes a hundred years.[255]

One cannot reach the Kaʿba without a proper guide, nor can an apprentice learn his art without being properly trained by a master.[256] These comparisons show that it was mainly the technical side of the path which Rumi had in mind when speaking of the mystical master. A story told by Aflaki about a dervish whose *zekr* was lost since it was not properly inspired by a *sheykh* illustrates this point quite well.[257] But Rumi knew also that the last step depends exclusively upon Grace and Love.

Mowlānā quotes, of course, the Prophetic tradition that the *sheykh* is like the prophet in his community,[258] and that he who has no *sheykh* will be guided by Satan. One has to find the *pir-e rashād*, the master who guides to the right path, and not rely upon the *pir-e gardun*, the 'old man of the sky', i.e. Fate. Therefore Mowlānā makes one of his heroes cry out:

> I seek a *pir*, I seek a *pir*, I seek a *pir*![259]

Still, even for those who are aware of the high veneration of the *pir* as it had developed in the course of the centuries, it is surprising to hear Rumi say:

> Who is an infidel? He who neglects the faith in the *sheykh*.
> Who is dead? He without knowledge of the *sheykh's* soul.[260]

This verse is in a certain way reminiscent of the Shia doctrine of the necessity of knowing the Imām.

The *morid,* the disciple, is admonished to trust the *sheykh*, who is the prophet of his time, and not to fly but with the wings of the spiritual master.[261] To quarrel with one's *sheykh* is utterly stupid;[262] even the dimwit of a *sheykh* is not inferior to a stone and an idol: all are made by God as means of devotion meant for Himself.[263]

The disciples are only vessels which preserve the light radiated by the *pir*,[264] they are nourished by his spiritual milk.[265]

And since the *sheykh* works through God's spiritual light, he is like a mirror placed in front of the novice to teach him right behaviour and to make him acquainted with spiritual truth, just as man puts a mirror before a parrot to teach him to talk.[266] The image of the mirror for the saint lost in the beloved is common in Sufism; it means that his whole spiritual state reflects the Divine Light, thus informing human beings of its glory. As Rumi sings:

> I am a mirror, I am a mirror, I am not a man of talking—
> My state becomes visible when your ear becomes an eye.[267]

Vision of the Divine Light, that is what the disciple can gain from the radiance of the master. In this quality, the master can be called the great elixir and alchemy which converts base material, i.e. the *nafs,* into gold;[268] his very shade kills the lower soul of those who approach him. Those who have reached this stage are no longer physicians who cure the sick with food and medicaments, but physicians of the soul who heal by means of acts inspired by the Divine Light,[269] through God's power; for their hands are 'under the hand of God'.[270] And Rumi sums up his thoughts on saintship with the line:

> O you who have considered the friends of God to be separated of God:
> How would it be, if you would have a good opinion about the saints?[271]

And who brings forth the living from the dead and the dead from the living . . .

THE STORY OF THE CHICKPEAS

Man's spiritual way from childish ignorance through periods of learning, fermentation, and suffering towards the goal of becoming a veritable 'man of God' is only part of the great movement in which everything created participates. For Rumi's central motif is the idea of *Stirb und werde,* the permanent interplay of *fanāʾ*, 'annihilation', and *baqāʾ*, 'eternal life' in God. The whole creation follows the law of dialectical movement. Yet, this movement is not only the necessary co-operation of positive and negative forces, of the alternation of day and night, summer and winter, the attraction of male and female, of *yang* and *yin,* it is, at the same time, an uprising movement which continues not only throughout the life of sensual experience, but also in the otherworld: death is brought forth from life, life from death, as the Koran repeatedly attests (cf. Sura 3/27). Only in the fathomless depth of the Divine Essence movement and rest, not-being and Being, becoming and annihilation, is one and the same.

This constant tension between negation and affirmation, of being naughted and being quickened, was symbolized by many Sufis, and thus by Rumi, in the words of the profession of faith. The formula *lā ilāha illā Allāh* 'There is no deity but God' offered itself to the poets and mystics as the best, indeed a Divine, symbol for expressing their spiritual journey. The *lā* points to the negation of everything besides God, including man's own wishes and ambitions, his own self; it is a fiery word which indeed 'burns the two worlds'.[1] The poet therefore calls man to dig out his heart and cast the net of the heart into the ocean of *lā.*[2]

As Sanāʾi already stated, *lā* is a broom[3] (its calligraphic form lends itself to this comparison):

> Clean this house from yourself, see that imperial beauty, go, take the broom No, for the No is good for sweeping the house.[4]

By negating one's own base qualities, by sweeping away everything besides God, all dust of worldliness, one will eventually find the majestic lustre that fills the clean house of the heart, which is then worthy to receive the highest guest, or to reflect, like a polished mirror, the Divine Light.

Rumi may also speak of the torrent '*lā*' which carries away joy and pain, gain and loss, fear and hope, body and soul.[5]

But this sweeping and cleaning is only the preparatory stage:

> Who knows God (*ilāh*)? Someone who is saved from the *lā*.
> And who goes from the *lā*, say? The lover who has experienced affliction, (*balā*).[6]

Love is the power which annihilates everything in the world. This is expressed in rather strong language in the story of the Queen of Sheba

> Gardens and castles and the water of the river
> became before the eye like an ash-house through love,
> Love in the moment of overpowering and anger makes lovely things hideous for the eye.
> The jealousy of love makes every emerald look like a leek: that is the inner meaning of *lā*.[7]

The very moment man is captured by Divine love, he sees nothing but God, everything is negated, cut off, swept away; only the Beloved—*illā Allāh*—remains. Then, the lover will 'cut the head of the *lā*, and reach the *illā*',[8] or will ask the beloved to consider him to be a *lā* and to transform him into an *illā*,[9] i.e. to see him as nothing and bring him to true existence in and through God. Later poets would explain this expression in more detail: the lover, being *lā*, becomes an *illā* when the beloved puts his slim slender stature, which resembles the letter *alef*, before him . . .

Rumi praises Shamsoddin by saying:

> Whoever found help from your hand,
> became an *illā'i* (a positive affirmant of God) without the vestige of *lā*;[10]

but in another verse he calls himself 'intoxicated by negation, not by positive affirmation',[11] which shows, once again, his inconsistency in the use of images, which change according to his spiritual stage.

To express this upward movement leading from the *lā* to the *illā*, Rumi has invented ever new images. One of the stories typical of his dealing with philosophical and theological problems in everyday words is that of the chickpeas.[12] As we have seen, he was fond of kitchen-imagery. The lowly vegetable can serve as a symbol of what Mowlānā found to be the deepest truth of life, and he writes the story:

> Comparison of the fleeing and the impatience of the true believer in the time of affliction to the agitation and restlessness of chickpeas and other pot-herbs when boiling in the pot, and to their running upwards in order to jump out.

The chickpeas, put into a kettle with boiling water, feeling uncomfortable in the heat try to jump out of the water. But the poet tells them that they have grown under the rain and water of Divine grace, therefore they have to suffer for a while in the fire of Divine wrath. Did not God say: 'My grace precedes my wrath?' (this well-known *ḥadith qodsi,* according to which God's mercy has precedence over His wrath, is here interpreted in quite a daring way in a temporal sense).[13] The housewife compares herself to Abraham and the chickpeas to Ishmael, who has to surrender to the sacrificial knife, for 'the pre-eternal goal is your surrender'. This being cooked and eaten is, indeed, the only way for the pea to reach a higher level of development.

> If thou has been parted from the garden of water and earth, (yet) thou hast become food in the mouth and hast entered into the living.
> Become nutriment and strength and thoughts! (Formerly) thou wert milk; (now) be a lion in the jungles!
> By God, thou grewest from His attributes in the beginning: go back nimbly and fleetly into His attributes.
> Thou camest from the cloud and the sun and the sky; then didst thou become (diverse) attributes and ascend to heaven.
> Thou camest in the form of rain and heat: thou wilt go into the goodly attributes.
> Thou wert a part of the sun and the cloud and the stars: thou becamest soul and action and speech and thought.

Thus, the pot-herbs are consoled in their suffering; for they have to learn that suffering and grief is absolutely necessary for spiritual growth. This is a topic common to all Sufis and mystical poets; but no one has invented a more poignant example than Rumi: the porters in the streets—and which visitor to the Middle East does not remember their shouting?—fight with each other as to who can carry the heaviest burden; for they know that the heavier the load, the higher will be the price they get; since they see gain in this pain, they try to snatch away the burden from each other.[14] Man should act like them, for he should know that the spiritual reward will be in exact relation to the grief and affliction he patiently, nay willingly, bears. Prophetic traditions were adduced to prove that the prophets are the most afflicted of men, then the saints, then the pious, and so on;[15] for 'Affliction is to saintliness as fire is to gold', a means of purification.[16]

> Grief cleans the house of the heart, and shakes off the yellow leaves from the branch of the heart, so that new green leaves can sprout,
> and it digs out old crooked roots to make room for a new one.[17]

Certainly, man will cry for a while in his grief, but does not the weeping of the cloud bring new greenery to the meadows and fields?[18] Does not the candle which weeps in melting become more radiant?[19] Did not God say 'Weep much!' so that the dried-up garden of the heart be filled with fruit?[20] So long as the child does not cry, his mother's milk will not flow to nourish it.[21] Tears shed in grief and affliction are as precious as the blood of the martyrs.[22]

Grief for God's sake is like a garden in which the sugar of happiness will eventually grow, provided man embraces grief with love and regards it as a good and trustworthy friend.[23] For only through grief and pain does man turn towards God, whom he tends to forget during the day of happiness.

It is by means of affliction and suffering that man can mature, when he sees that all friends leave him, and he is left to God alone.[24] How could cider develop into tasty wine unless it ferment for a while?[25] And raw hide has to undergo the painful process of tanning before it becomes lovely *ṭā'efi* leather.[26] The ordinary stone matures during long periods of suffering into a ruby, and the oyster laughs when it is broken . . .[27]

To be broken, is the prerequisite for new life: the nutshell has to be broken in order to find the kernel, for 'the kernel and the precious oil call silently for release'.[28] And once the vessel of human existence is broken, the wave of Mercy can embrace everything.[29] The Sufis and among them Rumi, relied upon God's promise: 'I am with those whose hearts are broken for

My sake'.[30] Therefore he tells his listeners with ever new variations about the necessity of breaking:

> Wherever there is a ruin, there is hope for a treasure:
> Why do you not seek the treasure of God in the devastated heart?[31]

The house has to be destroyed so that one may find the treasure hidden beneath, a treasure which is worth many, many houses;[32] the tree casts off its leaves in fall, practising spiritual poverty (*bi bargi*) and only thus it can open new and more beautiful blossom in spring.[33] Likewise the field has to be ploughed so that the seed can be sown which in turn will develop into corn, which will be crushed in the mill and made into bread, which will be destroyed by human teeth, until it becomes united with man and becomes soul.[34] Does not the tailor cut precious silk into pieces so that he may produce a lovely dress?[35]

Temporal destruction involves higher development: man destroys his base qualities in order to qualify himself with Divine attributes, or else he surrenders his own will to become invested with participation in the Divine will, and the more he gives up, the higher the reward, the deeper the annihilation, the more the gain.[36]

The Prophetic tradition *mutu qabla an tamutu* 'Die before ye die' is the focal point in Rumi's mysticism:

> The one whose neck the Beloved cuts, will become long-necked;
> The one whose harvest He burns, will gain a rich harvest.[37]

The candle shines better when its wick is cut,[38] and thus, death on the spiritual level and resurrection in spirit brings man, once for all into the Divine presence without the pangs or horrors of the general resurrection. Man is called to become winter so that he may see the coming of spring.[39] Out of apparent nothingness, creation appears: to be nothing, is the condition for God's new creative work. For God brings forth life from death, and spiritual death is like a bridge over which the caravan of souls passes, and is the goal of the wayfarer: a bridge towards higher stations.[40]

For nothing can return to its previous state, no mirror can become iron again, no bread again corn.[41] The movement, caused by dying through love, involves resurrection on a higher plane. In Rumi's lyrics we find wonderful descriptions of the state of man, who, after leaving this world, will experience true union and endless meeting with the Beloved.[42]

Therefore, why should man fear death? If he was wicked, his badness is finished all the earlier, and if he was good, he will reach home sooner.[43] Death is like breaking free of the prison of the body, out of the dark well of this world into a lovely garden, breaking the fetters of the material world.[44] The sensual light diminishes, and only the light of the soul radiates and leads him forwards.[45] The human being, who was like a beggar in the prison of grief, now reaches his royal castle.[46] The falcon returns to his lord, the nightingale to the rose-garden, and therefore the true faithful dies with a smile, like roses.[47] He knows: 'I was sugarcane, now I have become sugar . . .'[48]

Rumi dreams of the moment when the Beloved will pour death into a cup so that he can kiss the cup and die of intoxication,[49] and addresses his friends and disciples in enthusiastic repetitions: 'Die . . . die . . . !'[50] In one of his last ghazals, composed shortly before his death, he consoles them with the lines:

> Did ever a grain fall into the earth, that did not unfold beautifully?
> Do you think that the seed which is man would behave differently?[51]

In long chains of comparisons he tells them of the constant upward movement which lies beyond life and transgresses death: did not Alexander see the water of life in the darkest valley?[52] Life is a journey, the caravan of souls moves from one station to the other and has to overcome danger and fear, has to climb steep hills and to cross dark vales to reach the Kaʿba of the Beloved. Whatever seems lost on the path, will be found when the goal is reached. It is the journey towards Nowhere,[53] a journey into the country of inward meaning,[54] without rest, a journey by which the veils which still hide the heart are removed, the meeting-place of man and God.

Rumi sees, in accordance with the Sufi terminology, the whole spiritual life as a path, or a ladder; and the same holds true for life in general. There is no rest at any one of the stations:

Our cry is like the bell in the caravan,
or like the thunder's voice when the clouds are wandering:
Oh traveller, do not bind thy heart to any station,
that you may not become sleepy at the time of attraction![55]

The call, *ar-raḥil*, 'Start the journey!' is often heard in his poetry;[56] many are called to leave home and family and to set out on the spiritual journey. Only travelling brings everything to perfection; the lean crescent moon grows into a majestic being during his journey, and the sun appears more radiant in the morning after her journey at night.[57] Rain becomes transformed into pearls when entering the ocean, and the Prophet's hegira indicates the importance of leaving one's home and gaining a new kingdom on a higher level before returning home again. Matured in separation, the traveller returns home,[58] and the lover who has burnt himself in the flame of suffering, comes back and sees only his waiting friend, no longer himself, so that he is lovingly accepted into the house. Thus, every moment of human life is a step along the upwards journey which culminates in death—spiritual or corporeal—and then resurrection. The more man proceeds on this path, the deeper his longing to come closer to the mysterious abyss, the higher his ambition to soar to the summit of Mountain Qāf.

That holds true not only for the development of the individual seeker during the course of his life but for nature in general. It seems, that Rumi became more theoretically interested during the mid-sixties of the thirteenth century in the problem of the constant upward development of everything created, a development which starts in the lowest zones and finally ends in the 'journey in God'. During those years he tried to express this idea, which had been elaborated by Sanāʾi and ʿAṭṭār in philosophically tinged verses. Sanāʾi described the way of the soul through different stages in his small didactic *mathnavi*, *Seyr al-ʿebād ila'l-maʿād*. The feeling that one soul-principle permeates everything created and slowly rises upwards, after having become exiled in the lowest degrees of creation, is common with ʿAṭṭār as well. Both these predecessors of Rumi have spoken more than once of the slow upward development of the world: thousands of flowers have to be annihilated until a single rose can appear, millions of human souls have to be born and again to die until one day the highest manifestation of humanity, the Prophet, can appear.[59] The whole creation consists of a rising gamut of existences which culminates in mankind, and mankind, again, finds its highest expression in the Perfect Man, as later Sufis would call him, in the Prophet, or in the saint who has reached eternal life in God.

ʿAṭṭār perceived this upward movement also under the symbol of the musk-deer which eats grass and transforms it into precious musk: lower existences 'must be eaten'.[60] Rumi follows him in describing this movement, partly, with the image of eating and being eaten. Indeed, he even put the heading of one chapter in the *Mathnavi* as:

> Everything outside God is eating and eaten.[61]

Birds eat worms and are, in turn, devoured by cats.[62] This leads us back to the example of the chickpeas. Rumi sees the same truth also in the fate of corn, which is thrashed, baked, chewed, and thus transformed into power and sperm, which will become spiritual potencies.[63] In a fine pun, he speaks of the drop of sperm, *mani*, which has to give up its ego, *mani*, in order to become a cypress-like stature and lovely cheek.[64] Likewise, animals must be slaughtered to serve man as nourishment and become part of his higher existence:[65]

> To be broken is necessary for the unripe water-melon of the body which only then can be eaten.[66]

The *Mathnavi,* mainly in Books III to VI, contains many elaborations of this topic; in the *Divān* some allusions to the movement can also be detected, which were then taken up by Solṭān Valad in his poetry.[67] Rumi thus sings in soft, swinging rhythms:

> You have been in the station of dust, you have made a hidden journey:
> When you have reached the state of Adam, be careful lest you establish yourself there;
> You continue the journey, and you travel up to heaven,
> and you move bit by bit so that God may give you freedom.[68]

This is exactly the same idea which was expressed in the *Mathnavi* not long before Rumi invented the story of the chickpeas, namely the famous lines:

I died as mineral and became a plant,
I died as plant and rose to animal,
I died as animal and I was Man.
Why should I fear? When was I less by dying?
Yet once more I shall die as Man, to soar
With angels blest; but even from angelhood
I must pass on: all except God doth perish.
When I have sacrificed my angel-soul,
I shall become what no mind e'r conceived.
O let me not exist! For Non-existence
Proclaims in organ tones 'To Him we shall return'.[69]

This poem was first translated into German by Friedrich Rückert, but he left out the last, decisive line, which speaks of the return into ʿ*adam*, the positive Not-Being, the abyss of the *Deus absconditus.* Not too long after writing the just quoted lines, Rumi has taken up this very motif, though in different and more diffuse imagery:[70]

First he came into the clime of inorganic things, and from the
state of inorganic things he passed into the vegetable state.
(Many) years he lived in the vegetable state and did not remember
the inorganic state because of the opposition (between them)
And when he passed from the vegetable into the animal state,
the vegetable state was not remembered by him at all,
Save only for the inclination which he has towards that (state)
especially in the season of spring and sweet herbs—
Like the inclinations of babes towards their mothers: It does
not know the secret of its desire for being suckled;
Or like the excessive inclination of every novice towards the
noble spiritual Elder, whose fortune is young.
The particular intelligence of this disciple is derived from that
Universal Intelligence: the motion of this shadow is derived
from that Rose-bough . . .

Yet, the story then takes a different turn and explains the world as a dream out of which man awakes in the morning-light of eternity:

Thus did he advance from clime to clime, till he has now become intelligent, wise and mighty.
He hath no remembrance of his former intelligences; from this (human) intelligence also there is a migration to be made by him,
That he may escape from this intelligence full of greed and self seeking and may behold a hundred thousand intelligences most marvellous,

> Though he fell asleep and became oblivious of the past, how should they leave him in that self-forgetfulness?
> From that sleep they will bring him back again to wakefulness; that he may mock at his present state,
> Saying 'What was that sorrow I was suffering in my sleep?' . . .

This ending hints to another Prophetic tradition in which Moḥammad claims that 'Men are asleep, and when they die, they awake'.[71] R. A. Nicholson, discussing Rumi's poem 'I died as mineral' in detail in his commentary, has seen here a purely neo-Platonic doctrine: the Universal Soul working through the various spheres of being, a doctrine introduced into Islam by al-Fārābi (d. 950) and being related, at the same time, to Ibn Sinā's ideas about love as the magnetically working power by which life is driven into an upwards trend.[72]

This interpretation is possible; but other interpretations of these lines have been offered by almost everybody who has studied Rumi. It seems that in the Islamic world Mowlānā Shibli Noʿmāni, the great Indian Muslim scholar (d. 1914) was to first to stress the importance of the idea of *development* in the sense of *evolution* in these verses which he discusses at the very end of his Urdu biography of Rumi, issued in 1902. These lines seem to prove to the orthodox, but modern-minded Muslim that Darwin's theory of evolution was known to the Muslims as early as the thirteenth century: one more proof of the priority of Muslim thinkers over the Europeans, who had discovered this theory only recently.

In the year 1913, Friedrich Rosen, when writing his introduction to his father's German verse translation of the first two books of the *Mathnavi* (composed in 1849) remarked:

> We seem to hear here Darwin or Haeckel, but it is in reality Aristotle who is the predecessor of development theories.[73]

Shibli's words about the 'development of the species' have been adopted by quite a number of Indo-Pakistani scholars: Khalifa Abdul Hakim in his booklet, *The Metaphysics of Rumi*, has traced back the theory of evolution to the *Ikhvān aṣ-ṣafāʾ* which 'made them predecessors of Darwin and Spencer'.[74] He, like Muhammad Iqbal, considers the philosopher Ibn Miskaweyh (d. 1034) to be the true father of evolutionary theories. For Khalifa Abdul Hakim life

> is a product of the Will to Life: always disappointed with the present state, life creates new wishes which have to be fulfilled.

Life is a striving towards the First Beloved, to Eternal Beauty. That is certainly true, but the Pakistani scholar neglects the significant last line, the return to ʿ*adam*, which is higher than Beauty and Majesty. According to Hakim, the idea of progressive immortality is 'absolutely original' with Rumi.

I dare doubt this statement; it is a good Sufi idea, mentioned by Sanāʾi and ʿAṭṭār; al-Ghazzāli's chapter on 'Longing and Love' in the *Iḥyā ʿolum ad-din* points to the same goal. It seems more interesting that this very idea was, once more, brought to life at approximately the same time in East and West—by Muhammad Iqbal as a Muslim thinker who relied upon Rumi, and by the German philosopher Rudolf Pannwitz, a follower and critic of Nietzsche.[75]

The Pakistani writer and diplomat Afzal Iqbal has discussed the problem posed by the lines 'I died as mineral' as well. He quotes from Hakim the following passage which contains a useful approach to the problem:

> That a mystic should have shown the way to the scientists and the philosophers is one of the rarest phenomena in the history of thought. But the mystic neither begins with naturalism nor ends with it. His matter to start with, is not the matter of the materialist or the Darwinist. It was from the beginning only the outer form of the spirit, it consists rather of the monads of Leibniz than the atoms of Democritus. Then again Darwin ends with man but Rumi does not stop there. Nor do the mystic and scientist agree about the forces that lead to this evolution. Darwin's doctrine consists of struggle for existence, chance variation and natural selection. With Rumi there is no development by chance variations. For him development consists in the creation of an ever increasing need for expansion and by assimilation into a higher organism.[76]

Afzal Iqbal's own interpretation, however, denies an evolution with a destined goal: evolution must give man the free possibility of choosing the direction of his own development. This idea is, however, contradictory to Rumi and his predecessors in Sufism: what would be the meaning of evolution if it could take *any* form: It would end up in a cancer-like multiplication of dangerous and eventually fatal overdevelopments. For Rumi, the development in a Divinely ordered and hence meaningful direction with its final station in the abyss of Divine Love was unquestionable.

Khalifa Abdul Hakim has taken up the verses in question once more in an Urdu booklet (1955); but here, he stresses more the possible pantheistic interpretation of Rumi's 'stone-to-angel'—verses; human existence is nothing but God's existence. After being separated from God, man has to pass through all the stages of being until he reaches once more the only source and only reality, God.[77]

This was formerly the generally accepted interpretation of these verses. Muhammad Iqbal in his thesis of 1907, had made some statements pertaining to this explanation:[78] he develops the idea from the parable of sleep, e.g. out of *Mathnavi* IV 3637 ff. and sees everything besides God only as dream, shade, phantasy, out of which the soul returns into the Only Real. In his later work, however—and I would surmise that this happened under Shibli's influence—the same poet-philosopher has regarded these very verses as a most poignant expression of man's permanent striving towards perfection so that he could build them into his own dynamic world-concept.[79]

As for the Turkish scholar Abdulbaki Gölpınarlı. he sees in our verses an allusion to creation's being renewed every moment, and he stresses the acts of constant 'eating and being eaten', the struggle for survival as an element necessary to the development of higher strata of life.[80]

All these interpretations are possible, and perhaps intended by the variable applications of very similar words; but they seem to neglect two aspects of the story of the chickpeas, which stands here as a model for the whole complex of ideas. Rumi himself clearly thinks of this upwards movement as something taught by the Koran: the Lord can transfer a horse from the stable into his private pen, and there look after it better, if he finds it worthy;[81] and thus, the true miracle is that God should bring man from a lowly estate to a higher one, just as he developed a lovely human being out of a mean drop of sperm.[82] Rumi was certainly acquainted with the verses of Sanāʾi and ʿAṭṭār about the journey of the soul, and may have known the relevant philosophical doctrines as well. But his main interest lay in the spiritual interpretation of this act of development as he could see it every day in eating and growing in the persons surrounding him. The story of the poor chickpeas should be read in this context, all the more as the poet all of a sudden introduces Ḥallāj's verses: 'Kill me, o my trustworthy friends . . .', words which he always used when speaking of spiritual death and spiritual resurrection. It is not a cold magnetic force which produces the attraction and the upward movement in creation, but the free grace of God's creative love which enables the lower potencies to grow to higher levels, provided they follow the law of love which is, to sacrifice their small egos for the sake of something higher, i.e. finally, for the Beloved.[83]

> Only love produces this change: otherwise how would minerals be naughted in plants? . . .[84]
> Love makes dead bread into soul,
> Love makes the soul which was perishable, eternal.[85]

This love, dumb and unconscious on the lover levels of existence, becomes visible in man, who can through its fulfilment in willing sacrifice experience what Goethe has called, in his interpretation of Ḥallāj's story of Moth and Candle, the *Stirb und werde*.

He loves them, and they love Him

THE IDEA OF LOVE IN RUMI'S WORK

Rumi's poetry has been produced under the spell of Divine Love—

> Save love, save love, we have no other work![1]

This love, the veritable astrolabe of God's secrets, was kindled by his meeting with Shams, but differs from the experiences of those mystics who saw the Divine Beauty reflected in beautiful youths. His experience of love, separation, and spiritual union was dynamic; it overwhelmed him and burned him. Therefore, his words about love, which form the warp of his poetry from the first to the last page, are colourful and fiery.

He knows, like his predecessors in the path of mystical love, that earthly love is but a preparation for heavenly love. It is a step towards perfection: people give their little girls dolls to teach them their duties as future mothers and their boys wooden swords to get them accustomed to fighting;[2] likewise, man's heart can be educated through human love to perfect obedience and surrender to the friend's will. The happiness of such love, however, will soon vanish; real love should, therefore, be directed towards Him who does not die. This Divine love may start with a sudden rapture or take the form of a slow spiritual development: when the hook of love falls into a man's throat God most High draws him gradually so that the bad faculties and blood which are in him may go out of him little by little.[3]

Eventually, the lover is totally immersed in the ocean of Divine love and those people who are still fettered by hope and fear or think of recompensation for good and punishment for evil deeds, will never understand him.[4]

Love is a quality innate in everything created:

> Every animal knows what love is, wolf and rooster and lion;
> He who is blind to love, is lower than a dog.[5]

> All the particles of the world are loving,
> Every part of the world is intoxicated by meeting.[6]

This basic truth is explained once more in a letter of Mowlānā's:

> In the eighteen thousand worlds, everything loves something, is in love with something. The height of each lover is determined by the height of his beloved. Whose beloved is more tender and more lovely, his eminencc is also higher . . .[7]

But true love is, at the same time, the prerogative of man. He alone can express it and live through it in all its stages. Rumi, although sometimes using language influenced by the discussions of Avicenna and the theoreticians of Sufism concerning the nature of love, knows that this experience, as produced by Divine power, cannot be described in human words. He begins his *Mathnavi* with a praise of this love:

> How much I may explain and describe love,
> When I reach love, I become ashamed.
> Although the commentary by the tongue is illuminating,
> love without tongues is more radiant.[8]

More than a decade later, he still sings:

> Love cannot be described; it is even greater than a hundred resur-

> rections, for the resurrection is a limit, whereas love is limitless. Love has five hundred wings, each of which reaches from the Divine Throne to the lowest earth . . .[9]

Once man has reached the limits of love in this life, his journey continues in the Life Divine, in which he is faced with ever new abysses of love which induce him into deeper longing. Love and longing are mutually interdependent; love grows stronger the more the Divine Beauty unfolds in eternity, in ever new forms.

> Ever more shall I desire
> than time's bounded needs require.
> Ever as more flowers I pluck
> Blossoms new gay spring's attire.
> And when through the heavens I sweep
> Rolling spheres will flash new fire.
> Perfect Beauty only can
> True eternal love inspire.[10]

Mowlānā Jalāloddin sees the power of love everywhere:

> Love is like an ocean on which the skies are only foam,
> agitated like Zoleykha in her love for Joseph,
> and the turning of the skies is the result of the wave of love:
> if love were not there, the world would be frozen.[11]

One may explain these lines, and also many similar verses found in Rumi's work, as an expression of the almost magnetic force of love which attracts everything, sets it in action, and eventually brings it back to its origin. But Rumi's view is closer to the notion of love as 'the essential Desire' of God as defined first in Sufism by Ḥallāj, who was overwhelmed by the dynamic essence of God which caused the Creator to say: 'I was a hidden treasure, and I wanted to be known . . .'

Rumi emphasizes this dynamic character of love again and again in ever new images:

> Love makes the ocean boil like a kettle, and makes the mountains like sand.[12]

It is the only positive force in the world:

> The sky revolves for the sake of the lover, and for the sake of love is the dome turning,
> not for the sake of baker and blacksmith, not for the sake of superintendent and pharmatician.[13]

Love is the physician of all illnesses, Plato and Galen in one, and the cause and goal of existence:

> If this heaven were not a lover, its breast would have no purity,
> and if the sun were not a lover, in its beauty were no light,
> and if earth and mountain were not lovers, grass would not grow out of their breasts.[14]

As the sun changes doleful shades and destitute darkness into colourful beauty, love is the great alchemy which transforms life: 'love means to fall in a goldmine'.[15]

> From love bitternesses become sweet, from love copper becomes gold,
> from love the dregs become pure, from love the pains become medicine,
> from love the dead become alive, from love the king is made a slave,[16]

as Rumi says in his great hymn in honour of love's power. Much later, he continues in the same strain:

> Loves makes the dead bread into soul, and makes the soul which was perishable eternal—[17]

a verse which must be seen in connection with his thoughts on the constant upward development which traverses the whole gamut of existence from minerals to man and angel.

The same idea underlies an oft-quoted passage written towards the end of Mowlānā's life:

> When the demon becomes a lover, he carries away the ball,
> he becomes a Gabriel, and his demon-qualities die.
> 'My Satan has become a Muslim' becomes here conspicuous,
> Yazid became, thanks to his bounty, a Bāyazid.[18]

That means the base faculties of man, the *nafs,* seen here in accordance with the Prophetic tradition in the old Arabic image of the demon, can be fully conquered and educated only by love, not by loveless austerities and sheer asceticism. Eventually, man will be blessed with the Prophet's own experience: his demonic qualities become sanctified and serve him only in the way towards God. The stronger the 'demon' was previously, the higher will his rank be in the angelic world, once he has given himself to the power of love; even an accursed sinner like Yazid could, by such an alchemy, be transformed into a Bāyazid-like saint. Such an annihilation by love of the *nafs*, the personal representative of all evil of 'the world', as well as of independent, separate existence, can be seen in Koranic terms:

> Love is Moses who slays the Pharaoh of existence by means of his miraculous rod . . .[19]

and it is the police-officer who helps the soul to break down the door of the prison of the world.[20]

Love, which destroys the borders of separation, is the truly uniting force: it gives union to hundreds of thousands of atoms;[21] their faces which are at present directed towards various, and often conflicting, directions and to egotistic goals, are turned by love towards the One Eternal Sun. There, they will be united in the whirling, mystical dance and, lost to themselves, live in a higher unity, no longer distinct as rose and thorn, or as Turk and Hindu. For the religion of love knows no difference between the seventy-two sects:[22] it is different from all religions.[23]

But how to explain this love? Even examples and parables cannot help: did not Somnun the Lover say in early tenth century Baghdad:

> One can explain something only by a means subtler than itself. Now, there is nothing subtler than love; how, then, can it be explained?[24]

The *qāl*, 'word' conveys only a weak shade of this experience; what is required, is *ḥāl*, 'mystical state'. Love may be understood by the lover's behaviour when his pulse, beating irregularly, tells the secret of his illness,[25] and Rumi replies to his inquiring friends:

> Some asked: 'What is the state of a lover?'
> I said: 'Don't ask these meanings!
> The moment you become like me, you will see it,
> The moment He calls you, you will call!'[26]

Love defies any intellectual task of explanation. Intellect is indeed 'like the donkey that carries books' (Sura 62/5), as the mystics, and among them Rumi have often repeated with the Koranic expression. It is a lame donkey, not comparable to the winged Borāq, which carried Moḥammad into the divine Presence. 'Has anybody ever seen a lame Borāq?' asks the poet.[27] For:

> Love is ascension towards the roof of the Soltān of Beauty.[28]

The contrast of love and discursive reason was always a favourite subject of the mystics. Rumi, too, never tires of repeating the needlessness of not only reasoning,[29] but also of scholastic theology where love is concerned. Love flies towards heaven, but reason is required to learn science and correct behaviour.[30]

The poet introduces a charming discussion between love and reason into his lyrics:

> Reason says: 'The six directions are the limit, there is no way out!'
> Love says: 'There is a way, and I have gone it several times!'
> Reason saw a bazaar and began to commerce,
> Love has seen other markets beyond this market . . .[31]

And he teaches: 'Sacrifice intellect in love for the Friend!'[32] Intellect must become lean, when love becomes fat.[33] Or he sees intellect as a thief which must be hanged when love becomes the ruler of the country.[34]

> Far be the intellectuals from the lovers,
> Far be the smell of the ash-house from the morning-breeze![35]

It is typical that the verse:

> Abu Ḥanifa did not give lessons in love, Shāfeʿi has no traditions about it,

was attributed to Mowlānā.[36] although it is in fact Sanāʾi's invention.[37] Rumi alludes to it in the *Mathnavi,*[38] and describes the 'school of love which is closed to jurists, physicians, and astrologers',[39] a school in which one learns the *ʿelm-e ladoni*, immediate Divine knowledge without *madrasa* and paper,[40] a school made of fire in which the pupil has to sit and to mature.[41]

Intellect is not bad in itself; it is a stick which may help the blind to find his way in the darkness, for what would a blind man do with a candle? Such is he who has not seen the friend's beauty and takes intellect as his prayer-direction.[42] Or else reason may be compared to the moth, the Beloved to the candle.[43]

Just as the child cannot understand the acts of intellect, thus intellectuals are incapable of understanding love.[44] The numerous allusions to Majnun, completely beside himself in his passionate love for Leyla, point to this end: the fetters of intellect no longer hinder the loving soul in its frenzied roaming through the deserts of love.

Love is jealous;[45] it is a flame which burns the outward form, nay, everything save the beloved.[46]

> If the cold becomes rebellious, put firewood in the fire,
> You pity the wood? Is the wood better, or the body?
> The wood is the image of annihilation, the fire is God's love:
> Burn the figures, O pure soul![47]

Fire-imagery fills Rumi's poetry: love is a lightning bolt which destroys everything,[48] and the soul is like sulphur in the fire,[49] the spirit like oil for its flame.[50] Only Abu Lahab, the 'father of the flame', the prototype of infidelity has never tasted this fire.[51] Mowlānā sees:

> A face like fire, wine like fire, love is fire: all the three lovely.
> The soul in the midst of the fire full of lament: where is an escape?[52]

This is but a rhetorical question, for the soul does not want to flee from this fire. It feels like Abraham on Nimrod's pyre, which turned into a rose garden for him.[53] The lovers fly like moths towards the candle-like radiant face of the beloved, and dance in the flames like wild rue. Love's fire is better than the water of life itself,[54] or else the water of the ocean through which the lover swims is fire.[55] Later Persian-writing poets have added to this imagery new and highly exaggerated inventions which all point to the same focal point: Can one cross the fiery ocean of love with the wooden leg of 'intellect'?[56] Sitting in the midst of this fire, how could the lover be patient?[57]

> Love has cast fire into the station of patience;
> My patience died the night when love was born; it passed away—long live the present one![58]

Or Jalāloddin may sing in a lighter tune:

> Repentance started travelling with a lame foot,
> Patience fell into a narrow pit.
> None but me and the cupbearer remained
> When that harp made *taranga tarang.*[59]

Love is the police-master who puts a cauldron with the fire of separation on the breast of the spirit to torture him when he, for one moment, forgets his duty of rendering thanks to the

Preserved in the National Museum, Delhi.

Last page of a Mathnavi, written in India in 837/1433, one of the rare copies with miniatures.

beloved.[60] Or else love is, as we mentioned, a black lion, a crocodile,[61] a dragon,[62] man-eater.[63] Man should make himself sweet before this wild beast: so long as he is still sour and unripe, he is difficult for the animal Love to digest; but the saint is a sweet morsel, and therefore devoured by Love.[64] This somewhat strange image points again to Rumi's central idea that man has to become softened through love's afflictions. For:

> The blood of every soul which this lion has eaten is rendered alive and eternal;[65]

and the lovers are like 'blood in the vessel for love's dogs'.[66] For:

> Love means to become blood, to drink one's own blood.
> to live with the dogs on the door of faithfulness.[67]

Love is therefore not made for the weak; it is the occupation of heroes,[68] and even the two worlds could not bear the strength of love.[69] Its claws will definitely uproot every house, just as it was able to split the moon and make the earth tremble.[70]

Mowlānā knows that in love the normal rules of behaviour are suspended:

> The etiquette of love is completely without etiquette,[71]

as he says, following Joneyd's well-known dictum. The sharp dagger should cut the throat of shame,[72] and *towba*, repentance, is no longer required: this initial station was a huge male dragon, but its fault-finding eyes were blinded by the emerald of love.[73]

Love annihilates the lover, and thus tears the veils which hide the face of the Beloved: mystical death leads to union.

> What is love? To fly heavenward,
> to tear a hundred veils in every wink . . .[74]

This is the result of love—but one may ask how man can love at all? How can he dare turn towards the Eternal God with the feeling of love? The Sufis—like the mystics in other religions—have felt that love is a Divine gift; man in his weakness would never be able to attract it or to reject it: Bāyazid expressed his amazement that God should love such a destitute creature as he was; Yaḥyā ibn Moʿāẓ the Preacher always reminded God of his prior grace, and Ḥallāj spoke of the ᶜ*ināya azaliyya*, the pre-eternal kindness of God 'without which you would not have learned what is the Book nor what is faith'.[75]

This Love, which the Sufis understood from the Koranic word 'He loves them and they love Him' (Sura 5/59) manifested itself at the very first moment of creation. Its branch is in pre-eternity, its root in eternity, as Rumi says with a paradox.[76] This love began with the Divine address 'Am I not your Lord?' (Sura 7/171) at the festival of the pre-eternal covenant. Here, the mystics were granted the wine of love; that first sip from the eternal cup of happiness, suffering, and longing which should mark their lives until resurrection. For by answering *balā* 'Yes', they had accepted willingly to take upon themselves all the affliction, *balā*, which God would shower down upon them as signs of His grace. In the words of the prophets, in the *z̲ekr* of the dervishes, in the melodies of *samā*ᶜ, this primordial Divine address of love was brought to the common people that they might remember their former promise and be led towards God and His love.

This pure love was together with Moḥammad at the beginning of creation. Only for his sake the world was created, and when he assumed his earthly form, the Divine love once more became manifest for his community.[77]

Rumi rarely discusses theoretical problems connected with love. He simply knows, and repeats it everywhere:

> Not a single lover would seek union, were the beloved not seeking it.[78]

The seeker and the sought are mutually interdependent; the water is thirsty and longs for the seeker as much as he longs to find the water and slacken his thirst.[79]

> The lovers here are not seeking from their own initiative;
> In the whole world is no other seeker than He.[80]

Love originates in God; it is *qadim*,[81] co-eternal with Him. If man responds to the call of love, he can slowly be qualified with Divine qualities and thus reach proximity to his Beloved, for God's foremost quality is love, not fear.[82] And thus the lover reaches immortal happiness already in this life:

How many fruits has the green garden of Love!
The true lover is beyond grief and joy; he is fresh and happy without spring and fall.[83]

The relation between lover and Beloved is the central theme in both the *Divān* and the *Mathnavi*.

How beautifully has Rumi described the state of the lover who returned to Bokhara to see his friend, although he was forbidden to do so! But:

For the lovers, the beauty of the friend becomes the teacher,
their notebook and lesson and lecture is His face.[84]

Although the earthly beloved may be attractive, yet, Rumi takes up Shibli's verdict against a man who mourned the death of his friend: 'Why do you love someone who can die?'[85] One has to take into one's embrace a friend who cannot be embraced (a fine pun on *kanār*, 'breast' and 'limit').[86]

There is no end of praise for the Beloved in Mowlānā's work. He uses all the devices developed by Arabic and Persian poets, all the plays of rhetoric, all artistic forms to describe the One who is the only goal of man's life. Throughout long sequences of verses he asks:

O friend, is sugar better or He, who makes sugar?
Is the moon's beauty better, or He, who makes the moon? . . .[87]

and tells the Friend that he can bring spring into the heart of winter by his very loveliness and can bring the Festival on Friday if he would only come upon the pulpit to explain his own lofty qualities.[88] In the tradition of profane love-poetry he may sing:

Whoever sees your face, goes no more to the rose garden;
whoever knows your lip, does not speak of the goblet![89]

In between his tresses see the face like fire—
Say: Amidst musk and amber have I found a censer![90]

He longs for a dream image of the beloved, or describes his nocturnal visions in words full of fragile, romantic tenderness;[91] he sees him in the morning sun which rides proudly through the world, whereas the souls are walking, numerous as dust particles, to accompany him in his glory.[92] And the beloved is the moon beyond the horizons which takes his restplace (*qonuq*) in the lover's heart for just one night;[93] since the night regards itself as white and luminous during full moon, the lover, dark night himself, becomes enlightened by the moon-like beloved.[94] The Friend is everything, companion and cave, Noah and Spirit, Opener and Opened One,[95] and whatever man can imagine. He is father and mother, sun and moon, milk and sugar.[96]

My idol was yesterday radiant like the moon;
nay, nay, he added to the sun's splendour.
Beyond the realm of imagination: I know,
he *was* beautiful, but I do not know, *how* he was![97]

Whoever loves him and surrenders completely into his love becomes the elect prince (*khāṣṣbeg*) of the age;[98] a disciple whom He has recently accepted is immediately the *sheykh* of all *sheykhs* in the world.[99] Even if the lover be a king, he cannot be superior to the beloved master; even if he be honey, he is bound to chew the friend's sugarcane. The lover is only like a picture, his ideas are faint images, whereas the Friend's thought is truly soul.[100]

His moonlike face is reflected in the heart which is like a pure mirror: what else but a polished mirror could the lover bring as gift to Joseph?[101]

My heart is like water, pure and limpid,
and water is the mirror-holder for the moon![102]

This water gains lucidity only by the moon's reflection. The lover is therefore invited to follow the example of the dove, which always repeats its call *ku? ku?* 'Where, where?' in order to find this very goal of life.[103] For:

Where is a roof but Thy roof, where is a name but Thy Name?
Where is a cup but Thy cup, oh sweetly moving *sāqi*?[104]

With your face the mourning sessions become festivals,
Without your face, festival becomes mourning![105]

Even the thorn which grows in the Beloved's garden is a hundred times better than fragrant roses elsewhere,[106] and the most beautiful city in the world is that in which the friend lives.[107] The blame which reaches the lover from the friend's lips is as precious as a ruby, for 'sweet is every wind that passes through roses'.[108]

Rumi sings of the miraculous power of the beloved:

You come into the two eyes of the blind and give sight,
and come into the mouth of the dumb one, and become tongue.
You enter into an ugly demon and make him (a beautiful) Joseph,
and come into the form of a wolf and become a shepherd . . .[109]

Did not God promise to become man's hand by which he seizes, and his eye by which he sees?

To meet the beloved, is 'the answer to all questions, the solution to all problems'.[110] For he is the elixir and the alchemy which no one can find and without which nothing can exist. The lover may try and examine every possible way of life, investigate every wisdom and search in every corner, but nothing is better than the Friend,[111] for he is higher and more beautiful than everything imaginable. Therefore Rumi addresses him:

When you call the (luminous white) moon a (black) Abyssinian, she will prostrate herself before you;
When you call the (upright slim) cypress a circle, it will not cry aloud.[112]

Everything is worthless, compared with the absolute beauty and grandeur of the Beloved: the rubies of this world are ordinary pebbles compared to him; lions, donkeys, and the sun only a dust-particle.[113] He is indeed spring and everything else the month of December,[114] for he bestows new life on everything which was imprisoned in the hibernal world of matter, and 'his kindness is the cause for the soft touch of squirrel's fur . . .[115] His alchemy transforms the raw materials of the world into treasure, and leads the erring caravan again to the right path.[116] The beloved thus addresses the lover:

You are like a dry valley, and we like rain,
You are like a devastated city, and we like an architect.[117]

The friend can transform colocynth into sweet dates or sugar, but also sugar into bitterness.[118] Even though man's situation outwardly be hopeless, it can be illuminated by the presence of the Beloved: wherever this Joseph appears, the dark, narrow prison (i.e. the world of matter) turns into a paradise.[119]

His miraculous power not only transforms base qualities into higher ones; it completely uproots everything evil:

When Thy shade falls upon the sinful evildoer,
all his crimes become seclusion and ritual prayer.[120]

And:

If an infidel of a hundred years should see Thee,
he prostrates himself and quickly becomes a Muslim.[121]

Rumi, who has described the pangs of separation and yearning like no one else learned, finally, after Shamsoddin had left for ever, that the beloved cannot be separated from him: he is 'closer than reason'. He knows that he is like dust, moved by the wind of the friend without whom he cannot move and who carries him to loftier stations by his movement.[122] How could he ever feel himself absent from him?[123] He is like a mountain echoing the voice of the beloved[124] (an allusion to the poetical inspiration through Shams), speaking through his breath like the flute, moved by his hands like the harp. And he is straw in his fire. In a poem with Greek rhyme-words Mowlānā addresses the friend in elegant verse:

When I am on top of the mountain, like the monks I seek your love,
and when I am in the depths of the sea, you are in that ocean my *agapos* (beloved).[125]

The dream-image of the friend keeps him company after the other friends have departed like dreams,[126] although it may be difficult for the dream to cross the waves of blood which the longing lover's eye has shed at night.[127] The very name of Shams can bring back his youth in a magical process of spiritual rejuvenation.[128]

Out of this soft and sweet feeling Rumi has written verses which sound like sheer worldly love-poetry; in gentle rhythms has he invented images of great beauty to describe his bewilderment before the friend, and the silent conversation 'with eyebrows and eyes':[129]

Last night I went before him, full of heat—
He did not ask me, but sat calm and still.
I looked at him, that meant 'O please, do ask:
How have you been without my moonlike face?'
My friend, however, cast his eyes to earth:
'Be you like dust, so selfless and so low!'

I kissed the ground and fell upon my face;
That meant 'I am bewildered like the dust'.[130]

How lovely is his description of love's power:

The lady Spirit, sitting at home, began again to draw her veils, and to run about from the castle of the body out of love . . .
Sleeping on the roof of love, the shepherd 'Heart' began, out of love for the moon, again to count the stars, one by one . . .

Rumi knows that 'for the lover and the thief the night is wide and long':[132]

Take the Leyla 'Night' (*leyl*) on your breast, o Majnun:
The night is the secret chamber of *towḥid*, and the day idolatry (*sherk*) and multiplicity . . .[133]

This night should be used and not spent in the sleep of heedlessness:

It is fitting that I should not sleep at night, for secretly the moon gives a kiss every night to him who counts the stars.[134]

And he turns again to the fresh green meadow, spirited by the water's kiss:

I am a brooklet, and you the water, and the kiss of the water happens always on the lip of the brook;
from the water's kiss on the lip of the brook flowers and greenery come into existence.[135]

Rumi asks the beloved for a kiss to quicken him by putting his soul into his mouth.[136] That is the ages-old image of the exchange of souls through kisses: the soul being connected in primitive religious concepts with the breath. Therefore the poet can easily say:

If the prize of a kiss is one soul, it is a religious duty to purchase it.[137]

But eventually he tells the beloved, with whom he is fully united in spirit:

Give a kiss on your own face, tell the secret into your own ear,
Look at your own beauty, speak yourself your praise![138]

These are poems of happy days, days in which Rumi experienced the happiness of spiritual union and peace of soul after long periods of burning and yearning. Yet, the suffering in love occupies the larger part of his poetry: the whole complex of affliction as the true alchemy of life, and of growing through sacrifice belongs essentially to this chapter.

Jalāloddin may complain that the beloved did not care for him when he came to visit him,[139] or he tells how the friend left him in wrath:

> Confused he left the house and us; he took a porter and carried away his belongings;
> he put a heavy lock on the heart, went away, and handed over the key.[140]

But such is the friend's wish, and that counts, nothing else. And as the sun 'kills' the stars in the blood-red glow of dawn, the blood of the whole world can be licit for the beloved.[141]

> If he wants it, even death becomes sweet,
> thorn and lancet become narcissus and wild rose.[142]

It is only his exterior coquettery, the quality typical of the Beloved, which makes him say 'I don't care!', although in his essence he is compassionate.[143] He shows his mercy hidden in cruelty; and the lover who knows the secret of this action enjoys this suffering: at night, he boils in the fire of separation like a cauldron, whereas in the daytime he drinks blood—his own blood—like sand, hopeless and never saturated,[144] wanting more thirst, not water.[145]

> I have turned into blood, boiling in the veins of love,
> I have become humidity in the eyes of his lovers.[146]

When the lover proceeds towards this sea of blood, he will find the Divine table in that very blood,[147] for the heart's blood is his wine.[148] To be drowned in blood is one of the qualities of the true lover.[149] To be sure, Rumi's descriptions of the cruelty of the beloved and the sufferings of the lover cannot compete with the almost masochistic imagery of later Persians poets; but his complaints are more substantial and heartfelt than in the cases of many other poets, where suffering for the sake of love has congealed into a mere figure of speech which can only be exaggerated, but not deepened.

Love and suffering are inseparable:

> From my bent stature in the way of love
> one can make a bridge over my tears . . .[150]

and, in an ingenious combination of the garden-motif and contemporary politics:

> I do not find the peach's kiss when I flee from destitution (*bi-bargi.*)
> I do not smell Tartarian musk when I flee from the Tartars.[151]

In fact, the very essence of love is to suffer, to accept Ḥallāj's statement that 'suffering is God Himself, whereas happiness comes from Him'.

> What does the ascetic seek? Your mercy (*raḥmat*).
> What does the lover seek? Your pain (*zaḥmat*).[152]

For the lover is comparable to the women at Zoleykha's meeting, who, gazing at Joseph, cut their hands in bewilderment: one would be less than a woman if one would not sacrifice one's self and forget all suffering in the radiant beauty of the Majestic Lord![153] The lover should resemble St. George (*Jerjis*), killed and again revived a hundred times by love, or be like Isaac, sacrificed by God's order.[154] (It is remarkable that here Isaac, as in the Judeo-Christian, and not Ishmael, as in the Muslim tradition, is mentioned as the sacrificed son; perhaps the name of St. George in the first hemistich suggested this connection.) Such a death at the hand of love is indeed new life:

> I was dead and became alive, I was crying and became laughing,
> the happiness of love came, and I became a firmfooted happiness.[155]

For the lover knows that the beloved himself is the blood-money for those who are slain in his love;[156] thus, their outward melting is indeed growing and waxing stronger. So the afflicted lover can break out in the jubilant cry:

> No drink sweeter than this poison did I see,
> No health lovelier than this illness did I see.[157]

Even if his heart is burnt by the friend, the lover will dance in the flames like wild rue,[158] exuding sweet scent like aloes-wood.[159] The fire of love, manifested through the Beloved, is necessary to purify the gold: the sincere lover, then, can be recognized as unalloyed gold,[160] whose base and dark elements are burnt away in this trial[161] which constitutes, at the same time, spiritual nourishment for him.[162]

> If the whole world were filled with thorns,
> The lover's heart is always a rosegarden.[163]

It is a rule that lovers must not complain; for they do not remember any grief or pain as long as they behold the friend's face.

> How could you find the grief of the two worlds in the heart of the lover?
> How could the leader of the pilgrims' caravan be esteemed by the Meccans?[164]

Grief, though a guide during the spiritual pilgrimage, is no longer valued once the caravan has reached its goal; and those who dwell in the sanctuary itself, do not care for such a guide.

Neither should the lover think of the acts of obedience he has performed in the way of love. Rumi blames the person who enumerates all his virtues and acts of worship before the beloved[165] as much as him who reads a love-letter in the presence of his beloved: True love wants to reach the contents and is not satisfied with the 'box', the outward forms in which words play still a role.[166] The lover should prove his love by smilingly dying at the friend's order, for love is 'to give up free will'.[167]

Mowlānā has invented innumerable images to describe the lover's state. Following the examples of Nuri and other early Baghdad Sufis, he compares him to

> a cloud at the hour of crying, a mountain at the time of endurance,
> prostrating himself like water, lowly like the dust of the road:

the garden which he thus finds is the Beloved.[168]

The lover is conspicuous everywhere, comparable to the camel that thought it was invisible on the minaret: his behaviour tells his secret. Whatever he says bears the scent of love: when he pronounces the word *feqh*, 'jurisprudence', it turns into *faqr*, 'spiritual poverty', and when he says *kofr*, 'infidelity', the word bears the flavour of *din*, 'religion'.[169] Even should he commit an error out of love, this error is better than other people's righteous actions—to the same degree as the blood of the martyrs is better than water.[170] He should therefore avoid the company of uncongenial people: was not

Majnun grieved two-fold: by Leyla's absence and by the company of the gypsies?[171] And he should not mix with those who are grieved for worldly concerns lest dust fall on the pure brightness of his selflessness.[172]

Just as the lover talks exclusively through love and in love, he wants to hear the name of the beloved everywhere: he looks for the *aṭlāl*, the remnants of former dwelling-places of the beloved, to talk to them about happy memories, in the same way as the ancient Arabian poets would address the deserted resting-places of the friend's caravan in the introductory part of their poems.[173] Or else he wants to be a mountain to enjoy the name of the Beloved, repeated manifold by the echo:[174] the mountain has no will of its own and reiterates nothing but the melodious name.[175] Although the lover may try to hide the name of the beloved from others,[176] the name is the most precious treasure for him; he repeats it constantly; and when he writes it into the dust, every dust particle will become a houri . . .[177]

Certainly, Jalāloddin has never spoken about certain practices common with the mystics of his time, e.g. the concentration upon particular names of God; but his deep love of the name of the beloved belongs basically to the same category of experience. The permanent reiteration of the beloved name produces the feeling of proximity, and finally of union, in the lover's heart: the name of the friend makes the hungry satiated, the thirsty refreshed, and is the fur-coat in the time of cold.[178] Eventually 'when you speak his name and loose my name'[179] union is perfect – a union which is expressed in Rumi's attribution of his own poetry to Shamsoddin.

Only the friend is sought and found in every word.[180] Joseph, whose beauty became the nourishment of the soul in the time of famine,[181] is the centre of Zoleykha's words and thoughts: there are few passages which could compare in psychological truth with the description of the enamoured woman by whose every word her beloved is intended:[182]

> She concealed his name in all other names and made the inner meaning thereof known to (none but her) confidants.
> When she said, The wax is softened by the fire, this meant: My beloved is very fond of me,
> and if she said, Look the moon is risen; or if she said: The willow bough is green;

or if she said, The leaves are quivering mightily; or if she said, The rue-seed is burning merrily . . .

or if she said, How auspicious is Fortune; or if she said, Give the furniture a good dusting;
or if she said, The water carrier has brought the water; or if she said, The sun is risen,
or if she said, Last night they cooked a potful of food; or, The vegetables are cooked to perfection;
or if she said, The loaves have no salt; or if she said, The heavenly sphere is going in the contrary direction;
or if she said, My head aches; or if she said, My headache is better—
If she praised, t'was his caresses, and if she blamed, t'was separation from him (that she meant).
If she piled up a hundred thousand names, her meaning and intention was always Joseph . . .

Rumi knew from his own experience that lover and beloved are never without each other. Even if separated, even if outwardly far from each other, they act and react through each other. Although longing makes lovers thin and pale, like autumnal leaves, love shows itself in the beloved in glorious, springlike radiance.[183] The relation cannot be severed; willingly or unwillingly the straw is drawn towards the amber.[184] In fact, the beloved longs as much for the lover as the lover does for him. His love preceeded every other love. The lover is blinded by love, which is Light, before which people are like shadows;[185] he is blinded to anything but the Divine beloved,[186] and is killed by the sword *lā* 'No', as if he were a sacrificial lamb.[187] Then, only *illā Allāh* remains, nothing else.[188] The lover who has understood this mystery of the profession of faith, gives his soul with a smile like a rose.[189] He knows that:

Tomorrow, when the creatures will rise from the dust,
Poor me will rise, without choice, from your dust![190]

The lover has lost himself in the beloved; he has put his tent in non-existence,[191] and the angel of death has no power over him.[192] Nothing but his name has remained in him; everything else is filled with the beloved:

The beloved asked a lover for the sake of examination:
Do you love me more or yourself?

Whereupon the lover admitted that only his name had been left to him: how could he make a distinction in love?[193]

Lover and beloved are like two mirrors which gaze into each other,[194] an image dear to all love-mystics from the time of Aḥmad Ghazzāli; but the secret of this relation can never be explained by rational thought.[195] They experience a higher unity,[196] a comprehensive love which is incomparable and ineffable; even Gabriel would be an intruder in the intimacy of this love:[197] for the lover who has completely purified his heart's mirror, or who has matured by endless suffering, eventually feels, not as the expression of a philosophical truth, but as a personal *Erlebnis*:

> Everything is the beloved, and the lover is a veil,
> Living is the beloved, and the lover dead.[198]

Call, and I shall answer

THE PROBLEM OF PRAYER IN JALĀLODDIN'S WORK

In the West, one story from the *Mathnavi* has gained fame more than others: these are the touching verses in the third book of the *Mathnavi* about the man who prayed the whole night until Satan appeared before him and said:

> Prithee, O garrulous one, where is the response 'Here am I' to all this 'Allāh'?

Thereupon the man got quiet and distressed, but in a dream Khiżr appeared before him, informing him that God Most High had ordered to tell him:

> That 'Allāh' of thine is My 'Here am I', and that supplication and grief and ardour of thine is My messenger to thee.
> Thy shifts and attempts to find a means of gaining access to Me were in reality My drawing thee towards Me, and released thy feet.
> Thy fear and love are the noose to catch My favour; beneath every 'O Lord!' of thine is many a 'Here am I' from Me.[1]

This story has been brought to light by F. A. D. Thorluck, the first German to attempt to compile a historical survey of Sufism in his Latin booklet *Ssufismus sive theosophia persarum pantheistica*, published in Berlin in 1821. On p.12 he quotes the last lines of Rumi's poem under the heading: *Deus est qui in mortalium precibus se ipse veneratur, se ipse adorat*, 'God is it who venerates Himself and worships Himself in the prayers of mortals', and with the heartfelt antipathy of an orthodox protestant theologian toward anything that looks like pantheistic mysticism he comments upon these words: 'What more abstruse, what more audacious could be thought!'

Tholuck quoted the same verses once more in his anthology *Blüthenlese aus der morgenländischen Mystik* (1825),[2] and thus, the poem became known to all students of mysticism in nineteenth century Germany. As far as I can see, the first person to draw the attention of larger circles of philologists and theologians to these lines of Rumi was the Swedish orientalist K.V. Zetterstéen in the beginning of our century: he translated this passage from the *Mathnavi* for Nathan Söderblom's collection *Främmanda religionsurkunder,*[3] the great collection of religious texts by the pioneer of History of Religions in Europe. By that time, however, the scholars' attitude towards Rumi's story had completely changed. Söderblom wrote in his introduction to his collection in 1902 about Mowlānā Rumi:

> His is the wonderful word about prayer and the hearing of prayer whose consoling main idea is met with once more in religious literature, i.e. with Pascal.

The same statement was repeated by N. Söderblom in his new edition of Tiele's *Kompendium der Religionsgeschichte* in 1931.[4]

In the meantime, in 1914, R.A. Nicholson had inserted our story into his book *The Mystics of Islam*[5] in order to show that 'for Jalāloddin man's love is really the effect of God's love'. Both Söderblom's and Nicholson's dicta are quoted by F. Heiler who, in his standard work on prayer (*Das Gebet*, fifth ed. 1923) cites Rumi's verses[6] as the most beautiful proof of the fact that the *oratio infusa* is known not only in Christianity but also in Islam; and he repeated this statement—and often the quotation from the *Mathnavi*—in his numerous later publications; he loved to recur to it in his sermons.[7]

Through these channels, Rumi's story on prayer has gained fame among theologians and historians of religion. It seems, however, that these verses were often regarded in too isolated a way. In fact, they constitute only the quintessence of Rumi's innumerable sentences, verses, and whole poems on prayer which rank from simple ritual prayer and its obligations to the highest summits of mystical meditation. One of the finest examples is the story of the mystic Daquqi leading the congregational prayer, in which the poet describes ritual prayer as man's experience in God's presence at Doomsday[8]—the base soul is slaughtered as a sacrificial animal as soon as man utters the words *Allāhu Akbar* and the believer is totally engaged in self-examination and orisons:

> Daquqi advanced to perform the prayer: the company were the satin robe and he the embroidered border.
>
> . . . When they pronounced the *takbirs*, they went forth from this world, like a sacrifice.
> O Imām, the meaning of the *takbir* is this: 'We have become a sacrifice, O God, before Thee!'
> At the moment of slaughtering you say *Allāh Akbar*: even to (do) in slaughtering the fleshly soul which ought to be killed.
> The body is like Ismāʿil, and the spirit like Abraham: the spirit has pronounced the *takbir* over the noble body . . .

One may also think of Adam's great prayer, culminating in the praise and laud of the Creator:

> O Helper of them that call for help, lead us! There is no (cause for) pride in knowledge or riches.
> Do not let a heart stray that Thou hast guided by Thy grace, and avert the evil which the Pen has written . . .
> If Thou art upbraiding Thy slaves, that is suitable to Thee, O Thou whose every wish is fulfilled.
> And if Thou say that the sun and moon are scum, and if Thou say that the stature of the cypress is (bent) double,
> And if Thou call the empyrean and the sky contemptible, and if Thou say that the mine and the sea are poor—
> That is proper in reference to Thy perfection: Thine is the power of perfecting (all) mortalities,
> For Thou art holy (and free) from danger and from non-existence:
> Thou are He that brings the non-existent ones into beings and endows them (with existence) . . .[9]

We could add many other examples of touching, deep-felt

prayers which the poet put into the mouth of his heroes in the *Mathnavi*.

Rumi's work comprises every aspect of prayer life. Thus, he speaks of the ritual ablutions, for:

> None with face unwashed beholds the faces of the houris; he (the Prophet) said: There is no ritual prayer without the ablution.[10]

Although he may spiritualize the meaning of the externals he never denies their necessity for the correct performance of the ritual prayer.[11] In this connection we may remember his amusing story of the poor individual who mixed up the prayer formulas to be used when washing the different parts of the body, so that he said at the time of abstersion 'O God, unite me with the scent of Paradise!' instead of 'O God cleanse me from this defilement!'—a perfect model of doing the right thing in the wrong place, as well-meaning foolish people often do . . .[12]

Mowlānā himself may speak of performing his ablution with his tears,[13] as many poets and mystics have done in the course of time. The legend of Mary's bath during which she conceived Jesus, the Spirit of God, is utilized as a model for the lover who should perform his ritual bath in the veil of love.[14] But when the average Muslim cleans himself of outward impurities, the lover washes his hands of speaking, purifying himself of logical speech.[15]

Ritual prayer can become a symbol for man's whole life:

> Illuminate the lamp of your five senses with the light of the heart,
> The senses are the five prayers, and the heart is like the *sabʿ mathāni* (the seven verses),[16]

i.e. the opening *fāteḥa* without which no ritual prayer is complete, for:

> God has put a kingdom into the *fāteḥa*, for the sincere without trouble of spear and shield.[17]

The *fāteḥa* indeed opens for him the spiritual kingdom, for, as Rumi says on another occasion: when man says 'Lead us the right path', God takes his hand and transforms him into light.[18]

Rumi sees the words of the *fāteḥa* manifested even in the

attitude of the trees in the garden:

> 'We worship Thee' is in winter the prayer of the garden;
> In spring it says; 'To Thee we ask for help'.
> 'We worship Thee' (means): I have come to thy door,
> Open the portal of joy, don't keep me any longer distressed.
> 'We ask for help': (that means) from the wealth of fruits
> I have become broken — O Helper, watch me well![19]

The thought of the beloved, the absolute presence of the heart,[20] is as necessary in prayer as the *fāteḥa*. Somebody may boast of being engaged in prayer day and night — but what is the use, when his words are not fitting for prayer, and he lives not up to the high ideals of pious life?[21] Prayer should leave its mark on the character — even though man cannot hope to reach God's Essence by performing ritual prayer and recollection, yet it is as if he had touched a piece of musk through the lid of a box, and thus, his whole hand becomes perfumed . . .[22]

The outward ritual is a prerequisite for the inward approximation — that is true for prayer as it is true for every aspect of life: Rumi always kept the rules of etiquette and has admonished his disciples to correct behaviour, as we understand from a number of remarks in *Fihi mā fihi*. And when man follows the rules prescribed in the presence of the worldly ruler — how much more must he behave correctly with all his senses and limbs when entering into the presence of the Lord of the Universe!

> Our God says 'Prostrate and draw near!' (Sura 96/19)
> The prostration of our bodies became the proximity of the soul.

To be sure, Mowlānā may even include charming little jokes in his description of prayer: How could he perform a correct evening prayer since the face of his beloved — the Sun of Tabriz — grants him perpetual morning draught?[24] But utterances like this lead us merely to the state when the lover — as Ḥallāj had expressed it already in his famous poem — is so intoxicated by the presence of his beloved that he cannot count any longer the hours of prayer. For

> Whosoever is bewildered by Thee, He keeps him fasting in fasting, prayer in prayer.[25]

The intoxicated know neither time nor place in their ritual

prayers. Though love may outwardly transform the ascetic's rosary into song and poetry, and break his renunciation a thousand times,[26] the prayer of the lovers is perpetual—*fi ṣalātin dāʾimun*;[27] for, as we understand from the story in whose context this Koranic saying (Sura 70/23) is inserted, ritual prayer is the deepest and most tender conversation of lover and beloved (represented in Rumi's story by the enamoured mouse and the frog!). This definition—prayer as intimate conversation—goes back to early times of Sufi history, and Rumi himself certainly belongs to those whose mystical state was deepened by the experience of ritual prayer, not to those whose high spiritual flights were interrupted when turning to the prescribed formulas of the *namāz*, to use Hojwiri's definition of the different approaches to prayer.[28]

Sepahsālar quotes one of Mowlānā's most enraptured prayer poems, written in an intoxicated rhythm in which two long and two short syllables alternate:[29]

> When at evening prayer everybody lays candle and table,
> I am there with my friend's dream image, grief and sighing and lament.
> When I perform my ablution with tears, my prayer becomes fiery,
> It burns the door of my mosque, when my call to prayer reaches it . . .
>
> . . .
> I wonder at the prayer of the intoxicated! Tell me: is this correct?
> For he does not know time, nor is he aware of space.
> I wonder—are these two *rakʿas*? I wonder: is this my fourth one?
> I wonder which sura did I recite, since I have not got a tongue?
> How shall I knock at God's door, since neither hand remained in me, nor heart?
> Since Thou hast carried away heart and hand, O God, give pardon!
> By God, I do not know how I performed the ritual prayer,
> Whether my genuflexion is finished, or who was the Imam . . .

And Sepahsālār goes on telling that on a cold winter night—and winter in the Konya plains is very cruel! —Mowlānā once performed the prayer in the mosque, and wept so profusely during his prostration that the tears froze on his cheeks and in his beard which adhered, finally, to the ground; in the morning, his disciples had to dissolve the ice with hot water . . . Did the master not say:

> There are a hundred kinds of prayer, genuflexion and prostrations for him who has taken the Friend's beauty as his prayer niche?[30]

Love is Rumi's Imām, an Imām thanks to whom thousands of mosques are filled, and from the minaret comes the call 'Prayer is better than sleep'.[31] Love is such an Imām that, when it gives only half a *salām* (greeting formula) to man he will immediately utter the four *takbir* i.e. the funeral prayer, over eating and sleeping.[32]

Rumi sometimes alludes to some peculiarities of prayer: the free prayer of petition must be uttered only at the end of formal prayer;[33] during Ramadan, the prayer of the faithful is certainly well accepted,[34] as much as prayer in early morning time at the threshold of the Living and Self Subsistent is advisable;[35] though perhaps worthless in the eyes of the common people it is 'like a radiant candle' in God's eyes.[36] Not in vain does Jalāloddin turn several times to the example of the Prophet Jonah who prayed inside the fish—man should pray at midnight in the darkness of his existence, and should again render grace when entering the morning light, rescued from the belly of the fish 'Night'.[37]

Time and again has Rumi expressed his absolute trust in the effectiveness of prayer:

> Those who have no information about us say that prayer has no result.[38]

He praises the formula of *esteghfār*, 'I ask God for forgiveness' which certainly will yield good results:

> He makes all the sins of the trespassers fall like leaves in December;
> He inspires to the ear of those who speak ill the excuse for sin.
> He says: 'Say: O Faithful One, forgive a sin which is hidden'!
> When the servant enters prayer, He says in secret 'Amen'.
> His Amen is, that he grants him taste in his prayer
> and that He makes him inwardly and outwardly sweet and agreeable like a fig . . .[39]

Prayer is indeed 'the key of people's needs'.[40] For Rumi firmly relies upon the Koranic word (Sura 40/62) that God 'has tied invocation together with His promise "I shall answer"';[41] man's sigh, directed to God, may serve as a rope which carries him out of the deep well of his despair.[42] In fact, Jalāloddin believes, like most of the Sufis since at least the ninth century, that grief is a perfect means to draw man to God:

> Grief is better than the empire of the world, so that you may call unto God in secret,[43]

and he often repeats that most people forget their Creator in the time of happiness, but remember Him during the time of affliction—so what could be better for them than affliction, pain and grief?

The smell of burnt liver—like a burnt offering—can be felt from a lover whose liver is wounded by hundreds of sparks of grief,[44] and will certainly be agreeable to the Lord. To a modern mind, Rumi's comparisons may sound, at times, strange and even irreverent in their plain and sometimes crude anthropomorphism. He holds that God loves to test the believer by not answering his prayers immediately because he rejoices in listening to his voice—parrots and nightingales are put into a cage because their owner loves to listen to them.[45] Does not man likewise hesitate to give a piece of bread immediately to a lovely young beggar whom he wants to contemplate for a while, but sends away an ugly old wretch with some pennies to get rid of her the sooner the better . . .? Such is the way God is thought to act. Rumi seems to rely here upon a *ḥadith* quoted by Qosheyri which tells that God orders Gabriel not to answer the wishes of His beloved servants for the pleasure He takes in their voices.[46]

Perhaps, however, just some of these apparently childish stories in the *Mathnavi* reveal more of the strong living relation between Rumi and his Lord than high-soaring theoretical discussions about the meaning and end of prayer could do. How touching is the story of the old harp-player who eventually seeks refuge with God:

> For seventy years I have been committing sin, yet not for one day hast Thou withheld Thy bounty from me.
> I earn nothing—today I am Thy guest, I will play the harp for Thee, I am Thine . . .[47]

The destitute musician strives to thank God with his half-broken instrument and his shrieky voice; the shepherd, again, imagines his Lord to be a child for which he wants to care in order to prove his gratitude:

> Moses saw a shepherd on the way, who was saying: 'O God who choosest (whom Thou wilt),
> Where art Thou, that I may become Thy servant and sew Thy shoes and comb Thy head?
> That I may wash Thy clothes and kill Thy lice and bring milk to Thee, O worshipful One,
> That I may kiss Thy little hand and rub Thy little foot (and when) bedtime comes I may sweep Thy little room,
> O Thou to whom all my goats be a sacrifice, Thou in remembrance of Whom are my cries of ay and ah!'[48]

Moses, full of prophetic wrath at hearing this seemingly blasphemous prayer, chased him away: 'Stuff cotton into your mouth!'—but even he, the great prophet, had to learn that God preferred the sincere prayer of the spiritually poor to the highflown words of the intelligent and the learned: indeed, every Divine acceptance is an act of grace, no matter who the praying person be:

> This acceptance (by God) of your praise is from (His) mercy: it is an indulgence like (that granted in the case of) the prayers of a woman suffering from menorrhœa.
> Her prayers are stained with blood, your praise is stained with assimilation and qualification . . .[49]

Of course, there is a difference between the praying humans—the beggar, i.e. the infidel, calls God for the sake of bread, the devout says 'God!' from the depth of his heart.[50] Rumi has skillfully employed a story known already from ᶜAṭṭār's work, namely that of a dervish in Herat who was scolding God when he saw that the wordly ruler had conferred better clothes upon his servants than God had given to His faithful slave—but:

> God gave the waist and the waist is better than the belt;
> If anyone gives you a crown—He has given the head![51]

This is one of the very few instances in which the motif of 'Muslim Mystics' strife with God', so prominent in ᶜAṭṭār's poetry,[52] is used by Rumi—he always returns to the soul's deep, loving trust in God.

Thinking of the differences between the praying people, Rumi may warn his readers not to mix their prayer with that of the unworthy who will be rejected; and if one reads the *fāteḥa*, one should know that the words 'Lead us the right path' mean:

> O God, do not mingle my prayer with that of the erring or the hypocrites![53]

Jalāloddin knows that many prayers are not answered—however, God's eternal wisdom is revealed even here, for:

> Thanks be to God that this prayer was rejected: I thought it was loss, but it has turned out to be gain.
> Many are the prayers which are loss and destruction, and from kindness the Holy God does not hear them.[54]

The only prayer which will certainly be heard and answered is that for others, be they relatives, masters, friends, or enemies; for the true Muslim prays even for his enemies, the highway robbers, corrupters, and insolent transgressors, because:

> They wrought so much wickedness and injustice and oppression that they cast me forth from evil into good.
> I took refuge from the blows Yonder: the wolves were always bringing me back into the right way.
> It behoves me to pray for them.[55]

Such prayers—the prayers of true lovers—are like birds which certainly fly towards heaven.[56] Did not the Beloved promise:

> I shall bring you beyond heaven like the prayer of the lovers?[57]

Therefore the loving prayer can be compared to the Simorgh, the mythical bird at the end of the world.[58]

Such prayers—uttered by lovers and by 'dervishes with burnt heart'[59] are answered,[60] and Rumi never ceased to urge his companions to pray, incessantly and intensely.[61] God can turn even dried-up prayer into grain and fruitful trees and give man unexpected reward, just as the dry palm tree was quickened by Mary's sigh and showered down fruits upon her during her birthpangs[62] (Sura 19/25). Who would not think of Paul Valéry's wonderful poem *La Palme*, when reading these comparisons?

Jalāloddin claims that his prayers made even heaven lament during the time of separation[63]—and he makes one of his heroes say:

> Thou knowest (the truth), and the long nights (know it) during which I was calling unto Thee with a hundred supplications.[64]

With an ingenious allusion to the old mystic motif of the moth and the candle, he describes himself:

> My profession is to speak prayers . . .
> My prayers constantly turn around the candle (*shamᶜ*) of Thy hearing (*samᶜ*),
> therefore I possess burning prayers like the moth.[65]

The moth, casting itself into the flames, becomes united with it and thus gains new life: the burnt prayers of the poet's moth-like heart will certainly reach the place of union. Rumi claims several times that he, who has nothing but prayer,[66] has himself become prayer—so that everyone who looks at him wants prayers from him.[67] This is perhaps the most beautiful self-portrait we possess of him: completely transformed into that light which—according to the Sufi saying—surrounds those who pray at night when the Lord covers them with light from His Light.

It is therefore small wonder that Mowlānā was able to understand the prayer of everything created, as it is described so often in the Koran, and as it was experienced by the Sufis throughout the centuries: 'only adoration is intended in the world',[68] and everything recites words of praise, from the moon to the fish which carries the earth (*az māh to māhi*),[69] the minerals,[70] the birds, and the flowers; the fire stands upright in ritual prayer, and the water prostrates itself . . .[71]

> The trees are engaged in ritual prayer and the birds in singing the litany,
> the violet is bent down in prostration twice.[72]

Indeed, the trees open their arms in the gesture typical of the prayer of supplication, and particularly the plane-tree's hands are opened for prayer;[73] the lily with its sword and the jasmine with a white shield shout the call *Allāh Akbar* as if they partake in the religious war.[74] And once more combining the *bi-bargi* 'being without means' with *barg* 'leaf', Rumi sees the leaves supplicating out of destitution,[75] an expression inherited from Sanāʾi. Sanāʾi had also invented the 'Rosary of the Birds' *tasbiḥ-e ṭoyur*, a long qasida in which he interprets every sound uttered by the birds as a word of praise and prayer;[76] Rumi participated in the joy of understanding the secret language of the birds (which had been translated into epic poetry by ᶜAṭṭār), and he interpreted it many times in a variety of images. For he knew that the words and acts of praise are different in the world, and that they often are not even verbally expressed. But everyone who helps building the tent of God, is engaged in praise:

> There is one praise for the rope-maker, another for the carpenter who makes the tent-poles, another for the maker of the tent-pins, another for the weaver who waves the cloth for the tent, another for the saints who sit in the tent and contemplate in perfect delight.[77]

However even in their most eloquent hymns the creatures have to aver, knowingly or unknowingly, with the Prophet's word: 'I cannot reckon up Thy praise', or sing:

> If the top of every hair of mine should gain a tongue, yet the thanks due to Thee are inexpressible.[78]

Likewise the last goal of mystical prayer is inexpressible—it is not worldly bliss and human felicity but the hope for God's eternal beauty and love: when even the infidels cannot endure separation from Him, how much less the faithful![79] Rumi's *Divān* is replete with words of longing and hope—prayers which need not be expressed in words but are understood through the *lisān al-ḥāl*, the lover's 'mute eloquence' which speaks through all his limbs. God answers those unspoken prayers,[80] since He knows everything man needs. In fact, man does not know how to pray; be it that he dares not speak in the presence of the Almighty, or that his words are not convenient:

> As Thou has shown Thy power, show Thy mercy, O Thou who hast implanted feeling of mercy in flesh and fat.
> If this prayer increases Thy wrath, do Thou teach us to pray, O Lord![81]

It is He who lights the candle of prayer in the darkness;[82] it is He who makes the heart narrow, but also makes it green-fresh and rose-coloured; it is He who induces you into prayer and gives you the reward of prayer,[83] who turns the bitter dust into bread, the bread into soul, and guides the soul by the right path.[84]

Whenever man prays in the right way, moved by God, he will hear the Amen from God who dwells in his soul,[85] for:

> From Thee come both the prayer and the answer, from Thee safety, from Thee also dread.
> If we have spoken faultily, do Thou correct it; Thou art the corrector, O Thou Sultan of speech![86]

This idea, which brings our discourse back to our starting-point, is, however, not Rumi's invention. A Prophetic tradition—probably coined in early Sufi circles—promises:

> When the slave says *Yā Rabbi* (O my Lord!) God says *labbayka ya ʿabdi* (Here I am at your service, my servant), ask, and it will be given unto Thee.[87]

God's love preceeds man's love—that is how the mystics interpreted Sura 5/59 'He loves them and they love Him', and they knew that man cannot address God unless he has been addressed first. The Iraqian mystic Niffari (d. 965), whose work was apparently widely used in 13th century Egypt, has uttered many a daring word about the mystery of the *oratio infusa*, so much so that his modern interpreter could compare one of his *mavāqif* to Francis Thompson's *Hound of Heaven*:[88] he tells how Divine Grace follows him wherever he may flee—just as the psalmist had expressed this feeling of God's unceasing activity and utter proximity in the words of Psalm 139.

> Let us turn our heads from ourselves towards Thee, inasmuch as Thou art nigher unto us than we,
> even this prayer is Thy gift and lesson—else wherefore has a rosebed grown in an ash-pit?[89]

> Thou madest prayer flow like water from me—now fulfill it according to Thy promise![90]

That is what the faithful feel when submerged in prayer—and Rumi has described this mental change which is the result of prayer in many passages of the *Mathnavi*, the most beautiful verses among which are probably those describing Daquqi's prayer when he, completely annihilated in God, experiences that God prays in him and through him.

> Become silent, and go by way of silence towards non-existence, and when you become non-existent, you will be over and all praise and laud.[91]

This feeling has been expressed once more in Rumi's story of the Israelite who addressed God:

> To whom but Thee should Thy servant lift his hand? Both the prayer and the answer are from Thee.
> Thou at first givest the desire for prayer, and Thou at last givest likewise the recompense for prayers.
> Thou art the First and the Last, we between are nothing, a nothing that does not admit of expression.[92]

Here, prayer is both supplication, springing from the presence of God in the heart and answered by God, and *z̲ekr*, recollection, which culminates in the absorption of the recollecting subject in the recollected object, as Joneyd had put it.[93] Mowlānā Rumi knows this secret of constant recollection (although he has never given any fixed rules pertaining to *z̲ekr*):

> And think so intensely of God that you forget yourself, until you be annihilated in the Called One, where there is neither calling nor call —.[94]

He has touched this problem in a passage of *Fihi mā fihi*, which has been taken up by Sepahsālār.[95] Formal prayer, he says, has an end, but the constant prayer of the soul is unlimited, it is

> the drowning and unconsciousness of the soul so that all these forms remain without. At that time there is no room even for Gabriel who is pure spirit.

That is what the Prophet experienced when he stood in the Divine Presence and had 'a time with God' while even the angel of inspiration had to remain outside this most intimate discourse between Creator and creature. Annihilated in the Divine Presence, the praying person partakes of the Divine light. Rumi illustrates this point with an oft-repeated story according to which a certain saint (allegedly his own father) was completely absorbed in prayer and so united with God that those who bore him company were facing the direction of the Kaʿba, whereas those who had performed the ritual prayer without him, were seen turning their backs towards Mecca: God's light, as manifest in the praying master, is 'the soul of the Mecca-ward direction'. If someone would entrust himself and his wishes to such a saint, God would fulfill his request without his uttering a word.[96] And thus writes Rumi in one of his letters:

> The *faqih* knows the form of prayer, its beginning is *takbir*, its end *salām*. The *faqir* knows the . . . soul of ritual prayer. The condition of the soul of prayer is to be forty years in the greatest *jehād*, to make one's eyes and soul blood, to transgress the veil of darkness, to die from one's own existence, to be alive through God's life, to exist through God's existence.[97]

It is not difficult to understand that stories like those which highlight God's praying in man's heart could be interpreted in a pantheistic sense: later admirers of Rumi would find here the idea that there is nothing Existent but God who prays in Himself and through Himself. Yet, Rumi's own statement that faith is even better than prayer, since it is invariable, and is the very root of prayer, should be kept in mind when discussing his thoughts on prayer.[98]

The story which we discussed in the beginning of the chapter has often been echoed in the Muslim world—we know an almost verbal paraphrasing by the Persian poet Shāh Jehāngir Hāshemi who found shelter at the court of the Arghunids in Sind (he was murdered on his way to Mecca in 1539).[99] Other allusions are frequent in both high Persian, and popular Punjabi and Sindhi mystical poetry. In our century, Muhammad Iqbal has once more interpreted Rumi's idea of the dialogue between man and God[100]—a God who longs to be known, loved and worshipped and therefore creates the world and what is in it; a God who teaches man how to address Him, answering the way He considers it necessary for the course and the welfare of the world. But, more important: such prayers which are intimate conversations of the soul and God, cause a change in man's consciousness so that he, finally, conforms to the Eternal Will in loving surrender and experiences that his prayers—even though not answered verbally—have led him to a new level of experience, and thus yielded unexpected fruit for his spiritual life.

IV

Mowlānā Jalāloddin Rumi's Influence in East and West

Whosoever recites the Mathnavi *in the morning and evening,*
For him Hellfire be forbidden!
The spiritual Mathnavi *of Mowlānā*
Is the Koran in Persian tongue . . .

What shall I say in praising this lofty personality?
He is not a prophet, but he has a book!

That is how Mollā Jāmī (d. 1492), the last classical poet of Iran, has praised Mowlānā Jalāloddin. His two statements, that Jalāloddin's *Mathnavi* with its more than 26,000 verses is almost an integral translation of the Koran in Persian, and that Mowlānā has almost the status of a prophet who brought a sacred book for his community, have been repeated time and again by the admirers and followers of Jalāloddin Rumi in every corner of the world.

The admiration shown to Rumi in East and West reached a new culmination point in 1973, the seven-hundredth anniversary of his death. Not only in Konya, where the mystical poet is buried, and in Turkey in general international meetings were held, and learned and popular books published; Iran likewise celebrated the memory of the greatest mystical poet in Persian tongue. Numerous lectures on Rumi and the various aspects of his poetry and teachings were arranged in Pakistan and Afghanistan, but even more in Western countries. Scholars and lovers of Mowlānā gathered around them many admirers during the Rumi-year: the Netherlands and Germany, Great Britain and various universities in the United States participated in memorial meetings, as did orientalists in Italy, Switzerland, and other countries.

At such a moment we may ask ourselves why Rumi had such a deep impact on millions of people, and how his spiritual influence manifested itself through the centuries in East and West. Perhaps we may be able to find an appropriate answer to this question.

Long before Jāmi wrote his lines in the late 15th century, the admiration for Jalāloddin Rumi's work was widespread in the Muslim world. In fact, the first books composed about him in Konya itself show already all the traits of deep veneration and high respect for the master that were later to become commonplace. They virtually form the cornerstone of the whole literary output written about him and his poetico-didactic work in the seven centuries to follow.

Mowlānā's beloved eldest son Solṭān Valad (1226-1312) is not only the organizer of the Mevlevis into a proper order, known in the West as the Whirling Dervishes; he is also his father's first biographer.[1] He was able to record the events of his father's life as he witnessed them himself from his very childhood onward. The coming of Borhānoddin Moḥaqqeq to Konya impressed the six-year-old child,[2] and later, Solṭān Valad was sent to bring back his father's mystical beloved, Shamsoddin, from Syria;[3] it was he who was married to the daughter of Ṣalāḥoddin Zarkub to whom Rumi had turned in mystical love after Shamsoddin's disappearance. Solṭān Valad was a faithful disciple of his father-in-law through whom he was inspired to compose poetry.[4] He was likewise faithful to Ḥosāmoddin Chelebi, accepting him as his father's successor and obeying him in perfect devotion until this youngest friend of Mowlānā passed away and Solṭān Valad, 'orphaned', as he said, took the seat as the head of the Mevlevi order.[5] His poetical narratives are the most faithful interpretation of his father's life and teachings, although at times he tends to use historical data somewhat loosely. But with his unassuming style, and his simple way of explaining some of the most complicated ideas of Mowlānā while retelling his stories, he is an excellent source for the understanding of Jalāloddin's thought. The figure of Solṭān Valad himself would be worth investigating; after the weird and dark personality of his grandfather Bahā'oddin Valad and the radiant beauty and power of Mowlānā himself, this man of the third generation appears somewhat subdued. He was certainly not a creative mind but a faithful interpreter, not a fiery soul but a mirrorholder for those whom he loved and whose beauty his poetry tried to reflect.[6]

Two other authors in the Konya environment wrote memories of Mowlānā, one of them being Faridun Sepahsālār who had served the master for many years and died in 1319 at a great age; his *risāla* contains sober and reliable material. The younger Aflāki (d. 1356), no longer a personal witness of the events, introduces a considerable number of legends and tales into his *Manāqeb al-ʿārefin,* a book which gives the most detailed description of the religious life in Konya during and shortly after Mowlānā's lifetime. It has to be used with a certain amount of caution yet, it is the only early source available to Western readers in (a not very convincing) French translation.

It is small wonder that the Turks were and still are extremely fond of Mowlānā Jalāloddin who took his surname, *Rumi,* from the Romean, e.g. Anatolian, area where he spent most of his life. He was, as is claimed of Turkish origin. In the centuries following his death, during which the Mevlevi order consolidated and spread over the Ottoman Empire, innumerable poets, musicians, and artists were more or less closely affiliated with the order and honoured the master's spirit by their music, poetry, and calligraphy.

In a fine study, Shahābettin Uzluk has shown the role of Mevlevi calligraphers and painters in the history of Turkish art.[7] It is touching to see that even in contemporary Turkey young apprentices of vocational schools in Konya are able to produce new variations of the oft-repeated formula *Ya Hazret-i Mevlâna,* which, written in decorative calligraphy, adorns many houses.

Classical Turkish music is unthinkable without the Mevlevi tradition, and the tunes composed for the meetings of mystical dance (*samāᶜ*) are today as moving as they were centuries ago.[8]

Since the average Turks had little or no knowledge of Persian, a number of Mevlevi scholars took upon themselves the task of commenting upon the *Mathnavi*, or of translating it into Turkish.[9] The two best commentators of Persian literature in the heydays of the Ottoman Empire, Shamᶜi and Soruri, composed a commentary each in the years 1591 and 1592. Only a few years later, Ismāᶜil Rüsuhi Ankarali (d. 1631) wrote a commentary which is still regarded as the soundest introduction to the enormous work, and which was made known in Europe by the good analysis of its contents by the Austrian scholar Joseph von Hammer-Purgstall in 1851.[10]

One century after Ismāᶜil Ankarali Ismāᶜil Haqqi Bursali (d. 1724), a good mystical poet in his own right, produced his introduction called *Ruh-e Mathnavi*.[11] At approximately the same time, Süleyman Nahifi (d. 1738) succeeded in translating the *Mathnavi* into Turkish poetry in the original meter. In our day, many Turkish scholars work in the field of Mowlānā studies; the indefatigable Abdülbaki Gölpınarlı has contributed most valuable studies into the biographical data of Rumi's life and the history of the Mevlevi order; he has also transformed the poetry of the lyrics of the *Divān-e Shams* into modern Turkish and published a revised version of Veled Izbudak's translation of the *Mathnavi*. His two books,

Mevlâna Celâleddin Rumi and *Mevlâna'dan sonra Mevlevilik* certainly deserve translation into a Western language. Most recently, the noted mystical writer Samiha Ayverdi has begun with the publication of her long-awaited commentary.

A small anthology prepared by the former director of the Mevlâna Müzesi in Konya, Mehmet Önder, gives an impressive survey of poetry written during the centuries in honour of Jalāloddin Rumi.[12] The anthology begins with Gülsheni (d. 1534); we find verses by representatives of the most complicated Ottoman baroque style, like Nabi. Abu Bakr Qāniᶜ (d. 1792) belongs to the most unusual members of the Mevlevi order; his work ranges from religious poetry to social satire.[13] Special mention must be made of Ghalib Dede, the head of the Mevlevihane in Galata/Istanbul, who prematurely died in 1799. His involved poetry gives expression to the inward fire that animated the dervishes to spin around their axis. Many of the 19th century poets, like Fazil Enderuni, Kececizade ᶜIzzet Mollā, and Pertev, wrote in honour of Rumi: even more astounding is the great number of modern Turkish literary men who paid tribute to him: the name of Neyzen Tevfik, the flute-player and satirist, is well known to students of modern Turkish; Yahya Kemal (Beyatli), the last representative of classical poetry (d. 1958) has compared himself to the reed-flute which is played during the *samāᶜ*-meetings. The former minister of education in the Inönü era, Hasan-Âli Yücel, is as sincere in his admiration for Rumi as the deeply orthodox Kemal Edip Kürkçüoglu, and as Asaf Halet Çelebi, one of the truly modern lyrical poets of Turkey, whose poem on the *samāᶜ* faithfully interprets the mystical flight experienced by the whirling dervish.[14]

The *Mevlâna Bibliografyasi*, compiled by Mehmet Önder at the occasion of the 700th anniversary of Rumi's death, reflects the Turkish share in scholarly and popular studies very clearly. And if the long list of names of writers were not sufficient to show the love of the Turks for their Mowlānā Jalāloddin, the thousands of visitors who attend the celebration of the anniversary of Rumi's death in Konya every December, and those who come from all parts of Turkey to offer a prayer at his threshold, would prove how deeply this love is rooted in the hearts of the Turks even half a century after Ataturk closed the dervish lodges and strictly prohibited any activity of mystical fraternities.

The Mevlevi order remained restricted to the Ottoman Empire. A few branches were founded in the Arab countries which came under Turkish domination in 1517. However, the stylistic differences of Arabic and Persian are so great that the Arabs never became really interested in Rumi's work but rather remained faithful to their own tradition of mystical poetry. Still, in the early 19th century one of the members of the order, Sheykh Yusuf ibn Ahmad, composed a commentary of the *Mathnavi* in Arabic under the title *Al-minhāj al-qavi li-ṭullāb al-mathnavi*[15]

Recently, the University of Tehran published an Arabic verse translation of the *Mathnavi* under the title *Javāhir al-āthār* by a certain ᶜAbdol ᶜAziz Ṣāheb al-Javāhir. A few famous passages from Rumi's *Mathnavi* and his *Divan* have been rendered into Arabic by ᶜAbdol Vahhāb ᶜAzzām.[16] These few attempts notwithstanding it is impossible to speak of a real 'influence' of Jalāloddin Rumi's poetry on the Arabs or even of a proper knowledge of his name among them. Yet, along with the renewed interest in the Sufi tradition that is visible in the last years in modern Arabic poetry Rumi's name appears in unexpected places: in a tender poem about the complaining reed-flute, dedicated by the Iraqi poet ᶜAbdol Vahhāb al-Bayāti to the memory of the Turkish socialist poet Nāzim Hikmet, Rumi's spirit is all of a sudden present in perfect beauty . . .[17]

Very different is the situation in Iran and the countries east of Iran. It is told that Moṣleḥoddin Saᶜdi of Shiraz (d. 1292) was asked to select the best poem known to him, and he choose one of Rumi's ghazals. Even if this be a nicely invented story we can be sure that many Persians even today would pass a similar judgment.

Iran, like Turkey, can boast of a great number of commentaries on the *Mathnavi*: in the beginning of the 15th century, Kamāloddin Ḥoseyn ibn Ḥasan al-Khwārezmi al-Kobravi (d. ca. 1440) wrote his *Kunūz al-ḥaqāʾiq fī rumūz ad-daqāʾiq*, also called *Javāhir al-asrār u zavāhir al-anvār,* which is only partly preserved.[18] During the same age, Neẓāmoddin Maḥmud Dāᶜi collected his own mystical works which contain, among other poems, seven *mathnavis* in the style of Rumi, for whose *Mathnavi* he wrote scholia.

Jāmi, then, tells that in the 15th century the leader of the early Naqshbandiyya order in Eastern Iran, Moḥammad Pārsā, used to take prognostication from Rumi's *Divān-e Shams,* just as most people would use the *Divān-e Hāfez* for the purpose of telling the future.[19] The Naqshbandiyya, sober as they are, apparently maintained their interest in Rumi's work through the centuries; for Ḥoseyn Vāʿiẓ-e Kāshifi, the fertile didactic writer of Herat (d. 1506) also worked on the *Mathnavi.*[20]

Although during the Safavid and post-Safavid period the study of Sufism was no longer as popular in Iran as it had been formerly, some of the leading philosophers wrote extensive, and very difficult, commentaries on the *Mathnavi* in which they tried to find every possible wisdom; for the latest time, the commentary of Mollā Hādi Sabzavāri (d. 1872) is a typical example of this approach.[21]

In our day, the Persian interest in Mowlānā's work is manifested best in the magnificent edition by Badiʿozzamān Furuzānfar of the *Kolliyāt-e Shams* which comprise more than 3000 ghazals and about 2000 quatrains. Along with Furuzānfar's numerous other works on Rumi, the elucidation of his literary sources, as well as his editions of related books, the ten volumes of the *Kolliyāt* (or *Divān-e kabir)* enable the scholar for the first time to study Rumi's style intensively. The University of Tehran is engaged in two extensive projects of the same character, viz. the preparation of a vocabulary of the *Mathnavi* and an exhaustive commentary of the same work.

Besides, Rumi's work is continuously recited in the various mystical groups, orders and suborders in Iran, like the Khāksār, for whom it forms the centre of their spiritual life. The same growing interest in the work of Mowlānā as a source for the renewal of spiritual life can be witnessed in the book of a Persian born psychologist, Reza Arasteh, called 'Rumi the Persian, Rebirth in Creativity and Love'. As everywhere between Istanbul and Lahore, excerpts from the *Mathnavi*, children's editions, and popular versions are produced. The artistic recitation of Jalāloddin's poetry is as alive in Iran as the interest in his musical heritage.

However, the strongest influence of Rumi's work in the countries east of Suez is visible in the Indo-Pakistan Subcontinent. The Indian names on many old tombstones in

Konya bear witness of the pious pilgrims who spent part of their lives in the spiritual presence of Mowlānā. We may doubt the veracity of stories which tell of connections between the Indian Sufis and Rumi and his immediate successors: the poet Buʿ Ali Qalandar (d. 1324) is related to have visited Mowlānā, and his poetry doubtlessly shows traces of Rumi's influence. Another story tells that Sayyid Ashraf Jehāngir (d. 1404) paid a visit to Solṭān Valad to collect information about his father's life from him. But since Solṭān Valad died in 1312, we can dismiss this story. However, we have to admit that the interest of the Chishtiyya order in Rumi's work developed very early. The first great leader of this order in Delhi, Neẓāmoddin Owliyā (d. 1325) composed a commentary of the *Mathnavi* a small part of which is preserved in the Asiatic Society of Bengal.[22] His disciple and successor, Cherāgh-e Dehlavi, was thoroughly acquainted with Rumi's poetry, as is clear from a remark in his conversations.[23] The *Mathnavi* belongs to the fundamental books in the Chishtiyya tradition. Since this order, contrary to the Naqshbandiyya, is in favour of music and mystical dance, the enthusiastic lyrics of Rumi were congenial to the spiritual atmosphere.

But knowledge of the *Mathnavi* did not remain restricted to Northern India; even a Bengali historian in the late 15th century wrote: 'The holy Brahmin will recite the *Mathnavi*'.[24] At that time Rumi's poetry had become well known in East Bengal, this country being under Muslim rule since the late 13th century. The numerous saints and poets in Bengal sometimes blended the famous Song of the Reed, the first eighteen verses of the *Mathnavi*, with Hindu tales about Lord Krishna playing the flute: the longing tunes of the magic flute could well express love and yearning, whatever the cultural context might be. We may mention at random that commentaries of the *Mathnavi* were also composed in Bengali language, though only in later times. A poetical translation of the first part of the *Mathnavi*, made in 1888 by a certain Qazi Akram Ḥoseyn, has been printed in Calcutta in 1945; I once heard of a prose translation by Maulvi Fazli Karim but am not aware whether it has been published.

Interestingly enough, in the Subcontinent the name of Jalāloddin's mystical beloved and master, Shamsoddin of

Tabriz, is connected with another strong spiritual tradition: in the town of Multan, the tomb of a certain Shams-e Tabriz is a place of visitation for the pious. The simple building, decorated with blue and white tiles with stylized cypresses, belongs, however, to the famous Ismaili missionary Shams-e Tabriz, as W. Ivanow has shown. The legendary Shams has even attained the rank of one of the Panj Piriya, a group of five saints who have long been worshipped in parts of India and particularly in the Indus valley.[25]

Rumi's mystical master Shams has become a well-known figure in Indo-Muslim folk poetry. His name occurs in combinations with that of the great mystical poet Faridoddin ʿAṭṭār (d. 1220): both of them were martyred for their excessive love (although that cannot be proved in ʿAṭṭār's case). More often, Shams is praised in later Sindhi and Punjabi poetry as a martyr of love who, like 'Manṣur al-Ḥallāj' (d. 922) was cruelly killed by the theologians because they considered his ardent love and his claim to be 'the Beloved' dangerous and irritating. Sindhi literature, always confusing Rumi's beloved and the Ismaili missionary, knows several legends about Shams-e Tabriz; but the combination of Ḥallāj, Shams, and Jalāloddin Rumi has even inspired a Persian *taʿziya* (Passion play), called *The Majlis of al-Ḥallāj, Shams and the Mollā-ye Rum*. This interesting piece has been brought to light by the Afghan scholar and diplomat A. R. Farhadi.[26]

Afghanistan, by the way, cherishes the memory of Jalāloddin, here called 'Balkhi' after his birthplace Balkh; the recent poetical description *Az Balkh tā Qunyā* by Khalilollāh Khalili is not the only witness of the emotional appeal of Rumi to modern Afghans. Khalili has also edited some classical texts connected with Jalāloddin.[27] Pashto texts of an earlier period concerning Rumi's work have been recently edited by Professor ʿAbdul Ḥayy Ḥabibi; they show the influence of the *Mathnavi* in the Pashto speaking areas very well. The 700th anniversary of Mowlānā's death was most impressively celebrated by an international symposium, which was widely echoed in the Afghan Press.

In India, the love of Mowlānā Rumi was by now means restricted to the Sufi orders. We may say without exaggeration that the *Mathnavi* was accepted as authoritative throughout medieval India. The emperor Akbar (ruled 1556-1605) loved the *Mathnavi*,[28] and we read that the poet Sheyda at Shāh Jehān's court (ruled 1627-1658) 'quoted in self-defence the authority of Mowlānā Rumi' and was released.[28] The heir apparent of the Mughal Empire, Shāh Jehān's son Dārā Shikoh (d. 1659) copied a *mathnavi* of Solṭān Valad with his own hand. He, who in vain tried to 'unite the two oceans' of Islam and Hinduism by his attempts to promote a deeper understanding of Indian mystical tradition in the Islamic environment, was a great admirer of Rumi, so much so that one of his works consists largely of quotations from Mowlānā's verses.[29] Dārā's younger brother Aurangzeb (ruled 1658-1707), who persecuted and eventually executed him, was likewise fond of Jalāloddin's poetry to such an extent that his theological instructor, Mollā Jivān, composed an interpretation of the *Mathnavi*. One of his courtiers told Dārā Shikoh's mystical leader, Mollā Shāh Badakhshi:

> I have often had the honour of reading before Aurangzeb passages from the *Mathnavi* of Jalāloddin Rumi. The Emperor was often so touched that he shed tears.[30]

Other sources confirm this stern, orthodox ruler's admiration for people who were skilled in reciting the *Mathnavi* in an affecting way. Indo-Pakistani sources contain much information about famous *mathnavi-khwān's* who excelled in the recitation of Rumi's verses. Among them we may mention a certain Sayyid Saᶜdollah Purabi (d. 1726) who wrote a *resāla-ye chehel beyt-e Mathnavi*:[31] just as the pious Muslim selected forty traditions from the Prophet, thus the mystics chose forty verses from the 'Koran in Pahlavi tongue' and commented upon them.

The anthologies of Persian poetry written during the 17th and early 18th centuries supply us with allusions to Rumi and quotations from his work in the lyrical effusions of almost every major and minor poet. When the Kashmiri poet Ṣafyā, who wrote poetical pieces in the meter of Mowlānā's *Mathnavi*, tells us that:

> The *Mathnavi-ye Mowlavi-ye maᶜnavi* grants new life to one who has been dead for a hundred years,[32]

he is perfectly in harmony with many other Indo-Muslim poets who praised the *Mathnavi* as source of inspiration, or imitated it in various ways. The biographical handbooks speak of many poets who 'were possessed of an excessive love for the *Mathnavi*',[33] and the outstanding Persian poet of the 17th century, Ṣāʾeb, wrote quite a number of poems in imitation of Rumi's ghazals.[34] Since it had become fashionable to write *naẓiras*, 'counter-poems', to classical poems, the poets not only tried to imitate and emulate Ḥāfeẓ, Khāqāni and Anvari, but also Mowlānā. The last great representative of the Indian Style, and most admired poet of the 'Tajik' tradition, Bedil (d. 1721) is no exception to this rule; his variation upon Rumi's little ghazal:

> From every piece of my heart you can make a nightingale . . .[35]

is very successful; besides, allusions to the reed-flute, to the fire which it casts into the reedbed, and to other images from Rumi's poetry are found in Bedil's *Divān,* though often in very distorted form. His whole world view, centring around the idea of a constant upward movement of everything created, bears similarities with Rumi's dynamic world view; but these seeming similarities still await scholarly proof.[36]

That Rumi's *Mathnavi* inspired many poems is well known: the refugee from Afghanistan to the court of Sind, Jehāngir Hāshimi (d. 1539) offers a new variation of Rumi's famous story on prayer in his *Mathnavi maẓhar al-āthār.*[37] And when, one-and-a-half centuries later, Aurangzeb's daughter, the accomplished poetess Zeb un-Nisā asked her poet friends to compose a *mathnavi* in the style of Rumi's poetry, this should not be taken as an isolated instance; in fact, there were many such imitations produced around 1700.[38] Again, about a hundred years later, a Hindu writer called Anandagana Khwosh composed a *Mathnavi-ye kajkolāh* in the style of Rumi's *Mathnavi* (1794); it is important to note that he inserted in it the story of Dārā Shikoh's meeting with the Hindu sage Bābā Lāl Das to remind his readers of the attempt at reconciliation of Muslim and Hindu mystical tradition by the unlucky Mughal prince.[39] To glance through A. Sprenger's Catalogue of the manuscripts of the king of Oudh (1854) reveals not only how many copies of the *Mathnavi* were found in the libraries of Indian Muslim kings, but even more the extent to which Rumi's work influenced and was imitated by numerous early 19th century writers in both Persian and Urdu.

It goes without saying that Indian scholars and mystics wrote numerous commentaries of the *Mathnavi*; most of them date from the 17th century, the period of greatest scholarly and poetical activity in the Subcontinent. We could easily enumerate a dozen or more learned commentaries written during this period, besides special glossaries, and anthologies made from Rumi's poetry.[40] The amount of material is probably even larger than is known at present, since a thorough investigation into the catalogues and particularly into the treasures of uncatalogued libraries in India and Pakistan would give even more information about direct or indirect influences of Rumi's work on Indo-Muslim thought. Suffice it to mention that the most famous commentary of the *Mathnavi*, that of ʿAbd al-ʿAli surnamed Baḥr al-ʿolum was composed in Lucknow in the late 18th century; it has been considered by Western scholars the best introduction into Rumi's theology.[41] The useful analytical index known as *mirʾāt al-Mathnavi* and compiled by Telmidh Ḥoseyn, should not be left out in this connection; it gives an excellent survey of the contents of the *Mathnavi*.

Of special interest is the survival of Rumi's poetry in the Indus valley, in Sind, the first part of the Subcontinent that came under Muslim rule (711). The above mentioned poet Jehāngir Hashimi, though of Persian extraction, lived at the court of the Arghun rulers in Thatta, Sind; after him there came a great number of poets who 'kept warm the market of Divine Unity'[42] by reciting the *Mathnavi* in this province. Sind had been noted for the interest of its inhabitants in saint-worship and mystical poetry, and the historians enumerate the names of those who indulged in the recitation of Rumi's work which was regarded as 'the highway for those who attain Divine Reality'.[43] Some of them were able to recite the *Mathnavi* 'with sad voice so beautifully that all the listeners were brought to tears.'[44]

In Sind, as in other parts of Indo-Pakistan, the admiration for the *Mathnavi* was not restricted to a single mystical order. Not only the Chishtiyya but the Qadiriyya and the Naqshbandiyya relied largely upon this book. It is told that one of the 18th century leaders of the Naqshbandiyya in Sind, Moḥammad Zamān-e awwal, gave away his whole library and kept for himself only three books, namely the Koran, the *Mathnavi*, and the *Divān-e Ḥāfeẓ*.[45] This was apparently not unusual. As for Moḥammad Zamān's disciple, ᶜAbdor Raḥim Girhori, martyred when attempting to destroy a Shiva idol in a nearby village, he would quote from the *Mathnavi* in his letters of complaint which he sent to the rulers of his country.[46]

Mowlāna Rumi's influence on mystical poetry in the Indus valley is best revealed in the work of Shāh ᶜAbdul Laṭif of Bhit (d. 1752). His *Risālō* in Sindhi is for everyone who speaks Sindhi, be he Hindu or Muslim, the textbook of his Weltanschauung; verses from this collection of mystical poetry are still stock-in-trade in the country. Even the foreigner has to admit that the *Risālō* belongs to the most touching poetical expressions of Islamic mysticism, and that Shāh Laṭif's way of blending simple Sindhi folktales with highflown mystical speculations is remarkable.

Lilaram Watanmal, one of the first (Hindu) authors to write about the mystical poet of Bhit expressed the opinion that the Koran and the *Mathnavi* were always in the poet's hand, together with some Sindhi mystical poems, and:

> It is related that Nur Moḥammad Kalhora, the then ruler of Sind, from whom Shah Laṭif had become estranged, won back the poet's favour by presenting him with a fine copy of the *Mathnavi*.[47]

Fifty years later, the British civil servant H. T. Sorley, who has devoted a useful book to the Sindhi poet, went so far as to think that Shāh ᶜAbdul Laṭif's poetry is nothing but 'an Indian Muslim development of the philosophy of Jalāloddin Rumi' and 'that it would have been enough for the author of the *Risālō* to be familiar with the *Mathnavi* alone.'[48] Sorley is no doubt right, but he has not proved his theory in detail. This, however, would be easy. Shāh ᶜAbdul Laṭif has inserted into his poetry the famous motif of the blind men and the elephant,[49] and a couple of other allusions to the *Mathnavi*. The most touching instance is that in *Sur Sasui Abri* (I,8):

> Those, in whom is thirst—water is thirsty for them.

This quotation from the *Mathnavi* (I 1741) points to the truth that God and man act together—were not the Source of Love thirsty for man's longing, how could man dare to long for this unfathomable source of Life?

In a long sequence of verses in *Sur Yaman Kalyan* (V lo-15) the Sindhi poet openly acknowledges his indebtedness to

Rumi. Every verse begins with the statement: 'This is Mowlānā Rumi's idea . . .' and then explains theories of unity and plurality, of love and longing.[50]

It is also known that Shāh Laṭif was on very friendly terms with Shāh Ismāᶜil Sufi (d. 1732) who was famous as reciter of the *Mathnavi*.[51]

Among the later poets of Sind, all of whom knew Rumi's work very well, we may mention Bēdil of Rohri (d. 1872) who read the *Mathnavi* with one of the great mystical leaders of Sind, Pir ᶜAli Gowhar Shāh Asghar whose family has played an important role in the history of Sufism in the Indus valley. The historians tell us that Bēdil was comforted during his illness by the recitation of the *Mathnavi*, and his poetry in Sindhi, Siraiki, Urdu and Persian contains numerous allusions to Rumi's verses and to Shams-e Tabriz. He has even composed a strange book called *Mathnavi-ye delkoshā* which consists of a combination of Koranic quotations. Prophetic traditions, verses from the *Mathnavi* and verses from Shāh ᶜAbdul Laṭif's *Risālō*: these four elements were put together to show the way of higher mysticism.[52]

How strong the love for Mowlānā still is among the Sindhis can be understood from the fact that only a few years ago, beginning in 1943, an excellent Sindhi verse translation of the complete *Mathnavi* was written in Hyderabad/Sind; the author of this work, called *Ashraf al-ᶜolum,* was Din Moḥammad Adib, a teacher in Hyderabad (d. 1973).[53]

Similar is the situation in the Punjab. At least two commentaries on the *Mathnavi* in Punjabi have been printed, one of them being in Punjabi verse by Pir Imām Shāh (1911), which comprises, however, only a small part of the 26,000 verses of the original. Another Punjabi verse translation, by Mowlānā Moḥammad Shāhoddin, appeared in Lahore in 1939.[54]

As to Pashto I know of a poetical version of the *Mathnavi* which is being prepared by Mowlvi ᶜAbdul Jabbār Bangash from Kohat, and by Abdul Akhar Khan 'Akbar' of Peshawar. In the poetry of the Pathans we find as many allusions to Rumi's work as in the other languages of Muslim India and Pakistan or Turkey.[55]

The regional languages of the Subcontinent contain a large amount of material taken from the *Mathnavi*. It would be surprising if the literary language proper of the Indian Muslims, viz. Urdu, would not contain allusions to or translations from the work of Rumi.[56] How widely Mowlānā's work was read is illustrated by the fact that even the satirist Saudā (d. 1792), one of the 'four pillars of Urdu' in the 18th century, composed a very little *mathnavi* on a verse of Rumi about all-embracing unity.[57] That the great mystical poet of Delhi, Mir Dard (d. 1785). following his father Nāṣir Moḥammad ʿAndalib's example, quotes profusely from Rumi goes without saying. Even in the poetry of the last great master of Urdu and Indo-Persian poetry, Mirzā Ghālib (d. 1869) some images can be traced back to Rumi through the long chain of poets like Dard, Bedil, and ʿUrfi. Urdu translations of the *Mathnavi* are of course available. Munshi Mostaʿān ʿAli's poetical version, *Bāgh-e Iram,* was completed in 1826 and has been printed several times. The most recent, and probably most successful, Urdu verse translation, which like every good version in the Islamic languages preserves the original meter, is the *Pirāhan-e Yusofi* by Moḥammad Yusof ʿAli Shāh Chishti, lithographed in 1943. Its name 'Joseph's Shirt' (besides alluding to the author's proper name) invokes the image of the healing quality of Joseph's garment which, being part of him, conveyed sight to his blind father: should not the translation of the *Mathnavi* brighten the reader's eyes, filling them with spiritual insight?

The Indian Muslims also showed interest in Rumi's prose work *Fihi mā fihi:* ʿAbdur Rashid Tabassum translated this book into Urdu in our century, after ʿAbdol Majid Daryābādi had undertaken the task of editing it for the first time in 1922. He received inspiration for this work from the poet-philosopher Sir Muhammad Iqbal, the 'spiritual father of Pakistan'.

Iqbal himself is no doubt the most fascinating example of Rumi's influence on a contemporary Muslim poet and thinker.

Most commentaries in the Islamic languages interpreted Rumi's *Mathnavi* as a perfect expression of pantheistic mysticism, for the post 13th century writers had been largely under the influence of Ibn ʿArabi's (d. 1240) theosophy in which the philosophy of Unity of Being is brought to its final conclusions. The interpretations of Rumi's thoughts in the West generally followed their example. It is therefore natural

Photograph by Jeffrey Somers

The Ceremony of the Mevlevi (Whirling Dervishes).

than an Indian Muslim like Muhammad Iqbal (1877–1938) wrote in his doctoral thesis submitted to Munich University in 1907:

> All feeling of separation . . . is ignorance, and all 'otherness' is a mere appearance, a dream, a shadow, a differentiation, born of relation essential to the self-recognition of the Absolute.
>
> The great prophet of the school is 'the excellent Rumi', as Hegel calls him. He took up the old Neo-Platonic idea of the Universal Soul working through the various spheres of being, and expressed it in a way so modern in spirit that Clodd introduces the passage in his 'Story of Creation'.[58]

The verse which Iqbal quotes as proof for this theory:

> First man appeared in the class of unorganic things . . .

was to become later in his work the proof for the rising gamut of ego-hood which at present culminates in man and eventually leads to the Superman, the *insān-e Kāmel* (Perfect Man) of Muslim mysticism. The change in outlook which becomes visible in Iqbal's work after his return to Lahore in 1908 was probably caused by a small book, *Savāneḥ-e Mowlānā Rum*, a biography of Rumi by the great Indian orientalist Mowlānā Shibli Nuʿmani (d. 1914).[59] Shibli closes his booklet with a comparison of some of Rumi's ideas with modern theories of evolution and points out similarities with Darwin, quoting the passage:

> I died as mineral and became a plant . . .,

a passage which was central for modern pseudo-scientific interpretation of Rumi's thought (see Chapter III, 5).

After 1911, Mowlānā Rumi revealed himself to Iqbal no longer as an exponent of all-embracing pantheism but rather as the advocate of spiritual development, of the love-relation between man and a personal God, or of the infinite quest for God. These ideas can easily be detected in the *Mathnavi*, but even more in Rumi's lyrics, which Iqbal probably studied first in R. A. Nicholson's fine selection, published in 1898.

Iqbal's new orientation became visible in his first Persian *mathnavi*, called *Asrār-e Khudi* 'Secrets of the Self' (1915) where he relates 'How Jalāloddīn Rumi appeared in a vision and bade him arise and sing' (Chapter XI; the veracity of this experience has been confirmed by members of his family).

And, as R. A. Nicholson writes in his translation of the *Asrār*:

> As much as Iqbal dislikes the type of Sufism exhibited by Hafiz, he pays homage to the pure and profound genius of Jalaloddin though he rejects the doctrine of self-abandonment taught by the great Persian mystic and does not accompany him in his pantheistic flights.[60]

The connection established in the *Asrār-e Khudi*—Rumi as Iqbal's *pir*, his mystical guide—lasted till the very end of the poet's life. All his Persian *mathnavis* are composed in the easy flowing meter of Rumi's *Mathnavi*, which enables him to insert verses by Rumi into his own poetry without difficulty. The Koran and the *Mathnavi* were for Iqbal as for many mystical poets of Muslim India the two basic books for man's spiritual education; he therefore advised young scholars to read and re-read the *Mathnavi* and take inspiration from it.[61]

In the *Asrār-e Khudi*, Mowlānā Rumi appears not only as the poet's spiritual guide; in Chapter XVI his legendary first meeting with Shams-e Tabrizi is described, that will stand for the moment of inspiration through love. Rumi becomes Iqbal's Khiżr, the guiding genius of the mystical traveller, who is aware of the fountain of life toward which he leads his disciple. The same idea of Rumi being the *Khiżr-e rāh* is taken up once more in a dialogue in *Bāl-e Jibrīl*,[62] Urdu poetry published fifteen years after Iqbal's first great poem by this name in his first collection of Urdu verses, *Bāng-e Darā* (1922). In both instances Iqbal puts his difficulties before his master who solves them with aptly chosen verses from the *Mathnavi*.

> The Pir Rumi, the guide with shining heart,
> The leader of the caravan of love and intoxication,
> Whose place is higher than moon and sun,
> And who makes the Milky Way the rope of his tent . . . .[63]

Rumi, praised with these words in the introduction of the Persian collection *Pas che bāyad kard* (1932) is 'the lamp of the free man's way',[64] the master who discloses the secret of life and death,[65] since the light of the Koran is shining in the midst of his breast.[66] Rumi becomes, for Iqbal, the guide through the otherworld, and leads him in his mystical flight through the spheres as it is described in glowing colours in the *Javidnāma* (1932).[67]

Allusions to Rumi's verses are frequent in Iqbal's poetry:

The beauty of love gains from his reed
A share from the Majesty of Divine Grandeur . . .[68]

That is how the modern poet applied the symbol of the reed, whose voice is heard in the introductory verses of the *Mathnavi*. It is interesting to observe that Iqbal alludes here to the concept of *kibriyā*, Divine Grandeur, which is in fact one of the central words in Rumi's thought: this little instance shows the depth of Iqbal's intuitive understanding of his master's thought. The reed itself becomes a symbol for creativity through longing: separation from the reedbed enables the reed-flute to sing and to express its yearning. It stands for Adam who, far away from Paradise and its peace, began to work and to invent arts and crafts, since only separation makes man creative and inventive.

Rumi's famous poem with the rhyme-word *-m arzust*, 'is my wish' serves him as a kind of magical incantation, for it speaks of the longing for the man of God, the perfected saint, as he revealed himself to Iqbal under the form of Mowlānā.[69]

Rumi, the teacher of love and longing, became for Iqbal the counter-weight against the forces of cold reason and dry philosophy. His name and that of Avicenna, the philosopher, become mere ciphers for the contrast of heart and brain: he is the master of loving meditation which flies immediately into the Divine Presence while philosophy lags behind on dusty roads.[70] The only spiritual guide comparable to Rumi is in Iqbal's view, the German poet Goethe; he therefore invents a scene in Paradise where these two masters meet. Both of them are not prophets but have a book: Mowlānā the *Mathnavi*, Goethe the *Faust*, and both acknowledge the superiority of love, Adam's share, over satanic intellect.[71]

Iqbal knew that:

No other Rumi will rise from the tulip gardens of Iran,[72]

and therefore he took charge from his spiritual guide after having learnt the subtleties of love from him. He has burnt himself in his letters,[73] and now aims at opening again 'the tavern of Rumi',[74] since the Muslim community had forgotten the spiritual wine of Divine Love. For:

From the intoxicated eye of Rumi did I borrow
Joy from the rank of Divine Grandeur.[75]

That is how Iqbal transforms ᶜErāqi's famous line about the first wine that was borrowed from the intoxicated eyes of the eternal cupbearer.

Iqbal's admirers like to call him 'the Rumi of our age'; but such a comparison can only be made with a grain of salt.[76] For Iqbal lacks the strong, overwhelming experience of love which transformed Jalāloddin into a poet; he is, as he himself acknowledges, not as comprehensive as his mystical guide, and his verses can be interpreted in only one sense; they do not convey, as Rumi's poetry, an opalizing picture, filled with flames of different hues. Iqbal has, like a prism, singled out only rays of a certain wave-length from Rumi's poetry, concentrating them like a burning glass to kindle with them the heart of his compatriots.

Inspired by Iqbal's ideas, a number of Pakistani scholars have taken to interpreting Rumi's thoughts afresh. The only major English biography of Mowlānā was produced by a Pakistani diplomat, Afzal Iqbal. Among the productions of numerous scholars and admirers who, more or less successfully, composed a large amount of books and articles on Rumi, Rumi and Iqbal, Iqbal and Rumi . . . the studies of Khalifa Abdul Hakim, both in English and Urdu, deserve special mention.

However, the ingenious interpretation of Rumi by Iqbal remains unsurpassed. Not inappropriately Iqbal's Turkish admirers have honoured his memory by erecting a small but worthy memorial for him in the garden of Mowlānā's shrine, the Mevlâna Müzesi, in Konya, in order to testify the close spiritual union between the two poets who were so deeply animated by Divine Love. And a small alabaster vessel with dust from Konya stands on Iqbal's tomb in Lahore.

Rumi's influence did not remain restricted to the area of Islamic civilization. His work attracted the interest of European scholars at a rather early stage of Oriental studies.

Naturally enough, it was the external aspect of the Mevlevis, the whirling dance, that first impressed casual visitors to the Ottoman Empire, who did not fail to describe it in their itineraries. However, it took long, and will perhaps still take a while, for the Western spectator to realize that the whirling movement of the Mevlevis is not an irregular, ecstatic movement, but a harmonious art in which every step is prescribed according to a fixed ritual. There is nothing of the frenzied movement which is so often connected, particularly in German, with the expression *Tanzender Derwisch*. It is, however, fair to add here that the experience of the Whirling Dervishes has induced a few English writers to express their ideas of mystical flight by using the symbol of the mystic who, spinning around his axis, joins the cosmic dance.[77]

European diplomats were the first to attempt a deeper understanding of Rumi's work. A young Frenchman, J. de Wallenbourg (d. 1806) worked during his six years' residence in Istanbul on a French translation of the *Mathnavi*; his work was, unfortunately, completely destroyed during the great fire in Pera in 1799. He was followed in his attempts at making Mowlānā known in the West by the indefatigable Austrian diplomat and orientalist Joseph von Hammer-Purgstall (1774–1856) who first encouraged V. von Hussard (1788–1850) to translate selected passages from the *Mathnavi* for the journal *Fundgruben des Orients*, the first scholarly orientalist journal in German language.[78] Hammer-Purgstall himself was a great admirer of Mowlānā, and in his *Geschichte der schönen Redekünste Persiens*, the first comprehensive history of Persian literature, he deals at length with Rumi (p. 163 ff.) whose *Mathnavi* 'is the handbook of all Sufis from the borders of the Ganges up to the borders of the Bosphorus.'—Hammer was also the first to recognize the supreme importance of the *Divān-e Shams* of which he writes in highflown sentences that match Rumi's style at his most grandiose:

> Auf den Flügeln der höchsten religiösen Begeisterung, welche hoch erhaben über alle äusseren Formen positiver Religionen, das ewige Wesen in der vollkommensten Abgezogenheit von allem Sinnlichen und Irdischen als den reinsten Quell ewigen Lichtes anbetet, schwingt sich Mowlana nicht wie andere lyrische Dichter und selbst Hafiz, bloss über Sonnen und Monden, sondern über Zeit und Raum, über die Schöpfung und das Los, über den Urvertrag der Vorherbestimmung und über den Spruch des Weltengerichts in die Unendlichkeit hinaus, wo er mit dem ewigen Wesen als ewig Anbetender, und mit der unendlichen Liebe als unendlich Liebender in Eines verschmilzt . . .

The translations which Hammer offered, in the same book, from both the *Divān-e Shams* and the *Mathnavi*, are like his previous translations from Ḥāfeẓ without higher poetical merit; yet, they give a first impression of the rich symbolism, the glowing intensity of Mowlānā's lyrics. He has also published a few pieces from what he calls *Das Brevier der Derwische*, small poems sung during the *samā*ʿ-sessions.

Although Hammer's translation of the *Divān-e Ḥāfeẓ* had inspired Goethe to compose his *West-Östlicher Divan*, the specimens from Rumi's poetry offered by him did not attract Goethe at all. On the contrary, his judgment about the great mystical poet as noted in his *Noten und Abhandlungen* is rather critical. What disturbed him was the apparently pantheistic trend that made him think that Mowlānā had turned too much to strange and abstruse theories as a consequence of the confused situation in Near Eastern politics during the 13th century (an idea nowadays common among the orientalists of the Eastern Bloc). He then goes on to say:

> He has dealt with little stories, fairy-tales, legends, anecdotes, examples, problems in order to make understandable a mysterious doctrine of which he himself does not properly know what it is.

This judgment is certainly far off the mark.

A similar picture of Rumi as pantheist is, however, more or less explicitely visible in other publications which appeared at approximately the same time from the pens of Western orientalists: the British scholar Graham dwelt upon one ghazal ascribed to Rumi[79] which was considered for a long time one of his central poetic expressions:

> What shall I do, O ye Muslims, for I do not know myself anymore;
> I am neither Christian, nor Jew, nor Zoroastrian, nor Muslim . . .

This poem, which shows the mystic beyond time and space, beyond the created borders between races and religions, has often been repeated in the West; however it is not found in the critical edition of the *Kolliyāt-e Shams*, and resembles in its whole tenor rather the effusions of slightly later poets in the Persian and Turkish speaking areas, who would repeat similar ideas time and again.

Two years after Graham's publication, the German Protestant minister F. A. D. Thorluck published his short introduction to Islamic mysticism, called with a sonorous latin title *Ssufismus sive theosophia persarum pantheistica* (1821), which contains several quotations from the *Mathnavi*.

Tholuck's aversion to anything that looked like pantheistic mysticism is known, and Mowlānā became his crown witness for a 'mystical' interpretation of Islam. He quotes him as defender of the theory that *hic mundus carcer est animarum nostrarum*, 'This world is the prison for our souls', that means, for the old orphic tradition of *soma sema*. This, again, can be accepted only with a grain of salt; for as much as Rumi has talked about the soul in exile, his whole approach to the world of matter is much more complex than the few examples known to Tholuck can explain: matter is not evil in itself but is rather something which has to be made lucid and transparent by the power of love so that the divine light can shine through it.

Tholuck's *Blüthensammlung aus der morgenländischen Mystik*, an anthology of Sufi wisdom published in 1825, offers likewise a few translations from Rumi. But in the meantime a booklet had appeared which was to really introduce Mowlānā the poet in the German speaking world. It is the *Ghaselen* by Friedrich Rückert (1788-1866). In this small collection, Rückert, both gifted poet and learned orientalist, translated fortyfour ghazals of the mystical poet in the most congenial way and also introduced the Persian poetical form of the ghazal into German literature where it soon became an accepted lyrical form. In verses of unforgettable beauty Rückert speaks about love, longing, and unity, using Mowlānā's vocabulary, rhythmical structure, and imagery with such astonishing elegance that his work still provides the best introduction into Rumi's poetical genius. The fortyfour ghazals which reflect almost every mode of thought culminate in the grand hymn of Unity:

> Ich bin das Sonnenstäubchen, ich bin der Sonnenball,
> Zum Stäubchen sag ich 'Bleibe!' und zu der Sonn: 'Entwall!'[80]

A second collection of ghazals in the style of Rumi was published by Rückert in 1836. The German readers did not know what to make of these poems, asking themselves whether or not they were translations. A noted orientalist like Graf Schack considered them to be completely original German poetry; other critics agreed with him. Others regarded Rückert's verses as a perfect reflection of Mowlānā's spirit. A careful study reveals that Rückert, though able to understand the original Persian very well, has largely relied upon his teacher's, Hammer's translations in the *Geschichte der schönen Redekünste*. He transformed them into veritable poems, sometimes even preserving the first line, or the meter, of Hammer's version. Now and then he developed a single verse into a full poem. He rendered the raw material into poetry of such beauty that more than eighty years later, in 1903, a Scottish theologian, W. Hastie of Glasgow, produced an English translation of the *Ghaselen* in ghazal-form. Interestingly enough, Hastie saw in the 'Festival of Spring', as he called his adaptations, a powerful antidote against the lewdness and irreligious attitude of Omar Khayyam and his western admirers . . .

Hammer-Purgstall himself never ceased to be fascinated by Rumi. We owe him the first thorough review of the contents of the *Mathnavi* when it was published in Istanbul with the Commentary of Ismāᶜil Rüsuhi Ankaravi; his analysis of the main trends of this great poem is absolutely correct and conveys more of Rumi's spirit than many later, and certainly more scholarly articles and books, a few timebound judgments notwithstanding.[81] The Austrian orientalist even undertook to write a *mathnavi* himself; this book—not yet published—consists of seven long chapters in which the whole symbolism of Islam is poetically elaborated and in which Rumi plays a central role; sentences from the *Mathnavi* occur verbatim in this interesting imitation of Rumi.[82] Rückert later added a few anecdotes and translations of some passages from the *Mathnavi* to his poetical transformations of Rumi's ghazals. But it was the *Ghaselen* that deeply influenced the German reading public. Through these verses Hegel became acquainted with 'the excellent Rumi' who seemed to constitute for him a perfect model of pantheistic thought. The question, how far Hegel's dialectics can be compared with, or even derived from Rumi's ideas has been posed lately by scholars of the Eastern Bloc countries.[83] What ever the answer may be, Rumi remains since Hegel a favourite with European philosophers, historians of religion and historians of literature, although most of those scholars rely exclusively upon Rückert or, in our day, upon the selections made by R. A. Nicholson. The impact of his famous story concerning the prayer of grace, first discovered by Tholuck, upon European historians of religion (from Söderblom to Friedrich Heiler and their disciples) is discussed in Chapter III 7.

In the German speaking world, V. von Rosenzweig-Schwannau, an Austrian orientalist from the school of Hammer, published a selection from Rumi's poetry in 1838 (*Auswahl aus den Divanen Dschelaladdin Rumis*) which, despite its merits, is not comparable to Rückert's more poetical adaptation. In 1849, the German diplomat, Georg Rosen, offered the public a German verse translation of the first part of the *Mathnavi*, which was heavily attacked by Hammer-Purgstall. Since Rosen's book was printed only in a very limited edition, it never became popular; a new edition published by his son, Friedrich Rosen, with a learned introduction in 1913, was soon out of print.

In the meantime, scholars all over the Western world had become interested in Mowlānā Rumi's work. Hermann Ethé has praised him in *Grundriss der iranischen Philologie* (1898 1902) as 'the greatest mystical poet of the East and at the same time the greatest pantheistic poet all over the world'.[84] As much as one will applaud the first half of the sentence, the latter statement, though commonly accepted at the turn of the century, is barely acceptable today. Parts of the *Mathnavi* were made available to a large audience by the British scholars Sir James Redhouse (1881) and H. Whinfield (1887) who conveyed in their respective introductions much useful material about Mowlānā's life and work.

They were followed by R. A. Nicholson who began his scholarly career with the *Selected Poems from the Dīvān-i Shams-i Tabrīz*, published in 1898. This book is still one of the most useful and, at the same time, most delightful introductions into the peculiarities of Rumi's poetry and will remain one of the best books on Islamic mystical poetry, even though some of Nicholson's views are outdated. The learned author never turned away from Rumi, for all his scholarly work on other Arabic and Persian mystics and poets; his *magnum opus* is the edition and translation of the *Mathnavi* with his extensive commentary. This commentary is a veritable gold mine the depth of which the specialist appreciates more the longer he studies it.

With this edition, European orientalists have paid the highest possible tribute to Mowlānā Rumi's spiritual greatness, and have laid the foundations for further research into the details and subtleties of the immense ocean of the *Mathnavi*. Both R. A. Nicholson and his successor A. J. Arberry have publicized Rumi's poetry in numerous books; Arberry has also translated Mowlānā's prose work *Fihi mā fihi*, 'Discourses of Rumi', a most useful addition to the poetical works. That a number of second- and third-class scholars and devotees wrote and still write books on Mowlānā goes without saying; he seemed to offer no difficulties if read in the smooth translations available in English and German, and could be interpreted easily according to everyone's taste and understanding.

France and Italy did not lack in interest in Rumi's work. The French orientalist C. Huart was the first to translate Aflāki's *Manāqeb al-ʿārefin* into his mother tongue as *Les Saints des Dervishes Tourneurs* (Paris 1918 22), and though his translation is not too reliable it still serves its purpose. L. Massignon, in the course of his work on the martyr-mystic al-Ḥallāj (d. 922) used Rumi's poetry extensively. A biography of the great master was produced recently by Eva Meyerovitch who, however, stresses primarily the philosophical implications of Rumi's work. She has lately also translated Rumi's *Fihi mā fihi* as: *Le Livre du Dedans*.

In Italy, it is particularly Alessandro Bausani who has studied several aspects of Mowlānā's work; he, too, is mainly interested in the religio-philosophical contents of the *Mathnavi*, as he has proved in some thought provoking articles.

Translations of single poems by Mowlānā are nowadays available in almost every European language; full or abridged translations of the *Mathnavi* are found even in Swedish[85] and Dutch.[86] The first Czech versions of some ghazals were published as early as 1895,[87] and Rumi's poetry has inspired the modern Polish composer I. Szymanovski to his symphonic composition 'Song of the Night' where he used the translation by Micinski, which relies, in turn, on a German verse-rendering of one of Rumi's poems. Remarkable is the good Russian biography of Rumi by Radij Fish, which appeared in Moscow in 1972.

In Germany, the interest kindled by Rückert and Hammer continues up to our day. Hellmut Ritter's exhaustive review of Nicholson's edition of the *Mathnavi* is a major contribution to our understanding of the poem; the same author's weighty articles about the mystical dance of the Whirling Dervishes (first in 1933, then in 1965 after witnessing the celebrations in Konya) are as important for our knowledge of the technical side of Rumi's teachings as are Ritter's articles about manuscripts dealing with Mowlānā and his followers, and as his analyses of the first eighteen verses of the *Mathnavi* (1932), not to mention his numerous smaller contributions to the topic. Furthermore, a true understanding of Rumi's imagery is impossible without consulting Ritter's study on ʿAṭṭār, *Das Meer der Seele* (1955) which is a veritable ocean of knowledge. Ritter also translated a study by the Russian scholar E. E. Berthels about the development of the mystico-didactic *mathnavi* from Sanāʾi to Rumi (*Grundlinien der Entwicklungsgeschichte des sufischen Lehrgedichtes*).

The interest in the mystical dance which Ritter has expressed in his two articles was further deepened by the short but penetrating study of the Swiss scholar, Fritz Meier, about *Der Derwischtanz* (1954), and by the fine study by the Polish-French iranologist Marijan Molé in his articles in the volume of *Sources Orientales* devoted to the religious dance, *La Dance Sacrée*, (1963).

In German, Rumi's name came to stand for everything ecstatic and love-enraptured. Some of his verses were included, though in rather unsatisfactory translations, in Martin Buber's famous anthology *Extatische Konfessionen* (1909), and Otto Weinreich, the historian of classic religions, begins his review of this book by quoting Rumi's story about the lover who would no longer say 'I', a story that has always attracted the interest of historians of religions.[83]

Another aspect of Rumi which was touched less frequently by the orientalists was underscored by the Jewish philosopher, Constantin Brunner (d. 1934), in his doctrine of the genius as leader of mankind: Rumi is the ideal leader of those in need of a spiritual guide who is completely annihilated in God so that his words are inspired by God. Brunner, with his deep conviction of the necessity of a spiritual leader for the development of man, found in Sufism, and particularly in Mowlānā, what he needed: it is the genius, the instrument of Divine spirit and love, by whose activities the masses are kept alive. Rumi would call these geniuses 'saints', and their most perfect embodiment the *Pir*; but the idea underlying the different names is exactly the same, and highlights a decisive aspect of Rumi's teaching: no real life is possible without the mediation of the few elect, the veritable 'men of God' who alone are the interpreters of Divine Love. Brunner's sentence:

> Art shows how it loves, philosophy shows what it loves, mysticism knows only *that* it loves,

is strongly reminiscent of Rumi's sayings.[89]

As to the orientalists, they took up the task of explaining some of Rumi's stylistic and poetical expressions: H. H. Schaeder's article on the Perfect Man in Islamic Thought (1925) provides a deep interpretation of Rumi's lovely poem on the cup-bearer (see p. 151); Gustav Richter has given a first explanation of Rumi's style (*Stildeutung*) in three lectures (1932), a useful book which has been, unfortunately, out of print for a long time. The present writer submitted a first study into Rumi's imagery in 1949. This topic becomes indeed the more fascinating with continued study since there is no hope of exhausting the fabulous store of similes and images in Rumi's work.

Following Rückert, German poets never lost interest in Mowlānā's verses. W. von der Porten's rather free adaptations from Rumi were quite positively reviewed by an eminent scholar like Jan Rypka.[90] Ernst Bertram included some of Rumi's verses in his booklet *Persische Spruchgedichte* and has 'germanized' the dark harmonies of some of Rumi's verses better than he did with the lighter mood of other Persian-writing poets. Very interesting are the ghazals by Hanns Meinke (d. 1974) which convey something of the ecstatic flights of Rumi and, though relying upon earlier German versions, are faithful to Rumi's spirit in their frenzied love and absolute surrender; the poet never had them printed completely but gave them in beautifully illuminated and hand-written copies to his friends, a true spiritual alms. The present writer has also published, in 1948, a collection of ghazals and quatrains in the spirit of Rumi (*Lied der Rohrflöte*). Lately, J. Christoph Bürgel has manifested his deep interest in Mowlānā's work by his anthology *Licht und Reigen* (Bern 1974), German verse translations of a number of ghazals with a most welcome commentary, and has devoted some learned articles to the poetical art of Rumi, dwelling upon the poet's use of sound structures and word-plays.

We meet Mowlānā's name in histories of literature and studies on religion, and find it in the most unexpected places, thus in the book by Francis Brabazon, *Stay with God*, written in the interpretation of Meher Baba's mystical movement, and published in Australia:[91] Mowlānā, and the tragic death of his beloved master Shams play a prominent role among the mystics which the author quotes, and although the stories are rather distorted, the enthusiasm of love is still reflected in the long winding sentences of this modern mystical epic. And this feeling of the 'starkness of Rumi's love for Shams which overpowered the normal sense of intellectual detachment' (as one of my undergraduate students prefaced his term paper) is perhaps the aspect of Rumi that appeals most to the modern reader even through the veil of more or less successful translations. He may feel, as I was told recently, in the relation of Rumi and Shams of Tabriz something comparable to the grandeur of the friendship of the mythological heroes, Gilgamesh and Enkidu.

These are only a few aspects of his thought and his influence, and we do not claim to have covered all possible implications of his verses. Did not Rumi himself, in one of his lighter moods say in a charming quatrain in which he plays on the double-entendre of the word *beyt* which means both 'verse' and 'house':

> I spoke out a verse *(beyt)*; my Beloved became angry with me.
> He said; 'With the meter (or: weight, *vazn*) of the verse (or:
> the house) has he weighed me!'
> I said; 'Why do you destroy my verse/house?'
> He said: 'In which verse/house could I find room?'[92]

Indeed, in which verse, in which house, and in which book could Mowlānā Jalāloddin find room?

Perhaps only in the hearts of those who love him . . . .

Notes

My first intention was to document every concept and expression in full with all available verses; but I discovered that such an 'index of imagery' would constitute a book in itself. Therefore, only in cases which seem particularly important to me, full—or almost full,—documentation is given. I have likewise refrained from tracing back the symbols and images to previous poets; I hope to publish a detailed study of Persian poetical imagery soon.

Abbreviations:

AF	Aflāki, *Manāqeb al-ʿārefin*
AM	Furuzānfar, *Aḥādith-e Mathnavi*
D	*Divān-e kabir*, ed. *Furuzānfar.*
DT	the tarjiʿbands in D
DST	Selected poems from the *Divān-i Shams-i Tabriz*, ed. R. A. Nicholson
F	*Fihi mā fihi* in the translation of A. J. Arberry, Discourses of Rumi
M	*Mathnavi*, edition of R. A Nicholson
MC	Commentary by Nicholson
(N)	translated by Nicholson
R	*Robāʿiyyāt*, in the eighth volume of D
RE	*Robāʿiyyāt*, ms. Esad Efendi, Nr. 2693 (sometimes different from R).
S	Sepahsālār, *Risāla*, ed. Furuzānfar
VN	Soltān Valad, *Valadnāme*, ed. J. Homāʿi

THE OUTWARD SETTING

BIOGRAPHICAL NOTES

1. S 113; D 972/10285 10302.
2. D 656/6841, 6848.
3. F 181.
4. S 162. On the other hand, Bahā'oddin's praises of female beauty as expressed several times in his *Ma'āref* are quite remarkable.
5. D 2529/26819; cf. another allusion D 2282/24250; and D 3073/32743: 'The word is an arrow, and the tongue is the bow of the Khwarezmians'.
6. A. Gölpinarli, Mevlâna Celâleddin Rumi, Istanbul 1952, p. 54.
7. S 11; cf. VN 187 f.:

   'Like him there was noone in *fatvā*; he had surpassed the angels in piety . . . .

   What would Fakhr-e Rāzi and a hundred Avicenna say before that seeing one?

   All would come like children new in school every day into his service . . .'

From *Ma'āref* (ed. B. Z. Furuzanfar, Tehran 1338 sh.) p. 142, cf. 156 and 109 it is understood that Bahā'oddin had at least one more son (Hoseyn) besides Jalāloddin. AF I 16 mentions a certain 'Alā'oddin who was two years senior to Jalāloddin; the theologian seems to be slightly younger then generally accepted; for during the time he wrote the last part of the *Ma'āref*, his mother, an angry old lady, was still alive (id. p. 144). That the theologian was afflicted by *sels* (explained as an illness of the urinal tract; otherwise diabetes) is understood from id p. 4, 31, 49, 53, 90.

8. M V 4144
9. S 13; cf. VN 190 ascribes the Mongol invasion to God's wrath against the Balkhians who had hurt Bahā'oddin's feelings.
10. D 2784/29599.
11. For Kamāloddin Ibn al-'Adim (1193 1262) cf. GAL I 332, S I 568.
12. M VI 777
13. cf. H. Ritter, Maulānā Gelāladdīn Rūmī und sein Kreis, Philologika XI, in: Der Islam 26/1942. The fact that Ṣolṭān Valad bore his grandfather's name indicates that he was indeed the firstborn. Cf. VN 218:

    'Do not people call their son Moḥammad out of love for Aḥmad. Thus my father, out of love for his father, made me a namesake of that leading king'.

    and id. p. 3:

    'He gave me a special rank among my brothers and the disciples by the crown "you are closest to me of all people both in nature and character".'
14. The best introduction into the political history of this period is: Osman Turan, Selcuklular zamanīnda Türkiye, Istanbul 1971; further Speros Vryonis Jr., The Decline of Medieval Hellenism in Asia Minor and the process of Islamisation from the Eleventh to Fifteenth Century, Berkeley 1971.
15. VN 179 f. dramatically describes the arrival of Borhānoddin.

    'Even to a six years old child it became clear that the like of him never came to Anatolia'.

    Solṭān Valad was indeed six years old when the master, 'unique in love and '*elm-e ladonni*' arrived. – It would be worth while to study the exact influence of the *Ma'āref* on the formation of Rumi's thought as it was first attempted in an unpublished Ph.D. thesis by Maḥbūb Sirāj in Ankara University in the mid

1950s. Rumi takes stories from this book, like the one of the lover who fell asleep, and the beloved put some nuts into his pocket: *Maʿāref* p. 169 = M VI 594. Similar instances could be multiplied.—A few translations from Bahāʾoddin Valad's rather weird book, in which some extremely interesting visionary recitals are found, have been published by A. J. Arberry in Aspects of Islamic Civilization, University of Michigan Press 1967.

16. S 25. This is not corroborated by VN.
17. Gölpinarli, Mevlâna p. 65.
18. S 122.
19. AF I 68.
20. D 1921/20224.
21. S 172; cf. VN 237, further id. p. 355 with a poetical elaboration in the ensuing verses p. 356.
22. Gölpinarli, Mevlâna p. 6 ff.
23. D 1764/18491.
24. D 2187/23211; cf. D. 452/4784.
25. D 2670/28317.
26. D 2669/28310. For Shamsoddin cf. the whole fourth part of AF.
27. S 128.
28. Gölpinarli, Mevlâna p. 48.
29. AF II 616; cf. Jāmi, Nafaḥāt al-ons, ed. M. Tawhidipur, Teheran 1336 sh., p. 590.
30. Gölpinarli, Mevlâna, p. 50.
31. id. p. 52.
32. id. p. 49.
33. id. p. 58.
34. S 122; VN 197 and 287 f. about Shams as *maʿshuq* and the ranks of the lovers and the beloved.
35. S 126. About the reaction of the disciples cf. VN 43 f. who compares their attitude to that of the infidels at the Prophet's time. He gives the first period of Shams's stay as one year, id. 42.
36. D 227/2561.
37. D 2524/26754.
38. D 2572/27309 ff. The most famous letter is D 1760.
39. D 1493/157 27 40.
40. Cf. VN 48 the description of Valad's going besides Shamsoddin's horse, 'not out of necessity but out of sincerity'; for the meeting scene cf. id. p. 49. A poetical description: R 352.
41. M I 1741.
42. S 134; VN 52.
43. Gölpinarli, Mevlâna p. 78 f; AF II 683 ff. I thank Mr Mehmet Önder for informing me about all the details of his discovery. The great poem with the rhyme-word *bogristi* '. . . would weep' (D 2893/30712 42) was written after the tragic event, as Aflāki states.
44. D 336/3644, a very sinister poem.
45. D 2186/23190.
46. D 1568/16473; cf. VN 53:

    The sheykh became mad in separation, without head and tail like Zuʾn-Nun;
    The sheykh and mofti became a poet from love; he became drunk, although he was an ascetic;
    not from the wine which is in the grape—his lightful soul drank nothing but light. . . .'

47. The dramatic description of the process in VN 59 61 particularly p, 60; cf. also id. p. 290.
48. D 2968/31504.
49. D 1081/11369 72; cf. D 1978/20912.
50. D 2351/24875; R 616, 1293, 1134. As VN 57 says:
 'Not a moment he was without *samā*ᶜ and dance;
 He did not rest for a moment day and night—
 to such a degree that there remained no singer
 who had not become almost mute from singing. . . .
51. R 534, cf. 533.
52. Mektuplar Nr. XXXII.
53. Gölpīnarlī, Mevlâna p. 91; VN 41 uses the comparison of Jalāloddin to Moses and Shams to Khiḍr, which is certainly more fitting.
54. D 1768/18521.
55. Letters addressed to him: Mektuplar Nr. XXIII, LXXXIII, CXXVI
56. D 650/6778 f; the same expression in VN 64.
57. F 106 f. About the gossip cf. VN 72 74, and Ṣalāḥoddin's smiling reaction id. 75. Cf. S 137.
58. Cf. Gölpīnarlī, Mevlâna, p. 104 105. However, Solṭān Valad incessantly underscores his perfect love for his master and father-in-law to whom he was bound in unceasing loyalty (VN 97); he became annihilated in him and, forgetting intellectual speech, brought forth words from the sea of the heart (VN 107), and saw in Ṣalāḥoddin a manifestation of the '*mercy of kibriyā*' (VN 65).
59. D 31/400 413 and D 236/2660 2665.
60. Mektuplar Nr. LVI.
61. The marriage-song for Hadiyya Khātun is D 2667/28288 94.
62. AF I 261 and D 1327/14040 50. Allusions to the Tartars or Mongols: D 1609/16860; in D 1728/18109 he speaks of the 'Tartar Grief' against whom love fights. Cf. Note 24.
63. D 2364/24995 25005; cf. S 141. VN 109 speaks of ten years of companionship between Rumi and the goldsmith. That would date Ṣalāḥoddin's death to ca. 1262. Ṣalāḥoddin himself is said to have ordered a *samā*ᶜ to be held at his funeral, VN 112.
64. D 1823/19143.
65. M V 2238 f. cf. AM Nr. 179; VN 209.
66. About him cf. Nejat Kaymaz, Pervane Mu'in ud-Din Süleyman, Ankara 1970. Letters addressed to him in Mektuplar II, XVI, XXVI, XXVII, XXX, XXXI, XXXVII, XLII, XLIII, LI, LXIII, LXVIII, LXXII, LXXVIII, LXXXII, LXXXIV-LXXXVI, XCVI, XCIXX, CI, CXIV, CXVI, CXX, CXXXVII.
67. Gölpınarlı, Mevlâna p. 21.
68. AF I 339 = D 1623/16995 17008.
69. Mektuplar p. 248.
70. AF I 470; Gölpınarlı, Mevlâna p. 221.
71. Jāmi, Nafaḥāt p. 557.—For all mystical contemporaries of Mowlānā cf. Gölpīnarlī, Mevlâna 220 232.
72. Cf. E. G. Browne, A Literary History of Persia, III, Cambridge 1951, p. 124 ff; J. Rypka, History of Iranian Literatures, Dordrecht 1968, p. 254 f. ᶜIrāqi's *Divān* was edited by S. Nafisi, Teheran 1338sh; his ᶜ*usshāqnāma* 'Song of the Lovers' by A. J. Arberry, Oxford 1939.
73. Najmoddin Dāyā Rāzi died in 1256, cf. GAL I 448, S I 804, and Fritz Meier, Stambuler Handschriften dreier persischen Mystiker, ᶜAin al-Quḍāt al-Hamadāni, Naǧm ad-dīn al-Kubrā, Nagm ad-dīn ad-Dājā, in: Der Islam 24/1937.

74. Jāmi, Nafaḥāt p. 435.
75. AF I 257, cf. id. I 151; Gölpīnarlī, Mevlâna, p. 206.
76. AF I , Gölpınarlı, id.
77. Mektuplar Nr. LXII.
78. Mektuplar Nr. CXXIII. An interesting advice to a disciple who apparently had gone astray in a not very respectable place: id. LXX.
79. MVIII 517 f; cf. D. 1093/11509 ff; about the village-boy who disturbed the market (symbol of the base soul). The idea that life in the village renders people stupid goes, however, back to a *ḥadith* 'Dont live in the villages, for he who lives in the villages is like the one who lives in tombs (*kufūr—qubūr*), AM Nr. 205, which is also alluded to in the *Maᶜāref* (p. 283 in the commentary).
80. F 152.
81. F 158.
82. Mektuplar Nr. XLVI, cf. CXXVIII.
83. AF I 375; cf. Gölpınarlı, Mevlâna p. 182.
84. AF I 490.
85. AF I 425.
86. A. Gölpınarlı, Mevlânaᶜdan sonra Mevlevilik, Istanbul 1953, p. 246 ff.
87. AF II 621.
88. AF II 488 = D 570/6135 43.
89. Mektuplar Nr. LIV.
90. cf. Mektuplar Nr. CXXVI.
91. S 145
92. Mektuplar Nr. CXXX, CXXXI.
93. D 738/7761.
94. M I 2685. That would, however, not be sufficient for a stringent proof; since Baghdad as seat of the caliph occurs also in much later times as a poetical topos: Jāmi speaks of the 'Baghdad of beauty where you are the caliph' (Divān, ed. Hāshim Rezā, Teheran 1341 sh.), p. 786.
95. D 1839, a ghazal which deserves special study.
96. M I 125ff. The chronology is not complete established. VN places the investiture of Ḥosāmoddin immediately after Ṣalāḥoddin's death which, as we saw, according to him took place ca 1262. Cf. VN 113.
97. Mektuplar Nr. LXI.
98. cf. VN 121 for a detailed description.
99. D 683/7102 11.
100. Jāmi, Nafaḥāt p. 464.
101. VN 123 speaks of Ḥosāmoddin's attempt to make Solṭān Valad accept his father's seat, but:

 'I said: No! my father is certainly alive . . .

 During his time you were our *khalifa*, and no change is acceptable . . .'

 For the later development cf. A. Gölpīnarlī's excellent study: Mevlâna'dan sonra Mevlevilik, further J. Spencer Trimingham, The Sufi Orders in Islam, Oxford 1971.

POETICAL TRADITION

1. Mektuplar p. XII. The previous pages give a short survey of motifs taken from Sanāʾi and ᶜAṭṭār. Cf. also VN 257; AF I 220.
2. D 824/8620.
3. D 24/292.
4. D 60/735.

5. F 215; Solṭān Valad likewise quotes from Sanā'ī, thus VN 10, 226.
6. D 1007/10634 42.
7. Sanā'i, Divān, ed. M. Razavi, Teheran 1320 sh., p. 1059; for Rūdaki cf. ʿAufi, Lubāb, al-albāb, ed. E. G. Browne and M. Qazvini, London-Leyden 1903 1906, II p. 8. It should be remembered that Mowlānā has also written a *naẓira* to Rudaki's famous poem with the *radif āyad hamī*: D 2897.
8. M III 4229; for more examples vd. Index I (M VI p. 564) s.v. *ḥakim* (Sanā'i).
9. Thus M I 2035; D 2733/29064.
10. Thus M III 2771, 3750, IV 2566.
11. In D 1244/13181 an allusion to the Ḥadiqat al-ḥaqiqat, ed. M. Razavi, Teheran 1329 sh., p. 449, 1.4.
12. Sanā'i, Divān, p. 488.
13. D 1752/18364.
14. Sanā'i, Ḥadiqat, ch. VII p. 848.
15. Cf. H. Ritter, Das Proömium des Maṯnawi-i Maulawi, in: ZDMG 93/1932.
16. For the genesis of this story (M III 1259 ff) cf. F. Meier, Die Geschichte von den Blinden und dem Elefanten, in: Das Problem der Naturim esoterischen Monismus des Islam, Eranos-Jahrbuch XIV, 1946.
17. Sanā'i, Divān p. 987; cf. pp. 138, 393, 484, 509; about the expression cf. F. Meier, Der Geistmensch bei dem persischen Dichter ʿAṭṭār (Eranos-Jahrbuch XIII, 1946), p. 322 ad Ilāhināme 170, 6 7. Cf. also here, Ch. II, c, Note 59.
18. Sanā'i, Divān, p. 413, 465 etc.
19. id. p. 515.
20. M VI 1383 = Moṣibatnāme (ed. N. Fesāl, Teheran 1338 sh), p. 276 ff. Cf. H. Ritter, Das Meer der Seele, Leiden 1955, p.
21. Manṭeq oṭ-teyr, ed. M. J. Mashkur, Teheran 1341 sh., p. 241.
22. id. p. 222.
23. id. p. 243; for its elaboration in Rumi's poetry cf. III Ch. *God* note 103.—I wonder if ʿAṭṭār's expression 'The mowlā has become the Kaʿaba of the lovers' (oṣibatnāme p. 199) may have influenced the verse on Rumi's tomb according to which 'this place is the Kaʿaba of the Lovers'.
24. M IV 2203; cf. D 2944/31279.
25. M II 3615 ff.
26. cf. M IV 3463.
27. D 895/9369; 1747/18320.
28. For *Vis u Ramin* cf. J. Rypka, History of Iranian Literatures, p. 177 ff. and the translation: Vis and Ramin by Fakhr ud-Din Gurgani, transl. by George Morrison, Columbia University Press 1972. Allusions to this story: D 213/2385; 1932/20320; 2066/21824; 2160/22876; 2080/21965; 2551/27069; 3063/32628; M III 228, IV 1828, MV 1204: Read Vis and Ramin and Khosrow and Shirin: to mention only a few typical examples.
29. For this romance, first mentioned as a pre-Islamic story, cf. J. Rypka, History, p. 51, 132. Typical allusions: D 24/288; 65/777; 98/1103; 532/5661; 1961/20692; 3129/33442. Very charming is 64/765:
    Did you ever see a picture that fled from the painter?
    Did you ever see a Vāmeq who excused (ʿ*odhr*) himself from ʿAdhrā?
30. D 480/5109 and others.
31. D 1529/16090; 1530/16097.
32. D 742/7799.
33. For Khāqāni cf. F 33; D 110/1245.
34. D 32/414.
35. cf. D 33/426; 142/1617; 2039/21501. Perhaps, however, this is only a practical wordplay without any deeper meaning.

36. D 1493/15730.

37. D 3115/33238; 2266/24079; 103/1192; 1209/12872; M I 3039 (the lion's smile), F 20, F 23. AF II 623/4 tells how Shamsoddin cured Mowlānā from his love of the Arabic poet: he appeared to him in a dream, grasping poor skinny Motanabbi by his beard, shaking him in front of Jalāloddin whom he blamed for reading poetry of such a person . . .

38. D 2627/27830.

39. D 1499/15800.

40. D 1949/20587 88; F 84 f.

41. F 207.

42. D 1100/11640.

43. D 1547/16251.

44. D 2329/24655.

45. D 2938/31183. Here belong also utterances like D 3073/32742.

    Know that I am the servant of your poem, for the poem is spoken by you,
    who is the soul of Isrāfil's soul and the sound of the trumpet.

    i.e. the Beloved is equated with the angel of resurrection.

46. M I 1727

47. M I 28; cf. IV 2112 f. about inspiration by a jinni.

48. D 1344/14222.

49. M V 1897 ff.

50. M II 493.

51. D 468/4976.

52. For the whole problem cf. A. Schimmel, Mir Dards Gedanken über das Verhältnis von Mystik und Wort, in: Festgabe deutscher Iranisten zur 2500-Jahrfeier Irans, herausg. von W. Eilers, Stuttgart 1971.

53. D 771/8055; 1028/10840; 917/9653. But he claims also that this heavenly poetry is enjoyed even by superhuman beings:

    My word is the food of angels —; when I do not speak
    The hungry angel says: Talk! Why are you silent? (D 2838/30144)

    Cf. D 917/9653:

    Sing a ghazal which people will sing for a hundred centuries;
    The fabric which God has woven will not get rotten.

54. D 1856/19562; cf. 419/4415. Also the charming beginning of D 2080/21958 61 where he complains:

    I said four poems, but he said: 'No! (Produce something) better than this!'

55. D 2802/29742; cf. 2807/29787;

56. D 938/9896. Solṭān Valad (VN 53 f.) speaks in a long passage about the 'sacred' quality of Mowlānā's verses, and later writes:

    Whosoever is inclined towards the *divāns* of Anvari and other poets belongs to this world, and water and clay are prevalent in him; and whoever is inclined towards the *divāns* of Sanā'i and ʿAṭṭar and the spiritual benefits of Mowlānā which is the marrow of the marrow and the finest thing possible (*maghz-e maghz u naghz-e naghz*) and the cream of both Sanā'i's and ʿAṭṭar's words, then it is a sign that he belongs to the 'people of the heart' and to the class of saints. (VN 212).

57. D 8/106; M I 25.

58. D 895/9375; 38/486; cf. 589/6226 and M VI 160.

59. D 386/4118.

60. D 229/2593.

61. D 775/8093.

62. D 46/598, the following—last—verse has only the *moftaʿelon mofāʿelon* in the first hemistich, which shows that there was indeed need to 'shorten the qaṣida'.

63. D 132/1527.
64. M VI 695 f.
65. M V 2238 f. cf. AM Nr. 179; VN 209.
66. D 869/9092; cf. D 958.
67. M IV 2062.
68. D 2132/22570.
69. D 1799/18911.
70. D 2115/22338.
71. M I 135 f.
72. cf. M III 2120, i.e. the five senses and the seven heavens.
73. M V 228 f. The same idea in VN 180.
74. M III 1150.
75. M V 17 ff.
76. M III 3637, cf. VN 298.
77. M V 3597 f.
78. M IV 2069 f.
79. D 2568/27270.
80. M IV 420.
81. M III 2098.
82. D 402/4248. He continues in verse 4249 that the heart is like a cloud, the breasts like roofs, and the tongue like the spout through which the water flows to the ground, and then goes on elaborating this example.
83. M VI 4898.
84. M II 3622.
85. M IV 318, V 20, 1175 f.
86. D 921/9694 f.
87. M II 302 ff.
88. M II 3312.
89. M VI 84 ff.; cf. VI 4890.
90. M VI 104 ff.
91. D 1751/18363; cf. M I 577.
92. M II 29 f.
93. D 250/2804 ff.
94. M II 3581.
95. M III 3842; cf. D 3180/34105 a *molamma*ᶜ poem in which he reminds himself to talk in Persian, for 'one should not eat sugar alone'. Cf. also 2502/26481; 2700/28649; 3191/34253.
96. M II 3681 ff.
97. M III 1259 ff.
98. M I 1136.
99. M II 3291.
100. M VI 2248; cf. IV 789 f.
101. M I 514.
102. M III 4242 cf:
    'Suddenly a great booby popped his head out of ass-stable, like a railing woman, (saying) that this discourse, the Mathnavi, is low . . .' (N).
103. M III 3200 f.; cf. IV 32.
104. M VI 1525 f.
105. M III 4287 ff.: the reply to him who rails at the Mathnavi on account of his being deficient in understanding (N).

106. M III 1228.
107. M VI 66f.
108. M IV 789 f.
109. M III 4440 f.
110. M III 2110 f.
111. M I 3531 ff.
112. M III 3760 ff.
113. M III 3700 ff.
114. M VI 2044 ff.
115. Cf. D 1255/13284 ff.
116. D 310/3393.
117. D 463/4911 ff. with its climax in the word *ṣafāst*.
118. D 156/1785 91.
119. D 3007 is the most outspoken example of this style.
120. Thus D 2798/29715 21; D 1086; 1159.
121. D 2288/24316 24 with the rhyme-word *moṣādara* 'confiscation'.
122. D 1125/11876. The way Rumi personifies love is highly interesting: it is a police-master, a bleacher, a qādi, a carpenter, a physician.
123. F 73.
124. M III 792 f.
125. D 1198/12749; 2104/22216; 886/9277; 2948/31321; DT V/34821, etc.
126. D 1093/11509; cf. M III 517 f.
127. D 1060/11184 ff.; cf. R 575:
    When soul and world become polluted by sorrow,
    they become clean when love acts as bleacher.
128. D 1206/12852.
129. D 784/8191 ff.
130. F 52.
132. D 674/7017.
133. D 761/7973; cf. D 21/22970: 'my separation became fat from your blood which it drank, oh heart!'
134. D 2852/30282.
135. D 2895/30755.
136. D 757/7921 f.
137. D 3127/33407.
138. D 1444/15281.
139. D 500/5319.
140. D 500/5320. Maybe the wolf has torn sleep in pieces (R 842), or sleep flew toward the skies (R 384), or the moonlight has cut its throat . . . (R 80).
141. D 779/8126.
142. D 2728/28973.
143. D 697/7261; Sanāʾi, Divān p. 117:
    With your grace the heart has no soul,
    and without you, the soul has no goal.
144. D 688/7160.
145. D 928/9779.
146. D 1304/13785.
147. D 1643/17201.
148. D 1213/12907.
149. M V 2497 title of the story.

150. M II 2388 ff.
151. M III 1483.
152. M III 3014.
153. M II 203 ff; Rumi comes back to this story in M V 2518.
154. M VI 703 ff.
155. D 469/4981.
156. M IV 2377.
157. thus M IV 2222; D 482/ especially 5143, 44; etc.
158. D 2528/26808; cf. 27/314.
159. D 2776/29505 06.
160. Thus, we often find allusions to the dogs barking at the moon or at the caravan; among the Persian proverbs the more frequently used ones are 'beating the drum under the carpet', 'He found water and broke the vessel', 'He who seeks finds', 'When water rests it becomes stinking', 'a locust's leg', 'the excuse of the stupid is worse than his fault', 'The smell of wood becomes manifest from its smoke', 'Man is hidden under his tongue' (alleged *ḥadith*, both in Arabic and Persian) or in Arabic: *idhā jāʾa 'l-qaḍā, aṣ-ṣabr miftāḥ al-faraj, khair al-umūr ausaṭuhā, man jarrabaʾl-mujarrab ḥallat bihi'n-nadāma* (this also often in Sanāʾi), and many other sayings.
161. D 1203/12812; or the expression 'He remained in the mosque like dregs in the cup' M V 75.
162. D 1991/21050 f. The expression occurs very often, thus D 100/1138; 526/5589; 671/7003; 692/7198; 767/8019; 1608/16840; 2231/23654; M III 1565, IV 3502; V 3904; II 2061; cf. MC VI 312 'often applied to a lover whose secret passion has become evident to all.' Yet, Nicholson sometimes translates the expression as 'he fell into ecstasy'.

II RUMI'S IMAGERY

THE SUN

1. D 310/3398 (N)
2. M I 120.
3. M IV 577.
4. M III 2813.
5. D 1621/16967.
6. D 1436/15194.
7. M I 141.
8. F 47.
9. Cf. D. 2902/30842.
10. D 1947/20558; cf. 1940/20486 f.
11. D 1758/18427; 2010/21242; cf. 463/4917.
12. M II 2534.
13. DST Nr. 44, comparable is D 3038/32318.
14. D 464/4930.
15. M IV 16 ff.

16. M VI 90.
17. M VI 2010.
18. M V 2025 f.
19. D 2429/25592.
20. D 2784/29601 f.
21. M III 707 f.
22. D 1053/11113.
23. D 2054/21691.
24. M II 42 f.
25. D 911/9561 62.
26. M II 3014 f.
27. D 1940/20487.
28. M IV 506.
29. M I 117, 427; III 3718 f.
30. M I 425; D 1599/16732. The finest example of his claim to be only a shade of his Beloved is found in the ecstatic prayer-poem D 2831/30060 64.
31. M I 3555.
32. M II 2084 ff.; cf. III 3620 f; VI 3395: The sun of this world is a bat before the spiritual sun; cf. 'Animals', note 216 for more bats.
33. M II 793 ff.
34. M III 2719 ff.
35. M II 1611.
36. M V 9 f. Cf. VN 242. As Mowlānā says: 'He who praises the sun praises himself'.
37. M II 791.
38. M VI 40.
39. D 2408/25429.
40. M I 2500; cf. MC VII 214.
41. M V 1262 f.
42. M II 3411; VI 2693.
43. M VI 930 f.
44. D 1349/14265.
45. D 2702/28662.
46. D 2408/25430.
47. M II 45 f.
48. M II 1107.
49. D 2439/25727; for the problem cf. H. Corbin, L'homme de lumière dans le Soufisme Iranien, Paris 1971.
50. M V 2134.
51. D 1938/20395.
52. D 1480/15620.
53. M III 3671 ff.
54. M I 3656.
55. F 114.
56. M VI 691; an elaboration also in VN 5, in the very beginning of the Valadnāme.
57. M I 1128.
58. M I 1121.
59. M V 988 f.
60. M I 3958 f.
61. About the mystical meaning of colours in the Kubrāwīya cf. Fritz Meier, Die

fawāʾiḥ al-ğamāl wa fawātiḥ al-ğalāl des Nağm ud-Din al-Kubrā, Wiesbaden 1957, and the article by J. L. Fleischer, Ueber die farbigen Lichterscheinungen der Sufis, in: ZDMG 16/1862.

62. D 1407/14899 900.
63. D 2130/22533.
64. D 460/4879.
65. D 710/7440.
66. D 2258/23970
67. D 1052/11099 and the explanation in AF I 280 f., where Rumi's interpretation of colours in dreams is added: red = joy, green = asceticism, white = piety, dark blue or black = grief. Cf. further, H. Corbin, Quiétude et inquiétude de l'âme dans le Soufisme de Rūzbihān Baqlī de Shiraz (Eranos-Jahrbuch XXVII 1958) about the importance of red in Rūzbihān's mysticism.
68. M II 1097 ff.
69. M II 1597.
70. D 212/2366.
71. D 2168/22960.
72. D 2185/23179 80.
73. D 1177/12548 49.
74. M I 501.
75. D 1947/20549 ff: the *zar-e jaʿfari*, (cf. Sanāʾi, Ḥadiqa III 518, V 327) 'finest gold' is called after the Imām Jaʿfar aṣ-Ṣādeq, (d. 765) to whom alchemistic works are ascribed. Cf. also D 1092/11498, and R 1063 for an elegant contrast between the friend's sun-like face and moon and Saturn.
76. D 2807/29793; cf. M II 1709 f.
77. D 2723/28911.
78. D 778/8121; cf. M VI 4860 and MC VIII 403.
79. D 2519/26698.
80. D 785/8212; D 882/9241.
81. D 2280/24222.
82. D 1028/10837.
83. D 2276/24167.
84. D 1612/16886.
85. D 1092/11507.
86. D 409/4330; AM Nr. 159.
87. M II 2077.
88. D 2778/29549.
89. D 1430/15123; cf. D 1751/18362.
90. D 2758/29316.
91. D 33/433.
92. D 523/5563; cf. also D 991/10480; 1262/13368; 2548/27038; 2560/27176.
93. D 260/2948.
94. D 2339/24754.
95. D 754/7897.
96. D 110/1244.
97. D 2229/23640; cf. M V 2858 f.
98. M IV 3848; D 455/4816 and often.
99. Cf. D 2797/29712: The *jaʿfari*-gold laughs in the fire. It is, however, connected here with Jaʿfar aṭ-Ṭayyār, one of the early heroes and martyrs, not with Jaʿfar aṣ-Ṣādeq.
100. S 94. About Divine alchemy cf. M II 694.

101. DT 17/35349; D 1554/16327.
102. D 179/2009.
103. D 2239/23735.
104. M II 3473.
105. D 314/3430.
106. D 863/9023.
107. D 1848/19498.
108. M II 1350 f.
109. M I 716.
110. D 2163/22904.
111. D 2591/27487.
112. D 1877/19785.
113. D 70/827; cf. 1790/18749.
114. D 1633/17109.
115. D 2238/23730.
116. D 2015/21275 f.
117. D 2764/29376.
118. D 1324/14021.
119. D 551/5854; cf. MC VIII 68 ad M III 2548.

IMAGERY OF WATER

1. M II 1199.
2. M I 1145.
3. M V 199.
4. M II 1366 f.
5. M V 209 f.
6. M II 1075 f.
7. M I 2724 f.; cf. IV 2593 f.; IV 1051 speaks of the 'sweet water from the ocean of *ladon*'.
8. M V 3294.
9. M I 3338 ff.
10. M II 3297.
11. M VI 2028.
12. D 649/esp. 6773 77.
13. D 31/412.
14. D 921/9695.
15. M V 2907.
16. F 22.
17. M V 2907 ff.
18. M V 3622.
19. M VI 2298 ff.
20. M I 2675 f.
21. M II 3140 f.
22. M III 968.
23. D 1713/17939.
24. Iqbal, Payām-e Mashreq, Lahore 1923 (repr.), p. 151, German verse-translation by A. Schimmel, Botschaft des Ostens, Wiesbaden 1963, p. 62.
25. D 1667/17480.
26. D 193/2130.

27. M II 2813 f.
28. D 99/1118.
29. D 798/8343.
30. D 1142/12113.
31. Cf. MC VII 107 ad M I 1468.
32. D 602/6344, cf. 1341/14195.
33. M V 1084 f.; cf. II 2451 f.
34. M II 3292 f.
35. M I 2708 2864.
36. D 1740/18257 58.
37. Cf. D 2672/28334.
38. F 69. Solṭān Valad was particularly fond of this imagery which is used in VN 83, 137, 176.
39. M V 3431 f.
40. D 919/9677.
41. D 1387/14680 81; cf. 2914/30949; 3024/32136.
42. D 1033/10878 79; the 'snow of words' melts thanks to the Sun of Religion, D 132/1528.
43. D 2784/29602; cf. 2919/31000.
44. D 514/5499 ff.—For more ice-imagery cf. D. 1395/14790; 1410/14922; 2058/21746; 2239/23736; 2281/24235; 2429/25589; 2491/26341; 3071/32705; R 114, 965; cf. also MC VII 371 ad M I 520.

SYMBOLISM OF GARDENS

1. Joseph von Hammer, Geschichte der schönen Redekünste Persiens, Wien 1818, p. 177 = D 651/6785 86.
2. D 1093/11526.
3. D 1940/20461. The whole long poem (20411 92) describes the marvels of spring, ending in a praise of the Sun, Shamsoddin.
4. D 2147/22732.
5. D 2878/30553.
6. D 1378/14590.
7. D 758/7946.
8. D 1285/13570; cf. 1486/15672; 'the head is a gourd full of wine'.
9. M II 3231.
10. D 1167/12382 ff.
11. D 1339/14163.
12. DT 28/35781.
13. D 1121/11830.
14. D 2636/27971; cf. Sura 22/6 7 where the often used proof for the possibility of resurrection as derived from the awakening of the dead earth in spring is particularly clear.
15. M V 233; cf. III 3635.
16. M I 2786.
17. M I 1896.
18. M II 1592.
19. M I 1277.
20. DT 11/35041; cf. R 676.
21. D 993/10497; cf. 2320/24601.
22. F 46.

23. D 782/8162.
24. D 589/6223.
25. D 871/9107.
26. D 1940/20418 ff.; cf. M I 2019.
27. F 62; cf. D 2320/24606 f. For nine months of pregnancy of the earth cf. D 871/9108.
28. D 1056/11146.
29. D 1408/14906; a beautiful poem about autumn is D 1794.
30. D 1073/11291; cf. 2168/22964.
31. D 928/9777, the whole poem describes spring as loving union.
32. D 985/10428, a poem on expectation; cf. D 2319/24595.
33. D 1915/20152; cf. M IV 3020.
34. D 1298/13712; the whole poem describes the joy of spring.
35. D 1291/13548; cf. 2120/22425.
36. D 1672/17520.
37. M I 1341 f. About different kinds of rain cf. M I 2037.
38. D 2082/21977; 297/3245; 668/6978; R 214, 1604.
39. M I 820; cf. V 141.
40. D 181/2023 ff.
41. M V 138 41.
42. D 1832/19256.
43. M II 1655 ff. (N).
44. D 148/1674.
45. D 297/3245 ff.
46. D 2713/28795.
47. D 589/6219.
48. D 3048/32416, 18; another image D 1439/15225: both devour their children, like cats.
49. D 1308/13857.
50. M I 1911.
51. D 3041/32336.
52. D 1158/12289.
53. D 1958/20669; 1101/11649; 2138/22630; cf. Chapter 'Music'.
54. D 2120/22426.
55. D 2464/26051; M IV 3267 f.
56. F 74. The idea that the garden is so to speak the visible garment of the invisible breeze occurs in later Persian and Urdu poetry up to Mirzā Ghālib (d. 1869).
57. D 451/4763.
58. M I 2014 f.
59. D 2320/24601; 2433/25648; 1224/13009; 1429/15114; 2590/27483; R 1222; M II 1378 f; III 4761; IV 2055; MC VII 147 and M I 2237. Cf. 'Poetic Tradition', note 17.
60. D 928/9778; 2314/24554.
61. D (reference lost).
62. D 888/9315; 1847/19465.
63. D 1690/17705.
64. M II 1569; cf. II 2691.
65. D 1623/17003.
66. M II 1017.
67. M III 707.

68. M II 1244 f.
69. F 105.
70. M V 2052.
71. D 2242/23760.
72. D 1693/17738; cf. 2103/22211.
73. M II 1968 f; IV 525 ff.
74. M III 1128.
75. M III 1292 f.
76. M IV 2051 ff.
77. D 2308/24500.
78. D 933/9839; 2854/30301 08; 1990/21030; 2849/30248 65 a whole beautiful spring-poem.
79. D 1490/15702; cf. 1484/15650: 'The Beloved is a tree whose fruit we are'.
80. D 2185/23176.
81. D 2921/31015.
82. D 2444/25807; cf. 2160/22875.
83. D 968/10233.
84. Golestān, Part 5 (= Kolliyāt, ed. M. A. Forughi, Teheran 1342 sh Vol. I p. 139).
85. D 28/365.
86. M II 3394 f.
87. D 3181/34107.
88. M VI 4542.
89. D 2784/29593.
90. D 2975/31571.
91. D 1940/20443; 1592/16673 'blackhearted', the usual epithet of the tulip.
92. D 2242/23758.
93. DT 1/34691; cf. Irène Mélikoff, La Fleur de la Souffrance, JA CCXXV, 1967.
94. D 1624/17022.
95. D 3059/32573.
96. D 1590/16656; 2435/25676.
97. D 1790/18752.
98. D 2242/23760.
99. D 2200/23342; 2167/22947; 2493/26355.
100. D 1121/11828; cf. 2107/22245; a charming *robāᶜi*, Ṙ 1565, says:
    As much as the cypress has an incomparable stature,
    What a place has the cypress compared to my friend's stature?
    Sometime it says 'My stature is like his stature!'—
    O Lord—what a damaged brain has the cypress!
101. D 1044/11005 contrasting with the upright hyacinth and cypress.
102. D 2242/23758.
103. D 2930/31086.
104. D 2748/29223; 581/6147, a superb spring-poem.
105. D 1199/12764.
106. D 1961/20691.
107. Cf. L. Massignon, La vie et les oeuvres de Rūzbehān Baqlī, in: Studia Orientalia . . . J. Pedersen, Copenhaguen 1953; A. Schimmel, Rose und Nachtigall, in: Numen V 2, 1958.
108. M VI 1815 f.
109. D 2871/30473; 2632/27918; 759/7954; cf 2753/29272.

110. D 2823/29973; cf. R 1609.
111. D 1348/14259 and the explanatory footnote.
112. D 1348/14261 62.
113. D 2820/29944.
114. D 2389/25247.
115. D 1182/12595. The opening of the 'oppressed' sad bud into a happy smile which, at the same time, announces its death, is a favourite topic of Persian writing poets throughout the ages.
116. D 84/974; cf. R 240: the lover's soul is smiling like a rosegarden, his body trembling like leaves, as if he had fever.
117. DT 10/35029; D 549/5841; 1167/12383; 1913/20124; 2389/25249. Part of an Arabic romance where the rose claims to be the king surrounded by the army of grass is found in the inscription of a Persian fayence bowl, dated 1220, Museum für Islamische Kunst, Berlin-Dahlem, described in *Fikrun wa Fann* 7 1966, p. 32 33.
118. D 455/4813.
119. D 711/7449.
120. D 460/4877.
121. D 1460/15436.
122. D 1639/17161.
123. D 2948/31312; 1824/19155; M V 1256; R 1493.
124. M I 672.
125. D 914/9594.
126. M II 3286 ff.
127. M I 3076.
128. M I 2472.
129. D 1305/13807.
130. D 2195/23298.
131. D 946/9987.
132. D 864/9036.
133. D 1005/10619.
134. M II 154; cf. I 3007; D 445/4694. In R 579 Rumi applies the motif of *ṣoḥbat* 'spiritual company' to the rose and the thorn:
    By dint of the company of the rose, the thorn is safe from fire,
    By dint of the company of the thorn, the rose comes into the fire.
135. D 729/7652.
136. M I 3828.
137. D 3041/32340; 3029/32179.
138. D 326/3546; M I 763.
139. M I 2022.
140. D 1000/10565 66; cf. R 202, 203, 774: 'All these are pretexts—it is He Himself'.

IMAGERY INSPIRED BY ANIMALS

1. D 3048/32422 ff; cf. M IV 3389. About the camel's 'intoxication' e.g. heat, for forty days every year cf. Maʿāref p. 3. About the 'camel's dance' as 'unfitting and unharmonious actions which incite amazement' id. Notes p. 263.
2. D 1531/16107.
3. D 2828/30026.
4. D 1344/14219.
5. D 1894/19923; 2437/25703 with allusion to Sura 6/11; 3099/33022. For the

ḥādi cf. as-Sarrāj, *Kitāb al-lumaʿ fiʾt-taṣawwuf*. ed. R. A. Nicholson, Leyden-London 1914. ch. on *samāʿ* About the camel carrying the king's drum cf. the nice story M III 4090 ff.

6. D 1312/13892; 508/5418; 2170/22988; the pun consists in the confrontation of *ʿaql* 'reason' and *ʿiqāl* 'rope', cf. Maʿāref p. 59. Cf. also R 223 and often.
7. D 182/2032.
8. D 626/6539; 2993/31812 ff.; cf. 1563/16418.
9. D 1432/15146.
10. D 302/3296 f.
11. D 2252/23877.
12. D 2353/24906.
13. D 356/3832 34.
14. D 1624/17014 15.
15. D 474/5026; cf. M IV 187 the mischieveous man in women's dress is 'like a camel on the ladder'. Khāqāni speaks of the 'elephant on the ladder', Divān, ed. M. Sajjādi, Teheran 1338 sh, p. 343. The contrary is 'a camel on a water spout', i.e. on the brink of destruction; cf. M III 4539, 4731.
16. D 2356/24927.
17. D 2937/31168 69.
18. M III 4668.
19. D 2598/27558; 1847/19477.
20. D 2544/27002 ff.
21. M II 2975 ff.
22. D 3032/32229 30.
23. D 2252/23872.
24. M IV 1533 ff.; Mektuplar Nr. LXV.
25. D 1828/19217.
26. M VI 2476 ff.
27. M V 833 ff.
28. M V 2008.
29. M II 1436; III 2504; V 928, 2866 ff., cf. MC VIII 245 ad M V 928 ff.; A nice story about a peasant who rubbed the limbs of a lion in the dark stable because he thought it was his ox, in M II 503 ff. —The mythological cow that carries the earth is several times mentioned, thus D 1813/19050; 2662/28238.
30. D 972/10299.
31. M IV 1327.
32. D 2433/25650.
33. D 2777/29515; the story of the sea-cow elaborated in M VI 2922 f; MC VIII 372.
34. D 2464/26031.
35. According to a *ḥadith*, 'every servant is resurrected in the way he dies', AM Nr. 40; for the application of this idea in Sanāʾi's and ʿAṭṭar's work cf. Ritter, Das Meer der Seele, p. 102, 155.
36. M II 1413: The resurrection of the greedy vile eater of carrion will be in the shape of a hog.
37. Cf. 'History, Geography', note 117 119.
38. D 59/725.
39. D 3052/32483.
40. M V 3345.
41. M VI 4856.
42. D 2862/30380.

43. D 2881/30584; the 'wolf of annihilation' R 38.
44. Cf. D 2830/30037 ff.; M VI 3288.
45. M IV 228.
46. D 755/7904; M II 3700 f. (example of Solomon), M V 2286 f.
47. D 2818/29927.
48. D 1419/15020.
49. M III 2806.
50. M III 721 777: this jackal is a symbol of Pharaoh who claimed divinity.
51. D 1264/13381; cf. M II 2722 ff.
52. S 92, but not in D.
53. M VI 3001.
54. D 1527/16071; M II 2432; cf. 382.
55. D 2500/26453. Solṭān Valad uses the image of the mouse to explain that 'fear of God is the station of great people', for the mouse fears only the cat, not the lion, thus, the worldly, mouse-like people fear the police and the watchman, because God is too great for them (VN 235/6).
56. M VI 2632 2970.
57. M II 3532.
58. M V 2409 ff.
59. M VI 2428.
60. D 914/9630.
61. M VI 3042 ff.
62. D 2457/25957.
63. M III 3003.
64. M IV 1987 ff.
65. D 813/8497 9.
66. M V 194. The hypocritical 'pious' cat with the prayer beads is a traditional theme in folkstories; it occurs in high poetry in Persian and Turkish (cf. ʿObeyd-e Zakāni's *mush u gorba*) and is even represented on modern Mongolian postage-stamps.
67. M VI 582 f.
68. M III 3983 f.; but compare D 2861/30371 'Death is a mouse'.
69. D 1439/15225.
70. D 2854/30307.
71. D 1252/13256.
72. D 1298/13719.
73. D 2226/23622.
74. D 432/4556; 750/7869 70; 1354/14318; 1844/19405; 1887/19850 3171/33990; cf. also chapter 'History, Geography' note 25.—AF I 478 gives the background of this attribution: a snake threatened the Prophet and did not leave him notwithstanding his order; Abu Horeyra passed by and left a big black cat out of his bag; the cat killed the snake, and the *ḥadith* was issued 'The love of cats is part of the faith'.
75. M V p. 178 in the title.
76. D 1656/17358.
77. D 1887/19850; M VI 908.
78. D 2071/21866.
79. D 2223/23589 90; cf. F 67.
80. D 446/4696; 2855/30310; M II 416.
81. M VI 12 and others.
82. D 2769/29442; cf. 1710/17912; M III 4551 f.; AM Nr. 705.

83. D 2782/29579; 1006/10627. Famous is the story of al-Ḥallāj feeding the soul-dog, as told in Akhbār al-Ḥallāj, ed. L. Massignon et P. Kraus, Paris 1957, ch. 66. An allusion to resurrection in a dog's shape in VN 349, where also the saintly dog of the Seven Sleeprs is mentioned.

84. Cf. D 2170/23996; very poignant R 1249: even a necklace made of repentance does not help—as soon as the dog sees carrion, he tears the fetters.

85. M V 626 f.

86. D 482/5135; cf. 1422/15035; M V 2977.

87. D 958/10101.

88. D 298/3257.

89. M III 3498.

90. M VI 1663.

91. F 180.

92. S 83.

93. D 652/6809.

94. D 3135/33549.

95. D 2021/21325.

96. M VI 4856 f.

97. D 2883/30609; cf. 1875/19754; cf. also Maʿāref p. 100.

98. D 803/8406.

99. M I 830 ff: I am not less than a dog in devotion, nor is God less than a Turcoman in life.

100. M V 2940 ff.

101. D 2102/22199.

102. M III 287 324.

103. M III 567 ff., he even gave the dog pure sugar-julep to drink!

104. D 676/7030 34 is a praise of the dog; cf. M III 575 and often.

105. D 1174/12491; cf. the strange 136/1565; 2130/22529 claims

  'The lion sits with lowered tail before the dogs of His street' which fits into the story told AF I 335 f. about Mowlāna praising Ḥosāmoddin's dog who is better than a lion.

106. M I 1022.

107. D 101/1160; cf. A. Schimmel, Nur ein störrisches Pferd . . ., in: Festschrift für Geo Widengren, Leiden 1972.

108. D 1492/15721.

109. M III 4013.

110. M IV 464.

111. M II 729 f.

112. D 747/7843.

113. D 1427/15096. Day and night as two lame donkeys R 492. The image of day and night as a black and a white horse is common with Persian poets.

114. D 2944/31246. Donkeys' heads were used as scarecrows, cf. Maʿāref, p. 58. MC VIII 221 ad M IV 3821 f. Rumi uses the image rather often, thus D 1192/12685:

  We are like a donkey's head, you are like the kitchen-garden,
  Cf. also 2723/28905, and the amusing 529/5625:
  The immature goes into the kitchen-garden of the soul to eat melon (*kharbuz*)—
  Have you, or has anybody, ever seen that an ass (*khar*) ate a goat (*buz*)?

Donkey's head and *kharbuza* are also combined in 3060/32578.

115. D 1921/20228.

116. M V 2350 f.

117. D 1813/19045 f.; 1607/16829; 1332/14096; 215/2412.
118. D 666/6956; cf. 1558/16370; 606/6379.
119. M II 514 ff.
120. M I 115; D 298/3256; cf. R 364: Don't send anyone to the friend for whom a lame donkey and a swift horse are alike.
121. D 100/1144.
122. D 2416/25492 9; cf. 3030/32197 ff.
123. D 477/5060.
124. thus D 1300/13733.
125. M IV 2619.
126. D 1380/14608.
127. D 1172/12453.
128. D 1817/19087.
129. M V 2547 f.
130. D 916/9649; cf. 2137/22619; M V 924.
131. D 2464/26025; cf. 1332/14098; M III 3961.
132. D 1107/11698.
133. D 96/1071; cf. M III 2238.
134. D 1752/18364 ff; Sanā'i, Kārnāma'ye Balkh, in: Mathnavihā, ed. M. Razavi, Teheran 1348 sh, p. 175 l. 149. Cf. also M II 2358: 'The philosopher paid honor to the tail of an ass, and gave him the title of "noble" '.
135. D 618/6469; cf. R 819: 'Since the ugliest voice is that of the head of the donkey (Sura 31/19), imagine what kind of voice comes from the donkey's back'.
136. M V 1333 1392.
137. D 3030/32196 ff; 2435/25670.
138. D 1358/14356.
139. D 1313/13909; 1595/16694. D 862/8997 speaks of the 'Borāq of insight'. Cf. further D 2417/25501' the Borāq of Inner Meanings', 2503/26489; 2910/30917; 3038/32300.
140. D 1426/15081; 3/48 9.
141. D 3042/32356.
142. D 709/7437; 2894/30751.
143. D 684/7114.
144. M III 3618.
145. M I 3965.
146. Cf. MC VII 291 ad M II 1427. The lion as saint is contrasted to the hare as 'low soul' in verses like R 1342:

    I do not want a hare and do not catch a gazelle —
    I am only a lover and seeker of that lion.

147. M IV 414.
148. D 1330/14082; 604/6366; 1595/16702; cf. MC VIII 245.
149. D 2177/23073.
150. D 1799/18902; 1502/15827.
151. D 974/10321; 859/8967; 2518/26653.
152. M VI.
153. M I 3160.
154. D 2152/22787.
155. D 919/9674; the lover as lion: D 336/3640; 1713/17949; 2738/29110:

    All the lions seek moonlight — I am a lion, and the friend the moonlight.

156. D 674/7018; cf. 380/4067.

157. D 2191/23255; 1241/13152; 704/7362 (hare), 887/9286 (fox) 2904/30859; 1331/14087.

158. Ḥadiqa, Ch. VII pp. 427, Sanāʾi Divān p. 286, 323. He uses the older form *guz*.

159. D 2777/29517; 1612/16894; 2165/22929; 1533/16127; 1573/16504; 998/10545; 1183/12609; 1188/12655; 1199/12755. The gepard, *fahd*, was proverbial in the Arab countries for his sleepiness (cf. Damiri, Ḥayāt al-ḥayawān al-kubrā, Cairo 1956, II 156), but not for a special diet. For a reference to the cheetah and cheese, see Saʿdi, Bostan ch. II. 30.

160. D 1643/17209; 2029/21410 'gazelle of inner meanings'.

161. D 2162/22896; cf. 1439/15221; 541/5767.

162. D 741/7782.

163. D 847/8863.

164. D 1378/14589; 843/8832; 1875/19754.

165. M V 2473 f.

166. D 2685/28469 f.

167. Cf. MC VII 34 ad M I 321; cf. Sanāʾi, Divān, p. 935 and often in poems of Seljuk poets, like Anvari.

168. cf. D 424/4466.

169. D 1270/13438.

170. D 1209/12879; M I 3039.

171. D 1395/14800; M III 2818, II 3422; D 1904/20043.

172. D 2983/31678; M I 211.

173. Cf. ʿAṭṭār, Moṣibatnāme p. 74. The freeze in Konya is reproduced in P. Ettinghausen, The Unicorn, Washington D.C., 1950, pl. 3.

174. D 920/9688.

175. D 687/7149; cf. 2108; M V 2622.

176. R 142. Cf. MC VII 318 ad M II 2233; M III 4199; V 1892; VI 3561; D 735/7720; 1866/19674; 2138/22635; 3032/32232: 2005/21194. For parallels cf. Khāqāni, Divān, p. 171, 474 and often; Neẓāmi, Khosrow Shirin 94 = H. Ritter, Ueber die Bildersprache Nizamis, Berlin-1927, P. 68; ʿIrāqi ʿUshshaqnāma, ed. A. J. Arberry, p. 47. The topic is also known to Indian poets, cf. Ch. Vaudeville, Kabir Granthvali (Doha), Pondécherry 1957, p. 17.

177. M IV 3068.

178. M IV 3078.

179. M II 2233.

180. D 1791/18769; 2646/28074.—We may add here an animal which was left out from our enumeration, e.g. the porcupine, which occurs in a very strange combination in M IV 98: it appears as the model of the true believer since it grows fatter and stronger when beaten by a stick; in the same way, the believer thrives under the blows of affliction.

181. S 83.

182. M VI 2926 f; I 1009. About two kinds of bees cf. M I 268 f.

183. M V 1228 f.

184. F 228.

185. D 2390/25254.

186. D 1460/15438.

187. D 300/3274.

188. D 2924/31042.

189. D 724/7600.

190. M V 2509; contrary to the general use of the image this verse speaks rather of the greedy person who tries to get hold even of the blood of gnats.

191. D 1564/16432.

192. D 1894/19924.
193. D 651/6788; cf. 2408/25435.
194. M II 3471; cf. IV 2356.
195. M V 2067; cf. R 152.
196. D 1972/20847.
197. D 502/5336.
198. D 2727/28966.
199. D 2512/26576; cf. 355/3819; The fly in our sourmilk is a falcon and a ʿAnqāʾ! R 636.
200. F 55.
201. D 790/8271 f; cf. 482/5125.
202. D 846/8855.
203. D 802/8399.
204. D 922/9710, 12.
205. M V 303 ff.
206. M II 2321 f.
207. D 651/6790; cf. M I 1011, IV 2537 about the miraculous transformation of the worm.
208. D 1484/15652.
209. D 3134/33529 30.
210. D 1372/14504.
211. D 3141/33613 14.
212. D 1734/18182 83.
213. D 587/6205.
214. D 197/2172.
215. M II 791.
216. D 2276/24182. For more bats cf. M IV 856, II 3350 ff.; III 3620 ff.; M VI 3393; M VI 181 claims that God Himself has blindfolded the bat's eye in order to prevent it from seeing the unique sun. D 452/4786; 1211/12885; 1612/16888; 2928/31068.
217. D 304/2334.
218. al-Ḥallāj, Kitāb aṭ-ṭawāsīn, ed. L. Massignon, Paris 1913, *Ṭasīn al-fahm*; cf. H. H. Schaeder, Die persische Vorlage von Goethes 'Seliger Sehnsucht' in: Festschrift für E. Spranger, Berlin 1942
219. D 458/4856.
220. D 538/5730.
221. D 465/4945.
222. M V 2638.
223. D 3101/33068; 1838/19335 blinds the dragon 'sadness'.
224. M VI 3842; III 2548; VI 3060.
225. M V 1951.
226. D 1154/12245 46.
227. D 2039/21500.
228. D 2157/22836.
229. D 1311/13877.
230. D 500/5321. D 3059/32569 combines the panther (*palang*) Love with the crocodile (*nehang*) Poverty.
231. M VI 4086.
232. D 1631/17089.
233. D 2654/28160.

234. D 1455/15383 last line of a ghazal to show the importance of silence. Cf. also M I 21.

235. M I 17; cf. D 1597/16716.

236. D 1920/20213

237. D 2703/28567.

238. D 2171/23004; more salamandar, partly in combination with *qalandar* D 142/1621; 1033/10881; 2435/25680; 2479/26630; 2508/26535; 3015/32052; M V 229; and MC VIII 229; R 504.—Solṭān Valad explains that ordinary men can enjoy fire only through hot water, unless they be a *morgh-e samandar* which comes in the middle of the fire, 'and that is the saint of God' (VN 180). Still today among Muslims the reptile 'salamandar' is usually imagined to be a bird.

239. D 3010/31986.

240. M II 3758 f; IV 851; VI 4010.

241. D 2854/30308; M I 2292.

242. Sanāʾi, Divān, p. 29 ff.

243. M V 43 ff. Cf. the short article by Özgün Baykal, Mevlâna Celâleddin Rumi'nin Mesnevi ve Divan-i Kebir'inde Kuş Motifleri, in Dogu Dilleri I 1, Ankara 1964.

244. D 1390/14714 with the contrast of *lāhuti* 'divine' and *nāsuti* 'human' nature.

245. M I 2790.

246. M V 1411.

247. M I 583; cf. III 3957.

248. M III 3951 ff.

249. D 850/8885.

250. M I 317, 3356; II 2658.

251. MC VII 314 ad M II p. 326; cf. R 516.

252. D 410/4354.

253. D 627/6548.

254. M III 3508.

255. MC VII 276 ad M II 982.

256. D 1940/20489 91.

257. D 577/6108.

258. D 581/6150; DT 8/34901.

259. D 2046/21590. A charming winter—robāʿi (R 1037) says:
The birds went screaming to Solomon:
'Why don't you twist that nightingale's ear?'
The nightingale said: 'Don't get agitated:
I talk three months, and am silent for nine months!'

260. D 3135/33551.

261. D 1048/11050.

262. D 2608/27652.

263. D 684/7117.

264. M II 3624.

265. M I 1802.

266. M II 3755.

267. D 3073.

268. D 778/8117.

269. D 1626/17035.

270. D 827/8645.

271. M I 247 ff.

272. D 11/121.

273. MC VIII 255 ad M V p. 91. Cf. R 1857:

Hear the secrets from the Divinely inspired parrot (*rabbānī*):
You are a baby-parrot and know the language of parrots!

274. M VI 158 f. Cf. M I 247 the story of the shopkeeper's parrot and M I 1547 the story of the merchant and the parrots of India.
275. D 573/6080.
276. D 2864/30405; 1681/17621.
277. D 696/7246.
278. D 1526/16058.
279. M V 635.
280. D 2746/29193.
281. F 38.
282. Thus D 2536/26912 f; M I 3750.
283. M II 1131 ff.
284. D 1353/14300; cf. 3051/32462.
285. D 1354/14325 f.
286. D 313/2318/; RE 340 b. 4.
287. D 2713/28798.
288. M II 1131 ff; R 1385, cf. R 1563.
289. D 1394/14785.
290. M II 334.
291. M VI 136; cf. the flight of *happy* black crows and white falcons R 937.
292. M V 1154.
293. Thus D 1522/16027.
294. M I 1892.
295. D 166/1894.
296. M I 2332.
297. D 728/7641.
298. D 3069/32685.
299. D 2088/22044.
300. D 862/9006; also R 693.
301. D 2512/26581 85; cf. 2912/30932; RE 324 b. 2.
302. M II 3752.
303. Sanā'i, seyr al-ʿebād l. 754.
304. D 2817/29916.
305. D 649/6770; R 833.
306. Cf. D 3076/32775 f.
307. D 3094/33004.
308. D 2255/23910.
309. D 1283/13552.
310. D 1083/11401; 1140/12088.
311. D 535/5695; in a half Arabic quatrain Rumi takes up the topic of the complaining dove as interpreter of the lover's feelings, so common in Abbasid poetry (R 1981).
312. 'The Dove's Necklace' by the great Spanish theologian of the Zahirite lawschool, Ibn Ḥazm (d. 1046) is the most perfect handbook of chaste, ʿ*odhri*, love, and has been translated into almost all Western languages.
313. D 1673/11401; cf. 1721/18010.
314. D 791/8274.
315. D 410/4354.
316. D 2513/26595. The number of these pigeons in the Divān is too great to be

mentioned here in detail.

317. Cf. DT 18/35367; D 1589/16645, 1428/15101.

318. Mektuplar No. CV.

319. M V 4177.

320. M VI 3959.

321. D 1794/18838.

322. M V 395.

323. M III 4035.

324. M V 498 ff.

325. M I 208.

326. Cf. D 212/2358; 1372/14506; 1932/20325; 2626/27804.

327. M II 3503 f.

328. D 2368/25035.

329. D 1417/14990.

330. D 394/4168.

331. D 212/2358.

332. D 189/2099; in a description of his desolate state, the poet therefore complains: (R 874):

When I plant roses without you, only thorns grow,
and when I hatch a peacock's egg, a snake emerges. . . .

333. D 3031/32209.

334. M VI 4785.

335. D 1734/18179.

336. D 1207/12855 56.

337. D 1345/14225.

338. D 3071/32696; 619/6473.

339. M V 1974 ff.

340. M I 943; II 2524 f.; III 2168; MC VII 79.

341. D 2104/22218.

342. M II 3767.

343. D 1537/16154.

344. D 2654/28151.

345. M VI 1877 ff.; cf. AM Nr. 262 the cock calls to prayer.

346. D 570/6063; he says pulpit, but intends the minaret.

347. D 2120/22423.

348. D 2854/30301.

349. D 741/7788; 1940/20477; 1794/18853; cf. MC VII ad M II 1662.

350. M II 3753.

351. M II 2103.

352. D 1904/20043.

353. Thus D 2278/24200; M II 3751.

354. D 2788/29633.

355. D 2636/27964; 2690/28526; 1940/20417.

356. D 2622/27767 71. That the ostrich can devour burning charcoals without being hurt is stated by Damiri, Ḥayawān II 326. About a 'strange bird' cf. also R 686:

You are not a peacock that one would look at your beauty,
You are not a Simorgh that one would mention your name without you,
You are not a royal falcon that one would call you from the game—
Now, what kind of bird are you, and with what can one eat you?

357. M IV 847.

358. D 586/6198.
359. Cf. Ritter, Meer der Seele p. 359, ʿAṭṭār, Moṣibatnāme 16/1.
360. D 795/8320.
361. D 1665/17457; 2204/23380.
362. D 2174/23033; cf. 959/10124; 1248/13229; 2258/23968; 2856/30317; 3071/32696: O heart, you Homā of union, fly . . .
363. D 1256/13312; cf. 945/9965; 1413/14956.
364. D 2625/27789; 608/6392; cf. 2257/23937.
365. D 24/283. The acoustic similarity between ʿ*anqā* and ʿ*ankabut* 'spider' may have helped shaping this combination. In R 1056, the spider-like reproachful enemy is contrasted with the cheerful Simorgh.
366. D 609/6403.
367. D 343/3718; 2840/30178.
368. D 451/4758.
369. D 3006/31948.

CHILDREN IN RUMI'S IMAGERY

1. S 101.
2. F 118.
3. M III 325f (N); cf. III 1756 f.
4. M I 927.
5. M III 3562 f.
6. D 985/10427; 1852/19821.
7. M III 53 ff. (N).
8. D 1580/16578.
9. D 3070/32693.
10. D 1883/19821; 3095/33014.
11. M III 3560.
12. M VI 1804 07.
13. D 1372/14496.
14. M III 1285; cf. D 1306/13827: 'I am, my mouth closed, like the child in the womb of grief, nourished by the blood of the navel.'
15. D 2755/29287.
16. M IV 222 f.
17. AM Nr. 413. (This *ḥadith* is often used in Mevlevi circles to point to the close relation between Ṣolṭān Valad and his father.)
18. D 1472/15536.
19. M II 1; for the process of inspiration cf. D 2234/23679: 'The lady "thought" is pregnant from the light of Thy Majesty'.
20. D 401/4243; 143/1625; 2343/24793; M I 597; III 3213.
21. F 203.
22. Cf. M VI 4755
23. M II 1951: 2445/25825.
24. D 1156/12265.
25. M VI 4048. Cf. M II 2969 about the child Moses, refusing the nurses until he discovered his mother.
26. M III 4592. The intoxicating power of the beloved is once described in an image taken from this sphere: (D 254/2863)

    The two days old baby would turn the cradle towards the Friend if it would only taste his smell.
27. D 2631/27900; 507/5412; cf. 2405/25401:

If a child of one month would get for one moment milk from the breast of Love,
It would gain a stature like a cypress.

28. M I 2378 f. With a pun on *shir* 'milk' and *sher* 'lion' he says (D 2224/23602 03): 'The lovers are lion cubs, drinking lion's milk.'
29. M II 362.
30. D 1472/15536.
31. D 1234/13091. The nurses used to blacken their breast with pitch to wean the children. In D 200/2199 'fate' is compared to a nurse.
32. M I 581; cf. D 825/8634. Ṣolṭān Valad uses the same imagery to explain that God can be seen and 'tasted' only under veils according to man's capacity (VN 180):

    . . . As the mother eats food and bread so that it becomes milk in her, and makes the child eat the bread and meat in the form of milk. If she would put the same meat and bread into the child's mouth, the child would immediately die.

33. M I 555.
34. Mektuplar Nr. XXXVIII.
35. D 1639/17168.
36. M III 1820.
37. M V 3264 ff.
38. D 980/10374; cf. R 728.
39. D 3144/33656.
40. D 2370/25052.
41. D 2893/30725. The long poem was written in connection with Shams' final disappearing.
42. D 2375/25108.
43. D 2237/23713.
44. D 405/4292; cf. 2083/21988: The mother pricks the lip of the child with a needle when he talks too much nonsense.
45. M IV 2923.
46. M VI 3257.
47. D 1170/12409.
48. M VI 1433 ff.; cf. III 4015 about the orphan.
49. M I 923.
50. M I 1623.
51. M V 1289.
52. D 945/9972; in 1793/18827 applied to the Universal Soul which is a babe before the Prophet.
53. D 1439/15223.
54. M II 402.
55. M VI 453.
56. M III 2636; cf. III 2275 f.; VI 4734; D 1353/14306.
57. M II 2597 f.
58. D 629/6559.
59. M IV 1133 f.
60. D 1384/14656. This game is played by two rows of children, one of them forming a firm line with stretched-out arms; they try to catch children from the other group to add to their strength—hence the comparison with the constant influx of spiritual power. Cf. also VN 200:

    The affairs of this world are all play and game, and there is no use or result that comes from them. Just as children become one a king and the other one a vizier and one a prince and one a leader and others soldiers. . . . yet, by that (game) they do not gain a fortress or a country.

61. F 93.
62. M V 3342 f.
63. M V 3597.
64. M VI 4718.
65. F 240. Solṭān Valad explains the same truth with a story of the inhabitants of a besieged town, who threw stones back at the Mongols and thus increased their wrath, . . .
66. M III 2602 ff., a lovely description of children's tales and 'nonsense-verses'.
67. D 2003/21176.
68. D 2629/27860.
69. M III 4585.
70. M IV 2577 f.; cf. I 2792; D 1196/12725.
71. M III 3740; cf. III 511.
72. D 1705/17849.
73. D 1657/17366.
74. D 1523/16035; cf. 232/1608.
75. D 1065/11232.
76. D 1504/15844.
77. D 1957/20662; 882/9243; cf. M IV 2056.
78. D 105/1203.
79. D 2625/27797.
80. F 141.
81. D 2606/27630.
82. M IV 2017.
83. M IV 192.
84. M III 1522 ff.
85. D 1582/16589.
86. M III 550 f.

IMAGERY FROM DAILY LIFE

1. M VI 3921 ff.: how the learned doctor misbehaved. One should not forget that Bahā'oddin Valad's Maʿāref contain a number of very frank, almost obscene statements about sensual love and the role of women; cf. p. 10: 'A lustful (*shahiya*) woman is a most high mosque for God's obedience and worship', cf. also p. 116, 140, 35.
2. D 2003/21177.
3. D 1405/14877. Interesting is his use of the old Turkish word *yalvāj* 'messenger'.
4. M II 3150 and often; D 2878/30557. Cf. R 1784 where he describes all the wrong things one can do: to play ṭanbura before the deaf, to make Yusuf a roommate of the blind, to put sugar into the mouth of the sick, and to couple a *mokhannath* with a houri. . . .
5. The expression is probably by Jamāloddin Hansvi, cf. Zubaid Ahmad, The contribution of Indo-Pakistan to Arabic Literature. Lahore 1968, p. 96. The expression became proverbial in Indian Sufi circles.
6. D 2280/24218 19.
7. D 158/1812 a poem about the mixture of spirits, in strange language.
8. D 195/2147 f. He also alludes to the difficulties of polygamy in a ghazal on patience, D 1340/14179.
9. D 2409/25439.
10. D 2207/23419; another bath-image R 1558. Cf. S 104 about Rumi's frequent-

ing the *ḥamām*.

11. D 2234/23678.
12. D 3073/32732.
13. F 23; cf. M III 3545 f.; cf. for a similar logic VN 180.
14. F 218.
15. D 1099/11621.
16. M V 3663.
17. cf. H. Grotzfeld, Das Bad im arabisch-islamischen Mittelalter, Wiesbaden 1970. Cf. Sanāʾi, Divān p. 333; Ḥadiqa ch. II 174, VIII p. 556. General applications in Rumi: M I 2765; IV 800, 3000, 3479; D 1458/15408; 3013/32028; 1433/15170; 205/2288; 591/6244; 605/3671; 2627/27825; 568/6031.
18. M VI 142 f.; MC VII 173 ad M I 2770.
19. M V 3918.
20. M VI 1548.
21. D 2323/24622.
22. D 809/8454 ff.
23. D 788/8240.
24. M III 3545.
25. D 1095/11574 ff.; 2409/25442.
26. D 1534/17116.
27. D 2761/29351; 1965/20729; and very often, as in all early Persian poetry.
28. D 2490/26336.
29. D 1580/16574.
30. M I 3467 ff.; MC VII 202. The story goes back to Ghazzāli, Iḥyā-ʿolum ad-din III, in 'The Wonders of the heart'. Nezāmi uses it in the Sikandarnāme, 1077 ff.; Cf. Th. Arnold, Painting in Islam, New ed., New York 1965, p. 66 68. A fine miniature showing this contest is found in the Neẓāmi ms. Pers. 124, f. 242 b, in the Chester Beatty Library, Dublin.
31. D 2743/29160.
32. D 169/1916.
33. D 2400/25343; cf. 1473/15539; 1498/15795.
34. D 1379/14596. Cf. also D 358/3854; 396/4196; 655/6830; 1039/10955; 1392/14731; 1679/17600; 1802/18935; 3169/33971—The image is not novel: Aṭṭār uses it in a beautiful *maṭlaʿ* Divan Nr. 288:
    Those who walk in the Reality of Mysteries
    walk with turning head like the point of the compasses.
35. DST p. 282.
36. D 564/5978.
37. D 27/349 ff.
38. D 526/5592; cf. Ch. III, Chickpeas, note 65.
39. D 295/3221.
40. D 1473/15545; cf. 3004/31932, a poem in which the mystic complains of the constant repetition of the same events in the created world.
41. D 2496/26397.
42. D 181/2023 ff; AF I 370 f.; Cf. M V 2900; R 473; 'The body is like a mill, and Love is like its water'; F 183.
43. D 2575/27347.
44. D 583/6176.
45. D 2918/30988.
46. D 1242/13164.

47. D 303/3306.
48. D 1095/11564 65.
49. D 1139/12075.
50. F 35.
51. D 1591/16665.
52. M III 1163; plus MC VIII 31.
53. D 27/344; cf. 2437/25704.
54. D 671/7003; 2938/31184.
55. D 914/9625.
56. Cf. Ch. III, Love, note 158, and very often.
57. D 62/751; cf. 1607/16832 35; 2651/28129; 2706/28711.
58. D 561/5950; cf. 2988/31738; Cf. the amusing image in D 1100/11634:
    Repentance is a glass-bottle, His love is like the bleacher—
    What has a bottle-maker to do with a bleacher? (who will cast his good on the stony ground as bleachers do with the laundry)?
59. M V 324 ff.; Sanā'i mentions it Sanā'i'ābād line 219.
60. D 2650/28114; cf. R 1351.
61. D 1673/17528. A *fatvā* about *parī-khwānī* by Mowlānā's father in Ma'āref p. 3, cf. id. Hāshiya p. 189 with examples.—The dangerous jinni who has to be confined in the bottle forms the *maṭla'* of D 212/2356; cf. also M V 1211 ff. Cf. M III 471 plus MC VIII 14, and R 1161:
    The pupil of my eye became restless in (beholding) your face,
    That means, I saw a peri (fairy) and became obsessed.
    D 724/7598 f. connects it with the bath, which was regarded as a dwelling place of fairies and demons; so also R 285.—More *pari-khwānī*: D 2507/26528; 3011/32004; 484/5159; 423/4453; 2560/27174; 1467/15492; 233/2629; 1520/15995 f.; 2643/28041. Particularly charming is D 1466/15482 f.

THE IMAGERY OF FOOD IN RUMI'S POETRY

1. D 2152/22777. Ma'āref 174 uses also kitchen imagery. A very strange account of Bahā'oddin (Ma'āref 115) tells how he had eaten too much and received an inspiration that all the bread and fruits in his stomach were praising God . . .' and everything created is a nourishment', an idea elaborated by Rumi, too; cf. Ch. III The Chickpeas, note 60 ff.
2. D 1036/10929 30.
3. M VI 4706.
4. D 914/9591; 1827/19191; 1407/14894; cf. 2154/22798 f.
5. A study into Rumi's use of *bu*, 'smell, scent' would be highly interesting; it is known that at least in later times the Sufi masters, before accepting someone as disciple, used even to 'sniff' at him in order to find out whether or not he would fit into their spiritual circle, cf. Sha'rāni, quoted by C. Farah, 'The duties of the sheykh towards his disciples'. We may assume that this 'smelling' was in use already in earlier times as means of spiritual recognition.
6. D 1402/14845.
7. M VI 1212. Cf. also for the same purpose, R 689:
    O soul, sugar is procured from the reed with caution, and satin is made from the leaves of the muleberry tree—Slow! Do not hurry! Be Patient,
    For from our sour grapes ḥalvā is made in the course of time.
8. D 2574/27335; *yakhnī* is mentioned R 1521.
9. D 1417/14992 ff; cf. also 133/1537 in connection with the 'spiritual Bughrā Khān'. Khāqāni, Divān p. 758, connects *totmāj* with the Turks. Cf. M VII 408.
10. D 2372/25084.
11. D 2355/24916; cf. V 3460.
12. D 3171/33991.

13. D 805/8430.
14. D 581/6165.
15. D 2944/31249.
16. D 2255/23907.
17. D 3073/32731 (a pun on *bolghāri — bolghuri*).
18. D 1631/17089; M VI 719.
19. D 1071/11276.
20. D 1260/13350.
21. D 1450/15339.
22. D 2879/30565.
23. D 1695/17767.
24. D 1652/17310.
25. M IV 3030 f; the same image for the world of matter which contains the world of the spirit in D 2897/30793.
26. D 1239/13136.
27. DT 24/35603.
28. D 3101/33065.
29. Cf. D 1194/12707; 910/9555; cf. R 507. Sanā'i speaks with the same combination of someone being—'unveiled like the garlic, in the veil like onions', Divān p. 299, cf. id. p. 291.
30. M III 3355.
31. M IV 864.
32. M VI 4042.
33. D 1600/16746; cf. 1122/11844: God as the cook who sells all kinds of meat and edibles without outward fire.—Khāqāni sees the cruel sky = fate as a butcher's shop, Divān, qaṣida p. 61.
34. D 1380/14607.
35. D 1959/20676.
36. D 1141/12108.
37. D 2167/22949.
38. D 2872/30493.
39. D 1198/12739.
40. D 3074/32755.
41. D 344/3727; M I 167, III 3863.
42. D 2653/28146.
43. Cf. D 1417/14986; 3062/32611; 2431/25625; 2922/31022 the fire falls into the reed which thus becomes sweet. In R 213, and comparable R 219, 224 the poet uses related puns and speaks of the beloved whose burden is all sugar, and:
    I said: 'Do you not give me a portion of this sugar?'
    He said 'No!' (*ney*) and did not know that the *ney* ('no' and 'sugarcane') was sugar.
44. D 1393/14756, cf. 1527/16072 sugar sold by the druggist = ʿAṭṭār.
45. D 1593/16680.
46. D 2488/26320; cf. 2909/30903: 'When Intellect read the book of His love, the heart of the paper became full of sugar, yes.'
47. F 41.
48. D 1047/11035.
49. D 134/1545; cf. 2787/29626, M V 1966.
50. D 2595/27521.
51. D 945/9976.
52. D 1227/13045.

53. D 2096/22141.
54. D 1219/12960; cf. 3012/32023.
55. F 197.
56. D 125/1433; cf. 244/2751 'like milk in *zalubiyya*', a sort of pancake.
57. D 96/1080; 2230/23647; M II 393. The fondness of the Sufis for *ḥalvā* was notorious from the 10th century on as many satirical remarks from early Sufi literature show (cf. A. Mez, Die Renaissance des Islams, Heidelberg 1922, p. 275), and the topic of the Sufi whose object of worship is milk-rice and ḥalvā is used by Persian writing poets from Sanā'i to 17th century Indian poets. On the other hand, the ḥalvā ritual has a special place in the Bektashi tradition.
58. D 225/2541 48.
59. D 1372/14510; cf. 31/413; 371/3974.
60. D 106/1210. The whole poem speaks of ḥalvā and ends with the two lines:
    As proof that we are born from the Universal Intellect his call comes: 'O daddy's darling!'
    He always calls: 'Children, come! The table is laid, and the friend is alone!'
61. D 99/1128.
62. D 316/3450.
63. D 589/6225; 2120/22417.
64. D 2511/26562 63; cf. R 1953 and 1955 about the ḥalvā which comes from *ʿadam*, non-existence.
65. D 2431/25627.
66. D 2660/28222.
67. M V 1662 ff.
68. MC VII 137 ad M I 2003.
69. D 1749/18339.
70. D 2570/27283.
71. Cf. D 45/585.
72. M II 1344 (dead ass); VI 1858 f.; cf. D 3041/3243; 3100/33057; DT 10/34985. Cf. ʿAṭṭār, Divān, ghazal Nr. 516, and Muṣibatnāma p. 15; VN 222, to explain the *ḥadīth* 'Die before ye die' speaks of the 'saltmine of union'; cf. id. 292. The expression occurs still in Mir Dard (d. 1785) Dard-e del, in Chahār Resāla, Bhopal 1310 h., Nr. 161, cf. id. Nr. 302.
73. M I 2003; cf. R 540.
74. D 76/883; 2290/24339.
75. D 124/1425.
76. D 1071/11277.
77. D 1286/13589.
78. D 1422/15047.
79. D 1212/12901.
80. D 3057/32553.
81. D 3090/32967 69; cf. 971/10274: In the oven of affliction he made me baked and red (honoured).
82. D 2084/22000.
83. M VI 3946 ff.
84. D 1329/14056; 2683/28450; 2685/28475; R 1156 describes the 'kitchen of grief in which every moment the smell of burnt liver is felt'.
85. D 2150/22760 f.
86. D 2809/29828; R 1327 speaks of the kitchen of heaven with golden vessels and admonishes the disciple not to be content with hot water; cf. R 1213.
87. M V 387.
88. D 1439/15230.

89. D 970/10257; 1774/18585; 2838/30144.
90. D 1644/17224; 2065/21812.
91. D 2177/23082.
92. D 862/9005.
93. D 1602/16762.
94. ad-Daylami, ed, Juneyd-e Shirāzī, Sirat-e Ibn al-Khafif, ed. A. Schimmel, Ankara 1955, Ch. X p. 107.
95. M VI 4898; AM Nr. 129.
96. Thus Mir Jānullāh of Rohri, in H. Sadarangani, Persian Poets of Sind, p. 109.
97. D 1241/13145.
98. D 2685/28475.
99. D 59/728.
100. D 1023/10791; 1697/17781.
101. D 225/2546.
102. D 1691/17716.
103. ʿAṭṭār, Divān.
104. D 2939/31194.
105. D 2276/24175.
106. D 372/3987 f.
107. D 1358/14367.
108. D 683/7102 ff.; cf. R 791.
109. Cf. N. Söderblom, Rausch und Religion, in: Ur Religionens Historia, Stockholm 1915, and the extensively documented chapter in F. Heiler, Erscheinungsformen und Wesen der Religion, Stuttgart 1961 p. 249 ff.
110. M I 10.
111. D 1077/11336.
112. D 1930/20292; 2514/26607; M II 3723 ff.
113. D 1381/14612 f.
114. M I 3426 ff., elaboration of a saying by Sanāʾi.
115. M II 343; cf. V 4197 f.
116. M II 2392 ff.
117. D 488/5208; 2827/30011 ff.; cf. R 1307.
118. D 1371/14476.
119. D 1500/15804; cf. R 373.
120. D 713/7464.
121. D 1381/14617.
122. D 650/6781.
123. M V 3288 f.
124. D 2432/25630.
125. M V 372 f.
126. M III 4746.
127. D 1403/14869.
128. D 2395/25295 302 (N). This poem which describes the annihilation of the cupbearer in the Beloved whose mirror he was has been analyzed best by H. H. Schaeder, Die islamische Lehre vom Vollkommenen Menschen, in: ZDMG 79/1925.
129. Notwithstanding the more recent edition and translation of Ibn al-Fāriḍ's Divān by A. J. Arberry, the best introduction into his poetry is still R. A. Nicholson, Studies in Islamic Mysticism, Cambridge 1921, Ch. II. Even S 48 quotes Ibn al-Fariḍ's *Tāʾiyya*.

130. In the superb wine ode D 1966/20742. Another fine example of this style is the long poem D 1135. Cf. also R 1125.

131. M II 180 f., cf. M V 3456 f.

132. Ghālib, Kulliyāt-e Fārsi, Qaṣāʾid, Lahore 1976, No. 26; German verse-translation A. Schimmel, Rose der Woge, Rose des Weins, Zürich 1971, p. 61.

133. M III 2348; cf. R 1125.

134. Divān-e Ḥāfeẓ, ed. M. R. Jalāli Nāʾini and Dr. Nadhir Aḥmad, Teheran 1350 sh, Nr. 115 p. 134. AM Nr. 624.

135. D 2583/27425.

136. D 2319/24592; this line forms the basis of a chain of verses in Shāh ʿAbd al-Latif's Risālo (Sindhi), ed. K. Advani, Bombay 1957 Sur Yaman Kalyān VI 1 ff.

137. D 1542/16195.

138. M IV 2098.

139. M III 823 f.

140. M I 1812; cf. R 291 'today the goblet is intoxicated by us'.

IMAGERY CONNECTED WITH DISEASES

1. D 321/3486 ff.
2. M VI 4599.
3. D 2197/23319.
4. D 2133/22575.
5. S 81.
6. M V 1697 f.
7. D 1422/15037.
8. D 2605/27615. Further examples D 590/6230; 846/8855; 2511/26563.
   It is not the fault of the light when the blind neglect it,
   It is not the fault of the ḥalvā when it causes pain in the bile-affected.;
   2921/31018. —Sanāʾi uses the same imagery; Divān p. 56:
   God tells you: Do not drink in this world!
   The Christian says: Do not eat ḥalvā when you suffer from bile (*ṣafrā*).
9. D 106/1208.
10. M IV 180.
11. D 224/2532.
12. M I 17.
13. D 308/3377; cf. 2244/23775; 2120/22418; DT 24/35649.
14. Khaqāni, Divān qaṣida p. 54 speaks of the drum of the navel of those afflicted with dropsy.
15. D 2897/30785; 2919/31002 as quality of insatiable love.
16. D 1016/10721; cf. M V 285.
17. D 1652/17302.
18. D 2808/29820. *ʿillat-e sil* D 1345/14233.
19. D 908/9513.
20. M IV 149.
21. M III 1335.
22. D 1090/11471 74.
23. Cf. D 3148/33727; cf. also Sanāʾi, Divān 465.
24. D 656/6847; cf. M IV 342.
25. Cf. Ch. III Chickpeas, Note 27.
26. D 587/6206; M V 236 f.
27. M V 2879.

28. M I 103.
29. D 1134/11991.
30. D 865/9058.
31. MC VII 211 ad M I 3663. Rumi even describes the process of *fanā*ʾ 'annihilation' as the annihilation of vinegar in *angubin*, M V 2024.
32. M III 2346 f.
33. M I 3664.
34. F 205.
35. Opium is often mentioned either alone or along with wine as an intoxicant, thus 1931/20296: 'Reason ate opium from the hand of love'; 1855/19561; 1644/17216; 1215/12929; 1141/12100; 1113/11752; 89/1007; 245/2753; 855/8935; 1025/10800; 2161/22884; 2393/25279; 2398/25326; 1247/13216; DT 11/35901; R 1508, 1439.
36. D 702/7316.
37. D 2532/26850; the *ṭuzghū* in the text is probably the original form ('salted') of the word *turghu* as given in Steingass. It means 'salted and pickled food for provision'. — To help a person who has swallowed something rotten to vomit is an act of grace; cf. the story of the man who rescued somebody who unwittingly had swallowed a snake by making him vomit M II 1878 f., taken up VN 183 as model for the saint's seemingly cruel, but useful actions.
38. D 951/10032.
39. F 126.
40. Thus D 1475/15564 he describes himself as the miraculous physician; cf. M I 24. Cf. for this imagery R 1959, 827 (the physician himself needs a physician) and the amusing R 1513. Further D 2097/22148; 2521/26729.
41. D 1963/20715.
42. D 1474/15546 55.
43. M III 2701 Allusions to Galen and also to Plato in his capacity as physician occur frequently, though not always in a very flattering connection, cf. D 1161/12330:

   He whose pulse does not jump from love —
   Consider him an ass though he be Plato.

42. D 1513/15924: *isfantin*, wormwood, Wermut, *artemisia absinthium*, was used against many diseases, cf. G. Kircher, Die 'einfachen Heilmittel' aus dem 'Hand buch der Chirurgie' des Ibn al-Quff, Bonn, Ph.D. Diss. 1967, p. 65. Likewise the friend, even though of bitter taste, is a panacea for all diseases of the lover.
45. D 2658/28196; cf. 2940/31201; the *mofarreḥ* was generally produced by using precious stones as ingredients, mainly rubies, hence the connection with the friend's ruby-lips, Cf. B. Reinert, Khaqāni als Dichter, Berlin 1972, p. 19.
46. D 565/5996.
47. F 187. Solṭān Valad explains the whole medical imagery VN 167 f:

   Just as the body of water and clay has (its own) physicians, thus the heart and the soul have also physicians, and these are the prophets and saints. The physician says: 'Eat this and dont eat that so that your body be without pain and become strong', and the prophets and the saints say: 'Do this and dont do that, so that the soul becomes pure and nicely fat . . .'

WEAVING AND SEWING

1. D 133/1530.
2. D 46/592; 2710/28766.
3. D 1393/14754.
4. D 857/8943.
5. D 1230/13066.
6. About the symbolism of the garment cf. Heiler, Erscheinungsformen, p. 118 ff.

7. Cf. C.-G de Fouchécour, La description de la nature dans la poésie persane lyrique . . ., Paris 1969.
8. Farrokhi, Divān, ed. M. Dabir Siyāqi, Teheran 1335 sh, Nr. 169, p. 329.
9. D 666/6955.
10. D 2649/28108.
11. D 1554/16330; 3172/34005.
12. D 2939/31191.
13. M III 684 a *baghaltaq*, wide vest made of satin.
14. DT 36/36082.
15. D 2971/31534.
16. M III 2140.
17. D 954/10062; cf. 1201/12794: 'The lover's perfection gets a *ṭerāz* when he seizes Shamsoddin's hem.'
18. D 2519/26669.
19. D 2002/21165; cf. 2672/28335.
20. D 2632/27917.
21. For the idea cf. H. Zimmer, The King and the Corpse, ed. by J. Campbell (Bollingen Series XI) Paperback, Princeton 1971, p. 221.
22. D 2281/24236.
23. D 385/4104.
24. D 999/10549; cf. 783/8173; 2536/26921.
25. D 551/5852; cf. 2063/21787; 2203/23362.
26. M VI 4618.
27. D 218/2453.
28. D 2777/29512.
29. D 314/3436.
30. D 3128/33425 in a negative sense: talking is compared to weaving a coarse garment. For the spinning-imagery cf. L. Ramakrishna, Punjabi Sufi Poets, London-Calcutta 1938, Introduction.
31. D 2073/21893.
32. D 2087/22043.
33. D 2715/28823; cf. 1339/14176.
34. D 931/9812; 917/9655; 2650/28116.
35. D 2344/24803.
36. D 907/9504.
37. D 55/679.
38. D 2938/31182; 2939/31190; cf. 1852/19537 'the satin of inner meaning'.
39. D 1247/13220. *Aṭlas* and *iksun* are generally mentioned together, thus 1089/11460; 1215/12933; 1878/19793.
40. D 2897/30783; 853/8917; 364/3900.
41. Thus D 1573/16506.
42. M IV 1039.
43. D 3004/31934.
44. D 3029/32179; 3041/32340.
45. Cf. D 877/9178.
46. D 1958/20670; DT 11/35068.
47. DT 11/3569.
48. D 2376/25119.
49. D 2443/25784.
50. D 2494/26361.

51. D 2431/25623.
52. D 1847/19479.
53. D 2777/29514; cf. the *lebās-e qahr* 'garment of wrath' D 391/4154.
54. D 869/9081; the *maṭlaᶜ* is taken from Khāqani, Divān p. 765.
55. M VI 1650 1721; quoted also by Damiri (MC VIII 345); it must have been known among the Arab popular tales for many years.
56. M II 1311.
57. F 123.
58. D 216/2424 26.
59. D 482/5145 with an allusion, in the preceding verse, to the camel and the needle's eye (Sura 7/40).
60. D 1538/16172; cf. 1384/14650.
61. D 616/6454 5.
62. D 922/9710, 12. — A strange application of the motif of sewing in D 135/1554.

DIVINE CALLIGRAPHY

1. J. von Hammer-Purgstall, Sitzungberichte der K.u.K. Akademie der Wissenschaften, Wien, 1851, p. 58.
2. Cf. D 1215/12934; 562/5954; M VI 369. For the whole topic cf. A. Schimmel, Mystical Dimensions of Islam, Appendix I.
3. D 2205/23396.
4. D 460/4886.
5. D 947/9993.
6. M I 1514; cf. MC VII 110, 179.
7. D 1377/14584; cf. P. Nwyia, Exegèse Coranique et langage Mystique, Beirut 1970, p. 166.
8. Ghazaliyāt-e Shams-e Tabrizi, ed. M. Moshfeq, Teheran 1335 sh: p. 128.
9. D 2536/26917.
10. M V 3612.
11. M VI 2239 45. The idea is found in Sanāʾi, seyr al-ᶜebād, 1. 700, and Ḥadiqa Ch. II p. 187.
12. M VI 2329 ff.
13. D 3035/32274.
14. D 1188/12649. Another allusion to the *hamza* D 1463/15462.
15. D 1898/19962.
16. D 1744/18298.
17. D 1411/14932.
18. D 540/5755; R 442.
19. D 2/24; cf. 335/3625 *alif-nun*.
20. M V 2365.
21. D 145/1643.
22. D 931/9823; DT 23/35585.
23. D 430/4540; cf. R 1491.
24. D 1304/13796.
25. M VI 1650.
26. Cf. Sanāᶜi, Ḥadiqa Ch. IX p. 666: 'Their hearts narrow like a kufic *kāf*'.
27. D 1316/13935; cf. 4691/4986; 1461/15445; DT 33/36016; cf. R 443.
28. D 1948/20568.
29. D 1728/18106; cf. the beautiful description of the mystic's entering into the letters of *Allāh* until he is surrounded by the final *h*, in Nāṣir Moḥammad

ʿAndalib (d. 1758), Nāla-yi ʿAndalib, in: Schimmel, Mystical Dimensions p. 421.

30. M V 1316 ff and others.
31. DT 12/35117.
32. D 2499/26438; cf. 2366/25021.
33. D 2655/28165; cf. ʿAṭṭār, Manṭeq oṭ-ṭeyr, p. 291: 'I prefer the *kāf* of *kofr* there through the light of gnosis to the *fā* of *falsafa* (philosophy)'.
34. DT 32/35975.
35. M I 3457; cf. R 1047: the letters of ʿ*eshq* mean ʿ*ayn* = ʿ*ābed*, *sh* = *shāker*, *q* = *qāne*ʿ. Typical examples in Sanāʾi are Ḥadiqa Ch. V p. 330; cf. also ʿAṭṭār, Divān, ghazal Nr. 300: 'In the way of love one needs a heart (*del*) which is free from *d* and *l*'.
36. D 1418/15006 7.
37. D 1520/15993 4; cf. M I 3100.
38. D 684/7118.
39. D 66/791.
40. D 1497/15783.
41. D 1187/12645.
42. M I 292.
43. D 21/238.
44. DT 16/35293.
45. D 1419/15024.
46. I found it only in D 860/8987; cf. 1351/14288.
47. D 747/7848.
48. D 2578/27379; DT 26/35731; M I 2727.
49. D 2909/30901.
40. M III 1267.
51. D 2572/27310. The most famous letter written to Shams is D 1760/18449 60.
52. D 1351/14288; cf. 842/8816; 1224/13011; cf. Sarrāj, Kitāb al-lumaʿ, ed. R.A. Nicholson, p. 50 Shibli's verse.
53. D 2224/23595.
54. D 2251/23857.
55. M IV 3721 ff.
56. M II 159. Rumi uses even the image of the paper-shirt, the dress of the plaintiff at court, in connection with picture and colour D 2134/22582; the image, which is used in the first line of Ghālib's Urdu Divān in 19th century India, has generally puzzled the interpreters of Ghālib's poetry; it is, however, quite common in medieval Persian imagery.
57. M V 1961 ff.
58. D 926/8816.
59. AM Nr. 13; M V 1686; 2777 ff; D 1521/16016, 2778/29553; RE 336 a 1 and often.
60. D 2530/26824 5 (the whole poem deals with writing); cf. D 1487/15685; 2433/25649; where the ruler (*mosaṭṭar*) is mentioned.
61. D 2530/26829; cf. 538/5729.
62. D 2872/30510; 882/9236; cf. R 1291.
63. D 1915/20142; 1664/17442; cf. 1769/18526; M I 393 f.
64. D 2530/26828.
65. M I 2914 f.
66. M I 3334 f.
67. D 1291/13644.

68. Ḥaydar-e Āmoli, quoted by T. Izutsu, The Basic Structure of Metaphysical Thinking in Islam, in: M. Mohaghghegh and H. Landolt, Collected Papers on Islamic Philosophy and Mysticism, Teheran 1971, p. 66.
69. D 1076/11322.
70. D 1739/18239.
71. D 743/7808.
72. D 1425/15071.
73. D 1213/12911; cf. 2257/23930; 1669/17500; M V 4195.
74. cf. M IV 2972.
75. D 1497/15772.
76. M I 114.

PASTIMES OF THE GREAT

1. D 1932/20327 f; 364/3895; for shadowplay as a mystical symbol cf. Schimmel, Mystical Dimensions, Ch. VI c.
2. Cf. MC VII 259 ad M II 613; D 129/1481. Typical is M II 2600 2790.
3. D 1383/14634.
4. D 2417/25502.
5. D 1528/16083.
6. D 1558/16361 ff. Yaʿqubi (Taʾrikh I p. 103) mentions an Indian tradition according to which *nard* was invented to illustrate the doctrine of determinism, and chess to prove the doctrine of freewill.
7. D 2372/25079; 1233/13084.
8. D 2330/24664; M III 535, and often.
9. D 386/4113. The expression *miyān bord* is not clear to me.
10. D 1649/17273; cf. 525/5581.
11. D 2131/22559.
12. D 133/1536; 2918/30989; 2980/31633.
13. D 734/7710 19.
14. Resāla-ye hush-afzā, Ms. Ph 96 (1786) Punjab University Library, Lahore (unique ms.).
15. Such a game is found in the Institute of Islamic Studies, McGill University, Montreal.
16. D 1569/16475.
17. F 146.
18. Goethe, Noten und Abhandlungen zum West- Oestlichen Divān, Ch. *Despotie*.
19. D 397/4201.
20. D 28/361; M VI 926.
21. D 2226/23619 21.
22. D 994/10508 10.
23. D 2195/23299.
24. D 681/7083.
25. D 239/2691 in the Furuzānfar edition; DST Nr. II.

KORANIC IMAGERY

1. F 173.
2. M V 3128 f.
3. S 71; cf. VN 53 ff: 'The poetry of the saints is all Koranic exegesis and the secret of the Koran. . . .' and id p. 256: 'Its outward is poetry, and its inside exegesis'.
4. D 1948/20559 71.

5. M IV 2122.
6. M I 3860.
7. D 1481/15626.
8. D 2519/26703. This long ghazal belongs to a late period in Mowlānā's life; it speaks of Ḥosāmoddin and is filled with technical terms of theosophical mysticism.
9. D 2630/27884; cf. 2753/29268; D 1594/16685 addresses the beloved: 'You are the Koran-copy (*moṣḥaf*) of Inner Meaning.'
10. D 2807/29776.
11. D 2756/29292.
12. M V 1537 ff.
13. D 148/1675; cf. 1674/17544.
14. D 1665/17455.
15. D 1696/17773; 142/1620.
16. D 2809/29825.
17. D 1100/11642.
18. D 2120/22419 20.
19. D 2073/21892.
20. D 1894/19924.
21. D 1272/13459.
22. Especially in the long winding story beginning M IV 562.
23. M I 956 ff.; transl. R. A. Nicholson in: Rumi, Poet and Mystic, London 1950, p. 66, Nr. XXX. The sources of this story are given in H. Ritter, Das Meer der Seele, p. 37. This story was often retold in the West, even in Flemish (P. N. von Eyck, De Tuinman en de dood, 1926).
24. AM Nr. 320.
25. D 2649/28107.
26. Cf. H. Ritter, Muslim Mystics' Strife with God, in: Oriens V 1952.
27. D 3016/32064.
28. D 911/9564.
29. D 1142/12114; about Shamsoddin as absolutely superior to Yusuf cf. D 2782/29577.
30. D 3038/32306.
31. D 2800/29731.
32. M III 2334 f.
33. D 1932/20335; 1723/18041.
34. D 1712/17930.
35. D 859/8971.
36. Cf. D 2782/29572 82 about the problem of hiding the overwhelming light of the Sun.
37. D 2687/28500.
38. D 2236/23695.
39. D 1599/16733.
40. D 1329/14063.
41. S 93; cf. D 2176/23063; 3038/32305.
42. D 667/6965 (the allusion is, however, negative).
43. D 81/937; cf. AM Nr. 599 'There is no monkery in Islam'.
44. D 728/7642.
45. D 892/9350.
46. D 1826/19180.

47. D 189/2100.
48. D 1414/14962.
49. D 3090/32965.
50. D 2981/31654.
51. F 61.
52. D 3094/33001.
53. D 1509/15884 (allusion to Sura 2/61)
54. D 1427/15099.
55. D 2617/27726; for the terminology cf. R 1395; in a lighter mood: D 2439/25720.
56. D 2550/27055; The story is attributed to Ahmad Ghazzāli by Ibn-al Jauzi, Kitāb al-quṣṣās waʾl-mudhakkerīn, ed. M. S. Swartz, Beirut 1970, §.225.
57. D 2176/23064.
58. F 33.
59. M IV 4547; cf. R 914 for the process of inspiration in imagery taken from Mary who was 'virgin and pregnant'.
60. D 565/5990.
61. D 1594/16689.
62. D 122/1390.
63. D 933/9839; 2003/21177; 2849/30260; 1990/21030; 2854/30305; M VI 1807. The image was not novel; already Kisāʾi has used the comparison of blossoming trees with Maryam.
64. M III 3700 ff.
65. D 114/1283.
66. M I 335 ff.
67. M VI 493 f.; cf. his remarks F 98 (Ch. XX) about the problem of marriage and celibacy:

    The way of monks was solitude, dwelling in mountains and not taking women, giving up the world. God most High and Mighty indicated to the Prophet, God bless him and give him peace, a strait and hidden way. What is that way? To wed women, so that he might endure the tyranny of women and hear their absurdities.
68. M V 3255 ff.
69. D 693/7215.

IMAGERY TAKEN FROM HISTORY AND GEOGRAPHY

1. M II 922 ff.; D 2503/26494.
2. D 2220/23556; 2326/24638.
3. D 2173/23026; 2871/30472; R 1765.
4. D 2934/31129.
5. D 2175/23053.
6. M I 77; D 786/8216: VN 314, cf. Bo Utas, Ṭariq at -taḥqiq, Lund 1972, p. 169 Note ad 99 b.
7. D 2580/27400; cf. 786/8216; VN p. 314.
8. D 668/6982.
9. M V 843 ff.
10. D 810/8474.
11. M III 578 f.
12. M I 3944 ff.
13. D 2934/31133.
14. D 2840/30165 (in the first hemistich an allusions to the 'lonely' Isfandiyār).

15. D 718/7547.
16. D 1392/14734; 24/282.
17. D 338/3660.
18. D 879/9206.
19. D 230/2595. This etymology is, however, already found in the book *al-amāli wa'l-majālis* of the 10th century Shia theologian Ibn Bābuya (Qumm 1373 sh, p. 71), founded on an alleged *ḥadīth*.
20. D 2707/28715.
21. D 1621/16977; the Banu Qoḥāfa are the family to which the first caliph, Abu Bakr, belonged. Cf. also M II 2203 about the Khārijites.
22. Thus D 2710/28746 ff.
23. M III 177 ff. about Bilāl's mispronouncing the call to prayer; but 'a fault committed by lovers is better than the correctness of strangers', a topic often elaborated in Sufi lore.
24. D 2136/22613.
25. Thus M V p. 178 ff. and MC VIII 281; cf. D 485/5184; 3092/32985; 3005/31946; 1651/17295; 1845/19419; 1806/18983.
26. D 1246/13203 ff.
27. D 897/9394.
28. His name occurs in D 1024/10799; 808/8452; 1091/11482; 870/9103; 477/5065; 296/3233; 2337/24735; 2450/25877; 2797/29712; 733/7695; 784/8194; 1791/18771; 1456/15387; 2260/23989. A chapter in M VI 3029 ff. is devoted to his bravery during the attack at a fortress.
29. M III 3429 f.; D 2593/27501.
30. About the different versions of the Ḥamza-story in Persian, Turkish, Urdu, Hindi, Malay and Javanese cf. Ethé, in W. Geiger—E.Kuhn, Grundriss der irnaischen Philologie, Strassburg 1896 1903, Vol. II 318, and for the miniatures G. Egger, Der Hamza-Roman, Wien 1969. Manuscripts of Indian versions with miniatures in large size are found in almost every larger European and American museum.
31. Thus D 375/4026; 1638/17153; 1604/16795; 1940/20294.
32. Thus D 2807/29798; 2275/24153.
33. D 2710/28745 ff.
34. M III 4101: 'I am unafraid (of death) like the Ismailis . . .', He alludes to the Assassins or Hashāshiyun whose last stronghold was destroyed during his lifetime by the Mongols.
35. Thus D 1637/17142; 2319/24589; 11/131; 1221/12982; also several times in his letters.
36. Thus D 2207/23431; 2205/23386; 2516/26625; 2464/26027.
37. D 2531/26843.
38. D 2983/31679; cf. 3016/32062; 809/8463.
39. D 1373/14520; cf. 1374/14524.
40. D 787/8229.
41. Farrokhi, Divān, p. 161, Nr. 78.
42. Cf. H. Ritter, Das Meer der Seele s.v. Ayāz, G. Spies, Maḥmud von Ghazna bei Farīd ud-Dīn ʿAṭṭār, Basel 1959.
43. M V 1891 ff.; cf. MC VII 278; cf. also M VI 234; AM Nr. 529. For the genesis of this *ḥadīth* cf. F. Meier, ʿAziz-i Nasafi, WZKM 52.
44. The most typical allusions: D134/1550; 970/10265; 1202/12807; 725/7613; 1195/12716; 1565/16446; 1724/18052; 1854/19551; 2317/24579; 2455/25927; 2524/26760; 2472/26146; 2870/30469; 2218/23528; 2057/21727.—Solṭān Valad has elaborated the story as told in M V in VN 29 ff. and interprets it on

p. 34 ff. as: 'Meant with Solṭān Maḥmud is God, and with the princes the intelligent and scholars and philosophers and with Ayāz the prophets and saints and their essence.'

45. Cf. D 2529/26819; 2282/24250 alludes to the fact that the Khwarezmians as Muʿtazilites denied the possibility of the *visio beatifica, ruʾyā*, but:
    From your vision 'without how' (*bi chun ₇ bilā kaifa*) your Khwārezm has stamped the foot (in mystical dance)',
    i.e. the ineffable beauty of the Beloved intoxicated even those who deny this vision. Cf. Maʿāref, Ḥāshiya p. 284. For the Muʿtazilites cf. also D 948/10006; 3091/32974.
46. F 167.
47. M I 2684 f.
48. D 736/7735.
49. D 2284/24266.
50. D 2634/27941; 2862/30389; 2311/24531; 2326/24640. A contrast Baghdad-Abkhāz M V 1023.
51. D 1358/14360.
52. M VI 2823.
53. MC VIII 370 mentions also the explanation *aṭrāf al-maʿmura*.
54. Cf. for the concrete Qayrawān Sanāʾi, Divān p. 427: The setting sun will bring the ruler's order to Qayrawān, and id. 764; Khāqāni, Divan p. 402, and often in pre-Rumi poetry.
55. D 2519/26702 a pun with *qir*, 'pitch'.
56. D 1081/11362.
57. D 2000/21139; Silk from Istanbul M VI 1650 ff.
58. D 529/5627.
59. D 2214/23482.
60. D 2939/31193.
61. D 552/5866.
62. D 2922/31025.
63. D 3148/33272.
64. D 2494/26367.
65. D 1493/15727 40.
66. D 634/6610.
67. D 1690/17709.
68. D 800/8372.
69. D 567/6013; R 1204. About the 'beauties of Kashmir' in early Persian poetry cf. the introduction in M. Aṣlaḥ, Tazkere-ye shoʿarā-ye Kashmir, ed. H. Rashdi, 5 Vols, Karachi 1970.
70. But cf. R 1386:
    O Bulghar, make your house in Bulghar,
    O Arabic-speaking person (*tāzi-gu*), go to ʿAbbadān!
71. D 358/3853.
72. D 3101/33074; 2298/24408.
73. D 3101/33074.
74. M II 2620.
75. D 2031/21432; 2657/28188; cf. 1755/18396.
76. D 644/6717: thoughts and ideas which were as ugly as Gog and Magog become as beautiful as if they were Chinese dolls.
77. D 2031/21432.
78. Cf. DST p. 341.

79. D 372/3994; cf. 910/9554.

80. D 1921/20227; for Tabriz cf. also R 1373, contrasted with Marāgha.

81. D 2905/30872 and R 1375:
When Syria and Iraq and Luristan
by this Nuristan-like face have become illuminated,
then take Monkar and Nakir by the hand
so that the graveyard claps hands and dances.

82. D 1290/13633 8; cf. i.a. the 'Turk of joy' and the 'Hindu of grief' D 879/9200; M I 3525, MC VII 91 and very often. For the problem cf. A. Schimmel, Turk and Hindu, a poetical symbol and its application to historical facts, IV, Giorgio della Vida Conference, Los Angeles 1972 (Wiesbaden, 1974).

83. M I 2918; VI 4787.

84. M V 3157; the story M VI 1383 ff. is adopted from ᶜAṭṭār, Moṣibatname 30/11, cf. Ritter, Meer der Seele, p. 333, and MC VIII 337. Cf. also the story of the Hindu slave who had secretly fallen in love with his master's daughter M VI 249 ff.

85. D 750/7867.

86. D 1335/14126 and often.

87. D 2127/22496.

88. D 603/6347.

89. M VI 1650 ff.

90. M VI 643 ff.

91. D 832/8691.

92. D 2568/27265; cf. 58/714; 1385/14662; 1949/20587; the same classification is also used by Saᶜdi, Amir Khosrow, and later by Jāmi, cf. Schimmel, Turk and Hindu.

93. D 542/5770.

94. D 1741/18263.

95. D 524/5568.

96. D 525/5580.

97. D 1880/19808; cf. 1934/20360.

98. D 2320/24603.

99. DT 11/35032.

100. D 1940/20478.

101. D 570/6062.

102. D 1876/19765.

103. D 1439/15245.

104. D 2233/23669. To this imagery belongs R 1360:
I am not an enemy, as much as I look enemy-like
My origin is Turkish although I speak Hindi.
Cf. also R 1978.

105. M I 3521.

106. D 1458/15419.

107. D 2971/31542.

108. M VI 4709.

109. M I 2370.

110. M III 3440; cf. 3524 f.

111. Qāsim Kāhi, quoted in Mir ᶜAli Shir Qāniᶜ, Maqālāt ash-shoᶜarā, ed. H. Rashdi, Karachi 1956, p. 677. The verse itself, though generally ascribed to Rumi, is not found in D.

112. Cf. G. Rotter, Die Stellung des Negers in der islamisch-arabischen Gesellschaft bis zum XVI. Jahrhundert, Ph.D. Diss Bonn 1967.

113. M V 817; VI 1047.
114. Sanāʾi, Ḥadiqa p. 88.
115. M VI 4535.
116. D 3013/32030.
117. D 694/7227; 1211/12883; 2517/26632: The heart is like Jerusalem, and the wine like the Ferangis.
118. Khāqāni, Divān, Qaṣida Nr. 1.
119. D 361/3882.
120. D 1330/14073.

IMAGERY TAKEN FROM SUFI HISTORY

1. Cf. MC VII 283 ad M II 1203; AM Nr. 195.
2. D 1662/17422.
3. D 2222/23570.
4. Cf. D 3120/33325; 3144/33668; 2003/21180; 1990/21033.
5. D 640/6682; 598/6304; 1905/20059 with a combination with the 'greed of Azar'.
6. M IV 829 ff. (N), cf. VI 3983; cf. also VN 384.
7. D 527/5602 where the *adham* contrasts with *ashhab*; yet the interior connection can easily be made.
8. D 1135/12020; 2136/22612.
9. M IV 3078.
10. M IV 1357 ff.; cf. ʿAṭṭār, Moṣibatnāme 19/5, Tadhkirāt al-auliyā, ed. R. A. Nicholson, I p. 68. Rābeʿa occurs in AF likewise only as an appelative for extraordinarily pious women.
11. D 2512/26577 8.
12. D 1854/19552; cf. 879/9211. That such a claim was not a mere poetical exaggeration is understood from the fact that he himself considered himself to have reached the stage of the Beloved, cf. note 88.
13. D 1644/17225.
14. D 3099/33049.
15. M II 926 ff.
16. D 1597/16709.
17. D 1023/10788.
18. Thus D 2427/25572; 1507/15872; 2821/29955; 2550/27050 (where the Prophet Jonah may be intended; the limits are rarely completely clear).
19. D 3120/33331.
20. D 1247/13214.
21. M II 1386 ff. the story is related in other sources about Shibli, cf. Hujwiri/Nicholson, p. 313.
22. Thus D 1201/12791; a confusion between the two occurs in 2782/29559.
23. D 583/6179; 341/3687; M II 2182.
24. M IV 1803 ff.
25. M VI 2045 f.
26. D 1136/12048.
27. M II 2250 ff.; VI 2207; cf. M VI Index p. 562 cf. Bāyazid; Cf. D 2406/25415: a poem in honour of Ṣalāḥoddin.
28. M IV 2104 ff. (N); retold VN 172 f.
29. M VI 2548; VI 2207; D 2471/26137.
30. D 1006/10526; cf. 1417/14985; 987/10453; 3081/32841; M I 2275. The inverted sequence—Bāyazid becomes a Yazid by drinking 'devil's milk' in D

951/10032.

31. Hujwiri/Nicholson, p. 187; cf. Abu Nuʿaym al-Isfahāni, Ḥilyat al-auliyāʾ, Cairo 1930 ff., Vol. X p. 40.
32. D 824/8618.
33. D 858/8950; cf. 2781/29559; 2843/30204; M III 1699.
34. D 2946/31296.
35. D 3/48 9.
36. M V 3358 ff.
37. Iqbāl, Jāvidnāme, Lahore 1932, verse 1122; transl. by A. J. Arberry, Jāvidname, London 1966, p. 94: interestingly enough, this saying is put by Iqbal, into Ḥallāj's mouth, cf. note 39.
38. D 1834/19278.
39. D 370/3973. The combination of the two mystics is common at least since Sanāʾi, cf. Divān p. 686.
40. D 743/7805.
41. D 3152/33766.
42. W. Redhouse, Translation of the Mathnawi, Vol. I p. 92.
43. D 1135/12021.
44. Thus R 1322.
45. Thus D 1726/18069; R 1785.
46. DT 9/34959.
47. AF I 466; VN 172, 197 f., 299; cf. note ad D 1094.
48. D 1854/19550.
49. al-Ḥallāj, Kitāb aṭ-ṭawāsin, Ch. VI Tāsin al-azal waʾl-iltibās,p.41.
50. M II 2523.
51. M V 2035; cf. about the same problem VN 316.
52. F 55 f.; cf. 85.
53. F 202.
54. M VI 2095; cf. also R 422:
    He dived into the ocean of his own non-existence,
    and then pierced the pearl of *anāʾl-haqq*.
55. M II 1347 f. The comparison is common, cf. Chapter III, 'The Spiritual Ladder', Note 181.
56. M V 2534 f. A beautiful quatrain praises Ḥallāj, R 717:
    I am the slave of those who know themselves,
    and save every moment their hearts from error.
    They make a book of their essence and attributes
    and read as title of this book 'I am the Truth'.
57. D 738/7760.
58. M I 1809; cf. D 1130/11922.
59. D 81/931.
60. D 1318/13962.
61. D 2599/27561.
62. D 1094/11542.
63. Cf. D 452/4787; 1833/19268; 2275/24139 with the *radif avikhta* 'hanging'; 2400/25349; 3108/33154.
64. D 1288/13600; cf. 1257/13320; similar R 1172: *sard āram—sardāram—sar dāram—bar dāram*.
65. D 1719/18001.
66. D 3163/33882; Zuʾn-Nun was indeed imprisoned during the Muʿtazilite predominance.

67. D 2643/28035.
68. D 133/1533.
69. D 581/6164; cf. 864/9033; 784/8198; 758/7940. Even the *nafs-e nāṭeqa* is hanging on the gallows like Manṣur, D 2882/30598.
70. Sanā'i, Divān p. 208, 210, 247, 662, although barely in connection with Ḥallāj.
71. Ghālib, Kulliyāt, Lahore 1969, Divān-e Fārsi, ghazaliyāt, Nr. 83 p. 114.
72. D 132/1524; cf. 1374/14525; 1581/16581 (prison instead of gallows); 1918/20193. Cf. M III 3845: The lover will lecture on the gallows.
73. D 2365/25010.
74. M III 4214 (N).
75. al-Ḥallāj, Divān, ed. L. Massignon, JA 1931, qaṣida Nr.X.
76. Cf. M I 3934; III 3836; IV 109; D 386/4116.
77. First line of D 264/2984; al-Ḥallāj, Divān, muq. No. 32 v.2.
78. M III 3842.
79. M V 2675 ff.; cf. D 2086/22031; 2813/29859 f.
80. M V 4133.
81. M III 4187 ff.
82. M VI 4062.
83. D 2121/22456, Arabic verse in a poem with Greek, Persian and Arabic lines. Cf. R 1255. For the alleged *ḥadīth*: AM Nr. 408.
84. Cf. D 2012/21257. Cf. further—besides the allusions in M which can be checked in the Index—D 728/7643; 778/8120; 872/9122; 997/10532; 1459/15426; 1545/16222; 1513/15926; 1629/17065; 1658/17378; 2601/27587; 2430/25612; 3031/32207; 3073/32719; DT II/35087; R 562, 617.—A special study could be made of Rumi's use of Ḥallajian terms like *nāsut—lāhut*, thus M II 1787 ff., cf. Chapter II, 'Koran', Note 55.
85. M III 692.
86. D 246/2765.
87. D 2461/25997; 2429/25601. Poems rhyming in *-ur* usually contain an allusion to Manṣur; that is true for poetry up to the 19th century.
88. S 124; cf. Note. 47. Solṭān Valad has often returned to Ḥallāj, thus VN 161; 300; 80: 'Ḥallāj's infidelity is better than *towḥid* for he has seen the King without veil'.
89. For the whole problem vd. L. Massignon, La Passion d'al-Ḥosayn ibn Manṣour al-Ḥallāj, martyre mystique de l'Islam, Paris 1922, and Massignon's numerous studies. For his survival in Islamic poetry cf. A. Schimmel, al-Halladsch, Märtyrer der Gottesliebe, Cologne 1969.

THE IMAGERY OF MUSIC AND DANCE

1. Jāmi, Nafaḥāt al-ons, p. 462; cf. M IV 735 ff. The German version: F. Rückert, Erbauliches und Beschauliches aus dem Morgenlande, Gesammelte Werke in 12 Bänden, Frankfurt 1882, Vol. 6 p. 54. In this collection three more stories about Mowlānā are retold.
2. Cf. D 457/4837 ff.
3. D 332/3589.
4. R 616, cf. Chapter I, Biographical Notes, Note 50.
5. M I 1 18 (N).
6. Cf. H. Ritter, Das Proömium des Maṭnawi-i Maulawi, ZDMG 93/1932.
7. M I 27; cf. VI 2002 ff.; R 892.
8. Sanā'i'ābād 1. 236 41.
9. D 1628/17044; 1680/17609 (connection with sugarcane), 2499/26447; 2135/22608; 2134/22593; 2415/25491.

10. D 1949/20586; cf. the *ḥadith* AM Nr. 222 'The believer is like a flute; his voice is beautiful only when his stomach is empty', and R 880.
11. D 3001/31897; 2315/24564; R 438.
12. D 2902/30836 f.
13. D 2994/31825.
14. D 7/94 (allusion to Sura 3/26). Cf. R 361; R 1221: when the flute is silent, it does not want to sell the Friend's sugar to every mean person.
15. DT 12/35133.
16. M I 8; D 2994/31831.
17. D 831/8682; cf. 2249/23838.
18. D 2217/23512; R 859, R 1273.
19. D 2168/22971.
20. D 2677/28402; other typical verses D 59/722; 532/5664; 671/6999 f.; 1238/13125; 1417/15000; 1545/16223; 2168/22971; 2401/25357; 2392/25275; 2571/27298: the *sornā* complains in *tāzi* 'Arabic' and *soryāni* 'Syriac'.
21. A lovely example RE 318a 3.
22. D 2351/24878.
23. D 1352/14295.
24. ʿAṭṭār Divān, ed. S. Nafisi, Teheran 1339 sh., Nr. 759.
25. D 1405/14883; cf. also id. 14878.
26. D 1934/20363; cf. 1467/15494; other typical instances D 1621/16978; 2629/27856; 2779/29546; R 73, 75, 465, 1113.
27. D 313/3415 ff.
28. D 304/3317 ff. against the orthodox who disliked the *rabab*, cf. AF I 167.
29. Thus M II 1573, 1916; D 2636/27963; 1523/16037; D 2194/23282.
30. D 2315/24564.
31. R E 333 a 1.
32. D 1809/19015; 302/3294.
33. D 2223/23585.
34. D 741/7780; cf. RE 321 b 1.
35. D 1914/20133.
36. D 2168/22972; cf. 2480/26242.
37. D 2342/24780.
38. D 1458/15415.
39. M III 4603.
40. Cf. D 1308/13855 (*ṭabl-e shādi*).
41. D 1370/14467 speaks of the *ṭablkhāna-ye ʿeshq*, as if Love were an amir who has the drums beaten at his door at regular hours and in fixed number.
42. D 2747/29203; cf. 1308/13854; 552/5870.
43. D 2472/26144.
44. D 492/5241. R 1094: 'He who does not smile like the rose at the sight of the friend is empty like a drum without soul and reason.
45. M VI 2573.
46. M III 4346.
47. Thus D 1605/16814.
48. D 1704/17826 7;
49. M III 3890; cf. D 2120/22418; 653/6813; Cf. Khāqāni about the drum of the navel of those afflicted with dropsy, Divān, Qaṣida p. 54.
50. D 1509/15885.
51. D 1358/14353 f.

52. D 1513/15932; further 159/1818; 1862/19628; 1168/12397; 2453/25904 (the connection with the humming of bees, *zanbur*).
53. D 2212/23452; cf. 1173/12483. Such negative statements about the *barbaṭ* are also part of Khāqāni's musical imagery.
54. D 1561/16405.
55. DT 16/35304. Sometimes a quatrain combines comparisons of the human heart with three or four different instruments, thus R 1196.
56. M I 2187 ff.; D 457/4837 ff.; 2963/31444 ff.; further good examples D 2937/31174; 2968/31494; 2971/31537; 3032/32226; 3171/33997; M I 2201 f.
57. D 2472/26144.
58. D 146/1662; 738/7750.
59. D 788/8244.
60. M I 6.
61. D 1832/19257 8.
62. D 94/1045.
63. Relying on M IV 742 and earlier Sufi sayings.
64. Cf. Hujwiri/Nicholson, Chapter XXV, and the bibliography given by A. Schimmel, Mystical Dimensions, Ch. IV d. The best introduction is the article by M. Molé, La Dance Exstatique an Islam, in: La Danse Sacrée, Sources Orientales VI, Paris 1968.
65. Jāmi, Nafaḥāt al-ons, p. 590.
66. Cf. A. Gölpīnarli, Mevlânaᶜdan sonra Mevlevilik; the best description in a Western language: H. Ritter, Der Reigen der Tanzenden Derwische, Zeitschrift f. Vgl. Musikwissenschaft I, 1933, and id., Die Mevlâna Feier in Konya vom 11 17. December 1960, in: Oriens XV, 1962.
67. Often also in the Robāᶜiyyāt, thus RE 318 a 1, 335 b 4.
68. D 2395 (for a translation cf. supra p. 151).
69. R 279, 1141 (with a pun on *parda*), 703; cf. D 1100/1627.
70. R 1206.
71. D 466, cf. 611, 229.
72. D 1760/18457; cf. 1295/13681 90 *radif samāᶜ*, 1296/13691 7 *radif samāᶜ*; cf. R 910: *samāᶜ* in the friend's presence is like ritual prayer in the Prophet's company.
73. M I 1346 ff. (N).
74. Cf. Heiler, Erscheinungsformen p. 240.
75. D 326/3550.
76. D 1936/20379 80; cf. 548/5829. Cf. also ᶜAṭṭār, Moṣibatnāma p. 148.
77. D 1355/14329.
78. D 804/8416.
79. D 2327/24645.
80. M I 867.
81. D 624/6523 ff.
82. D 797/8332; cf. R 278, 702.
83. D 686/7132.
84. M IV 3265. Cf. Chapter II, 'Gardens', note 53 55.
85. Thus D 211/2345; 886/9279; 1124/11863.
86. D 782/8158; cf. 1101/11649; 2563/27210; 2138/22630; 2158/22854 5.
87. D 2150/22759; 1452/15353.
88. D 2849/30259.
89. D 2120/22426.
90. D 2960/31423.

91. D 189/2089 2101 with the *radif be-raqṣ* 'enter the dance'; 1195/12713.
92. D 1867/19687.
93. D 2282/24252.
94. M II 1942.
95. D 1295/13686, 1296/13695.
96. RE 322 a 5.
97. D 624/6519.
98. D 1734/18177.
99. D 1832/19255.
100. D 186/2061 2.
101. D 1978/20912 (a dancing poem), cf. 2299/24421.
102. M III 96; cf. r 1375. For more dancing-quatrains cf. 191, 195, 254, 1043, 1044, 1045, and the ecstatic 1046.
103. D 441/4645.
104. W. Hastie, The Festival of Spring, Glasgow 1903, Nr. 6.
105. H. von Hofmannsthal, Gedenkwort für Sebastian Melmoth.

RUMI'S THEOLOGY

GOD AND HIS CREATION

1. M II 3544 ff.
2. D 2296/24392; AM Nr. 70.
3. M IV 3025 ff.
4. DT 23/35575 f.
5. F 238.
6. M II 364.
7. D 2172/23022.
8. D 1683/17644.
9. D 28/375, 1309/13860 and often in M.
10. M II 1622 ff.
11. M III 2520; cf. also II 1842 f.; 3786; III 3153; VI 1315.
12. F 161.
13. M V 2560 ff.
14. M III 3107.
15. M IV 738.
16. M III 3109.
17. Daylami-Joneyd-i Shirazi, Sirat Ibn al-Khafif p. 179; Jāmi, Nafaḥāt p. 220.
18. M III 1359. The idea has been expressed by Ghazzāli several times in his Iḥyāʾ ʿolum ad-din.
19. D 1044/11000.
20. M IV 2406.
21. M II 3275.
22. M II 1627 ff.
23. D 484/5169.
24. M III 3068 ff.; particularly 3072.
25. M IV 1498 ff.
26. M II 1964 ff.

27. M III 3562 f.
28. M IV 1211.
29. M III 3500 ff.; Rumi often alludes to the alleged *ḥadīth* 'Hurry is from Satan', AM Nr. 271.
30. M I 3070 f.
31. M V 57 ff.
32. M I 2591 f.
33. M III 4129 f.
34. M III 2903.
35. M III 330 ff.
36. M IV 2823.
37. M III 26 ff.
38. M VI 3126.
39. M V 494 f.
40. M IV 1169 ff.
41. M I 613.
42. M II 2684.
43. M IV 1343; cf. H. Ziai, The principle of bi-polarity of all things in the Mathnavi of Jalāl ud-Din Rumi, in: Mevlâna Güldestesi, Konya 1971. The oft-quoted verse 'By their contrast are things made clear' is a quotation from Rumi's favourite poet Motanabbi, cf. Maʿāref p. 68 and Ḥāshiya p. 269.
44. M V 598.
45. M VI; for the whole concept cf. R. Otto, Das Heilige (The Concept of the Holy), which couches in scientific terms—tremendum and fascinans—the two aspects of the Experience of the Holy, as they had been known to the Sufis for centuries.
46. M VI 1847 f.
47. M V 2128.
48. M VI 3576 f.
49. M I 3863 f.
50. M IV 3695 f.
51. M V 512; D 181/2023 and footnote; cf. M V 2900.
52. M IV 3051.
53. M V 1028 f.; cf. II 1281; III 383; VI 1459; D 2688/28511; F 34.
54. D 2690/28529.
55. M I 1133.
56. M III 1899.
57. M I 3905.
58. M I 245.
59. M V 106; the whole chapter, beginning on p. 28, discusses this problem.
60. M II 4387; AM Nr. 133.
61. M VI 2660.
62. M V 3294.
63. M IV 2816 ff.
64. M IV 71.
65. M III 3210 ff.
66. M IV 2884 ff.
67. M II 2535 ff.
68. M III 1372 f.
69. M IV 2881f. cf. Chapter 1. 'Biographical Notes' note 85.

70. M I 1570.
71. M I 3856.
72. Some examples M II 2438 f.; III 4115; V 1463; VI 879 f. 1265.
73. F 28.
74. M V 1665.
75. M V 1666 f.
76. M V 2158.
77. F 43.
78. F 184.
79. F 188.
80. F 224.
81. M VI 1739 ff. (N).
82. M I 837.
83. M V 1591.
84. M IV 1075.
85. M II 590 f.; cf. I 312.
86. F 18; AM Nr. 116.
87. M V 1566; D 1372/14505; 1046/11027.
88. M I 1066; cf. D 724/7601.
89. M V 1569 87; VI 3269.
90. M IV 3700 ff.
91. M II 2933.
92. F 220.
93. M II 1741.
94. D 2072/21881 2.
95. DST Nr. XXXI, this famous ghazal is not found in D.
96. M IV 215 f.
97. Cf. al-Ghazzāli, al-maqṣad al-asnā fi sharḥ maʿāni asmā Allāh al-ḥusnā, ed. F. A. Shehadi, Beirut 1971.
98. M IV 113 ff.
99. M I 1134.
100. M III 1318 ff.
101. M II 1745 ff.
102. M III 1151 ff.
103. M II 3637; cf. IV 2034; VI 3220 ff.; D 2167/22951; 1337/14137; cf. 1799/18910, 1145/12158; 2242/23762 and often; R 1168, 1263. The nicest story in this respect is told in M I 326 ff. about the squint-eyed and the 'two' bottles.
104. M I 3078.
105. M I 766; II 1345.
106. M IV 3281 f.
107. Sanāʾi, Ḥadiqa Ch. I. p. 60.
108. M I 3008.
109. M II 190 ff.
110. M IV 3163 f.
111. M II 3107.
112. D 900/9434 ff.
113. M I 2653 ff.; AM Nr. 63.
114. D 1337/14140; About the concept of *ʿadam* cf. A. Bausani, Persia Religiosa,

Milano 1959, p. 273 f,; Ismail Hüsrev Tökin, Mevlâna da yok oluş Felsefesi, in: Türk Yurdu, Mevlâna Özel Sayısı, Ankara 1965: Besides the instances mentioned in the notes, I counted more than sixty verses in the Divān (and there may be lines which have escaped my attention) in which ʿ*adam* was used either as general contrast to *hasti* 'being' or *shey*ʾ 'thing', as prerequisite of creation, or as final state of man. A detailed study of this central concept would be most welcome.

115. D 2824/29984.
116. D 1019/10753.
117. D 1122/11842.
118. D 1432/15143.
119. D 2436/25684.
120. M I 522; cf. the lovely R 1955.
121. M I 1886.
122. D 451/4763.
123. M V 1023 f.
124. M VI 1366 ff.; cf. D 873/9136 and often: for only when man has become non-existent, God can make him anew.
125. D 2935/31145.
126. M V 1026 f.
127. D 1902/20010.
128. M V 1018.
129. M I 1448.
130. M V 4213 ff.
131. M I 606 f.
132. The Universe rests on this ocean like foam, or moves in it like a fish: D 1420/15027; cf. 1384/14649.
133. D 155/1773.
134. M I 1889.
135. M V 4236f.
136. D 2234/23683.
137. M VI 2772 f.
138. D 435/4578 and previous verses.
139. M I 1242 f.
140. M V 1016 f.
141. M I 602 f.
142. D 107/1216.
143. D 2501/26469; cf. 158/1814 that the ʿ*adam's* are in degrees.
144. D 2373/25091.
145. D 1716/17968 73; other positive evaluations: D 709/7425; 1704/17834; 1769/18528; 2086/22027; 1585/16622; R 1306; 113; 673; 46; 1946; 1672; 961.
146. D 771/8051.
147. D 2663/28250.
148. M III 3901 ff.
149. D 734/7707. The whole poem deals with ʿ*adam* in its different aspects.
150. D 3032/32229.
151. M III 3552 ff.
152. M III 3024; cf. 1821/19122 'make your nest in ʿ*adam*'.
153. D 381.
154. D 2628/27850.

155. D 863/9015.
156. D 950/10025 ff.
157. D 498/5294; for the verse cf. Hujwiri/Nicholson p. 297 (*ḥayāt* instead of the generally acepted *wujūd*).
158. D 1019/10754 and previous lines.
159. M VI 36 ff.
160. M III 1008.
161. D 96/1072 (a dunghill), 655/6833 and often; R 1544; AM Nr. 96.
162. M IV 3259 ff.
163. M III 1729 ff; AM Nr. 222, 436.
164. D 771/8053.
165. D 2239/23739.
166. D 2501/26470; cf. RE 341 b 5.
167. M V 1109.
168. M IV 3062 ff.
169. M II 1670.
170. M III 1737.
171. M IV 3654 ff.
172. F 193.
173. M V 1720 f.
174. M II 3547; AM Nr. 188.
175. D 14/160 1.
176. M V 1686 ff.
177. D 765/8001.

MAN AND HIS POSITION IN RUMI'S WORK

1. F 118.
2. D 463/4912.
3. D 2781/29560.
4. M V 3574; cf. the *ḥadīth-é qodsi*: 'O son of Adam, I have created you for me, and the things for you', AM Nr. 575.
5. D 313/3422.
6. M V 3375 f.
7. M VI 138.
8. D 2951/31346. Maʿāref p. 163 explains this *amānat* as *mani* 'Ego', the conscious thought which distinguishes man from minerals and plants.
9. F 27; almost verbatim repeated VN 309.
10. M VI 2648.
11. M I 1234.
12. M IV 2969 ff.
13. M V 1563 ff.
14. M I 1238 44.
15. M VI 4021 ff; VI 1750 f.
16. The best analysis is found in R. C. Zaehner, Hindu and Muslim Mysticism, London 1960, p. 139 ff. in the chapter on Joneyd.
17. D 2242/23763.
18. M II 1667 f.
19. M III 2348; AM Nr. 624.
20. Nwyia, Exégèse Qoranique p. 46 after H. Corbin, Histoire de la philosophie islamique, p. 16.

21. D 703/7323.
22. M II 2970 f.
23. D 1688/17694.
24. D 1117/11796.
25. D 463/4921.
26. D 1477/15576 cf. ʿAṭṭār, Moṣibatnāme p. 133. Cf. further D 2741/29144; 2396/25310; 548/5833; M III 2344 53, V 174, 600, 830, 2124 f.
27. D 251/2818.
28. D 930/9805.
29. D 68/814.
30. M I 2010 ff.
31. M II 17.
32. D 1203/12809; cf. Sanāʾi, Divān, p. 188: 'Peacock and serpent were Iblis' leaders'.
33. M I 1634 f.
34. D 2082/21976; 2041/21521 speaks only of forty years.
35. D 1794/18840.
36. D 1372/14494.
37. M IV 1874 f.
38. M III 3291 f.
39. D 918/9669. The whole poem deals with man's situation.
40. D
41. John Donne, Devotions upon emergent occasions, Nr. XVII.
42. F 61.
43. M III 1001.
44. M V 2547.
45. Mektuplar Nr. XXX; cf. D 10/118; Sanāʾi, Divān p. 656.
46. D 2497/26403.
47. D 2984/31697.
48. D 2433/25652.
49. M I 1031 f.
50. M I 3311 ff.
51. M II 1353.
52. M III 4258 ff.
53. M IV 521; cf. AM Nr. 346.
54. F 22; M VI 3138.
55. F 42.
56. D 1669/17499.
57. D 441/4639; cf. also M V 2887, II 2221 f; the motif has been taken up in our day by M. Iqbal in the poem of his *Jāvidnāme*, and recently by the Egyptian poet Ṣalāḥ ʿAbduṣ Ṣabūr in his poem on the Sufi Bishr al-Ḥāfi.
58. M V 2113 ff.
59. M VI 2155.
60. For a bibliography of works on Satan cf. A. Schimmel, Gabriel's Wing, Leiden 1963, and id. Mystical Dimensions of Islam, p. 193 f. Interestingly enough, VN 246 underscores Iblis's obedience which was not blended with love of God: love of God is more important than sheer obedience.
61. Sanāʾi, Divān p. 871.
62. M II 2614 ff.
63. Ritter, Das Meer der Seele, p. 538.

64. M V 520.
65. M II 2661 f.
66. M I 3396.
67. M VI 259; IV 1617.
68. M IV 1402; cf. Iqbāl, Payām-e Mashriq, p. 246 7, transl. A. Schimmel, Botschaft des Ostens, p. 97.
69. M VI 2799 f.
70. M VI 4471 f.
71. M I 2956; AM Nr. 74.
72. M VI 4320 f.
73. D 160/1827.
74. F 98.
75. M VI 2050.
76. M VI 1222 ff.
77. M I 2433 f.; cf. MC VII 155.
78. M III 3300.
79. Cf. for the problem W. M. Watt, Free Will and Predestination in Early Islam, London 1948.
80. D 3071/32708.
81. M III 1501 (N).
82. D 545/5812.
83. M I 637.
84. D 2002/21167.
85. D 1134/11991.
86. M V 3050 ff.
87. M I 624 f., esp. 635.
88. M VI 210 ff.
89. M V 3039.
90. M V 3077 99; cf. F 160.
91. M V 3151 ff.; AM Nr. 97.
92. F 60; AM Nr. 338.
93. F 21.
94. M V 1801 f.
95. D 1337/14140; cf. 3047/32410: cf. also M II 1062. Rumi likes Sura 2/263 about the ears which bring sevenfold fruit, and 21/47 about the mustard-seed of action. Solṭān Valad follows him VN 306.
96. M V 3181.
97. M VI 419 f.
98. M IV 1317 f.
99. M IV 1201.
100. Mektuplar Nr. LIV.
101. M I 3931.
102. M V 1791.
103. M III 3438 ff.; D 2037/21480 ff. This whole poem deals with the beautiful death of the believer.
104. M II 1413; acc. to AM Nr. 40; cf. Ritter, Das Meer der Seele p. 102, 155, and Chapter II, 'Animals', note 35.
105. D 385/4099 4104; cf. 402/4245.
106. D 2978/31610; 1940/20436.

107. AM Nr. 134; M II 1247 ff.
108. M IV 2420; cf. D 1145/12149.
109. M V 1537 f.
110. M I 929 ff.
111. M V 3112 f.
112. M V 2967 ff.
113. M V 3004; cf. F.
114. M V 3102.
115. M V 3093.
116. M I 838.
117. M V 1731; cf. AM Nr. 42.
118. M V 3187 f.; I 1468 f.;
119. M I 1328; cf. II 30; D 1535/16137; 2498/26416, AM Nr. 104.
120. M II 2187; I 215; the same VN 387.
121. F 200.
122. M I 8.
123. M III 3417; cf. F.
124. M III 4426.
125. M III 3572 f; cf. D 2519/26676 ff., a poem which belongs to the later period of Rumi's life (allusion to Ḥosāmoddin 26699 f.) and speaks of the macrocosmos and other technical terms, otherwise rarely found in Mowlānā's lyrics.
126. D 2433/25657.
127. M III 527.
128. M II 199 ff.; V 1942.
129. M III 1388 f.
130. M I 1019 f.; F 223.
131. M V 3935 f.
132. M IV 423 ff.; cf. IV 1840.
133. M VI 650 f.
134. M VI 2735 f.
135. D 1590/16657; 2341/24769 (a man is sleeping like an anchor but should give himself to the wind of *samāʿ*); 2521/26735: this anchor can be broken by Khizr.
136. D 2723/28905.
137. M V 1098.
138. M V 1089 f.
139. D 3020/32106.
140. D 1177/12538. The word *taḍrib*, translated here as 'patches' means originally 'quilting'. But cf. Maʿāref 214 *ḍarb-e kherqa* means 'to tear the kherqa during *samāʿ* and throw it away'.
141. M IV 3576.
142. M IV 1011.
143. cf. D 2961/31434 'the verdigris of existence'.
144. M IV 3045 f.
145. D 1460/15434.
146. M I 3514
147. D 1353/14308
148. D 600/6321-22.
149. M I 2666 f.
150. M IV 2535 f.

151. M VI 2391 f.
152. M VI 77.
153. M V 1901 ff.
154. D 3110/33178.
155. M IV 3259 ff.
156. M I 2515 f.
157. D 1528/16082-83.
158. D 1077/11336.
159. M V 2477; cf. V 296; cf. Maᶜāref p. 14, and often in M.
160. M IV 3607.
161. M V 3644 f.
162. M IV 431 f.
163. M I 3445 f.
164. M IV 2388
165. M IV 2394 f.
166. M II 3236 f.
167. M III 1834 ff.
168. M II 1285-95.
169. M III 1826 f.
170. M II 61 f. (N), cf. D 3091/32974 'You will see God inspite of the Muᶜtazilites'.
171. M III 374 ff. The Koranic allusion is to Sura 2/54 and 4/66.
172. M II 1227 ff.
173. M III 4066; III 3786; II 2473 f; Cf. AM Nr. 17.
174. M VI 4862 f.
175. D 941/9931 f; cf. 102/1176; AM Nr. 352.
176. D 658/6859 for the body, but explained by '*nafs*'.
177. M I 1351; cf. the whole chapter on Animal Imagery.
178. M II 1445; cf. Chapter II Animals, Note 107.
179. M IV 3621.
180. M III 2548, 1053.
181. M VI 1431; II 2272; I 2618 ff; cf. D 2664/28261; 3072/32710. In D1313/13901 the *ruḥ* 'spirit' is called 'mother'; *ruḥ*, like *nafs*, is feminine in Arabic. Cf. AM Nr. 541.
182. D 1656/17358.
183. D 778; M I 1377f. insatiable.
184. M III 3197; cf. II 15 f.
185. M III 2554 ff.
186. D 52/642; 610/6412.
187. D 1353/14300.
188. D 864/9047.
189. M V 557 f.
190. M VI 1607.
191. M I 2497 f.
192. M III 2557.
193. D 3057/32545; M III 3193.
194. M III 4053 f.
195. M V 2461 f.
196. M III 2507.
197. M II 26 f.

198. M III 2547; V 737.

199. M IV 2301 f; Cf. the tradition, AM Nr. 532, and its elaboration by VN 27 f:

> When God created reason (ʿ*aql*) He said to him 'Sit', and he sat down; then He said to him 'Get up', and he got up, then He said to him 'Come near', and he came, then He said to him 'Go away', and he went away, then He said to him 'Stand upright', and he stood upright, then He said 'Look', and he looked; then He said 'speak', and he spoke. . . . etc.
>
> Then He said to him: 'By my Glory and Majesty and Greatness and My being upright on my Throne—I have not created any creature which is nobler for Me than you, or more beloved to me than you! By you I am known, and worshipped, and obeyed, and through you I give and it is you whom I blame. Verily the recompensation is for you, and for you is the punishment.'

200. D 2981/31643.

201. M II 1850 f.

202. Sanāʾi, Ḥadiqa Ch. IV p. 305.

203. M IV 3727 f.

204. M I 2051 f.

205. M III 4312.

206. M I 3690 f.

207. M II 2324 ff; cf. D 918/9664 where ʿ*aql* is contrasted with 'nature', *ṭab*ʿ.

208. M I 3114.

209. M VI 4075 f.

210. M V 3350 f.

211. M VI 4138 f.

212. M IV 1986.

213. M V 459.

214 M VI 4649 f.

215. D 914/9621 ff.

216. D 2019.

217. D 1333/14104

218. D 1799/18898.

219. D 878/9190 (last line), cf. 2556/27129; 2130/22530, 1374/14533 (last line), 103/1184; 24/280; M III 1558; V 2585 f. R262. The ʿ*aql-e koll* as father 106/1214.

220. M III 1144.

221. D 2989/31761.

222. D 1130/11920.

223. M IV 1923 f.

224. D 2678/28410.

225. D 812/8494; cf. 353/3792.

226. D 1374/14533 (last line).

227. M V 1258 f.

228. M IV 1309.

229. M IV 1294 f.

230. D 732/7687.

231. M IV 1960 ff (N).

232. M IV 1256 ff.

233. M III 2531.

234. D 1793/18827; cf. 2113/22306 f; 1388/14689; 810/8478; 731/7680 'Before that *nafs-e koll* was an architect in water and clay, our joyful life was flourishing in the taverns (*khārābat*, contrast with *me 'mar*) of Divine Realities'. Cf. also Utas,

Ṭariq at-taḥqiq, transl. p. 152: 'The Universal Soul is sitting in the hindmost row at the Universal Reason's banquet in order to gain perfection'.

235. D 840/8797.
236. D 202/2239 qadi.
237. M IV 2110.
238. D 689/7174.
239. RE 320 a 4.
240. M IV 568.
241. F 123.
242. D 1440/15251; cf. 1082/11378 ff; 987/10448; 335/3632.
243. D 2430/25608.
244. D 52/641 ff.
245. M I 1477.
246. M VI 153 f.
247. D 830/8676; cf. 454/4802 'the body as guest-room of the soul'.
248. M IV 2820.
249. M II 3326 ff.
250. M III 2536, Koran Sura 39/31.
251. M V 680 f.
252. M III 2402 ff.
253. M IV 408.
254. D 972/10285 ff.
255. M VI 148 f.
256. M VI 3306.
257. D 615/6444.
258. F 68.
259. D 213/2389.
260. M I 1974. Rumi develops this out of Moḥammad's address to A'isha 'O Homeyra, talk to me', AM Nr. 47.
261. M II 3238 ff.; cf. I 1785.
262. M I 725.
263. D 968/10241.
264. M II 1369 f.
265. M V 146.
266. D 673/7113; cf. R 52:
What is the soul? A tiny babe in our cradle!
What is the heart? Our roaming stranger!
267. D 574/6088.
268. D 898/9402; cf. RE 322 b 2.
269. D 310/3397.
270. MC VII 90 ad M I 1126 f.
271. M I 3665 f.
272. M VI 2882 f.
273. M V 874 f.
274. M I 3459
275. D 2031/21432.
276. M IV 1852 f; II 72.
277. M V 2878 f; II 3129.
278. D 1683/17641; 1460/15433; 1052; M C VII 90.
279. Cf. Nwyia, Exégèse Qoranique p. 316 ff.

280. AM Nr. 63—cf. the imagery of the fairy in the bottle as symbol for the beloved in the heart! Ch. II, Daily Life, Note 61.
281. AM Nr. 466; D 3104/33110 ff, the whole poem deals with the broken heart.
282. D 576/6098.
283. R E 323 b 1.
284. M I 3064.
285. M III 515 ff; cf. Nwyia, l.c.
286. M IV 1383 f.
287. D 2142/22691.
288. D 332/3590.
289. D 1690/17705.
290. D 1673/17528 with an application of Sura 2/109.
291. D 2130/22527.
292. D 923/9721. The scent which then exudes from the fire will show the quality of the burnt heart.
293. D 574/6089.
294. M I 3574 ff.
295. D 898/9402.
296. D 1001/10570.

MOWLĀNĀ'S PROPHETOLOGY

1. D 2275/24155; 901/9452.
2. D 1560/16381.
3. D 490/5217. Praise of the Prophet also in R 107, 1173 seems to be written in self-defence:

    I am the servant of the Koran as long as I am alive,
    I am the dust of the road of the elect Moḥammad . . .

4. D 2198/23328; cf. 3104/33119.
5. M VI 1659 ff; 2102 f; cf. II 974; AM Nr. 546.
6. AM Nr. 301.
7. F 211.
8. M I 3086.
9. M II 574 f.
10. M IV 976.
11. M V 75 281. For the stories about Moḥammad cf. the index in M VI. Cf. AM Nr. 449.
12. D 1142/12115.
13. M II 366.
14. D 1690/17705.
15. D 2131/22556; 1414/14963; cf. 526/5594.
16. M VI 858.
17. M III 3110 ff.
18. D 1348/14259. According to the tradition quoted in the footnote, this happened during the Prophet's ascension.
19. ad M I 1397.
20. D 676/7031; 82/953; AM Nr. 459.
21. F 143.
22. D 16/187.
23. D 1300/13740.
24. D 1205/12825; 1274/13485; D 444/4675 contains an allusion to Moḥammad's

saying that he repented seventy times every day.

25. M VI 165 f. (N).
26. D 2443/25786.
27. D 984/10420; cf. M VI 3197.
28. D 1954/20631.
29. M II 420 f.
30. D 463/4916.
31. D 638/6656.
32. M IV 1019 f; cf. II 920 ff; D 938/9904.
33. DT 18/35373.
34. M VI 1156.
35. M VI 2643; AM Nr. 44.
36. M IV 1464.
37. D 2967/31491.
38. Cf. AM Nr. 342: 'The first thing that God created was my light'.
39. D 882/9231.
40. Sanā'i, Divān p. 34, an extempore qasida in explanation of Sura *Wa'z-zohā*.
41. D 792/8288.
42. D 1137/12052.
43. M VI 676; cf. IV 3788.
44. D 3.
45. M VI 1861; cf. III 1212 f.
46. M C VII 66.
47. D 1158/12296.
48. D 1354/14323; cf. AM Nr. 48 'O Bilal, quicken us with the call to prayer!'
49. D 2400/25345.
40. D 258/2914, refers to Sura 28/73.
51. D 288/2572; cf. Chapter II Animals, Note 139.
52. D 112/1264.
53. M I 1066; cf. D 724/7600 01; DT 9/34953.
54. Cf. AM Nr. 100, cf. Nr. 445. Sanā'i, Ḥadiqa Ch. V. p. 328 says:

    Love is higher than reason and soul—
    'I have a time with God' belongs to the true man.

    Cf. also Sanā'i, Divan p. 191. This story belongs to the favourite topics of mystical poetry, and has been re-evaluated by M. Iqbal in his philosophy of serial and Divine Time.
55. M I 727 f.
56. M I 1106.
57. This tradition is not found in AM; for documentation cf. Schimmel, Mystical Dimensions, Ch. V 3.
58. D 144/1632; cf. 1578/16553; M I 228; 782.
59. F 226.
60. MC VII 26.
61. D 409/4342.
62. D 1966/20745 6 a beautiful wine-ode.
63. D 1135/12019.
64. M I 529.
65. F 151 f; That the *'aql-e avval* is at times interchangeable with the Muhammadan Light, has been shown by L. Massignon, Passion II 830 ff.
66. M III 3132.

67. M II 3710.
68. M II 2091.
69. M IV 538.
70. M III 1209.
71. M IV 990 f.
72. M V 1234.
73. D 1245/13194.
74. D 3135/33536 7.
75. D 463/4915.

THE SPIRITUAL LADDER

1. M IV 2556. It seems that Rumi has inherited the frequent use of the word *nardebān* from Sanāʾi, cf. Ḥadiqa I 123, 73; IV 299; V 323, 318; VI 372; VII 440, 441, 456, 474, 490, 491, 500, to quote only some prominent examples. The relation between the concept of *nardebān* and its Arabic equivalent *meʿrāj* deserves a special study.
2. M I 303.
3. M VI 4125.
4. M VI 724.
5. D 1295/13686; 1296/13695.
6. D 196/2161; cf. 965/10205.
7. D 13/155.
8. D 1940/20470.
9. D 2180/22110.
10. Mektuplar Nr. CVI.
11. M V 183 f.
12. D 1602/16767 8.
13. DT 2/34711.
14. D 1602/16759. The whole poem consists of thirty verses.
15. D 2266/24070 a *molammaʿ* poem, Arabic verse; cf. 2307/24480 92 with the radif *ruza*.
16. D 925/9742.
17. D 892/9345 ff.
18. D 925/9744 ff.
19. D 2520/26717.
20. D 302/3301.
21. D 350/3774; cf. 875/9154 65.
22. D 977/10355 a lovely *ʿid*-congratulation; cf. 1525.
23. D 112/1257; 2685/28477; 858/8955.
24. D 1394/14784.
25. D 617/6465.
26. D 2997/31865.
27. D 199/2179 ff; 3104/33105.
28. D 648/6762 ff.
29. D 617/6466.
30. D 2205/23384 f.
31. M VI 1896 ff (N). These verses were so well known that Mrs Meer Hasan Ali could quote them in her *Observations on The Mussulmauns of India*, London 1832, I 159 as words of 'a commentator of the Khoraun'. For a German version cf. F. Rückert, Erbauliches und Beschauliches, p. 70.
32. D 1661/17410.

33. D 2114/22314 15.
34. D 1689/17699; cf. 3152/33764; 2162/22899.
35. D 2906/30878.
36. D 2977/31601.
37. D 129/1477.
38. D 728/7635.
39. D 1027/10823.
40. D 2223/23577.
41. DT 8/34926 and others.
42. D 736/7740; about Rajab and Shaʿbān D 668/6975, 634/6607.
43. Mektuplar LXXV.
44. M VI 507 f.
45. Mektuplar CXXXII.
46. M IV 2373 ff.
47. M IV 3382.
48. M IV 1449 ff. Rumi even quotes an alleged Divine word in which the Lord ordered Moḥammad to sit only with the lovers, for:

    The world may be well heated by your fire—
    but fire dies in the company of the ashes, R 898.

49. M IV 1710.
50. cf. M IV 1446 ff.
51. M IV 333 f.
52. M III 2095.
53. M VI 855.
54. M III 787.
55. M II 1038; cf. I 2024.
56. M I 640-41, cf. Sura 83.
57. M III 2735 f.
58. M IV 301.
59. M III 2595 f.
60. M VI 1423 f.
61. M
62. MC VII 196 ad M I 3309.
63. M V 120; cf. V 2818; IV 1189.
64. M III 166.
65. M V 31 ff.
66. M III 2609 ff.
67. M VI 2935.
68. M I 717.
69. M V 2762.
70. M IV 1402.
71. M IV 1407.
72. M VI 3878 f.
73. M IV 1510.
74. M I 2830 ff.
75. M II 3200.
76. M I 1088.
77. AM Nr. 303; R 1578 speaks of those who are *ablah* through love; but cf. AF I 396 where Mowlānā explains this ḥadith to his wife: 'If they were not stupid, would they be content with Paradise and rivers? What has the place where the

Friend is seen to do with Paradise?'

78. VN 209.
79. M IV 1418.
80. M III 1130.
81. M I 3278.
82. M I 3283.
83. M VI 2353.
84. D 42/537.
85. D 1093/11521 7; cf. M V 3807 ff. He speaks also of the imposter, *ṭarrār*, in the shape of ascetics, D 2169/22981. (The expression *ṭarrār* occurs not infrequently in his lyrics.)
86. M II 3508 ff.
87. D 879/9198.
88. M V 363.
89. D 105/1204.
90. M III 3261; cf. R 600: 'A dervish is not he who seeks bread—a dervish is he who gives his soul.'
91. M VI 2653 f.
92. D 78/1907.
93. D 496/5269-70. In R 1747, the candle is skilfully compared to a true Sufi: it gets up at night with lightful face and pale countenance, with burning heart, weeping eye and wakeful.
94. M III 4234 ff. (N).
95. D 959/10114.
96. M I 3484.
97. D 75/874.
98. M III 1173; AM Nr. 390.
99. M I 1435.
100. M VI 464. But *towba* is like glass-making: difficult to make and easy to break, R 183.
101. M V 2227 ff; cf. MC VIII 271.
102. M IV 829 ff.
103. M IV 2504.
104. M VI 1222 ff.
105. D 2303/24445.
106. D 3156/33822.
107. AM Nr. 705; Mektuplar LX; D 2769/29442 and often.
108. D 2213/23474.
109. A good example D 1004/10606.
110. D 2710/28763.
111. D 2728/28978; 2646/28068 (*radif na khospi*), and the numerous ghazals with the rhyme *ma-khosp* 'Do not sleep!'
112. D 3171/33991; AM Nr. 460.
113. D 1739/18239. The whole poem deals with 'keeping the stomach empty'; cf. R 880. M VI 4213 cf. AM Nr. 728: 'The believer is like a flute whose voice becomes good only when his stomach is empty'.
114. D 777/8111.
115. M V 1756; VN 168 ff.
116. AM Nr. 89; D 488/5209.
117. M III 6 f; cf. V 1727 f; 2838 f; VI 4726 ff.
118. D 2728/28977-8.

119. RE 322 b 4; cf. D 1523/16035: The lovers assume the qualities of *al-ḥayy al-qayyum* by abstaining from food and sleep. (Allusion to the Throne-verse, Sura 2/256.)
120. M I 1644 f.
121. F 132; cf. Hujwiri/Nicholson, p. 365 f.
122. M I 914; AM Nr. 20
123. M VI 4913 — these are almost the last words of the Mathnavi.
124. M II 3145.
125. M III 1852.
126. M III 1853. This expression is particularly common in Indian Sufi literature.
127. M II 1276; cf. III 410 f.
128. M V 2469.
129. D 2285/24285; the imperial horse would be ashamed if little bells were put around it, i.e. if it were to make noise. That is left to the watercarrier's horse. Cf. M II 3074 ff; VI 1408.
130. M III 1847.
131. M I 3002 ff.
132. D 1126/11886.
133. D 2142/22694.
134. M I 1271 f.
135. M I 1525.
136. M III 2895 f.
137. Mektuplar Nr. 1.
138. F 87; cf. AM Nr. 122: He who lacks patience lacks faith.
139. D 1845/19429.
140. D 33/420.
141. D 395/4186.
142. D 1253/13270.
143. D 2526/26791.
144. M III 3734 ff.
145. AM Nr. 54; thus D 223/2527; 1069/11260; 1239/13132; DT 25/35695.
146. Jami, *Nafaḥāt* p. 464.
147. D 1069/11261; cf. 963/10168.
148. M I 2374.
149. D 2119/22404. There are numerous verses about *faqr* in the Divān, some of great depth and beauty.
150. D 2352/24893; cf. the fine Arabic quatrain R 1042.
151. D 2492/26346; cf. 1715/17960.
152. D 2015/21275.
153. D 2479/26234. In the same poem (26230) *faqr* is compared to a salamander which alone is able to survive in the fire of love.
154. D 3102/33079; cf. 3082/32852.
155. D 890/9326 f; cf. Sanāʾi, Divān p. 139, where he speaks of the 'Bāyazid of *faqr*'.
156. D 3010/31989.
157. M IV 1856.
158. cf. M V 672; D 863/9019. In ʿAṭṭār's Manṭeq oṭ-ṭeyr, the last valley is that of *faqr u fanā*, poverty and annihilation; cf. R 811: 'If one hair from Existence remains on him, this hair appears to the eye of *faqr* like an infidel's girdle (*zonnār*).
159. D 863/9026.

160. D 1948/20567, the contrast *faqir—faqih*.

161. M I 133 f.

162. D 261/2959; 2498/26422.

163. M III 1426-34.

164. DT 11/35113.

165. M I 2625.

166. D 357/3839.

167. D 910/9548.

168. M III 3669 f.

169. M VI 823 f.

170. M II 3321.

171. M III 4662.

172. M I 3051 f.

173. Cf. Nwyia, Exégèse Qoranique, p. 248 (saying by Kharrāz).

174. M I 3056 ff. (N).

175. M III 4659; cf. his R 800 about *towḥid* which is not *ḥolul*, 'indwelling, incarnationism' but 'becoming annihilated from self'.

176. M IV 398; V 1895.

177. M VI 1522 f; cf. VI 732 f; D 1954/20631 and often.

178. M V 683 f.

179. D 1443/15274.

180. M III 3921.

181. M II 1350. The comparison is found, among others, in the logos speculations of Origines; in the Greek medieval mystic Symeon the New Theologian, d. ca. 1040, (cf. M. Buber, Ekstatische Konfessionen, Jena 1909, p. 48), Richard de St Victor, in his De Quatuor Gradibus Caritatis, and Jacob Boehme, Vom dreifachen Leben des Menschen, VI 84-6 (cf. E. Underhill, Mysticism, New York 1956 (Paperback), p. 421; further in the saying of Baba Lal Das, Dara Shikoh's Hindu friend in the mid 17th century, (cf. L. Massignon et Cl. Huart, Les entretiens de Lahore, in JA CCIX, 1926, p. 325).

182. D 2306/24472; M VI 730.

183. M III 3669.

184. M III 3683 f.

185. D 1389/14705.

186. F 144.

187. M III 1985 ff.

188. S 89 on the authority of Kera Khatun. AF tells more stories about Mowlānā's miracles and ecstatical states.

189. D 649 (N)/6769 ff.

190. D 463/4911—464/4923. Here, the inspiration seems to taper off. The rhythmical structure and the internal rhyme are unfortunately lost in the translation.

191. D 33/431.

192. M II 3129 f.

193. D 959/10115.

194. M VI 232.

195. D 2673/28347.

196. D 2723/28917.

197. D 2968/31503.

198. D 2473/26156.

199. D 2406/25412.
200. AM Nr. 404.
201. D 240/2707.
202. D 2275/24166; cf. 197/2170; 155/1779.
203. D 1576/16526.
204. D 1215/12936; cf. 927/9766, its contrast with ᶜ*aql* 'reason'.
205. M I 2445.
206. This combination is found in 2765/29405; 774/8077; 839/8782; 23/267; 251/2817; 2276/24176; in 2451/25888 is this *kibr* satanic.
207. Thus D 114/1280. Further typical instances of *kibriyā*: D 202/2254; 47/600; 27/341; 1016/10718; 766/8013; 1321/13997; 1824/19157; 2854/30305; 2944/31247; 909/9545; 2856/30329; 2839/30154; 2786/29615; 2758/29313; 197/2181 etc. R 1127; 1470—Interesting is Bahā'oddin Valad's remark, Maᶜāref p. 150, when he connects the *Allāhu akbar* with *kibriyā* (*allāhu akbar, yaᶜni kibriyā*). VN 65 and 75, then, uses the term in connection with Ṣalāḥoddin, in whom the *Mercy of kibriyā* was manifest.
208. D 2762/29354.
209. D 2371/25070.
210. DST Nr. VIII, but not in D.
211. M I 1425.
212. M VI 2120 f.
213. M II 3225 ff; otherwise attributed to Ẕu'n-Nun.
214. M III 79 ff; cf. AM Nr. 193.
215. M III 1879.
216. M V 2339 f.
217. M I 2042 f.
218. M VI 3190.
219. D 3006/31949; cf. also Chapter II Animals, Note 328; R 804 claims: As long as madrasa and minaret are not destroyed, the 'state' of the qalandar will not become flourishing.
220. M V 2802.
221. D 587/6204.
222. M V 3613 f.
223. D 38/485.
224. M VI 2075 f.
225. M III 4369 ff.
226. M V 3066.
227. M II 1250; IV 2712; VN 185.
228. Cf. also VN 289:
    They wield the sword without hands,
    they read the unwritten letter . . . .
229. M I 3146 f; IV 606.
230. M II 3216.
231. M VI 1481 f.
232. M VI 1357 f.
233. M VI 2024 f.
234. M V 3609 ff.
235. M VI 3210 f.
236. M III 3352.
237. M V 2484.

238. D 929/9794 7.
239. M I 3187 f.
240. M I 1669.
241. M III 2221 f.
242. M I 2969 f.
243. M II 2816.
244. M III 2934 f; VI 3447.
245. M II 412 f.
246. M IV 1770.
247. M VI 1893 f.
248. M III 3331 f.
249. AM Nr. 131; Mektuplar Nr. XXII; cf.,the description VN 90:
 'It is easier to know and recognize God than to know the saints; for God Most High is more manifest than the sun . . . But to recognize the saints is difficult; for their art and craft is hidden like they themselves . . .
250. F 133.
251. M I 721.
252. AM Nr. 635; M II 2163; F 153; cf. VN 172, 324 ff.
253. M IV 3370; cf. VN 89.
254. M I 2522.
255. M III 588 f; cf. VN 217, and 346: 'The saint of God is like Noah, and his mercy like the ark—and the flood of ignorance is worse than the flood of water . . .'.
256. F
257. AF 517.
258. AM Nr. 224; M III 1774; AM Nr. 73.
259. M VI 4121 ff.
260. M II 3325.
261. M IV 540 f.
262. M IV 374 f.
263. F 168; cf. M V 2348.
264. MC VII 342 and M II 2969.
265. M V 1430 ff.
266. D 38/492.
267. M II 3343 f; cf. II 1567.
268. M II 2528 f.
269. M III 2703; cf. for similar praise VN 105.
270. M I 2975.
271. D 844/8841. A beautiful description of the saint is D 730.

THE STORY OF THE CHICKPEAS

1. D 155/1768.
2. M VI 1376.
3. Sanāʾi, Ḥadiqa Ch. I p. 139.
4. D 587/6204; 1876/19771.
5. D 152/1743.
6. D 2406/25415.
7. M IV 865; other examples M I 1925; D 2366/25023; 872/9122; love kills everything; 1674/17542; DT 28/35792.
8. D 212/2372.
9. D 1912/20116.

10. D 2725/28944.
11. D 336/3640.
12. M III 4158 ff. The same image in DT 30/35887.
13. The same formulation occurs also in D 896/9382; cf. AM Nr. 64.
14. M III 3755 ff.
15. AM Nr. 320; M IV 2009 f. and often.
16. AM Nr. 138; M I 232 f; cf. IV 97 f. the comparison of the true believer's soul with a porcupine which is made stout by the blows of tribulations.
17. M V 3678.
18. M V 3697 f.
19. M II 479 f.
20. M VI 1579 ff; I 818.
21. M V 134 f.
22. M V 1617; II 373, VI 2343 etc.
23. M III 3751.
24. M V 3206.
25. DST Nr. IV, not in D.
26. M IV 102.
27. D 1989/21015; cf. D 1847/19471, M IV 342.
28. M V 2143 ff.
29. M V 2276.
30. AM Nr. 466.
31. D 141/1613; cf. 1715/17961.
32. M IV 2540 f; cf. III 3555; IV 2350.
33. M I 2237.
34. M IV 2344 f; I 1532; IV 343, 2352; I 2932.
35. M IV 2348 f.
36. M VI 1468 f; cf. III 3760; VI 3837; AM Nr. 352.
37. D 2263/24015; cf. R 313.
38. M VI 4067.
39. M V 551.
40. M VI 751 f; VI 1452; non-existence as prerequisite for existence D 873/9136; 831/8685 6; 498/5294, cf. Chapter III God, Note 114 ff. on ʿ*adam*.
41. M II 1317 ff; cf. R 1575.
42. D 911/9557 65.
43. M V 606 f; cf. VN 36.
44. M V 1712 f.
45. M II 940 ff.
46. M III 3535.
47. D 2948/31312; 1824/19155; M V 1256.
48. D 2573/27325 7.
49. D 1639/17163.
50. D 636/6628 ff.
51. D 911/9563.
52. M III 3907 ff.
53. D 1789/18727.
54. D 1620/16961.
55. D 304/3323 4.
56. D 1347/14242 ff. (rhyme-word).

57. D 1142/12110 18 in praise of journeying (the same *maṭla*ʿ was already used by Abu'l-Faraj Runi, (d. 1191), cf. ʿAufi, *Lubāb*, vol. II 238); M III 533; cf. III 1974; cf. D 214/2397 for the same topic with a different rhyme.
58. M I 3066 f.
59. Cf. Manṭeq oṭ-ṭeyr 232; the whole of Moṣibatnāme, and Sanāʾi's *al-*ʿ*ebād* deal with the slow upward movement.
60. ʿAṭṭār, Divan, ghazal Nr. 655; cf. also Maʿāref p. 115.
61. M V p. 47; cf. III 36 f.
62. M V 719.
63. M II 1093 ff; V 3980; cf. also VI 125 ff; V 782 ff; VI 2900.
64. D 863/9021.
65. M I 3872; cf. III 3897.
66. D 3017/32074.
67. Thus the poem in DST Nr. XI.
68. D 2837/30125 f.
69. M III 3901; cf. V 800 ff; cf. also D 543/5784 about the development from sperm-drop to intelligence, or 1789/18732 'You were clay (*gel*) and became heart (*del*)'.
70. M IV 3637 ff.
71. AM Nr. 222.
72. MC VIII 214 ff.
73. F. Rosen, Mesnevi, München 1913; Introduction p. 18.
74. Khalifa Abdul Ḥakim, The Metaphysics of Rumi, Lahore 1933, Ch. IV; for the whole problem cf. R. Pannwitz, Der Aufbau der Natur, Stuttgart 1961 and the documentation in A. Schimmel, Gabriel's Wing.
75. Tor Andrae, Die letzten Dinge, deutsch von H. H. Schaeder, Leipzig 1940.
76. Afzal Iqbal, The Life and Thought of Rumi, Lahore s.d (ca. 1955); p. 158, quotation from Ḥakim, l.c. p. 32 ff.
77. Khalifa Abdul Ḥakim, *Ḥikmat-e Rumi*, Lahore 1955, p. 151 ff.
78. Shaykh Muhammad Iqbal, The Development of Metaphysics in Persia, London 1908, p. 116 17.
79. cf. Schimmel, Gabriel's Wing, esp. p. 128.
80. Gölpinarli, Mevlâna Celâleddin, p. 167.
81. F 32.
82. F 129.
83. M III 4098 f.
84. M V 3853 f.
85. M V 2014. Cf. C. Rice, The Persian Sufis 22: Rumi is the supreme exponent of the Sufi path, and his writings have only faint traces of emanationist speculation.

THE IDEA OF LOVE IN RUMI'S WORK

1. D 1475/15557; cf. R 49 and 728 where Love is called man's mother.
2. D 27/337; M V 3597; cf. R 166:
   The beloved woman is a pretext—the Beloved is God:
   whosoever thinks they are two is either a Jew or a Christian.
3. F 127.
4. D 313/3424.
5. M V 2008.
6. D 2674/28365.
7. Mektuplar I.

8. M I 112 f.
9. M V 2189 f.
10. Hastie, Festival of Spring Nr. 38, though not an authentic verse it expresses very well the centre of Rumi's thoughts. Ghazzali, Iḥyā ʿolum ad-din IV 277 f. has expressed similar ideas on *longing*.
11. M V 3853 f.
12. M V 2735.
13. D 1158/12293 4.
14. D 2674/28369 ff.
15. D 1861/19618.
16. M II 1529 f; cf. R 805.
17. M V 2014.
18. M VI 3648 f; cf. D 1012/10675.
19. D 1970/20807.
20. D 1643/17199; or love is the carpenter who builds a ladder leading to the Friend, D 2897/30784.
21. M II 3727.
22. M III 4719 ff.
23. M II 1770 f; V 3276.
24. Hujwiri/Nicholson p. 137; about Sumnun's theory of love id. 308.
25. M I 166 f; III 3678, and often in D.
26. D 2733/29050 f; cf. R 1881 'Love has to come and is not to be learned'.
27. D 1997/21109.
28. D 133/1532.
29. M I 1982 f.
30. D 317/3455.
31. D 132/1522 3. In this poem, v. 1524, the juxtaposition of gallows and pulpit occurs.
32. M IV 1424.
33. D 2190/23246.
34. D 429/4520.
35. D 172/1950. Cf. the threefold pun (*tajnis*) in the rhyme of R 716:
    The day when your love makes me mad (*divāna kunad*)
    I produce a madness which even the jinn does not produce (*div ān nakonad*).
    The order of your pen does with my heart that
    which with the top of his pen the administrator of the Divan will not do (*khāja-ye divān nakonad*),
    For the tradition says that the Pen is not valid over the madman, i.e. the madman is not responsible for his actions.
36. D 498/5287.
37. Sanāʾi, Divān p. 605.
38. M III 3832.
39. D 790/8259; cf. 478/5089. 429 a whole poem about the uselessness of intellect.
40. D 1478/15593.
41. D 1657/17366.
42. D 1087/11437.
43. F 47; cf. D 2806/29768:
    The steadfast intellect becomes a vagabond through love, and thousand-toothed wrath a teethless old man by its grace.
    Cf. also 615/6450: 'The madman is pregnant with the soul'. Cf. R 569:
    When could the sun reach your countenance,
    or the swift-feeted wind (reach) your hair?

Reason which acted as khwāja in the city of Existence
became mad when it reached the corner of your street.

44. M V 3932 f. In R 151, Rumi speaks of the frenzied lover who knows no sleep and is therefore 'a sleep-companion of God', since God is seized neither by slumber nor sleep.
45. M V 2765; cf. III 4755.
46. M V 588; III 1136 f.
47. D 2043/21538 9.
48. D 2401/25367.
49. D 1304/13788 ff; 1573/16502.
50. D 176/1975.
51. D 1690/17705.
52. D 1077/11333; cf. R 1026.
53. M III 3919 and very often in D.
54. D 785/8201; R 6, 105. Cf. D 449/4734 'The fire of love is a *kowthar*'.
55. D 1096/11582.
57. D 1105/11681.
58. M VI 4162.
59. D 1332/14091 2.
60. M VI 1995.
61. D 1331/14086.
62. D 471/5055 ff; 2919/31001.
63. M V 2726 ff, it eats everything except love.
64. D 1136/12039 40.
65. DT 11/35063 f.
66. D 1531/16110.
67. D 2102/22199.
68. D 1082/11389.
69. D 2919/31002—they are a small morsel of bread for unsatiable love!
70. M V 2734 f.
71. D 317/3458; cf. R 795.
72. D 213/2379; cf. 2445/25816 'When I finished the cup, I threw away the garment of shame'.
73. DT 38/36133; cf. 1478/15592 'we have left behind fasting and *chella*' in a poem on spiritual liberation.
74. D 1919/20201.
75. Cf. Massignon, Passion, p. 610.
76. D 395/4183.
77. M V 2737.
78. M III 4393.
79. M I 1704.
80. D 425/4471.
81. D 991/10479.
82. M V 2186 f.
83. M I 1793.
84. M III 3846: he teaches on the gallows.
85. M V 3590; cf. III 547; cf. 'Aṭṭār, Tadhkerat-al-owliyā, ed. R. A. Nicholson, II p. 172.
86. D 455/4812.
87. D 628/6551 ff.

88. D 2078/21941 2.
89. D 787/8227.
90. D 1600/16744.
91. Thus D 1962/20697 702.
92. D 2331/24670.
93. D 321/3407.
94. D 2195/23297.
95. D 37/477 83; cf. R 317:
He is our sun and stars and full moon,
He is our garden and He is our qebla and fasting and patience,
He is our ʿ*id* and Ramadan and Night of Might . . .
which then culminates in the *hama ust* 'He is everything'; cf. R 321: but the context shows that this *hama ust* is the feeling of the lover, not a metaphysical speculation.
96. D 1690/17710.
97. RE 328 a 5.
98. Rumi uses this word in D 656/6850; 782/8161; 1020/10765; 2465/26069.
99. D 557/5920.
100. M II 1985 f.
101. M I 3192 ff; cf. F 195.
102. R 334.
103. M II 1987 f.
104. D 7/83.
105. D 705/7365.
106. D 1926/20270.
107. M III 3808 ff.
108. RE 328 a 4.
109. D 2980/31629 30.
110. M I 97.
111. D 770/8039.
112. D 1090/11465
113. D 33/434.
114. M III 507.
115. D 2336/24726.
116. M VI 1064; cf. II 53.
117. D 3055/32518.
118. M III 537.
119. M III 3811.
120. D 766/8010.
121. D 1005/10617.
122. D 1694/17751; cf. 1350/14273 ff; and 1565/16436 as fine examples of the lover's complete surrender.
123. D 1053/11106 f.
124. D 940/9921.
125. D 2542/26985.
126. D 1596/16704.
127. D 1408/14910.
128. D 207/2317.
129. RE 345 b 4.
130. D 1236/13112 15.

131. D 1198/12744, 48.
132. D 1201/12779.
133. D 947/9995.
134. D 97/1087.
135. D 704/7350 f.
136. R 1289; 110.
137. D 1888/19857.
138. D 2148/22738.
139. D 2820/29938.
140. D 2348/23835 6.
141. M I 1749.
142. M III 1424.
143. D 2718/28861.
144. M III 3893; cf. D 2690/28533 vice versa:
    I am that water which the sand of Love has swallowed.
    What sand? Rather a boundless ocean!
145. D 1751/18353.
146. D 1661/17401.
147. D 1388/14696.
148. M V 3485.
149. DT 23/35562.
150. D 684/7113.
151. D 1429/15114.
152. D 1804/18955.
153. M V 3237 f; cf. 2199/23330: 'O Sanāʾi, the lovers need pain—where is pain?'
154. D 2213/23465; cf. M VI 1541 f.
155. D 1393/14742.
156. M II 2439; D 1594/16686; cf. II Sufis, Note 83.
157. M VI 4599.
158. D 2401/25366; 1630/17070; cf. 1607/16832; and often.
159. D 716/7514; 1560/16376; *ʿud* occurs often in connection with *ʿid*.
160. M II 1458.
161. D 1848/19498
162. M V 2713 f.
163. D 662/6914. Cf. R 44: With the beloved, one thorn is better than a thousand dates.
164. D 133/1531.
165. M V 1242 f.
166. M III 1414 ff.
167. D 455/4809.
168. D 3041/32335 6.
169. M I 2880; cf. the contrast *faqih-faqir* in Mektuplar XIX.
170. M II 1765 ff.
171. D 3060/32581.
172. D 2775/39498.
173. M III 1345.
174. M III 1349 f.
175. D 237/2672.
176. RE 323 b 1.

177. D 364/3902.
178. M VI 4034.
179. D 1156/12272 in a poem addressing the singer during the *samāʿ*; cf. R 325.
180. M IV 758.
181. D 2230/23644.
182. M VI 4023 ff. The same R 1019, also, in a different setting, in R 643.
183. cf. M III 4445 ff. The lover is autumn, the beloved is spring, RE 330 b 6.
184. D 2163/22907; cf. 22905; M III 4445.
185. M VI 983.
186. M III 2362.
187. M III 4098.
188. M V 589.
189. M V 1255; cf. Ch. II, Garden, Note 123.
190. DST 209; cf. 1697/17780. Cf. R 346 when he says in a joking mood, playing with the usual addresses to the beloved 'My soul, my two eyes':

    My Beloved said: 'How can that person be alive?
    When I am his soul—strange that he can live without soul!'
    I began to cry; He said: 'This is even stranger:
    Without me, who is his two eyes, how can he weep?'

191. M III 3023 f.
192. D 728/7638.
193. M V 2020 f.
194. M VI 1083 f. A thorough study into Rumi's symbolism of mirrors—a favourite image of almost all Sufi poets—would be most welcome.
195. M I 1740.
196. M V 3547.
197. M I 1066; cf. Chapter III Prophet. Note 53.
198. M I 30. In R 1905, Rumi uses an expression which was to become very popular with later poets:

    Neither am I I, nor are you you, nor are you I,
    Yet I am I, and you are you, and you are also I;
    O Beauty of Khotan, I am with you so
    That I am in doubt whether I am you or you are I!

THE PROBLEM OF PRAYER IN JALĀLODDIN'S WORK

1. M II 189 ff. A shorter version of this chapter was published in Yādnāme-yi Jan Rypka, Prague 1967. Cf. for the same topic also VN 249.
2. Tholuck, Ssufismus, p. 116.
3. Främmande Religionsurkunder, Uppsala 1908, Vol. II, 2, p. 981. Reprinted 1954 under the title: Om Religionsurkunder.
4. Tiele-Söderblom, Kompendium der Religionsgeschichte, Berlin 1931, p. 128.
5. R. A. Nicholson, The Mystics of Islam, p. 113.
6. Das Gebet, München [5] 1923, p. 225.
7. Thus in: Erscheinungsformen und Wesen der Religion; and in: Das Gebet in der Problematik des modernen Menschen, in: Festschrift für R. Guardini, Würzburg 1964, p. 243, and often.
8. M III 2140 ff. (N).
9. M I 3899 ff. (N).
10. M III 3033; AM Nr. 253.
11. Cf. D 686/7134:

    This pleasure-full happy life was like prayer,

and those dregs of pain became like an ablution.

For a fine description of ritual prayer as a vineyard the door of which is the formula *Allāhu akbar*, the walls the parts of prayer (*qiyām, sojud, roku*ᶜ), and the key ritual purity, cf. Maᶜāref p. 17.

12. M IV 2213 ff.
13. D 2831/30054; 3091/32977.
14. D 2807/29784.
15. D 1418/15011.
16. D 3038/32313; cf. 56/691.
17. D 2984/31692.
18. M IV 3420. But compare also his sigh D 1459/15425: 'I am sick of the *Fāteḥa*'.
19. D 2046/21580 1.
20. M I 381; cf. AM Nr. 10 'No ritual prayer without the presence of the heart'.
21. D 2971/31532.
22. F 182 f.
23. M IV 11.
24. D 1525/16052.
25. DT 17/35336.
26. D 940/9918 f.
27. M VI 2669.
28. Hujwiri/Nicholson, Ch. XIX.
29. S 41 ff = D 2831/30053 65
30. R 81; cf. also R 941:

    As long as I am with you, my *majāz* (metaphorical act) is all *namāz* (prayer),
    When I am without you, my prayer is all metaphorical.

    Cf. also VN 88 about the one content and different forms of prayer.
31. D 915/9638.
32. D 1735/18195.
33. D 1194/12706.
34. D 2344/24804.
35. D 2339/24749.
36. M III 2374 f.
37. M VI 2305; D 3061/32602.
38. D 696/7251.
39. D 528/5619 21.
40. D 3063/32628; cf. 346/3740 2, a tender little prayer-poem.
41. M III 2304.
42. M V 2311.
43. M III 203.
44. M V 2259.
45. M VI 4227 ff; the same in F 49.
46. AM Nr. 730.
47. M I 2083 ff. (N).
48. M II 1720 ff. (N); cf. V 3320 f.
49. M II 1797 (N). During her monthly impurity a woman is not allowed to perform the ritual prayer, to recite or touch the Koran, or to enter a mosque. But God accepts even her prayer.
50. M II 497.
51. M V 3165 73.
52. Cf. H. Ritter, Muslim Mystics' Strife with God, in Oriens V 1953.

53. M I 2290; cf. D 2781/29570.
54. M II 139 f; cf. III 169; 2469.
55. M IV 56 ff.
56. D 2478/26213; 19/213.
57. D 322/3499.
58. D 1633/17105; cf. 226/2559: The messiah went to the fourth heaven on the wing of prayer.
59. D 1237/13117.
60. D 2227/23629.
61. Cf. D 2944/31258.
62. M V 1184 f.
63. D 949/10015.
64. M III 2374 f (N).
65. D 1425/15069 70.
66. D 767/8029.
67. D 903/9470; 942/9944.
68. M III 1495 ff.
69. D 573/6082; cf. M II 3136.
70. D 413/4370.
71. D 873/9138.
72. D 805/8422.
73. D 927/9757; 581/6155; 1000/10561.
74. D 1000/10557.
75. D 2590/27483; for the expression cf. supra Chapter II Gardens. Note 59.
76. Sanā'i, Divān, p. 29 ff.
77. F 104.
78. M V 2315; cf. AM Nr. 3.
79. M III 405.
80. M V 309.
81. M II 2495 ff, here 2505 f. (N).
82. M III 2215 f.
83. D 21/237.
84. M V 780 ff; cf. II 1992; III 2173.
85. D 2223/23584; 1853/19542.
86. M II 691 ff. (N).
87. M I 1578; MC VII 113.
88. Mawāqif and Mukhāṭabāt, ed. and transl. A. J. Arberry, London 1935, Mawqif XI, 16.
89. M II 2443 f. (N).
90. M V 4162; VI 1438 ff; 2295 f, 2317 ff.
91. D 2628/27850; cf. M I 517 f; V 2243 f, about the prayer of the mystical leader; M III 2200 ff; VI 1438.
92. M IV 3498 ff. (N).
93. Cf. ʿAṭṭār, Tadhkerat al-owliyā, II p. 32.
94. DST Nr. IV verse 11.
95. F 24.
96. S 25 f; cf. A. Gölpinarli in the Introduction of *Mektuplar*.
97. Mektuplar Nr. XIX.
98. F 43.

99. Jehangir Hāshmi, Maẓhar al-āthār, ed. H. Rashdi, Karachi 1957.
100. Cf. A. Schimmel, The Idea of Prayer in the Thought of Iqbal, MW XLVIII, July 1958.

Other important prayers or discussions related to prayer, in the Mathnavi are: I 1196; 1880 ff; 3391 f; II 2552; f; 2443 f; 2495 ff; III 2209 f; 2364 f; V 1197 ff; 1451 f; 3990 f; VI 560 ff; 2298 ff; 2887 ff.

MOWLANA JALĀLODDIN'S INFLUENCE IN EAST AND WEST

1. Cf. H. Ritter, Maulānā ğalāluddīn Rūmī und sein Kries, Der Islam 26/1942—Solṭan Valad's Turkish and Persian Divāns as well as his *Valadnāma* (VN) (written in the meter of Sanā'i's *Ḥadiqa*) have been edited, but have rarely attracted the interest of Western scholars although they, as Ritter has pointed out, contain most important material for the history of Mowlānā's life and interpretation of his thought.
2. VN 179 ff.
3. VN 48 ff.
4. VN 72 74, 97, 107, and often.
5. VN 158 ff. Solṭān Valad claims that the three mystical friends of his father were not in themselves great personalities but became important only through their relation with Mowlānā, and through being immortalized by his, Solṭān Valad's books.
6. It would be interesting for religious psychology to analyse the relation Bahā'oddin Valad—Mowlānā—Solṭān Valad on the one hand, the relation Nāṣir Moḥammad ʿAndalib (d. 1758) and his son Khwāja Mir Dard (d. 1785) on the other hand.
7. Şehabettin Uzluk, Mevlevilikte resim, resimde Mevleviler, Ankara 1957.
8. The *Mevlevi ayinlari* were published by the Conservatorium in Istanbul in the late thirties; a UNESCO record and a record made in Turkey are available; other records have been produced in Iran; they show the various modes of recitation.
9. The first translation into Turkish, dedicated to Sultan Murad II (d. 1451) was recently discovered by Dr. Hasibe Mazioglu, Ankara. cf. her contribution to *Bildiriler*, Ankara 1973.
10. His *fātiḥ al-abyāt* was first printed in Cairo 1251/1835, then 1289/1872 in Istanbul, and was described by J. von Hammer-Purgstall in 1851. For more Turkish translations and commentaries see Hammer-Purgstall, *Geschichte des Osmanischen Reiches* III 77. Sometimes a seventh volume was added to the *Mathnavi*, since its imitation in a simple meter was comparatively easy. One of the compilers of a seventh volume is Ismāʿil Farrukhi (d. 1840). For more information see H. Ethé, Neupersische Literatur, in: *Grundriss der iranischen Philologie* II, p. 290 ff, and R. A. Nicholson in his introduction to his commentary of the *Mathnavi* p. VII, XII.
11. The *Ruḥ al-Mathnavi*, being an incomplete commentary, was printed in Istanbul 1287/1870. Other important printed commentaries on the first book of the *Mathnavi* are those by Sàri ʿAbdullāh Efendi (d. 1071/1660 1), called *javāhir-e bavāḥir-e Mathnavi*, printed in five volumes Istanbul 1288/1871, and that of Abidin Pasha in six volumes, Istanbul 1887 8. Besides, many unpublished manuscripts exist in the mystical traditional circles in Turkey. At present, the commentary of Kenân Rifai (d. 1950) appears in print.
12. *Mevlâna Şiirleri Antolojisi*, Konya 1956 and often.
13. About him see *Encyclopaedia of Islam* s.v. Kāniʿ; particularly interesting seems his *hirrenamesi*, social criticism under the disguise of letters written by a cat. For more poets with Mevlevi inclinations see Gibb, History of Ottoman poetry II

374 (Gülsheni who wrote a *mathnavi* in response to Rumi's *Mathnavi*), further III 337; IV 198 ff., 238 ff.; 312 ff.; 333 ff.; VI 208.

14. Asaf Halet Çelebi has translated Rumi's quatrains into Turkish in 1939 and into French in 1950; Hasan-Âli Yücel has produced translations of the same poems in 1932; many other free adaptations of Rumi's poetry can be found in modern Turkish, out of which we mention the selection by M. Nuri Gencosman, *Mevlâna*ʿ*dan Seçme Rubailer*, Ankara 1964. The fact that the journal *Türk Yurdu* published a Special Mevlâna Number in July 1965 shows Rumi's popularity very well. Scholarly work about him is being carried on in Ankara and Istanbul Universities; Dr. Meliha Tarikâhya has translated several works of Mevlevi literature into Turkish; her colleagues Dr. Hasibe Mazioglu and Dr. Tahsin Yazīclī belong to the most active scholars in the field of Mevlâna studies in Turkey.

15. Yusof ibn Aḥmad belonged to the mevlevi *tekke* in Beşiktaş, Istanbul, cf. Nicholson, Commentary, p. XII.

16. *Foṣūl min al-Mathnavī*, Cairo 1946.

17. Dīvān, Beirut 1972, p. 572; cf. also the special Mowlānā-issue of *Fikrun wa Fann* 21, 1973, with contributions about Mowlānā in Arabic.

18. For the Persian commentaries see Ethé, l.c. II 291 f. The *javāhir al-asrār* was printed in Lucknow 1894.

19. Jāmi, *Nafaḥāt al-ons* p. 393; cf. also the allusions to Rumi in Jāmi's Divān, thus p. 696 to Shamsoddin, further p. 248 Nr. 301 and p. 321 Nr. 390.

20. *Lobb-e lobāb-Mathnavi*, ed. Said Nafisi, Tehran 1344/1965.

21. *Sharḥ-e Mathnavi*, Tehran 1285/1868.

22. Royal Asiatic Society of Bengal, Proceedings, 1870.

23. *Khayr al-majālis*, ed. K. A. Nizami, Aligarh 1968.

24. M. Enamul Haq, *Muslim Bengali Literature*, Karachi 1957, p. 42.

25. cf. Sir Thomas Arnold, *Saints and Martyrs, Muhammadan*, ERE X 68 ff.

26. For examples see A. Schimmel, *The martyr-mystic Hallaj in Sindhi folk-poetry*, in: Numen IX 1961. The combination of Shams with Ḥallāj is common in the poetry of Sachal Sarmast and Bedil Rohrīwārō.

27. Thus the *Nā*ʾ*īnāma*, Kabul 1956.

28. Cf. Abdal Ghani, *Persian Language at the Mughal Court* III 10 f., based on Abuʾl-Fazl, *Akbarnāme* I 271.

29. Qanungo, *Dara Shukoh*, Calcutta 2 1952, p. 382; See also B. J. Hasrat, *Dara Shikuh*, p. 143 f. The *Ṭarīqat al-ḥaqiqat* consists three quarters of quotations from Rumi; in the *Sakinat al-owliyā*, ed. M. Jalāl Nāʾini, Dārā Shikoh mentions a certain Miān Abuʾl-Maʿāli as Mathnavi-specialist in Miān Mir's entourage. See further JRAS of Bengal, 1870, p. 272.

30. C. Field, *Mystics and Saints of Islam*, 1910, p. 186.

31. Mir ʿAli Shir Qāniʿ, *Maqālāt ash-shuʿarā*, ed. H. Rashdi, p. 122.

32. Moḥammad Aṣlaḥ, *Tadhkira-ye shuʿarā-ye Kashmir*, ed. H. Rashdi, Karachi 1967 68, Vol. II 658.

33. Qāniʿ, Maqālāt p. 470; see also Qāniʿ, *Tuḥfat ul-kirām*, Sindhi translation, Karachi 1958, p. 547, 557, and Dara Shikoh, *Sakina* p. 30, 33.

34. Moḥammad Aṣlaḥ, *Tadhkira* II 597 (twelve poems by Ṣāʾeb). The influence of Rumi's diction of Ṣāʾeb has still to be studied.

35. *Kolliyāt-e Bedil*, Kabul 1964 ff., Vol. I 151.

36. id. 251, 141, 607; p. 105: 'I have become full of complaint since fire was cast into the reedbed', and often.

37. *Mathnavi maẓhar al-āthār*, ed. H. Rashdi. On p. 103 we find verses on the flute and mystical dance in the spirit of Rumi.

38. A certain Mirzā Afzal Sarkhosh (d. 1714) wrote six *mathnavi* after Rumi's example, one of them being called *Nūr ʿalā nūr* (Storey, Persian Literature Nr.

1132). ᶜĀqil Khān Rāzi, too, composed a book (*moraqqa*ᶜ) imitating the model of the *Mathnavi-ye ma*ᶜ*navi* 'in a gnostic manner' (M. Aṣlaḥ, *Tadhkira* I 252). ᶜĀqil Khān's son-in-law Shukrullāh Khān wrote also a commentary on the Mathnavi (W. Ivanow, *Catalogue of the Curzon Collection*, p. 211). Aziz Aḥmad, *Studies in Islamic Culture in the Indian Environment*, Oxford 1964, p. 235, speaks about Rumi's influence on Bhopal Rai of Jammu (d. 1719). It is remarkable that the great theologian of Delhi, Shāh Valiollah (d. 1762) quotes Rumi rather frequently in his Persian writings (thus *Tafhimāt* II). — A number of copies of the *Mathnavi* as well as of Indian variations of this work are mentioned by A. Sprenger, Catalogue of the Library of the Kings of Oudh, Calcutta 1854, Nr. 360 375; on page 490, he calls 'Shams Tabryz a most disgusting cynic'. See Sprenger esp. Nr. 468, A mathnavi by a certain Rāzi 'in which he imitates Jalal aldyn Rumy'; Nr. 154, Bahā' oddin Amoli's *Nān u halvā*, (d. 1030/1621) which is 'considered to be an introduction to Rumi's *Mathnavi*'; Nr. llo ᶜAshiq's *'Eysh u ṭarab* of 1071/1668, which 'seems to be an imitation' of Rumi's *Mathnavi*, and Nr. 163 Bāqir ᶜAli Khān's *Romuz aṭ-ṭāhirin*, 1139/1796 7. — A Persian commentary of the Mathnavi by Hajji Emdād ᶜAli (d. in Mecca 1899) was published in Cawnpore 1896 1903.

39. Ethé, *Neupersische Literature* II 3ol, the two volumes are preserved in the India Office Library, Nr. 2914

40. Cf. Ethé, l.c. p. 291, and Nicholson, Commentary p XII f. Among the Indian commentaries those by ᶜAbdol Laṭif ibn ᶜAbdallah al-ᶜAbbāsi (d. 1638) are worth mentioning; they are called *laṭā'ef al-ma*ᶜ*navi* and *mir*ʾ*āt al-mathnavi;* the same author published a critical edition of the *Mathnavi* in 1623, further a special glossary, *laṭā*ʾ*ef al-loghāt* (lithographed Lucknow 1877 and 1905). Sayyid ᶜAbdol Fattāḥ al-Ḥoseyni alᶜAskari wrote a commentary of the *Mathnavi* under the title *meftāḥ al-ma*ᶜ*āni* and an anthology from the same work called *ad-dorr al-maknun*. There is further the *Mokāshafāt-e Rezavi* by Mowlvi Ahmad Rezā (1673, printed Lucknow 1877), and the *Sharḥ-e Mathnavi* by Mowlvi Vali Moḥammad Akbarābādi (1727, printed Lucknow 1894).

41. ᶜAbduʾl-Âli Baḥr al-ᶜolum, d. 1810; his commentary was lithographed Lucknow 1876, Bombay 1877.

42. Qāniᶜ, *Maqālāt* p. 73.

43. Qāniᶜ, *Tuḥfat ul-kirām*, p. 573 quote from a certain Shāh Moḥammad Vilhāri.

44. Ibrāhim Khalil, *Takmilat Maqālāt ash-shu*ᶜ*arā*, ed. H. Rashdi, p. 36 (the reciting person is a certain Aṣaf, d. 1287/1870).

45. G. M. Qāsimi, *Hāshimiya Library*, in: Mihrān ja moti, Karachi 1959, p. 309.

46. U. M. Daudpota, *Kalām-e Girhori*, Hyderabad/Sind, p. 45 (note), 47 (note), 50.

47. Lilaram Watanmal, *The Life of Shah Abdul Laṭif*, Hyderabad 1889, p. 11.

48. H. T. Sorley, *Shah Abdul Laṭif of Bhit*, London 1940, p. 243, 281, 174.

49. Sur Asā III 31 in the edition of K. B. Adwāni, Bombay 1957.

50. Cf. A. Schimmel, *Schāh* ᶜ*Abdul Laṭifs Beschreibung des wahren Sufi*, in: Festschrift für Fritz Meier, Wiesbaden 1974; cf. Dr. N. A. Baloch, *Maulānā Jalāluddin Rumi's influence on Shāh* ᶜ*Abdul Laṭif* (publication of a paper at the International Mevlâna Seminar, Ankara 1973); the text of the crucial verses varies from that in Adwāni's edition. See also A. Schimmel, *Pain and Grace*, Leiden 1976.

51. Qāniᶜ ,*Tuḥfat al-kirām*, p. 572 f. This recitor was a disciple of Shāh ᶜInāyat Shahid (d. 1718), the martyred Sufi leader of Sind, and a descendant of ᶜAbdallah-i Ansāri, the saint of Herat (d. 1089).

52. Also *Mihrān jā moti*, p. 244, 256, 261.

52. Bedil Rohriwārō, *Divān*, Karachi 1954: Introduction p. 10 and 57, in the text see p. 145, 125, 216, 437.

53. Published Hyderabad 1960 ff. Another translation in Sindhi, again in the

original meter, has been undertaken by Moḥammad Aḥsan China; see the journal *Naien Zindagi*, June 1960, p. 19. The Sindhi Adabi Board has also published in the series of children's magazines, *Gul Phul*, numerous tales from the *Mathnavi* in simple Sindhi.

54. L. D. Barnett, *Panjabi Printed Books in the British Museum*, London 1961, p. 39. The Panjabi verse translation by Mowlānā Moḥammad Shāhoddin was published with an Urdu introduction by Nur Aḥmad Khalaf Moḥammad Maḥbub in Lahore 1939.

55. See G. Raverty, *Selections from the popular poetry of the Afghans*, London 1862, p. 227 (Khushḥāl Khān Khattak).

56. Cf. S. Naʿimuddin, *Influence of Rumi on Urdu Poetry*, XXVI. International Congress of Orientalists, Delhi 1967; further: *Urdu zabān men Mathnavi-yi Rumi kā attibāʿ*, Karachi 1962. It would be worth while to collect the allusions to Rumi and to the *Mathnavi* from the various sources in Indo-Persian and early Urdu. A. S. Nadvi, *Sheʿr al-Hind* 2/210 mentions that the Urdu poet Mir Ḥasan (d. 1782) had composed a mathnavi *romuz al- ʿarefin* after Mowlana's model. Garcin de Tassy, *Historie de la Littérature Hindoue et Hindoustani* II 594 deals with two Urdu translations of the Mathnavi, that by Ilāhi Bakhsh Neshāṭ, *Majmaʿ feyz al-ʿolum*, and by Shah Mostaʿān, Bāgh-i Iram (s. a. Sprenger Nr. 670), printed Bombay 1875. Sprenger Nr. 207 f. mentions an Urdu Mathnavi by Aʿẓam of Agra imitating Rumi, and Shah Shāker ʿAli of Delhi, who works on the Mathnavi (p. 287)—Gholam Ḥeydar'r selections, *Shajara-ye maʿrefat* was printed Lucknow 1885, Mohd. Yusof ʿAli Shāh's *Pirāhan-e Yusofi* Lucknow 1889, and Abdol- Majid Polbhabati's commentary, *Bustān-e maʿrefat*, Lucknow 1894-96.

57. Khaliq Anjum, *Mirzā Saudā*, Aligarh, 1965.

58. Muḥammad Iqbal, *The Development of Metaphysics in Persia*, London 1908, p. 117.

59. *Savāneḥ-e Mowlānā Rumi*, Lucknow 1902.

60. R. A. Nicholson, *The Secrets of the Self*, London 1920, p. XI.

61. *Iqbālnāme*, ed. Sheykh ʿAṭāʾullāh, Lahore s.d., Vol. I p. 284 (letter written in 1935), cf. I 27.

62. *Bāl-e Jibril*, p. 180.

63. *Pas che bāyad kard* p. 5 ff.

64. *Bāl-e Jibril* p. 180.

65. *Payām-e Mashriq* p. 17.

66. *Pas che bāyad kard* p. 5.

67. *Jāvidnāme*, Lahore 1932; English, German, French, Italian, and Turkish translations available (see bibliography).

68. *Armaghān-e Hijāz*, p. 106.

69. *Jāvidnāme*, Introduction p. 12, in Arberry's *Javidname* p. 28, in Schimmel, *Buch der Ewigkeit*, p. 25; the poem is Nr. XVI in Nicholson's *Selected Poems from the Divān-i Shams-i Tabriz*.

70. *Payām-e Mashriq* p. 122; cf. also the two poems on Hegel id. p. 242 and 245: in both of them, Rumi saves the poet from boring and useless philosophy. German translation: A. Schimmel, *Botschaft des Ostens*, p. 48, 94. It is interesting to notice that Goethe is linked with Rumi in Iqbal's thought, although the German poet disliked Mowlānā, whereas Mowlānā's admirer Hegel is transformed into Rumi's antagonist.

71. *Payām-e Mashriq* p. 246, Schimmel l.c. p. 97; the verse is M IV 1402.

72. *Bāl-e Jibril* p. 7.

73. *Pas che bāyad kard* p. 36.

74. *Musāfir* p. 30.

75. *Armaghān-e Hijāz* p. 180.

76. Thus the book by Khwāja ʿAbdul Ḥamid ʿIrfāni, Tehran 1332 sh/1953. For the whole problem cf. A. Schimmel, *Gabriel's Wing*, last chapter.

77. Thus Edward Dowden, *The Secret of the Universe*; Arthur Symons, *The Turning Dervish*; cf. also S. Waddington, *A Persian Apologue*, in: *The Oxford Book of English Mystical Verse*, p. 341, 367, and 476.

78. *Fundgruben des Orients* I 429 brings some excerpts from Jāmi's *Nafaḥāt al-ons* about Rumi; later issues contain translations by Valentin Freiherr von Hussard. In the Yïldïz Kiöşk Library, Istanbul, a copy of a selection from the *Divān-e Shams*, calligraphed by this Austrian scholar, is preserved as Asar-e nefise Nr. 23.

79. About him and his article in the Bombay Transactions, London 1819, see A. J. Arberry, *History of Sufism*, London, 1940, p. 11-14.

80. For Rückert's adaptations of Rumi and other Oriental poetry cf. A. Schimmel, *Orientalische Dichtung in der Uebersetzung Friedrich Rückerts*, Bremen 1963.

81. *Sitzungsberichte der Österreichischen Akademie der Wissenschaften*, Wien 1851; although Hammer mentions the previous translations from Rumi's work, all of which were produced by German scholars (Hussard, Rosenzweig, Tholuck, Georg Rosen, and himself), he omits the name of his one-time pupil Rückert. Cf. A. Schimmel, Zwei Abhandlungen zur Mystik und Magie des Islams.

82. Cf. A. Schimmel, *Ein unbekanntes Werk Joseph von Hammer-Purgstalls*, in: *Die Welt des Islam*, NS XV, 1974.

83. R. Kodve-Khorb, *Maulavis Mystik und seine Dialektik*; in: *Trudi XXV mezhunar. Kongr. Vostokovedov*, Moskau 1963, II 362/64.

84. Ethé, *Neupersische Literatur*, p. 309

85. By Axel E. Hermelin, Lund 1933/36.

86. By R. Van Brakell-Buys, 1952.

87. The first translation by P. Hajek and Dr. Jan Aksamit was published in *Kvety* 24/II, 1902, p. 462-69: Z divánu Dzeláluddína Rumiho. Some of Rumi's quatrains have been translated by Vera Kubičková, a ghazal in very free adaptation in Slovak translated by I. Kupec in *Perly a ruze*, Bratislava 1962. The first article on Rumi was composed by Rudolf Dvořák in 1904. (I thank Dr. Jiří Bečka, Prague, for detailed information).

88. In 'Literatur und Wissenschaft' Nr. 11, Heidelberg, November 1910.

89. Cf. Lotte Brunner, *Constantin Brunners Genielehre und der Sufismus*, Berlin 1927.

90. *Aus dem Rohrflötenbuch*, Jacob Hegner, Hallerau, 1930, and the review by Jan Rypka in OLZ 1931/883.

91. F. Brabazon, *Stay with God*, Woombye, Queensland 1959, p. 28f. and 38. For the whole problem and more details see A. Schimmel, *Mevlâna Celâlettin Rumiʾnin Sark ve Garpʾta tesirleri*, Ankara 1963, and the article; *Maulana Jalaluddin Rumi's influence on Muslim literature*, in Güldeste, 1971.

92. Rubāʿi 839.

Bibliography

Since the manuscript of this book was completed in 1974, not all publications which appeared after that date have been included.

Jalāloddin Rumi, *Mathnawi-yi maᶜnawi*, edited with critical notes, translation and commentary by R. A. Nicholson, Vol. 1–8, London 1925–40; cf. the reviews by Hellmut Ritter in OLZ 1928, 1935, and 1941. A one-volume reprint of this edition: Tehran 1350 sh/1971.

Kolliyāt-e Shams yā Divān-e kabir, edited by Badi ᶜozzamān Furuzānfar, Tehran 1336 sh/1957 ff., in ten volumes.

Maktubāt, ed. Ahmad Remzi Akyürek, Istanbul 1937; ed. Yusuf Jamshidipur u Gholāmḥoseyn Amin, Tehran 1956; Turkish Translation by Abdülbaki Gölpınarlı, Istanbul 1963.

Fihi mā fihi, edited ᶜAbdol Majid Daryābādi, Aᶜzamgarh 1929, edited Badi ᶜozzamān Furuzānfar, Tehran 1330 sh/1951.

Majāles-i sebᶜa, (Yedi Meclis) Turkish translation by Abdülbaki Gölpınarlı, Konya 1965.

A full documentation of the printed literature about Rumi is found in Mehmet Önder, *Mevlâna Bibliografyası, I: Basmalar*, Ankara 1973.

Abdal Ghani, *A History of Persian Language and Literature at the Mughal Court, Allahabad 1929–30*, repr. 1972.

ᶜAbdol ᶜAziz Ṣāḥib al-javāhir, *Javāhir al-āthār* (Arabic verse translation of the *Mathnavi*), University of Tehran, s.d. (after 1955).

Abdul Hakim, Khalifa, *The Metaphysics of Rumi*, Lahore 1933, ^{2}1948.

id. *Ḥikmat-e Rumi*, Lahore 1955 (Urdu).

ᶜAbdul Laṭif, Shāh, *Risālo,* edited Kalyan B. Adwani, Bombay 1958 (Sindhi)

ᶜAbdaṣ Ṣabur, Ṣalāḥ, Dīvān, Beirut 1971 (Arabic).

Adib, Din Moḥammad, *Ashraf al-ᶜolum*, Hyderabad/Sind 1960–5 (Sindhi verse translation of the *Mathnavi*).

Aflāki, Aḥmad ibn Moḥammad, *Manāqeb al-ᶜārefin*, ed. Agra 1897; edited Tahsin Yazıcı, Ankara 1959–61, 2 Vols; Turkish translation: *Ariflerin menkibeleri*, by Tahsin Yazıcı, Ankara 1964. See also: Huart.

Ahmad, Aziz, *Studies in Islamic Culture in the Indian Environment,* Oxford 1964.

Ahmed, Zubaid, *The Contribution of Indo-Pakistan to Arabic*

Literature, Lahore 2nd edition 1968.

Ali, Mrs Meer Hassan, *Observations on the Mussulmauns of India*, 2 Vols. London 1832.

ʿAndalib, Moḥammad Nāṣir, *Nāla-ye ʿAndalib*, 2 Vols. Bhopal 1309 h/1891.

id. *Risāla-ye hush-afzā*, Ms. Panjab University Library, Lahore.

Andrae, Tor, *Die person Muhammads in lehre und glauben seiner gemeinde*, Stockholm 1918.

id. *Die letzten Dinge*, deutsch von H. H. Schaeder, Leipzig 1940.

id. *I Myrtenträdgarden*, Uppsala 1947 (German translation: Islamische Mystiker, by H. H. Canus-Kredé, Stuttgart 1960).

Arasteh, Reza, *Rumi the Persian: Rebirth in Creativity and Love*, Washington 1965.

Araz, Nezihe, Aşk Peygamberi Mevlâna, Istanbul 1972.

Arberry, Arthur John, *Catalogue of the India Office Library*, Vol. II, London 1937.

id. *An Introduction to the History of Sufism*, London 1942.

id. *Classical Persian Literature*, London 1958.

id. *The Rubāʿiyāt of Jalaluddin Rumi*, London 1959.

id. *Tales from the Mathnavi*, London 1961.

id. *More Tales from the Mathnavi*, London 1963.

id. *Discourses of Rumi,* London 1961.

id. *Mystical Poems of Rumi*, First Selection, Poem 1-200, Chicago 1968.

id. *Aspects of Islamic Civilisation*, University of Michigan, 1967.

Arnold, Sir Thomas, *Saints, Muhammadan, India, in*: Hastings, Encyclopaedia of Religions and Ethics, X, 68 ff.

Aṣlaḥ, Moḥammad, *Tadhkira-ye shoʿarā-ye Kashmir*, edited and completed by Sayyid Hussamuddin Rashdi, Karachi 1967-8, 5 Vols.

ʿAṭṭār, Faridoddin, *Tadhkerat al-auliyāʾ*, ed. Reynold Alleyne Nicholson, Vol. 1-2, London-Leyden 1905-7, repr. 1959.

id. *Manṭeq oṭ-ṭeyr*, ed. M. Javād Shakur, Tehran 1961.

id. Moṣibatnāma, ed. N. Feṣāl, Teheran 1338 sh/1959.

id. *Divān-e qaṣāʾed u ghazaliyāt*, ed. Saʿid Nafisi, Tehran 1339 sh/1960.

ʿAufi, Moḥammad, *Lubāb al-albāb*, ed. Edward G. Browne and Moḥammad Qazvini, London 1903-6.

ʿAzzām, ʿAbdulvahhāb, *Foṣul min al-Mathnavi*, Cairo 1946.

Bahāʾoddin Valad, *Maʿāref,* ed. Badiʿozzamān Furuzānfar, Vol. IV, Tehran 1338 sh./1959.

Baloch, Nabibakhsh A., *Maulana Jalaluddin Rumi's Influence on Shah Abdul Latif,* Hyderabad/Sind 1973; (paper read at the Mevlâna conference in Ankara 1973).

Barnett, D., *Panjabi Printed Books in the British Museum*, London 1961.

Bausani, Alessandro, *Persia Religiosa*, Milan 1959.

id. *Storia della letteratura persiana* (together with Antonio Pagliari), Milano 1960.

id. *Il Pensiero religioso di Maulânâ Gialâl ad-Din Rûmî*, in: Oriente Moderno XXXIII, April 1953.

al-Bayāti, ᶜAbdul Vahhāb, *Divān*, 2 vols. Beirut 1972.

Baykal, Özgün, *Mevlâna Celâleddin Rumi'nin Mesnevisi ve Divan-i Kebir' inde kuş motifleri*, in: Dogu Dilleri I 1, Ankara 1964.

Bečka, Jirí, *Gazel v české poezii*, in Česká literatura 2/1976

Bedil, Mirzā ᶜAbdol Qāder, *Kolliyāt*, 4 vols., Kabul 1963 ff.

Bedil Rohriwārō, *Divān*, ed. ᶜAbd al-Ḥoseyn Shāh Musawi, Karachi 1954 (Sindhi).

Berthels, E. E., *Grundlinien der Entwicklungsgeschichte des sufischen Lehrgedichtes*, in: Islamica III 1, 1929.

Bertram, Ernst, *Persische Spruchgedichte*, Insel-Bücherei, Leipzig 1940.

Bildiriler: Mevlâna'nin 700 ölüm yıldönümü dolaysiyle uluslararası Mevlâna semineri (Papers read at the International Mevlâna Seminar in Ankara, December 1973), Ankara, Türkiye Iş Bankası, 1973.

Binā, Ḥoseyn Sh., *Shakhṣiyat-i Mowlavi*, Tehran 1937.

Bogdanov, *The Quatrains of Jalal ud-Din Rumi and two hitherto unknown manuscripts of his Divan,* Journal of the Asiatic Society of Bengal, Calcutta 1953.

Brabazon, Francis, *Stay with God. A Statement in Illusion on Reality,* Woombye, Queensland 1959.

R. van Brakell Buys, Djalalu'ddin Rumi, Fragmenten uit de Mashnawi, 'sGravenhage 1974.

Brockelmann, Carl, *Geschichte der arabischen Literatur*, 3 vols. and supplements, Leiden 1937 ff.

Browne, Edward Granville, *A Literary History of Persia*, 4 vols. London 1902, Cambridge, 1920 ff.; repr. 1957 f.

Brunner, Lotte, *Constantin Brunners Genielehre und der Sufismus*, Berlin 1927.

Buber, Martin, *Ekstatische Konfessionen*, Jena 1909.

Bürgel, Christoph, Licht und Reigen. Auswahl aus dem Diwan, Bern 1974.

id. Lautsymbolik und funktionelles Wortspiel bei Rumi, in: Der Islam 51/2, Berlin 1974.

Büyükkörükçü, Tahir, Hakiki Veçhesiyle Mevlâna ve Mesnevi, Istanbul 1972.

Çelebi, Asaf Halet, *Mevlâna'nin Rubaᶜileri*, Istanbul 1939.

id. *Roubâyât, traduit du Persan*, Istanbul 1950.

Chelkovski, Peter, (ed.), The Scholar and the Saint, al-Biruni and Rumi (collection of lectures), New York 1975.

Chester Beatty Library, *Catalogue of the Persian Manuscripts and*

Miniatures, 3 volumes, Dublin 1959 ff.

Chirāgh-e Dehlavi, *Khayr al-majālis*, ed. Khaliq Ahmed Nizami, Aligarh 1959.

Chishti, Muhammad Yusuf Shāh, *Pirāhan-e Yusufi*, Delhi 1943.

Chittick, William C., The Sufi doctrine of Rumi, an introduction. With a foreword by Seyyed Hossein Nasr. Teheran 1974.

Corbin, Henri, *L'homme de lumière dans le Soufisme Iranien*, Paris 1971.

id. *Quiétude et inquiétude de l'âme dans le soufisme de Rûzbihān Baqli dė Shiraz,* in Eranos-Jahrbuch, XXVI, 1958.

ad-Dailami, *ʿAli ibn Aḥmad, Sīrat-i Ibn al-Hafīf aṣ-Ṣīrāzi*, in the Persian translation of Cuneyd-i Şirāzi, ed. A. Schimmel, Ankara 1955.

ad-Damīrī, Kamāluddin Moḥammad, *Ḥayāt al-ḥayawān al-kubrā*, Cairo 1950.

Dārā Shikoh, *Sakinat al-auliyāʾ*, ed. M. Jalāli Nāʾini, Tehran 1965.

Dard, Khwāja Mir, *Chahār risāla*, Bhopal 1310 h/1892.

id. , *ʿIlm ul-kitāb*, Bhopal 1309 h/1891.

Daudpota, ʿUmar Muḥammad, *Kalām-i Girhōri*, Hyderabad/Sind 1956 (Sindhi).

Davis, F. Hadland, *The Persian Mystics: Rumi*, London s.d. (ca. 1908), repr. Lahore s.d.

Donne, John, *Poems by John Donne*, edited with an introduction by Hug I'Anson Faussett, London 1931 and often

id. *Devotions upon emergent occasions,* ed. Izaak Walton, Ann Arbor Paperbacks, 1959.

Drewes, G. W. J., *Sjamsi Tabriz in de Javaansche hagiographie*, TITLW 70/1930.

Egger, Gerhard, *Der Hamza-Roman*, Wien 1969.

Ethé, Hermann, *Neupersische Literatur*, in: W. Geiger und E. Kuhn, *Grundriss der iranischen Philologie II*, Strassburg 1896/1904.

Ettinghausen, Richard, *The Unicorn*, Washington 1950.

Farah, Cesar, *The etiquette of the sheykh/murshid toward his disciple, murid,* in: Numen XX 1974.

Farhadi, A. R., *Le Majlis de al-Ḥallāj, de Shams-e Tabrezi et du Mollā de Roum,* in: Revue des Études Islamiques 1954, based on Ms. Vatican Persian Cerulli 724.

Farrokhi, *Divān*, ed. M. Dabir Siyāqi, Teheran 1335 sh/1956.

Field, Claude, *Mystics and Saints of Islam*, London 1910.

Fish, Radij, *Dschelāladdin Rumi*, Moscow 1972.

Fikrun wa Fann, Zeitschrift für die arabische Welt, herausgegeben von Albert Theile und Annemarie Schimmel, Hamburg 1963-72. München 1972-3. Nr. 21, 1973 is devoted to Jalāloddin Rumi.

Fleischer, Johann Leberecht, *Über die farbigen Lichterscheinungen der Sufis*, in: ZDMG XVI 1862.

de Fouchécour, C.-G., *La description de la nature dans la poésie lyrique persane du XIe siècle*, Paris 1969.

Friedländer, Ira, *The Whirling Dervishes*, New York s.d. (1975).
Fundgruben des Orients, herausgegeben von J. von Hammer, Wien 1809-14.
Furuzānfar, Badi ʿozzamān, *Risāla dar taḥqiq-e aḥvāl u zendegāni-ye Mowlāna Jalāloddin Moḥammad, mashhur be-Mowlavi*, Teheran 1312 sh/1933.
id. *Aḥādith-e Mathnavi*, Tehran 1334 sh/1955.
id. *Maʾākhes-e qeṣaṣ u tamthilāt-e Mathnavi*, Tehran 1333 sh/1954.
See also Bahāʾoddin, Rumi.
Garbett, C., *Jalalu'ddin Rumi, Sun of Tabriz.* A lyrical introduction to higher metaphysics, 1956.
Garcin de Tassy, J. H., Histoire de la Littérature Hindoue et Hindoustani, Paris 1870-1, 3 vols.
Ghālib, Mirzā Asadullāh, *Kulliyāt,* 17 volumes, Lahore 1969.
al-Ghazzāli, Abu Ḥāmid, *Iḥyā ʿolum ad-din*, Vols. 1-4, Bulāq 1289 h/1877.
id. *al-Maqṣad al-asnā fi sharḥ maʿāni asmāʾ Allāh al-ḥusnā*, edited with introduction by F. A. Shehadi, Beirut 1971.
Ghazzāli, Ahmed, *Sawāniḥ, Aphorismen über die Liebe*, edited by Hellmut Ritter, Istanbul 1942.
Gibb, E. J. W., *A History of Ottoman Poetry*, 6 volumes, London 1900 ff.
Gölpınarlı, Abdülbaki, *Mevlâna Celâleddin, hayatı, felsefesi, eserlerinden seçmeler*, Istanbul 1952 and often
id. *Mevlâna'dan sonra Mevlevilik*, Istanbul 1953.
id. *Mevlânaʾnin Mektuplari*, Istanbul 1963.
id. *Divan-i Kebir*, 7 volumes, Istanbul 1957-60.
id. *Mesnevi*, revised edition of Veled Izbudak's Turkish translation, Istanbul 1956 ff.
Goethe, Johann Wolfgang von, *Noten und Abhandlungen zum West-Östlichen Divan*, 1819 and often.
Gramlich, Richard, Die schiitischen Derwischorden Persiens, Teil II: Glaube und-Lehre, Wiesbaden 1976.
Grotzfeld, Heinz, *Das Bad im arabisch-islamischen Mittelalter*, Wiesbaden 1970.
Güldeste, a collection of articles on Rumi, ed. by A. Schimmel, Konya 1971.
Güven, Rasih, Mawlānā Jalāluddin and Shams Tabrizi, in Indo-Iranica XVII 4, 1964.
Gurgāni, Fakhrud-Din, *Vis u Ramin*, translated by George Morrison, Columbia University Press, New York 1972.
Ḥabibi, Abdul Ḥayy, Sharḥ beyteyn-i Mathnavi, az sardār Mehrdel Khān Mashreqi, (d. 1271/1854 in Kandahar), Kabul 1351 sh.
al-Ḥallāj, Ḥusain ibn Manṣur, *Kitāb aṭ-ṭawāsin, texte arabe . . . avec la version persane d'al-Baqli*, édit et traduit par Louis Massignon, Paris 1913.
id. *Divan, Essai de reconstitution*, par Louis Massignon, in:

Journal Asiatique, 1931.

Hammer, Joseph von, *Geschichte der schönen Redekünste Persiens*, Wien 1818.

id. *Bericht über den zu Kairo im Jahr d.H. 1251 (1835) in sechs Foliobänden erschienenen türkischen Commentar des Mesnewi Dschelaleddin Rumis.* Sitzungsberichte der Oesterreichischen Akademie der Wissenschaften, Phil.-Hist. Kl. 1851; repr. in: *Zwei Abhandlungen zur Mystik und Magie des Islam*, herausgegeben von Annemarie Schimmel, Wien 1974.

Haq, Enamul, *Muslim Bengali Literature*, Karachi 1957.

Hāshimi, Jihāngir̄, *Maẓhar al-āthār*, edited Sayyid Hussamuddin Rashdi, Karachi 1957.

Hasrat, Bikram Jit, *Dara Shikuh*, Shantiniketam 1953.

Hastie, William, *The Festival of Spring from the Divan of Jalâl ed-Dîn*, Glasgow 1903.

Heiler, Friedrich, *Das Gebet*, München,[5] 1923.

id. *Erscheinungsformen und Wesen der Religion*, Stuttgart 1961.

id. *Das Gebet in der Problematik des modernen Menschen*, in: Festschrift für Romano Guardini, Würzburg 1964.

Huart, Clement, *Les saints des dervishes tourneurs*, Paris 1918-22. (translation of Aflāki's *Manāqib al-ʿārifīn*), see the review in: Der Islam XVIII 380.

al-Hujwiri, ʿAli ibn ʿUthmān, *Kashf al-maḥjub*, ed. V. A. Zukovskiy, Leningrad 1926, repr. Tehran 1336 sh/1957. *The Kashf al-Maḥjub, The Oldest Persian Treatise on Sufism*, translated by R. A. Nicholson, London-Leyden 1911, repr. 1959.

Humā'i, Jalāloddin, *Tafsir-i mathnavi-i Mowlavi*, Tehran 1349 sh/1960.

Ibn Babuyā, *Al-āmāli waʾl-majālis*, Qumm 1373 h/1953.

Ibn Ḥazm, ʿAli, *Ṭauq al-ḥamāma*, ed. D. K. Pétrof, St. Petersburg/Leyden 1914, English translation by R. A. Nykl.

Ibn al-Jauzi, *Kitāb al-quṣṣāṣ waʾl-mudhakkirīn*, ed. Merlin S. Swartz, Beirut 1970.

Iqbal, Afzal, *The Life and Thought of Rumi*, Lahore s.d. (1956).

id. The Impact of Mowlānā Jalāluddin Rumi on Islamic Culture, Tehran 1974.

Iqbal, Shaikh (later Sir) Muhammad, *The Development of Metaphysics in Persia*, London 1908.

id. *Asrār-i khudi*, Lahore 1915, English translation by R. A. Nicholson: *Secrets of the Self*, London 1920.

id. *Bāng-i Darā*, Lahore 1922.

id. *Payām-e Mashriq*, Lahore 1923, German verse translation by A. Schimmel (*Botschaft des Ostens, Wiesbaden 1963).

id. *Jāvidnāme*, Lahore 1932, English translation by A. J. Arberry, 1965 London, German verse translation by A. Schimmel, 1957, Italian translation by A. Bausani, French

translation by E. Meyerovitch.
id. *Pas che bāyad kard*, Lahore 1933.
id. *Musāfir*, Lahore 1933.
id. *Bāl-i Jibril*, Lahore 1936.
id. *Armaghān-i Ḥijāz*, Lahore 1938.
id. *The Reconstruction of Religious Thought in Islam*, Lahore 1930 and often.
Iqbālnāme, Letters, ed. Sheykh ᶜAṭāʾullāh, Lahore s.d.
ᶜIrāqi, Fakhruddin, *Divān*, ed. Said Nafisi, Tehran 1338 sh/1959.
id. *The Song of the Lovers (ᶜushshaqnāme)*, ed. and translated by A. J. Arberry, Oxford 1939.
Irfani, Khwāja ᶜAbdul Ḥamid, *Rumi-yi ᶜaṣr*, Tehran 1332 sh/1953.
al-Iṣfahāni, Abu Nuᶜaym, *Ḥilyat al-auliyā*, Cairo 1932 ff.
Izutsu, T., *The Basic Structure of Metaphysical Thinking in Islam*, in M. Mohaghghegh and H. Landolt, Collected Papers on Islamic Philosophy and Mysticism, Tehran 1971.
Jāmi, ᶜAbdur Raḥman, *Divān-e kāmel*, ed. Hāshem Reżā, Tehran 1341 sh/1962.
id. *Nafaḥāt al-ons*, ed. M. Towhidipur, Tehran 1336 sh/1957.
Kandhāri, Mowlawi Ṣāleḥ Moḥammad, Pashto Mathnavi, Kabul 1350 sh.
Kaymaz, Nejat, *Pervane Muᶜinud-Din Süleyman*, Ankara 1970.
Keklik, Nihat, *Sadreddin Koneviʾnin Felsefesinde Allah, Kâinat, ve insan*, Istanbul 1967.
Khalil, Makhdum Ibrahim, *Takmilat maqālāt ash-shuᶜarā*, ed. Sayyid Hussamuddin Rashdi, Karachi 1958.
Khalili, Khalilollah, *Az Balkh tā Qunyā*, Kabul 1346 sh/1967.
id. *Neynāma*, Kabul Nov. 1973.
Khāqāni, *Divān*, ed. Z. Sajjādi, Tehran 1338 sh/1959.
Kircher, Gisela, *Die 'einfachen Heilmittel' aus dem 'Handbuch der Chirurgie' des Ibn al-Quff*, Phil. Diss. Bonn 1967.
Kove-Khorb, R., *Maulawis Mystik und seine Dialektik*, Trudi XXVI Mezhdunarodni kongressa vostokovedov, Vol. II, Moskau 1963.
Lukach (Luke), H. C., *City of Dancing Dervishes*, London 1914.
Macdonald, Duncan B., *Emotional Religion in Islam as affected by Music and Singing*, JRAS 1901.
Majāles-i Mowlānā Balkhi, collection of papers delivered at the International Mowlānā Seminar October 1974 in Afghanistan, Kabul 1353 sh.
Massignon, Louis, *La Passion d'Al-Ḥosayn ibn Manṣour al-Ḥallāj, Martyre mystique de l'Islam executé à Bagdad le 26 Mars 922*, Paris 1922, 2 vols. new ed. 4 vols., Paris 1976.
id. *Interférences philosophiques et percées metaphysiques dans la mystique Hallajienne: Notion de l'Essentiel Désir'*, Mélanges Maréchal, Vol. 2, Brussels 1950.
La Vie et les oeuvres de Ruzbehan Baqli, Studia Orientalia . . . Joanni Pedersen dicata, Copenhagen 1953.

Massignon, Louis, et Paul Krauss, *Akhbār al-Ḥallāj*, Paris 1936, 3rd edition 1957.
Massignon, Louis, et Clement Huart, *Les entretiens de Lahore*, JA CCIX, 1926.
Meier, Fritz, *Die fawāʾih al-ǧamāl wa fawātiḥ al-ǧalāl des Naǧmuddīn al-Kubrá*, Wiesbaden 1957.
id. *Stambuler Handschriften dreier persischen Mystiker, ʿAin al-Quḍāt al-Hamadānī, Naǧm ad-dīn al-Kubrá, Naǧm ad-dīn ad-Dāja*, in: Der Islam 24/1937.
id. *Der Geistmensch bei dem persischen Dichter ʿAttār*, in: Eranos-Jahrbuch XIII 1946.
id. *Das Problem der Natur im esoterischen Monismus des Islams*, in: Eranos-Jahrbuch XIV, 1946.
id. *Die Schriften des ʿAzīz-i Nasafī*, WZKM 52/1953.
id. *Der Derwischtanz*, in: Asiatische Studien 8/1954.
id. *Zum 700. Todestag Mawlānās, des Vaters der Tanzenden Derwische*, in: Asiatische Studien XXVIII 1, Bern 1974.
Mélikoff, Irène, *La Fleur de la souffrance. Recherche sur le sens symbolique de* lâle *dans la poésie mystique Turco-Iranienne*, in: JA CCXXV 1967.
Mevlevi Ayinleri 1 38, Istanbul Konservatuari neşriyati 1933/9 (the tunes used in the Mevlevi ritual).
Meyerovitch, Eva, *Mystique et poésie en Islam, Djalâl-ud-Din Rumi et l'Ordre des Dervishes tourneurs*, Paris 1972.
id. (transl.) Rumi, *Le Livre du Dedans*, Paris 1976.
Paris 1976.
Mez, Adam, *Die Renaissance des Islam*, Heidelberg 1922.
Molé, Marijan, *La Danse Exstatique en Islam*, in: Sources Orientales, VI, La Danse Sacrée, Paris 1963.
Mills, Margaret Ann, *Exploring an Archetype*, in: Güldeste, Konya 1971.
Naʿimuddin, S., *Influence of Rumi on Urdu Poetry*, Proceedings of the XXVI International Congress of Orientalists, Delhi 1968.
Nasr, Seyyed Hossein, *Jalāl al-Dīn Rumi, supreme Persian poet* and sage, Tehran 1974.
Nicholson, Reynold Alleyne, *The Mystics of Islam*, London 1914.
id. *Studies in Islamic Mysticism*, Cambridge 1921, repr. 1967.
id. *Selected Poems from the Dīvān-i Shams-i Tabrīz*, Cambridge 1898, repr. 1961.
id. *Tales of Mystic Meaning*, London 1931.
id. *Rumi, Poet and Mystic*, London 1950.
id. *The Table-Talk of Jalâluʾ-d-Dîn Rûmî*, JRAS 1924, Suppl. 225.
id. *The Idea of Personality in Sufism*, Cambridge 1923.
id. *The Secrets of the Self*, London 1920 (cf. Iqbal)
ad-Niffarī, Moḥammad ibn ʿabdi'l-Jabbār, *The Mawāqif and Mukhāṭabāt . . . with other fragments*, ed. A. J. Arberry, London 1935.

Nwyia, Paul, *Exégèse Coranique et Langage Mystique,* Beirut 1970.
Otto, Rudolf, *Das Heilige*, München 1917,[28] 1958.
The Oxford Book of English Mystical Verse, Oxford 1917 and often.
Önder, Mehmet, *Mevlâna Şiirleri Antologjisi*, Konya 1956, 3rd ed. 1973.
id. *Mevlâna Şehri Konya*, Konya 1962.
id. *Mevlâna,* Ankara 1971.
id. *Mevlâna'nin ve Mevlevilerin Kiyafeti,* in: Anıt 20 1, Konya 1957.
id. *Mevlâna bibliografyasi.* 1. Basmalar, Ankara, Is Bankası, 1973.
id. *Mevlâna Bibliografyasi* II, Yazmalar, Ankara 1975.
Pannwitz, Rudolf, *Der Aufbau der Natur*, Stuttgart 1961.
von der Porten, Walter, *Aus dem Rohrflötenbuch*, Hallerau 1930.
Qāni^c, Mir ᶜAli Shir, *Maqālāt ash-shuᶜarā,* ed. Sayyid Hussamuddin Rashdi, Karachi 1957.
id. *Tuḥfat al-kirām*, Sindhi translation by Makhdum Amir Ahmad, Hyderabad/Sind 1957.
Qanungo, K. R., *Dārā Shukoh*, Calcutta 1935.
Qāsimi, Ghulām Muṣṭafā, *Hāshimiyya Library*, in: Mihrān jā Moti, Karachi 1959.
Qureishi, Maulvi Moḥammad Shāh Din, *Mathnavi Sharif*, Lahore s.d. (1939) (Panjabi verse translation of the *Mathnavi*).
Raverty, G., *Selections from the popular poetry of the Afghans*, London 1862.
Redhouse, James W., *The Mesnevi . . . of Mevlâna (Our Lord) Jalâl-u'd-Din Muhammad, er-Rumi . . . Book the First*, London 1881.
Reinert, Benedikt, *Die Lehre vom tawakkul in der älteren Sufik*, Berlin 1968.
id. *Ḫāqānī als Dichter*, Berlin 1972.
Rice, Cyprian, *The Persian Sufis*, London ²1969.
Richter, Gustav, *Persiens Mystiker Dschelalad-Din Rumi: eine Stildeutung in drei Vorträgen*, Breslau 1933.
Ritter, Hellmut, *Das Meer der Seele. Gott, Welt und Mensch in den Geschichten Farīduddīn ᶜAṭṭārs*, Leiden 1955.
id. *Muslims Mystics' Strife with God*, Oriens V, 1952.
id. Die Flötenmystik ǧalāladdīn Rumis und ihre Quellen in: ZDMG 92/32*
id. *Das Proömium des Maṯnawī-i Maulawī*, ZDMG 93/1932.
id. *Der Reigen der 'Tanzenden Derwische'*, Zeitschrift für vergleichende Musikwissenschaft 1/1933.
id. *Die Mevlânafeier in Konya vom 11. 17. Dezember 1960*, Oriens XV, 1962.
id. *Maulânā ǧalāluddīn Rūmī und sein Kreis*, Philologika XI, in: Der Islam 26/1942.
id. *Neuere Literatur über Maulānā Calāluddin Rūmī und seinen Orden*, Oriens XIII-XIV, 1960-1.

id. *Über die Bildersprache Nizamis*, Berlin 1927.

Rypka, Jan, *History of Iranian Literature*, s'Gravenhage 1968.

Rotter, Gernot, *Die Stellung des Negers in der arabisch-islamischen Gesellschaft bis zum XVI. Jahrhundert*, Phil. Diss. Bonn 1967.

Rosen, Georg, *Mesnevi oder Doppelverse des Scheich Mevlâna Dschalaladdin Rumi*, herausgegeben von Friedrich Rosen, München 1913.

Rosenzweig Schwannau, Vinzens von, *Auswahl aus den Divanen des grössten mystischen Dichters Persiens, Dschelaladdin Rumi*, Wien 1838.

Rückert, Friedrich, *Ghaselen*, 1819.

id. *Erbauliches und Beschauliches aus dem Morgenlande*, in: Gesammelte Werke in 12 Bänden, Frankfurt 1882, Band 7.

Rumi Herdenking, catalogue of an exhibition held in Leiden 1973, ed. by J. T. P. de Bruyn and A..C. M. Hamer.

Sachal Sarmast, *Risālō Sindhi*, ed. O. A. Anṣāri, Karachi 1958.

id. *Siraiki kalām*, ed. Maulwi Ḥakim M. Ṣādiq Rānipuri, Karachi 1959.

Sadarangani, H., *Persian Poets of Sind*, Karachi 1956.

Saᶜdi, Moṣleḥoddin, *Kolliyāt*, ed. M. A. Foroughi, Tehran 1342 sh/1963, 4 volumes.

San'ā i, Abuʾ l-Majd Majdud, *Divān*, ed. Modarris Rażavi, Tehran 1320 sh/1941.

id. *Ḥadiqat al-ḥaqiqat va shari ᶜat aṭ-ṭariqat*, ed. Mudarris Rażavi, Tehran 1329 sh/1950.

id. *Mathnavihā* (including *Sanāʾi ābād, Kārnāma-ye Balkh, Seyr ol ᶜebād,* and others), ed. Mudarris Rażavi, Tehran 1348 sh/1969.

as-Sarrāj, Abu Naṣr, *Kitāb al-lumaᶜ fi't-taṣavvuf*, ed. R. A. Nicholson, Leyden-London 1914.

Sepahsalār, Faridun ibn Ahmad, *Resāla dar ahvāl-e Mawlānā Jalāloddin Rumi*, ed. Badi ᶜozzamān Furuzānfar, Tehran 1325 sh/1946.

Söderblom, Nathan, *Främmande Religionsurkunder*, Uppsala 1907.

id. *Rausch und Religion*, in: Ur Religionens Historia, Stockholm 1915.

Sorley, H. T., *Shah ᶜAbdul Laṭif of Bhit*, Oxford 1940, repr. 1968.

Spies, Gertrud, *Maḥmūd von Ghazna bei Farīduʾd-Dīn ᶜAṭṭār*, Basel 1959.

Schaeder, Hans Heinrich, *Die persische Vorlage von Goethes Seliger Sehnsucht*, in: Festschrift für Eduard Spranger, Berlin 1942.

id. *Die islamische Lehre vom Vollkommenen Menschen, ihre Herkunft und ihre dichterische Gestaltung*, ZDMG 79/1925.

Şerefeddin, Mehmet, *Mevlâna'da Türkçe kelimeler ve türkçe şiirler*, Istanbul 1934.

Shibli Nuᶜmani, *Sawāneḥ-e Mowlānā Rumi*, Lucknow 1902;

Persian translation by Mohammad Taqi Fakhr Dāʿi Gilāni, Tehran 1333 sh/1954.

Schimmel, Annemarie, *Die Bildersprache Dschelaladdin Rumis*, Walldorf 1949.

id. *The Symbolical Language of Maulānā Jalāl ad-Din Rumi*, in: Studies in Islam I, New Delhi 1964.

id. *Mevlâna Celâlettin Rumi'nin Şark ve Garp'ta tesirleri*, Ankara 1963.

id. *Dschelaladdin Rumi, Aus dem Diwan*. Übertragen und eingeleitet, Stuttgart, Reclam, 1964.

id. *Zu einigen Versen Dschelāluddin Rumis*, in: Anatolica I, Leiden 1967.

id. *Jalāluddin Rumi's story on Prayer*, in: Yādnāme-yi Jan Rypka, Prague 1967.

id. *Ein unbekanntes Werk Joseph von Hammer-Purgstalls*, in: Die Welt des Islams, NS XV, 1974.

id. *Pain and Grace*, A study of two Indian Muslim mystical poets of the 18th century, Leiden 1976.

id. Friedrich Rückert und Dschelaluddin Rumi, in: Miscellanea Suinfurtensia Historica VI, Schweinfurt 1975.

id. Feiern zum Gedenken an Maulāna ğalāluddin Balḫī-Rūmī. in: Die Welt des Islams, NS XVI 1 4, 1975.

id. *Schāh ʿAbdul Laṭifs Beschreibung des wahren Sufi*, in: Festschrift für Fritz Meier, Wiesbaden 1974.

id. *The martyr-mystic Ḥallāj in Sindhi folk-poetry*, in: Numen IX, 1961.

id. *al-Halladsch, Märtyrer der Gottesliebe*, Cologne 1969.

id. *Gabriel's Wing. A Study into the religious ideas of Sir Muhammad Iqbal*, Leiden 1963.

id. *Muhammad Iqbal, Botschaft des Ostens,* Wiesbaden 1963.

id. *The Idea of Prayer in the thought of Iqbal*, MW XLVIII, 1958.

id. *Orientalische Dichtung in Übersetzungen Friedrich Rückerts*, herausgegeben und eingeleitet, Bremen 1963.

id. *Nur ein störrisches Pferd . . .* , in: Ex Orbe Religionum, Festschrift für Geo Widengren, Leiden 1972.

id. *Mir Dard's Gedanken über das Verhältnis von Mystik und Wort*, in: Festgabe deutscher Iranisten zur 2500-Jahr-Feier Irans, herausgegeben von Wilhelm Eilers, Stuttgart 1971.

id. *Turk and Hindu. A poetical image and its application to Historical facts.* Proceedings of the IV Levi della Vida conference, Wiesbaden 1975.

id. *Mystical Dimensions of Islam*, University of North Carolina Press, Chapel Hill 1975.

id. *Lied der Rohrflöte*, Ghaselen. Hameln 1948.

Soliman, A. D. *Le Mevleviisme*, in: Abr Nahrain, XIV 1973 4.

Sprenger, Aloys, Catalogue of Library of the Kings of Oudh, Calcutta 1854, Vol. I.

Tholuck, G. F. D., *Ssufismus sive theosophia Persarum pantheistica*, Berlin 1821.

id. *Blüthensammlung aus der morgenländischen Mystik, Berlin 1825.*

Tiele-Söderblom, *Kompendium der Religionsgeschichte, herausgegeben von Nathan Söderblom*, Berlin 1931.

Tilmidh Ḥusain, *Mirʾāt al-Mathnavi*, Hyerabad 1292 h/1875.

Tirmizi, Seyyid Burhaneddin Muhakkik, *Maarif*, translated into Turkish by Abdülbaki Gölpinarli, Ankara 1971.

Tökin, Ismail Hüsrev, *Mevlâna'da yok oluş felsefesi*, Turk Yurdu 52/3, July 1965.

Trimingham, J. Spencer, *The Sufi Orders in Islam*, Oxford 1971.

Turan, Osman, *Selcuklular Zamanında Türkiye*, Istanbul 1971.

Underhill, Evelyn, *Mysticism. A Study in the Nature and Development of Man's Spiritual Consciousness*. London New York 1911, paperback New York [4]1956.

Ünver, Süheyl, *Sevâkib-i Menakib, Mevlâna'dan Hatiralar*, Istanbul 1973 (a study of miniatures illustrating events from Mowlānā's life).

Utas, Bo, *Ṭarīq at-taḥqīq. A Sufi Mathnavi ascribed to Ḥakīm Sanāʾī of Ghazna and probably composed by Aḥmad ibn al-Ḥasan ibn Muḥammad an-Nakhchavānī*, Lund 1972.

Uzluk, Ṣehabettin, *Mevlevilikte Resim, Resimde Mevleviler*, Ankara 1957.

Valad, Solṭān, *Valadnāma*, ed. Jalāl Homāʾi, Tehran 1315 sh/1936.

id. *Divān-i Sultan Veled*, ed. Feridun Nafiz Uzluk, Istanbul 1941.

id. *Divān-i Turki*, ed. Kilisli Muallim Rifᶜat, Istanbul 1341 h/1922.

Vaudeville, Charlotte, *Kabir Granthvali (Doha)*, Pondécherry 1957.

Vryonis, Speros, *The Decline of Medieval Hellenism in Asia Minor and the process of Islamization from the Eleventh through the Fifteenth Century*, University of California, Berkeley 1971.

Watanmal, Lilaram, *The Life of Shah Abdul Latif*, Hyderabad/Sind 1889.

Watt, W. Montgomery, *Free Will and Predestination in Early Islam*, London 1948.

Whinfield, H., *Masnavi-i Maᶜnavi, Spiritual Couplets.* Translated and abridged . . . , London 1887.

The Whirling Dervishes, A Commemoration, London 1974.

Zaehner, R. C., *Hindu and Muslim Mysticism*, London 1960.

Zimmer, Heinrich, *The King and the Corpse*, ed: J. Campbell, Princeton 1971.

INDEX OF PROPER NAMES

INDEX OF CONCEPTS AND TECHNICAL TERMS

(Words like 'love', 'heart' and other central concepts are not included)

INDEX OF KORANIC QUOTATIONS AND PROPHETIC TRADITIONS

Persian Heritage Series

Volumes Published

Varavini, *The Tales of Marzuban* (No. 1), tr. Reuben Levy
Indiana Univ. Press, 1959 (Reprint 1968)

Tusi, *The Nasirean Ethics* (No. 2), tr. G.M. Wickens
London: George Allen & Unwin, 1964

Ferdowsi, *The Epic of the Kings* (No. 3), tr. Reuben Levy
University of Chicago Press, 1967 (Reprint 1973)

Nezami, *Le Sette Principesse* (No. 4), tr. A. Bausani
Rome: Leonardo da Vinci, 1967

Attar, *Muslim Saints & Mystics* (No. 5), tr. A.J. Arberry
University of Chicago Press, 1966 (Reprint 1973)

Nezami, *Chosroès et Chîrîne* (No. 6), tr. Henri Massé
Paris: Maisonneuve et Larose, 1970

Rumi, *Mystical Poems I* (No. 7), tr. A.J. Arberry
University of Chicago Press, 1974

Aruzi, *Les quatre discours* (No. 8), tr. I. de Gastines
Paris: Maisonneuve et Larose, 1968

Anon., *The Letter of Tansar* (No. 9), tr. M. Boyce
Rome: IsMEO, 1968

Rashid al-Din, *The Successors of Genghis Khan* (No. 10)
tr. J.A. Boyle, Columbia University Press, 1971

Mohammad ibn Ibrahim, *The Ship of Sulaiman* (No. 11)
tr. J. O'Kane, Columbia University Press, 1972

Faramarz, *Samak-e Ayyar* (No. 12), tr. F. Razavi
Paris: Maisonneuve et Larose, 1972

Avicenna, *Metaphysics* (No. 13), tr. P. Morewedge
Columbia University Press, 1973

Gurgani, *Vis and Ramin* (No. 14), tr. G. Morrison
Columbia University Press, 1972

Persian Heritage Series

Volumes Published

Fasai, *History of Persia Under Qajar Rule* (No. 15)
tr. H. Busse, Columbia University Press, 1972

Aturpat-e Emetan, *Denkart III* (No. 16), tr. J. De Menasće
Paris: Libarie Klincksieck, 1974

Sa'di, *Bustan* (No. 17), tr. G.M. Wickens
University of Toronto Press, 1974

Anon., *Folk Tales of Ancient Persia* (No. 18)
tr. F. Hekmat & Y. Lovelock, Delmar, N.Y.: Caravan Books, 1974

Bighami, *Love and War* (No. 19), tr. W. Hanaway Jr.
Delmar, N.Y.: Scholars' Facsimiles & Reprints, 1974

Anon., *The History of Sistan* (No. 20), tr. M. Gold
Rome: IsMEO, 1977

Manichaean Literature (An Anthology) (No. 22), tr. J. Asmussen
Delmar, New York: Scholars' Facsimiles & Reprints, 1974

Rumi, *Le Livre du Dedans* (No. 25), tr. E. de Vitray-Meyerovitch
Paris: Edition Sinbad, 1975

Rumi, *Licht und Reigen* (No. 26), tr. J. Ch. Bürgel
Bern: Herbert Lang Verlag, 1974

Samarkandi, *Le Livre des sept vizirs* (No. 27), tr. D. Bogdanovic
Paris: Edition Sinbad, 1975

Attar, *Ilahiname* (No. 29), tr. J.A. Boyle
Manchester University Press, 1977

Hafez, *Divan (Hafizu-Shishu)* (No. 30), tr. T. Kuriyanagi
Tokyo: Heibosha Ltd., 1977

Nezami, *Khosrau and Shirin* (No. 33), tr. A. Okada
Tokyo: Heibosha Ltd., 1977

Persian Heritage Series

In Press

Rumi, *Mystical Poems II* (No. 23)
tr. A.J. Arberry

Eskandar Beg Monshi, *History of Shah 'Abbas* (No. 28)
tr. R.M. Savory

Anon., *Iskandarnama* (No. 31)
tr. M. Southgate

Nizam al-Molk, *The Book of Government* (No. 32)
tr. H. Darke

Forthcoming

Razi, *Mersad al-Ebad*
tr. H. Algar

Nishapuri, *History of the Saljuqs*
tr. A. Luther

Mohammad b. Monavvar, *Asrar al-Tawhid*
tr. J. O'Kane

Naser-e Khosrow, *Safarnama*
tr. W. Thaxton

Tabari, *Annals 774-809 A.D.*
tr. J.A. Williams

Anon., *Myths and Legends of Ancient Iran*
tr. E. Yarshater

Anon., *Sasanian Law Book (Matikan-i hazar datastan)*
tr. A. Perikhanian and N. Garsoian

Aturpat-e Emetan, *Denkart III*
tr. S. Shaked

Ferdausi, *Anthologie du livre des rois*
tr. J. Mohl, edit. G. Lazard

Anon., *Le livre d'Ardaviraz*
tr. P. Gignoux

Gardizi, *History*
tr. A. Pontecorvo

Khayyam, *The Ruba 'iyat*
tr. P. Avery and Heath-Stubbs

Persian Studies Series

Published

Reuben Levy, *Introduction to Persian Literature*
Columbia University Press, 1969

Ali Dashti, *In Search of Omar Khayyam* (No. 1), tr. L.P. Elwell-Sutton
London: George Allen and Unwin, 1971

James Pearson, *A Bibliography of Pre-Islamic Persia* (No. 2)
London: Mansell Information and Publishing Ltd., 1975

M.H. Tabataba'i, *Shi'ite Islam* (No. 5), tr. S.H. Nasr
State University of New York Press, 1975

J. Ch. Bürgel, *Drei Hafis Studien* (No. 6)
Bern: Herbert Lang Verlag, 1975

Biruni: A Symposium, ed. E. Yarshater (No. 7)
Columbia University Press, 1976

Christopher J. Brunner, *A Syntax of Western Middle Iranian* (No. 3)
Delmar, New York: Caravan Books, 1977

John Yohannan, *Persian-Literature in England and America* (No. 4)
Delmar, New York: Caravan Books, 1977

In Press

A. Schimmel, *Rumi: A Study of His Life and Works* (No. 8)
London: Fine Books

M.J. MacDermott, *The Theology of al-Shaikh al-Mufid* (No. 9)
Beirut: Dar el-Machreq

Edward C. Bosworth, *The Later Ghaznavids* (No. 10)
Edinburgh University Press

All inquiries about the Persian Heritage and Persian Studies Series should be directed to Mr. Felix Weigel, Harrassowitz, P.O. Box 2929, P-6200 Weisbaden, Germany.